Third Edition

Visions
of the Heart

CANADIAN ABORIGINAL ISSUES

**David Long
& Olive Patricia
Dickason**

OXFORD
UNIVERSITY PRESS

OXFORD
UNIVERSITY PRESS

8 Sampson Mews, Suite 204, Don Mills, Ontario M3C 0H5
www.oupcanada.com

Oxford University Press is a department of the University of Oxford.
It furthers the University's objective of excellence in research, scholarship,
and education by publishing worldwide in

Oxford   New York

Auckland   Cape Town   Dar es Salaam   Hong Kong   Karachi   Kuala Lumpur   Madrid   Melbourne
Mexico City   Nairobi   New Delhi   Shanghai   Taipei   Toronto

With offices in

Argentina   Austria   Brazil   Chile   Czech Republic   France   Greece
Guatemala   Hungary   Italy   Japan   Poland   Portugal   Singapore
South Korea   Switzerland   Thailand   Turkey   Ukraine   Vietnam

Oxford is a trade mark of Oxford University Press in the UK and in certain other countries

Published in Canada
by Oxford University Press

Library and Archives Canada Cataloguing in Publication

Visions of the heart : Canadian aboriginal issues / [edited by] David Long, Olive Patricia Dickason.—3rd ed.

Includes bibliographical references and index.

ISBN 978-0-19-543377-7

1. Native peoples—Canada—Textbooks. I. Long, David Alan, 1958–   II. Dickason, Olive Patricia, 1920–

E78.C2V58 2011   971.004'97   C2010-907706-7

Cover image: Doug Plummer/Getty Images

Oxford University Press is committed to our environment.
This book is printed on permanent (acid-free) paper ♾.

Printed and bound in Canada

1 2 3 4 -- 14 13 12 11

Contents

Elders' Teachings in the Twenty-first Century: A Personal Reflection *Marlene Brant Castellano*   35

Foundations: First Nation and Métis Families *Kim Anderson and Jessica Ball*   55

Learning from Indigenous Knowledge in Education *Jan Hare*   90

6 Aboriginal Languages in Canada: Generational Perspectives on Language Maintenance, Loss, and Revitalization
Mary Jane Norris   113

7 Aboriginal Demography
Don Kerr and Roderic Beaujot   149

11 From Paternalism to Partnership: The Challenges of Aboriginal Leadership *Brian Calliou*   258

12 Moving Beyond the Politics of Aboriginal Well-being, Health, and Healing *Martin Cooke and David Long*   292

13 Urban Aboriginal People in Canada: Community Trends and Issues of Governance *Kevin FitzMaurice and Don McCaskill*   328

14 The Canada Problem in Aboriginal Politics
David Newhouse and Yale Belanger   352

15 Rekindling the Fire: Indigenous Knowledge and New Technologies *Simon Brascoupé*   381

Conclusion: Reconciliation and Moving Forward
A Dialogue between David Newhouse and David Long   403

Important Features of This Edition

David Long and Olive Dickason have once again assembled an outstanding collection of essays by some of the most respected scholars of Aboriginal issues today: Marlene Brant Castellano, David Newhouse, Don McCaskill, Mary Jane Norris, Don Kerr, Jessica Ball, Augie Fleras, Martin Cooke, and Patricia Monture, to name only a few. This third edition offers a wealth of insight into the questions of concern to Canada's First Nations, Inuit, Métis, and non-status Aboriginal people—questions that should be of no less concern to mainstream Canadians. More than half of the contributors are new, and material from the second edition has been thoroughly revised to reflect recent developments. In addition, the pedagogical features—glossary, suggested readings, and thought-provoking discussion questions—have been revised and updated.

Highlights

- **New!** New contributions include a study of First Nations and Métis families, an examination of media representations of Aboriginal peoples, a personal reflection on the teachings of Elders, and a dialogue between David Newhouse and David Long on the transformative change that is required to make the vision of the Royal Commission on Aboriginal Peoples (RCAP a reality.
- **New!** For the first time, two on-line resources are available to accompany *Visions of the Heart*: a student study guide complete with learning objectives, study questions, timelines, chapter outlines, and links between chapters, and, for instructors, a test bank containing hundreds of questions that will make exam planning easy.

Contributors

Kim Anderson is a Cree/Métis writer and educator. After working as a consultant in social and health policy for many years, Kim returned to school and graduated with her doctorate from the Department of History, University of Guelph, in 2010. Kim has an interest in indigenous feminism, motherhood, indigenous research ethics, and indigenous women and leadership and has published in all of these areas. Her books include *A Recognition of Being: Reconstructing Native Womanhood* and *Strong Women Stories: Native Vision and Community Survival* (co-edited with Bonita Lawrence). Kim has also co-edited special editions of *Atlantis: A Women's Studies Journal* (2005, 29 [2]) and *Canadian Woman Studies* (winter/spring 2008, 26 [3/4]).

Jessica Ball, MPH, PhD, is a professor in the School of Child and Youth Care at the University of Victoria. She is a third-generation Canadian of English and Irish descent and has the privilege of raising her son and daughter on the traditional territories of the Coast Salish peoples. She has an interdisciplinary, grant-funded program of research on the cultural nature of child and family development (www.ecdip.org). Projects in Canada and internationally address indigenous children's health, language development, early screening and intervention, program evaluation, father involvement, and child care capacity-building in rural and remote communities. Dr Ball has authored or co-authored more than 100 journal articles and book chapters as well as three books. Her work has been recognized through several awards for research in the service of communities.

Roderic Beaujot is professor of sociology at the University of Western Ontario, academic director of the University of Western Ontario Research Data Centre, and director of Population Change and Lifecourse, a Strategic Knowledge Cluster funded by the Social Sciences and Humanities Research Council of Canada (SSHRC). He is also chair of the Statistics Canada Advisory Committee on Demographic Statistics and Studies. His most noteworthy publications are *Population Change in Canada* (Oxford University Press 2004, second edition with Don Kerr) and *Earning and Caring in Canadian Families* (Broadview 2000).

Yale D. Belanger is associate professor of Native American studies (NAS), University of Lethbridge, Alberta. He is the author of *Gambling with the*

Future: The Evolution of Aboriginal Gaming in Canada (Purich 2006), *Aboriginal Self-Government in Canada: Current Trends and Issues* (Purich 2008), and *Ways of Knowing: An Introduction to Native Studies in Canada* (Nelson 2010). He has an edited volume entitled *First Nations Gaming in Canada: Perspective* scheduled for publication with the University of Manitoba Press in 2011 and is finalizing an edited compilation with P. Whitney Lackenbauer entitled *Blockades or Breakthroughs? Aboriginal People Confront the Canadian State, 1973–2008.*

Simon Brascoupé, Kitigan Zibi Anishinabeg, is adjunct research professor of sociology and anthropology, Carleton University, and adjunct professor, indigenous studies, Trent University. He has taught at Queen's University, McGill University, and the University of Manitoba. He has a BA and an MA from State University of New York at Buffalo, where he is completing his PhD. He has a strong interest in traditional knowledge and sustainable development and has written on development, environment, and art. He was an official delegate at the UN Conference on the Environment and Development (UNCED) in June 1992 and successfully negotiated an alternative treaty between non-governmental organizations and indigenous peoples.

Brian Calliou is the director of the Banff Centre's Aboriginal Leadership and Management program area, which designs and delivers leadership development and organizational development programs and applied research for indigenous leaders. Brian is Cree and a member of the Sucker Creek First Nation in the Treaty 8 area of northern Alberta. Brian is married, a father of two grown children, and grandfather of two grandsons. Brian holds a BA in political science, an LLB and an LLM from the University of Alberta. Brian's research interests include Aboriginal leadership, self-government, economic development, Aboriginal and treaty rights, and legal history.

Marlene Brant Castellano is a Mohawk of the Bay of Quinte Band and professor emeritus at Trent University, where she provided leadership in the development of the emerging discipline of indigenous studies (1973–96). She served as co-director of research with the Royal Commission on Aboriginal Peoples (RCAP). Professor Castellano's teaching, research, and publications are deliberately bicultural, promoting discourse between indigenous and Western cultures. She has been honoured with LLDs from Queen's, St Thomas, and Carleton universities, induction into the Order of Ontario, and a National Aboriginal Achievement Award. In 2005, Dr Castellano was named an Officer of the Order of Canada.

Martin Cooke is an associate professor jointly appointed in the departments of Sociology and Legal Studies and Health Studies and Gerontology at the University of Waterloo, where he teaches in the master of public health and master of public service programs. His research interests are in social policy and the life course and the social demography of Aboriginal populations. Current research projects examine the labour market experiences of older workers and the dynamics of social assistance receipt. He is currently the principal investigator of a SSHRC-funded study of the health and social conditions of Aboriginal peoples across the life course.

Joseph E. Couture was an Alberta Métis of Cree ancestry. His PhD training and experience were in the areas of Native development, psychology, and education. His work experience included teaching, addictions counselling, community development, and research. Although deeply appreciated as an Elder, Joe had always expressed profound gratitude for the opportunity to have been apprenticed to Elders from 1971 until his passing in 2007. A collection of Joe's writing is currently being published by his widow, Ruth, and co-editor Dr Virginia McGowan in a book entitled *A Metaphoric Mind: Selected Writings of Dr. Joseph Couture*.

Olive Patricia Dickason is professor emeritus of history at the University of Alberta. Her best-selling *The Myth of the Savage* (1984) and *Canada's First Nations* (1992) fostered widespread recognition of indigenous peoples as this country's founding civilization. A member of the Order of Canada and recipient of the Canada Medal 125, Olive holds an Aboriginal Lifetime Achievement Award and in 1992 was named Métis Woman of the Year. She served as the Aboriginal peoples history consultant for CBC's 2000 broadcast of 'Canada: A People's History', and in 2002 her own life story was televised nationally in the one-hour documentary 'Olive Dickason's First Nations'.

Kevin FitzMaurice has been teaching in the discipline of Native studies for the past 13 years. He is a graduate of Trent University's indigenous studies doctoral program and an ongoing student of Anishinaabe/Cree knowledge. Kevin began teaching as an instructor in Trent's Indigenous Studies Department and is now an assistant professor, Native studies, at the University of Sudbury, where he specializes in Canadian politics and Aboriginal peoples, child welfare, criminal justice, urbanization, and Native critical theory. He brings an interdisciplinary approach to his research, which is predominantly community-based and informed by Western critical theory in conversation with indigenous knowledge and practice.

Augie Fleras has a PhD in Maori studies and anthropology from Victoria University in Wellington, New Zealand. He is the author of numerous articles and more than 25 books, including *The Politics of Race in Canada* (Oxford University Press Canada 2009). His areas of specialization include the politics of indigeneity (especially for Aboriginal peoples and indigenous Maori iwi), race and ethnic relations in Canada, Canadian and international perspectives on multiculturalism, and mass media communication.

Jan Hare is an Anishinaabe member of the Mchi'ging (West Bay) First Nation in Ontario. She is currently associate professor in the Department of Language and Literacy Education at the University of British Columbia and has published widely in the areas of indigenous education, Aboriginal literacy practices, Aboriginal early childhood education, indigenous research methodologies, and Aboriginal youth issues. She was recently awarded a federal grant to provide culturally sensitive literacy training for early childhood educators in Aboriginal urban and northern communities across BC, a project dedicated to building the capacities of Aboriginal communities and organizations to provide programs and services for Aboriginal people based upon indigenous knowledges and approaches to learning.

Don Kerr is a professor of sociology at King's University College at the University of Western Ontario. He is also a research associate at the Population Studies Centre at the University of Western Ontario. His areas of interest are population studies and Canadian demography. His research has focused on social demography, population estimates and projections, the Aboriginal population, and most recently on issues relating to population change and environmental sustainability.

David Long, who is of Anglo-Celtic descent, is professor of sociology at King's University College, Edmonton. David has been on faculty at King's since he and Karen moved with their children to Edmonton in 1989. Along with his teaching and research interests in Aboriginal/non-Aboriginal relations, men's health and well-being, and fathering, David works with a variety of men's groups, human service organizations, and government in promoting the development of support services for disadvantaged populations. He currently serves on a national steering committee to establish a network of support for dads and their families throughout Canada.

Don McCaskill has taught in the Department of Indigenous Studies at Trent University for 38 years. He was chair for 12 years and was the founding director of the indigenous studies PhD program, the first such program in Canada. He has edited seven books in the fields of Aboriginal education, community development, Elders, cosmology, and international indigenous peoples. He has written numerous government reports that have had a significant impact on policy and programs. He is the director of the Indigenous Studies Thailand Year Abroad program.

Patricia Monture is a citizen of the Mohawk Nation, Grand River Territory. In the Department of Sociology at the University of Saskatchewan where she teaches, Professor Monture is also the academic coordinator of the Aboriginal Justice and Criminology program. In 2008, she received the Sarah Shorten Award from the Canadian Association of University Teachers and the Human Rights in Action Award from the Canadian Association of Elizabeth Fry Societies. She is a prolific author, and her books include: *Thunder in My Soul: A Mohawk Woman Speaks*; *Journeying Forward: Dreaming First Nations Independence*; and *First Voices: An Aboriginal Women's Reader*.

David Newhouse is Onondaga from the Six Nations of the Grand River near Brantford, Ontario. He is chair of the Department of Indigenous Studies at Trent University and an associate professor in the Business Administration program. His research interests focus on the emergence and development of modern Aboriginal society. He lives in Peterborough, Ontario, in Ashburnham Village, now East City, on land mysteriously acquired from the British Crown by the Burnham family in the mid-1850s.

Mary Jane Norris is a demographer and consultant who has specialized in Aboriginal research over the past 35 years and has held a number of senior research positions within the federal government, including Indian and Northern Affairs Canada, Statistics Canada, and Canadian Heritage. She has published in the areas of Aboriginal demography, including mobility, migration, and population projections, Aboriginal languages, and education. She is of mixed Aboriginal and non-Aboriginal ancestry, with family roots in the Algonquins of Pikwàkanagán (Golden Lake) in the Ottawa Valley. Mary Jane holds a masters degree in sociology and a BA (Honours) in sociology and economics from Carleton University.

Cora Voyageur is a sociology professor at the University of Calgary. Her research interests explore the Aboriginal experience in Canada, including leadership, employment, community and economic development, women's issues, and health. She is the author of the books *Firekeepers of the 21st Century: Women Chiefs in Canada and My Heroes Have Always Been Indians*. She is co-editor of *Hidden in Plain Sight: Contributions of Aboriginal Peoples to Canadian Identity and Culture*, volumes I and II. She is a member of the Athabasca Chipewyan First Nation from northern Alberta.

Preface and Acknowledgements

Given the public fanfare surrounding such landmark 'events' as the 1996 Royal Commission on Aboriginal Peoples (RCAP), the 'New Relationship' discussions involved in the 2005 Kelowna Accord, and Prime Minister Stephen Harper's 2008 apology for the Canadian government's full complicity in the history of Indian residential schooling, some people may wonder why there would still be a need for post-colonial dialogue and action in this country. Indeed, anyone familiar with the previous edition of *Visions of the Heart* may recall that the book opened with the following statement:

> The post-colonial age in which we live is a fundamental turning point in human history. The hallmark of this age is the movements throughout the world of diverse people seeking to challenge the basic ethnocentric tenet of colonialism: that one people's way of thinking and acting is 'the way' for all people.

Those who view human history as linear and progressive would reasonably assume that in the 10 years since the above statement was written, relations between Aboriginal people and representatives of the Canadian state would have become more respectful and democratic, that individually and collectively Aboriginal people in this country would have more control over their lives, and that the material conditions of life for Aboriginal people in varied geographical contexts would have improved significantly.

As is evident in the following collection, however, things are rarely if ever as we think they should be. For example, Canada has a relatively long-standing international reputation as somewhat of a 'peaceable and prosperous country of order and good government'. It is evident throughout *Visions of the Heart* that this notion is easily dismantled if one looks at past and present conditions in this country with a careful and critical eye. However, because this reputation continues to be cultivated in many different ways and contexts, it is understandably difficult for those who have little direct knowledge of Aboriginal life in Canada to believe that the experiences and circumstances of Aboriginal individuals, communities, and Nations throughout the country could be all that bad. For example, anyone who watched the inspiring and joyful celebration of

Canada's Aboriginal peoples throughout the opening ceremony of the Vancouver Olympics might easily assume that such a display reflects the current status and circumstances of Aboriginal people throughout the country. They may well have thought (and preferred to believe) that the story televised from Vancouver's BC Place Stadium on 12 February 2010 *is* the story of Canada's Aboriginal peoples. It is certainly a far more pleasant and thus *palatable* story than the everyday reports of Aboriginal people throughout this country experiencing widespread poverty and other expressions of material disadvantage, injustice at the hands of the country's criminal justice system, serious health conditions, and loss of cultural traditions, ancestral languages, and other means of maintaining and cultivating their identity. Contributors to this collection are not by any means of the mind that all is bleak for Aboriginal peoples in Canada, and indeed it remains a hallmark of *Visions of the Heart* that we focus attention throughout our writing on much that is good and hopeful in their lives. Nonetheless, it is to bring clarity and understanding to honest, forward-looking dialogue that *Visions of the Heart* has been written.

Our commitment and vision is, however, not only to help tell the story of relations between Aboriginal peoples and the rest of Canada. We are also committed to walking and working with Ovide Mercredi and others who seek to understand as well as effect positive, transformational change in this country:

> The greatest ambitions of aboriginal peoples are to restore and reclaim their assaulted cultures and languages, to own land and resources, to re-build their economy, and to re-establish governments based on indigenous concepts of consensual democracy that will provide their people with the legacy of good government Canada has failed to offer.

> Our vision includes respect for civil and human rights, and the freedom of individuals to participate in Canada's national life, free from discrimination, racism, or poverty. It is a vision that would allow our people to be themselves, to advance as distinct peoples, and yet remain active and contributing citizens of a country that has finally stopped hurting them (Ovide Mercredi).[1]

The vision for the future of Aboriginal people in Canada as expressed by Ovide Mercredi can be found in all post-colonial discourse that seeks positive,

[1]Retrieved on-line at www.greatquestions.com/e/q3_mercredi_2.html.

transformational change. As David Newhouse and Yale Belanger note in their discussion of Aboriginal politics, it is a vision of social justice and reconciliation that can only be realized through collaboration, cooperation, accommodation, coexistence, and acceptance of diversity. In the Canadian context, it is a vision for Aboriginal people and the rest of Canada that, according to Marlene Brant Castellano in her observations on recent developments surrounding Elder wisdom, seeks to 'realize *pimatziwin*, living well in Anishinaabe tradition, and *peace*, the ideal of respect and mutual responsibility valued in Iroquois tradition'. Although contributors to this collection express a degree of optimism regarding recent developments involving Canada's Aboriginal people, they also recognize that ours is not fully a time of *pimatziwin* and *peace*. It is our hope that *Visions of the Heart* will help in some way to bring us closer to that time.

Acknowledgements

Editing this edition of *Visions of the Heart* has been a challenging though once again thoroughly rewarding experience. The reason it was a challenge was largely because the second edition was published more than 10 years ago. Much has happened in Canada during that time, so 'doing justice' to all that has happened is no small task. Moreover, providing editorial guidance to those who had previously contributed to *Visions of the Heart* was potentially hazardous, given that each of them had become somewhat older and wiser since the last edition. For some contributors who had moved on to different projects and concerns, the timing for 'revisiting' *Visions of the Heart* was less than ideal. Nonetheless, along with the many previous contributors who welcomed the opportunity to take part in this renewed project, a number of new contributors joined our project with enthusiasm and a wealth of experience and insight. I am therefore once again grateful to each of them for bringing their wisdom, insight, and commitment to the hopeful vision that informs *Visions of the Heart*. Olive and I are thankful that Katherine Skene and Phyllis Wilson of Oxford University Press were both thoroughly pleased to welcome us to the task of putting this book together for OUP. Undoubtedly, my editorial burden would have been much heavier had not Peter Chambers of OUP been as supportive, encouraging, and professionally skilled as he was in helping to bring *Visions* to production. I would also like to express appreciation for the way that Dorothy Turnbull's copyediting acumen provided proper flow to the reading. I continue to be thankful to my colleagues and students at The King's University College, who challenge as well as inspire me on a daily basis to think critically, deeply, and inclusively about the social world we inhabit as well as the one we envision as possible.

On a more personal note, there are two people I would like to thank not only for their contribution to my understanding and work but more significantly for their dedication and wisdom in guiding us into a much more deep and broad understanding of the ways and histories of Aboriginal people in Canada. They are Dr Joseph Couture and Dr Olive Dickason. I had the privilege of first meeting with Joe Couture in 1994 when I was putting together the collection of contributions to the first edition of *Visions of the Heart*. I was quite familiar with his writing in the area of Aboriginal Elders and sensed that his contribution was vital to both the spirit and the vision of our book. In our first conversation, I rather naively asked Joe about the vision of his own heart and what it meant for him to be an Elder. He paused for moment, looked at me with a glint in his eye, and then replied in his rather matter-of-fact way: 'Oh no, I'm not an Elder. I'm still an Elder in training. There are those who are wise, and I still have much to learn from them.' We were honoured that Joe gave permission to include his timeless article on Elders in that first edition, and I am grateful that his wife Ruth gave us permission to include it once again in this one. It should also please us all that Ruth and co-editor Dr Virginia McGowan are in the process of publishing a collection of Joe's writings in a book entitled *A Metaphoric Mind: Selected Writings of Dr. Joseph Couture*, as his ability to make clear sense of the practical relevance of deep truths and the wise vision he had for the future of Canada deserve as wide a reading as possible.

I would also like to acknowledge my deep appreciation, respect, and love for my mentor and friend Olive. It is now more than 15 years since I rather brashly phoned Dr Olive Dickason with an idea for a book that 'needed her guidance and contribution'. I admit now that I was nervous in approaching her, for I was very aware of the discrepancy between the accomplishments of my early scholarly career and the significance of Olive's groundbreaking contributions to our understanding of Native history in Canada. Thankfully (and I know now not surprisingly), Olive was thoroughly gracious and invited me to send her my outline to look over. I called her the next day and was quite humbled when she responded that she would be honoured to be part of *Visions of the Heart* and that she looked forward to working with me on this very interesting project 'and maybe learning a thing or two'. As I look back on our relationship, my feelings are somewhat bittersweet when I think of my visit with Olive at her home in Ottawa in the summer of 2009 to talk about this edition of *Visions of the Heart*. I learned just prior to our meeting that she had experienced a minor stroke that had affected some of her memory. Olive was gracious and humorous as ever in welcoming 'the esteemed Dr David Long'. As we talked about everything from her growing up on a trap line in northern Manitoba to her thoughts about 'that rather misguided fellow Columbus' and how she felt that 'it is simply time that Canada sets things right with its original people', I came to realize that while her feisty and celebratory personality may have faded from the public scene, Olive was still very present and very much a gift to me. It is unfortunate that personal discomfort often prevents academics (and others) from publicly acknowledging when 'one of their own' moves out of the limelight because of the reality of aging and human frailty, for in some ways this indicates how impersonal and non-communal our relations with one another are. Along with receiving the gift of graciousness from Olive during the time I have known her, I have learned much about the necessity of dogged determination, serious discipline and rigor, and commitment to integrity and justice in scholarship. While dedicating a book pales in comparison to the gift that she has been to me, I wish to dedicate this edition of *Visions of the Heart* and all that is good that comes from it to my friend, Elder, and fellow sojourner, Olive Patricia Dickason.

In peace and hope,
David Long

Introduction

David Long

Indigenous people have had more than one hundred years of experience with outsiders who have come into their communities to conduct research framed by 'The Indian problem'. . . . Today 'The Indian Problem' paradigm continues to problematize Indigenous peoples by studying Indigenous poverty, the justice system, education, health, and a host of other complex issues as 'Indian' problems rather than as systemic problems inherent in a society that historically treats Indigenous peoples as outsiders or others.[1]

Saskatchewan Indian Federated College

Contributors to *Visions of the Heart* agree that the 'The Indian Problem' paradigm is colonial through and through. And while we also agree that post-colonial analysis and action is the way forward, we recognize that engaging readers in post-colonial dialogue is no easy task. Most significantly, post-colonial dialogue challenges participants to pay critical attention to colonial attitudes, relations, processes, and structures that have disaffected and even destroyed the lives of many. The challenge for many readers is that the attitudes, relations, processes, and structures they are asked to examine critically happen to have built and maintained the very system that grants them privilege. While post-colonial dialogue may well be uncomfortable, it is also the case that there are different ways of seeing the problems it points to and envisioning a way forward. In *Visions of the Heart*, we take the hopeful, visionary lead of those who wrote the following in the final report of the Royal Commission on Aboriginal Peoples (RCAP):

> The new partnership we envision is much more than a political or institutional one. It must be a heartfelt commitment among peoples to live together in peace, harmony and mutual support. For this kind of commitment to emerge from the current climate of tension and distrust, it must be founded in visionary principles. It must also have practical mechanisms to resolve accumulated disputes and regulate the daily workings of the relationship.[2]

It is in light of this vision that contributors to *Visions of the Heart* invite readers to reflect critically on a wide variety of forward-looking questions surrounding Aboriginal issues in Canada. Given the diversity of perspectives surrounding Aboriginal issues in Canada and the complexity of the subject matter, it should come as little surprise that the articles in this collection do not flow in a smooth and uniform manner from beginning to end. We recognize that even the ordering of chapters in a collection such as this is somewhat arbitrary and that other editors might well have decided, contrary to the order of presentation we have chosen, that 'the first should have been last and the last should have been first.'

This is not to say that we are presenting a haphazard and disconnected array of articles, for a number of key themes thread their way throughout the collection. Briefly, these themes include the purpose of seeking positive transformational change, the necessity and challenge of working toward positive transformational change, the unique touchstone of positive transformational change in Canada in the form of the RCAP, and the means by which contributors to *Visions of the Heart* give account of positive, transformational change in this country. The remainder of this introduction provides a detailed description of each theme as well an explanation of how and why they inform the articles in this collection.

The Purpose of Seeking Positive Transformational Change: Affirming Aboriginal Identity

In our cultures, to vision quest is strong and good medicine. To have a vision for the people is powerful and to fulfil a vision for the people is sacred. Our ancestors were given visions by the Creator, which lead the people to govern themselves.[3]

Morningstar Mercredi

Where there is no guiding vision, a people will run unrestrained and perish.

Proverbs 29:18

The main theme that runs throughout *Visions of the Heart* is that questions and issues surrounding identity are at the centre of all post-colonial discourse. As noted by Morningstar Mercredi and the writer of the Proverbs, vision is a sacred gift that is at the heart of a people's identity, and where there is no vision a people perish. Whenever a people understand and follow the vision of their hearts, they have guidance, direction, and hope.

Unfortunately for Aboriginal people in Canada, the relatively brief history of colonialism in this country is a history of the denial of their Aboriginal identity. In contrast, in her discussion of Aboriginal history in this volume and elsewhere, Olive Dickason presents clear evidence that Aboriginal peoples in all their diversity lived and moved throughout the land of Turtle Island (i.e., present-day North America) for thousands of years prior to the arrival of Europeans. Out of their 11 indigenous language families emerged 53 different languages, and as noted by Mary Jane Norris in her 'demography of language' discussion, each of them has been given unique expression by people living in different times and places. Jan Hare notes similarly in her discussions of Aboriginal education that the varied complexity of Aboriginal communities, settlements, and Nations was evident in their unique knowledge systems, cultural traditions and values, economic and political arrangements, familial and kin relationships, and languages. In short, each and every Aboriginal community, settlement, band, and Nation has its own unique history that has shaped its present-day culture and relations with the rest of Canada. As Olive Dickason asserts, to ignore the rich histories of Aboriginal peoples before and after European settlement is to ignore an essential element of this land's identity.

Perhaps the most significant challenge in putting together a collection of articles on Aboriginal issues in Canada is honouring the complexity of issues surrounding Aboriginal life in Canada both past and present. A related challenge is acknowledging that while it is possible to generalize to a certain extent about 'Aboriginal issues in Canada', there are significant historical, linguistic, cultural, political, economic, and legal differences among First Nation, Inuit, and Métis people that simply should not be glossed over or ignored—not to mention the tremendous diversity that exists among bands and communities within each of these major Aboriginal population groups. Notwithstanding the challenges of doing so, *Visions of the Heart* invites readers to reflect critically on past and present developments that involve a wide variety of Aboriginal population groups in this country. Apart from Cora Voyageur, who focuses most of her analysis on First Nation women, the articles in this collection provide insight into the issues facing Aboriginal people in Canada in general as well as circumstances and issues that are specific to certain First Nations, Métis, and Inuit populations and groups throughout this country. Most notably, they draw attention to the various ways and contexts in which Aboriginal people are reclaiming their identity by (re)turning to indigenous wisdom, which Jan Hare notes is contributing to the revitalizing and in many instances re-establishing of traditional knowledge systems, cultural traditions and values, and ancestral languages. This points to the fact that while post-colonial discourse and action often focus on deconstructing and dismantling the ways and means of colonialism, their *raison d'être* is the affirmation of a people's identity. It is vital to remember this when trying to make sense of the 'movements' of Aboriginal peoples in Canada. As Olive Dickason (1997, 412) notes:

> If any one theme can be traced throughout the history of Canada's Amerindians, it is the persistence of their identity. The confident expectation of Europeans that Indians were a vanishing people, the remnants of whom would finally be absorbed by the dominant society, has not happened. If anything, Indians are more prominent in the collective conscience of the nation than they have ever been, and if anyone is doing the absorbing it is the Indians. Adaptability has always been the key to their survival; it is the strongest of the Amerindian traditions. Just as the dominant society has learned from the Indians, so the Indians have absorbed much from the dominant society, but they have done it in their own way. In other words, Indians have survived as Indians and have preferred to remain as such even at the cost of social and economic inequality.

We therefore think it essential that readers understand that the underlying concern of Aboriginal people in Canada is not simply to *become* more Aboriginal in a highly Western context. Rather, their concern is to (re)claim and revitalize their Aboriginal identity in a manner that will positively transform their individual lives, families, communities, organizations, and Nations as well as their relations with the rest of Canada. Those who embrace this 'way forward' share the conviction that post-colonial dialogue and action is necessary to transform Canada in ways that benefit us all.

Accordingly, contributors to *Visions of the Heart* examine current issues and activities involving Aboriginal people at a number of levels and in a wide variety of historical and current contexts. For example, Cora Voyageur and Simon Brascoupé, as well as Kim Anderson and Jessica Ball, invite readers to reflect on the everyday, grass-roots experiences and perspectives of Aboriginal people in particular communities. Joe Couture and Marlene Brant Castellano offer engaging accounts of the re-emergence of Aboriginal Elders that illustrate particularly well the lesson that guiding wisdom serves best those who are patiently committed to one another over time. Also, Augie Fleras's insightful analysis of the relationship between media representations and Aboriginal identity, Kevin FitzMaurice and Don McCaskill's insights into the complex developments and questions surrounding Aboriginal identity in urban areas, Jan Hare's as well as Kim Anderson and Jessica Ball's moving analyses of transformational changes taking place in educational and familial contexts, Patricia Monture's perceptive analysis of Aboriginal (in)justice in the context of international human rights, and Simon Brascoupé's insights into the effects of an indigenous vision of economic and technological development all demonstrate that critically hopeful analysis of different levels of Aboriginal life can deepen our appreciation of the creative determination that is fundamental to Aboriginal identity, as well as provide insight into uniquely Aboriginal ways of bringing about positive, transformational change.

Unlike the authors of most historical and social scientific accounts of Aboriginal life in Canada, contributors to *Visions of the Heart* also invite as well as challenge readers to reflect critically on how they and others make sense of Aboriginal issues in Canada. A significant benefit of doing so is that readers are forced to confront the fact that even the most sensitive and respectful dialogue can cultivate diverse and sometimes even competing 'versions' of experiences, circumstances, and events. As much post-colonial dialogue makes clear, each particular version gives concrete expression to the identity of the one who is telling the story. Thanks in particular to Olive Dickason, we are now much more aware of how and why taking 'the Native factor' seriously can both broaden and deepen our understanding of Canada's history. We invite readers to reflect in a similar way on which particular 'version' of Canada's past and present history they identify with and what this says about their vision for the country's future.

The Meaning of Transformational Change: Cultivating Post-colonial Dialogue

As Olive Dickason notes, Europeans from France and England ventured across the ocean roughly 500 years ago to explore and discover lands on which to settle and resources and possibly people to exploit. While history attests to countless destructive visions based on a belief in the superiority of some and the inferiority of others, the ethnocentric vision that Europeans sought to impose on the Aboriginal people of this land was also fundamentally colonizing in nature. By and large, this vision was informed by a perspective that regarded the Aboriginal inhabitants of the lands they 'discovered' as *l'homme sauvage*. Consequently, whether colonizers viewed the 'savages' they sought to assimilate or exterminate as noble or hopelessly inferior, their new world vision had little if any room for indigenous ways of thinking and acting. Unfortunately for their many generations of descendants, the spirit and imprint of a colonizing vision continues to be evident in virtually every spiritual, physical, cultural, relational, and structural area of Aboriginal life in this country. The result, as is discussed throughout *Visions of the Heart*, is a history of painful and even deadly experiences, broken and unhealthy relations, and deeply embedded and thoroughly oppressive cultural attitudes and institutional structures.

Engaging in serious post-colonial dialogue that seeks a hopeful way forward is therefore vital to positive, transformational change, since it challenges and enables those who are involved to understand and seek to change the circumstances, social attitudes, processes, and structures that privilege some at the expense of 'others'. Post-colonial dialogue that envisions positive transformational change therefore seeks to not only deconstruct and dismantle social relations and conditions that breed social injustice and inequality but also to effect liberating social change by giving voice to the experiences, perspectives, and visions of those whose lives have been disadvantaged and in many respects destroyed by colonization. It is this very vision that informs our analyses of issues surrounding Aboriginal Elders, language, women, leadership, education, family, identity and urban mobility, health, justice, and technological change. And while contributors to *Visions of the Heart* agree that there are clear indications over the past 50 or so years of a 'post-colonial turn' in Canada, we disagree with those who argue that the age in which we live can properly be called post-colonial. Two of the most obvious reasons for this are that: (1) there is clear evidence that colonizing experiences, relations, processes, and structures continue to abound in Canada and that Aboriginal individuals, communities, and Nations in this country have to fight each and every day for the right to have control over most areas of their lives and (2) quite apart from such official statements as the prime minister's 2008 apology for the Government of Canada's role in Indian residential schools[4] and the lofty sentiments of the 'New Relationship' expressed in the 2005 Kelowna Accord, there appears to be little evidence that official representatives of the Canadian state are sincerely committed to treating Aboriginal people in terms of equality, dignity, and respect. In commenting on the lack of governmental action in the five years since the Kelowna meetings, National Chief Phil Fontaine stated that 'When we met here many years ago, it was quite a moment—I thought we were finally going to turn a corner. It set out real outcomes based on real targets . . . but it has been a missed opportunity.'[5]

Referring to this or any other age as post-colonial assumes not only that large-scale movements of diverse people have managed to successfully challenge the basic ethnocentric tenet of colonialism but also that these movements resulted in a fundamental restructuring of colonial relations in ways that brought liberation to the oppressed and resulted in them gaining meaningful control over the social and material conditions of their lives. Certainly there is much evidence presented throughout this volume of significant and very positive changes in the physical, social, political, legal, and economic conditions of Aboriginal peoples' lives in this country. However, the existence of post-colonial dialogue and developments does not necessarily indicate that we live in a post-colonial age. As you engage the following collection of articles, we thus invite you to reflect on how you think a post-colonial Canada would look and whether or not you think the evidence we present supports the view that the Canada in which we live can properly be termed post-colonial.

The Touchstone of Transformational Change in Canada: The Royal Commission on Aboriginal Peoples

The third theme connecting the articles in this collection is the RCAP. Contributors to *Visions of the Heart* share the critically hopeful vision for relations between Aboriginal people and the Canadian state expressed in the following excerpt from the RCAP final report (1996). According to the commissioners,

> [A] vision of a balanced relationship has been a constant theme in our work as a Commission. . . . [W]e rejected the idea that the past can simply be put aside and forgotten as we seek to build a new relationship. What we should strive for instead is a renewed relationship. The concept of renewal expresses better the blend of historical sensitivity and creative initiative that should characterize future relations among Aboriginal and non-Aboriginal people in this country. It would be false and unjust to suggest that we start entirely anew, false and unjust to attempt to wipe the slate clean, ignoring both the wrongs of the past and the rights flowing from our previous relationships and interactions.

Throughout this collection, authors highlight numerous ways in which the RCAP represents the first real watershed of hope for relations between Aboriginal people and the rest of Canada. For one, they note that it was a unique occurrence in Canada's history as thousands of Aboriginal people from all across Canada shared their deeply personal stories with all Canadians. The fact that so many were willing to open their hearts and speak their truth signified that they felt safe to publicly tell of their experiences and share their insights in relation to the history, place, and circumstances experienced by Aboriginal people in Canada. Together, RCAP submissions testified to the resilience, resourcefulness, courage, strength, understanding, trust, and wisdom of Aboriginal people and their supporters. The RCAP thus foreshadowed a Canada quite different and much more hopeful than the one it testified to, since it not only envisioned a Canada in which Aboriginal people have confidence and pride in themselves, their communities, their cultures, and their place in Canadian society but also a Canada in which Aboriginal people have autonomy and control over their individual and collective lives (RCAP 1996, 12).

While all contributors to this collection share this vision of Canada, we recognize, as Augie Fleras notes in his analysis of the politics of representation, that it clearly requires much more than a general agreement by different people to live together separately. This is particularly obvious when we listen carefully to the many accounts presented to the RCAP, which included: deeply personal and often painful stories of abuse, addiction, poverty, violence, and loss; complex statistical analyses of health and social status indicators and demographic transitions that indicated not only difference but also significant measures of inequality between Aboriginal and non-Aboriginal people in Canada; impassioned outbursts by sometimes enraged and often profoundly sad individuals who had experienced the loss of their native languages, their traditions, their cultural identity, their legal status, their means of subsistence and livelihood, and/or their immediate as well as extended familial relations. There were those who presented detailed historical analyses of socially devastating developments in pre- as well as post-Confederation relations between Aboriginal and non-Aboriginal people in this country, while others provided insightful and wide-ranging critique of the many ways that fundamentally racist legislation, policies, and programs have long affected the lives of Aboriginal individuals, families, communities, and Nations.

Given the experiences and historical status of Aboriginal people in Canada, it is hardly surprising that there had been relatively few comprehensive examinations of Aboriginal issues in this country prior to the RCAP. While a large number of national and provincial task forces, non-government organizations, and individual researchers had examined many different areas of Aboriginal life in Canada, none of them had sought to provide a 'big picture' perspective that also honoured the everyday lives and experiences of Aboriginal people across the country. As highlighted throughout *Visions of the Heart*, that changed with the Royal Commission on Aboriginal Peoples. As a compendium of individual and collective stories, questions, experiences, and insights, the final report of the RCAP instantly became an invaluable resource for Aboriginal and non-Aboriginal leaders, researchers, students, policy-makers, lawyers, and community activists, to name a few. And while the report contains a wealth of information, valuable insights, and concrete recommendations for change, in an important respect it embodies something much more significant than the words, statistics, and ideas printed on its pages. A close reading of the transcripts and reports indicates that there was something that informed the many submissions by Aboriginal people to the RCAP that was far deeper than even the many expressions of frustration, lament, and anger. Rarely did those who spoke to the RCAP commissioners merely express anger or focus strictly on critiquing and blaming Canada and/or representatives of the Canadian state. Regardless what story they told or how they told it, those who contributed to the RCAP expressed their commitment to a new way forward in Aboriginal–non-Aboriginal relations.

Although the final RCAP report is now almost 15 years old, the social and historical significance of the RCAP is that it embodies the shared vision and commitment of those whose hope is to realize justice, peace, and wellness for Aboriginal people in Canada. As discussed in the concluding dialogue between David Newhouse and David Long, the way forward for this vision involves the cultivation of relationships between Aboriginal and non-Aboriginal people based on mutual respect, dignity, and an appreciation of difference. While there may be those who say it is time to look beyond the RCAP to more recent developments, it is our conviction that all who are truly interested in moving forward would do well to (re)acquaint themselves with the principles, personal accounts, in-depth analyses, and forward-looking policy statements that comprise the five-volume RCAP final report. To ignore it and say it is simply time to move on would be to ignore one of the most significant historical moments and documents in Canadian history.

Framing Our Stories of Transformational Change: Issues of Interest and Levels of Analysis

The diverse sources and types of data the RCAP drew upon helped to provide a picture of the past and present life of Aboriginal people that was both broad and intimate. The same can be said for *Visions of the Heart*, for the research discussed in this collection draws upon a wide variety and number of quantitative and qualitative sources of data. Quantitative data used by Mary Jane Norris, Patricia Monture, Don Kerr and Roderick Beaujot, Kevin FitzMaurice and Don McCaskill, as well as Martin Cooke and David Long, come from a large number and variety of sources including their own research; submissions to the RCAP; government-sponsored national, provincial, and territorial task forces and surveys; a variety of federal and provincial ministries; other academic and non-government studies; and numerous reports and discussion papers. Although their analyses provide important insight into 'big picture' trends and issues, these contributors recognize the dangers of generalizing from data that has been drawn from regions, cities, reserves, settlements, and towns with vastly different geographical, historical, and social characteristics. Even Mary Jane Norris, as well as Don Kerr and Roderick Beaujot, who draw upon sophisticated national-level demographic data, caution against generalizing their findings to all First Nation, non-status, Métis, or Inuit people in this country.

As an important complement to statistical analysis, qualitative research serves to 'flesh out' our understanding of human experiences and relationships. The contributions of Joe Couture, Marlene Brant Castellano, Jan Hare, Kim Anderson and Jessica Ball, Simon Brascoupé, and Patricia Monture illustrate that giving voice to the unique of experiences and perspectives of Aboriginal people deepens our understanding of the individual as well as the collective aspects of their lives. Moreover, research that honours the diverse and subtle character of human experience and relations challenges readers to reflect critically on the role of different kinds of storytellers and the validity of their stories. This is fundamental to all post-colonial discourse, since it highlights not only that social analysis is a highly interpretive act but also that the stories told by academics may sometimes cloud rather than clarify our understanding.

Our hope is that readers will join this and other similar conversations that seek to challenge and enable them to put their own understandings and perspectives of Aboriginal life in Canada to the test. To encourage dialogue beyond this book, questions specific to each contribution are included at the end of each chapter. Beyond these specific questions, we encourage readers to reflect on the more general questions of who should be responsible to initiate change and how they should go about their tasks. The glossary at the end of the book is intended to clarify how contributors understand key terms, while the further readings section at the end of each chapter offers suggestions should readers want to pursue an issue area in more depth. *Visions of the Heart* thus continues to be more than a collection of articles by individuals writing on a common theme in their area of expertise. Together, the chapters in this collection embody the kind of dialogue that values contributions from people with different experiences and sometimes quite divergent perspectives. The intent is to highlight that openness to different experiences, insights, and voices is essential to cultivating a hopeful way forward. The diverse character of this collection thus represents our way of both promoting inclusive dialogue and challenging the perspectives and activities of those who esteem unity of literary or methodological style and oneness of voice.

Fortunately, there have been significant changes over the past 50 years in the experiences of Aboriginal people in Canada and in writing by and about them.

Prior to the early 1960s, those who supported the dominant social scientific perspectives of the time assumed that social disorganization, cultural conflict, and feelings of inferiority experienced by racial and ethnic minority group members reflected their inability and/or unwillingness to adjust to rapid social and cultural change. The assumption underlying the perspectives of main(white) stream social scientists, who were apparently blind to their own ethnocentrism, was in some respects the same as that held by those whose vision it had been to colonize the 'New World'; it was the taken-for-granted superiority of those who viewed it as their right and even destiny to dominate whatever individuals, groups, and societies they deemed inferior. Consequently, in much early writing about Aboriginal people in Canada, they were blamed for having inadequate skills, for lacking understanding of European ways, and for an apparent unwillingness to do anything to alleviate their personal and social problems. Scholars, government officials, and others perpetuated this 'blaming the victim' perspective through their interpretations of the data they had gathered on everything from Aboriginal peoples' rates of physical and mental illness, family violence, suicide, homicide, incarceration, unemployment, and standards of living. Moreover, many academic and government representatives assumed that little would change, since along with blaming Aboriginal people for their own problems, they also saw them as lacking adequate technical and interpersonal skills as well as the commitment needed to address their own problems in constructive ways.

A different set of theoretical assumptions began to take hold during the 1960s in relation to the personal and social problems experienced by Aboriginal people in Canada. According to those writing out of this emerging post-colonial perspective, the different levels and contexts of colonizing social structures and processes needed to be examined in light of the experiences and perspectives of those who had been disadvantaged by colonization. In their analysis of issues affecting Aboriginal people in Canada, they noted that the 'colonizing project' of Europeans had formally (re)organized all aspects of Aboriginal life through policies and legislation that primarily served the economic, political, legal, and cultural interests of the colonizers. Their analysis of Eurocentric cultural ways and means of colonialism clearly identified how they gradually, though sometimes quite forcefully, displaced the diverse cultural ways and means of Aboriginal people in this country. In doing so, they drew attention to the fact that colonization represents a 'totalizing' phenomenon in that it leaves no area of social life unscathed, including the way that academics and others give account of the experiences and circumstances of Aboriginal people as well as their relations with the rest of Canada.

For example, it would be naive and socially unjust to ignore the personal and social significance of research studies and reports that indicate disproportionately high rates of suicide, certain types of addiction and illness, unemployment, incarceration, and interpersonal violence among certain segments of the Aboriginal population in Canada. However, it would be equally naive and unjust to assume that these reports and statistics provide a clear and fully informed sense of what life is like for Aboriginal people in this country. We all clearly need to be careful not to assume that life is as bleak as many statistics and news stories would seem to indicate. However, it is also important to recognize that there are numerous problems and even dangers in assuming that 'all is well' for Aboriginal people in this country. It is in this light that a 'critically and cautiously hopeful' spirit of post-colonial dialogue and analysis weaves its way throughout the articles in this collection.

It is also in this spirit that *Visions of the Heart* invites readers to become aware of issues surrounding the history of research and writing about Aboriginal people. One of the most basic of these issues is that historical and social scientific analysis does not merely provide an impersonal, detached approach to understanding social life in Canada. Contributors to this collection are therefore of the mind that in this somewhat tumultuous age of de/reconstruction, both academic writers and readers must take seriously our role in storytelling. We agree that open, constructive dialogue depends on those involved having a sense of how and why they view the relationship between academic research and storytelling in particular ways. While this does not necessarily require everyone to tell their own personal story every time they speak or write, it does require those involved to reflect honestly on certain fundamental philosophical, methodological, and theoretical issues in research involving human subjects. The issues that contributors to *Visions of the Heart* engage in various ways include: (1) the challenges, benefits, and drawbacks of using certain types of data, such as oral and ethnographic accounts, interviews, surveys, and archival information, to name a few; (2) the challenges of conveying the inner workings of personal relationships, families, communities, and societies to 'outsiders'; (3) general difficulties in doing cross-cultural research; (4) honouring the different experiences, concerns, and perspectives that Aboriginal and non-Aboriginal people have in relation to the lives of Aboriginal people; and (5) politically charged questions surrounding voice appropriation, all of which are fundamentally a question of the appropriateness and validity of telling another's story. Not all contributors articulate their position on all of these issues, nor would they answer them in the same way. However, all agree that their different experiences, perspectives, styles of writing, and approaches to exploring Canadian Aboriginal issues are important to the inclusive spirit and vision that animates this collection.

Concluding Remarks

Contributors to *Visions of the Heart* agree that it is the commitment of Aboriginal people to the visions of their hearts that has long animated their willingness and ability to seek personal and social justice, healing, and a hopeful way forward. It is their hope that *Visions of the Heart* will contribute to visionary post-colonial dialogue and positive, transformational change in at least two ways: by offering a critically hopeful examination of past and present sources of oppression and injustice in the lives of Aboriginal people in Canada and by challenging/enabling readers to see the many ways that Aboriginal people in this country have, in the face of these experiences, sought to realize the visions of their hearts. We are convinced that it is only by speaking about and listening to our different experiences and perspectives that truthful, hopeful dialogue can occur. The solemn importance for all of Canada to listen carefully to the words and actions of Aboriginal people is stated rather prophetically by Olive Dickason (this volume):

> Canada's First Nations (and all other Aboriginal peoples) are a vital part of our national persona, both present and future. The challenge for us all is to take a broader and deeper view of Canada's past, which will not only change our understanding of our history but will enormously enrich it. Because our sense of history is fundamental to our sense of ourselves, both as individuals and as a nation, it arms us for the formidable task of working out solutions to the social and political problems that are developing not only as a result of our rapidly evolving technology but also from our changing ideological position.

Our hope is that this collection will contribute in some small way to building a Canada in which all people live well and are able to experience a society that is truly one of peace, order, and good relations among its peoples. We share the conviction that the way forward for Aboriginal people and the rest of Canada requires us to understand and affirm that it is the inherent right of all people to govern themselves. The way forward also requires Aboriginal people and the rest of Canada to work together in cultivating a shared vision, passion, and commitment to bring justice, healing, and positive transformational change to all of Canada. As we trust is evident throughout *Visions of the Heart*, (re) examining, (re)defining, and revitalizing all our relations in this good way is the way forward.

Notes

1. Retrieved on-line at http://old.fedcan.ca/francais/pdf/issues/indigenousresearch.pdf.
2. Retrieved on-line at www.ainc-inac.gc.ca/ap/pubs/rpt/rpt-eng.asp.
3. Retrieved on-line at http://aboriginalsportcircle.ca/en/the_north_american_indigenous_ games.
4. Retrieved on-line at www.cbc.ca/canada/story/2008/06/11/pm-statement.html.
5. Retrieved on-line at www.kelowna.com/2009/10/28/near-anniversary-of-kelowna-accord-former-national-chief-phil-fontaine-spoke-about-a-country-divided.

References

Dickason, Olive Patricia. 1997. *Canada's First Nations: A History of Founding Peoples from Earliest Times*. Toronto: Oxford University Press.

Report of the Royal Commission on Aboriginal Peoples. 1996. www.collectionscanada.gc.ca/webarchives/20071115053257; www.ainc-inac.gc.ca/ch/rcap/sg/sgmm_e.html.

Saskatchewan Indian Federated College. *A Brief to Propose a National Indigenous Research Agenda*. Submitted to the Social Sciences and Humanities Research Council.

Toward a Larger View of Canada's History: The Native Factor[1]

Olive Patricia Dickason

A major lesson for many Canadians that followed from events as disparate as the Oka confrontation of 1990, the 52-day occupation of a southwestern Ontario construction site by members of the Six Nations confederacy in 2006, and Prime Minister Stephen Harper's 2008 apology for the government's role in Indian residential schools was the realization of how little they knew about their own history. It continues for many to be a most unsettling revelation to learn that the conflict evident in each event, far from being a flash in the pan, has roots that go deep into our national past—easily to the first meetings between Amerindians and Europeans and by extension even beyond, if the attitudes that both sides brought with them are included. Nothing in our standard national histories prepared Canadians for this lesson. To this day, the accepted historical approach in elementary, secondary, and post-secondary school textbooks used throughout Canada begin with the voyages of Jacques Cartier, give a brief summary of his relations with the Amerindians of the St Lawrence Valley, go on to discuss the fur trade and missionary activity that were described as radically altering the Amerindian way of life, and perhaps include something about the role of Amerindians in the colonial wars of the seventeenth and eighteenth centuries. Once launched into the political and constitutional development of our country, historians have habitually left the Amerindians far behind as picturesque but irrelevant relics of the past. Not even mentioned are the numbered treaties of the West and North by which the federal government acquired enormous areas of Amerindian lands for white settlement and industrial development, paving the way for the creation of the Canadian confederacy ('confederacy' is a common—and in this case more correct—term used by historians and others to describe a political entity). Until well into the twentieth century, Canadian historians habitually depicted Natives as barbarians much in need of the civilizing influence of whites. And while many viewed the 1996 Royal Commission on Aboriginal Peoples as a historic opportunity to meaningfully engage 'the Native Factor' in Canada's history, many others continue to question the legitimacy of examining the Amerindian side of the story.[2]

History as Defined in the Western World

History as developed in the Western world during the nineteenth century is based upon written documentation, particularly when derived from official sources (Dickason 1997, xi). Oral tradition was not considered reliable (or even pertinent) for historical purposes and so was categorically dismissed. Further, until the past few decades, the emphasis was almost exclusively on public affairs, where the powerful and important dominated; not only were the rank and file who made up the bulk of society largely excluded, but preliterate or tribal societies were almost completely ignored. Such societies were labelled prehistoric or perhaps protohistoric; the best they could hope for was to become historical by extension when they came into contact with literate societies. Since this meant that history began with the arrival of Europeans, Canadians considered theirs a young country, a land of much geography and little history.[3] As H.H. Trevor-Roper, Regius professor of modern history at Oxford University, maintained when discussing Africa, the period before the arrival of Europeans 'is largely darkness, like the history of pre-European, pre-Columbian America. And darkness is not a subject of history' (*The Rise of Christian Europe*, cited in Krech 1991, 345).

In the case of Canada, the meeting of the French and Amerindians on the North Atlantic coast in the sixteenth century was very poorly documented, because with few exceptions (principally Jacques Cartier, who made three official voyages during 1534–42), early visitors came over on their own initiative, attracted by the profits to be made from fishing and whaling. Keeping records was not a concern, except perhaps for commercial reasons, and the survival rate of those records has reflected their low official importance. It should also be remembered that these meetings were not a first, either for the French or for the Natives. The French had been trading with Amerindians in Brazil for nearly a century before they began seriously to develop the northern fur trade toward the end of the sixteenth century. By that time, northern Amerindians and Inuit had been dealing with Basque and Breton fishermen for almost as long and before that may have encountered Norse. The earliest accounts we have indicate prior familiarity on both sides (except perhaps for the Norse); nowhere in the documented Canadian experience do we find Amerindians reacting toward Europeans as they did in the Caribbean toward the Spanish, whom they at first regarded as returning spirits. The closest approximation of this that has been recorded for Canada was Cartier's reception by the people upriver on the St Lawrence above Stadacona (today's Quebec City), especially at Hochelaga (today's Montreal). There is some indication that they regarded Cartier as a shaman, with curing powers; however, their joy seems to have been mainly inspired by the French breach of Stadacona's control of the river and the consequent prospect of direct trade with the new arrivals. Known documentary sources about these contacts, patchy as they are, in most cases have not been thoroughly searched by historians with Native history in mind. Surviving records, early published material, and Native traditions all need to be re-examined with this in view. A point to remember is that written accounts, no matter how apparently objective they may seem, are always influenced by the attitudes and beliefs (not to mention the cultural outlook) of the writer. It is not unusual for these reports to differ, sometimes widely, even when dealing with the same event. This can be a particular problem with printed material, when texts have not only been edited differently in various editions but have also been changed from the original manuscript. To complicate the matter even further, many of these manuscripts are now lost. Sorting out the biases and misinformation from facts is rarely simple, no matter what the source.

Points of Departure

Obviously, undertaking a history of Canada's Aboriginal peoples is not a simple matter. Two points of departure suggest themselves. First, despite the rich variety of their cultures, there is an underlying commonality in Amerindian world views that is evident in their myths.[4] Central to the myths, wherever they are found, is the concept of the interconnectedness of all living things, all of whom are 'people' and some of whom are human. Humans are seen as part of the world system, with some advantages but also with responsibilities, rather than as the dominating force, as in the European view. These underlying assumptions meant that Amerindians and Europeans each shared a basic civilization, even though it was expressed in a multitude of ways. The 'formidable originality' of Amerindian civilizations has led some scholars to place them on a par with those of the Old World, the Han, the Gupta, and the Hellenistic age (Needham and GweiDjen 1985, 64). Canada was in the northern zone of a hemispheric civilization, just as the American hemisphere would later be on the western periphery of European civilization.

Second, it is important to keep in mind the fundamental importance of the early encounters between Europeans and Amerindians. As already noted, they set the pattern for Amerindian–white relationships that has influenced policies to this day. The general sixteenth-century European impression that Amerindians were 'sans foi, sans loi, sans roi' stemmed from first reports that New World people lacked churches and marketplaces and lived according to nature 'like beasts in the woods'. Columbus, for one, could not see that Amerindians had government, since in warm latitudes they wore little, if any, clothing. When he spoke with an elderly chief 'who seemed respectable enough although he wore no clothes', Columbus was surprised to observe 'sound judgment in a man who went naked' (Anghiera 1912, vol. 1, 1:102–3). Leading European thinkers concluded that Aristotle's doctrine 'that some men are by nature free and others servile' applied to Amerindians—in other words, that they were not yet fully developed as human beings although capable of becoming so, like children. The custom of referring to Amerindians as children, or even worse as 'savages', would endure until well into the second half of the twentieth century. Such a people were obviously not qualified to run their own affairs; besides, the rights of Christians had priority over those of non-Christians. On both these counts, Europeans had no doubts about their right to claim New World lands for themselves. As we learn more about Amerindian societies, it becomes clearer all the time how wrong these European impressions were; New World societies met individual and community needs very well and had worked out solutions to problems of living that are still viable today.

Lack of official documentation for the early contact period, at least as far as Canada is concerned, is offset to some extent by the publicity to which the discoveries gave rise. Columbus's letter making his sensational announcement was disseminated with unheard of speed, thanks to the printing press. It heralded new fashions in literature: cosmographies, particularly popular during the second half of the sixteenth and the first part of the seventeenth century, and travel tales, much in vogue during the seventeenth into the eighteenth century until they were overtaken by explorers' accounts, which hit their stride during the eighteenth and continued through to the early twentieth century. Cosmographers, as their name indicates, set themselves the task of describing the whole world and everything in it, particularly its peoples and their societies; travel accounts concentrated more on adventure, while explorers' accounts developed a scientific bent, particularly during the nineteenth and twentieth centuries. Not to be overlooked are the accounts written for special purposes, such as promoting colonization and its attendant commercial prospects. This varied literature is invaluable for the researcher because it opens a window onto the type of information that was being disseminated, as well as reactions to the wonders of worlds previously unknown to Europeans. For the student of Amerindian–white relations, this literature is in some ways more useful than official records, since it reflects more clearly the general level of knowledge and the interests of the time. As always, however, caution must be exercised, particularly when generalizing.

Early Interactions

What this literature reveals, although not always directly, is the highly charged nature that so often characterized early interactions. Far from overwhelming simple savages, Europeans often found themselves in complex and difficult negotiations from which they did not always emerge the winners. Recollet friar Gabriel 'Theodat' Sagard (fl. 1614–36) tells of one such confrontation at Tadoussac, which occurred when a chief felt the French had insulted him by offering inappropriate gifts during pre-trade ceremonies. He told his people to help themselves to whatever French trade goods they wanted, paying what they wished. Although the French were not in a position to resist, the Amerindians, on thinking the matter over, later brought extra furs to make up the value of what had been taken. Both sides agreed to forget the incident and 'to continue always in their old friendship'. As Sagard saw it, the French were more concerned about offending the Amerindians than the Amerindians were of antagonizing the French (Sagard 1939, 45–6; Dickason 1997, 82). Both the seventeenth-century entrepreneur Nicholas Denys (1598–1688) and the eighteenth-century Jesuit historian Pierre-François de Charlevoix (1682–1761) reported that some Sagamores took a haughty tone when dealing with the French; in the words of Charlevoix, they made it clear 'they were honoring the Great Sagamo of the French by treating him as an equal' (Denys 1908, 195–6; Charlevoix 1744, part I, 128).

An important factor that has been all too often overlooked by historians was the role of religion in these early encounters. Ritual was traditionally very important to Amerindians, whose most respected leaders were also shamans. A major factor in the success of the French with their Amerindian alliances was their identification of the centrality of religion in Amerindian leadership and their enlistment of these sentiments in their favour. This was of considerable consequence to the role of the missionaries, who besides functioning in their evangelical capacity also operated as agents of the state. In this, the French conformed to Amerindian political reality; as one eighteenth-century colonial governor observed, 'It is only these men [the missionaries] who can control the Savages in their duty to God and the King.'[5] Without an appreciation of how spiritual sensibilities shaped Amerindian politics, it is not possible to understand Native behaviour in relation to Europeans or, for that matter, in any other field of action. As noted previously, treaties illustrate this, as well as the roles of reciprocity and the principle of family connections.

The Role of Treaties[6]

The importance of treaties would be difficult, if not impossible, to overestimate; as long as people have lived in organized societies, treaties have been fundamental to inter-group relationships. Among Amerindians, as with tribal societies in general, treaties were major instruments for stabilizing inter-group relations. Without treaties and their resulting alliances, the situation was one of latent, if not outright, hostility. Accords were worked out on the basis of kinship and reciprocity. Fictive kinships were established through the use of family terminology to delineate relationships, and gift exchanges ('I give to you that you might give to me') symbolized the obligations incurred, which usually had social and political ramifications beyond the immediate purpose of the treaty. For the treaty to be effective, the basic exchanges had to be equal. Rituals, often both extensive and elaborate and always with spiritual ramifications, ceremonially sealed the commitments. Both rituals and exchanges had to be repeated from time to time if the treaty was to be kept alive, a recognition that changing circumstances could affect the agreements. This did not mean that treaties were by their nature short-lived; quite the contrary, some endured through the generations so that the resulting alliances came to be considered traditional.

With the arrival of Europeans, two approaches developed for negotiating treaties: to follow the Amerindian custom or to rely upon written agreements, which were supposed to be binding without further ado once they were signed. The French, armed with a century of experience in trading with Brazilian natives, favoured the former, while the later-arriving English, with less experience in dealing with Amerindians, favoured the latter. As the French saw it, negotiating within the framework of Aboriginal custom more effectively engaged the loyalty of the Natives for which written texts were unnecessary; in the British view, the written texts were a legal confirmation. The British treaties habitually included an Amerindian acknowledgment that they were now subjects of His Britannic Majesty, a provision not likely to have had its counterpart in the Amerindian-style treaties entered into by the French.[7] Whether written or unwritten, for the Amerindians the treaties were ritualized compacts that established the reciprocal balance within which relations with Europeans could evolve in harmony (Friesen 1986, 51). For the Western-trained historian, the Aboriginal approach has meant considering treaties by their results rather than by their actual terms, since these agreements were unwritten and usually unrecorded. Still, their historical importance is beyond question, as the Amerindian role in the colonial wars makes abundantly clear.

Another point for the historian to consider is the nature of the treaties themselves. All of those entered into with the French can be classified as 'peace and friendship' treaties, as can those entered into by the British until the Proclamation of 1763. They reflected the need for peaceful relations to carry on commercial activities such as trade and fisheries, as well as for European settlement. Land was negotiated for as needed on an individual basis—a procedure, however, that soon led to disputes that were augmented by the fact that Amerindians had no concept of outright individual ownership. The Proclamation, issued after the defeat of the French in North America, sought to remedy this by reserving to the British government the right to acquire Amerindian lands. This shifted the emphasis of treaties from peace and friend-ship and acknowledgment of British suzerainty, although they were still present, to negotiating terms by which lands were freed for increased European settle-ment. In effect, treaties became real estate deals—but with a difference: because of reserving to itself the sole right to acquire Amerindian lands, the British government in effect put itself in a fiduciary position toward Amerindians. In other words, the British had implicitly accepted the responsibility of ensuring that Amerindians were dealt with fairly.

Here, another dichotomy of views quickly revealed itself. The British now looked upon the treaties as a tool for extinguishing Aboriginal land rights once and for all. Ironically, they resorted to Amerindian-style metaphors to express the binding nature of the obligations incurred by these surrenders: the phrase 'as long as the sun shines and the rivers flow' first appears in a written treaty in 1794, and it was used by the British to assure the Mi'kmaq signers that they would always be provided for (Wildsmith 1985, 200). Amerindians, for their part, looked upon the treaties as reciprocal arrangements by which they agreed to allow the British to share their lands in return for a guarantee that their rights would be protected. For them, the treaties provided leeway to adapt, within the framework of their own traditions, to the demands of a changing world. Consequently, in areas where European settlement was expanding, most of the pressure for treaties came from the Amerindians themselves. The government, for its part, only entered into treaties where the lands involved were foreseen as needed either for settlement or for industrial development. Post-Proclamation treaties were first signed in southern Ontario, beginning in 1764.

In all, close to 500 treaties and agreements have been negotiated between Canada and more than half of its Aboriginal peoples. Negotiations are ongoing; an outstanding agreement that came into effect on 1 April 1999 resulted in the creation of Nunavut, which was carved out of the Northwest Territories. This new territory has a population of 25,000, of which 80 per cent are Inuit. Its first premier was Paul Okalik, an Inuit lawyer who represents Iqaluit West in the legislature. Agreements entered into in the recent past are those of the Western Arctic (with the Inuvialuit in 1984) and the James Bay Agreement of 1975. Land claims are flourishing across Canada, particularly in regions not covered by treaty but in other areas as well, such as those where the government is charged with not honouring its treaty obligations. These claims have been given a collective boost through the 1998 decision of the Supreme Court of Canada allowing oral history and tradition as legal evidence. The Supreme Court ruled that the oral history of the Gitksan Wet'suwet'en bands supporting their claim to having inhabited their British Columbia lands since time immemorial had not been given proper weight when their claim was rejected in 1991. This decision signals a fundamental change in attitude from the long-standing position of the courts that oral history and tradition were hearsay and therefore not acceptable as evidence. The implications of this shift are profound, not only for the courts but also for historians. They will take years to unfold, and historians as well as the courts would thus do well to listen to other voices and evidence.

Toward a Broader Conception

Despite the difficulties, this century has seen a move toward a broader view of history, a move that has meant, among other things, that historians have begun to pay more attention to tribal nations. Because these nations were oral rather than literate peoples (even those who did possess a form of writing had not developed it into a widely shared form of communication), reconstructing their pre-contact history in the Western sense of the term is a daunting task. The inadequacy of written sources means that researching such a history calls for an interdisciplinary approach, one that draws from geology, archeology, anthropology, linguistics, oral traditions, and the arts. Each provides insights that when pieced together with whatever documentary evidence exists help to fill in the picture. A principal problem for this approach has been the development of critical techniques to evaluate the information; crosschecking can be difficult, if possible at all. On top of that, the type of information provided by oral history does not necessarily fit the requirements of Western-style history.[8]

Before delving into research methods, two questions should be answered: why is an understanding of prehistory important, and why should historians concern themselves about first contacts if the information is so difficult to come by? To begin with the second question, first contacts set the pattern for what was to follow in Amerindian–white relationships. The first impression of Europeans that Amerindians were 'a remarkably strange and savage people, without faith, without law, without religion' (Thevet 1878, 135) crystallized into attitudes that determined patterns of relationships, which in turn influenced policies.

It is comparatively simple to trace this sequence in today's sometimes problematic relations between First Nations and mainstream society. Two clear examples are the confrontation at Oka in 1990 over land that the Mohawk claim to be theirs since time immemorial and Justice Allan McEachern's rejection in 1991 of the Gitksan and Wet'suwet'en claim to 58,000 square kilometres of traditional lands in northern British Columbia, a resource-rich area about the size of Nova Scotia. Justice McEachern denied the existence of Aboriginal rights of ownership and jurisdiction,[9] drawing on arguments that had been developed originally from the sixteenth through the eighteenth century to justify the European takeover of Aboriginal lands. According to these arguments, a sedentary lifestyle based on farming within a nation-state is a prerequisite for proprietary and sovereign rights; since hunter-gatherers changed their abodes with the seasons, they had no legitimate claims to either. The Mohawk faced the added challenge of proving that they were the first, and continuous, occupants of the lands they were claiming. Although Justice McEachern's decision was reversed on appeal, it should be clear from these and many other examples why it is important to understand the nature and history of pre-contact societies in Canada, at least as far as we are able. As Renaissance Europe had debated, were these fully formed societies, although of models very different from those of Europe? Or were they living according to nature and thus with no more property rights (or rights of any kind, for that matter) than panthers or bears, to use a nineteenth-century journalistic expression?

What Geology Has to Say

Geology is included among the disciplines that contribute to our knowledge about our First Nations because it tells us what the ecological conditions were and thus when and where humans could survive. Since Canada was largely icebound until about 14,000 to 10,000 years ago, human habitation appears to have been first confined to the few areas that escaped glaciation, such as the Yukon. In regions south of the glaciers, it has been estimated that ecological conditions have been suitable for human habitation for about 50,000 years or more. It is widely believed by scholars (although passionately disputed by many Natives) that Amerindians first crossed over from Siberia on foot during periods when intensification of the glaciation lowered the sea level, transforming the Bering Strait into a grassy strip some 2000 kilometres wide, dotted with clumps of birch, heath, and willow ('What the stone tools tell us', cited in Dickason

1997, 3). Geologists inform us that this land bridge, called Beringia, emerged several times during the late Pleistocene geological age (the Wisconsin stage) between about 75,000 and 14,000 years ago (Young 1988). It provided a rich habitat for such animals as mammoth, mastodon, giant bison, saiga antelope, and the predators that preyed on them. That the herds attracted human hunters is a reasonable assumption that is supported by archeological evidence from both sides of the Bering Strait.

However, the presence of land game does not necessarily imply that the rich marine life off the coasts was ignored. Nor did the convenience of the pedestrian route mean that it was the only one that was used. In fact, the evidence is to the contrary; early campsites tend to be by seacoasts and waterways, probably because of the comparative ease of harvesting marine resources, not to mention that of water travel. This is supported by mounting archeological evidence indicating the use of coastal water routes. As well, the Japanese Current, sweeping straight eastward across the Pacific to the Americas, provided a natural aquatic highway that would not have presented any great problems. We know that sea voyages were being undertaken as early as 50,000 years ago, since that was the time that humans reached the island continent of Australia. The argument that Arctic conditions were too dangerous for early seagoing technology is tenuous at best; the seagoing Beothuk canoe, for example, was well adapted for use among the ice floes.

Archeology Lends a Hand

Archeology has been history's tool principally in tracing the first settling of the Americas. But here also difficulties abound. Because bones do not preserve well in New World soils, the evidence of very early human presence has been based on artifacts rather than skeletal remains, a situation unique to the Americas (Dillehay 1991, 13). Rather than providing sure answers, dates established so far for human habitation have given rise to more questions, since the oldest ones have come out of unglaciated South America and the most recent ones for pre-contact migration have come from the icebound Arctic. This, of course, argues for first arrival by sea. Attempts to prove an American genesis for modern Amerindians on archeological evidence have not been successful.[10] For most Amerindians, this is not important, because scientific evidence is not needed to convince them that this is the land of their origin.

Archeology has been described as 'simply another process for understanding the past' (Devine 1991, 21). No more than other types of knowledge does it give us final answers; what it does do is provide fresh insights as new data and new dating and interpretive techniques become available, which they are at an increasing rate (Trigger 1985, 52). Dating and, especially, interpretation have always been particular problems for archeologists, who even under the best of circumstances must work with non-perishable material remains, a tiny percentage of the data that would have been available from the site when it was active. It is extremely rare for sites to be preserved as they were used. Pompeii, buried under a volcanic eruption in 79 CE, is probably the best known; in the Americas, there is Ozette, a Makah village on the Olympic Peninsula in the state of Washington, which was buried under a mudslide about 500 years before Columbus. Since Makah still live in the area, archeologists have been able to work with the people to reconstruct the village's lifestyle. More often there is little, if any, apparent connection between ancient sites and present-day inhabitants. The best that can usually be hoped for is to be able to deduce the broad outlines of the social dynamics of the communities that once occupied them. As Bruce Trigger has observed (1985, 52), archeology studies what humans made or used; while such data can sometimes suggest what people thought and did, they are inadequate for fleshing out the intricacies of social interactions. Nor, where writing is absent, can archeology pinpoint languages, except perhaps in very general terms. Even where writing in whatever form is present, unlocking its information can offer formidable challenges. Such has been the case with the hieroglyphs of the Maya of Central America, which only recently have begun to yield to long-standing and persistent efforts to reveal their secrets.

In spite of these difficulties, archeology is still our main source of information about the distant past. For one thing, it can reveal much about trade patterns by tracing the sources of non-local plants, as well as non-local materials used in the manufacture of such items as tools. For another, it can tell us much about the tools themselves. Tools as such do not reveal methods or systems of use, but as archeologists learned when they began to involve Native communities in their projects, knowledge of these ancient technological systems has not entirely disappeared. An example of what can happen through such cooperation occurred recently when archeologists and villagers of the Koani Pampa in the Bolivian altiplano cooperated to reconstruct and put into practice ancient agricultural techniques for growing potatoes and were rewarded with a dramatic increase in yield.[11] In this case, recovering an ancient technology brought material benefits to the natives concerned and satisfaction to the archeologists for having proved a point. In Canada as well, cooperation between archeologists and the Native communities affected by their work has already brought benefits, not the least of which is a much wider and deeper understanding of the complexity and creativity of our Aboriginal societies and, consequently, of ourselves as a multicultural nation.

Anthropology's Contribution

Anthropology, as a discipline, is closely connected to both archeology and history. In the widest sense, anthropology is the science of humans in their myriad diversities. Whereas history looks for its evidence principally in documents and archeology looks to artifacts and material remains, anthropology relies mainly on direct observation of living societies; it is the study of humans in terms of their time and place. History and archeology are concerned with the past, anthropology with the present, although within the framework of what went before. Physical anthropology illustrates one type of linkage with both history and archeology. Since physical characteristics are influenced by cultural behaviour, skeletal remains can tell us something about ways of life: height, for instance, can be influenced by nutrition, diet can affect jaw conformity and the condition of teeth, diseases can affect bones, and injuries can point to occupational hazards or war.

Each of these approaches to the study of humans is supplementary to the other, as was demonstrated above in the case of archeology. Historians are capitalizing more and more on anthropology as they look for information to help them understand Native behaviour as reported in the documents. Some call this partnership between anthropology and history 'ethnohistory', but the term is not universally accepted; history is history, say some historians, even if in some cases they have to turn to other than documentary evidence. The term 'ethnohistory' came into use in the 1950s following a proposal by anthropologist William N. Fenton to the Institute of Early American History and Culture that ethnologists and historians get together on the 'common ground' of Indian–white relations to enhance our understanding of the past (Merrell 1989, 94). That historians were slow to respond reflected, at least in part, hesitancies about entering unknown territory.

Language, Oral Tradition, and the Arts

Yet another discipline that contributes to this holistic approach is linguistics. Studies have shown that prehistorically unglaciated North America contained by far the greatest proportion of languages, 93 per cent, along with a higher degree of differentiation than did the glaciated areas (Dickason 1997, 5). The two most widely diffused languages in the prehistoric Americas were Cree in the once-glaciated north and Inuktitut in the icebound Arctic. The latter still shows clear traces of its Asiatic connections. Of the 500 or so languages spoken in North America, the greatest concentrations were in California and on the coast of the Gulf of Mexico; in South America, the number totalled more than 1500. It has been proposed that such a wealth of languages more likely evolved in many localities over a very long span of time rather than having been brought in by separate migrations (Gruhn 1988, 77–9). It has even been theorized that all Amerindian languages, except for NaDene (Athabascan) and EskimoAleut, developed from a single prototype called Amerind. This highly controversial hypothesis postulates three founding migrations, the first of which brought Amerind, by far the largest, most widespread, and most diversified of the three proposed basic groups (Greenberg 1987, 331–37). Such theorizing has received some support from recent genetic studies, which suggest that Amerindians have all descended from four primary maternal lineages, although this is vigorously disputed by advocates of a multiplicity of migrations (Schurr et al. 1990).[12]

As Europeans initially saw it, these riches of language were not paralleled by systems of writing. While Amerindians did not have alphabetic script, they had other means of recording information, such as using drawings, symbols, glyphs, and knotted, coloured strings. Eighteen of these systems have now been identified as being in use when the Spaniards arrived. As understanding of pictographic symbolism and various types of glyphs slowly grows, the distinction between oral and written traditions is becoming less and less clear. Such forms of communication were also once widely used in Canada. A modern example is the syllabic script developed by Methodist missionary James Evans (1801–46) at Norway House, Manitoba, which was quickly adopted across the Cree-speaking North. Evans drew on symbols already used by the Cree as well as shorthand to create the script, which was soon adapted to other Aboriginal languages as well. Today it is in wide use across the North, both by Amerindians and Inuit, and is taught in schools. A still earlier example was that of Abbé Pierre-Simon Maillard (ca. 1710–62), who by building on the work begun by earlier missionaries adapted Mi'kmaq symbols to develop a hieroglyphic script for that language (Dickason 1997, 214).

As understanding develops, so does acceptance by ethnohistorians of oral history as a source of evidence, particularly for the recent past. More controversial is such evidence for the distant past, particularly when there are different versions of the same event. In that case, independent confirmation is needed. Myths are in another realm; with their different conception of time and nature, they deal with the interconnecting patterns of the spiritual and material worlds, whereas history deals with humans within the time and space of the material world. Myths tell us about a people's view of themselves and how they relate to the world around them; history records the actions by which humans work out their destiny. Mythic descriptions of how humans came to be here are many and varied, abounding in metaphors; what these stories have in common is their emphasis on and confirmation of the peoples' place in the web of the universe as well as their fundamental attachment to the land. Besides myths and story-telling, rituals and the visual arts also have roles in explicating and recording these relationships. Orally and visually, they are all part of the dialogue by which peoples create their cultural contexts and thus define themselves. In all, their underlying message is clear: whenever Amerindians came to be here, this is their homeland; they have no bonds with any other.

Some Concluding Remarks

Recent confrontations between Amerindians and the dominant society, of which Oka, Ipperwash, and Caledonia are but the most dramatic examples, and the rise of Amerindian participation in constitutional and other national-level political debates give witness to the continuing strength of Native cultures. In treating the Native factor within a narrow focus and dismissing it as a relic of the past, historians have impoverished Canada's history. However, when reassessing the evidence, particularly for the early period, historians will have to do more than just keep the Native factor in mind: they will have to make the effort to under-stand Native concerns and above all to appreciate Native perceptions and inter-nalize them as part of Canadian history. In doing so, they will continue to learn that the Native contribution to the formation of modern Canada has been both much greater and more multifaceted than has previously been acknowledged.

   It is therefore clearly an understatement to say that Native peoples are still an active element in our society today. Amerindians have been in the forefront of the environmental movement and are increasingly playing a key role in cultural, political, and economic development initiatives across the country. It is recog-nized by many, for example, that Vancouver would not have been granted the right to host the 2010 Winter Olympics if the Lil'wat, Musqueam, Squamish, and Tsleil-Waututh First Nations, now collectively known as the Four Host First Nations, had not given their full support and worked together to present a detailed plan of how indigenous history and culture would be incorporated and honoured throughout the Games.[13] These and many other examples illus-trate that Canada's Native people are a vital part of our national persona, both present and future. The challenge that faces historians is to take a broader and deeper view of Canada's past, which will not only change our understanding of our history but will enormously enrich it. Because our sense of history is fundamental to our sense of ourselves, both as individuals and as a nation, it arms us for the formidable task of working out solutions to the social and political problems that are developing not only as a result of our rapidly evolving technology but also from our changing ideological position. As the ante rises, so does the importance of understanding our history.

Discussion Questions

1. Outline the attitudes that contribute to the view that Canada is a young country of much geography and little history. Do you think these attitudes remain prevalent today?
2. How important were first impressions in the development of European attitudes toward Amerindians? What was the effect on subsequent relations and policies?
3. What do you think is the benefit of drawing from a wide range of disciplinary perspectives such as archeology, anthropology, and geology in tracing Canada's early history?
4. What is 'ethnohistory'? Would you put it in a separate category from standard history? Why or why not?
5. How do written and unwritten treaties compare with each other?
6. In what ways do you think the Royal Commission on Aboriginal Peoples contributed to renewed interest in the history of Amerindian peoples in Canada, particularly in terms of how and why their history is told?
7. Do you think historians will play a more significant or a diminishing role in the future unfolding of Canada, and why do you see their role in the way you do?

Further Readings

Calloway, Colin. 1997. *New Worlds for All: Indians, Europeans, and the Remaking of Early America*. Baltimore: Johns Hopkins University Press.

Chiappelli, Fred, ed. 1976. *First Images of America*. 2 vols. Berkeley, CA: University of California Press.

Dickason, Olive P., with David T. McNab. 2009. *Canada's First Nations: A History of Founding Peoples from Earliest Times*. Toronto: Oxford University Press.

Josephy, Alvin M., Jr. 1992. *America in 1492*. New York: Alfred A. Knopf; Ottawa: Canadian Museum of Civilization.

McLeod, Neil. 2007. *Cree Narrative Memory*. Saskatoon: Purich Publishing.

Ray, Arthur J. 1996. *I Have Lived Here Since the World Began*. Toronto: Lester Publishing.

Weatherford, Jack. 1991. *Native Roots*. New York: Crown Publishers.

Notes

1. An earlier version of this chapter appeared in Riewe and Oakes, 1993, pp. 1–10, and some of its material is drawn from Dickason 1992 (particularly Chapter 1).
2. See James W. St G. Walker's pioneering 1971 study, 'The Indian in Canadian historical writing'. See also his follow-up article (Walker 1983).

3. On 18 June 1936, William Lyon Mackenzie King, Liberal prime minister of Canada 1921–6, 1926–30, and 1935–48, observed in the House of Commons 'that if some countries have too much history, we have too much geography' (Colombo 1974, 306).
4. Claude Levi Strauss (1988; 1981) is particularly strong on this point.
5. National Archives of Canada, Archives des Colonies, C11B 12:37 v. Saint-Ovide à Maurepas, 25 novembre 1731.
6. This section is reworked from materials published elsewhere.
7. During the colonial wars, the French repeatedly denied responsibility for the actions of the Amerindian allies on the grounds that they were independent. The Indians enthusiastically endorsed this; for example, the Abenaki in 1715 declared that the French monarch was not their king, since they already had their own natural leaders (letter of Michel Begon, cited in Dickason 1976, 13).
8. Some of these problems are described by Rowley (1993).
9. 'Land claim dismissed', *Edmonton Journal* 8 March 1991; 'Judge heard 100 witnesses, read 10,000 documents', *Edmonton Journal* 8 March 1991; 'Natives hit another dead end', *Gazette* (Montreal) 15 March 1991.
10. See, for example, Goodman 1981. Some of the various approaches to the study of early man in the Americas are found in Laughlin and Harper 1979.
11. 'Archeology makes edible impact', *Christian Science Monitor* 9 October 1991: 12. Not only did potato yields rise from 2.5 tons to 70 tons per hectare, but weather damage to crops was minimized. All this was achieved without the use of artificial fertilizers or large infusions of capital.
12. For a different interpretation of the evidence, see Milford H. Wolpoff's article in Trinkaus 1989.
13. Jack Poole, VANOC board chairman, www.vancouver2010.com/more-2010-information/aboriginal-participation/partnerships-and-collaboration/four-host-first-nations.

References

Anghiera, Pietro Martire d'. 1912. *De Orbe Novo*. 2 vols. tr. Francis Augustus MacNutt. New York: Putnam's.

Charlevoix, Pierre François. 1744. *Histoire et description generale de la Nouvelle France*. 3 vols. Paris: Giffart.

Colombo, John Robert, ed. 1974. *Colombo's Canadian Quotations*. Edmonton: Hurtig.

Denys, Nicolas. 1908. *The Description and Natural History of the Coasts of North America (Acadia)*. ed. William Ganong. Toronto: Champlain Society.

Devine, Heather. 1991. 'The role of archeology in teaching the Native past: Ideology or pedagogy?' *Canadian Journal of Native Education* 18 (1): 11–22.

Dickason, Olive Patricia. 1976. 'Louisbourg and the Indians: A study in imperial race relations, 1713–1760'. *History and Archaeology* 6: 1206.

———. 1997. *Canada's First Nations: A History of Founding Peoples*. 2nd edn. Toronto: Oxford University Press.

Dillehay, Tom D. 1991. 'The great debate on the first Americans'. *Anthropology Today* 7 (4): 12–13.

Friesen, Jean. 1986. 'Magnificent gifts: The treaties of Canada with the Indians of the northwest 1869–70'. *Transactions of the Royal Society of Canada*, ser. 5 (1): 41–51.

Goodman, Jeffrey. 1981. *American Genesis*. New York: Summit Books.

Greenberg, Joseph H. 1987. *Language in the Americas*. Stanford, CA: Stanford University Press.

Gruhn, Ruth. 1988. 'Linguistic evidence in support of the coastal route of earliest entry into the New World'. *Man* 23 (2): 77–100.

Krech, Shepard, III. 1991. 'The state of ethnohistory'. *Annual Review of Anthropology* 20: 345–75.

Laughlin, William S., and Albert B. Harper, eds. 1979. *The First Americans: Origins, Affinities, and Adaptations*. New York: Gustav Fischer.

Levi Strauss, Claude. 1981. *The Naked Man*. tr. J. Weightman and D. Weightman. New York: Harper and Row.

———. 1988. *The Jealous Potter*. tr. Benedicte Charier. Chicago: University of Chicago Press.

Merrell, James H. 1989. 'Some thoughts on colonial historians and American Indians'. *William and Mary Quarterly* 3rd ser. 46 (1): 94–119.

Needham, Joseph, and Lu GweiDjen. 1985. *TransPacific Echoes and Resonances: Listening Once Again*. Philadelphia: World Scientific.

Riewe, Rick, and Jill Oakes, eds. 1993. *Human Ecology Issues in the North*, vol. 2. Edmonton: Canadian Circumpolar Institute.

Rowley, Susan. 1993. 'Frobisher Miksanuc Inuit accounts of the Frobisher voyages'. In William W. Fitzhugh and Jacqueline S. Olin, eds, *Archaeology of the Frobisher Voyages*, 27–40. Washington: Smithsonian Institution Press.

Sagard, Gabriel. 1939. *The Long Journey to the Country of the Hurons*. tr. H.B. Langton. Toronto: Champlain Society.

Schurr, Theodore G., et al. 1990. 'Amerindian mitochrondrial DNA have rare Asian mutations at high frequencies, suggesting they derived from four primary maternal lineages'. *American Journal of Human Genetics* 46: 613–23.

Thevet, André. 1878. *Les singularitez de la France Antarctique*. ed. Paul Gaffarel. Paris: Maisonneuve (reprint of 1558 edition).

Trigger, Bruce G. 1985. *Natives and Newcomers: Canada's Heroic Age Reconsidered*. Montreal and Kingston: McGill-Queen's University Press.

Trinkaus, Erik, ed. 1989. *Emergence of Humans: Biocultural Adaptations in the Late Pleistocene*. Cambridge: Cambridge University Press.

Walker, James W. St G. 1971. 'The Indian in Canadian historical writing'. *Canadian Historical Association Historical Papers* 1971: 21–51.

———. 1983. 'The Indian in Canadian historical writing, 1971–1981'. In Ian A.L. Getty and Antoine S. Lussier, eds, *As Long as the Sun Shines and Water Flows*, 340–61. Vancouver: University of British Columbia Press.

Wildsmith, Bruce H. 1985. 'PreConfederation treaties'. In Bradford W. Morse, ed., *Aboriginal Peoples and the Law*, 200. Ottawa: Carleton University Press.

Young, Steven B. 1988. 'Beringian: An Ice Age view'. In William W. Fitzhugh and Aaron Crowell, eds, *Crossroads of Continents: Cultures of Siberia and Alaska*, 106–10. Washington: Smithsonian Institution.

2 The Role of Native Elders: Emergent Issues

Shorn of the various surface features from different cultures, Coyote and his kin represent the sheerly spontaneous in life, the pure creative spark that is our birthright as human beings and that defies fixed roles or behavior. He not only represents some primordial creativity from our earlier days, but he reminds us that such celebration of life goes on today, and he calls us to join him in the frenzy. In an ordered world of objects and labels, he represents the potency of nothingness, of chaos, of freedom—a nothingness that makes something of itself.

Erdoes and Ortiz 1984, 39

In discussing the relationship of humankind to the Earth, we must understand the basic difference between the Navajo view of Mother Earth, and what the Western European or contemporary American mind means when it tosses around poetic metaphors like 'mother nature' or 'mother earth'.

The contemporary American means that the earth and all of nature is like his natural mother. But the Navajo (and other American Indians) means that his natural mother is the closest thing he will ever know that is like his real mother—The Earth.

Begay 1979, 28

There are those who say that the Native Way holds a key, if not the key, to the future survival of mankind. They say that it is in the nature of the Native's relationship to the cosmos, the land, to all life forms, to himself, manifest in ritual and ceremony. They say that to learn the 'how and why' of the traditional Native stance is to find the key, to discover a 'saving grace' of insights and a creative power beyond any rationality, all crucial to human continuance (see Berry 1987a; Brumble 1980; Steinmetz 1984). If that is so, as I know it to be, then central to this discovery, and primary to the Native existential positioning, is the presence and function of Elders. This chapter is dedicated as a tribute to their contemporary emergence.

To that end, comments to situate somewhat my experience with Elders and some of the difficulties in writing about them are presented, some events are highlighted and interpreted, the importance of a number of Elder teachings are underscored, and the relevance of Elder inner and outer behaviours is set forth. A discussion of several other Elder-related issues leads to a conclusion to this chapter.

Introductory Remarks

I agree with Brumble (1980, 34), who says that Elders have become the focus of a 'cultural dialectic'. Involved are Elders in treaty and non-treaty communities, as well as Natives and non-Natives. Included are social scientists of all stripes pushing to observe and analyze, striving for their syntheses, as well as increasing numbers of Natives engaged in a return to their roots. Both tend to look indiscriminately to Elders, wherever they can be found, for insights and guidance (see Brown 1982, 119, for similar views). Both experience difficulties in this endeavour, the former hardly aware that what they expect to observe is restricted by the conditions necessary for their presence as observers (Carter in Rothman 1987, 71) and the latter confused by the rarity of top or true Elders and by the relative immaturity and unsteadiness of younger spiritual teachers and ceremonialists.

It is true, in my view, that Elders themselves, of whatever type and development, form an unusual phenomenon. Like all other Natives, they too have been influenced by the forces and consequences of 'contact'. Early on, they were, so to speak, hammered back into the woodwork. Long proscribed and banned by governments and churches, now barely emerged from decades of withdrawn, underground activity, they are perceived not as harbingers of a lost Eden but as the oral historians, guardians of the secrets, as interpreters of the life of the people, as unusual teachers and way-showers to the people.

In the late 1960s, triggered by a sudden, strong wave of seekers, Elders, although flattered and grateful, were initially flustered and were forced to rethink and redefine themselves and their roles. They were faced with dire and unsettling questions about identity and survival and with the basic paradoxes regarding the nature of the Native world and the fundamental issues about the world in which humans live.

My views on Elders derive in general from experiences with a number of true Elders over the years since 1971 and particularly from apprenticeship with several Medicine Elders initiated that same year.

Use of the term 'Native' herein connotes inclusivity. It refers to all Original

Peoples in Canada. In the context of this kind of discussion, by choice I favour this broad connotation, since Elders themselves of all tribes stress Native identity as being a state of mind, as it were, centred in the heart. The late Abe Burnstick's frequent reply to 'Who is an Indian?' was to exclaim, with finger stabbing his heart area, 'An Indeeyin is Indeeyin rawt heah!'[1]

A difficulty confronting Native writers is to write for print-literate readers, especially of social science and professional education perspectives, as though these readers will somehow respond as to an oral literature.

To so write requires, for one thing, keeping in hand an immense oral 'reference bibliography'—i.e., the stories, legends, prophecies, ceremonies, songs, dance, language, and customs of the people. To so write also requires that the qualitative dimensions of these sources be expressed and conveyed with integrity—e.g., the non-verbal of the storyteller and the ceremonialist—and that is virtually impossible. And although Elders have declared that the '. . . time has come to share the secrets . . . ,' its achievement remains most awkward, if not painful.

Nonetheless, in my view and that of Brumble, the task of written sharing and communication, at this time in our history, must resolutely begin (Brumble 1980, 42; see also Buller 1980; Gould 1988; Lincoln 1980). There is a need in the contemporary Native world to articulate traditional views and to transmit with discernment and discretion, to the extent possible, something of the fullness of the traditional experience and story—as embodied in the highest, most evolved Elders—in its intricacies, beauties, and ineffability. Further, in the view of Berry and others, there is a worldwide human need to survive to which Native North Americans have something significant to contribute (see Fox 1972, 1983; Hausman 1986; Steinmetz 1984).

There is therefore a challenge, and the tentative solution followed here is to write as a storyteller as much as possible, from a general, social science perspective. In other words, as I now proceed, the best I can, with the expression and sharing of my thoughts and feelings regarding my experience with Elders, my endeavour attempts to circumscribe that experience and amplify it to some extent by deliberate association with Western social science and education constructs.[2]

In so doing, the hope is to avoid what someone has called the 'barbarism of reflection'—i.e., the over-refinement that is unable to sustain the poetic wisdom and imagination that establishes and sustains true Elders—and better yet, to suggest something of how normal and natural it is for Elders to think and behave a certain way.

My proposition assumes that traditional values are dynamic[3] and can be and are being re-expressed in new forms. This is being brought about, as it should be, by Elders now coming to grips with an ever-increasing flow of Natives and non-Natives seeking advice and counsel, healing and inspiration, interpretation of the past and present, in their apprehension and concern over future survival.

Some History

The late 1960s and early 1970s witnessed the political emergence of Native organizations in Alberta. The opening round of activity by both political and service leaders and organizers, initially enthusiastic, climaxed in early 1969 in much discouragement and deep, angry frustration. Both deliberate and unplanned obstacles to program development were formidable. In negotiations, mutual distrust predominated. Confrontation was required and frequently resorted to, and conflict became a working condition in the drive to break open bureaucratic and political doors. It was also a time when programs were exceedingly difficult to start and maintain, largely for lack of adequate core and development monies and partly for lack of skill and insight on both sides. Nonetheless, in the midst of this period of dismaying hurt and resentment, a major shift in consciousness slowly dawned. It started that same year with Native leaders seeking out Elders and continued subsequently when others also began the trek back to the Elders of their tribes.

Amazingly, and concurrently, and virtually everywhere in North America, signs of revitalization appeared. However, because the challenges of past and current efforts to resolve the enormous cultural, socio-economic, and political difficulties were stark, these efforts were unsettling failures.

So began a period of intense introspection, induced by a sharp perception of disheartening results and encouraged by an intuitive sense that Natives, through a return to cultural origins, might allay their profound consternation and anger and find answers to the basic question of 'How can we change the direction of the destructive currents? The white man hasn't got any answers. What can we do for our children and our children's children? Maybe, if we talked to some old people. . . .' That incipient awareness became the theme of the beginning struggles, a theme soon variously played across the country.

A second event, also paralleled subsequently in other areas of the continent, such as the Smallboy and Mackinaw camps in the Alberta Rockies, the Rolling Thunder camp in Nevada, occurred in the fall of 1972. It is most noteworthy, for it presents clear, milestone evidence of ominous stirrings within Native consciousness.

Elders from six different tribes in Alberta gathered for 12 days on the West

Coast of Vancouver Island under the leadership of the Indian Association of Alberta. After two days of discussion on education-related issues, the following was declared:

> In order to survive in the 20th century, we must really come to grips with the White man's culture and with White ways. We must stop lamenting the past. The White man has many good things. Borrow. Master and use his technology. Discover and define the harmonies between the two general Cultures, between the basic values of the Indian Way and those of Western civilization—and thereby forge a new and stronger sense of identity. For, to be fully Indian today, we must become bilingual and bicultural. We have never had to do this before. In so doing we will survive as Indians, true to our past. We have always survived. Our history tells us so.[4]

In discussion of that statement, the following comment was made by an Elder:

> On a given day, if you ask me where you might go to find a moose, I will say 'if you go that way you won't find a moose. But, if you go that way, you will.' So now, you younger ones, think about all that. Come back once in a while and show us what you've got. And we'll tell you if what you think you have found is a moose.[5]

Because of its obvious, singular importance, one particular event has been under-scored. However, and once again, that one incident is to be understood within a continental context of similar contemporaneous events throughout 'Indian Country'. Since that era, and understandably, attention to Elders continues to accrue, especially both to their role and function and to the relevance of their teachings to contemporary Native identity and survival.

Some Teachings

A few recurring sayings reveal characteristic simplicity, range, and richness. For example:

> Don't worry. Take it easy. Do your best. It will all work out. Respect life. Respect your Elders. It's up to you. You have all the answers within you.

> Listen to what Mother Earth tells you. Speak with her. She will speak to you.

What is Life but a journey into the Light? At the centre of Life is the Light.

Soon I will cross the River, go up the Mountain, into the Light.

These typical sentences set forth a deep, strong, moral and spiritual vision and understanding. These interrelated principles are corollaries or facets of a unitary, primary traditional insight that is variously stated. For example:

The centred and quartered Circle is the sign of wholeness, of inclusiveness of all reality, of life, of balance and harmony between man and culture (traditional saying).

There are only two things you have to know about being Indian. One is that everything is alive, and two is that we're all related (Anonymous Indian).

Comment

One sees here the classic themes of holism and personalism, of relationality, of an environment and cosmos that are alive. A broad characteristic goal of traditional education has always been that the whole person in the whole of his or her life be addressed. In the traditional setting, one effectively learns how to become and be a unique expression of human potential. These same traditional processes, in the context of extended family and community Elders, describe a strong sense of responsibility both toward self and toward the community.

Such statements also, in my view, provide reference points to the seeker in his or her journey 'back' and suggest something of the richness of the spirit of tradition, as well as providing 'memory-bank data', as it were, for Elder reinterpretations, of which the 1972 declaration is a prime example.

The 1972 statement is several-fold in its importance. For example, for the first time since the signing of the western treaties, top Elders responded in assembly as the historians of their tribes, as philosophers and teachers of tradition. They expressed anew for the people the meaning of their history, in light of present conditions, and pointed out a saving and safe direction to pursue so that the people's history be sustained and forwarded.

Crucial as well is that to describe the behaviour needed, Elders focused on needed connections between the two general cultures, urging discerning openness and selectivity over distrusting and closed defensiveness. A further emphasis of the declaration is the redefinition of Native identity—a landmark moment—for becoming bicultural is designated as a positive, warranted, existential act. At that meeting, it was clearly understood that to be bilingual would always be 'better' and 'richer', but what the Elders affirmed is that bilingualism is not essential for a core-sense of self as Native, thus keeping open the possibility of authentic Nativeness to those large numbers of Natives who, for whatever reason, do not speak a Native language.

Thus, criteria were defined whereby the survival movement could judge whether or not it has found a 'moose'. That day, Elder mediation empowered, sanctioned, formalized, and redirected the struggling emergence of the people.

Grown men cried that day. . . .

Traditional Native holism and personalism, as a culturally shaped human process of being/becoming, is rooted in a relationship with Father Sky, the cosmos, and with Mother Earth, the land—a characteristic that has led comparative religionists to rank Native American religion as a fifth classical world religion. These experts point to the centrality of land in Native spiritual and religious experience as its distinctive dimension (see Hultkranz in Capps 1976, 86–106; see also Berry 1987b; Fox 1972, 1983). This relationship with the land/cosmos is personalized and personal and marked by a trust and a respect that stems from a direct and sustained experience of the oneness of all reality, of the livingness of the land.

The richness of this holism and personalism extends further. When one looks beyond or behind the externals of local and regional custom, language, and history, more of the core dynamic of the Native way of life is revealed. In the West, classical existentialism stresses the utter validity of subjectivity—i.e., of the feeling, reflective subject who has the freedom to make choices and to thus determine his or her life. Therefore, what one does is of keystone importance. The doing that characterizes the Native way is a doing that concerns itself with being and becoming a unique person, one fully responsible for one's own life and actions within family and community. Finding one's path and following it is a characteristic Native enterprise, which leads to or makes for the attainment of inner and outer balance. This is in marked contrast with general Western doing, which tends and strains toward having, objectifying, manipulating, 'thingifying' every one and every thing it touches (see Couture 1987, 180–2).

Behavioural Features

The exemplars of such a way of living, relating, and perceiving, of course, are the most evolved, or 'true', Elders. The preceding references to typical sayings may now be usefully supplemented by a description of a number of Elders' behaviours.

It is no simple matter to describe Elder behaviour because of the deep inter-connectedness of all facets of their behaviour. The observations that follow are not rigorously organized in pyramidal fashion but rather as one link leading to the next, in cyclical fashion up and around a single conceptual axis—Elders.

Comment

I am of the opinion that true Elders are superb embodiments of highly developed human potential. They exemplify the kind of person that a traditional, cultur-ally based learning environment can and does form and mould. Elders also are evidence that Natives know a way to high human development, to a degree greater than generally suspected. Their qualities of mind (intuition, intellect, memory, imagination) and emotion, their profound and refined moral sense manifest in an exquisite sense of humour, in a sense of caring and communica-tion finesse in teaching and counselling, together with a high level of spiritual and psychic attainment, are perceived as clear behavioural indicators, deserving careful attention if not compelling emulation.

To relate to Elders, to observe and listen carefully, and to come to understand the what, why, and how of such behaviours grounds, or enroots, one, so to speak, in the living earth of Native tradition.

It is not possible to study and examine Elders in the conventional sense, simply because that is not the 'way'. One learns about Elders by learning from them over a long period of time, by becoming comfortable with a learning-by-doing model. Their counselling and teaching focus on learning from one's experience. Thus, through respectful and patient observation, evidence of remarkable, incisive intellect, of tested wisdom, of sharp and comprehensive ability, allied with excellent memory recall, and of well-developed discursive ability is eventually perceived.

Further signs of Elderhood are found in their level of trust both of life itself and of their own experiences, in their being into true feelings (i.e., into the spiritual side of feelings, without sentimentality), in their art of being still, quiet, unafraid of darkness and nothingness, in their ability to laugh at one another as well as at self. All that characterizes them because they are trained in the lessons of how the very nature of our being is in at-one-ment with the cosmo-genesis. And so they hold to the land, ceremony, medicine, linked to the past, in Spirit (see Cordova 1938, 23–4; Buller 1980, 166).

What is the 'secret', if any, behind those admirable multi-behaviours?

My experience suggests that it is their knowledge of and skill in 'primordial experience'.[6] Primal experience for true Elders, in my view, is centred in the pervasive, encompassing reality of the Life-Force, manifest in 'laws'—the Laws of

Nature, the Laws of Energy, or the Laws of Light (Couture 1989, 82–3). In other words, true Elders are familiar with energy on a vast scale, in multiple modes— e.g., energy as healing, creative, life-giving, sustaining. Both the experience and perception of such manifestations, the manifestations themselves, reveal that all is one, is natural, and is the realm of creative Spirit—the mysterious 'Life-Force' (the WakanTanka of the Sioux). There is no 'between'—between the God-Creator, Source and Sustainer-of-Life, and the cosmos, the environment, all life forms, and Native soul (see Couture 1989).

Such outstanding qualities, levels of insight and skill, testify to an inner and personal, fundamental, consistent, and unchanging process, to a capacity to respond to life as its conditions invariably change. 'We have always survived. Our history tells us so.'

Elders represent an invitation to taste existence within the functioning of the natural world, to experience the mystique of the land. They are, Berry says, in '. . . fascination with the grandeur of the North American continent . . .' (Berry 1987a, 185). They acquire knowledge and insight into the nature of the universe. For centuries, they have wondered over the revelation of the universe.

It strikes me that their 'wisdom' is rooted in Immanence and Transcend-ence—i.e., this wisdom is attuned to the Immanent in time and space, in the dimensions and seasonal rhythm of the universe, and to the Transcendent, the Above of the confines of historical space and time. This timeless positioning makes for the Story, as carried down through the ages to its being retold and reshaped in the present day, leading to the discovery of new forms needed to transform current conditions of Native individuals and groups and thereby of humankind.

Elders hold the secrets of the dynamics of the New Vision. They are propelled by the past, are drawn absolutely to the future. Theirs is a bioconcentric vision— i.e., a vision of Earth and community, an ecological vision of an enduring Mother Earth and the people, a relationship intertwined in a single destiny. In other words, Elders hold a deep insight into the structure and functioning and manifestation of the entire ecological process (Berry 1987a, 185).

The powerful and awesome beauty of Elder vision and experience includes the contemporary state of the ecology—a deep point of agony, for Mother Earth and Father Sky are in a worldwide, unprecedented state of ecological devasta-tion and disintegration.[7]

Elders have what Berry calls 'an earth response to an earth problem' (Berry 1987a, 186). 'We need only to listen to what Mother Earth is telling us,' the Elders repeatedly utter. Their 'earth response' is the Story that has never ceased, that carries the dream of the Earth as our way into the future. In a sense, this Story holds the 'genetic and psychic encoding' needed by humankind for survival.[8] Their 'earth response' is processive through and through, and the only immutable reality is the Life-Force itself.

True Elders are as they are and do what they do because they have shamanic personalities—that is, they have a non-romantic, brilliant sensitivity to the dimensions and patterns of manifestations of the natural world in its most challenging demands and delights. As humans, as one of the Earth's life-forms, they are capable of relations so that all others can equally flourish. Their power and personality hold the ability to shake us and lead us out of the current global cultural pathology and bring us along into and through a healing and restructuring at a most basic level. They facilitate healing because they have sensitivity to the larger patterns of nature—in its harsh and deadly aspects as well as in its life-giving powers, always in balance with all life-forms.[9]

More can be said about Elder perception. Once again, their perceived world is radically, entirely relational—that is, all realities are constituents of that perception. These are what Fontinell (1988, 138) calls 'fields' of being and what Fox refers to as 'isness'.[10] Therefore, their 'faith', if that is an appropriate term, or their 'knowledge' and their 'wisdom', is of these 'fields'. Theirs is a 'faith' founded in what they experience. Characteristically, their 'faith' is a fundamental mode of experience rather than an intellectual grasp and understanding of concepts. It is also necessarily a 'knowing' that is ongoing, an open-ended task, because for one grounded in nature, there can be no once and for all determination of just what is authentic (as opposed to that which is apparent, absolute revelation) .

Elders should not be considered as concerned, therefore, with a Western sense of 'belief'—i.e., a going beyond that for which there is evidence at the present moment—but as having 'faith'—i.e., experiential knowing, an integrating experience '. . . whereby all modes of experience are brought together in a relatively cohesive whole which is expressed in the life of the person, thus rendering human life meaningful' (Fontinell 1988, 140).

I suspect that the traditional Elder capacity to accommodate change, upon contact with Western Christianity forms, readily led them to become Christian, but in a way that allowed not only transformation of perception but sustained a full continuity with the faith of the people.[11] My hypothesis is that conversion was a simple instance of new growing out of the old, forming a new syncretism congruent with their 'faith'.

Summary

I concur with Gravely, who says that a true Elder is not classifiable as a 'passive informant on the traditional past' but as 'a creative theologian, open to the possibilities of his situation, to new ideas and symbols, and to a dialogue between the traditions' (Gravely 1987, 11). Elders manifest consistency in the life process and in relationship to several worlds, moving in and out as shamans are wont to do, with seriousness and humour, with persistent attention and awareness.

Elders possess keys to a classic journey of human and Earth ecological transformation. In this era, they are being called upon to reinterpret and to apply the tradition, the Story, in a new way. There is urgency to this task, for Mother Earth is no longer looking after herself naturally but is an Earth looked after, and badly, by man. Elders are now so engaged.

Some Issues

Every turn in this chapter raises questions, or issues, that deserve more extensive exploration but which an overview description such as this precludes. Nonetheless, in this last section, aspects of either a practical or an academic concern are reviewed.

The rapid decrease in numbers of true Elders is most alarming. Who is to replace them? For some decades now, significant numbers of communities across Canada have lost all traditional Elders. Many individuals, forced to seek out Elders in other tribal traditions, initially encounter some difficulty because of differences in ways. This is a two-way pressure on both Elder and seeker.

The range of kinds of Elders also is bothersome. An Elders' prediction states that these times of emergence are to be marked by chaos and confusion before changing into a time of light and peace. Certainly a significant part of this difficult phase is attributable to 'instant' Elders, overnight wonders who, with limited ceremonies and an abundance of clichés, confuse and stall many in their personal journey. The mantle will fall to those spiritual people, less evolved, of less ability and knowledge. 'True' Elders are those who have gone through a painful encounter with spiritual realities and who thus become, in the perception of the people, an intermediary between their respective cultural communities and the spiritual forces of the universe and defenders of the community's psychic integrity. They are those who have enacted and sustained a personal relationship with nature.

Elders constitute a national issue because of their qualities and rarity (see Phillips, Troff, and Whitecalf 1976; Phillips and Troff 1977). The needs of the people require guiding wisdom as assurance of a continuing, living Native presence in Canada and during the time needed to acquire a 'faith' about the real possibility of survival.

The practical requirements of establishing and maintaining a relationship with Elders are not readily perceived. First of all, at the level of individual need and change, much time and patience is required. There are no shortcuts to attitudinal and spiritual change, no possible end-runs around phases of inner change. A complete and enduring commitment is required. Secondly, the 'return' is not only to 'primal roots', to the living core of the tradition itself, but is conditional on personal achievement so as to arrive at presenting to the world an authentic mode of living (see Berry in Hausman 1986, 7). And that is not an easy matter.

The 'knowing' of Elders is problematic to those who, for a range of reasons, were not schooled in oral tradition. Elders as 'knowers' know intimately and directly and are non-dualistic in their perceptions and understandings. Western-trained people are inherently scholastic and dualistic in perception and thinking. True, the sense of identity of Elders is marked by an ordered consciousness. However, at the same time, it is unbounded by space and time, all the while remaining in direct consideration of both dimensions of historical time and space. Again, attaining that state of development is a basic challenge.

Problematic also, and for that same kind of mind, is that Elders have consistency, continuity, and clarity of insight and skill regarding paradigmatic alteration (i.e., reinterpreting the Story), which, in my view, as Grim declares 'germinates understanding of the creative role of imagination and intuition in human history' (Grim 1987, 235). Elders are positioned, I would suggest, to contribute to facilitating what Wilson (1985, 55) calls 'quantum leaps' in developing new models of thought.

It would seem that currently, there are growing numbers of Western academic approaches hinting at hitherto unknown possible amenability with the Native mind. Keutzer, commenting on the work of such physicists as Bohm, Einstein, and Capra, suggests that such physicists are becoming students of consciousness itself (see Keutzer 1984). Their concepts of 'flow' and 'hologram', for example, and statements that 'everything is alive' are very suggestive. To Keutzer's list I would add the names of such theologians and historians as Fox and Berry and of the physicist-philosopher Swimme.

A corollary to the issue of 'knowing' is mysticism (currently a much abused and misapplied concept, in my view). From a Native spiritual standpoint, as I see it, mysticism is a question of becoming/being rooted or grounded in relationships with all constituents or dimensions of reality. I like Fox's description of mysticism because it is congruent with my understanding of Native spiritual experience. He holds that 'the essence of the mystical experience is the way we are altered to see everything from its life-filled axis, to feel the mysteries of life as they are present within and around us' (Fox 1972, 77). That's Indian!

To arrive at a direct experiential understanding of that definition is a primary learning task. To discover how ceremonies, for example, mediate helping energy and teaching takes some doing. Prayer, ritual, and ceremony ground one in life, for 'It's all deah in de sereernonees!'[12]

To acquire an awareness of all Earth forms as having a life of their own, to become aware of all as Spirit-bearing, as Spirit-expressing, also takes some doing. To become steeped in, adept in Native mysticism is to enter into the beautiful, the truth, the oneness, in balance against all negativity and absence. It is to activate and sustain personal discovery, which leads to a true sense of self-understanding, to a sense of future time through awareness of the past—which leads to learning how to intuit the close relationship between one's culture and one's genetic impulses.

Elders have teaching challenges to deal with. One is with regard to non-Natives. They are aware of the currently unfolding prophecy that 'The White brother will come to the Red brother for teaching.' There is acceptance of the non-Natives who come to them. However, they find themselves struggling with a different mindset and affectivity, as well as with language barriers. Also, because of the knowledge level of both Native and non-Native seekers, many are not grounded in a sense of the real but mysterious power of nature in mountains, rivers and lakes, rocks, life-forms, all enmeshed in the web of the universe. So the legends and stories require pedagogical adaptation. The stories have to be retold, reshaped, and refitted to meet contemporary seekers' changed and changing needs.

Such encounters are but necessary moments in the retelling and reshaping of the Story, as in the case of the 1972 declaration. New legends are emerging across the continent, sparked by Medicine Elders' dreams and visions. Tradition through Elders is converging on the present, revealing forgotten depths of perception and understanding.

Current Elder endeavour is in a tensional context. Elders are aware of the tensional exchange between the Story of the people and the need for a new direction, as we have seen. They are aware of the tensional exchange between immanent direction within living matter itself and the transcendent source of the creative impulse. They are aware of the tensional character of awakening, of the inner dynamics of spiritual and socio-political life.

Conclusion

We look to Elders for the way words are used, for the structural devices they employ, for the teaching and counselling approaches they utilize, for their philosophical and spiritual perspectives on the world, experienced and envisioned.

We look to them to show us the 'the archetypal essences appearing in animal forms', as Brown says (1982, 7). In other words, to show us the Way.

We look to them to tell us about the 'Moose'.

Daniel Deschinney, a Navajo Blessingway singer, explains how a Navajo experiences the sacred mountains' inner forms:

> When a Navajo experiences the sacred mountains' inner forms kindling new strength within himself, he says, 'I am invincible. I am beautified.' To be invincible is masculine. To be beautified is feminine. These two concepts together are a powerful entity. There is no strength from only one. Power comes from the interaction between them. When you have strength, you recognize your opportunity, you know what you must do, and you have the grace to do it (quoted by Johnson 1988, 47).

Discussion Questions

1. Why were Elders so important to Native communities in the past, and what contributed to the waning of their roles?
2. How would you explain the re-emergence of different types of Elders within and outside Native communities?
3. In what respects have Elders become the focus of a cultural dialectic? What difficulties do you think this might pose for Elders and the communities in which they live?
4. Do you know someone who is acknowledged by others as a true Elder? If you do, in what ways is this person similar to and/or different from the ideal, true Elder outlined in this chapter?
5. In what respects might the bio-centric vision of Elders benefit humanity in the future? Can you think of other ways of thinking and doing that could hinder the continued re-emergence of Elders?

Further Readings

Bouchard, Dave (text), and Roy Henry Vickers (images). 1990. *The Elders Are Watching*. Vancouver: Raincoast Books. Combined images and texts that convey lessons from Native Elders past and present. A call to reflect and dream, to imagine and envision the meaning and hope that can be drawn from the wisdom of all of our Elders.

Brown, Joseph Epes. 1982. *The Spiritual Legacy of the American Indian*. New York: Crossroad. Brown asserts that ignoring or denying the spiritual legacy offered by Native Americans contributes to the impoverishment of all peoples. He invites readers to appreciate the ways in which the living religions of Native Americans can inform and enrich our everyday lives, our cultural sensibilities, and our social, economic, legal, and political structures.

Cardinal, Douglas, and Jeanette Armstrong. 1991. *The Native Creative Process*. Penticton, BC: Theytus Books. Douglas Cardinal and Jeanette Armstrong share their understanding and vision of 'our Native way' by blending conversational commentary with striking images.

Patt, Neal, ed. 1991. *Place Where the Spirit Lives: Stories from the Archaeology and History of Manitoba.* Winnipeg: Pemmican Publications. Seven stories of Native people in Manitoba based on the writings of archeologists are combined with seven teachings from Native Elders and teachers. An example of the way in which legend and science can complement and enrich one another.

Wolfe, Alexander. 1989. *Earth Elder Stories: The Pinayzitt Path.* Saskatoon: Fifth House. Stories belonging to the descendants of Pinayzitt that tell of how Earth Elder and his people survived sickness, participated in treaty-signing, obtained the grass dance, and lived in relation to Indian agents and other non-Native people. Invites the reader into a mystical encounter with history and an historical encounter with mysticism.

Notes

1. The late Elder Abe Burnstick, Stoney Nation, Paul's Band, Duffield, Alberta, was pre-eminent as an orator and teacher.

2. This position (take regarding the difficult issue of the oral-literate mind versus the print-literate mind) finds support in the views of Geertz and Jules-Rosette, for example. Geertz holds that the main task in interpreting cultures is 'explicating explications' (Geertz 1973, 18). In other words, it is imperative to acquire the feel for the 'homely in homely context', for to fail to do so is a failure to place common-sense thought within the context of its use. The development of the 'thickest descriptions' possible becomes therefore both an ideal and necessary objective.

    It also means, as Jules-Rosette points out, dealing frontally with the problems of subjective interpretation (1978, 563). The 'veil of objectivity' masks an inability to grasp another interpretive system or style of perception. Objectivity has 'totally falsified our concept of truth' (Polanyi in Jules-Rosette 1978, 289)—the 'veil of objectivity' is a protective shield of one's own oracular structure. It covers what G. Wilson calls 'profound parasitic lay assumptions' (1987, 118). This difficulty is illustrated by the case of Carlos Casteneda. His construct of reality was so impenetrable that drugs were needed to forcefully assault it so that he could receive spiritual insight.

3. For more detail about the creative capacity of Native culture, see Couture 1987, 80–4.

4. Declaration rendered by Elder Louis Crier, Cree Nation, Ermineskin Band, Hobbema, Alberta.

5. Observation made by the late Elder Charlie Blackman, Chipewyan Nation, Cold Lake Band, Cold Lake, Alberta.

6. Huston (1953, 276) claims that 'there is, first, a Reality that is everywhere and always the same; and second, that human beings always and everywhere have access to it.'

7. See *Akwasasne Notes.* This internationally established Iroquois journal of social comment, over two decades now, has reported on ecological deterioration abundantly and consistently. With special attention to Aboriginal regions worldwide, its regular columns, in cause–effect terms, describe the autistic relationship between the ecological vision and the industrial vision.

8. See Berry 1987b for a provocative, insightful discussion of this concept.

9. See Berry 1987b, 211–12, and Kelsey 1978 for more detail on shamanic personality and qualities.

10. 'Isness' is frequent in all of Fox's writings.

11. See Gravely 1987 for discussion of the adaptability of Black Elk.

12. Elder Abe Burnstick.

References

Begay, I. 1979. 'The relationship between the people and the land'. *Akwesasne Notes* summer: 28–30.

Berry, T. 1987a. 'Creative energy'. *Cross Currents* summer/fall: 179–86.

———. 1987b. 'The dream of the Earth: Our way into the future'. *Cross Currents* summer/fall: 200–15.

———. 1987c. 'The new story: Comment on the origin, identification and transmission of values'. *Cross Currents* summer/fall: 187–99.

———. 1987d. 'Twelve principles for reflecting on the universe'. *Cross Currents* summer/fall: 216–17.

Brown, J.E. 1982. *The Spiritual Legacy of the American Indian*. New York: Crossroad.

———. 1982. 'The bison and the moth: Lakota correspondences'. *Parabola* 8 (2): 6–13.

Brumble, D. 1980. 'Anthropologists, novelists and Indian sacred material'. *Canadian Review of American Studies* 11 (spring): 31–48.

Buller, G. 1980. 'New interpretations of Native American literature: A survival technique'. *American Indian Cultural Research Journal* 4 (1 and 2): 165–77.

Capps, W., ed. 1976. *Seeing with a Native Eye*. New York: Harper and Row.

Cordova, Viola. 1938. *Philosophy and the Native American: The People before Columbus*. Albuquerque: Southwest Indian Student Coalition, University of New Mexico.

Couture, J. 1987. 'What is fundamental to Native education? Some thoughts on the relationship between thinking, feeling, and learning'. In L. Stewin and S. McCann, eds, *Contemporary Educational Issues: The Canadian Mosaic*, 78–91. Toronto: Copp Clark Pitman.

———. 1989. 'Native and non-Native encounter: A personal experience'. In W. Cragg, ed., *Challenging the Conventional: Essays in Honour of Ed Newsberry*, 123–54. Burlington, ON: Trinity Press.

Erdoes, R., and A. Ortiz, eds. 1984. *American Indian Myths and Legends* New York: Pantheon Books.

Fontinell, E. 1988. 'Faith and metaphysics revisited'. *Cross Currents* summer: 129–45.

Fox, M. 1972. *On Becoming a Musical, Mystical Bear: Spirituality American Style*. New York: Paulist Press.

———. 1983. *Meditation with Heister Eckhart*. Sante Fe, NM: Bear and Co.

Geertz, C. 1973. *The Interpretation of Cultures: Selected Essays*. New York: Basic Books.

Gould, Janice. 1988. 'A review of Louise Erdrich's *Jacklight*'. In *The People before Columbus*, 11–14. Albuquerque, NM: Southwest Indian Coalition, University of New Mexico.

Gravely, W. 1987. 'New perspectives on Nicholas Black Elk, Oglala Sioux Holy Man'. *Illif Review* 44 (winter): 1–19.

Grim, J. 1987. 'Time, history, historians in Thomas Berry's vision'. *Cross Currents* summer/fall: 225–39.

Hausman, G. 1986. *Meditation with Animals*. Albuquerque, NM: Bear and Co.

Huston, S. 1953. 'Philosophy, theology, and the primordial claim'. *Cross Currents* 28 (3): 276–88.

Johnson, T. 1988. 'The four sacred mountains of the Navajos'. *Parabol* winter: 40–7.

Jules-Rosette, Benetta. 1978. 'The veil of objectivity: Prophecy, divination, and social inquiry'. *American Anthropology* 80 (September): 549–70.

Kelsey, M. 1978. 'The modern shaman and Christian belief'. *Transcend* 22: 1–6.

Keutzer, C. 1984. 'The power of meaning: From quantum mechanics to synchronicity'. *Journal of Human Psychology* 24 (winter): 80–94.

Lincoln, K. 1980. 'Trans—To the other side of, over, across'. *American Indian Cultural and Research Journal* 4 (1 and 2): 1–17.

Philips, Donna, and R. Troff, eds. 1977. *Elders*. Saskatoon: Saskatchewan Indian Cultural College.

Philips, Donna, R. Troff, and H. Whitecalf, eds. 1976. *Kataayuk: Saskatchewan Indian Elders*. Saskatoon: Saskatchewan Indian Cultural College.

Rothman, T. 1987. 'A what you see is what you beget theory'. *Discovery* (May): 90–6, 98–9.

Steinmetz, P. 1984. *Meditation with Native Americans: Lakota Spirituality*. Santa Fe, NM: Bear and Co.

Swimme, B. 1987. 'Berry's cosmology'. *Cross Currents* (summer/fall): 218–24.

Wilson, G. 1987. 'What is effective intercultural communication?' *Canadian Ethnic Studies* 18 (1): 118–23.

Wilson, R.A. 1985. 'Quantum Leaps'. *New Age* (June): 52–5, 80.

3

Elders' Teachings in the Twenty-first Century: A Personal Reflection

Marlene Brant Castellano

No one has the range and depth of knowledge that Jake had but there are many of us who carry some of his knowledge. If we work together we can do a lot to ensure that his teachings continue.

Paul Williams, on the passing of Chief Jake Thomas, 1998

The rapid decrease in the numbers of true Elders is most alarming. Who is to replace them? . . . The mantle will fall to those spiritual people, less evolved, of less ability and knowledge.

Joe Couture

The request from the editors of this third edition of *Visions of the Heart* to contribute an article on Elders prompted the response: 'I'm not the person to write about Elders.' While I have taken to heart teachings received first-hand or by report over the years from various Elders, I do not have the authority to speak of sacred knowledge. I count myself among those 'less evolved' humans who are called upon to share what First Nations world view and knowledge have to contribute to well-being in the twenty-first century.

When I relay received wisdom, I carefully qualify my interpretations as coming out of the experience of a Mohawk woman and an academic, located in a particular context and generation, with no claim of authority to represent the real tradition. I know from reports of colleagues and friends that there are gifted individuals engaged in the rigorous and lengthy process of forma-tion to become 'intermediaries between their respective cultural communities and the spiritual forces of the universe' (Couture 2000, 42). This essay is not about those successors of 'true Elders' described in Joe Couture's paper in this volume.

The pages that follow map some of the ways that knowledge rooted in traditions as received from Elders is being shared, interpreted, applied, and transmitted outward to effect transformation in multiple domains and, perhaps, in society at large. Changes in modes of teaching are cited and in particular the concepts developed in written form.

In the last quarter of the twentieth century, a relatively small cadre of Elders firmly rooted in their respective indigenous cultures and communities in Canada and the United States became magnets for knowledge-seekers from many regions. As stories of their power to awaken identity and restore balance to body and mind were told, as kernels of their teachings were shared, these Elders reached iconic status. I suggest that with the passing of many of that generation of Elders we have entered a period of transition characterized by uncertainty about the authenticity of new messengers and hence the validity of the messages they bring.

Traditional ceremonies, indigenous languages, and community validation are proposed as reference points to help navigate through uncharted waters, complemented always by the personal responsibility of seekers to discern whether particular mentors are helping them move toward wholeness.

Viewing the Landscape from a Particular Place

I speak and write from the vantage point of a Mohawk woman and an academic who has been a witness and participant in the extraordinary process of reclaiming and affirming indigenous ways of knowing that has engaged individuals and communities across Canada over the past 40 years. My direct experience with Elders, ceremonies, and cultural teachings has centred around the Trent University community, where I have had the opportunity of extended association with Elders on faculty and periodic meetings with visiting Elders and traditional people. My understanding has been stimulated and enhanced by exchanges with colleagues and students who are on a similar path of learning, and I have been challenged in particular to translate my insights and apply them to the practice of research.

Selecting terminology to represent streams of knowledge is difficult. Ceremonies and instructions come from specific peoples—Cree, Ojibway, Mohawk—but their relevance is much broader. Aboriginal is a collective term including First Nations, Inuit, and Métis peoples in Canada, but use of the term may inappropriately gloss over the distinctiveness of peoples and their cultural heritage. Indigenous knowledge is used in international discourse to refer to the streams of knowledge from First Peoples around the world, but the term is not in common use in many communities. The adjective 'traditional' acknowledges the ancient origins of teachings but obscures the dynamic nature of those teachings as they are experienced and adapted in contemporary settings. My perspectives have been greatly influenced by socialization in a Mohawk community, association predominantly with Iroquoian and Ojibway Elders, and interpretation through the medium of the English language.

I have learned from many people, but I am particularly indebted to Chief Jake Thomas, who was a colleague and mentor at Trent University for a decade and who shared many of the teachings introduced in this essay by way of illustration. Reflections and writing of Ross Hoffman and David Newhouse have contributed to articulating key ideas that frame the paper.

Uncovering Layers of Meaning

My first remembered encounter with traditional teaching was in the early 1970s at Trent University. Chief Jake Thomas had been invited to deliver a series of public lectures on Iroquois traditions. Jake was later to become a Condoled (Hereditary) Chief[1] of the Six Nations Confederacy. He was already a linguist fluent in five Iroquoian languages and English, a speaker in demand to lead ceremonies in Canadian and American traditional communities, a carver of masks that had been gifted to royalty on behalf of Canada, an artisan who had devoted years of his life to replicating symbols of traditional life—wampum belts, the ceremonial condolence cane, and rattles—and a teacher with a wealth of stories.

In a lecture on male and female roles, Jake talked about the protocol for gathering medicine:

> When you go out to gather medicine you must prepare yourself with prayer and cleansing, otherwise the medicine will hide from you. When you find the medicine it will be growing in families and you must leave the babies because they are the next generation. You must be careful to gather both the male and the female, otherwise your medicine will have no power. When you collect water to prepare the medicine you must dip your bucket with the flow of the stream. Otherwise your medicine will have no power.[2]

Jake's words resounded deep within me. I had a sense of knowing that what he said was true, with meaning on multiple levels. He was providing a prescription for harvesting medicine plants, acknowledging the spirit of the plants and the conditions on which they would share their power. He was consciously presenting a metaphor for ordering respectful, complementary relationships between men and women. He was relating the particular human act of preparing medicine with a flow of power in the universe with which humans can align themselves. And he spoke with authority that was not his own but that of the law of life that he was conveying to us.

Jake subsequently joined the faculty of Native Studies at Trent and became a teacher of teachers as well as of students. After a lecture one day, when Jake was being bombarded with questions about traditional teachings, he chuckled: 'Everyone has so many questions about culture, and it's so simple. It's all about respect and appreciation.'

The words stayed with me but without any rich unfolding of meaning at the time. They came back powerfully in a dream. I was invited to lead a three-day workshop involving a class of social work students at the University of Manitoba, comprised of Aboriginal and non-Aboriginal practitioners. At the end of the first day of professionally organized content, the students informed me that this was not what they had come to the workshop to learn. They wanted to know how traditional culture could help them in their work. I went to sleep that night with the dilemma of what to do with the next two days unresolved.

At 3:00 a.m. I awoke with a visual image of computer paper unfolding (as it used to do) to reveal lecture notes, headed by the titles 'Respect' and 'Appreciation' in bright letters, sketching out how these Iroquoian principles correlated with good practices I had learned in social work training. At the workshop, I announced that with reassurance in a dream I was ready to share some teachings from my own culture but I would need help in connecting them to the experience of the students who were working in Cree, Ojibway, Saulteaux, and Dakota settings. One of the participants revealed that she too had had a dream in which she was instructed to do what was asked of her that day. The seven or eight First Nations students, who had scarcely spoken the previous day, accepted my invitation and took seats on each side of me to become co-leaders for the rest of the workshop.

Learning from that experience has stayed with me. The meaning of a teaching may not be evident immediately, but it will come into focus when the time is right. We need to be ready to let go of our preconceived notions of what will work and take some risks. Help is available if we are willing to reveal our need. Teachings that we receive don't tell the whole story; we have to discover the sense that they make in new circumstances. Something that took hold in my own teaching was the approach of speaking from where I sit, not trying to project my insights into others' experience. Aboriginal people, especially those of older generations, are adept at lateral learning, absorbing messages imbedded in a story and transferring them to their own context to make meaning.

When the capacity to listen deeply to stories has been disrupted by schooling that asks direct questions and demands direct answers, students of any age may need lengthy or abrupt re-orientation to actually hear the teachings of Elders.

Sites of Learning

When Aboriginal people lived on the land, members of a community from childhood and throughout their lives were instructed in the laws of life through daily experience. Language that has evolved over many generations carries the code for interpreting reality. Language is learned within the family, and the world view embodied therein is reinforced by relationships and practices of the community. Public ceremonies and private rituals give shared expression to understandings that are implicit as well as explicit. In turn, communal experiences become incorporated in the language of family and community. The mutually reinforcing influence of each of these learning sites—language, family, community, and ceremony—is like a medicine wheel, always in motion, with each quadrant drawing from and enriching all the others.

A central feature of experience in traditional Mohawk society was the recital of the Thanksgiving Address, the words that come before all others, at the opening of any communal event. After acknowledging those who have come from different directions, the speaker invites all the assembly to put our minds together as one and give thanks to Mother Earth who supports our feet and brings forth all manner of life upon the Earth. The speaker then proceeds to give thanks to the waters that are essential to life; to the plants that give medicines, nourishment, and shelter to the people and all other life; to the birds that mark the passing of the seasons and please our ears with beautiful songs; to the animals of fields and forest who sacrifice their lives for our sustenance; to our elder brother the Sun who gives warmth and light to all creatures and marks the times upon the Earth; to our Grandmother the moon whose concern is for the faces of future generations coming to us from the Earth; to the stars and unseen forces of the four directions.

In each cycle of thanksgiving, the speaker affirms that all of those named have been faithful to the instructions given to them at the creation. The Thanksgiving Address concludes with the words: 'So we look deep into our hearts and find the finest thoughts and the finest words, and we put all of these together as one and give thanks to the Creator of all.'[3]

The Thanksgiving Address now figures centrally in language learning in communities where learners of multiple generations are engaged in recovering facility in the Mohawk language. Students are not only learning a mode of communication: they are gaining awareness of their place in an interdependent web of life; they are learning that, like all creatures, they have responsibilities and that they benefit from the responsibilities fulfilled by others; they are being reminded that 'putting our minds together as one' is a sacred act; they are being affirmed as persons who have deep in their hearts 'the finest thoughts and the finest words' that are worthy of offering up to the source of life. They are learning the deep meanings of respect and appreciation.

The devastating impact of colonialist interventions in Aboriginal lives is addressed elsewhere in this volume. Political structures, land-based economies, family cohesion, languages, and cultural transmission from one generation to another have been systematically undermined. Over the past 40 years, Aboriginal individuals across Canada have been returning to the teachings and ceremonies of their own ancestors or of related cultures.

The sites of learning extend beyond the family hearth and the village council of former times. Language instruction in elementary and secondary schools and oral history and culture courses in colleges and universities reinforce or re-introduce elements of cultural education to students. Sceptics say that such fragments of cultural education are only shadows of the real thing. Jake Thomas's response to critics of his taking traditional knowledge to the university, in classes open without discrimination to Aboriginal and non-Aboriginal students, was: 'I can only give our own students a taste of the culture. It will be up to them to go back to the Longhouse to learn more. According to the Great Law of Peace[4] anyone of any nation is welcome to follow the White Roots of Peace to their source and take shelter.'

For instruction situated in traditional contexts, adults and whole families from reserves and cities make pilgrimages to camps to take part in ceremonies, fasts, language immersion, and teaching sessions. Then they return to daily lives that may be quite distant from the tribal past. Whereas in the past Elders were reluctant to have their words recorded, oral histories and interpretations of symbols carved on rock and wood or etched on birch bark are now published. The texts of speeches are transcribed and studied. Knowledge deemed to be sacred, particularly that of a ceremonial nature, is still not disclosed except to those who have been initiated into the sacred circle.

As teachings of Elders and the impact of ceremonies are carried outward from the traditional camp and integrated into contemporary lives, the shape of the knowledge and the means of transmission change, as anticipated by Joe Couture, referring to both Native and non-Native seekers:

[S]o many are not grounded in a sense of the real but mysterious power of nature in mountains, rivers, lakes, rocks, life-forms, all as enmeshed in the web of the universe. So, the legends and stories require pedagogical adaptation. The stories have to be retold, reshaped, and refitted to meet contemporary seekers' changed and changing needs (Couture 2000, 43).

Selected examples of the ways in which Elders' teachings are being adapted and applied are presented in the next section.

Teaching Methods and Key Concepts

In a traditional, land-based lifestyle, the student learns about reality by direct encounter with his or her environment and personal observation. Older relatives are available to model behaviour and to help make sense of perceptions. Stories recounted in the lodge present social and historical context and ethical imperatives.

When learners are immersed in an environment that lacks experiential reinforcements and tends to contradict the world view represented by Aboriginal traditions, teachers have to be more explicit in their approach to affirming Aboriginal ways. Formal learning in public schools is secular and directed to preparing students for social and economic participation in settler society. The disconnect between Aboriginal culture and formal education has been identified as an impediment to learning and development of positive identity. In response, a number of urban and reserve communities have introduced 'survival schools'. The Joe Duquette High School in Saskatoon is one these schools, which builds its program around the cosmology of the regional culture, in this case Plains Cree.

> The school's spiritual perspective is sustained by daily sweet grass cere-monies, feasts on special occasions, special ceremonies, and sweat lodges. Teachers conduct talking/healing circles to build trust so that students can speak about their feelings and lives. . . . Drumming and dancing circles introduce students to aesthetic dimensions of culture that unify psyches and social relations through celebration. Support circles for stu-dents generate peer backing in dealing with abuse (Regnier 1995, 314).

Modifying and transferring selected practices from the traditional camp and inviting Elders into the classroom are means of introducing successive genera-tions to the contemporary value of traditional teachings. Another adapta-tion is the articulation of key concepts and processes inherent in indigenous knowledge. David Newhouse of the Department of Indigenous Studies at Trent University makes the point that learning *about* indigenous knowledge is not the same as engaging experientially with indigenous ways of coming to knowledge (Newhouse 2008). Nevertheless, the discourse proceeding in the literature and seminars and the introduction of structured field-based learning with Elders pave the way for further direct engagement with indigenous knowledge. A new generation of students and graduates is in the forefront of demonstrating that higher education can open a path to deepening consciousness of indigenous knowledge and identity.[5]

Joe Couture, a Cree Métis trained as a psychologist, and Leroy Little Bear, a Blackfoot scholar and lawyer, have been very influential in translating indigenous world view into conceptual, philosophical language. Joe quotes anonymous traditional sources as declaring: 'There are only two things you have to know about being Indian. One is that everything is alive, and two is that we're all related' and 'The centred and quartered Circle is the sign of wholeness, of inclusiveness of all reality, of life, of balance and harmony between man and culture' (Couture 2000, 36). His experience and insights are elaborated further in the same article.

Leroy sets out the axiom that 'In Aboriginal philosophy, existence consists of energy. All things are animate, imbued with spirit, and in constant motion.' He goes on to explain:

> The idea of all things being in constant motion or flux leads to a holistic and cyclical view of the world. If everything is constantly moving and changing, then one has to look at the whole to begin to see patterns. For instance, the cosmic cycles are in constant motion, but they have regular patterns that result in recurrences such as the seasons of the year, the migration of the animals, renewal ceremonies, songs, and stories. Constant motion, as manifested in cyclical or repetitive patterns, emphasizes process as opposed to product (Little Bear 2000, 78).

Marie Battiste, a Mi'kmaq educator whose research has focused on the patterns of Mi'kmaw language, confirms the concept of constant flux reflected in verb-based linguistic forms that emphasizes the centrality of relationships, whether between humans or with other members of the natural order (Battiste and Henderson 2000, 73–85).

A common feature of the knowledge systems of diverse Aboriginal peoples is the responsibility of humans to contribute to maintaining balance in the world. Little Bear explains:

Creation is a continuity. If creation is to continue it must be renewed. Renewal ceremonies, the telling and retelling of creation stories, the singing and re-singing of the songs, are all humans' part in the maintenance of creation. Hence the Sundance, societal ceremonies, the unbundling of medicine bundles at certain phases of the year—all of which are interrelated aspects of happenings that take place on and within Mother Earth (Little Bear 2000, 78).

In the field of Aboriginal health, the holistic understanding that well-being flows from a balance among physical, emotional, intellectual, and spiritual aspects of the whole person has become widely recognized, although biomedical treatment continues to focus on physical interventions. As in education, alternative, culture-based services give a place to spiritual dimensions of healing.

The medicine wheel, which brings together several key concepts of Aboriginal knowledge systems, has become probably the most recognized and widely used symbol in conveying traditional understandings. The centred and quartered circle can exemplify balanced awareness of wholeness that encompasses particulars, the holistic nature of well-being, the multiple domains of learning, the repeating cycle of life from infancy through youth, adulthood, and old age to a return to dependency and the spirit world.

Elders' teachings are concerned with personal development of apprentices as well as knowledge acquisition. Moral precepts for personal behaviour and ethical precepts governing relationships are codified in principles such as kindness, honesty, sharing, and strength in Anishinaabe tradition (RCAP 1996, 1:654) or the Good Mind that is fundamental to achieving peace, power, and righteousness in personal experience and community relations, as prescribed in the Iroquois Great Law of Peace (Newhouse 2008). Unbundling the meaning of moral and ethical values encoded in ceremonies and traditional teachings is the lifetime pursuit of those who are destined to become Grandmother and Grandfather to the whole community, not just to their own kin.

Interpreters of indigenous world view and ways of coming to knowledge consistently affirm that traditional teachings do not advocate an insular mind, shutting out alternative ways of perceiving reality and organizing perceptions. Battiste and Henderson encapsulate the tension involved in being open to new knowledge and maintaining the integrity of indigenous knowledge:

> Indigenous educators . . . must balance traditional ways of knowing with the Eurocentric tradition. . . . They must embrace the paradox of subjective and objective ways of knowing that do not collapse into either inward

or outward illusions, but bring us all into *a living dialogical relationship with the world* that our knowledge gives us (Battiste and Henderson 2000, 94; emphasis added).

David Newhouse uses the concept of 'complex understanding' to elaborate how traditional knowledge fosters harmonious relationships in a social and physical universe in constant motion.

Complex understanding occurs when we begin to see a phenomenon from various perspectives. Complex understanding doesn't seek to replace one view with another but to find a way of ensuring that all views are given due consideration. It doesn't work in an either-or fashion. A phenomenon is not one thing or another but all things at one time. Complex understanding allows for our understanding to change depending upon where we stand to see or upon the time that we look or who is doing the looking. Complex understanding is grounded in a view of a constantly changing reality that is capable of transformation at any time (Newhouse 2002).

As traditional teachings are carried outward from the tribal camp and village, across geographic space and generations, the modes of transmission are being adapted to the needs of learners who may not be grounded in an ecological consciousness, who need guidance in interpreting the stories and applying teachings to their life situation. Core concepts are being articulated in publications and integrated in teaching approaches and professional practice of Aboriginal professionals and non-Aboriginal colleagues. Symbols such as the medicine wheel, which were developed in specific contexts, are being shared and adopted across tribal and cultural boundaries. The content of traditional knowledge and the processes by which it is transmitted are becoming a focus of research by both Aboriginal and non-Aboriginal scholars.

Catalysts for Institutional Change

Ross Hoffman is an apprentice in traditional ways, of English and German origin. In his PhD dissertation (Hoffman 2006), Ross researched the impact of the teaching and ceremonial guidance of a gifted Arapaho Elder and healer located in Wyoming. For more than a decade, from 1969 until his passing in 1981, Raymond Harris welcomed knowledge-seekers from Alberta and Saskatchewan, principally Cree individuals and families, to his camp. Hoffman documented how the first wave of apprentices became catalysts for re-introducing ceremonies that had been suppressed in their communities by prohibition under the Indian Act and aggressive resocialization of children in residential schools. These apprentices in traditional ways also became key figures in transforming the values and practices of Aboriginal organizations and services. The roster of Cree leaders in social change interviewed by Hoffman is not proposed as a representative sample; it is derived from personal contacts pursued by the researcher. Nevertheless, the individuals' activities and recorded thoughts illustrate the rippling impact of Elders' teachings across geographical boundaries, institutions, and generations.

Harold Cardinal was a prominent figure in First Nations politics from the publication of his book *The Unjust Society* in 1969 until his passing in 2005. He was an advocate for the necessity of cultural and spiritual rebirth as a complement to the recovery of self-government and self-determination of First Nations. In interviews recorded by Hoffman, Cardinal recalled the influence of his encounter with tradition and ceremony under the guidance of Raymond Harris:

> I remember having a conversation with him one morning in Wyoming at the breakfast table, over morning coffee. Raymond said 'I'm only giving you a start so you can go back and find out the ways of your people, because they exist there. I can't make you an Arapaho—you are a Cree. You must go back and talk with your own people, the traditionalists'. . .
>
> [T]he traditions were still alive. Some of the old people had kept them underground because of the pressure of the church and law. People had kept them alive secretly. It was the generation, like myself who had been to residential school, the one or two generations who had been indoctrinated and who were Christians who felt that those traditions were evil because we had been separated from them, the culture, the spiritual traditions. . . .
>
> For many political leaders the Harris/Smallboy[6] influence was that it validated our core identity. It legitimated who we were. It validated that our direction was the right one—our political direction. Not only in this province, but nationally (Hoffman 2006, 114, 111, 145).

Others mentored by Raymond Harris had public impact. Eric Shirt, one of the founders and executive director of the Nechi Training Institute in Alberta was a key figure in the movement breaking new ground in culture-based treatment for addictions. Douglas Cardinal, a Cree–Métis architect, has acknowledged that his vision for the Canadian Museum of Civilization was received in a sweat lodge and that ceremonial practice is an ongoing source of personal renewal. Pauline Shirt was a founder of Wandering Spirit Survival School in Toronto, one of the first urban-based survival schools in Canada.

Joe Couture, another member of the group journeying regularly to the Harris camp, was a towering figure, stimulating cultural awareness and renewal in post-secondary education, mental health, restorative justice, ceremonial practice, and philosophy over a period of 35 years. His influence continues after his passing in 2007. As chair of the Native Studies (now Indigenous Studies) Department at Trent University from 1975 to 1978, Joe encouraged faculty and students to explore culturally based experiential learning, which is now part of the department's academic approach, represented specifically in the vision and mission of the PhD program. Joe's background in psychology and philosophy moved him to make connections in his writing with parallel streams of knowledge in contemporary philosophy and theology. His assertions that perceptions of reality opened up by traditional teaching are on a par with the great religious and intellectual traditions of the world have been taken up by younger scholars, providing a complement to the exploration of traditional environmental knowledge (TEK) that also gained recognition in the latter decades of the twentieth century.

The ongoing exploration of traditional perceptions of reality and application of these insights in contemporary life is evident in the work of scholars and teachers across Canada. Willie Ermine, a Cree from Saskatchewan who is an apprentice in traditional ways, wrote in 1995:

> The being in relation to the cosmos possessed intriguing and mysterious qualities that provided insights into existence. In their quest to find meaning in the outer space, Aboriginal people turned to the inner space. This inner space is that universe of being within each person that is synonymous with the soul, the spirit, the self, or the being. . . .
>
> Aboriginal people found a wholeness that permeated inwardness and that also extended into the outer space. Their fundamental insight was that all existence was connected and the whole enmeshed the being in its inclusiveness. . . . The tribal ceremonies display with vivid multidimensional clarity the entries and pathways into this inner world of exciting mystery that has been touched by only the few who have become explorers of sacred knowing. Rituals and ceremonies are corporeal sacred acts that give rise to holy manifestations in the metaphysical world. Conversely, it is the metaphysical that constructs meaning in the corporeal (Ermine 1995, 103, 106).

Currently, as an ethicist and faculty member of the First Nations University of Canada, Ermine envisages the possibility of creative dialogue between Aboriginal knowledge systems and researchers operating from the perspectives of Western scientific culture. He proposes that a pre-condition for such exchanges is the creation of ethical space where the undercurrents that have disrupted reciprocal exchange are addressed by acknowledging differences in history, modes of thought, and values. In this ethical space, the assumption that norms in Western society are appropriate models for knowledge creation in different cultural environments is deliberately suspended. Re-orientation of ethics of engagement is essential, because 'Western mind' incorporates images of indigenous peoples that are rooted in oppressive historical relationships (Ermine, Sinclair, and Jeffery 2004, 22–34; Ermine 2008).

Gail Guthrie Valaskakis, a communications specialist of Chippewa and European background, elaborates on the implications of the identities constructed by outsider perceptions of Aboriginal peoples:

> North Americans' representations of themselves and of Indians are linked in articulation to ways of knowing and experiencing otherness. . . . Drawn in literature and art, social imaginaries emerge and recede, inscribing Indians as primitive and pagan, heroic and hostile, exploited and defended. These politicized images are woven into policies—colonial and current—that not only isolate and identify Indians but also construct and position Indian identity, creating unsteady circles of insiders and outsiders (Valaskakis 2005, 213).

In his doctoral dissertation, John-Paul Restoule, an educator of Ojibway and French ancestry, explored identity formation by Aboriginal men in urban contexts. He documented the multiple identities of participants who juggled, negotiated, and adapted their presentation of self to themselves and to others as they moved from city to rural reserve, from private to public domains, and back again, fulfilling varied social roles (Restoule 2004).

Communicating wisdom of the Elders requires at least two-pronged initiatives to affirm Aboriginal identity in an environment that offers fragmented and distorted images of Aboriginal people and devalues traditional ways of knowing. Engaging in discourse with the non-Aboriginal public can effect a shift in the mindset of the majority society and create a more hospitable environment for Aboriginal people struggling to give expression to their core identity. New formulations of Elders' teaching can also affirm for Aboriginal people themselves the legitimacy of their exploration of language, tradition, and inner space.

In his research on the impact of Raymond Harris's work with the Plains Cree, Hoffman describes the core group of Cree traditional practitioners that he interviewed as 'the first wave' who learned from 'the Old Ones' and went on to become respected as Elders and mentors in their own right. Similar movements were emerging in other regions and Aboriginal communities across Canada. The social and institutional change initiated by the first wave of reborn traditionalists in the latter part of the twentieth century has been taken up by a second wave of knowledge-seekers and knowledge-holders who are animated by the conviction that indigenous ways of knowing have intrinsic value for non-Aboriginal as well as Aboriginal peoples in Canada and around the globe. In discourse and practice in politics, health, education, the arts, and research in every domain, these new traditionalists are working to give indigenous knowledge *visibility* as a way of being that is entirely relevant to the twenty-first century.

The necessity of giving expression to wisdom gained and the varied ways that it is communicated are underlined by Viviane Gray, a Mi'kmaq visual artist, citing Black Elk and Maria Campbell:

> A human being who has a vision is not able to use the power of it until after they have performed the vision on earth for people to see (Black Elk in Gray 2008, 275).
>
> [I]n the Plains Cree language, art is part of the mind or *mon tune ay chi kun*, which translates to 'the sacred place inside each one of us where no one else can go'. It is [in] this place that each one of us can dream, fantasize, create and, yes, even talk to the grandfathers and grandmothers. . . . The thoughts and images that come from this place are called *mom tune ay kuna*, which mean wisdoms and they can be given to others in stories, songs, dances and art (Campbell 2005 in Gray 2008, 268).

Preserving the Integrity of Traditional Knowledge

As traditional teachings become more widely diffused and incorporated in publications, practices, and statements of values in classrooms and organizations, applications of knowledge will become the responsibility of adherents who are physically and culturally distant from the 'true Elders' who led the process of renewal. As many observe, true Elders were always rare, and they are passing away at an alarming rate. Who can be trusted to interpret the wisdom of the Elders? Joe Couture quotes an Elder's prediction that these times of emergence are to be marked by chaos and confusion before changing into a time of light and peace (Couture 2000, 41).

While I have a sense that the quest for certainty in a universe characterized by constant change is doomed to fail, I suggest that there are touchstones that can help us avoid being tossed about by divergent and even competing interpretations of 'the way'. The touchstones are: ceremony, language, and community validation.

Ceremonies have stability over time. The reliability of oral tradition validated ceremonially has been recognized in Canadian law with the *Delgamuukw* decision of the Supreme Court in face of argument to the contrary. While particular features of protocol in a sweat lodge may differ from place to place, the core efficacy of sweat ceremonies to facilitate healing and transformation continues to be validated by participants. Jake Thomas, working as an oral historian of treaties and councils with ethnologist Michael Foster at the Museum of Civilization, demonstrated that his performance of council protocols illuminated what was recorded in colonial records reaching back close to 300 years (Foster 1984, 183–207). Participation in traditional ceremonies that reliably mediate connection to the Earth, to the community, and to one's own inner being are a critical counterbalance to the variability of concepts and interpretations that abound.

Indigenous languages reveal in their structure and content the values that have served the people over generations. Cardinal and Hildebrandt conducted research for the Treaty Commission of Saskatchewan on the language used by Cree, Saulteaux, Dene, and Assiniboine Elders in recalling and talking about the treaties. The researchers found a remarkable correspondence among the recollections, concepts, and terms of the different language groups. Based on collaborative interpretation with the Elders, they published a book exploring nine words or phrases that illuminated the view handed down in oral tradition of the sacredness of agreements undertaken, the means of securing good relations, and the commitments to respect future needs for a livelihood from the land (Cardinal and Hildebrandt 2000). Willie Ermine writes:

> The idea of our progenitors was to try to gain understanding of many of the greatest mysteries of the universe. They sought to do this by exploring existence subjectively; that is, by placing themselves in the stream of consciousness. Our Aboriginal languages and culture contain the accumulated knowledge of our ancestors, and it is critical that we examine the inherent concepts in our lexicons to develop understandings of the self in relation to existence. The Cree word *mamatowisowin*, for example, describes the capability of tapping into the 'life force' as a means of procreation. This Cree concept describes a capacity to be or do anything, to be creative (Ermine 1995, 104).

In quite personal terms, Caroline VanEvery-Albert describes her own journey of learning her ancestral language:

> The Mohawk language is polysynthetic. This means that it is made up of small grammatical elements each of which has a specific meaning. These grammatical pieces are linked together to create words, which are equal to an entire sentence in English. Another interesting element of the language is that it is verb-based and nouns are incorporated. Below is an example of the complexity and beauty of the Mohawk language. [Gives an example of the elements making up a word.] This word, which when translated into English means I want or need something, literally means the earth will provide for me or give me benefit. . . . I was amazed by the relationship between the Mohawk language and Rotinonhsyon:ni world view (VanEvery-Albert 2008, 43).

Having the facility to consider a teaching as it is expressed in our ancestral language is a fundamental way of reflecting on its meaning and its consistency with the values inherent in the culture and the language.

The third touchstone that I propose is community validation. While charismatic leaders and visionary holy men and women have existed in various cultures, Aboriginal societies value collective knowing rather than expert knowing. In another paper, congruent with Newhouse's description of 'complex understanding', I wrote:

> The personal nature of knowledge means that disparate and even contradictory perceptions can be accepted as valid because they are unique to the person. In a council or talking circle of Elders you will not find arguments as to whose perception is more valid and therefore whose judgement should prevail. In other words, people do not contest with one another to establish who is correct, who has the 'truth'. If a decision affecting the well-being of the community is required it will be arrived at through a process of discussion considering the several perspectives put forward and negotiating a consensus (Castellano 2000, 26).

Women speaking to the Royal Commission on Aboriginal Peoples warned of the dangers of naively putting trust in healers who lack community validation:

> We have also come across many self-proclaimed healers who have abused and exploited traditional spirituality in their own Aboriginal people. . . .

For controlling the spiritual malpractice, I guess it would be through all the Elders in each community. They would know the ones who are abusing the sweat lodge and abusing the medicines (Lillian Sanderson in RCAP 1996, 3:72).

Attachment to traditional lands formerly contributed to continuity of communities over generations. Mobility of individuals now makes the identification of persons and teachings that carry moral authority more complex, more dependent on effective communication networks.

Conclusion

Over the past two generations, First Nations, Inuit, and Métis people, the Aboriginal peoples of Canada, have been actively engaged in conserving and recovering our cultural heritage. Cultural renewal is not about going back to living in tipis and longhouses or a hunting and gathering lifestyle, as critics would suggest. The goal is to uncover those deep life-affirming values that are part of our heritage and to reconstruct in contemporary form the relationships that give expression to those values. Resistance and reconstruction continue to be necessary to rebuild cohesive communities in which the stabilizing elements of language, family, community, and ceremony have been systematically undermined by colonizing forces.

Many of the Elders who gave vitality and guidance to the wave of renewal that gained momentum over the past 40 years are passing into the spirit world. It is not clear who will be their successors. Younger generations continue to look for 'the wisdom of the Elders', which is repeated, reformulated, and interpreted at many sites, by many teachers. Young scholars are turning their attention to probing the depths of meaning imbedded in the languages, ceremonial forms, and ethical instructions that have been passed on. Connections are being made with traditions of indigenous peoples in other parts of the world. A small stream of non-Aboriginal people are seeking to learn from the wisdom of the Elders in matters as diverse as the environment, restorative justice, conflict resolution, and holistic healing.

There is much work to be done to restore wellness in our own communities and just relationships with the peoples with whom we share this land. This paper is an attempt to broaden the basis for dialogue within our communities and with our neighbours on how to realize *pimatziwin*, living well in Anishinaabe tradition, and *peace*, the ideal of respect and mutual responsibility valued in Iroquois tradition.

Nia:wen. Thank you for your attention.

Discussion Questions

1. Do Elders' teachings referred to in this article have relevance in the environment where you live, learn, and work?
2. Are there points of convergence between indigenous world views and other philosophies or belief systems with which you are familiar? Elaborate.
3. Is oral communication necessary to the transmission of Elders' teachings? Why or why not?
4. Who are the legitimate teachers of indigenous knowledge in contemporary times?
5. Do traditional teachings of particular indigenous societies constitute an authoritative canon of knowledge? Provide a rationale for your view.

Notes

1. On the passing of a hereditary chief of the Six Nations Confederacy, a Condolence Ceremony for the clan of the deceased chief is held, and the candidate who has been endorsed in councils to assume the vacated title is then installed. Chiefs thus confirmed are called Condoled Chiefs. The condolence cane mentioned later is a symbol of the authority of the Confederacy Council. It is carved with mnemonic markings and 'read' in the roll call of chiefs at the opening of council meetings.
2. As with other teachings attributed to Jake Thomas in this essay, this is my memory of what I heard. While I acknowledge and honour Jake as the source of the wisdom cited, any error in interpretation is my responsibility.
3. Ernie Benedict, Mohawk Elder, speaking at the opening of a meeting of the Canadian Psychiatric Association Section on Native Mental Health on the Native Family: Traditions and Adaptations, London, Ontario, 1983. Transcribed with permission.
4. The Great Law of Peace is both the constitution of the Iroquois Confederacy and the formulation of how members of the Five (later Six) Nations should maintain peaceful relations. The centre of the Confederacy is symbolized by a great white pine tree whose roots, the white roots of peace, go out from the tree in the four directions.
5. See 'Indigenous knowledges and the university', special theme issue of the *Canadian Journal of Native Education*, vol. 31, no. 1 (2008).
6. Robert Smallboy was a Cree Elder in Alberta who led a return to tradition and life on the land around 1968.

References

Battiste, Marie, and James (Sa'ke'j) Youngblood Henderson. 2000. *Protecting Indigenous Knowledge and Heritage*. Saskatoon: Purich Publishing.
Campbell, Maria. 2005. *Achimoona*. Saskatoon: Fifth House. First published in 1985.
Cardinal, Harold, and Walter Hildebrandt. 2000. *Treaty Elders of Saskatchewan*. Calgary: University of Calgary Press.
Castellano, Marlene Brant. 2000. 'Updating Aboriginal traditions of knowledge'. In George Sefa Dei, Budd Hall, and Dorothy Goldin Rosenberg, eds, *Indigenous Knowledges in Global Contexts: Multiple Readings of Our World*, 195–210. Toronto: University of Toronto Press.

Couture, Joseph E. 2000. 'The role of Elders: Emergent issues'. In David Long and Olive
    Patricia Dickason, eds, *Visions of the Heart: Canadian Aboriginal Issues*, 2nd edn, 31–48.
    Toronto: Harcourt Canada. Reprinted in this volume.

Delgamuukw v. British Columbia, [1997] 3 S.C.R. 1010.

Ermine, Willie. 1995. 'Aboriginal epistemology'. In Marie Battiste and Jean Barman, eds, *First
    Nations Education in Canada: The Circle Unfolds*, 101–12. Vancouver: University of British
    Columbia Press.

———. 2008. PowerPoint presentation on ethical space at the Ninth Global Forum on
    Bioethics in Research, 3–5 December, Auckland, Aotearoa/New Zealand. http://gfbr9.hrc
    .govt.nz/index.php/presentations.

Ermine, Willie, Raven Sinclair, and Bonnie Jeffery. 2004. 'The ethics of research involv-
    ing indigenous peoples'. Report of the Indigenous Peoples' Health Research Centre
    to the Interagency Advisory Panel on Research Ethics. www.iphrc.ca/Upload/ethics_
    review_iphrc.pdf.

Foster, Michael. 1984. 'On who spoke first at Iroquois–white councils: An exercise in the
    method of upstreaming'. In Michael K. Foster, Jack Campisi, and Marianne Mithun,
    eds, *Extending the Rafters: Interdisiplinary Approaches to Iroquoian Studies*. Albany: State
    University of New York Press.

Gray, Viviane. 2008. 'A culture of art: Profiles of contemporary First Nations women artists'.
    In Gail Guthrie Valaskakis, Madeleine Dion Stout, and Eric Guimond, eds, *Restoring the
    Balance: First Nations Women, Community and Culture*, 267–81. Winnipeg: University of
    Manitoba Press.

Hoffman, Ross. 2006. 'Rekindling the fire: The impact of Raymond Harris's work with the
    Plains Cree'. (Trent University, Peterborough, ON, PhD dissertation).

Little Bear, Leroy. 2000. 'Jagged worldviews colliding'. In Marie Battiste, ed., *Reclaiming
    Indigenous Voice and Vision*, 77–85. Vancouver: University of British Columbia Press.

Newhouse, David. 2002. 'The promise of indigenous scholarship'. (Keynote address to the
    First Aboriginal Policy Research Conference, Ottawa).

———. 2008. 'Ganigonhi:oh: The Good Mind meets the academy'. In 'Indigenous know-
    ledges and the university', special theme issue of the *Canadian Journal of Native Education*
    31 (1): 184–97.

RCAP (Royal Commission on Aboriginal Peoples). 1996. *Report* vol. 1, *Looking Forward,
    Looking Back*; vol. 3, *Gathering Strength*. Ottawa: Canada Communications Group.
    www.collectionscanada.gc.ca/webarchives/20071115053257; www.ainc-inac.gc.ca/ch/rcap/
    sg/sgmm_e.html.

Regnier, Robert. 1995. 'The Sacred Circle: An Aboriginal approach to healing education at
    an urban high school'. In Marie Battiste and Jean Barman, eds, *First Nations Education in
    Canada: The Circle Unfolds*, 313–29. Vancouver: University of British Columbia Press.

Restoule, Jean-Paul. 2004. 'Aboriginal identity in urban areas: Shifting the focus from defin-
    ition to context'. (Ontario Institute for Studies in Education, University of Toronto, PhD
    dissertation).

Sanderson, Lillian. 1996. Oral presentation cited in Report of the Royal Commission on
    Aboriginal Peoples, vol. 3, *Gathering Strength*. Ottawa: Canada Communications Group.

Thomas, Jake. Personal communication.

Valaskakis, Gail Guthrie. 2005. *Indian Country: Essays on Contemporary Native Culture.* Waterloo, ON: Wilfrid Laurier University Press.

Valaskakis, Gail Guthrie, Madeleine Dion Stout, and Eric Guimond, eds. 2008. *Restoring the Balance: First Nations Women, Community and Culture.* Winnipeg: University of Manitoba Press.

VanEvery-Albert, Caroline. 2008. 'An exploration of indigenousness in the Western university institution'. In 'Indigenous knowledges and the university', special theme issue of the *Canadian Journal of Native Education* 31 (1).

Credits

4

Foundations: First Nation and Métis Families

Kim Anderson and Jessica Ball

When teaching about the state of indigenous[1] communities today, Cree/ Métis Elder Maria Campbell (2008) sometimes calls upon an image provided to her by the late Anishinaabe Elder Peter O'Chiese. Campbell recalls that O'Chiese used to liken colonization to someone dropping a complex and snugly fitting puzzle, causing it to shatter into a million pieces. This shattered puzzle is an evocative way to describe the impact of settler intrusion into the worlds of indigenous peoples. O'Chiese used the image to encourage younger generations like Campbell and her students to go back and pick up the pieces of cultures, world views, families, and communities that were left scattered along the way. Decolonization can thus be seen as the process of bringing those scattered pieces back together to rebuild indigenous peoples and worlds and make them whole again. How do Aboriginal families fit into this process?

If we think about the puzzle as indigenous America, one of the central components was relationships: relationships between individuals, families, and communities as well as relationships with the land and the ancestral and spirit worlds. Campbell talks about the teachings she received from O'Chiese regarding the shattering of *Wahkohtowin*, a Cree word that can be defined as kinship relative, relationships, or the act of being related to each other and all things in creation. Of all the abuses that indigenous people experienced, the attack on indigenous relationships was perhaps the most devastating, for healthy indigenous communities depended on how they managed relationships and systems of relations.

The alarmingly high levels of crisis and poverty in many Aboriginal communities, identified in the final report of the Royal Commission on Aboriginal Peoples (RCAP 1996) and in recent findings of demographic and social surveys (e.g., Statistics Canada 2003) are evidence of the collateral damage from ruptured relationships on a number of levels—social, environmental, and spiritual. But as many contributors to RCAP and current community members note, the strength of relationships still holds in many families and communities, and many people are actively engaged in picking up the pieces of indigenous families, communities, and cultures and putting them back together. Family relations are a core element of *Wahkohtowin*, and the shattering and subsequent rebuilding of Aboriginal families are the subject of this chapter.

The authors acknowledge the challenge of writing broadly about 'Aboriginal families', since First Nation, Métis, and Inuit peoples are so diverse, both between and also within these categories. First Nation coastal cultures are, for example, very different from Plains cultures, as are Métis people who come from different geographies, and so on. Some common values, practices, and histories can be called upon, however, to construct a cohesive portrayal of the past, present, and anticipated future of Aboriginal families. Writing about Native American family systems, John Red Horse has asserted that 'the essence of traditional life is captured through important markers such as spirituality and relationship patterns among kin.' He adds, 'Indeed, these may serve as vital concepts in any general theory of American Indian culture' (Red Horse 1997, 243). A look at the shared characteristics of Aboriginal family systems can therefore tell us a lot about some of the fundamental elements or foundations of indigenous America, both past and present.

In this chapter, we focus on Aboriginal families using First Nation and Métis examples. We have not included the Inuit because we lack direct experience with Inuit families and we are not personally familiar with their distinct family practices and systems. Our chapter builds specifically on our understanding and experiences with mostly Algonquian, Haudenosaunee, and west coast peoples. We begin by examining the family's historical function and colonization's shattering effect on it, before moving into a profile of contemporary Aboriginal families and future directions.

Looking Back

Foundations: Kinship and Historical Aboriginal Societies

Family, as it was known in land-based or 'traditional'[2] Aboriginal communities, was significant because it was the core societal unit. People lived and worked in extended family groups that allowed them to harvest and share resources through hunting, trapping, fishing, gathering, and agriculture. These groups often changed in size depending on the season and the resources available. This comes across in the following description of the Ojibway:

> Ojibwa familial units would have looked rather different to an observer at different times of the year. In early autumn, in shallow water areas where wild rice grew, extended-family groups gathered canoes full of grain and processed it for winter use. After the rice harvest, Ojibwa groups both

shrank in size and multiplied in number as people scattered to hunting and trapping areas inland from main bodies of water. The more northerly the environment, the smaller the winter camps tended to be, but no group could easily survive without at least two male hunters and two or more women to care for children, process food and furs, make clothing and moccasins, and net snowshoes, among other things (Peers and Brown 2000, 532).

Peers and Brown point out that the family was 'the primary unit of economic production within Ojibwa culture' (532), and the same could be said of other traditional Aboriginal societies (Volo and Volo 2007). Indeed, the RCAP report begins with a focus on family 'because it is our conviction that much of the failure of responsibility that contributes to the current imbalance and distress in Aboriginal life centres on the family' (RCAP 1996). Because so much of the economy depended on family well-being, marriages were considered in terms of how the extended family might ensure survival through resource procurement. Historians of the fur trade have demonstrated that the intermarriage of Aboriginal women with traders was considered beneficial to Aboriginal communities as well as to traders, since these unions cemented alliances that served the trade (Brown 1980; Van Kirk 1980). Business was family business, and survival was a matter in which everyone in the family played a part. Marriages were often arranged because this allowed families to match skills and needs for community well-being.

Prior to the implementation of the Indian Act, Aboriginal communities were governed by families and family alliances. In hunting societies such as the Ojibway, extended families were typically led by elder men, and often there were different types of 'chiefs'—for hunting, warfare, and so on (Peers and Brown 2000). Métis communities had chiefs and captains of the buffalo hunt, which were organized along family lines. In many west coast societies, hereditary chieftainships were passed to men or women. As leaders of the 'house', Aboriginal women also held political authority as clan mothers, through women's councils, or as leaders of extended families (Anderson 2000). First Nation and Métis Elders talk about 'head women' in their families, women who governed large extended families through the authority they had earned during their lifetime. This authority came from recognition that the elderly women made decisions based on the best interest of the family and future generations, a principle that is evident in a number of Aboriginal societies (Anderson 2000).

Spiritual responsibilities were also often managed through family networks. Different families were keepers of different bodies of knowledge and practice, which were passed down through biological family members or to people who were adopted into their families for that purpose. Some families were known as healers or medicine people; some held sacred stories or songs. Collectively, these groups of families kept sacred knowledge and practices alive over the generations.

Dickason (2009) has described the changing and varied social structures among First Nation peoples over the past 600 years. Before contact, many Aboriginal peoples were organized according to clans, which represented broader kinship ties, both among humans and with the natural world (i.e., bear clan, eagle clan). Depending on the culture, clan membership passed through the mother (matrilineal) or the father (patrilineal). Clans were an important part of communities' social, political, and spiritual organization; they were the vehicle through which many Aboriginal societies governed themselves. Clans were led by 'head men' and 'head women' who ensured adherence to community laws. One law was that people could not marry within their clan, which prevented marriage between 'relatives'. Aboriginal societies often also organized collective and community responsibilities according to clan—one clan might be responsible for overseeing health, others for negotiating with outsiders, and so on. The family and clan one was born into thus prescribed one's greater role in society and the way in which one built family and community into the future.

Child-rearing was typically shared in family groups; traditional Aboriginal communities were the prototypical model of 'it takes a village to raise a child'. Children were raised with siblings, cousins, aunts and uncles, grandparents and great-grandparents, great-aunts and great-uncles. Although children knew their biological siblings, parents, and grandparents, other members of the extended family could be equally considered a parent, grandparent, or sibling. The names people used to refer to one another are telling in this regard: a child might refer to any elderly person in his or her community simply as 'grandmother', *Kohkom*, or 'grandfather', *Mosom* (to use Cree as an example). Likewise, elders would refer to young people in the community as 'grandchild', *Nosim*, and treat them accordingly. In Algonquian and Haudenosaunee societies, similar words could be used to address one's mother and her sisters (*ni kowi*, 'mother', and *nikowis*, 'little mother' or aunt in Cree), and the offspring of one's mother's sister or father's brother would be considered a sibling. Thus, a child could have many mothers and fathers, grandparents, and sisters and brothers who played intimate roles in their upbringing. Roles relating to discipline, teaching, and play were divided up in a systematic way among kin so that children received comprehensive and balanced guidance as they moved towards adulthood.

Through ceremonies, children were both challenged and celebrated as they moved through different life-stage milestones, and these events were grounded in community support. Babies were held and passed around at naming ceremonies, children were collectively celebrated at walking out ceremonies (first steps), and youth were taught by various community members in puberty fasts and seclusions.[3] These practices contributed to children's sense of belonging and responsibility.

It was considered vital to educate children about their roles and responsibilities in relationships because community survival depended on how well the family worked together and how well they managed their relationships with the animals and the land. Maria Campbell has explained the significance of interconnecting roles within family and community by calling on a diagram shared by O'Chiese (see Figure 4.1). Within this system, Campbell explains, children were at the heart of the community. Everyone worked together for the children's well-being because children represented the future and the survival of the people. Elders sat next to the children because they were their teachers and typically their caregivers. It was understood that elders and children had a special bond, since they were closest to the spirit world on either side. Women looked after the circle of home and community. It is important to note that women were not caregivers in the Western patriarchal sense of being the family servant. Rather, it was women's job to manage the home and community in the most effective way. Men were charged with protecting and providing. They travelled outside the communities and brought in resources that women distributed and managed.

In this system, everyone was involved in ensuring the health and well-being of present and future generations. Responsibilities were organized according to gender and age so that everyone cared for their relations and was also cared for. Reciprocity in relationships was important and can be seen, for example, in the relationships between elders and children: elders were teachers to children, who were expected in turn to help their elders. People also carried responsibilities to animals and plants, to the natural and spirit worlds, and were cared for in turn by these entities. These interconnecting responsibilities created a comprehensive web of relationships, and children were raised to know their responsibilities to this web.

This brief overview demonstrates the significance of families and family systems in traditional Aboriginal societies. Family underpinned everything from economics to politics, law, and social order, so the health of the family and family systems was paramount. 'Family' meant life itself, as Nuu-chah-nulth hereditary chief Richard Atleo has expressed:

In the Nuu-chah-nulth worldview it is unnatural, and equivalent to death and destruction, for any person to be isolated from family or community. Nuu-chah-nulth life, therefore, is founded by creating and maintaining relationships (Atleo 2004, 27).

The following section will demonstrate how relationships, and thus life itself, were violated for Aboriginal peoples.

Dismantling the Foundation

From the earliest encounters, Aboriginal peoples were coerced and threatened by European newcomers to change the way they managed their families. This was not simply because the newcomers didn't like the way indigenous peoples raised their children (although indigenous child-rearing practices were radically different from those in seventeenth-century Europe). Aboriginal family systems came under attack because they stood in the way of colonization.

In seventeenth-century New France, the Jesuits complained that Aboriginal children enjoyed the liberty of 'wild ass colts' and noted an 'excessive love of their offspring' among the peoples they encountered (Miller 1996, 46, 55). This was problematic to the Jesuits because the autonomy and respect afforded to children in Aboriginal societies made it difficult for them to 'train' and assimilate children through the schools they were trying to establish. These early missionaries had ascertained that working with children held the most potential for converting Aboriginal populations to Christianity, but they were thwarted by the strength of the Aboriginal family. Parents were reluctant to give up their children, and women were hostile to patriarchal family structures that would rob them of their power (Anderson 1991; Miller 1996). Yet these efforts to displace Aboriginal women and appropriate the education of Aboriginal children were not easily abandoned; they formed a central part of church and state policy and practice well into the twentieth century.

Pressures to change Aboriginal family systems intensified toward the end of the nineteenth century as Canada became a nation and settlers were encouraged to move west. Rose Stremlau connects the dismantling of kinship and removal from the land in the United States. She describes how reformers during the late nineteenth century campaigned for allotment, the subdivision of tribal lands into individual homesteads, as a way to dismantle 'the kind of societies created by different systems of property ownership' (Stremlau 2005, 276). Kinship systems supported indigenous relationships with the land and vice versa, and all of these relationships would need to be dismantled to get rid of 'the Indian problem'. Stremlau writes:

Reformers concluded that kinship systems, especially as they manifested in gender roles, prevented acculturation by undermining individualism and social order, and they turned to federal Indian policy to fracture these extended indigenous families into male-dominant, nuclear families, modelled after middle-class Anglo-American households (Stremlau 2005, 265).

During this period, 'field matrons' were sent out by the Office of Indian Affairs in the US to train Native American women in the ways of Victorian womanhood (Emmerich 1991), and female missionaries in Canada took on a primary role in trying to convert Aboriginal women to Euro-Western standards of conjugality and domesticity (Perry 2005; Rutherdale 2002). At the same time, indigenous motherhood came under attack through public discourse in which indigenous mothers and indigenous women in general were cast as dirty, lax in discipline, and in need of training (Carter 1997). With these tools and pretexts, the patriarchal nuclear family was forced upon indigenous peoples across North America.

All of these incursions were damaging to Aboriginal families, but two twentieth-century strategies in particular caused an implosion that sent communities reeling: residential schools and the child welfare system. Beginning in 1879 and operating until 1996, residential schools took over the role of raising Aboriginal children in Canada. Although they resisted, many communities lost whole generations of children; by 1930, almost 75 per cent of First Nation school-aged children were in residential schools (Fournier and Crey 1997, 61). Many of these children were abused physically, sexually, emotionally, and spiritually. Many never returned to their communities, and many found themselves alienated from their families, lands, and cultures when they did. When residential school survivors became parents, many struggled because they had not experienced positive parental role modelling, having been raised in abusive institutions. Residential schools thus blew *Wahkohtowin* apart in a way that no policy or practice had done before. In the wake of this devastation, child welfare authorities removed Aboriginal children from their homes in record numbers in what has come to be known as the (1960s) 'Sixties Scoop' (Miller 1996). By the early 1980s, Native children represented less than 4 per cent of the population but made up 50, 60, and 70 per cent of the child welfare caseloads in Alberta, Manitoba, and Saskatchewan, respectively (Bennett and Blackstock 1992).

O'Chiese and Campbell would link colonization, residential schools, and child welfare interference by referring to the aforementioned diagram of social

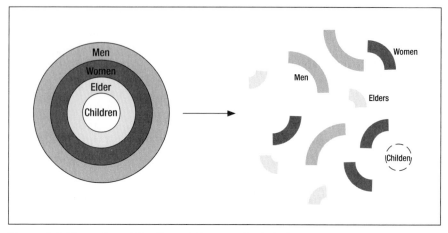

Figure 4.1 Shattering of Family and Community Relations

relations (Figure 4.1). In this narrative, men were the frontline of resistance to colonization through warfare and negotiations, and when these lines broke down, women protected the culture and family by resisting change. But in spite of colonial inroads made among indigenous men and women, strong kinship systems and relationships with the land persisted into the twentieth century. State authorities came to the same conclusion the Jesuits had centuries earlier: the fastest way to overtake Aboriginal communities, deal with 'the Indian problem', and gain access to land was to assume the education and rearing of Aboriginal children. Ojibway educator Sally Gaikezheyongai explains that the mass removal of children from Aboriginal communities was akin to ripping the heart and centre out of indigenous worlds (Wemigwans 2002). Once the heart was taken, everything else began to shatter and fall away: elders had no one to teach, women had no one to care for, and men had nothing to protect and provide for. This created the conditions for an unravelling that communities struggle with to this day (see Figure 4.1).

The ongoing repercussions of these colonial intrusions are evident in the material presented in the next section.

First Nation and Métis Families Today

We begin this section with some basic demographic and socio-economic information about contemporary First Nation and Métis families. This information will be followed by a discussion of the current quality of life and emerging trends among Aboriginal families. This discussion lends itself to observations about the general character of Aboriginal families today and an understanding of where they might go in the future.

Basic Characteristics of First Nation and Métis Families[4]

Between 1996 and 2006, the total population of First Nation, Métis, and Inuit peoples in Canada grew by 45 per cent, nearly six times faster than the 8 per cent increase of the non-Aboriginal population over the decade (Statistics Canada 2006). Table 4.1 shows the number of residents in Canada who reported having a primary Aboriginal identity in the 2001 and 2006 censuses (Statistics Canada 2006).

Table 4.1[5]   Aboriginal Populations in Canada, 2001 and 2006

	Number	Percent of Canadian Population	Percent of Aboriginal Population
Aboriginal identity			
2001	976,305	3.3	
2006	1,172,790	3.8	
Aboriginal ancestry			
2001	1,300,000	4.0	
2006	1,700,000	5.4	
North American Indian	698,025		60
Métis	389,785		33
Inuit	50,485		4
Mixed Aboriginal identity	34,495		3

Source: Statistics Canada, census of population, 2001 and 2006.

The population of First Nation people on reserves is growing at a rate of 2.3 per cent annually, which is three times the overall rate for Canadians. The most remarkable trend can be found in the growth of Aboriginal children and families. With an overall median age of 27 years, the Aboriginal population is very young compared to the overall median age of 40 years. Table 4.2 provides available data on the youth of Inuit, Métis, and First Nations (registered and non-status Indians who make up this group are shown separately) in 2001 and projections for 2026. In 2006, about 9 per cent of the Aboriginal population was under five years, and 10 per cent was five to nine years old (Statistics Canada 2006). The proportion of Aboriginal people under five is approximately 70 per cent greater than the proportion of non-Aboriginal youngsters of that age.

Table 4.2   Median Age and Population under 25 for Aboriginal Groups*
and Canada**, 2001 and 2006

Year	Population	Median age (in Years)	Percent Population 0–14 Years	Percent Population 15–24 Years
2001	Inuit	20.1	40%	19%
	Métis	26.8	29%	18%
	Registered Indian	24.0	35%	17%
	Non-status Indian	23.8	35%	17%
	Canadian population	37.2	19%	14%
2026	Inuit	25.3	32%	18%
	Métis	34.1	23%	14%
	Registered Indian	32.1	24%	15%
	Non-status Indian	22.2	35%	20%
	Canadian population	43.3	15%	11%

*Indian and Northern Affairs Canada and Canada Mortgage and Housing Corporation 2007.
**Statistics Canada 2001.

Statistics Canada indicates that 40 per cent of First Nation people currently live on reserve, but First Nation people also experience a great deal of mobility. A steady migration of Aboriginal families into urban centres has been noted over the last three censuses: 54 per cent of Aboriginal families live in urban areas with a concentrated population of 1000 or more. Winnipeg, Edmonton, and Vancouver have the largest Aboriginal populations. Another one-third live on reserves, in self-governing First Nations, and in Métis settlements.

Aboriginal peoples suffer disproportionately from poverty, as the average household income of Aboriginal families in Canada in 2006 was little more than one-third of that of non-Aboriginal families. The 2006 census data estimated that 41 to 52.1 per cent of Aboriginal children live below the poverty line (depending on criteria for defining poverty and whether estimates include children with Aboriginal identity or ancestry). One in four First Nation children living on reserve lives in poverty, compared to one in six Canadian children as a whole. The gap between Aboriginal and non-Aboriginal adults in average annual incomes has increased over the past quarter-century (Cooke, Beavon, and McHardy 2004). Aboriginal unemployment rates exceeded the jobless rate of the population as a whole in every province, with rates in Saskatchewan and Manitoba more than triple the overall rate.

Related to employment and household income, average educational attainment among Aboriginal parents, though improving, is lower than that among non-Aboriginal parents. This gap seems to be narrowing; for example, the proportion of Aboriginal people who have attained a high school diploma or education beyond high school increased from 38 per cent in 1981 to 57 per cent in 2001. Yet by 2001, the proportion of Aboriginal people who had not attained a high school diploma was 2.5 times higher than the proportion among non-Aboriginal Canadians.

Quality of Family Life

While some First Nation and Métis families are thriving, the evidence related to poverty and other socio-economic factors indicates that a majority of these families are not. Aboriginal leaders and scholars have asserted that the deteriorated quality of life for First Nation and Métis families is a direct consequence of the extent to which their parents and grandparents were negatively affected by colonization (RCAP 1996). These scholars make particular reference to the negative and intergenerational repercussions of residential schooling.[6] Many of today's First Nation parents and grandparents did not learn parenting skills because they were institutionalized from a young age (Dion Stout and Kipling 2003; Mussell 2005). Many lost confidence in their capacity to engage in the kinds of nurturing social interactions with young children that promote attachment and intimate social interaction (Wesley-Esquimaux and Smolewski 2003). These interactions are the primary vehicles for promoting self-esteem, positive cultural identity, empathy, language development, and curiosity about the world during infancy and early childhood.

Child welfare involvement exacerbated the disruption of Aboriginal families that began in residential schools, and this legacy continues today. Children who were removed from their homes and communities often suffered not only from a lack of nurturing but also from a crippling loss of identity because of being displaced from their homes, communities, lands, and cultures (Newhouse and Peters 2003). In addition to these losses, Aboriginal families have experienced trauma because of forced relocation of villages, the dispersion of clans, and urbanization.

Aboriginal peoples also suffer from the ongoing and pervasive influences of government policies and variations in access to supports and services. These conditions result in a very different quality of life for most First Nation and Métis families compared to most non-Aboriginal families in Canada. First Nation and Métis family life is a function, in large part, of the quality of the environments in which they are embedded, including social, economic, political, and physical conditions. Many of the risks and difficulties facing First Nation and Métis parents and their children arise from ongoing racism, political oppression, and structural factors. The latter include poverty, environmental dispossession and degradation, and lack of community-based education, health, and family support programs that incorporate First Nation and Métis knowledge and are relevant to local circumstances (Salee 2006). All of these factors contribute to the quality of life indicators discussed below.

Shattered Families and Lone-Parent Households

The pattern of shattered families that started with disruptive government policies is evident today in the reportedly high rates of lone-parent families. Census data indicate that more First Nation and Métis mothers are lone parents and, overall, more Aboriginal children (35 per cent) than non-Aboriginal children (17 per cent) live in lone-parent households. Lone parenting is even more common among Aboriginal families living in urban areas, where more than 50 per cent of Aboriginal children live in single-parent homes compared to 17 per cent of non-Aboriginal children. Most lone-parent households are headed by mothers, although there are also more Aboriginal single-father-headed households (6 per cent) compared to non-Aboriginal single-father households (3 per cent) (Health Canada 2003).

It is possible that census data convey a distorted picture of life in First Nation and Métis communities, where households may include a varied and changing array of relations. Parents who are co-parenting may not be legally married and therefore not recognized. While census data are suggestive, there is no direct measure of fathers or mothers, and the numbers of lone parents may be overestimated. Individuals counted as lone parents may, in fact, be supported by extended family networks. Nonetheless, the reported high incidence of lone parenthood is a concern because of the potential impacts on the social and economic well-being of all family members; lone parenting is associated with a greater probability of living in poverty (Weitzman 2003). This is particularly likely for adolescent mothers, a phenomenon that is much more common among First Nation and Métis women than among non-Aboriginal women (Statistics Canada 2006). The number of First Nation children born to adolescent women has remained high since 1986 at about 100 births per 1000 women, a rate that is seven times higher than the rate for other Canadian adolescents and comparable to the adolescent fertility level in the world's least developed countries such as Nepal, Ethiopia, and Somalia (Guimond and Robitaille 2008).

Statistical data and anecdotal reports from First Nation and Métis communities and family-serving agencies indicate that many First Nation and Métis fathers are elusive when it comes to family life. Increasing alarm about this pattern motivated an inaugural study involving interviews with 80 First Nation and

Métis fathers of young children (Ball 2010). Statistical data sources show that as a group, and compared to non-Aboriginal men, First Nation and Métis men have a higher prevalence of living in poverty, homelessness, and unemployment (Statistics Canada 2003), nine times more incarceration (Correctional Service Canada 2006),[7] and higher rates of suicide, mental and physical health problems, and injuries resulting in hospital admission (Health Canada 2003). Combined with negative social stigma, media stories, and expectations for their roles as fathers, First Nation and Métis men face formidable obstacles to positive involvement as fathers. The vast majority of the 80 fathers interviewed reported three or more of these problems as creating difficulties for connecting with their children, playing a role in family life, or sustaining connection with their children across changes in their relationships with their children's mother or other changes in their lives (Ball 2010). Virtually all of the 80 men described past or current challenges with mental health or addictions, and most were struggling to generate a living wage and to secure adequate housing. Research about non-indigenous fathers shows significant correlations between father involvement and developmental outcomes for children, mothers, and fathers (Allen and Daly 2007). Father absence is associated with more negative developmental and health outcomes for children and fathers (Ball and Moselle 2007). Grand Chief Edward John of the BC First Nations Summit contends that 'Aboriginal fathers may well be the greatest untapped resource in the lives of Aboriginal children and youth' (John 2003).

As Claes and Clifton (1998) and Mussell (2005) point out, the frequent lack of involvement of First Nation and Métis fathers in their children's lives tends to be widely interpreted as reflective of their indifferent attitudes. There is little acknowledgement in family support programs of the unique challenges faced by these men, most of whom have no memories of positive experiences with a father or father figure in their own lives as children and youth. And while there is a trend toward increasing numbers of lone-father-headed households, there are no programs specifically designed to help First Nation and Métis men become effective supports for their children's health and development (Ball and George 2007).

Aboriginal Child Welfare

One of the direst consequences of structural inequities confronting Aboriginal peoples and the legacies of colonial disruptions is that Aboriginal children continue to be greatly overrepresented among children in government care. An early study estimated that in the late 1990s, Aboriginal children represented between 30 and 40 per cent of children in Canada in out-of-home care in the late 1990s (Farris-Manning and Zandstra 2003). In 2005, analysis of child welfare data in three provinces revealed that a total of 10.23 per cent of First Nation children on reserves had been apprehended by child welfare agencies or placed voluntarily by parents in government care compared to 0.67 per cent of non-Aboriginal children (Blackstock et al. 2005). Currently, approximately 27,000 First Nation children under 17 are in government care, three times the number enrolled in residential schools at the height of their operations or at any time in Canada's history (Blackstock 2003). In some provinces, Aboriginal children outnumber non-Aboriginal children in care by a ratio of 8 to 1, and removals of Aboriginal children from home into child welfare custody appear to be increasing.

The *Canadian Incidence Study of Reported Child Abuse and Neglect* (Trocme et al. 2005) has shown that the primary reason Aboriginal children enter the child protection system is neglect, including physical neglect, lack of supervision of a child at risk of physical harm, or other examples of inadequate provisions for a child's health, safety, or education. The study found that among children coming to the attention of the child protection system, Aboriginal children are twice as likely as non-Aboriginal children to be part of a family that survives on social benefits and lacks full-time employment and to live in public housing or housing that is unsafe or overcrowded and many times more likely to have family members engaged in chronic patterns of substance misuse (Trocme et al. 2005). As Blackstock and other scholars argue, these factors indicate the grave socio-economic conditions of Aboriginal peoples. A child welfare study (Trocme et al. 2006) indicates that First Nation children are not overrepresented among reports for child abuse compared to other children for whom a child welfare investigation is carried out, suggesting some protective factors at work in families, however impoverished.

The Assembly of First Nations (2006a) has commented that there is insufficient funding to support some First Nation families to keep their children safely at home, coupled with seemingly unlimited funds to remove them. Shortfalls in funding for prevention and early intervention programs within child welfare services on reserves have been acknowledged by the Department of Indian and Northern Affairs (Blackstock et al. 2005). In addition, no program within the department actively funds and monitors family support programs and early intervention services that are understood in Canada as important for promoting the transition to parenthood, effective parenting, and family stability—services that are available to First Nation children living off-reserve, Métis families, and all other Canadian families through provincial systems (Blackstock et al. 2005; McDonald and Ladd 2000).

Health Consequences of Poverty and Shattered Families
First Nation and Métis families experience frequent and often serious health problems causing loss of family members, long absences of family members for health care in cities far from home, frequent disruption of family routines in order to travel to health services, and accommodations within the home environment and household routines to meet the needs of a family member with a physical disability, psychiatric disorder, or chronic disease (Ball 2008; de Leeuw, Fiske, and Greenwood 2002). Research reviews have found evidence of poorer health outcomes on almost every health indicator among Aboriginal compared to non-Aboriginal children (Canadian Institute for Health Information 2004) and adults (Adelson 2005). For example, they are more likely to be born prematurely, to be diagnosed with fetal alcohol spectrum disorder (FASD), to have a physical disability, or to suffer accidental injury. First Nation and Métis children have a 1.5 times greater probability of dying before their first birthday (Health Canada 2005) and a higher rate of hospitalization for acute lung infections (Canadian Institute for Health Information 2004).

The Aboriginal Peoples Survey conducted by Statistics Canada (2001) asked First Nation parents living off-reserve about the health of their children. This survey found that parents rated their children's health lower than that of all children in the general population; the gap in ratings was largest for children under five. The survey showed that compared to all Canadian children, First Nation and Métis children living off-reserve are more likely to have been born with a birth weight under 2500 g (8 per cent of First Nation and Métis infants compared to 6 per cent of all Canadian infants), more likely to be accidentally injured (13 per cent compared to 11 per cent for all children), and less likely to eat breakfast.

In 1999, a First Nations and Inuit Regional Health Survey Committee (1999) reported that First Nation parents living on reserves and Inuit parents reported nearly twice the rate of severe disabilities among their children compared to non-Aboriginal parent reports. Prevalent disabilities included FASD, hearing loss, attention disorders, and learning disabilities. The highest rates were among First Nation children living on versus off-reserve. Health inequities such as these have been attributed to poverty, low-quality and overcrowded housing, limited education resulting in low health literacy, and high unemployment (Cooke, Beavon, and McHardy 2004). Adding a chronological perspective to these ecological determinants of health, the First Nations Centre (2005) reported that in 2002/3, six of 10 First Nation and Métis respondents to a regional health survey identified the legacies of residential schools as a significant contributor to their own and their children's poorer health status. Data analysis indicated that First Nation respondents' health improved as a function of the number of years since family members were involved in residential schools (First Nations Centre 2005). Insufficient access to healing programs and other treatment options, particularly for First Nations living on reserves, was identified by parents as another contributor.

Chronic disease, severe learning disabilities, frequent illness, and overall poor health of children place enormous burdens on their caregivers in terms of financial implications, time and effort, parents' sense of adequacy in being able to meet their child's needs, and parents' overall experience of stress. Coupled with a widely recognized lack of access to needed screening, diagnostic assessment, early intervention programs, treatment, and occupational therapy programs, particularly on reserves and in rural areas, many First Nation and Métis parents face enormous challenges on a daily basis with few resources.

Families in Motion

One noteworthy feature of life in First Nation and Métis families is the frequency with which they move. First Nations living off-reserve and Métis families move nearly twice as often as non-Aboriginal families (Statistics Canada 2006). First Nation families living on reserves move less often. Norris and Clatworthy (2006) refer to this high mobility as 'churn':

> 'Churn' refers to the very high rates of mobility and migration within urban areas, with high rates of in- and out-migration (to and from cities, between reserves and cities), and high rates of residential mobility within cities. These high rates of mobility and migration can impact in a number of ways, affecting the delivery of programs and services, and having disruptive effects on families and children. This is particularly relevant in the area of education, with indications that high mobility and change can negatively affect children's educational outcomes.

Additional negative impacts identified by Norris and Clatworthy include the potential for family instability and dissolution and weak social cohesion in First Nation and Métis communities and neighbourhoods. The National Council of Welfare (2007) points out that the potential for these negative impacts is exacerbated when the family is headed by a lone parent and/or has low income and high needs, as do many First Nation and Métis families.

At the same time, First Nation and Métis parents often relocate as a strategy for gaining access to needed resources, including professional services and specialized programs for children with disabilities or health conditions, or education or employment for an adult family member (Ball 2006). Another phenomenon that sometimes accounts for relocating is that the boundaries of First Nation and Métis family units tend to be permeable and family members often transition from one home or town to another, one set of relationships to another, or divide their time among more than one place they call home. Sometimes an adult family member may leave the family unit temporarily or permanently because of difficulties in the primary–couple relationship. The remaining parent may welcome a new partner and one or more of his or her children or other relatives. Families may informally adopt a niece or nephew or even a neighbour. Families in urban centres may expand to include more distant relatives from rural or remote communities who come to the city for school, work, or special programs. The 'open doors' found in many First Nation and Métis families no doubt stem from the traditional extended family structures that were ubiquitous before colonization.

Summary of Basic Characteristics and Quality of Life Indicators

The quality of life of children everywhere depends not only on having necessary resources for survival and health but also on the well-being of their primary caregivers. No doubt some First Nation and Métis parents and their children draw on the many strengths of their cultural traditions and personal experiences of being raised in healthy families. Their cultures hold wisdom for child-rearing and positive predispositions toward children and youth. Values and approaches that inform socialization in many Aboriginal families include a recognition of children's varying abilities as gifts, a holistic view of child development, promotion of skills for living on the land, respect for a child's spiritual life and contributions to the community's cultural life, transmission of a child's ancestral language, and building upon strengths more than compensating for weaknesses. There is also evidence that many families still operate with the extended and fluid family structures and models that are part of *Wahkohtowin* in traditional indigenous cultures. For example, data collected by Statistics Canada (2009) through an inaugural Aboriginal Children's Survey[8] indicate that the growing population of Aboriginal children is being raised in a wider variety of caregiver arrangements than are non-Aboriginal children. These findings demonstrate that some Aboriginal children continue to be supported through the extended family model of care: as shown in Table 4.3, Aboriginal children to age 14 are more likely to live with a grandparent or other relative than are non-Aboriginal children.

In spite of this promising evidence that remnants of *Wahkohtowin* still hold, trends found in the 2006 census portray many challenges, including large

Table 4.3   Living Arrangements of First Nation, Métis, and Non-Aboriginal Children Less Than 15 Years of Age, Canada, 2006

Living Arrangements of Children	First Nations Population (%)			Métis Population (%)	Non-Aboriginal Population (%)
	Total	On-Reserve	Off-Reserve		
Total	100	100	100	100	100
Total living with at least one parent	92	92	91	96	99
Living with two parents	54	59	50	65	82
Living with a lone mother	31	26	35	27	14
Living with a lone father	6	7	6	4	3
Living with a grandparent (no parent present)	3	4	3	2	0.4
Living with another relative	5	3	6	2	0.5
Living with non-relatives	0.4	0.4	0.4	0.2	0.2

Source: Statistics Canada, census of population, 2006. Adapted from Statistics Canada, 2006 Census: Analysis series, 97-558-XIE2006001, 2008. www.statcan.gc.ca/bsolc/olc-cel/olc-cel?catno=97-558-XIE2006001&lang=eng.

numbers of lone-parent households, very young parents, and families living in poverty. Many First Nation and Métis parents are struggling to hold their families together and to support their children's health, development, and educational achievement.

A review of the data presented here draws attention to a few salient characteristics relevant to understanding First Nation and Métis families today, including the following:[9]

1.   The Aboriginal population of children under five is growing exponentially.
2.   First Nation and Métis families tend to move much more often than non-Aboriginal families.
3.   Families are increasingly urban-based.
4.   Except for Aboriginal families living in urban census metropolitan areas, the average size of Aboriginal families is larger than the average size of non-Aboriginal families, with the largest families in rural areas off reserves.
5.   While a majority of First Nation and Métis children live in two-parent homes, there is a much larger population of lone parents than among non-Aboriginal households. This trend is likely to continue.
6.   Many First Nation and Métis families live in poverty, with low employment, education, and overall quality of life. Related to poverty, many families struggle to provide adequately for their children—a predicament

that is the most frequent justification given by child protection agencies for removal of children from family to government care.

These characteristics depict circumstances that many Aboriginal families find themselves in as they work toward rebuilding their communities today.

Putting the Pieces Back Together

We will raise a generation of First Nations, Inuit and Métis children and youth who do not have to recover from their childhoods. It starts now, with all our strength, courage, wisdom and commitment.

Declaration of a collective of national Aboriginal organizations, quoted in Blackstock, Bruyere, and Moreau 2005, 1

As the previous section demonstrates, First Nation and Métis families suffer the consequences of shattered families and communities in their everyday lives, and there is plenty of work to be done. In addition to reconsidering our relationships to the animals and the land, rebuilding *Wahkohtowin* will need to include ways to rebuild our human relations through residential-school healing programs, education and support for mothers and fathers during the transition to parenthood, infant development programs, quality child care, family-strengthening initiatives, family literacy, community development, employment, and social justice. Efforts are being undertaken in all of these areas, but it will take time and resources to rebuild healthy communities. To use residential-school healing initiatives as an example, Canadian government investments in the Aboriginal Healing Foundation (2006) have enabled important programs, tailored to local community groups, to aid in the healing process. Yet given the time needed to reconstitute strong cultural communities and family structures, federal government contributions to healing programs, administered by Aboriginal organizations, need to be recommitted for some time to come. Aboriginal people often assert that it took 'seven generations' to erode Aboriginal families, cultures, communities, and territories and it will take seven generations to rebuild their strength (Castellano 2002). This principle must be recognized in any dialogue around initiatives to rebuild the human relationships within *Wahkohtowin*.

Family healing is complex. Difficulties facing many First Nation and Métis families, such as high mortality and morbidity among infants and young children, apprehension of First Nation and Métis children into state care, early school leaving, and family dissolution, cannot be reduced simply by investing in more medical care, parenting programs, and targeted school-based interventions. In the face of historically conditioned barriers, First Nation and Métis community representatives, leaders, advocates, practitioners, and investigators emphasize the need for adequately resourced, sustained, and culturally based strategies at every level of government to improve supports for First Nation and Métis families and particularly for young children and parents. Leaders have called for support to be delivered within the contexts of children's families and cultural communities through community-driven programs operated by Aboriginal practitioners (Assembly of First Nations 1988; RCAP 1996). In other words, Aboriginal people are calling for strategies that, together, address a broad scope of issues and goals, co-ordinated holistically across sectors, to form a circle of supports to increase positive outcomes for First Nation and Métis children and their parents and to help rebuild a sense of community and positive cultural identification.

Although many initiatives could be highlighted to illustrate the good work of rebuilding indigenous families and communities, this chapter will conclude with examples that pertain specifically to children. For if the dismantling of families, communities, and lives really set in when the heart—the children— was ripped from the core, perhaps one of the most effective ways of rebuilding Aboriginal communities is to put the heart back in its place. A focus on children is particularly relevant considering the exponential growth of children in Aboriginal communities.

Early Childhood as a Strong Foundation for Family Strengthening

National organizations representing First Nation and Métis peoples have identified early childhood care and development (ECCD) training and services as priorities within a holistic vision of social development, population health, and economic advancement (see Canada Council on Learning 2007). In 1990, the Native Council of Canada (1990) undertook the first national effort to define Native child care and the meaning of cultural appropriateness with respect to the delivery of child care services. The council's report, *The Circle of Care*, conceptualized a direct link between culturally relevant child care services that are controlled by First Nations and the preservation of First Nations cultures. First Nations scholar Margo Greenwood summarized:

> Aboriginal early childhood development programming and policy must be anchored in Indigenous ways of knowing and being. In order to close the circle around Aboriginal children's care and development in Canada, all levels of government must in good faith begin to act on the

recommendations which Indigenous peoples have been articulating for early childhood for over 40 years (2006, 20).

In many First Nation and Métis communities and community-based organizations such as friendship centres, ECCD is seen as essential for protecting and enhancing the physical health, psychosocial well-being, and positive cultural identity of indigenous children and their families.

A review of non-formal and program literature, websites, newsletters, and agency reports yields a plethora of examples of community-based and community-involving Aboriginal ECCD programs that have been initiated in the past decade across the country. Steps that have been taken to develop First Nation and Métis capacity in the ECCD sector encompass training First Nation and Métis infant development and child care staff, mostly of a short-term, non-accredited nature, as well as creation of child care spaces, parent education resources and programs, and organizations that enable networking and resource exchange. Many of these programs reach out especially to families seen as needing extra support to provide adequate supervision, nutrition, and nurturance for their children to stop the cycle of recurrent removal of children by welfare agencies. Some programs reach out to children with health or developmental challenges. Many individual communities have developed their own approaches to home visiting programs, nurseries, and preschools, creating culturally based program elements and drawing upon curriculum found in early childhood programs, such as music and movement, storytelling, pre-literacy and pre-numeracy games, as well as parenting skills programs. A common objective of these programs is to reinforce the positive cultural identity of Aboriginal youngsters and their families. For example, program activities and materials often draw upon traditional motifs in arts and crafts, drama, dance, and stories and provide opportunities to engage with positive Aboriginal role models in child care and teaching roles.

Aboriginal Head Start

A significant contribution to family strengthening has come in the form of the federally funded Aboriginal Head Start (AHS) programs, which provide preschool and other kinds of early childhood programs to approximately 9100 First Nation children on reserves and approximately 4500 First Nation, Métis, and Inuit children in urban and northern communities (Indian and Northern Affairs Canada 2008). In total, about 8 per cent of Aboriginal children aged three to five attend AHS. A key feature of the AHS programs is the strong emphasis on parent involvement and family support. A community group that receives funding for program delivery works with parents and other stakeholders to decide on program specifics, and the programs are managed in consultation with parent advisory committees. Some programs require parental commitment to volunteer or to make a monetary contribution. Overall, AHS programs deliver culturally based, community-specific programs embodying six components: (1) parent/family involvement; (2) education and school readiness; (3) health promotion; (4) nutrition; (5) social support; and (6) culture and language.

AHS programs help to fill gaps in services to support families during the early stages of family formation, when parents—many of them very young and with few resources—need social support and practical assistance (Ball 2008; Minister of Public Works and Government Services 2002). AHS programs have the flexibility to develop in ways that are family-centred, family-preserving, and delivered within a community development framework. The programs are informed by the communities' internally identified needs and vision for improving the quality of life of young children and their families.

Some AHS programs have the potential to reduce the high rates of removal of children from their families and communities. Anecdotal reports in the non-formal literature and at gatherings often describe how the programs help the families of participating children to gain access to food, warm clothing, income assistance, and health, mental health, and social services. This is a uniquely promising aspect of AHS: one challenge for ensuring Aboriginal children's access to needed supports and services is that they often do not make it as far as the entry point in mainstream service delivery systems set up to meet needs of children in middle-class families in urban centres (e.g., families with ready access to transportation as well as knowledge of how service systems work and how to advocate to get their child's needs met). The potential for early childhood programs to become an entry point for young children and their caregivers, gradually introducing families to a range of other services and opportunities, has been documented in First Nations early childhood programs in BC (Ball 2005).

In view of a preponderance of lone-parent households, more investment is needed in quality, centre-based child care both to provide stimulating, safe environments for infants and children and to enable parents to further their education and training and to generate income. AHS and similar programs that are family-centred, holistic, preventive, and community-driven are one way that Canada can act to promote the health and development of young children who are the next generation of parents. Investments in AHS should be doubled to enable access by at least 20 per cent of eligible children. Expanded investments are also needed in First Nation and Métis community economic development, child welfare programs such as family support and parent education, and education outreach to children as well as adults.

Reconnecting First Nation and Métis Children with Their Families and Cultures of Origin

Significant numbers of First Nation and Métis children spend much of their childhood living in a series of foster homes or in adoptive families. Approximately one-quarter of children waiting for adoption in Canada are First Nation and Métis children (Adoption Council of Canada 2009). Across Canada, child and family service agencies operated by First Nation and Métis councils are innovating programs to reconnect children with their families of origin and/or with their cultural communities. For example, in British Columbia, the Métis Community Services Society operates a 'Roots' program to ensure that each Métis child and youth in government care has a plan that respects and preserves their Aboriginal identity and ties to their community and heritage. Another Métis program in BC is called The Circle of Life: Honouring the Spirit of the Family. This family preservation program works closely with families to provide education and support for Métis culture-based parenting, teachings from the Medicine Wheel, loss and grief counselling, family violence prevention, conflict resolution, life skills, and healing and spiritual growth. A third example is a program called *Nong Sila*, a Lekwungen term meaning 'many grandparents, many grandchildren'. This program arose in response to the fact that most First Nation and Métis children are placed with non-Aboriginal parents and these adoptees risk losing their cultural roots in their communities. The goal of *Nong Sila* is to promote adoption strategies that are grounded in the needs and cultural traditions of urban indigenous peoples.

Child welfare policy reforms and expanded funding are needed to create effective systems of in-community placements for Aboriginal children needing temporary out-of-home care (e.g., kinship guardians and Aboriginal foster care) so that Aboriginal children and youth can maintain their identities and not be bereft of family, community, and the life that family and community provide, as described earlier in the quote by Chief Atleo.

Outstanding Work

On the whole, programs that serve Aboriginal children exist because Aboriginal people have advocated and worked tirelessly to secure the supports they perceive as necessary for change. Their successes are tempered by the knowledge that much work remains. Although Canada has an Aboriginal Action Plan (Minister of Indian Affairs and Northern Development 1997), there is no legal framework for implementing it and no mechanism for monitoring the extent to which it is implemented (Assembly of First Nations 2006b). Federal, provincial, and territorial governments have failed to mobilize a thoughtful and co-ordin-ated response to improve the quality of life of First Nation and Métis families, beyond the level of the apology offered by the Canadian Government on 11 June 2008 (Office of the Prime Minister of Canada 2008) for the multigenerational impacts of years of colonial interventions on First Nation and Métis children born into families today.

In terms of overall healing and support for adult caregivers, Ojibway investi-gator Chantelle Richmond and her colleagues (2008) find that First Nation and Métis adults report relatively high levels of social support. Yet it appears that colonial legacies have engendered some negative forms of social support in the form of relationship violence and peer pressure to engage in health-damaging behaviours (Richmond 2009). Low social status, socio-cultural disruption, and the material deprivation of many First Nation and Métis families appear to com-bine to reduce their access to the kinds of social support and social networks that have been shown to be health-promoting in research with non-Aboriginal peoples (Link and Phelan 1995). It is imperative to find ways of providing sup-ports to Aboriginal mothers and fathers to regain the strengths of their ances-tors in raising children and youth and caring for elders. A program of action research involving First Nation and Métis community groups could explore ef-fective components of culturally based initiatives to support Aboriginal women and men during the transition to parenting and early family formation.

Investments in programs to prepare Aboriginal youth for parenthood are also imperative, given that many Aboriginal men and women begin having chil-dren early and have more children than non-Aboriginal Canadians. The United Nations Population Fund and countries with high adolescent fertility such as the United States implement strategies to reduce adolescent fertility and to meet some of the unique needs of adolescent parents. Few programs in Canada spe-cifically assist individuals and communities to address high adolescent preg-nancy rates or meet the needs of First Nation and Métis adolescent parents and their children. Sustained investments are needed to promote the success of Aboriginal youth in education, training, and transitions to the labour force, especially for girls. Research around the world has shown that employment that promotes social inclusion, a sense of purpose, and gender equality are the most effective measures to encourage young people to delay having children.

Regarding First Nation families living on reserves, whose well-being is the fiduciary responsibility of the federal government, the First Nations Child and Family Caring Society (2005) and the Assembly of First Nations (n.d.) have called for funding for quality child care, family support, prevention, and early intervention programs *at par* with provincial services for children living off reserves and settlements. Regarding First Nation and Métis children living off reserves primarily in urban centres, the National Association of Friendship Centres, the Congress of Aboriginal People, and the Métis National Council have called for implementation of policies to expand access to quality, culturally fitting ECCD and early intervention programs.

With respect to child welfare, the Wen'de report (Blackstock et al. 2005) draws on evidence from the *Canadian Incidence Study of Reported Child Abuse and Neglect* to demonstrate the need to improve the funding formula for First Nations delegated child and family service agencies to support primary, secondary, and tertiary intervention services in First Nation communities on reserves. This would enable implementation of a policy of least disruptive measures for a child at risk of maltreatment or neglect (i.e., in situ rather than out-of-community foster placement or adoption). Examples of less disruptive measures include support for improved parenting, more supervision of children through placement in child care during the day, local access to services that the child or parent needs, supplementary food resources, or foster care with a relative instead of outside the community where the child cannot remain in contact with family members.

Among the efforts that First Nations and Métis organizations and communities are making to put the pieces of the family and community systems back together, many communities are forming their own child and family serving agencies. The range of programs and the scope of delegated authority for child welfare varies among these new agencies, from cultural consultation to mainstream agencies to a full range of family support, prevention, and early intervention services, as well as foster and adoption placement (Bala et al. 2004). The issues facing this agenda and ways forward are beyond the scope of the current discussion. The challenges are especially acute for communities on-reserve, partly as a result of federal funding shortfalls, a lack of credentialed First Nation and Métis child welfare practitioners, and difficulty recruiting qualified practitioners to work in settings with few support services or alternatives for children (Blackstock et al. 2006).

Finally, rebuilding *Wahkohtowin* will only succeed if poverty among First Nation and Métis children and their families is adequately addressed. The National Council of Welfare (2007, 26) links the high impoverishment of many Aboriginal families to their 'tremendous programming needs, reliance on food banks, and cyclical poverty'. Poverty makes the health and development problems of Aboriginal children both more prevalent and more entrenched

(Canadian Institute of Child Health 2000). In turn, poverty and a lack of practical supports for families make it difficult for parents to meet children's needs, contributing to a continuation of the time-worn pattern of government apprehension of First Nation and Métis children and their placement in foster and adoptive homes.

Conclusion

Aboriginal families will never look like they did in the past, when family was the foundation for indigenous economies, governance, social systems, and law. But the notion of *Wahkohtowin* can be reconstructed so that strong families and kinship systems and healthy relations with the natural world will make Aboriginal peoples strong again. As Aboriginal peoples and their allies come together to reconstruct the puzzle, many strengths exist to build upon; new pieces will be added and others adapted to fit new circumstances. Maria Campbell teaches that rebuilding piece by piece can involve something as small as a song, a story, or a gesture, working with traditional ways to reconstruct families and communities into the centuries to come.

Many Aboriginal children still have opportunities to be cared for by extended kin networks as they would have been in the past. But if we look at the structure of contemporary Aboriginal families and communities, we can also see a creative and adaptive process happening in the absence of blood kin. Marlene Brant Castellano (2002) notes that the extended family's traditional role is being assumed in many communities by Aboriginal agencies, many of which have borrowed from mainstream practice models and adapted them to reflect the community's culture. She describes how some Aboriginal adults, working on recovery, are finding their way 'home' not by returning to their original families but by knitting together connections in an urban environment with Aboriginal people who come from diverse nations, creating 'families of the heart' (2002, 1). This kinship model is evident in a story shared by Métis writer Joanne Arnott, who participated in a 'traditional parenting skills' program in Vancouver that was facilitated by 'Grandmother Harris'. Arnott's experience was one of 'home making' in which she was able to benefit from kinship support through the program's 'family of the heart' (Arnott 2006).

Another strength that will lend itself to rebuilding is the flexibility and accommodation to changing family configurations and new surroundings that many First Nation and Métis families have demonstrated over time. As was suggested by findings of the 2006 Aboriginal Children's Survey (Statistics Canada 2009), First Nation and Métis children may enjoy the benefit of multiple caregivers, of being raised by a community rather than in the nuclear and patriarchal family model that was imposed by colonial authorities. Ball's research on Aboriginal fathers is evidence of the complex, fluid, and mobile nature of Aboriginal families. Although this has often been cast in a negative light, it may also be seen as a strength to build on. Another strength is that Aboriginal families continue to work together to face adversities such as poverty. As the daughter–mother team of D. Memee Harvard-Lavell and Jeannette Corbiere-Lavell point out:

> Even in its contemporary manifestation, as opposed to the more historical notions of communal tribal living, for most members of the Aboriginal community everyday survival is still dependent on extensive networks of family and friends who support and reinforce one another. Unlike the non-aboriginal middle-class whose adult members can generally afford to pay others to assume their familial responsibilities, such as child and elder care, those who have almost no economic opportunity, much less actual economic security, must rely heavily upon the help of others (2006, 189).

Between extended families and 'families of the heart', Aboriginal peoples have worked to meet the needs of children in their communities, and they call upon the genius of their cultures to do so. The Ontario Federation of Indian Friendship Centres (2002), for example, demonstrates how families and communities work with children and youth on FASD by tapping into kinship models, working with the land, using traditional parenting techniques, participating in ceremonies, and drawing on the Aboriginal family as medicine. Other families are holding onto or reclaiming practices to strengthen individuals and rebuild families and communities. Naming ceremonies, walking out ceremonies, puberty seclusions, fasts, and traditional infant care practices (e.g., using a cradle board) reinforce these vital relationships.

In closing, we share a story told by Lakota scholar John Red Horse:

> The Anishinaabe family drove its station wagon into a tight parking space at the Regional Native American Center in Minneapolis. Everyone in the family above the age of toddler joined in unloading suitcases, folding chairs and bustles. A celebratory dance was being held tonight—the Wild Rice Festival—and the family was there to dance, sing, and visit kin as well as old friends. Once in the building, those family members who would dance this evening went to the dressing area and changed from street clothes to regalia. One daughter carried her 3-year-old son back to

the dance area; he was dressed in the regalia of a grass dancer. They got to their chairs, and the mother laid out a star quilt. She put her son on the quilt, and this was the first glimpse that any stranger had of the boy outside his mother's arms. These strangers looked at him with a sympathetic expression. The boy was disabled from the waist down.

As the evening wore one, the strangers were taken aback with the circle of care and concern organized around the boy by family and friends. He was the centre of attention. Elders, including grandparents and older aunts; older brothers, sisters, and cousins; and a host of teenage and adult friends joined together to meet the boy's needs: holding him when he became restive, carrying him around to retail stands, entertaining him with play, and supervising him when his mother was dancing. The strangers beamed with pride because the boy danced in his own way—from the waist up, with head and shoulders keeping time to the beat of the drums. He participated in every inter-tribal dance and entered the dance contest for little boys (Red Horse 1997, 243).

Like all Aboriginal stories, this one has many lessons and levels. The first observation might be that in many cases, extended family and community still work together, with children at the heart and centre. The significant presence of children in community gatherings comes across here; anyone who has spent time in an Aboriginal community will know that children are always around, even in business venues that might be considered off-limits in a mainstream setting. As with stories of FASD gathered by the Ontario Federation of Indian Friendship Centres, Red Horse's story demonstrates that Aboriginal communities often recognize and honour children with different abilities and that cultural activities can be a way of providing them with a place and a way to participate. Red Horse's story, then, is the story of Aboriginal families, now and into the future—one of strengths and challenges; of time-honoured systems and cultures; of modern settings, emergent tools and techniques; of children at the heart and a resolute *Wahkohtowin* falling into place.

Discussion Questions

1. Why do you think family was identified as the most fundamental area of concern and the starting point for healing and hope in the report of the Royal Commission on Aboriginal Peoples?

2. Who took care of you as you grew up, and how did your experiences as a child contribute to how you view family now? In what ways is this similar to or different from the ways that Aboriginal peoples may have raised their children in the past?

3. What are Aboriginal and non-Aboriginal child and family serving agencies in your region doing to contribute to rebuilding the strength of First Nation and Métis families?

4. What challenges and opportunities do you see in your community or area of work that may affect the opportunities for First Nation and Métis families to a secure quality of life?

5. How might the growth of 'families of the heart' as discussed by Marlene Brant Castellano contribute to the development of new kinds of 'kinship' networks and communities for Aboriginal peoples living in urban areas?

Further Readings

Anderson, K. 2007. 'Giving life to the people: An indigenous ideology of motherhood'. In A. O'Reilly, ed., *Maternal Theory: Essential Readings*, 761–81. Toronto: Demeter.

Ball, J. 2008. 'Promoting equity and dignity for Aboriginal children in Canada'. *IRPP Choices* 14 (7): 1–30.

Blackstock, C., et al. 2005. 'Wen'de: We are coming to the light of day'. www.fncfcs.com/docs/WendeReport.pdf.

Castellano, M. Brant. 2002. *Aboriginal Family Trends: Extended Families, Nuclear Families, Families of the Heart*. Contemporary Family Trends Series. Ottawa: Vanier Institute of the Family.

Mussell, W.J. 2005. *Warrior-Caregivers: Understanding the Challenges and Healing of First Nations Men*. Ottawa: Aboriginal Healing Foundation.

Wesley-Esquimaux, C.C., and M. Smolewski. 2003. *Historic Trauma and Aboriginal Healing*. Ottawa: Aboriginal Healing Foundation Research Series.

Notes

1. In this chapter, 'Aboriginal' is used to refer to First Peoples in Canada, which include First Nations, Inuit, and Métis as recognized in Section 35 of the Canadian Constitution. The term 'indigenous' (as used here) is inclusive of First Peoples internationally and, in particular, Native Americans.

2. We use 'traditional' in this paper to signify communities that were living in close relationship with the land. It is important to note that traditions and traditional ways are not static and that many of the values, principles, and practices that come from 'traditional' Aboriginal ways still operate in contemporary communities. Many traditional ways are also now being reclaimed to suit current generations.

3. These examples refer to Algonquian peoples.

4. Each source of data about Aboriginal peoples in Canada offers an incomplete set of information because of widely differing sampling opportunities and methods and different ways of asking questions, analyzing data, and reporting findings across data collecting agencies (e.g., Statistics Canada, Indian and Northern Affairs Canada, Health Canada, National Aboriginal Health Organization). Thus, constructing a picture of First Nation and Métis families' quality of life and their health and development requires a synthetic process relying largely on proxies and anecdotal

and non-formal reports, along with a handful of program evaluations that are far from conclusive.

5. Several communities on reserves, including some with comparatively large populations such as the Mohawks of Akwesasne and Six Nations of the Grand River, did not participate in the 2006 census. The number of residents in Canada who report Aboriginal identity is considerably smaller than the number who report Aboriginal ancestry. Sources of population-level data about Aboriginal peoples are often conflicting and contested, and all are incomplete in terms of which populations of Aboriginal children have been surveyed.

6. To find bibliographies of information on the impact of residential schools, visit the Aboriginal Healing Foundation, www.ahf.ca.

7. Aboriginal offenders are increasingly overrepresented in the Canadian justice system. While Aboriginal people make up 3.3 per cent of the Canadian population, they account for 18 per cent of the federally incarcerated population and 16 per cent of people sentenced (Correctional Service Canada 2006).

8. The Aboriginal Children's Survey is the first repository of Aboriginal parents' reports on developmental milestones, health, and quality of life of young Aboriginal children in Canada (see Statistics Canada 2009). In 2006/7, more than 10,000 First Nation, Métis, and Inuit parents of children aged six months to five years participated in this new post-census survey conducted by Statistics Canada and guided by a group of Aboriginal and non-Aboriginal advisors. The survey yielded quantitative data enabling disaggregated and combined analysis of development trends, estimates of health problems and developmental difficulties, and information on the perceived accessibility and frequency of utilization of programs and services for Inuit, Métis, and First Nation children living off-reserve across Canada.

9. The summary material presented here highlights some general characteristics and trends among First Nation and Métis families overall. However, as noted, there are many cultural groups among First Nation and Métis peoples and many variations among individuals within them. As well, many families today are composed of some children and adults with Aboriginal ancestry and some without, as couples with mixed ancestry have children and as family composition changes with separation, divorce, death, formal and informal adoption, and so on. Recognizing the diverse and hybrid character of First Nation and Métis families today is as important as knowing general trends when developing understandings, policies, and programs to support quality of life improvement and goal achievement among First Nation and Métis individuals, families, or communities.

Acknowledgements

For their helpful comments during the writing of this chapter, we are grateful to Sharla Peltier, Cathy Richardson, John Red Horse, and David Long. We thank Maria Campbell for permission to share her metaphor about the shattering of Aboriginal families and communities and John Red Horse for permission to share his story.

References

Aboriginal Healing Foundation. 2006. *Final Report of the Aboriginal Healing Foundation: Promising Healing Practices in Aboriginal Communities*, vol. 3. Ottawa: Aboriginal Healing Foundation.

Adelson, N. 2005. 'The embodiment of inequity: Health disparities in Aboriginal Canada'. *Canadian Journal of Public Health* March/April: 45–61.

Adoption Council of Canada. 2009. 'Canada's waiting children'. www.adoption.ca.

Allen, S., and K. Daly. 2007. *The Effects of Father Involvement: A Summary of the Research Evidence*. Research review for the Public Health Agency of Canada Population Health Fund Project: Fathers Involvement. Ottawa: Fathers Involvement Initiative.

Anderson, Karen. 1991. *Chain Her by One Foot: The Subjugation of Native Women in Seventeenth-Century New France*. New York: Routledge.

Anderson, Kim. 2000. *A Recognition of Being: Reconstructing Native Womanhood*. Toronto: Canadian Scholars Press.

Arnott, J. 2006. 'Dances with cougar: Learning from traditional skills parenting programs'. In D.M. Harvard-Lavell and J. Corbiere-Lavell, eds, *Until Our Hearts Are on the Ground: Aboriginal Mothering, Oppression, Resistance and Rebirth*, 94–104. Toronto: Demeter.

Assembly of First Nations. n.d. 'Fact sheet: The reality for First Nations in Canada'. www.afn.ca/article.asp?id=764.

———. 1988. *Tradition and Education: Towards a Vision of Our Future*. Ottawa: Assembly of First Nations.

———. 2006a. *Leadership Action Plan on First Nations Child Welfare*. Ottawa: Assembly of First Nations.

———. 2006b. *Royal Commission on Aboriginal Peoples at Ten Years: A Report Card*. Ottawa: Assembly of First Nations.

Atleo, E.R. 2004. *Tsawalk: A Nuu-chah-nulth Worldview*. Vancouver: University of British Columbia Press.

Bala, N., et al. 2004. *Canadian Child Welfare Law: Children, Families and the State*. Toronto: Thompson.

Ball, J. 2005. 'Early childhood care and development programs as hook and hub for inter-sectoral service delivery in indigenous communities'. *Journal of Aboriginal Health* 1: 36–49.

———. 2006. 'Developmental monitoring, screening and assessment of Aboriginal young children: Findings of a community–university research partnership'. Paper presented at the Aboriginal Supported Child Care Conference, Vancouver, November.

———. 2008. 'Promoting equity and dignity for Aboriginal children in Canada'. *IRPP Choices* 14 (7): 1–30.

———. 2010. 'Indigenous fathers reconstituting circles of care'. *American Journal of Community Psychology* special issue on Men, Masculinity, Wellness, Health and Social Justice–Community-Based Approaches. DOI 10.1007/s10464-009-9293-1.

Ball, J., and R.T. George. 2007. 'Policies and practices affecting Aboriginal fathers' involvement with their children'. In J.P. White, S. Wingert, D. Beavon, and P. Maxim, eds, *Aboriginal Policy Research: Moving Forward, Making a Difference*, vol. 3, 123–44. Toronto: Thompson.

Ball, J., and K. Moselle 2007. *Fathers' Contributions to Children's Well-being*. Research review for the Public Health Agency of Canada Population Health Fund Project: Fathers' Involvement. Ottawa: Fathers' Involvement Initiative.

Bennett, M., and C. Blackstock. 1992. *A Literature Review and Annotated Bibliography Focusing on Aspects of Aboriginal Child Welfare in Canada*. Winnipeg: First Nations Child and Family Caring Society.

Blackstock, C., et al. 2005. 'Wen'de: We are coming to the light of day'. Ottawa: First Nations Child and Family Caring Society of Canada. www.fncfcs.com/docs/WendeReport.pdf.

Blackstock, C., et al. 2006. *Reconciliation in Child Welfare: Touchstones of Hope for Indigenous Children, Youth, and Families*. Ottawa: First Nations Child and Family Caring Society of Canada.

Blackstock, C., with M. Bennett. 2003. *National Children's Alliance: Policy Paper on Aboriginal Children*. Ottawa: First Nations Child and Family Caring Society of Canada.

Blackstock, C., D. Bruyere, and E. Moreau. 2005. 'Many hands, one dream: Principles for a new perspective on the health of First Nations, Inuit and Métis children and youth'. www.manyhandsonedream.ca.

Brown, J.S.H. 1980. *Strangers in Blood: Fur Trade Company Families in Indian Country*. Vancouver: University of British Columbia Press.

Campbell, Maria. 2008. Personal communication (summer).

Canada Council on Learning. 2007. *State of Learning in Canada: No Time for Complacency*. Report on Learning in Canada 2007. Ottawa: Canada Council on Learning.

Canadian Institute for Health Information. 2004. 'Aboriginal peoples' health'. In Canadian Institute for Health Information, eds, *Improving the Health of Canadians*, 73–102. Ottawa: Canadian Institute for Health Information.

Canadian Institute of Child Health. 2000. *The Health of Canada's Children*. 3rd edn. Ottawa: Canadian Institute of Child Health.

Carter, S. 1997. *Capturing Women: The Manipulation of Cultural Imagery in Canada's Prairie West*. Montreal: McGill-Queen's University Press.

Castellano, M. Brant. 2002. 'Aboriginal family trends: Extended families, nuclear families, families of the heart'. www.vifamily.ca/library/cft/aboriginal.html.

Claes, R., and D. Clifton. 1998. *Needs and Expectations for Redress of Victims of Abuse at Residential Schools*. Ottawa: Law Commission of Canada.

Cooke, M., D. Beavon, and M. McHardy. 2004. 'Measuring the well-being of Aboriginal people: An application of the United Nations Human Development Index to registered Indians in Canada, 1981–2001'. In J.P. White, P. Maxim, and D. Beavon, eds, *Aboriginal Policy Research: Setting the Agenda for Change*, vol. 1, 47–70. Toronto: Thompson.

Correctional Service Canada. 2006. 'Strategic plan for Aboriginal corrections: Innovat-ion, learning and adjustment'. www.csc-scc.gc.ca/text/prgrm/abinit/plan06-eng.shtml.

de Leeuw, S., J. Fiske, and M. Greenwood. 2002. *Rural, Remote and North of 51: Service Provision and Substance Abuse Related Special Needs in British Columbia's Hinterlands*. Prince George: University of Northern British Columbia Task Force on Substance Abuse.

Dion Stout, M., and G. Kipling. 2003. *Aboriginal People, Resilience and the Residential School Legacy*. Ottawa: Aboriginal Healing Foundation.

Dickason, O.P. 2009. *Canada's First Nations: A History of Founding Peoples*. Toronto: Oxford University Press.

Emmerich, L. 1991. '"Right in the midst of my own people": Native American women and the field matron program'. *American Indian Quarterly* 15 (2): 201–16.

Farris-Manning, C., and M. Zandstra. 2003. 'Children in care in Canada: A summary of current issues and trends with recommendations for future research'. Ottawa: Child Welfare League of Canada. www.cecw-cepb.ca/publications/574.

First Nations and Inuit Regional Health Survey National Steering Committee. 1999. *First Nations and Inuit Regional Health Survey: National Report 1999*. First Nations and Inuit Regional Health Survey National Steering Committee.

First Nations Centre. 2005. 'First Nations Regional Longitudinal Health Survey (RHS) 2002/03: Results for adults, youth and children living in First Nations communities'. www.naho.ca/firstnations/english/regional_health.php.

First Nations Child and Family Caring Society of Canada. 2005. 'A chance to make a difference for this generation of First Nations children and young people: The UNCRC and the lived experience of First Nations children in the child welfare system of Canada'. Submission to the Standing Senate Committee on Human Rights, 7 February. www.fncfcs .com/docs/CommitteeOnHumanRightsFeb2005.pdf.

Fournier, S., and E. Crey. 1997. *Stolen from Our Embrace: The Abduction of First Nations Children and the Restoration of Aboriginal Communities*. Vancouver: Douglas and McIntyre.

Greenwood, M. 2006. 'Children are a gift to us: Aboriginal-specific early childhood programs and services in Canada'. *Canadian Journal of Native Education* 29 (1): 12–28. www.accel-capea.ca/pdf/FinalGreenwood.pdf.

Guimond, E., and N. Robitaille. 2008. 'When teenage girls have children: Trends and consequences'. *Horizons* 10 (1): 49–51.

Harvard-Lavell, D.M., and J. Corbiere-Lavell, eds. 2006. *Until Our Hearts Are on the Ground: Aboriginal Mothering, Oppression, Resistance and Rebirth*. Toronto: Demeter.

Health Canada. 2003. *A Statistical Profile on the Health of First Nations in Canada*. Ottawa: Health Canada, First Nations Inuit Health Branch.

———. 2005. 'First Nations comparable health indicators'. www.hc-sc.gc.ca.

Indian and Northern Affairs Canada. 2008. 'Early childhood development: Programs and initiatives'. www.ainc-inac.gc.ca/hb/sp/ecd/index-eng.asp.

Indian and Northern Affairs Canada and Canada Mortgage and Housing Corporation. 2007. *Aboriginal Demography: Population, Household and Family Projections, 2001–2026*. Ottawa: Indian and Northern Affairs Canada and Canada Mortgage and Housing Corporation.

John, E. 2003. Presentation to the Aboriginal Leadership Forum on early childhood development, University of British Columbia, Vancouver, 10–11 March.

LeClaire, N., and G. Cardinal. 1998. *Alberta Elder's Cree Dictionary*. ed. E. Waugh. Edmonton: University of Alberta Press.

Link, B.G., and J. Phelan. 1995. 'Social conditions and fundamental causes of disease'. *Journal of Health and Social Behaviour* 35: 80–94.

McDonald, R.J., and P. Ladd. 2000. *First Nations Child and Family Services Joint National Policy Review: Final Report*. Ottawa: Assembly of First Nations, First Nations Child and Family Service Agency Representatives, and Department of Indian Affairs and Northern Development.

Miller, J.R. 1996. *Shingwauk's Vision: A History of Native Residential Schools*. Toronto: University of Toronto Press.

Minister of Indian Affairs and Northern Development. 1997. 'Gathering strength: Canada's Aboriginal action plan'. www.ainc-inac.gc.ca/gs/chg_e.html.

Minister of Public Works and Government Services. 2002. *Aboriginal Head Start in Urban and Northern Communities: Program and Participants 2001*. Ottawa: Minister of Public Works and Government Services.

Mussell, W.J. 2005. *Warrior-Caregivers: Understanding the Challenges and Healing of First Nations Men*. Ottawa: Aboriginal Healing Foundation.

National Council of Welfare. 2007. *First Nations, Métis and Inuit Children and Youth: Time to Act*. Ottawa: National Council of Welfare Reports (vol. 127).

Native Council of Canada. 1990. *Native Child Care: The Circle of Care*. Ottawa: Native Council of Canada.

Newhouse, D., and E. Peters, eds. 2003. *Not Strangers in These Parts: Urban Aboriginal Peoples*. Ottawa: Indian and Northern Affairs Canada.

Norris, M.J., and S. Clatworthy. 2006. 'Aboriginal mobility and migration in Canada: Factors, policy implications and responses'. Paper presented at the Second Aboriginal Policy Research Conference, Ottawa, March.

Office of the Prime Minister of Canada. 2008. 'Prime Minister offers full apology on behalf of Canadians for the Indian residential schools'. Press release, 11 June. http://pm.gc.ca/eng/media/asp?id2149.

Ontario Federation of Indian Friendship Centres. 2002. 'Aboriginal approaches to fetal alcohol syndrome/effects'. www.ofifc.org/page/FAS_MAG_ED1.pdf.

Peers, L., and J.S.H. Brown. 2000. 'There is no end to relationship among the Indians: Ojibwa families and kinship in historical perspective'. *The History of the Family* 4 (4): 529–55.

Perry, A. 2005. 'Metropolitan knowledge, colonial practice, and indigenous womanhood: Missions in nineteenth-century British Columbia. In K. Pickles and M. Rutherdale, eds, *Contact Zones: Aboriginal and Settler Women in Canada's Colonial Past*, 109–130. Vancouver: University of British Columbia Press.

RCAP (Royal Commission on Aboriginal Peoples). 1996. *Report of the Royal Commission on Aboriginal Peoples*. Ottawa: Canada Communication Group.

Red Horse, J. 1997. 'Traditional American Indian family systems'. *Family Systems and Health* 15 (3): 243–50.

Richmond, C. 2009. 'Explaining the paradox of health and social support among Aboriginal Canadians'. *Canadian Issues* winter: 65–71.

Richmond, C., and N.A. Ross. 2008. 'Social support, material circumstance and health behaviour: Influences on health in First Nation and Inuit communities of Canada'. *Social Science and Medicine* 67: 1423–33.

Rutherdale, M. 2002. *Women and the White Man's God: Gender and Face in the Canadian Mission Field*. Vancouver: University of British Columbia Press.

Salee, D., with D. Newhouse and C. Levesque. 2006. 'Quality of life of Aboriginal people in Canada: An analysis of current research'. *IRPP Choices* 12 (6): 1–38.

Statistics Canada. 2001. *A Portrait of Aboriginal Children Living in Non-reserve Areas: Results from the 2001 Aboriginal Peoples Survey*. Cat. No. 89-597-XIe. Ottawa: Statistics Canada.

———. 2003. *Aboriginal Peoples of Canada: Highlight Tables, 2001 Census*. Ottawa: Statistics Canada.

———. 2006. 'Census of population 2006'. www.statcan.gc.ca.

————. 2009. 'Selected findings from 2006 Aboriginal Children's Survey. First Nations people, Métis in Canada, Inuit in Canada'. *Canadian Social Trends* special edition. Catalogue no. 11-008. Ottawa: Statistics Canada.

Stremlau, R. 2005. 'To domesticate and civilize wild Indians: Allotment and the campaign to reform Indian families, 1875–1887'. *Journal of Family History* 30 (3): 265–86.

Trocme, N., et al. 2005. *The Experience of First Nations Children Coming into Contact with the Child Welfare System in Canada: The Canadian Incidence Study on Reported Child Abuse and Neglect.* Ottawa: First Nations Child and Family Caring Society.

————. 2006. 'Mesnmimk Wasatek—Catching a drop of light. Understanding the over-representation of First Nations children in Canada's child welfare system: An analysis of the Canadian Incidence Study of Reported Child Abuse and Neglect'. CIS-2003. www.fncfcs.com/docs/mesnmimk_wasatek.pdf.

Van Kirk, S. 1980. *Many Tender Ties: Women in Fur-Trade Society in Western Canada, 1670–1870.* Winnipeg: Watson and Dwyer.

Volo, J.M, and D.D. Volo. 2007. *Family Life in Native America.* Westport, CT: Greenwood.

Weitzman, M. 2003. 'Low income and its impact on psychosocial child development'. In *Encyclopedia on Early Childhood Development,* 1–8. Centre of Excellence for Early Childhood Development.

Wemigwans, J. (producer/director). 2002. *Seven Fires* (Feature video). Available from V-tape. org, 401 Richmond Street West, Suite 452, Toronto, ON M5V 3A8.

Wesley-Esquimaux, C.C., and M. Smolewski. 2003. *Historic Trauma and Aboriginal Healing.* Ottawa: Aboriginal Healing Foundation Research Series.

5 Learning from Indigenous Knowledge in Education

Jan Hare

The educational landscape for Aboriginal children and families in Canada has undergone many changes since Europeans first settled in our country. But no matter how the educational landscape has been transformed, the transmission and continuity of indigenous knowledge has been at the foundation for learning that Aboriginal families, communities, and Nations have always maintained for their children. It has been our knowledge systems, cultural traditions and values, and ancestral languages that have ensured the survival of Aboriginal people since time immemorial and affirmed our place within the Canadian context. They are the sources of strength Aboriginal children and youth draw upon as they navigate the educational challenges they face, whether they attend schools on-reserve or in rural or urban communities. Aboriginal families and communities are well aware that navigating the educational terrain of community-controlled, public, and private schooling requires their children to experience Western forms of knowledge but have always asserted that educational approaches should never be to the exclusion of our own knowledge systems. We know that our future generations of Aboriginal children will walk in 'two worlds' and need to be armed with a strong sense of who they are as Aboriginal people, contributing to their families and communities, while at the same time ensuring our participation in the social, economic, and political fabric of Canadian society. This chapter describes the role of indigenous knowledge in education, examining how Canadian educational policies and practices have moved from the denigration of indigenous knowledge in learning institutions to finding spaces in learning settings where indigenous knowledge as a foundation for learning is having a positive impact on the educational outcomes of Aboriginal children and youth, giving way to hope and healing for Aboriginal people. Just as important are the new learning opportunities that indigenous knowledge and approaches to education provide for all learners.

Aboriginal children and youth do not experience the same success with schooling as their non-Aboriginal counterparts. Only half of Aboriginal children living in non-reserve areas reported attending an early childhood education program (Statistics Canada Housing, Family and Social Statistics Division 2001). More than 60 per cent of Aboriginal peoples, ages 16 years and older, taking part in the International Adult Literacy Survey (Statistics Canada 2003) failed to meet the basic standard level 3, compared to 42 per cent of Canadians overall failing to meet this basic standard. These lower levels of literacy are also observed in young Aboriginal children (Cowley and Easton 2004). In high school, 48 per cent of Aboriginal youth fail to attain a diploma, compared to 31 per cent of non-Aboriginal youth (Statistics Canada and Council of Ministers of Education 2001). For First Nation youth living on reserve in 2001, only 29 per cent had graduated, a decrease from 32 per cent in 1996 (Indian Affairs and Northern Development 2005). While Aboriginal enrolment in post-secondary education is increasing, entrance and completion rates remain relatively low compared to those of non-Aboriginal students enrolled in university and college (Mendelson 2006).

Too often, Aboriginal learners and their families bear the blame for their failure to achieve in educational systems that do little to value their culture, values, and languages. The education of Aboriginal people must be understood within the larger colonial enterprise historically aimed at eliminating the 'Indian problem' in this country and in the context of the systemic inequalities inherent in the current education system that pose significant challenges to the educational success of Aboriginal children and youth. The legacy of schooling for Aboriginal people must be understood by all Canadians as we strive for equality and mutual respect for all learners in our schools today and improve relationships with Canada's Aboriginal peoples.

Improved educational outcomes for Aboriginal learners are also critical to improving more general social, health, and economic indicators for Aboriginal people. The Aboriginal population has been steadily increasing, and Aboriginal youth, ages 16 to 24, represent the fastest-growing segment of the Aboriginal and overall Canadian population (Statistics Canada and Council of Ministers of Education 2006). Currently, Aboriginal people are more likely to reside in urban and rural areas than on reserves. As noted in the Royal Commission on Aboriginal Peoples final report (RCAP 1996), education is the means by which Aboriginal people will strengthen their identities, families, communities, and economies. It is through the inclusion of indigenous knowledge that Aboriginal people will find meaning and relevance in educational opportunities. Moreover, attention to indigenous knowledge will benefit all Canadians as economic, environmental, and educational issues form an essential part of the ongoing nation-building agenda of this country.

The Role of Indigenous Knowledge in Traditional Education

Indigenous knowledge represents the local and culturally specific knowledge of a people that is dynamic, adapting over time and place (Battiste 2005). For indigenous people, their knowledges are derived from their ways of living, knowing, and being in this world. Indigenous knowledge emerges from the values, beliefs, and practices associated with their world views (Barnhardt and Kawagley 2005). Mi'kmaq scholar Marie Battiste (2005, 8) tells us that

> Indigenous peoples have their own methods for classifying and transmit-ting knowledge, just as they have Indigenous ways of deriving a liveli-hood from their environment. Information, insight, and techniques are passed down and improved from one generation to another.

Indigenous knowledge is intimately connected to land (Barnhardt and Kawagley 2005; Battiste 2002, 2005; Cajete 2000), where meaning and identity are con-structed through landscapes, territory, and relationships with the natural world. As indigenous peoples, our knowledges include processes that are intergenera-tional, experiential, tied to narrative and relational as ways of ensuring the con-tinuity and relevance of our knowledge systems.

Barnhardt and Kawagley (2005, 10) tell us that traditional education processes

> were carefully constructed around observing natural processes, adapting modes of survival, obtaining sustenance from the plant and animal world, and using natural materials to make their tools and implements. All of this was made understandable through demonstration and observation accompanied by thoughtful stories in which the lessons were embedded.

The emphasis on learning by watching, listening, and then doing is under-scored by many Aboriginal elders reflecting on their childhoods. Agnes Alfred (2004, 83–5) recounts of her Kwakwakewak childhood on the northwest coast of British Columbia:

> I watched my grandmother in her daily activities, whether cooking, pre-paring fish, digging roots or clams, weaving baskets or making rope. . . . I also followed my grandmother around when she was stripping bark off the trees so I would know how to do it myself.

Innu Elder Elizabeth Penashue shares her parents' hands-on approach to learning: 'When I was old enough as a little girl my mother encouraged me to work, cleaning beaver and other animals. My mother would perform and the children would sit around and watch, so that they can learn (Kulchyski, McCaskill, and Newhouse 1999, 200).

Storytelling provides Aboriginal children with valuable teachings about how things came to be and how to live in this world in a 'good way'. Pueblo poet and writer Simon Ortiz (1992, 7) tells us:

> Oral tradition of Native American people is based upon spoken language, but it is more than that too. Oral tradition is inclusive. It is the actions, behaviors, relationships, practices throughout the whole social, economic, and spiritual life process of a people. In this respect, the oral tradition is the consciousness of a people.

Storytelling was always part of children's daily living, as shared by Mary Lou Andrew in her interview with Sto:lo scholar Jo-ann Archibald (2008, 73):

> Stories were told when children were being taught how to sew, how to do laundry . . . in my childhood, my grandmother, my grandfather, always had stories . . . [when] walking through the fields or if you went to gather fruit or food, or just going from point A to point B, there was a story to be told. . . . You got not only the history about the place, the land; you were taught [other] lessons. . . . You got social studies . . . sometimes even science was thrown in, when you had to deal with herbs and medicines. You learned the importance of why you do something.

Anishinaabe children learn they came to the world by being lowered from above after a union of Mother Earth's four elements, wind, air, fire, and water. When the Earth was flooded, it was Nanaboozho and other animals floating on a log that searched below the waters for any sign of Earth. It was Muskrat who was successful in the animals' attempts to bring up the dirt from the depths below. And it is Turtle who bears the weight of the Earth, which expands on the turtle's shell to form what we know today as Turtle Island, or more familiar to non-Aboriginal people, North America. It is through the amusing, and sometimes serious, antics of the trickster that Aboriginal children learn important life lessons. Known as Raven or Coyote among First Nations communities in British Columbia, Glooskap among the Mi'kmaq, Nanaboozho to the Anishinaabe, and Wesakechak in Cree oral traditions, this character takes on many transformations, providing us with new understandings of the world.

Accompanying oral tradition were other communicative practices containing indigenous knowledge. Song, dance, and drumming were part of celebration and ceremony. Whether the handheld drums played among the Cree, the water drums used by the Anishinaabe or the wide and light-held drums of the Innu, their beat and rhythm go together with song, story, and dance. Aboriginal dances tell stories whereby the movements, style, and regalia of the dancer come together to give meaning. Some dances were considered prayers to give thanks. Some are shared at powwows or feasts. Other dances are more sacred, such as spirit dancing among northwest coastal groups or curing dances among the Haudenosaunee, remaining private when and where they are danced. The house posts and totem poles are another narrative 'text' that may honour a family or clan. These texts are every bit as committed to meaning-making as the written word that is privileged in schools (Hare 2005). Aboriginal children learn to read these alternative texts and know the protocols and teachings associated with them.

Ancestral languages are intimately connected to the world view of Aboriginal people (Battiste 2000). As the very means by which indigenous knowledge is contained and transmitted, ancestral languages convey cultural values, shape thought and identity, and describe relationships to people and place. Odowa Elder Liza Mosher explains the visceral connection to thought and feelings that ancestral languages provide:

Native language is very important because our teachings are in the language. You miss out on the meaning when you talk about it English. . . . What I understand is when I hear the teachings in the Lodge, how beautiful and sacred it is when it reaches people in the language I can't even describe how it feels. But when you talk about it in English, it is not the same, you don't have that feeling as you have in the language (quoted in Kulchyski, McCaskill, and Newhouse 1999, 160).

For Aboriginal people, the language expresses their distinct relationship with land (Task Force on Aboriginal Languages and Culture 2005). Place names, land-based experiences, custodial responsibilities to landscapes, and traditional territories and identity are given expression and meaning through ancestral languages. The transmission of language from one generation to another ensures the continuity of indigenous knowledge.

Living and learning have always been interwoven for Aboriginal people. Family and community were responsible for making sure that children learned the necessary skills and knowledge to ensure their survival. Elders and other traditional people in the community, such as healers, two-spirited and medicine people, and knowledge carriers, also had specific roles. All are important sources of indigenous knowledge. For example, Elders are revered for their role as holders of traditional and sacred knowledge and maintain the responsibility for sharing that knowledge. Leaders among their people, they help guide, teach, and care for children and families. Traditional healers took a holistic approach to helping the mind, body, and spirit. They drew on the natural world of plants and medicines, as well as the guidance of prayer and ceremony and wisdom of the Elders, to provide healing. Extended family is also highly valued. It was not unusual for children to live with grandparents, aunties, and cousins, who shared responsibility for caring for children.

Indigenous knowledge has always been at the heart of traditional educational approaches. Children learned through looking, listening, and experiential learning (Miller 1996). They came to understand who they were and their place in this world through the stories inscribed in landscape and other narrative texts in their lives (Hare 2005). Learning experiences took place in meaningful contexts, such as on the land or within celebration and ceremony. Family and community members were teachers and caregivers to children. Ancestral languages were the mode of communication for transmitting our knowledge through the generations. These sources of indigenous knowledge prepared children for a sustenance lifestyle, thus enriching families, communities, and Nations. It is our ways of knowing and being in this world that have made us strong vibrant Nations, where our knowledge systems thrived, giving rise to proud, prosperous children and families.

Colonizing Indigenous Knowledge in Education

Missionaries were the first outsiders to take on the task of providing a formal education system for Aboriginal people, with the primary goal of civilizing 'Indians' to Christian and newcomer ways. Schooling options offered by missionaries included day and boarding schools, early integration experiments, and schooling for alliances (Hare 2003). Missionaries set up day schools and boarding schools where Aboriginal children could attend daily or live for a certain length of time. These schools were established as early as the 1600s, with the first known boarding school set up by the Recollects in 1620. The Jesuits followed suit shortly thereafter (Miller 1996), and residential schools eventually became the norm across Canada as settlement expanded westward. Barman's (2003) case study of All Hallows School in British Columbia demonstrates that in some early instances Aboriginal children attended schools alongside the children of white settlers and newcomers. Needing access to indigenous peoples for conversion in their evangelistic endeavours, missionaries set up schools that attracted local First Nations groups, such as that begun by Thomas and Emma Crosby on the northwest coast of British Columbia (Hare and Barman 2007). Most of these early schooling arrangements allowed for indigenous peoples to carry on with their seasonal living and maintain their cultural practices and traditions. Interestingly, missionaries themselves gained knowledge of ancestral languages in the locales where they established their missions to indigenous peoples, who, for the most part, accepted missionaries for their own purposes and gains in their newly changing worlds.

It was only when Aboriginal people came to be viewed as a threat that the government of Canada constructed Aboriginal people as a problem to formulating the Canadian nation (Hare and Barman 2000). The government deemed the assimilation of Aboriginal people to settler society as a necessary means of gaining access to land and resources that would benefit settlers and newcomers and as a way of ridding themselves of the 'Indian problem' in this country. It was believed that if Aboriginal people gave up their seasonal lifestyle and rid themselves of their cultural practices, values, and languages, they could be persuaded to take up sedentary pursuits among white settlers in towns and villages and on farms. As historian John Milloy (1999, 4–5) describes in his comprehensive review of the residential school system in Canada: 'Aboriginal knowledge and skills were neither necessary nor desirable in a land that was to be dominated by European industry and, therefore, by Europeans and their culture.'

Since Aboriginal people were deemed inferior to the newcomers of this land, it was assumed that Aboriginal people needed to be assimilated through strict indoctrination into Christian ways in the most expedient and aggressive manner. Day and boarding schools were ineffective as part of the assimilation agenda, since children were permitted to remain with their families, clans, and villages, essentially keeping indigenous knowledges intact and giving Aboriginal people choices about schooling and even whether to take part.

In order to move toward the goal of assimilation so as to 'do away with the tribal system and assimilate the Indian people in all respects with the inhabitants of the Dominion' (Sir John A. Macdonald in 1887, quoted in Milloy 1999, 6), it was necessary to remove Aboriginal children and youth from the influences of their families and to prevent the transmission of indigenous knowledge passed on through families and across the generations. Motivated by Indian policy in the United States that saw Native American children confined to segregated residential institutions, Canada soon adopted a similar approach based on the recommendations put forward by Nicholas Davin in his report to the government. By 1880, residential schools had become the model of schooling for Aboriginal children and youth across Canada, and the government decided that Aboriginal people would from then on be required by law to send their children to these schools. The number of residential schools in Canada hit its peak in 1923 with 72 schools in operation. There is widespread agreement that the entire history of residential schools has left a painful legacy that belongs to all Canadians.

From the very beginning, the government gave responsibility for 'civilizing' Aboriginal children and youth through education to various Christian denominations and ecclesiastical traditions. Government and religious representatives were convinced that full transformation of the Indian child called for indoctrination into Christianity alongside a basic education. Institutional routines were established that included giving children a number aligned to their Christian name, school uniforms, strict rules governing all behaviour, and a rigorous program of prayer, in-class learning, and labouring. Recalling her early mornings at Kamloops Indian Residential School in the 1930s, Sophie shared:

> We marched from there down to the chapel and we spent over an hour in the chapel every morning, every blessed morning. And there they interrogated us on what it was all about being an Indian. . . . He [the priest] would get just get so carried away; he was punching away at the old altar rail . . . to hammer it into our heads that we were not to think or act or speak like an Indian. And that we would go to hell and burn for eternity if we did not listen to their way of teaching (quoted in Haig Brown 1988, 59).

Manual labour was not a necessary part of the educational curriculum. Rather, it was deemed necessary because government funding provided to the schools was minimal. Schools therefore needed children to help with the daily operation of schools as well as to provide paid services for neighbouring towns. This resulted in children spending limited time in the classroom, which is the origin of the notion of the 'half day' schooling system. Children and youth would attend classes for part of the day and provide labour for the school in another portion of the day. Clara Campbell, who attended the St Mary's Mission located on Sto:lo territory in British Columbia, recalls:

> think we maybe only had two hours of school in the morning. We didn't have much school. The bigger girls sort of were working. They did two or three hours of work, and then in the afternoon they had two or three out of school. That's the way it was when I was there (Glavin 2002, 30).

In previous work, my colleague Jean Barman and I argued that the emphasis on domestic and labouring work and moral training and the resulting short amount of time allotted to learning in a classroom with poorly trained teachers ensured that Aboriginal children and youth could not participate socially or economically in a dominant society. It also prevented Aboriginal children and youth from being able to return to their traditional ways of life (Hare and Barman 2000).

In personal accounts as well as in comprehensive reviews of residential schooling in Canada (Assembly of First Nations 1994; Fournier and Crey 1997; Furniss 1995; Glavin 2002; Grant 2004; Haig Brown 1988; Ing 1991; Jaine 1993; Knockwood 1992; Miller 1996; Milloy 1999; Nuu-chah-nulth Tribal Council 1996; Secwepemc Cultural Education Society 2000), writers agree that the most destructive feature of these schools was the denigration of indigenous knowledge that was embedded within traditional cultural practices, values, ways of living, and languages. It was forbidden for Aboriginal children to speak their ancestral languages in the schools. They were expected to take up English, or French in Quebec, immediately upon their arrival at school. The fact that children only spoke an Aboriginal language on their arrival made adjusting to the expectations of the institutions and learning in the classroom extremely difficult. A member of the Nuu-chah-nulth Nation, Ambrose Maquina, recalls just how difficult it was when he came to Old Christie Residential School (at what is now known as Tofino, BC):

> We ended up in a school room. I didn't know what A.B.C. was. I never spoke English. I didn't understand English . . . I couldn't even speak English . . . I felt really lost! Yeah, really, really lost (quoted in Nuu-chah-nulth Tribal Council 1996, 45).

What stands out most for survivors of the residential school experience is the abuse doled out as punishment if they were caught speaking their languages. Children were hit, strapped, whipped, and beaten by priests and nuns who refused to accept their languages as valid. In her memoir of her time at Shubenacadie Residential School in Nova Scotia, Isabelle Knockwood (1992, 98) observed, 'when little children first arrived at school we would see bruises on their throats and cheeks that told us they had been caught speaking Mi'kmaw.' One Aboriginal woman's unsettling recollection reveals the extent of the punishment:

> Today I understand quite a few words in my language. But every time I try and talk it, my tongue hurts. I didn't know why. I ran into another woman

who went to residential school with me and we were talking about it. She asked me if I remembered how they would stick a needle in our tongue if we got caught talking our language. . . . Maybe that's why my tongue hurts whenever I try to talk my language (quoted in Assembly of First Nations 1994, 25).

The widespread prohibition against speaking one's ancestral language was devastating, for ancestral languages are at the very heart of Aboriginal peoples' culture and are the primary means by which indigenous knowledge is expressed, cultivated, and learned. The loss of Aboriginal languages by a majority of students who attended these institutions was inevitable, and it has had severe consequences for indigenous knowledge, family relations, identity, and language continuity among Aboriginal people. Knockwood (1992, 99) explains:

> The punishment of speaking Mi'kmaw began on our first day at school, but the punishment has continued all our lives as we try to piece together who we are and what the world means to us with a language many of us had to re-learn as adults.

Many students resisted the English-language policy by continuing to speak their language among those within their language group while making sure they were out of earshot of those who ran the institutions, keeping to their language when returning home in the summer allowed for it, or simply keeping silent in the face of pressure or ridicule.

Expressions of indigenous knowledge in the form of social practices, cultural traditions, and values also suffered irreparable damage as a result of the assimilation policies and practices of residential schools. Outward appearance was altered by way of dress and grooming. Girls had their hair cut to 'respectable' lengths, and boys had their heads shorn, which ignored the fact that many young Aboriginal children had been raised to understand the sacredness and the status associated with how their hair was kept. For example, among the Anishinaabe, a braid in the hair is a symbol of strength and unity whereby mind, body, and spirit, represented in the three strands of the braid, are woven together. As a result, their pride and dignity was taken away when the hair was cut. The consequences for those who attempted to maintain aspects of their culture were the same as for speaking the language. Recalling her time at Kamloops Indian Residential School in the interior of British Columbia, one woman explained just what could happen if children took to their traditional ways:

We were not allowed to speak our language; we weren't allowed to dance, sing because they told us it was evil. It was evil for us to practice any of our cultural ways . . . Some of the girls would get some Indian food . . . they'd take it away from us and just to be mean they'd destroy it right in front of us (quoted in Haig Brown 1988, 58).

The forced separation of children and youth from families and members of their communities also prevented the passing on of indigenous knowledge from one generation to another. Whereas parents, Elders, extended family, and community members shared the collective responsibility of helping children make sense of their world and how to live in it, residential schools all but took away their involvement in the schools and ultimately in their children's lives as children attended these schools during their formative years into young adulthood. The schools provided an environment that was devoid of family interactions as children were separated from their own siblings. The result was that many children never returned to their families after attending a residential school. The former Grand Chief of the Assembly of First Nations, Phil Fontaine, attended the Fort Alexander Residential School north of Winnipeg. He describes how even his most basic emotional needs were not met in the 10 years he attended:

At home I learned certain things about love and how it was expressed, but that was cast aside when I went to residential school. There, I was completely cut off from my parents and I lost a lot. I lost my sense of family. I didn't develop the kind of love one should experience in a family (Jaine 1993, 53).

Remembering his time with his family, another residential school survivor shared that 'I learned my language from my dad, I learned about the medicine, I learned about the land, some of the old stories' (quoted in Secwepemc Cultural Education Society 2000, 167). The connections to family and community were intentionally severed by law so that children and youth could be under the complete control of government and church. Children and youth could no longer learn the traditional ways of their families, nor could they return to them.

There is clear evidence that Aboriginal families and communities have suffered greatly from the disparaging of indigenous knowledge at these institutions. Our traditional approaches to living and learning have been eroded as the policies and practices of these schools emphasized preparing children and youth for agricultural, industrial, and domestic pursuits patterned on white ways, diminishing the place of land-based relationships and learning. Children and youth were unable to maintain their cultural traditions, since they were prevented throughout their school years from listening to the stories of their people and learning from parents and Elders. The banning of cultural practices such as ceremony, singing, smudging, and drumming meant that children were unable to carry their meaning forward to future generations. The emotional and spiritual toll on children and their families from being punished for expressions of indigenous knowledge has left their identities in a fragile state. As one Aboriginal survivor of the Kamloops Indian Residential School relates about the conflict the messages of the schools created:

> They took away my belongings, they took away everything from me. Everything that's important to me, mother, father, culture. . . . And they put what they wanted in us, made us ashamed of who we are. Even right to this day, it still affects me. Like I really want to get in to Indian things and I just can't because of them telling us it was of the devil. Every time I try, something blocks me. I can't, because I am afraid (quoted in Secwepemc Cultural Education Society 2000, 29).

The Intergenerational Legacy of Residential Schooling

What cannot go untold is the legacy of abuse children and youth suffered at these institutions, resulting in intergenerational trauma for individuals, families, and communities. The personal recollections of those who attended these schools reveal dehumanizing experiences marked by isolation, hunger, humiliation, hypocrisy, shame, and fear, all carried out through spiritual, emotional, physical, and mental abuse (Hare 2007). Residential school survivors have also revealed the sexual abuse rampant in these institutions. Sadly, the abusive practices of many adults who ran these schools also turned many of the youth into aggressors against their fellow students. The tragic results of this legacy have spilled back into Aboriginal families and communities.

Recent court proceedings, in which many former students have brought criminal charges against school administrators and teachers, have provided an opportunity for school survivors to share their experiences and for healing to begin. Following the public disclosure of abuse against former students in the 1980s, churches began to publicly apologize for their role in the schools. The Royal Commission on Aboriginal Peoples (1996) called for a public inquiry to investigate and document the totally devastating impact that residential schools had on Aboriginal peoples. The federal government responded soon after with a statement of reconciliation. The statement expressed profound regret for past actions of the government and announced a healing fund to support community initiatives that would provide aid to residential school survivors and their families. As residential school survivors continued to seek redress through the courts, the government and churches eventually signed a settlement agreement that promised to provide compensation to residential school survivors. The Assembly of First Nations has also assisted survivors throughout the compensation process. A key component of the Indian Residential Schools Settlement Agreement is the newly established Truth and Reconciliation Canada, whose goal is to prepare a comprehensive historical review on policies and operations of the schools.

Most significant in the offering of reparations by the government to Aboriginal peoples was the formal apology given by Prime Minister Stephen Harper on 11 June 2008. The apology statement recognizes:

> The burden of this experience has been on your shoulders for far too long. The burden is properly ours as a Government, and as a country. There is no place in Canada for the attitudes that inspired the Indian Residential Schools system to ever prevail again. You have been working on recovering from this experience for a long time and in a very real sense, we are now joining you on this journey. The Government of Canada sincerely apologizes and asks the forgiveness of Aboriginal peoples of this country for failing them so profoundly.

Many Aboriginal people hope that this apology will enable them to move forward in their relationship with Canada in a positive and concrete way, although there have been varying responses to Canada's apology (Aboriginal Healing Foundation 2009). Canadian writer John Ralston Saul (2009) believes that reconciliation with Aboriginal people must occur through a major paradigm shift in education. For non-Aboriginal people, Saul insists that reconciliation requires them to accept that the future of this country and their place in it must be inspired more by Aboriginal views than by Eurocentric ones.

Creating Space for Indigenous Knowledge in Education Today

Residential schools first began to fade from the Canadian educational landscape in the early 1950s when educational policy promoted Aboriginal children attending schools alongside non-Aboriginal students. There was increasing support for a number of educational options, including schools on reserves under government control and children attending public schools off-reserve. Yet these schooling options failed to accommodate indigenous knowledge in their curriculum and teaching approaches. Schools relied on provincial curriculum, which did not reflect the histories, experiences, or perspectives of Aboriginal people. Families and communities remained on the margins of their children's education, since on-reserve schools were governed by policies set out by the Department of Indian Affairs. Moreover, provincial school boards did not consider the participation of Aboriginal parents as necessary or valuable. In sum, many of these early efforts to integrate Aboriginal children with their non-Aboriginal peers failed to enhance Aboriginal student success. This was evidenced in high incidences of school leaving, low parental participation, streaming of Aboriginal children and youth in special education, and age–grade lags.

Despite these attempts to provide a wider range of educational opportunities for Aboriginal students, efforts to assimilate Aboriginal peoples through federal government policies continued throughout the 1960s. Then in 1969, the federal government attempted to do away with the Indian Act by passing responsibility for Aboriginal affairs to provincial governments through its now infamous White Paper. In a varied set of political responses exemplified in the Red Paper (Indian Chiefs of Alberta 1970) and the Union of British Columbia Indian Chiefs' Brown Paper, Aboriginal groups overwhelmingly rejected the proposed policy that would see their political and legal rights to self-determination relegated to the status of other Canadians. A clear Aboriginal response came from the National Indian Brotherhood in a policy focused on education for self-determination and fostering a positive Aboriginal identity. Their document, *Indian Control of Indian Education* (ICIE), remains a landmark in Aboriginal education, for it proposed that Aboriginal peoples had the right to determine how best to meet their educational goals. Along with providing a vision for the future of Aboriginal education in Canada, the policy document was highly critical of the state of educational facilities for Aboriginal students, the quality of teacher training, and the limited way that the curriculum included Aboriginal perspectives, pedagogies, and histories. In effect, it insisted that indigenous knowledge must be at the core of all learning experiences for Aboriginal children and youth.

Subsequent reports and reviews of Aboriginal education have been critical of the slow response by governments, schools, and post-secondary educational institutions to advance the goals of Aboriginal families and communities (Abele, Dittburner, and Graham 2000; Assembly of First Nations 1994; British Columbia Human Rights Commission 2001; Indian Affairs and Northern Development Canada 2002; Kuokkanen 2007; RCAP 1996). Together, they highlight that educational programming, curriculum, learning materials, and teaching and evaluation approaches clearly fail to honour the proper place of indigenous knowledge in the educational experiences of Aboriginal students. They note that Aboriginal children and youth confront racism on a regular basis in their interactions with peers and teachers (Schissel and Wotherspoon 2003; St Denis and Hampton 2002; Timmons et al. 2009). They struggle to find relevance in the curriculum, and Aboriginal families and communities strive to right the imbalance of power in their relationships with schools, in both on- and off-reserve school settings. Consensus is strong that

> another study is not required, but an adjustment in attitude on the part of the government, First Nations and all Canadians is necessary in order to put into use all of the work that has been done over the last century to effect a much needed revolution in Canada's approach to First Nations education (Martineau 2002, 13).

The responsibility rests with all of us to create space for indigenous knowledge in learning settings; we must all open our minds as well as our hearts to the different ways knowledge is constructed, shared, and valued if education is to benefit all students.

Current educational trends that draw on indigenous knowledge to support learning experiences for Aboriginal children and youth are encouraging. One of the most promising is Aboriginal Head Start (AHS), a nationally funded early childhood education program that is locally designed and delivered by the Aboriginal communities the program serves. In 1995, the AHS program was implemented to support First Nations, Métis, and Inuit children living in urban and rural communities. Three years later, the program expanded to include on-reserve First Nations communities. The program supports families with children up to six years of age. It takes a holistic approach to preparing young Aboriginal children and their families for schooling by nurturing emotional, social, cognitive, and spiritual development. Family and community work together to help realize the operating principles of the program, which include family involvement, health promotion, nutrition, social support, culture and language, and school readiness. Currently, there are 125 AHS projects located in urban and northern communities and nearly 350 projects serving up to 380 First Nations communities across Canada. It has been reported that some children participating in an Aboriginal Head Start program maintained reading and language achievement gains made in the program up to grade five (O'Sullivan and Goosney 2007). Another study indicated that while 18 per cent of six- to eleven-year-old First Nations children living on reserves had repeated a grade, that number dropped to 12 per cent for children who had attended a preschool Aboriginal Head Start program (Canadian Council on Learning 2007; First Nations Centre 2005).

Increasingly and all across Canada, conversations about indigenous knowledge are becoming part of the dialogue about mainstream education (Brayboy and Maughan 2009). In British Columbia, efforts to enhance the academic performance of Aboriginal children and youth have brought together Aboriginal communities, provincial school districts/boards, and the Ministry of Education to develop goals and strategies that will serve the educational needs of Aboriginal learners (Morin 2004). These Aboriginal Education Enhancement Agreements emphasize the role of indigenous knowledge and therefore seek to incorporate Aboriginal culture, language, history, and perspectives into the learning experiences of Aboriginal students. In their review of 10 schools that foster success among Aboriginal learners in British Columbia and central Canada, Bell et al. (2004) observed that these schools were deeply committed to providing culturally relevant programming that honours Aboriginal student identity, including language and cultural classes and engaging the Aboriginal community as school resources. Elsewhere in Canada, the Ontario Ministry of Education implemented an Aboriginal education strategy in 2007. The First Nations, Métis, and Inuit Education Policy Framework (Ontario Ministry of Education 2007) describes several strategies that are based on a holistic and integrated approach to improving Aboriginal student learning outcomes. It places the onus on the province's Ministry of Education, school boards, and schools to create space for indigenous knowledge, recognizing that

> factors that contribute to student success include teaching strategies that are appropriate to Aboriginal learner needs, curriculum that reflects First Nations, Métis, and Inuit cultures and perspectives, effective counseling and outreach, and a school environment that encourages Aboriginal student and parent engagement (Ontario Ministry of Education 2007, 6).

The policy initiatives include alternative secondary school programs in Ontario Aboriginal Friendship Centres, new training opportunities and resources for teacher education programs, and the establishment of an Advisory Council on Aboriginal Education to direct the Ontario government in its implementation of the policy framework.

Post-secondary institutions are also making efforts to accommodate indigenous knowledge and approaches to learning that reflect Aboriginal history and perspectives. Both the University of Toronto and the University of British Columbia have developed strategic plans to expand the Aboriginal presence at these institutions, with the goal of increasing recruitment and retention of Aboriginal learners. Both institutions recognize the valuable contributions that indigenous knowledge systems offer in research, teaching, and learning to prepare all students for living in a global society. Initiatives include appropriate policy, program, and engagement strategies that affect classroom learning, university social and living spaces, university administrative policies, and research opportunities and partnerships. Concerns about ownership of traditional knowledge, appropriate methodologies for teaching and research, and relevant content have contributed to growth in the number of Aboriginal-controlled post-secondary institutions (Aboriginal Institutes' Consortium 2005). One such institution is the First Nations University of Canada, formerly Saskatchewan Indian Federated College, which provides students with a nationally recognized and transferable university education while offering them culturally appropriate programs and services designed and delivered by indigenous peoples (Jenkins 2007).

Hermes (2007) asserts that Aboriginal language immersion programs offer the greatest promise in indigenous language revitalization, while others describe them as the most effective means of ensuring the intergenerational transmission of indigenous knowledge (McCarty 2003; Reyhner, Trujillo, Carrasco, and Lockard 2003). Across Canada, immersion language programming is taking hold slowly as communities struggle with loss of language speakers and communities and governments offer staggered support for language revitalization initiatives. There are, however, some hopeful signs of success. Immersion programs exist from preschool to Grade 3 in Onion Lake, Saskatchewan, and Kanawa:ke, Quebec. Adams Lake in British Columbia hosts a 'language nest' for preschool children as well as a full language immersion program from kindergarten to Grade 7 in their community school (McIvor 2009). The benefits of immersion programming go well beyond education achievement. Hallet, Chandler, and Lalonde (2007) report that First Nations communities in British Columbia with higher knowledge of ancestral languages among their members have had fewer incidences of suicide compared to First Nations communities with lower levels of ancestral language fluency. Clearly, ancestral language is not only a prime expression for indigenous knowledge, it is also a fundamental means by which Aboriginal people cultivate a shared sense of identity and hope.

The Way Ahead

Once the very foundation of the learning experience of Aboriginal children and youth, the sharing of indigenous knowledge was severely disrupted by schooling policies and practices that aimed to assimilate Aboriginal people, with the goal of ridding them of their Aboriginal identity. For well over a century, residential schools were the primary means by which governmental and religious bodies attempted to systematically eradicate Aboriginal languages, cultures, and values. In short, they sought to fully alter the way Aboriginal children and youth came to understand their world. Schooling for Aboriginal children and youth still presents challenges and barriers to success. It is when expressions of indigenous knowledge find their way into the curriculum, pedagogical approaches, and policies of schooling that Aboriginal children and youth will find meaning and success in their educational experiences. It is through educational approaches that recognize the place of indigenous knowledge in learning, such as the examples I have described and many others that are making their mark on the educational landscape, that Aboriginal people will find solutions to the challenges they face in their lives. Indigenous knowledge is concerned with issues of power, place, and relationship and as such promises to offer support to children and to bring improvement and hope to Aboriginal people and communities (Villegas, Neugebauer, and Venegas 2008). Put simply, each and every learning experience that affirms indigenous knowledge systems enhances the quality of life for Aboriginal people.

The future benefits of indigenous knowledges to our Canadian society cannot be overestimated. The inclusion of Aboriginal world views, values, languages, culture, and approaches to learning in the country's overall educational agenda will broaden the learning experience for all students. Reconciliation between Aboriginal people and the rest of Canada requires both widespread awareness and understanding of the colonial history we must now all struggle to overcome as well as a deep respect for the future that Aboriginal people hope to build for our children, families, and communities. More and more educators have begun to recognize the limitations of Eurocentric views that dominate our learning institutions. As Barnhardt and Kawagley (2005) note, 'Our challenge now is to devise a system of education for all people that respects the epistemological and pedagogical foundations provided by both Indigenous and Western cultural traditions.' Increasing respect and understanding for other cultures and their knowledge systems offers hope and healing to all of us.

Discussion Questions

1. How do traditional approaches to education relate to current practices and policies in Aboriginal education?
2. Compare Aboriginal peoples' sources of knowledge with your sources of knowledge or those valued in schools today. How are they similar? How are they different?

3. What has been the legacy of residential schooling for Aboriginal people today?
4. Give other examples of educational initiatives that have successfully integrated indigenous knowledge.
5. What might Aboriginal peoples' vision of education in the contemporary world look like?

Further Readings

Canadian Council on Learning. 2007. *Redefining How Success is Measured in First Nations, Inuit and Métis Learning*. Ottawa: Canadian Council on Learning. Drawing on research and statistical data, this report describes the key characteristics that define successful approaches to education for Aboriginal learners.

Castellano, M. Brant, L. Davis, and L. Lahache. 2001. *Aboriginal Education: Fulfilling the Promise*. Vancouver: University of British Columbia Press. This book represents a collection of essays based on the reports and recommendations about Aboriginal education that were made to the Royal Commission on Aboriginal Peoples. The chapters address policy, program, and practices issues in Aboriginal education today.

Hall, B., G. Sefa Dei, and D.G. Rosenberg. 2000. *Indigenous Knowledges in Global Contexts: Multiple Readings of Our World*. Toronto: University of Toronto Press. This collection of essays looks at how indigenous knowledge is taken up across cultures, challenging our ideas of what constitutes knowledge. All readings describe the various sources of indigenous knowledge and the complexities associated with them.

Highway, T. 1999. *Kiss of the Fur Queen*. Toronto: Anchor Canada. This novel describes the lives of two Cree boys taken from their families and placed in a Catholic residential school. As young men, they both turn to artistic pursuits, struggling to survive while estranged from their family and culture.

Miller, J.R. 1996. *Shingwauk's Vision: A History of Native Residential Schools*. Toronto: University of Toronto Press. A comprehensive examination of the history of residential schools in Canada, this analysis spans three and half centuries to describe their origin in the early seventeenth century through to the final phase in the 1960s. The interests and perspectives of the government, the church, and Aboriginal people are shared in each phase.

References

Abele, F., C. Dittburner, and K.A. Graham. 2000. 'Towards a shared understanding in the policy discussion about Aboriginal education'. In M.B. Castellano, L. Davis, and L. Lahache, eds, *Aboriginal Education: Fulfilling the Promise*, 3–24. Vancouver: University of British Columbia Press.

Aboriginal Healing Foundation. 2009. *Response, Responsibility and Renewal: Canada's Truth and Reconciliation Journey*. Ottawa: Aboriginal Healing Foundation.

Aboriginal Institutes' Consortium. 2005. *Aboriginal Institutions of Higher Education: A Struggle for the Education of Aboriginal Students, Control of Indigenous Knowledge, and Recognition of Aboriginal Institutions. An Examination of Government Policy*. August. Canada: Canadian Race Relations Foundation.

Alfred, A. 2004. *Paddling to Where I Stand*. ed. M.J. Reid; tr. D. Sewid-Smith. Toronto: University of Toronto Press.

Archibald, J. 2008. *Indigenous Storywork: Educating the Heart, Mind, Body, and Spirit*. Vancouver: University of British Columbia Press.

Assembly of First Nations. 1994. *Breaking the Silence: An Interpretive Study of Residential School Impact and Healing as Illustrated by the Stories of First Nations Individuals*. Ottawa: Assembly of First Nations.

———. 1998. *Tradition and Education: Towards a Vision of Our Future*. Summerstown, Ottawa: National Indian Brotherhood/Assembly of First Nations.

Barman, J. 2003. 'Schooled for inequality: The education of British Columbia Aboriginal children'. In J. Barman and M. Gleason, eds, *Children, Teachers and Schools in the History of British Columbia*, 2nd edn, 55–79. Calgary: Detselig Enterprise.

Barnhardt, R., and A.O. Kawagley. 2005. 'Indigenous knowledge systems and Alaska Native ways of knowing. *Anthropology and Education Quarterly* 36 (1): 8–23.

Battiste, M. 2000. *Reclaiming Indigenous Voice and Vision*. Vancouver: University of British Columbia Press.

———. 2002. *Indigenous Knowledge and Pedagogy in First Nations Education: A Literature Review with Recommendations*. Ottawa: National Working Group on Education, Indian Affairs and Northern Development Canada.

———. 2005. 'Indigenous knowledge: Foundations for First Nations'. World Indigenous Nations Higher Education Consortium Journal. www.win-hec.org/docs/pdfs/Journal/Marie%20Battiste%20copy.pdf.

Bell, D., et al., eds. 2004. *Sharing Our Success: Ten Case Studies in Aboriginal Schooling*. Kelowna, BC: Society for the Advancement of Excellence in Education.

Brayboy, B.M.J., and E. Maughan. 2009. 'Indigenous knowledges and the story of the bean'. *Harvard Educational Review* 79 (1): 1–21.

British Columbia Human Rights Commission. 2001. *Barriers to Equal Education for Aboriginal Learners: A Review of the Literature*. Vancouver: British Columbia Human Rights Commission.

Cajete, G. 2000. *Look to the Mountain: An Ecology of Indigenous Education*. Durango, CO: Kivaki Press.

Canadian Council on Learning. 2007. *Redefining How Success Is Measured in First Nations, Inuit and Metis Learning*. Ottawa. Canadian Council on Learning.

Cowley, P., and S. Easton. 2004. *Report Card on Aboriginal Education in British Columbia*. Studies in Education Policy Occasional Paper. Vancouver: The Fraser Institute.

First Nations Centre. 2005. *First Nations Regional Longitudinal Health Survey (RHS): 2002/2003*. Ottawa: National Aboriginal Health Organization.

Fournier, S., and E. Crey. 1997. *Stolen from Our Embrace: The Abduction of First Nations Children and the Restoration of Aboriginal Communities*. Vancouver: Douglas and McIntyre.

Furniss, E. 1995. *Victims of Benevolence: The Dark Legacy of the Williams Lake Residential School*. Vancouver: Arsenal Pulp Press.

Glavin, T. 2002. *Among God's Own: The Enduring Legacy of St. Mary's Mission*. Vancouver: New Star Books.

Grant, A. 2004. *Finding My Talk: How Fourteen Native Women Reclaimed Their Lives after Residential School*. Calgary: Fifth House.

Haig-Brown, C. 1988. *Resistance and Renewal: Surviving the Indian Residential School*. Vancouver: Tillacum Library.

Hallett, D., M. Chandler, and C. Lalonde. 2007. 'Aboriginal language knowledge and youth suicide'. *Cognitive Development* 22 (3): 392–9.

Hare, J. 2003. 'September 11 and its aftermath: A roundtable. Is the bingo palace burning?' *Journal of Women in Culture and Society* 29 (2): 589–91.

———. 2005. 'To know papers: Aboriginal perspectives on literacy'. In J. Anderson, M. Kendrick, T. Rogers, and S. Smythe, eds, *Portraits of Literacy across Families, Communities and Schools: Tensions and Intersections*, 243–63. Mahwah, NJ: Lawrence Erlbaum Associates.

———. 2007. 'Aboriginal education policy in Canada: Building capacity for change and control'. In R. Joshee and L. Johnson, eds, *Multicultural Education Policies in Canada and the United States*, 51–68. Seattle, WA: University of Washington Press/University of British Columbia Press.

Hare, J., and J. Barman. 2000. 'Aboriginal education: Is there a way ahead?' In D. Long and O. Dickason, eds, *Visions of the Heart: Canadian Aboriginal Issues*, 2nd edn, 331–59. Toronto: Harcourt Brace.

———. 2007. *Good Intentions Gone Awry: Emma Crosby and the Methodist Mission on the Northwest Coast*. Vancouver: University of British Columbia Press.

Hermes, M. 2007. 'Moving toward the language: Reflections on teaching in an indigenous-immersion school'. *Journal of American Indian Education* 46 (3): 54–71.

Indian Affairs and Northern Development Canada. Minister's Working Group on Education. 2002. *Our Children—Keepers of the Sacred Knowledge Final Report*. Ottawa: Indian Affairs and Northern Development Canada.

———. '2004 Basic departmental data'. Ottawa: Indian Affairs and Northern Development Canada. www.ainc-inac.gc.ca/pr/sts/bdd04/bdd04_e.htm.

Indian Chiefs of Alberta. 1970. *Citizens Plus*. Edmonton: Indian Association of Alberta.

Ing, N.R. 1991. 'The effects of residential schools on native child-rearing practices'. *Canadian Journal of Native Education* 18: 65–118.

Jaine, L., ed. 1993. *Residential Schools: The Stolen Years*. Saskatoon: University Extension Press, University of Saskatchewan.

Jenkins, A. 2007. 'Indigenous post-secondary institutions in Canada and the US'. http://hep.oise.utoronto.ca/index.php/hep/article/viewFile/635/692.

Knockwood, I. 1992. *Out of the Depths: The Experiences of Mi'kmaw Children at the Indian Residential School at Shubenacadie, Nova Scotia*. Lockeport, NS: Roseway Publishing.

Kulchyski, P., D. McCaskill, and D. Newhouse, eds. 1999. *In the Words of Elders: Aboriginal Cultures in Transition*. Toronto: University of Toronto Press.

Kuokkanen, R. 2007. *Reshaping the University: Responsibility, Indigenous Epistemes, and the Logic of the Gift*. Vancouver: University of British Columbia Press.

McCarty, T. 2003. 'Revitalising indigenous languages in homogenising times'. *Comparative Education* 39 (2): 147–63.

McIvor, O. 2009. 'Strategies for indigenous language revitalization and maintenance'. http://literacyencyclopedia.ca/index.php?fa=items.show&topicId=265.

Martineau, C. 2002. 'Issues of control, appropriateness, and efficacy in band-controlled First Nations schools: Too many chiefs?'. www.ucalgary.ca.

Mendelson, M. 2006. *Improving Education on Reserves: A First Nations Education Authority Act.* Ottawa: The Caledon Institute of Social Policy.

Miller, J.R. 1996. *Shingwauk's Vision: A History of Native Residential Schools.* Toronto: University of Toronto Press.

Milloy, J.S. 1999. *A National Crime: The Canadian Government and the Residential School System, 1879 to 1986.* Winnipeg: University of Manitoba Press.

Morin, H. 2004. 'Student performance data and research tools to ensure Aboriginal student success'. www.bced.gov.bc.ca/abed/research/ab_student_success.pdf.

National Indian Brotherhood. 1972. *Indian Control of Indian Education.* Ottawa: National Indian Brotherhood.

Nuu-chah-nulth Tribal Council. 1996. *Indian Residential Schools: The Nuu-chah-nulth Experience: Report of the Nuu-chah-nulth Tribal Council Indian Residential School Study 1992–1994.* Port Alberni, BC: Nuu-chah-nulth Tribal Council.

Ontario Ministry of Education. 2007. 'First Nations, Metis and Inuit (FNMI) Education Policy Framework'. www.edu.gov.on.ca/eng/aboriginal/fnmiFramework.pdf.

Ortiz, S. 1992. *Woven Stone.* Tucson: University of Arizona Press.

O'Sullivan, J., and J. Goosney. 2007. *Get Ready, Get Set, Get Going: Learning to Read in Northern Canada.* Thunder Bay, ON: Centre of Excellence for Children and Adolescents with Special Needs.

RCAP (Royal Commission on Aboriginal Peoples). 1996. *Report of the Royal Commission on Aboriginal Peoples*, vol. 1, *Looking Forward, Looking Back.* Ottawa: Minister of Supply and Services Canada.

Reyhner, J., O. Trujillo, R. Carrasco, and L. Lockard, eds. 2003. *Nurturing Native Languages.* Flagstaff: Northern Arizona University.

Saul, J.R. 2009. 'Reconciliation: Four barriers to paradigm shifting'. In *Aboriginal Healing Foundation, Response, Responsibility and Renewal: Canada's Truth and Reconciliation Journey*, 311–20. Ottawa: Aboriginal Healing Foundation.

Schissel, B., and T. Wotherspoon. 2003. *The Legacy of School for Aboriginal People: Education, Oppression, and Emancipation.* Don Mills, ON: Oxford University Press.

Secwepemc Cultural Education Society. 2000. *Behind Closed Doors. Stories from the Kamloops Indian Residential School.* Kamloops, BC: Secwepemc Cultural Education Society.

St Denis, V., and E. Hampton. 2002. *Literature Review on Racism and the Effects on Aboriginal Education.* Prepared for the Minister's National Working Group on Education. Ottawa: Indian Affairs and Northern Development Canada.

Statistics Canada. 2003. *International Adult Literacy Survey.* Ottawa: Statistics Canada.

Statistics Canada. Housing, Family and Social Statistics Division. 2001. *Aboriginal Peoples Survey 2001—Initial Findings: Well-being of the Non-reserve Aboriginal Population.* Catalogue no. 89-589-XIE2003001. Ottawa: Statistics Canada.

Statistics Canada and Council of Ministers of Education. 2001. *Education Indicators in Canada: Report of the Pan-Canadian Education Indicators Program 1999.* Ottawa: Statistics Canada.

———. 2006. *Education Indicators in Canada: Report of the Pan-Canadian Education Indicators Program 1999.* Ottawa: Statistics Canada.

Task Force on Aboriginal Languages and Cultures. 2005. *Towards a New Beginning: A Foundational Report for a Strategy to Revitalize First Nation, Inuit, and Métis Languages and Cultures.* Ottawa: Canadian Heritage, Aboriginal Affairs.

Timmons, V., et al. 2009. 'Retention of Aboriginal students in post-secondary institutions in Atlantic Canada: An analysis of supports available to Aboriginal students'. www .atlanticuniversities.ca.

Villegas, M., S.R. Neugebauer, and K.R. Venegas, eds. 2008. 'Indigenous knowledge and education: Sites of struggle, strength, and survivance'. *Harvard Educational Review* 44.

6

Aboriginal Languages in Canada: Generational Perspectives on Language Maintenance, Loss, and Revitalization

Mary Jane Norris

Introduction

Generational perspectives are relevant to many aspects concerning the state and prospects of Aboriginal languages in Canada. Language maintenance, loss, and revitalization entail the transmission, rupture, or revival of traditional languages across all generations of Aboriginal people, from children and youth to young adults, the middle-aged, and elders. Generational perspectives on language survival can comprise various dimensions, such as historical, cultural, and socio-economic, as well as the demographics of family, community, and city. In this study, demographic approaches are used to explore patterns of language acquisition and learning, whether as a mother tongue (first language) or as a second language, and the processes of language learning in relation to aspects such as sources of learning and the domains and cultural context of language use.

The state and prospects of Aboriginal languages vary considerably. According to UNESCO's *Atlas of the World's Languages in Danger*, 86 different individual languages are currently spoken in Canada by First Nations, Inuit, and Métis (UNESCO 2010; 2009), reflecting a diversity of distinctive histories, cultures, and identities and linked to family, community, the land, and traditional knowledge. While many languages are endangered or nearing extinction, others are flourishing and viable. One estimate of Aboriginal language survival in Canada suggests that 'about a third of Aboriginal languages originally spoken in Canada have a good chance of survival. Fewer than half of the remaining languages are likely to survive for another fifty years' (Kinkade 1991).

Language transmission from one generation to another is the major factor in Aboriginal language survival and maintenance. Unlike other heritage languages in Canada, Aboriginal languages are indigenous to the country and cannot rely on immigration to maintain their numbers. The survival and maintenance of Aboriginal languages in Canada depend on their transmission from generation to generation, since Aboriginal children are the future speakers of their languages.

The extent to which different generations of Aboriginal people can speak their traditional language varies considerably across the many Aboriginal languages and their hundreds of communities. Some of the more viable languages are learned as a first language by most generations, young and old, and continue to be passed on to children, and hence there is a good prospect of future generations of speakers. For the more endangered languages, however, intergenerational transmission as a mother tongue has eroded, with aging and declining populations of first-language speakers. And among endangered languages, the impact of language erosion varies across the generations to the extent that the UNESCO atlas incorporates a generational perspective in its assessment of the degree of language endangerment: 'definitely' endangered languages are no longer being learned by children as their mother tongue in the home; 'severely' endangered languages are understood but not used among the parent generation although spoken by grandparents; while for 'critically' endangered languages, the youngest speakers are grandparents and even older generations. The atlas also includes the more viable Aboriginal languages, which while not currently endangered nevertheless have the potential to become so, given the relatively small populations that use them. As such, they are classified as 'vulnerable'—spoken by most children but often restricted to certain domains (UNESCO 2009; 2010).

Yet many endangered languages show signs of revitalization, especially among youth as they strive to learn their traditional languages as second languages, often with the aid of older generations and elders, within communities and cities. Comprising almost half of the Aboriginal population (median age of 27 in the 2006 census), children and youth represent a potentially significant factor in language survival.

This chapter explores, from a generational perspective, the factors, demographic processes, and outcomes that underlie the maintenance, loss, and revitalization of Aboriginal languages and their communities and the implications of that loss and revival for culture and identity across generations. Highlights include second-language learning, the contributions of youth in the revitalization of endangered languages, and the potential for 'secondarily surviving' languages. The developments and challenges, as well as the prospects, considerations, and implications of cultural continuity and identity, of keeping Aboriginal languages alive from generation to generation are illustrated through the example of the Cowichan community of British Columbia as its members strive to preserve their traditional language of Halkomelen. Concluding thoughts address the outlook, prospects, and considerations involved in keeping Aboriginal languages alive for future generations.

Generational Perspectives on the Loss and Revival of a Language

A language is not just about speaking as a way of communication—it is much more than that: it represents a way of thinking, of perceiving the world, interwoven with the knowledge, culture, and identity of a people. Language remains a critical component in maintaining and transmitting Aboriginal cultural integrity and identity, from generation to generation, and reflects a unique world view specific to the culture to which it is linked (Norris 2000). So losing a language is not just losing a way of communicating: it is like losing a world.

Importance of Language—More Than a Means of Communication

Language is not only a means of communication but a link that connects people with their past and grounds their social, emotional, and spiritual vitality—its importance to indigenous people is immense (Norris 1998). Language is often recognized as one of the most tangible symbols of culture and group identity to the extent that language and identity are often inseparable: 'Language embodies the intellectual wealth of the people who use it' (Hale 1992, cited in Abley 2003). Although loss of language doesn't necessarily lead to the death of a culture, it can severely handicap transmission of that culture. When these languages vanish, they take with them unique ways of looking at the world, explaining the unknown, and making sense of life (Norris 1998).

What Is Lost When You Lose a Language? Connections across Generations

Many Aboriginal communities have experienced the devastating impacts of cultural alienation and language loss, of children being raised without their culture, language, and traditions, losing connection with their past, history, traditional knowledge, and the land. Without the language of one's ancestors, both individual and collective identity can be weakened, and cultural loss can occur—loss of words, of meanings and understandings—in many aspects of daily life, in traditional ceremonies, and in spiritual teachings.

What Is Gained When You Revive a Language? Connections across Generations

Trends suggesting renewed interest in the vitality of Aboriginal languages among Aboriginal youth—signs of revitalization—are good news not only for the survival of endangered languages but also for bridging the connections across generations. The ability to speak the language of their ancestors affords youth opportunities to communicate with older family members in their traditional language, which can contribute to the maintenance of traditional cultures across generations.

Strong cultural attachment and a strong sense of identity are important components of well-being. There is growing evidence of links connecting language maintenance and revitalization with health, well-being, positive educational outcomes, and improved life chances. It is thought that the process of learning an Aboriginal language may also contribute to increased self-esteem among youth, community healing and well-being, and cultural continuity (Ball 2009; Chandler 2006; Chandler and Lalonde 2008; Canadian Heritage 2005).

Aboriginal Language Maintenance, Loss, and Endangerment: Forces, Processes, and Outcomes across Generations

Forces: A Multiplicity of Factors in Language Loss

Many indigenous languages are in danger of disappearing around the world, not only in Canada. Yet the causes and factors underlying the endangered state of these languages are complex and far from few.

> It would be naïve and oversimplifying to say that the big ex-colonial languages, English or French or Spanish, are the killers and all smaller languages are the victims. . . . There is a subtle interplay of forces (Moseley 2009).

Indeed, a multiplicity of factors—historical, societal, economic, geographic, and demographic—can contribute to the decline of languages. In the case of Aboriginal languages in Canada, historical factors include events associated with the forces of colonization and the legacy of the residential school system, which saw the prohibition of indigenous language use among Aboriginal children. The fact that most Aboriginal languages were predominantly oral may also have diminished, in an already difficult environment, their chances of survival. And today, the forces of larger mainstream languages and globalization can significantly affect less widely used languages. As well, the challenges of language maintenance and survival can be further exacerbated in an urban environment, outside of Aboriginal communities, as well as by the demand and need for mainstream language use in daily life in school, work, and the marketplace. As with other minority languages, individuals' continual exposure to more dominant languages, along with the need to use them in everyday life, is a powerful catalyst in the decline of Aboriginal languages (Norris 1998; 2007; 2008).

Language transmission from one generation to another is the major factor in Aboriginal language survival and maintenance. But over the past 25 years, many of Canada's Aboriginal languages have seen long-term declines in intergenerational transmission of language as a mother tongue or first language.

Processes of Language Maintenance and Loss across Generations

For purposes of analyzing and assessing the processes and states of Aboriginal languages, a number of demographic indicators and measures have been developed based on language variables from the census, the main ones being 'mother tongue', 'home language', and 'knowledge' of an Aboriginal language. Indicators refer to various aspects of language maintenance, loss, and revitalization, including:

- The size of the population with an Aboriginal mother tongue.
- The 'continuity' of language: Continuity refers to the natural transmission as mother tongue from generation to generation, parent to child, through language use in the home. Language maintenance or intergenerational transmission is related to language use in the home, which enables children to acquire an Aboriginal mother tongue.
- Average age of the population with an Aboriginal mother tongue (first language): Age is an important indicator of the state and viability or endangerment of any language—basically, the younger the first-language speakers, the healthier the language.
- Language revitalization: The 'ability to speak, or knowledge of, the language' provides some clues as to how speakers of different generations have learned their language, either at home as a mother tongue or later in life as a second language.

Children are the major source of growth for the Aboriginal mother-tongue population in Canada. However, decreased use of Aboriginal languages as a major language in the home has effectively lowered the chances that younger people will acquire their traditional language as a mother tongue, which is leading to an aging mother-tongue population. Over the past 25 years, from 1981 to 2006, census data show that many Aboriginal languages in Canada, especially endangered ones, have undergone long-term declines in intergenerational transmission and mother-tongue (first-language) populations, as reflected in rising average ages of endangered first-language speakers and shrinking numbers of speakers overall.

The impact of the long-term erosion of Aboriginal languages from generation to generation is evident today, with some 220,000, or about one in five (19 per cent), of Canada's 1.2 million people who identified as Aboriginal (First Nation, Métis, or Inuit) reporting an Aboriginal language as their mother tongue in the 2006 census. A greater number—252,000, or 21 per cent of Aboriginal people—said they could converse in an Aboriginal language, implying that other speakers had learned their traditional language as a second language. Fewer— just 17 per cent—reported speaking an Aboriginal language at home: 12 per cent said it was the language they used most often at home, and 5 per cent said it was a language they used on a regular basis at home

Language use at home is an important factor in transmission of Aboriginal languages to children—the next generation of speakers: the less a language is spoken at home, the less it is transmitted to children as a mother tongue. Language differences between younger and older generations of Aboriginal people in 2006 reflect long-term declines in intergenerational transmission. Overall, among those aged 65 and over, 33 per cent had an Aboriginal language as their mother tongue compared to just 15 per cent of children and youth. This overall low proportion of first-language speakers among younger generations points to endangerment, given that in general a language can be considered endangered if it is not learned by at least 30 per cent of the children in a community (UNESCO 1996, 23).

Many of the factors affecting the intergenerational transmission of an Aboriginal mother tongue are associated with its continued use as a major home language. As stressed in the recommendations of the Royal Commission on Aboriginal Peoples (RCAP 1996), the long-term viability or continuity of a language is dependent on its daily use—ideally as one 'spoken most often' in the home—if it is to be transmitted as a mother tongue to the next generation. Yet there are various dynamics that can affect the use of traditional languages in the home—for example, the life cycle and the transition from youth into adulthood; residence within or outside Aboriginal communities or in urban areas; migration to or from communities; family formation and linguistic out-marriage or parenting; and entry into the labour force. A census-based cohort analysis over the 1981 to 1996 period demonstrated that practically all age groups, both males and females, experienced a decline in continuity or home language use among those with a mother tongue, with a shift in home use from an Aboriginal to a non-Aboriginal language. Furthermore, this decline was most pronounced for women, especially during their childbearing and working years, which has important implications for intergenerational transmission, since these are the very years when women are raising children and possibly future speakers (Norris 1998).

The distinction between endangered and viable languages is also relevant to the prospects of home language use. Some of the demographic and geographic situations of endangered language speakers tend to be less conducive to intergenerational transmission of an Aboriginal mother tongue. For example, speakers of endangered languages, compared to speakers of viable languages, are more likely to marry or parent with people who do not speak an Aboriginal language, to live outside Aboriginal communities, and to be more urbanized. On average, if they are first-language speakers, they tend to be older, while younger speakers of endangered language are more likely to have learned their traditional language as a second language (Norris 2003). Furthermore, among those who do speak an endangered language at home, the language is much less likely to be 'spoken most often in home' and more likely on a 'regular' basis. For example, among home language speakers of the endangered Haida language in 2001, 10 per cent reported that Haida was 'spoken most often', and 90 per cent said it was spoken 'regularly'. In contrast, the more viable languages of Inuktitut and Cree were 'most often' spoken by 82 per cent and 69 per cent, respectively. However, regular use of a language at home, even if it is not the major home language, may help to maintain it as a first language and may also contribute to its being learned as a second language (Norris and Jantzen 2002; Norris 2008).

The index of continuity[1] measures the prospects of transmitting a language as a mother tongue from one generation to the next by comparing the number of persons speaking the language at home to the number who have the language as their mother tongue. From 1981 to 2001, the steady decline in the index of continuity indicated long-term erosion in home language use, corresponding to an aging mother-tongue population, whose average age rose by five and a half years to 33 years in 2001. However, the most recent 2006 census suggests some stabilization of these trends at least for the short term (Figure 6.1, see page 121) (Norris and Snider 2008).

Long-term declines in continuity and home language use effectively contributed to a decrease in the natural transmission of Aboriginal languages as a mother tongue to children. The effects of these trends can be seen in the increasingly older age composition of the mother-tongue population over the past 25 years. The proportion of children (age 0 to 19) in the Aboriginal mother-tongue population fell from 41 per cent in 1986 to just 32 per cent in 2001. In contrast, the percentage of older adults (age 55 and over) increased from 12 per cent to 17 per cent. In 2006, the proportion of children appeared to have stabilized at

32 per cent, although the proportion of adults aged 55+ continues to increase through the aging of middle-aged speakers (Figure 6.2, see opposite) (Norris and Snider 2008).

As noted earlier, there is a significant range in the state and continuity across the many different Aboriginal languages. For example, home language use and continuity is still relatively strong for Inuktitut languages overall, with a continuity index of 86 persons speaking Inuktitut at home for every 100 persons with an Inuktitut mother tongue—meaning that Inuktitut is highly likely to be passed on to the next generation. In sharp contrast, many of the smaller endangered languages, especially in British Columbia (for example, Haida, with only six persons speaking it at home for every 100 persons with Haida as a mother tongue), have an extremely low chance of being passed on to the younger generation as a first language. Yet other small languages, such as Attikamek and Montagnais-Naskapi, show good prospects for intergenerational transmission, with continuity indexes of greater than 90 (Norris 1998; 2008).

The average age of those who have an Aboriginal mother tongue reveals the extent to which language transmission has been successful—the younger the speakers, the healthier the language. High language continuity is associated with 'young' mother-tongue populations (e.g., Inuktitut, with an average age of about 23 years.) Low continuity is associated with 'old' mother-tongue populations, as evidenced by a high average age (e.g., for Haida, an average age of some 50 years indicates that few young people have learned Haida as a mother tongue and implies that it is used as a first language mostly by speakers of the grandparental and great-grandparental generation) (Figure 6.3, see page 122).

Outcomes of Endangerment of Aboriginal Languages across the Generations

The long-term processes of language maintenance and loss over the generations are reflected in the current states of the 86 different Aboriginal languages in Canada. With long-term declines in intergenerational transmission over the past 25 years and aging mother-tongue populations, endangered languages are no longer the mother tongues of children but are spoken mostly as first languages by the parental, grandparental, or great-parental generations, depending on the extent of aging. For some endangered languages, there are now fewer than 100, mostly elderly first-language speakers. Today, the 86 various languages and their communities differ widely in their size, state, and levels of vitality and endangerment—some relatively flourishing, others endangered, some critically (close to extinction). From a longer-term and more international perspective, even the largest and most viable of Canada's indigenous languages can be considered

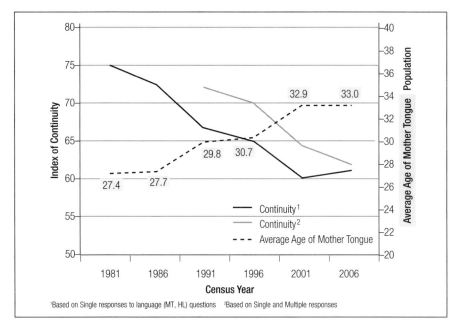

Figure 6.1   Declining continuity implies decreasing prospects for children learning their parent(s)' Aboriginal language

Source: 1981–2006 Census, Statistics Canada, author's calculations from Norris and Snider, 2008.

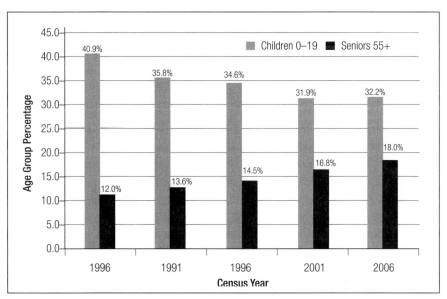

Figure 6.2   Decreasing shares of children learning an Aboriginal mother tongue and aging mother tongue populations.

Source: 1981–2006 Census, author's calculations, Statistics Canada, Norris and Snider, 2008.

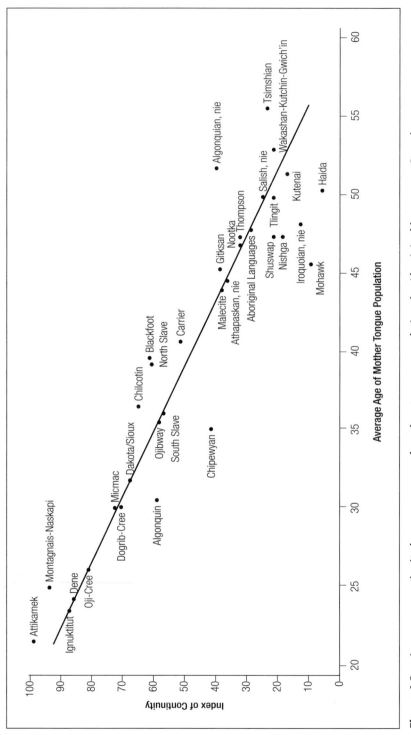

Figure 6.3   Language continuity by average age of mother-tongue population, by Aboriginal languages, Canada

Source: 2001 Census of Canada, Statistics Canada, author's calculations, from Norris, 2008.

potentially 'vulnerable' or 'unsafe', and hence all Aboriginal languages in Canada are included in the UNESCO *Atlas of the World's Languages in Danger* (UNESCO 2009; 2010).

In terms of assessing the degree of language endangerment of different languages, there are various approaches and criteria that can be considered. For example, in a five-category classification of language survival, the linguist Kinkade (1991) classified viable and endangered Aboriginal languages mainly on the basis of speaker populations, as follows:

- already extinct;
- near extinction: beyond the possibility of revival (spoken by only a few elderly people);
- endangered: spoken by enough people to make survival a possibility if sufficient community interest and concerted educational programs are present;
- viable but small: more than 1000 speakers and spoken in isolated and/or well-organized communities with strong self-awareness;
- viable: large enough population base that long-term survival is relatively assured.

In a more comprehensive approach, UNESCO's framework (2003) for assessing language vitality and endangerment incorporates a generational perspective within a set of nine major evaluative factors (recognizing that no single factor alone can be used to assess a language's vitality). Of these, there are six major evaluative factors (three demographic*) specific to language vitality, including:

*1. intergenerational language transmission;
*2. absolute number of speakers;
*3. proportion of speakers within the total population;
4. trends in existing language domains;
5. response to new domains and media;
6. materials for language education and literacy.

For purposes of determining degrees of language endangerment, the UNESCO *Atlas of the World's Languages in Danger* employed 'intergenerational language transmission' as the major factor, as outlined in Table 6.1. The atlas classifies the 86 different Aboriginal languages of Canada by these levels of language endangerment (not including two extinct since the 1950s), based in part on census data on Aboriginal language–speakers residing in Aboriginal communities

(UNESCO 2009, 2010; Norris 2009a). These generational classifications and their results for Canada are also summarized in Table 6.1.

On the whole, then, 24 (or 28 per cent) of Aboriginal languages in Canada classified as 'vulnerable', although still relatively healthy or viable, are spoken as first languages by young generations of Aboriginal speakers. However, the vast majority of Aboriginal languages in Canada (the remaining 62, or 72 per cent) are endangered—that is, Aboriginal children are no longer learning these traditional languages of their parents, grandparents, or great-grandparents as their mother tongues. In the case of 14 (or 16 per cent) of Aboriginal languages that are definitely endangered, children are no longer learning the language as

Table 6.1   UNESCO Factor 1: Intergenerational Transmission: Generational Measures of Language Vitality and Endangerment

UNESCO Degree of Endangerment	Intergenerational Language Transmission	Distribution of Languages in Canada by Degree	
		Number	% Distribution (excluding extinct)
Safe	Language is spoken by all generations; intergenerational transmission is uninterrupted. (N.B. not included in the atlas)	0	0
Vulnerable (viable but potentially endangered)	Most children speak the language, but it may be restricted to certain domains (e.g., home).	24	28
Definitely endangered	Children no longer learn the language as mother tongue in the home.	14	16
Severely endangered	Language is spoken by grandparents and older generations; while the parent generation may understand it, they do no speak it to children or among themselves.	16	19
Critically endangered	The youngest speakers are grand-parents and older, and they speak the language partially and infrequently.	32	26
Extinct	There are no speakers left. (N.B. included in the atlas if presumably extinct since the 1950s)	2	n/a

Source: UNESCO 2009. www.unesco.org/culture/en/endangeredlanguages/atlas. Copyright © UNESCO 1995–2008.

a mother tongue in the home. Another 16 (or 19 per cent) of Aboriginal languages, which parents understand but don't speak among themselves or to their children, are spoken by grandparents and older generations. Finally, there are 32 'critically' endangered Aboriginal languages in Canada—just over one in four (26 per cent)—spoken only partially or infrequently by grandparents and older generations, the youngest speakers.

According to the UNESCO classification, the 32 per cent of Aboriginal languages that are critically endangered are spoken by only 1200 persons (or 1 per cent of first-language speakers) from the grandparental and older generations; conversely, the 28 per cent of languages (24) that are 'vulnerable' or viable (not considered endangered) are spoken by the vast majority, some 134,000 persons (or 90 per cent) (Norris 2010) from all generations.

Revitalization of Aboriginal Languages: Generational Perspectives

There are signs of revitalization among Aboriginal languages, especially with youth who are learning the traditional but endangered languages of their parents or grandparents as second languages, at home or in school. Many Aboriginal communities are striving to preserve their traditional culture and languages by involving the participation of all generations, young and old—children, youth, adults, and elders. These efforts can also contribute to an increased awareness of Aboriginal languages among Canadians in general.

Certainly, census data attest to the ongoing efforts at revitalization through second-language learning. In both the 2001 and 2006 censuses, second-language learners accounted for a significant percentage of the speaking population among some of the most endangered languages. In 2001, they accounted for more than half of the speakers of Tlingit, Haida, and smaller Salish languages (Norris 2007). Shares of second-language speakers in 2006 also remained high at 30 to 40 per cent for some of the endangered languages with very few speakers (e.g., Shuswap, Tsimshian, and Tlingit) (Statistics Canada 2008; Norris and Snider 2008).

Census data also point to efforts at language revitalization among communities where intergenerational language transmission has been in decline with aging and decreasing mother-tongue populations, many beyond child-bearing years. Between 1996 and 2001, the proportion of communities where most Aboriginal speakers had learned the language as their mother tongue dropped from two-thirds to less than half, whereas the proportion of communities where most speakers had acquired it as their second language doubled from 8.5 to 17 per cent. Fully one-third of communities enumerated in 2001 could be classi-fied as being in transition from a mother-tongue population to a second-language population (Norris 2006; 2007).

From a demographic perspective, second-language learning is a critical counterbalance to mother-tongue decline and a necessary response for the revival of endangered languages, reflecting two phenomena: first, that many mother-tongue populations are aging beyond child-bearing years; and second, that for most children the ideal family and community conditions for mother-tongue transmission (that is, living within Aboriginal communities in families where both parents have an Aboriginal mother tongue) are becoming more the exception than the norm. In 2001, just over 10 per cent of Aboriginal children and youth lived in such 'ideal' conditions. Demographic data show that the children most likely to learn an Aboriginal language as a second language are from linguistically mixed families and live in urban areas (Norris 2003, 2007, 2008; Norris and Jantzen 2003).

Outside Aboriginal communities or settlements and in urban areas, where the intergenerational transmission of an Aboriginal mother tongue is much less likely, young people are significantly more likely to acquire their traditional language as a second language compared to youth on reserve. For example, among registered Indian children aged 10 to 14 who were able to speak an Aboriginal language in 1996, proportionately more of those living off-reserve had learned their traditional language as a second language (with an index of 165 able to speak an Aboriginal language for every 100 who had an Aboriginal language as their mother tongue) compared to their counterparts on-reserve with an index of 115 (Norris and Jantzen 2003).

Extent of Second-Language Learning among Youth

In general, Aboriginal youth are considerably less likely than their elders to speak an Aboriginal language, and among those who do, it appears that the likelihood that they have acquired it as a second language has increased (Norris 2003; 2007; 2008). While Aboriginal children and youth under the age of 25 represent 38 per cent of Aboriginal mother-tongue speakers, they make up a larger share of second-language speakers (about 45 per cent, double the percentage of those 45 years and older (Norris 2007). The index of second-language acquisition, which compares the number of people who report being able to speak the language with the number who have that Aboriginal language as a mother tongue, provides some idea of the degree of language revival. If for every 100 people with a specific Aboriginal mother tongue, more than 100 persons in the overall population are able to speak that language, then it implies that some must have learned it as a second language either in school or later in life. For example, in 2001 for every 100 Aboriginal youths in Canada who had an Aboriginal mother tongue, there were more—121—who could speak an Aboriginal language, implying that some youth must have learned their language as a second language. This index for youth is higher than the index for speakers aged 65 and over, which was 107. Among all Aboriginal language speakers, the second-language index rose from 117 in 1996 to 120 in 2001 (Norris 2006, 2007, 2008; Norris and Jantzen 2002).

While both viable and endangered languages share similar patterns of younger second-language learners and older first-language learners, generational differences in language learning are most pronounced among speakers of endangered languages. Although second-language learners make up the highest proportion of speakers of both viable and endangered languages in the younger age groups, they make up a substantially higher share of young people speaking endangered Aboriginal languages, much less than for viable languages. In the case of endangered languages, second-language learners constitute the majority of younger speakers able to speak the language. Among children under 15 who could speak an endangered language in 2001, 71 per cent had learned it as a second language; in contrast, only about one in five (some 20 per cent) of young speakers of viable languages learned their language as a second language (Norris 2007; 2008).The prevalence of second-language learners declines with increasing age among both endangered and viable language speakers, a pattern that is not surprising, since older generations of Aboriginal peoples are more likely to have an Aboriginal mother tongue (see Figure 6.4 on page 128).

Contribution of Youth in Revitalization of Endangered Languages through Second-Language Learning

The language development of today's Aboriginal youth has significant implications for the future prospects of Canada's Aboriginal languages, particularly endangered ones. Given the long-term decline in language continuity and natural transmission of endangered languages, rise in second-language acquisition is promising—particularly where speaker population may be growing because of an increase in youth population. Young second-language speakers make up an increasingly important segment of the endangered language speakers, and their contribution is critical to the growth and long-term viability of many endangered languages.

For example, from 1996 to 2001 the smaller Salish languages experienced a 5 per cent drop in mother-tongue population while simultaneously posting an impressive 17 per cent increase in total number of speakers because of an increased number of younger second-language learners. In 2001, the average age of all Salish speakers was notably younger at 42 years of age compared to

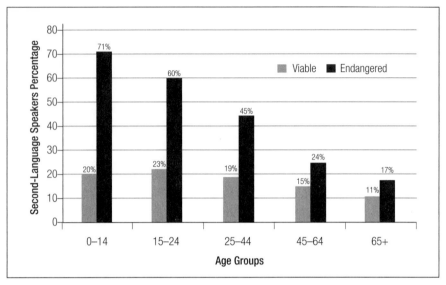

Figure 6.4   In younger age groups, second-language learners make up the
majority of those who speak endangered languages.

Source: 2001 Census of Canada, Statistics Canada, author's calculations, from Norris, 2007.

50 years for the population with a Salish mother tongue. Similarly, the Tlingit
language family had one of the oldest Aboriginal mother-tongue populations
in 2001, averaging close to 54 years, but its index of second-language acquisition (219) and the average age of all speakers (41 years) suggests that younger
generations are more likely to learn Tlingit as a second language (Norris 2007).

However, a high proportion of second-language speakers does not always
imply younger speakers: e.g., a third of the 500 people who could speak
Tsimshian in 2001 were second-language speakers, yet virtually none were
under the age of 25. Older populations of second-language speakers could
either imply the aging of current second-language speakers or, perhaps, people
starting to learn an Aboriginal language at an older age (Norris 2007).

Most Recent (2001–6) Trends: Possible Signs of New Cohorts of Children Acquiring Their Traditional Mother Tongue

According to Statistics Canada (2008), the 2006 census reveals that the share
of First Nations people who speak an Aboriginal language remains steady, even
among younger generations, and that First Nations languages are being learned
as second languages. And while Inuktitut remains strong, its use has declined,
with some Inuit learning Inuktitut as a second language. In the case of Métis,
older generations are more likely to speak an Aboriginal language.

A preliminary analysis of 2001–6 intercensal trends in language learning yields new insight into patterns that suggest some positive signs, particularly for mother-tongue transmission of some Aboriginal languages. Census figures adjusted for comparability between 2001 and 2006 indicate a 9 per cent increase from 2001 in the population with an Aboriginal mother tongue (Statistics Canada 2008), whereas the previous 1996 to 2001 intercensal period saw a slight decrease (although caution in interpreting these patterns and trends is required, since data have not been adjusted for comparability across all three censuses).

As well, these two intercensal periods display somewhat different patterns of growth between mother-tongue and total-speaker populations, with perhaps positive signs for some languages, possibly even endangered ones, that new cohorts of children may be starting to learn their languages through intergenerational transmission as a mother tongue. Over the 1996 to 2001 period, growth in mother-tongue populations of some Aboriginal languages tended to be outpaced by growth in their total-speaker populations such that gains in second-language speakers offset the declines in their mother-tongue populations. The more recent 2001–6 patterns for selected First Nation languages show more similar growth between mother-tongue and total-speaker populations. A few languages even experienced higher growth in their mother-tongue populations than in their overall speaker populations. In the case of the smaller Salish languages combined, their mother-tongue population increased by 6 per cent, while their total-speaker population remained effectively the same (Statistics Canada 2008), possibly implying that new cohorts of children may be starting to learn their language as a mother tongue or that older generations are relearning the traditional mother tongue that they once lost.

Though not directly comparable, 2001 and 2006 measures nevertheless suggest a continuation of trends and generational patterns in second-language learning, with younger generations of endangered-language speakers still remaining more likely than older speakers to have learned their traditional language as a second language, in contrast to more viable languages where the impact of second-language acquisition is relatively minimal across all ages (although still higher among youth). However, the levels and contrasts in language learning between younger and older ages appear to have lessened since 2001, which may reflect increases in mother-tongue transmission. This appears consistent with the fact that both the proportion of children in the total mother-tongue population and the index of continuity had not continued its long-term decline since 1981 but rather remained steady in 2006. Higher indices of second-language acquisition among older adults most likely reflect the impact of the aging of

cohorts of second-language speakers or possibly, to a lesser extent, people starting to learn an Aboriginal language at an older age (Norris and Snider 2008).

'Secondarily Surviving' Endangered Languages:
Impact of New Generations of Speakers

As new generations of Aboriginal people learn to speak the endangered languages of their elders, they could make a significant contribution to keeping
their Aboriginal languages alive even as the few remaining elderly first-language
speakers die off. Second-language learning has special relevance to the future
prospects of critically endangered languages, especially in Canada, since as the
Encyclopedia of the World's Endangered Languages observes, 'most efforts among
North American Indians to preserve some knowledge of their traditional languages have focused on second language learning' (Moseley 2007). In the event
that second-language learning contributes to an increase in speakers of the language while no first-language speakers are left, such languages may be best described as 'secondarily surviving' languages.

> A language that has no first language speakers, but that is being actively
> taught as second language and has a definable heritage speech commun-
> ity, may be better considered to be secondarily surviving rather than ex-
> tinct. . . . Since many of the North American languages that are on the
> verge of extinction as first languages are often associated with (often vig-
> orous) heritage communities it can be anticipated that the number of
> secondarily surviving languages will grow considerably in the next few
> decades. In addition, some languages that at present must be considered
> extinct may attain secondary survival status as communities of heritage
> learners create and learn codes on the extant documentation (Hinton
> 2001, in Moseley 2007).

In Canada, Huron could be an example of a 'secondarily surviving' language.[2]
    Clearly the relevance of second-language learning and the possibility of 'sec-
ondarily surviving' increases the more critically endangered the language is,
since with few and aging speakers its natural transmission as a mother tongue
is practically nil. In communities where endangered languages are spoken,
second-language learning accounts for a growing share of all speakers as degree
of endangerment increases. In communities where traditional languages are not
endangered, second-language learning accounts for less than half (45 per cent)
of the main form of language acquisition, whereas it tends to be the main form

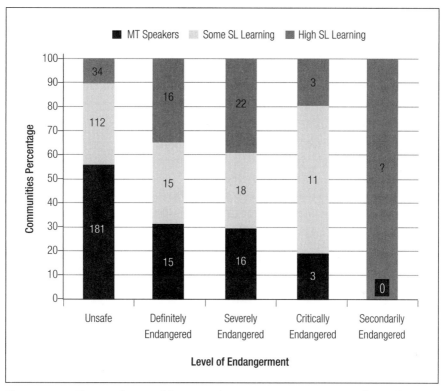

Figure 6.5   First- and second-language learning in communities with speakers
by degree of endangerment (UNESCO): Secondarily Surviving
Languages

Source: 2001 Census of Canada, Statistics Canada, author's calculations, adapted from UNESCO (2009, 2010); Norris, 2009b.

of language acquisition in the majority of the communities where languages are
clearly endangered: 56 per cent in communities where languages are 'definitely
endangered', 71 per cent in those with 'severely endangered' languages, and 83
per cent in those with 'critically' endangered languages (Figure 6.5).

Developments and Challenges in Keeping Aboriginal Languages Alive from Generation to Generation

Desire among All Generations to Learn and Maintain Aboriginal Languages

Trends in second-language learning suggest a growing awareness of Aboriginal
culture and identity and are consistent with findings from the post-censal

Aboriginal Peoples Surveys (APS), conducted since 1991, which suggest that the survival and maintenance of their traditional languages is important to all generations of Aboriginal people, young and old. According to the 1991 APS, nine in 10 Aboriginal adults would like to relearn the Aboriginal language they once knew, while the great majority of Aboriginal adults and nearly three-quarters of urban residents, who never spoke an Aboriginal language, would like to learn one. The 2001 APS indicates that speaking an Aboriginal language is important to all generations within and outside Aboriginal communities (Norris 2007; Statistics Canada 2003, 32).

Children, Parents, Grandparents, Extended Family, Educators, and Others: All Generations Are Teachers and Learners in Communities and Cities

Second-language acquisition by today's youth reflects an increasing interest in and desire to learn their traditional languages and opportunities for renewal and support. Even in the case of relatively strong languages like Inuktitut, Inuit youth say that they do not want to lose their ability to speak Inuktitut well, recognizing the importance of support through family, community, and education, with opportunities to learn, hear, and use it (Tulloch 2005; 2008). The ability to speak their ancestral language gives youth the opportunity to communicate with older family members in their traditional language and thereby can contribute to the maintenance of traditional cultures. In order to foster language learning, whether as a mother tongue or as a second language, it becomes increasingly important to consider the access youth have to sources of learning and the domains, such as home, school, and work, where they may use their language, whether within or outside Aboriginal communities.

For Aboriginal languages, the family and the community together play critical roles in the transmission of language from parent to child, affecting whether the child learns the Aboriginal language as a mother tongue or as a second language or speaks it at home. On their own, neither family capacity nor community support is sufficient to ensure the adequate transmission of an Aboriginal mother tongue. As noted earlier, many Aboriginal children, especially those in urban areas or with an endangered linguistic heritage, have not experienced ideal conditions for learning an Aboriginal mother tongue—i.e., they have not lived within an Aboriginal community in a family where either both parents or the lone parent has an Aboriginal mother tongue, let alone had any parent with an Aboriginal mother tongue.

Yet in the face of the challenges confronting Aboriginal people in the maintenance and revival of their traditional languages, there is evidence of ongoing concerted efforts on the part of all generations. Census data show that for some endangered languages, there appears to be a strong tendency among parents to ensure that their children have at least some knowledge of their ancestral language, even if transmission as a mother tongue is weak. For example, while 70 per cent of children with Salish-language parentage could speak the traditional language, only about 10 per cent had acquired it as a mother tongue (Norris and MacCon 2003). Furthermore, in passing the traditional language to the younger generation, it is not only the parental generation but extended family, teachers, and community members who are important sources of language learning and teaching. While APS results reinforce the importance of parents and home use of languages, they also point to other important sources of learning for children, including their extended family of aunts, uncles, grandparents; teachers in schools; other persons; and the community itself. As well, depending on the language knowledge or ability of parents, others (such as grandparents or teachers) may serve as the major source of language learning for children, whether within or outside Aboriginal communities.

Sources of Learning for Aboriginal Children in Winnipeg and Toronto

An example of the relationship between language ability and language sources for children can be illustrated through 2001 APS data for Winnipeg and Toronto. Winnipeg has the largest number of people with an Aboriginal mother tongue (4700) of any Canadian city and the largest proportion of Aboriginal adults (49 per cent) with the ability to speak an Aboriginal Language very well or relatively well. In contrast, in Toronto, which has one of the smallest populations with an Aboriginal mother tongue or ability to speak an Aboriginal language, only 19 per cent of Aboriginal adults are able to speak an Aboriginal language very well or relatively well. As a consequence, the two cities differ significantly with respect to the major sources of help for Aboriginal children learning their traditional languages. In Winnipeg, parents and grandparents are the major sources of learning for children, with at least half of the children receiving help from parents (52 per cent) and grandparents (54 per cent), whereas relatively smaller percentages of children receive help from teachers (6 per cent) and other persons (18 per cent). In Toronto, children learning an Aboriginal language are much more likely to receive help from teachers (39 per cent) and other persons (62 per cent), since only a minority of Toronto's Aboriginal adults in the parental and grandparental generations can speak an Aboriginal language.

As well, APS data demonstrate the importance of both family and community and the role of all generations in language transmission such that the more sources children have for help in learning their Aboriginal language—family, community, and schools—the better they fare in terms of the degree of difficulty they experience in understanding the language. The 2001 APS identifies the major sources from which at least half of the children in a community receive help in learning their Aboriginal language. On average, in Aboriginal communities where children receive help from only one major source, the vast majority (80 per cent) have difficulty in understanding the language. In contrast, in communities where children receive help from the five different sources (parents, grandparents, aunts and uncles, teachers, and other persons), on average just under 30 per cent have low proficiency in understanding the language (Norris 2004).

Community Example: How Cowichan Generations Are Preserving Their Traditional Language

In many communities where language revival is underway, all generations of family and community members are necessarily involved in the teaching and learning of the ancestral language. The importance of involving all generations in preserving the language is illustrated in the reserve community of Quw'utsun (Cowichan 1) of the Cowichan First Nation in British Columbia, which is striving to preserve and revive its severely endangered Salish language of Halkomelen, spoken as a first language by the grandparental and older generations. Statistics from the 2006 census clearly show that second-language learning among youth is well underway in this community. In both 2001 and 2006, more people could speak Halkomelen (hul'qumi'num) than had it as a mother tongue, whereas in 1996 those who knew their language were all older first-language speakers. By 2006, about 18 per cent of youth had a Halkomelen mother tongue, but even more, nearly one in four, had the ability to carry on a conversation in Halkomelen. The impact of youth in the revitalization of their traditional language is significant, especially in light of the fact that although youth represented about half of the community population of 1800, they accounted for the majority, some 70 per cent, of the community's second-language speakers in 2006.[3]

The concerted and ongoing efforts to save the Cowichan community's ancestral language of Halkomelen were profiled in a special CBC television feature on 'The National' (originally broadcast on CBC-TV and CBC Newsworld, 19 June 2009: www.cbc.ca/national/blog/video/aboriginal_issues/saving_aboriginal_languages.html).

This feature, entitled 'The Words of the Elders', provided significant insight into the involvement and contributions of all generations in the community as they attempted to preserve their endangered language and their race against time with only a few remaining Elders who knew the language.

Generations Preserving the Links: Language, Identity, and the Land

As with so many other endangered languages, the involvement of older generations in the preservation and revitalization of the Cowichan language of hul'qumi'num encompasses not only teaching the critical component of vocabulary but also the meanings, beliefs, values, and knowledge in the traditional language that link to culture, identity, place, land, traditional knowledge, and history.

Clearly, the Cowichan experience demonstrates that preserving a traditional indigenous language that respects the culture is more than just preserving words: it is all about 'maintaining the links: language, identity and the land' (Blythe and McKenna Brown 2003). Cowichan members stressed the links of language, identity, and land, the hope of language bringing back their culture and teachings, and the need for older generations to share their knowledge of the land and community history, as the following interview excerpts attest.

Identity:
If you don't know your language, you lose your culture and your identity. We need to keep our identity. . . . I hope one day that our language will come back and, along with it, our culture and teachings. This is my dream that one day we'll be speaking fluently and that all our teachings, all our sacred values will come back and be alive. (Arvid Charlie, community Elder)

Our traditions are maintained through the use of our language. I heard another uncle of mine say younger people misinterpret teachings because we don't understand the language, and I say 'we' because I am of the same age of a number of people who don't understand the language. So it has to be driven home, and that's where we need to focus is with some of the young adults. Kids, they pick it up, no problem. (Chuck Seymour, language coordinator for the Cowichan Tribes)

Traditional knowledge and the land:
This is the land of the Cowichan Tribes, and every mountain, every inlet, every creek has a story and a name in the language known as hul'qumi'num. . . . It was Arvid who taught Chuck the language orally. . . . Chuck's parents didn't speak hul'qumi'num, but Arvid chose him to share his knowledge of the plants and the trees. . . . For five years they

walked the territory, Arvid testing him every step of the way. . . . That sharing gave Chuck a connection to medicines and family histories and traditions he now carries into the spiritual ceremonies of his people, all conducted in hul'qumi'num. (Duncan McCue, CBC reporter)

Honestly at the time, the importance of what was being shared with me didn't fully sink in. Only through where we were going in the sharing that made me realize the importance of what it is that I'm carrying, and I need to share the names of these plants and trees. (Chuck Seymour, language coordinator for the Cowichan Tribes)

Generations Saving Old Words and Creating New Words: Embracing Technology and Curricula

Many communities trying to preserve and revitalize their traditional languages are confronted not only with the task of preserving the words of the traditional language but also with the challenge of creating new vocabulary so that the language can be used in the day-to-day world of home, school, work, and the marketplace. The processes of language preservation, maintenance, and revitalization also require the application of new technology in both documentation, development, and delivery of language references and school curricula. Often, the challenges of these language activities require the input of not only the oral traditions of the older generations of speakers but also the skills of everyone in the community, young and old, as the Cowichan experience demonstrates:

This fight against forgetting is . . . a responsibility they must share with everyone in the community. From his mother's house, Arvid Charlie takes his precious words to the office of his nephew Chuck Seymour, the language coordinator for the Cowichan Tribes. Arvid recalls each word and describes its meaning. Chuck enters them into a database. Not only do they bring old words to life, they create new ones too. . . . Oral tradition, it isn't, but language preservation these days means embracing new technologies. And all that painstaking work has resulted in this. They've printed two editions so far. Now they're assembling a phrase book, and they've even built a website to help new speakers wrap their tongues around unfamiliar sounds. (Duncan McCue, CBC reporter)

Every day my mother is coming up with words that I haven't heard in our Native language. But also we need other words in our hul'qumi'num language that is said in English, and I'll jot down that English phrase and then approach mom or some other elders to match a phrase to it or a word. It's all part of bringing back our language to life. . . . Today there's collapsible buckets or containers, collapse it, especially camping stuff. (Arvid Charlie, community Elder)

It's with Cowichan kids that the future of hul'qumi'num now rests. At Koksilah Elementary, children learn their language a half hour every day using a curriculum developed by the tribe, taught by members of the community. Nearly 800 students are now part of the program. (Duncan McCue, CBC reporter)

Bridging Connections across Generations: Past, Present, and Future

As children and youth learn the endangered languages of their elders, of the grandparental or great-grandparental generations if the language is severely or critically endangered, they are often learning languages their own parents have never learned or do not speak. And as children, parents, grandparents, and great-grandparents strive together to preserve and revitalize their language, they bridge new connections and communications across the generations. Each generation has an important role to play in the community endeavour.

Elders: 'Keepers' of the Languages

Clearly the elders play critical roles in the preservation and revitalization of their endangered language, since they are the only remaining generations with knowledge of the language and they are indeed the 'keepers of the language'. And for the elders themselves, their involvement renews their own connections with their past and the language of their ancestors.

. . . for the keepers of the language here, it's a race against time to revive the language one word at a time, which is why nearly every day Arvid Charlie goes on a quest. He's searching for those words in the home of his mother, Violet. She's 84 years old now. Their talks are pleasant, often funny, but throughout Arvid scribbles down what she says. . . . Sometimes it's a struggle to remember the past, but Violet can still evoke a time when all the people spoke or sang hul'qumi'num. To her, these recollections are a comforting and necessary connection to her elders. (Duncan McCue, CBC reporter)

It's not my words. It's our elders'. It's not mine. They gave it to me just for safekeeping to pass on. And he can pass it on to whoever is interested, will keep it. If they're not interested, we're just going to lose it. I told him a long time ago all the words. I've got no more. He comes in and I find another word in my head. I give it to him right away before I forget. (Violet, Arvid Charlie's mother)

Children: Learners and Teachers

As is often and understandably the case in the preservation and revitalization of severely and critically endangered languages that are generally known only by the grandparental generation and up, children are learning a language (usually at school) that their parents never acquired. As a consequence, when children who are learning their traditional language as a second language are at home, they can sometimes become the teacher in sharing what they have learned with their parents, which may lead to the language being used in the home at least on a 'regular basis'. And in that sense, it also provides a connection to the generations who grew up not speaking.

> When kids go home to talk to their parents, they are teaching them. So even though we're not focusing on those adults directly, the kids bring it home to the parents. . . . And they can't even talk with their parents in some cases. But the seed is planted. It's planted with the parents. So the learners become the teachers. . . . It's far from fluency, but it is a bridge to the generations who grew up not speaking. (Chuck Seymour, language coordinator for the Cowichan Tribes)

Parents: Importance of Seeing Children Learn Their Traditional Languages
In the case of severely or critically endangered languages, parental generations either have not learned or do not generally speak their traditional language for a variety of reasons. For some, it may be that during their childhood, conditions were not conducive to the acquisition of an Aboriginal mother tongue (e.g., they may have resided in an urban area). Others may have been discouraged from using their languages, or those who attended residential school may have been prohibited from or punished for speaking their languages. Thus, for parents to have their own children learn their ancestral language is significant, inspiring pride and hope for the future and contributing to community healing and well-being. Certainly, the following comments of Cowichan parents reinforce findings that the revitalization of Aboriginal languages contributes to community well-being and bonding with family and community (Chandler 2008; Tulloch 2008; Fonda 2009).

> It does wonderful things to my heart. It's just wonderful to see, and I want them to be fluent in the language. It's very, very important to me.
> Having our daughter here for me brings great pride in knowing that she's got more than I ever did.
> I get emotional because we growing up, we never had that opportunity. We were always told we were stupid and wouldn't amount to anything.

We've lost so much, so much of that has been taken away from us with residential schools that this feels like a complete circle in that our youth now can learn the language of our elders and carry that on because there are whole generations that have lost out on that, that's been stripped from them and stolen from them. So to have our young ones starting to learn that and be fluent in that, it's just wonderful to see, and it's healing for our community.

Children: Transmission to the Next Generation

Finally, as for all languages and communities, today's generation of children are the future, and it will be critical that they learn the language well enough, especially as second-language speakers, to ensure that another generation of speakers follows. And certainly the language planners and educators of Cowichan recognize that need when considering the prospects for their community's traditional language.

The people here know that if hul'qumi'num is to survive, this generation of learners will have to pass on their knowledge to the next. For that to happen successfully, a lot more effort is required. Some here dream of a hul'qumi'num immersion program in the schools. That means developing advanced curriculum and more language instructors . . . (Duncan McCue, CBC reporter)

Outlook, Prospects, and Considerations in Keeping Aboriginal Languages Alive for Future Generations

Certainly, the outlook and prospects for Aboriginal languages in Canada depend on inter- and intra-generational patterns of language use and learning that shape language maintenance, loss, and revitalization. Good prospects for currently viable languages require the continued transmission of the traditional language as the mother tongue of each successive new generation of children. Any rupture in that transmission can eventually lead to language loss and endangerment. In the case of endangered languages, clearly the involvement of all generations is essential to the revival of the language. And the challenges facing each generation in preserving and revising their language increase with the greater the degree of endangerment.

For languages that are critically endangered, with few remaining and elderly speakers, it is a race against time to prevent the language dying with them. Yet although many critically endangered languages will undoubtedly see their last remaining generations of older first-language speakers die, current trends in

revitalization and second-language learning suggest that they may not necessarily become 'extinct', since younger generations of second-language speakers
could ensure their continuation as 'secondarily surviving' languages.

Children and Youth of Today Are the Parents of Tomorrow

Aboriginal children and youth of today, in their role as future parents, will be
charged with passing on the language to the next generation. And certainly this
task is not without its challenges, given the various factors that can erode home
use of their traditional language, such as migration from Aboriginal communities, residence in cities, linguistic intermarriage (all tending to be higher for
women than for men), and the prevailing influence of English and French in
daily life (Norris 2007). Furthermore, the nature of the challenges they will face
as parents will also depend on how they themselves learned their traditional
language, whether as a mother tongue or second language.

> For those youth who are first-language speakers of more viable languages,
> their challenge lies in maintaining their mother tongue as a home lan-
> guage as they enter their family formation years, to ensure their language
> becomes the mother tongue of their children. . . . The crucial question for
> Aboriginal youth who are second-language speakers, especially in rela-
> tion to the revitalization of endangered languages, concerns the extent to
> which they as parents will be able to transmit knowledge of their language
> to their own children. They may face particular difficulties depending
> on their degree of fluency and the day-to-day use of the language within
> home and community: if home use as a 'major language' erodes, then so
> do the chances of it being passed on as the mother tongue of their chil-
> dren. However, it may be that even speaking an Aboriginal language on a
> 'regular basis' could contribute to continuity to some extent (Norris and
> Jantzen 2003) or at least provide children with knowledge of their ances-
> tral tongue as a second language (Norris 2008).

For some languages, recent 2001–6 trends suggest positive signs that new cohorts of children could be acquiring their traditional language as a mother tongue.
This trend could possibly reflect a revival in mother-tongue transmission among
younger generations of new parents who in learning their traditional language,
as either a mother tongue or second language, may also have support for and a
strong awareness of the importance of transmitting it to the next generation.

Passing Aboriginal Languages to the Next Generation: Considerations of Cultural Continuity, Identity, Family, and Community within Today's World

It is the reality that in today's world, Aboriginal youth must know the mainstream language of English or French, given the prevailing influence of these major languages through the mass media, popular culture, and other aspects of their daily lives such as education and work. At the same time, their traditional language can serve a different role than that of mainstream languages: it can be a means to 'express the identity of the speakers of a community . . . fostering family ties, maintaining social relationships, preserving historical links' (Crystal 2000; Norris 2007, 2008).

The maintenance, loss, or revitalization of a language can have significant implications for all generations, within family and community, given its strong ties with culture, identity, traditions, and history. In her study of Inuit youth and their language, Tulloch explains: 'language brings and binds community members together. Without it some Inuit feel disconnected; they miss acceptance and the opportunity to participate fully in their community.' In the case of language loss or declining fluency, 'Breakdowns in language competence are linked to interruptions in the social network', while in the case of revitalization, 'increased language competence can result in increased opportunities for community engagement . . . learning their traditional language is not a luxury for youth any more than communicating with one's parents and grandparents, knowing where one comes from and being able to gain the kind of education one values' (Tulloch 2008, 73–5). As Fonda (2009, 76) states, youth learning their traditional language is an essential contributor to social capital and cohesion.

There is a growing recognition in research of the importance of traditional languages in the educational success and well-being of Aboriginal children (Ball 2009; Guèvremont and Kohen 2008). Ball (2009) addresses the importance of language for cultural identity and belonging and in securing children's long-term academic, economic, and social success. She also stresses the need for language development and learning programs that are culturally appropriate if they are to contribute to a child's positive development and ability to communicate across generations in families and communities: 'Programs that help Aboriginal children learn their heritage language, rather than treating European-heritage language skills as normative, can support their cultural identity formation, cultural knowledge and connectedness with their cultural community (Crystal 1997; Hebert 2000; Ignace 1998)' (from Ball 2009, 39). And she recommends family- and community-driven approaches for young children: 'A national strategy that includes a stream for supporting Aboriginal early language development should support implementation and evaluation of culturally grounded approaches developed in consultation with families and communities as demonstration projects.' (Ball 2009, 41)

In this respect, Aboriginal women play a critical role in cultural and language continuity and revitalization within communities as well as families (Norris 2009b).

> On many education and policy fronts, success in Aboriginal education is being redefined and expanded with the increasing recognition of the need for an education that recognizes the importance of language and cultures, . . . and . . . the strengthening of Aboriginal peoples identity '. . . emphasizing language, cultural and traditional knowledge, and the effective reincorporation of elders and women in educating younger generations' (National Association of Friendship Centres 2007, 12) (from Norris 2009b).

The need for culturally grounded language learning and the contribution of all generations within families and communities toward preserving and revitalizing their languages raises important considerations for new generations of learners with respect to the context within which language learning takes place. For example, how appropriate or useful is the application of technology for language learning outside of a cultural context or setting or without the input of Aboriginal teachers or elders? Is it possible or meaningful to attempt to learn a language in isolation from the culture, traditions, and land? Can culturally appropriate or land-based knowledge be properly acquired within urban settings that are outside of Aboriginal communities? And to what extent can 'secondarily surviving' endangered languages contribute to cultural continuity, identity, and traditional knowledge?

In conclusion, generational perspectives are critical to an understanding of the dynamics and demographics of Aboriginal language maintenance, loss, and revitalization and to their broader implications with respect to cultural continuity, identity, family, and community. Furthermore, the developments, challenges, and prospects of keeping Aboriginal languages alive for generations to come clearly depend on the contributions of all generations. Finally, efforts to preserve, maintain, and revitalize traditional languages can significantly contribute to the cultural continuity and identity of Aboriginal people, to connections across their generations, to the well-being of their families and communities, and ultimately to the vision that they are indeed 'here to stay'.

Discussion Questions

1. Aboriginal languages in Canada differ significantly from each other in their state and prospects. The extent and level of their endangerment can be described with respect to their degree of intergenerational transmission. What are some of the challenges facing different generations of Aboriginal people in their efforts to preserve their traditional and ancestral languages, and how do these challenges vary according to the degree of vitality and endangerment of their particular language?
2. Prospects and challenges of Aboriginal people learning and using their traditional Aboriginal language vary across generations, families, and their locations in communities and cities. What types of family and location characteristics are most conducive to generations of children acquiring an Aboriginal language as their mother tongue or first language?
3. While ideally a language is best transmitted as the mother tongue of the next generation of speakers, for many endangered Aboriginal languages, second-language learning is often demographically the only option for younger generations. What are some of the ways, activities, and types of domains, within and outside families, schools, and communities, in which different generations can work together as participants, teachers, and/or learners in preserving their languages and cultures?
4. Languages that have no first-language speakers but that are being actively taught as a second language can be considered to be 'secondarily surviving'. What are some of the considerations concerning the prospects of current generations of second-language learners passing on 'secondarily surviving' languages to future generations of speakers? What approaches and factors in language learning and transmission might affect the extent to which 'secondarily surviving' languages contribute to cultural continuity, identity, and traditional knowledge?

Further Readings

Moseley, Christopher. 2007. *Encyclopedia of the World's Endangered Languages*. London and New York: Routledge. Endangered languages make up 90 per cent of the world's 6000 or more distinct languages. This encyclopedia provides an international perspective on the situation of the many endangered languages in countries throughout the world and explores the reasons why so many are not being passed on to future generations.
UNESCO. 2009. 'UNESCO's interactive atlas of the world's languages in danger'. http://portal. unesco.org/ci/en/ev.php-URL_ID=28377&URL_DO=DO_TOPIC&URL_SECTION=201. html. UNESCO launched the electronic version of the new third edition of its *Atlas of the World's Languages in Danger* in 2009. This interactive digital tool provides updated data about approximately 2500 endangered languages around the world, including the 88 different Aboriginal languages for Canada (two of the 88 becoming 'extinct' within living memory). The atlas provides searches on these 2500 endangered languages according to several criteria and ranks their degree of endangerment according to five levels of

vitality based on the extent of intergenerational transmission: vulnerable, definitely endangered, severely endangered, critically endangered, and extinct. As the interactive site notes, 'Some of the data are especially worrying: out of the approximately 6,000 existing languages in the world, more than 200 have become extinct during the last three generations, 538 are critically endangered, 502 severely endangered, 632 definitely endangered and 607 unsafe ("vulnerable").'

UNESCO. 2010. *Atlas of the World's Languages in Danger*. 3rd edn. ed., Christopher Moseley. Paris: UNESCO Publishing. This print edition of the third edition of the atlas provides discussion on the state and situation of endangered languages, including their degree of endangerment in relation to intergenerational transmission, for different countries and regions around the world. The atlas includes a chapter on the situation of Aboriginal languages in Canada.

UNESCO. 2003. *Language Vitality and Endangerment*. Prepared by UNESCO Ad Hoc Expert Group on Endangered Languages. Paper submitted to the International Expert Meeting on UNESCO Programme Safeguarding of Endangered Languages, Paris, March. Also available on-line at www.unesco.org/culture/ich/doc/src/00120-EN.pdf. The third edition of the atlas designates the degrees of endangerment according to UNESCO's Language Vitality and Endangerment framework that establishes six degrees of vitality/endangerment based on nine factors, of which the most salient is that of intergenerational transmission: 'In 2002 and 2003, UNESCO asked an international group of linguists to develop a framework for determining the vitality of a language in order to assist in policy development, identification of needs and appropriate safeguarding measures. This Ad Hoc Expert Group on Endangered Languages elaborated a landmark concept paper entitled "Language Vitality and Endangerment", which established nine criteria in establishing degrees of endangerment' (www.unesco.org/culture/ich/index.php?pg=00142). This paper discusses the nine factors that form the basis for assessing language vitality and endangerment. The nine factors include: intergenerational language transmission (scale); absolute number of speakers (real numbers); proportion of speakers within the total population (scale); trends in existing language domains (scale); response to new domains and media (scale); materials for language education and literacy (scale); governmental and institutional language attitudes and policies, including official status and use (scale); community members' attitudes toward their own language (scale); and amount and quality of documentation (scale).

Horizons. 2008: 'Hope or heartbreak: Aboriginal youth and Canada's future'. This special issue of *Horizons* dedicated to Aboriginal youth was a joint collaboration between the Government of Canada's Policy Research Initiative and the Research and Analysis Directorate at Indian and Northern Affairs Canada, http://policyresearch.gc.ca/doclib/HOR_v10n1_200803_e.pdf. With respect to Aboriginal languages, this issue contains four articles that address different aspects of the relationship between today's generations of Aboriginal youth and their traditional languages:

1. Chandler, M.J., and C.E. Lalonde. 'Cultural continuity as a protective factor against suicide in First Nations youth'.
2. Tulloch, Shelley. 'Uqausirtinnik annirusunniq—Longing for our language'.
3. Coley, Miali-Elise, and S. Tulloch. 'Emerging leaders: The Inuit Circumpolar Youth Council—A voice for the future of Inuit'.

4. Norris, M.J. 'Voices of Aboriginal youth today: Keeping Aboriginal languages alive for future generations'.

Notes

1. The prospects of transmitting a language as a mother tongue can be assessed using an index of continuity, which measures the number of people who speak the language at home for every 100 persons who speak it as their mother tongue. A high measure of 80 to 100 indicates high continuity, while a measure below 30 indicates very low continuity and the language is not likely to be transmitted to the next generation.
2. 'While Huron-Wendat is extinct in the sense that the last Aboriginal speakers died in the first half of the 20th Century, there are efforts to bring the language back to life' (John Steckley, professor, Humber College, personal communication, July 2002, in Norris and Jantzen 2002).
3. Some caution in interpretation over the 1996, 2001, and 2006 censuses is advised, since at the time of writing, available data were not adjusted for complete comparability across all three censuses, meaning that trends between 1996 and 2001 may not be comparable to those between 2001 and 2006.

References

Abley, Mark. 2003. *Spoken Here: Travels among Endangered Languages*. Toronto: Random House of Canada.

Ball, Jessica. 2009. 'Aboriginal young children's language development: Promising practices and needs'. *Canadian Issues* winter.

Blythe, J., and R. McKenna Brown. 2003. *Maintaining the Links: Language, Identity and the Land*. Proceedings of the 7th Conference of the Foundation for Endangered Languages, Broome, Western Australia, 22–4 September.

Canadian Heritage. 2005. *Towards a New Beginning: A Foundation Report for a Strategy to Revitalize First Nation, Inuit and Métis Languages and Cultures*. Report to the Minister of Canadian Heritage by the Task Force on Aboriginal Languages and Cultures, June 2005. Catalogue no. CH4-96/2005. Ottawa: Canadian Heritage.

Chandler, M.J. 2006. *Cultural Continuity in the Face of Radical Social Change: Language Preservation as a Protective Factor against Suicide in First Nations Youth*. University of British Columbia, Paper presented at Raising Our Voices, Language Conference, Cornwall, ON, 15 August.

Chandler, M.J., and C.E. Lalonde. 2008. 'Cultural continuity as a protective factor against suicide in First Nations youth'. In special issue of *Horizons*, dedicated to Aboriginal youth, a Policy Research Initiative (PRI) publication. http://policyresearch.gc.ca/doclib/HOR_v10n1_200803_e.pdf.

Crystal, David. 2000. *Language Death*. Cambridge: Cambridge University Press.

Fonda, Marc. 2009. 'Towards cultural well-being: Implications of revitalising traditional Aboriginal religions.' *Canadian Issues* winter.

Guèvremont, Anne, and Dafna Kohen. 2008. 'Success in the formal education system: Impact of the ability to communicate in an Aboriginal language, school context, and gender'. Paper presented at session on Aboriginal Issues: Physical Activity, Education and Wellness at the Statistics Canada Socio-economic Conference.

Hinton, L. 2001. 'The use of linguistic archives in language revitalization'. in L. Hinton and K. Hale, eds, *The Green Book of Language Revitalization in Practice*, 419–23. San Diego and London: Academic Press.

Kinkade, M.D. 1991. 'The decline of Native languages in Canada'. In Robert H. Robins and Eugenius M. Uhlenbeck, eds, *Endangered Languages*. Published with the Authority of the Permanent International Committee of Linguists (CIPL), Berg.

Moseley, Chris. 2007. *Encyclopedia of the World's Endangered Languages*. London and New York: Routledge.

———, ed. 2009. *UNESCO Atlas of the World's Languages in Danger*. Paris: UNESCO Publishing.

National Association of Friendship Centres. 2007. 'Urban Aboriginal women: Social determinants of health and well-being'. www.naws-sfna.ca/pdf/NAFC-Urban Aboriginal Women.pdf.

Norris, M.J. 1998. 'Canada's Aboriginal languages'. *Canadian Social Trends* 51 (winter). Catalogue. no. 11-008. Ottawa: Statistics Canada.

———. 2000. 'Aboriginal peoples in Canada: Demographic and linguistic perspectives'. In D.A. Long and O.P. Dickason, eds, *Visions of the Heart: Canadian Aboriginal Issues*, 2nd edn. Toronto: Harcourt Brace Canada.

———. 2003. 'From generation to generation: Survival and maintenance of Canada's Aboriginal languages within families, communities and cities'. In J. Blythe and R. McKenna Brown, eds, *Maintaining the Links: Language, Identity and the Land*. Proceedings of the 7th Conference of the Foundation for Endangered Languages, Broome, Western Australia, 22–4 September.

———. 2004. Poster: 'Status, use and accessibility of Canada's Aboriginal languages within communities and cities'. Foundation for Endangered Languages, VIII International Conference with UNESCO Chair on Languages and Education, Institute d'Estudis Catalans, On the Margins of Nations: Endangered Languages and Linguistic Rights, Barcelona, 29 September–4 October.

———. 2006. 'Aboriginal languages in Canada: Trends and perspectives on maintenance and revitalization'. In J.P. White, S. Wingert, D. Beavon, and P. Maxim, eds, *Aboriginal Policy Research: Moving Forward, Making a Difference*. Toronto: Thompson Educational Publishing.

———. 2007. 'Aboriginal languages in Canada: Emerging trends and perspectives on second language acquisition'. *Canadian Social Trends* 83 (summer): 19–27. www .statcan.ca/english/freepub/11-008-XIE/2007001/pdf/11-008-XIE20070019628.pdf.

———. 2008. 'Voices of Aboriginal youth today: Keeping Aboriginal languages alive for future generations'. In 'Hope or heartbreak: Aboriginal youth and Canada's future'. A joint collaboration between the Government of Canada's Policy Research Initiative and the Research and Analysis Directorate at Indian and Northern Affairs Canada. http://policy-research.gc.ca/doclib/HOR_v10n1_200803_e.pdf.

———. 2009a. 'Linguistic classifications of Aboriginal languages in Canada: Implications for assessing language diversity, endangerment and revitalization'. *Canadian Diversity: Quarterly Journal of the Association for Canadian Studies* 7 (3): 21–34.

————. 2009b. 'The role of First Nations women in language continuity and transition'. In Gail Guthrie Valaskakis, Madeleine Dion Stout, and Eric Guimond, eds, *Restoring the Balance: First Nations Women, Community and Culture*. Winnipeg: University of Manitoba Press.

————. 2010. 'Canada and Greenland'. In Chris Moseley, ed., *Atlas of the World's Languages in Danger*. Paris: UNESCO Publishing.

Norris, M.J., and L. Jantzen. 2002. Poster: 'From generation to generation: Survival and maintenance of Canada's Aboriginal languages within families, communities and cities'. http://dsp-psd.pwgsc.gc.ca/Collection/R2-234-2002E.pdf.

————. 2003: 'Aboriginal languages in Canada's urban areas: Characteristics, considerations and implications'. In David Newhouse and Evelyn Peters, eds, *Not Strangers in These Parts: Urban Aboriginal Peoples*, 93–117. Ottawa: Policy Research Initiative.

Norris, M.J., and Karen MacCon. 2003. 'Aboriginal language transmission and maintenance in families: Results of an intergenerational and gender-based analysis for Canada, 1996'. In Jerry White, Paul Maxim, and Dan Beavon, eds, *Aboriginal Conditions: The Research Foundations of Public Policy*. Vancouver: University of British Columbia Press.

Norris, M.J., and M. Snider. 2008. 'Endangered Aboriginal languages in Canada: Trends, patterns and prospects in language learning'. In Tjeerd de Graaf, Nicholas Ostler, and Reinier Salverda, eds, *Endangered Languages and Language Learning*. Proceedings of the XII Conference of the Foundation for Endangered Languages, Fryske Academy and Mercator European Research Centre, Leeuwarden, The Netherlands, 24–7 September. http://recherchepolitique.gc.ca/doclib/AboriginalBook_e.pdf.

RCAP (Royal Commission on Aboriginal Peoples). 1996. *Report*, vol. 3, *Gathering Strength*, and vol. 4, *Perspectives and Realities*. Ottawa: Minister of Supply and Services Canada.

Statistics Canada. 2003. *Aboriginal Peoples Survey 2001 Initial Findings: Well-being of the Non-reserve Aboriginal Population*. Catalogue no. 89-589-XIE. Ottawa: Minister of Industry. www.statcan.gc.ca/pub/89-589-x/89-589-x2003001-eng.pdf.

————. 2008: *Aboriginal Peoples in Canada in 2006: Inuit, Métis and First Nations, 2006 Census*. Catalogue no. 97-558-XIE. Ottawa: Minister of Industry. http://www12.statcan.ca/english/census06/analysis/aboriginal/pdf/97-558-XIE2006001.pdf.

Tulloch, Shelley. 2005. 'Inuit youth: The future of Inuktitut'. In R.O. van Everdingen, comp., *Proceedings of the 14th Inuit Studies Conference*, 11–15 August 2004, p. 285–300. Calgary: The Arctic Institute of North America, University of Calgary. http://pubs.aina.ucalgary.ca/aina/14thISCProceedings.pdf.

————. 2008. 'Uqausirtinnik annirusunniq—Longing for our language'. In special issue of *Horizons* dedicated to Aboriginal youth, a Policy Research Initiative (PRI) publication. http://policyresearch.gc.ca/doclib/HOR_v10n1_200803_e.pdf.

UNESCO. 1996. *Atlas of the World's Languages in Danger of Disappearing*. ed. Stephen A. Wurm. Paris: UNESCO Publishing.

————. 2003. *Language Vitality and Endangerment*. Paper prepared by UNESCO Ad Hoc Expert Group on Endangered Languages submitted to the International Expert Meeting on UNESCO Programme Safeguarding of Endangered Languages, Paris, March. www.unesco.org/culture/ich/doc/src/00120-EN.pdf.

——— 2009. 'UNESCO's interactive atlas of the world's languages in danger: Statistics by country or area'. February 17. www.unesco.org/culture/ich/UNESCO-Endangered Languages-Statistics-20090217.xls.

——— 2010. *Atlas of the World's Languages in Danger*. 3rd edn. ed. Christopher Moseley. Paris: UNESCO Publishing.

7

Aboriginal Demography

Don Kerr and Roderic Beaujot

Canada has witnessed some remarkable demographic changes of late. Toward the end of the first decade of the twenty-first century, there are very few countries in the world with a higher life expectancy, whereas fertility has fallen to a very low level. International comparisons suggest that Canada ranks fifth in life expectancy at birth, after only Japan, Iceland, Sweden, and Switzerland (Milan and Martel 2008). As far as the birth rate is concerned, Canada entered the twenty-first century with its total fertility rate falling to a historic low—at only about 1.5 children per woman in 2005—prior to rebounding somewhat more recently, up to 1.66 by 2007 (Statistics Canada 2009a).

Related to these changes have been continuing improvements in Canada's social and economic development. As an indicator of this progress, the United Nations Development Programme (UNDP 2009) has consistently placed Canada at or near the top of its annual ranking of countries according to its Human Development Index. Meant to capture differences in life expectancy, per capita gross domestic product, and level of education, this ranking has been widely portrayed to the Canadian public as suggesting that Canada is 'one of the best countries in the world to live in'. Throughout most of the 1990s, Canada ranked first in this listing, only to slip more recently to rank fourth among nations owing to the relative gains made by Norway, Australia, and Iceland (UNDP 2009).

As demonstrated through an innovative application of this index to the First Nations peoples of Canada, Aboriginal Canadians have clearly not shared equally in this affluence. In considering persons designated as 'status Indian' by the Canadian government and in focusing exclusively on those who live on reserves, Beavon and Cooke (2003) rank the First Nations as 79th, only slightly above Mexico and Brazil. While living conditions are known to be better 'off-reserve' than 'on-reserve', Beavon and Cooke rightfully highlight the frustration of the First Nations' political leaders. Ovide Mercredi, a former Grand Chief of the Assembly of First Nations (AFN), has condemned the wide circulation of the UNDP ranking, emphasizing that Canada is certainly not among the 'best countries in the world' to live in for its First Nations (Mercredi 1997). More recently, Grand Chief Phil Fontaine, as a successor to Mercredi, emphasized that if we isolate the situation of Aboriginal peoples in Canada, 'First Nations rank no better than Third World countries' (Eggertson 2007). Unemployment remains very high, housing conditions are often substandard, and health care and educational services are often inadequate.

In this context, it should not come as a surprise to find that the demographic dynamics underlying the Aboriginal population are also quite different from those of Canada as a whole. In particular, mortality continues to be significantly higher, with major challenges in terms of population health. Birth rates also tend to be relatively high, with childbearing often beginning at a younger age relative to other Canadians. In turn, the growth rate of the Aboriginal population continues to outpace that of the overall population, resulting in a younger age/sex structure. This leads to a somewhat unique set of challenges compared to those of the broader society. For example, policy debates relating to slowing growth and population aging in Canada are not particularly relevant to many First Nations communities, since the age structure of these communities remains relatively young, with a significant share of children and young adults.

Because the demography of Aboriginal peoples is unique in Canada, there is some utility in beginning with the broader historical context. The history of European/Aboriginal contact has included much conflict and social tension. In reviewing Canada's history, the current Grand Chief of the AFN, Shawn Atleo (2009), emphasizes a few facts often neglected or downplayed by the broader society, including 'the well documented theft of Indian lands and forced relocations of First Nations communities; the criminalization and suppression of First Nation languages and cultural practices; the chronic under-funding of First Nations communities and programs; and the denial of Treaty and Aboriginal rights'. The demographic situation that characterizes the present can better be understood by beginning with this colonial past, since this history continues to reverberate for many First Nations peoples.

We begin this chapter with a brief overview of the demographic history of Aboriginal peoples in Canada—from the period before contact with Europeans through to the depopulation and excessive mortality that occurred during the eighteenth and nineteenth centuries. From there, we broadly sketch the dramatic demographic recovery that characterized Aboriginal Canadians from the later nineteenth century onward. The chapter then considers the many definitional issues involved in studying the demography of this population. Given that much confusion and inadequate information characterizes public discussions of Aboriginal peoples, it is useful to first clarify the terms used to identify Aboriginal peoples in the Canadian census in order to elucidate the nature of the demographic data currently available in the study of Canada's Aboriginal population.

The discussion of definitions is followed by an overview of what is currently known of present-day population size, fertility, and mortality, as well as some of the implications of recent trends for population structure and composition. This will all be related to evidence on the evolving social and economic conditions of Aboriginal Canadians as well as to the broader context of Canada's demographic development.

Pre-Contact Demography

Most accounts of Canada's demographic history begin with European contact. Historical research is highly reliant upon the survival of historical records and documents, and for that reason there have been large obstacles to research into the early history of the peoples of the Americas. Nonetheless, the evidence that is available on the demography of North America before European contact has been pieced together through the efforts of archeologists, physical anthropologists, and ethno-historians. Physical anthropologists make estimates of the living conditions, diet, fertility, morbidity, and mortality of pre-contact peoples through the systematic study of skeletal remains and burial sites. Archeologists can inform demographers about settlement patterns and technology use before contact. Ethno-historians attempt to make sense of the scattered and incomplete documents left behind as the first Europeans came into contact with the Aboriginal population. In combination, this information makes possible a number of inferences about the demography of the original inhabitants of Canada before and after contact with Europeans.

When the Portuguese, the Basques, and the French were first navigating the waters off Newfoundland, about 50 distinct languages (as opposed to dialects) were spoken within the boundaries of modern-day Canada. This number, which has been called a conservative estimate, includes only those that have been relatively well documented and classified (Goddard 1996). As a result of decades of exhaustive historical study, historians and linguists have approximated the locations and distributions of these languages at the time of contact and have also been able to categorize them according to their structure (Sturtevant 1996). Linguists have classified them into 11 major linguistic families, further indicating the high level of linguistic diversity (Figure 7.1). In fact, most of these languages would have had less in common with each other than did the European languages that were establishing themselves on the eastern coast of North America at this time, all of which belonged to the same major linguistic family (Indo-European), with the exception of the Basque language (which has been classified as a linguistic isolate).

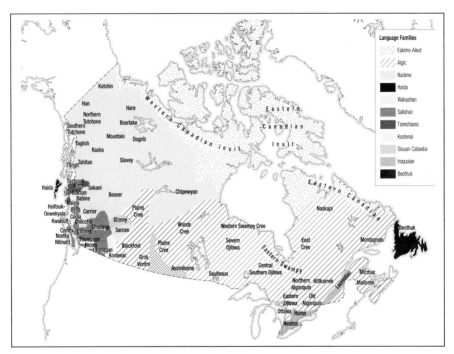

Figure 7.1   Native Languages and Language Families of North America: Pre-Contact Canada.

Source: Beaujot and Kerr, *Population Change in Canada*, 2nd ed., p. 20.

Although there are certainly obstacles to any effort to reconstruct population distribution so long ago, it is well established that the most densely populated region in the country at that time was along the west coast of British Columbia. Of the 50 languages spoken in Canada, approximately one-half were located within present-day British Columbia. Thanks to the abundance of food and the mild climate, population densities were higher than in any other region of the country, including the Iroquoian territories of southern Ontario and Quebec. What is clear is that Canada's west coast pre-contact peoples depended largely on the sea for subsistence as aquatic foragers, whalers, and fishermen. They also exploited the salmon runs that were once so abundant. In addition, this part of North America is noted for a greater supply of flora and fauna than other parts of Canada.

With this sedentary way of life, the peoples of the west coast of Canada were among the most densely populated 'non-agricultural' peoples ever documented by anthropologists (Boyd 1990). The second-most densely populated region of Canada before the arrival of the Europeans consisted of the territories of the Iroquoians of the St Lawrence River and Great Lakes. Yet unlike the peoples of

British Columbia, these farmer-hunters mostly practised slash-and-burn agriculture. The 'typical' pre-contact Iroquoian village was occupied year-round, only to be abandoned every few decades when the land was no longer fertile (Saunders, Ramsden, and Herring 1992). Consequently, we have been left with physical evidence of the various settlement patterns in this region during the pre-contact period, as well as evidence of early regional trade routes and likely socio-economic and political alliances.

As one moves farther north, population densities declined owing to the climate and physical characteristics of Canada's North. The northern boreal forest, also called the taiga or northern coniferous forest, spread across much of modern-day Canada, is noted for its ability to withstand particularly long and severe winters. In such forests in northern Quebec and Ontario, populations were low, and there is little evidence of permanent settlements before the arrival of the Europeans. In the absence of agriculture, the Algonquin, Montagnais, Ojibway, and Cree had adapted to an often difficult environment by acquiring an intimate knowledge of the food to be found in the boreal forest and by hunting and trapping the many mammals and birds. Resources were used extensively (that is, over a wide area) rather than intensively (as for example, in the more temperate regions of North America that allowed for some form of agriculture). Both the fauna and flora of the boreal forest are much less rich than those found in the deciduous forests farther south. The scarcity of food probably limited the population densities.

A relevant concept used by demographers and physical anthropologists in the study of non-agricultural peoples is the 'carrying capacity' of a specific region—in other words, the number of people that can be supported in an area given the available physical resources and the way that people use those resources (Boserup 1965; Harris and Ross 1987). Obviously, the carrying capacity of these northern regions would have been much lower than that of the south, and just as in modern Canada, population was concentrated in the most habitable regions of the country.

In the western provinces, the northern plains were relatively thinly populated with smaller communities whose main source of food was bison and other game, which were hunted communally. In the Arctic, the Inuit were spread extremely sparsely across an enormous landmass from Greenland to present-day Alaska. Owing to their remote location, some isolated bands of Copper and Netsilik Inuit were unknown to the Canadian government until the 1920s (Morrison 1984). Whereas the Beothuk of Newfoundland encountered Europeans in the sixteenth century, it would be 400 years before some isolated bands of Inuit first encountered people of European descent.

Although some historians have portrayed pre-contact America as a 'disease-free paradise' (Stewart 1973; Dobyns 1983), more recent research by physical anthropologists have shown that description to be inaccurate (Verano and Ubelaker 1992). In fact, pre-contact North American samples of skeletal remains suggest that mortality was high, particularly among the young; there is evidence of various contagious diseases, including respiratory infections, gastrointestinal illnesses, and a variety of parasites (Ubelaker 2000). The high mortality of pre-contact Canada paralleled that of Europe at that time. This is not a surprise to historical demographers, since it is well known that throughout most of human history, life expectancy probably fluctuated between 25 and 30 years (Wiess 1973). While mortality was high—by contemporary standards—on both sides of the Atlantic, it worsened dramatically in North America with European contact and the introduction of new lethal diseases that devastated the Aboriginal populations.

In populations with high mortality, the risk of death is highest among infants and young children. If, for example, life expectancy in North America were about 30 years on average, the chances of dying before one's first birthday would have been about one in four, with at least 40 per cent of all children not surviving to adulthood. And in fact, excavations by physical anthropologists in North America have repeatedly demonstrated that childhood mortality was very high, with many of the skeletal remains being that of infants and children (Ubelaker 2000). Under these circumstances, population numbers could only have been maintained from one generation to the next through relatively high fertility. This appears to have been the situation in pre-contact America, just as it was true of pre-modern Europe or, for that matter, most populations throughout human history.

The scattered evidence available suggests that before European contact in Canada, childbearing started early in a woman's life and continued until menopause (Charbonneau 1984). Involuntary infecundity was more common than it is today owing to untreated disease as well as lower levels of nutrition and the periodic shortage of food (Romaniuc 2000). Women would mostly breastfeed their children for as long as two years, which lowered the fertility but enhanced the survival chances of the young by widening the spacing of births. It is well known that breastfeeding lengthens the intervals between pregnancies and thus lowers birth rate (Jain and Bongaarts 1981).

European Contact, Excessive Mortality, and Population Decline

Romaniuc (2000) describes the pre-contact stage as most likely a quasi-stationary demographic state characterized by high mortality offset by moderately high fertility. Due to the constraints on fertility mentioned above, the birth rate was not exceptionally high, but it was high enough to assure continuity from one generation to the next. In all likelihood, the population grew in some regions of the country during certain historical periods, whereas disease and natural disaster periodically reduced numbers. Yet with contact, the Aboriginal population of Canada underwent an almost three-century-long depopulation, a tragedy that befell the Aboriginal populations of all the Americas and that has few parallels in modern demographic history.

A recurrent theme for historical demography in the study of pre-modern populations is the so called 'crise de mortalité'—that is, a sudden and pronounced rise in the death rate, with devastating consequences for local or even national populations (Meuvret 1965; Charbonneau and Larose 1979). Throughout much of human history, deaths from famines and epidemics would periodically have a devastating impact on populations, the best documented example, perhaps, being the Black Death (bubonic plague) in fourteenth-century Europe, which is thought to have killed 25 million people, or as much as a quarter of Europe's population at that time. By most accounts, European contact in America and the introduction of new, deadly diseases was even more devastating. The extent to which Canada was depopulated is certainly open to debate, but by all accounts this was an enormous disaster in human and cultural terms. With European colonization, the mortality of Aboriginal peoples climbed, often dramatically, first in eastern Canada and eventually across the vast territory of Canada. It was not until the late nineteenth century that population numbers among the Aboriginal population finally stabilized and began slowly to recover (Charbonneau 1984).

A variety of factors were responsible for three centuries of population decline, although the most important was the introduction of Old World diseases. With no previous exposure to these diseases, the original inhabitants of Canada had no acquired immunity. As described by Thornston (2000), new diseases introduced into North America often resulted in what are termed 'virgin soil epidemics' in which a new virus could spread to virtually all members of a population. The diseases that had a devastating impact on the peoples of America were numerous, including smallpox, measles, cholera, typhoid, diphtheria, scarlet fever, whooping cough, pneumonia, malaria, and yellow fever (Thornston 2000, 14). The records compiled by priests, soldiers, traders, and early settlers over a span of several hundred years contain innumerable examples of diseases taking on epidemic proportions and decimating entire peoples (Jenness 1977; Dickason 2002).

In a well-documented example, Boyd (1992) describes a smallpox epidemic that hit the Queen Charlotte Islands of British Columbia in the 1860s. Smallpox was not completely new to the northwest coast of North America, for it had been introduced almost 100 years earlier after initial contact. The first outbreaks were of unknown magnitude, and descriptions are limited to the oral reports of empty villages, but the later epidemics are well documented in 'Indian censuses' compiled by the Hudson's Bay Company and government officials. Working with reliable records, Boyd describes how in 1862 an infected ship docked at Victoria and the disease spread quickly to the crowded encampment on the city's outskirts. Instead of quarantining all those infected, the authorities evicted the encampment, sending Kwakiutl, Haida, Tlingit, and Tsimshian traders back to their villages. Consequently, over a two-year period, records from the Hudson's Bay Company indicate a 60 per cent decline in the Aboriginal population in this coastal region of British Columbia. It was not an isolated event but rather the fifth known outbreak of smallpox in this region after the initial contact, and depopulation continued through to the late nineteenth and early twentieth century.

In addition to disease, the causes of the depopulation included the intensification of conflict and warfare resulting from the efforts of the British and French to establish control over contested territory in their colonies. Romaniuc (2000) emphasizes that in addition to disease, European colonialism introduced wars, forced removals, and the destruction of traditional economies. Through the early accounts of Europeans, it is possible to document cases of total social disorganization brought by excessive mortality and colonization. In Newfoundland, the Beothuk disappeared completely by the early nineteenth century as a result of disease and continuous feuding with early settlers. Armed conflict with the British and Iroquois almost led to the disappearance of the Huron, who had also been weakened by disease. The opening of the west and the settlement of the prairies for farming resulted in forced removals and the destruction of the traditional economic base of this region, partly through the near extinction of the buffalo. At one time or another, the Aboriginal populations in all parts of present-day Canada were affected by varying degrees of serious depopulation.

Although there is little disputing this population decline, there is less agreement about the extent of the decline, owing to the lack of direct information on the size of the pre-contact population. The estimates vary widely, largely because of differences of opinion as to the accuracy and completeness of the earliest population figures recorded by colonial administrators (Daniels 1992). Since much of the information first obtained from priests, soldiers, traders, and government officials was compiled many years after initial contact, historians disagree about the extent to which depopulation might have started before 'direct' European contact (Thornston 2000; Ubelaker 2000). The obvious difficulty faced by ethno-historians in trying to piece together the pre-contact situation is that in many of the earliest accounts, some communities were already in a state of social disorganization and epidemic, whereas others had remained intact and largely isolated from European influence. When one examines the scattered historical evidence from over three centuries, it is virtually impossible to determine the extent to which depopulation may already have occurred; hence all efforts at demographic reconstruction become highly speculative and open to debate. The problems are further compounded by what were probably gross inaccuracies in population figures compiled several centuries ago by authorities who were far from being trained census-takers. Even today in the modern census in Canada, the undercount has been estimated to be several times higher among Aboriginal people than among the population in general.

Dickason (2002) proposed that 'the most widely accepted estimate is about 500,000' for pre-contact Canada, a figure later adopted by the Royal Commission on Aboriginal Peoples (1995) in its brief appraisal of the demographic history of Canada. It is unclear why the royal commission decided to rely on this estimate, since absolutely no references are provided in support of the figure. Earlier estimates had placed the pre-contact population at less than half that number; for example, Mooney (1928) gives a very conservative approximation of just under 200,000. This latter figure was based on a systematic review of the earliest written accounts available, which were very partial or imprecise, and virtually no adjustments were made. The physical anthropologist Ubelaker (1976) estimates that Canada's pre-contact population was about 270,000; this estimate was obtained by compiling and adding together regional estimates of specialists affiliated with the Smithsonian Institution. The Canadian historical demographer Charbonneau (1984) estimates the pre-contact population at about 300,000 by upwardly adjusting the earlier work of Mooney and others to take into account the most serious omissions or understatements. At the opposite extreme, a few estimates suggest that the pre-contact population may have been many times higher than Dickason's figure, perhaps as high as 1.5 million, on the assumption of major depopulation that could not possibly be detected from early colonial records (Dobyns 1983; Thornston 1987). In a sense, Dickason's 'guesstimate', based on informed judgment and considerable knowledge of the history of Aboriginal Canadians, can be considered a midrange figure.

Population Decline and Recovery

If we accept Dickason's figure of 500,000, it would be some 250 years after Jacques Cartier first sailed into the Gulf of St Lawrence before a similar number of Europeans had established a foothold in the territories of modern-day Canada and almost two full centuries after the establishment of the first permanent settlement in New France. As emphasized by Charbonneau (1984, 24), this basic observation is far too often overlooked in historical accounts of the demography of Canada. For instance, Charbonneau quotes an observation made by the historian L.E. Hamelin that it took many decades for the population of Canada to establish itself after the founding of the city of Quebec. As Charbonneau points out, this observation completely excludes the original inhabitants of the land.

With the excessive mortality that accompanied the diseases brought to North America, Aboriginal peoples experienced negative natural increase (births minus deaths) for probably at least 250 years, if not longer. From the highly uncertain estimate of 500,000 persons prior to European contact, the nadir in terms of population size has been documented in the 1871 census at only about 103,000 persons (see Figure 7.2). While this latter figure is in all likelihood an undercount—for reasons that we will outline below—there is no doubt of the preceding demographic disaster. Figure 7.2 portrays impressionistically the wide range of estimates that have been published on the size of Canada's pre-contact population, from Dickason's (2002) midrange estimate through to the more conservative numbers proposed by Mooney (1928) and Charbonneau (1984). Thornston's (1987) pre-contact population estimate of about 1.5 million is also included, merely as an extreme example in the opposite direction. In this context, Dickason's midrange estimate implies a depopulation ratio of about 5:1, with the pre-contact population of 500,000 down to only about 100,000 by 1871. If in fact Canada's Aboriginal population had declined over this period at roughly a constant rate, this implies a depopulation rate in the order of –0.6 per cent annually.

In this context, the basic fact remains: roughly modest differences in terms of the rate of depopulation over an extended period can imply large differences in terms of the size of the pre-contact population. In reference to the United States and Central America, where population densities were originally quite high relative to those of Canada, historical demographers have debated depopulation ratios as high as 10:1 or even 20:1 in comparing original population size with the nadir (Snipp 1989; Dobyns 1983). While such a dramatic depopulation might be considered a minority opinion among historical demographers in Canada, the fact remains that there is virtually no empirical evidence to easily verify what happened in reality. Nonetheless, Dickason's depopulation ratio of about 5:1 still implies a major disaster in human and demographic terms.

In the demographic evolution of Aboriginal peoples in Canada, the late nineteenth century can be thought of as pivotal. After about 250 years of demographic

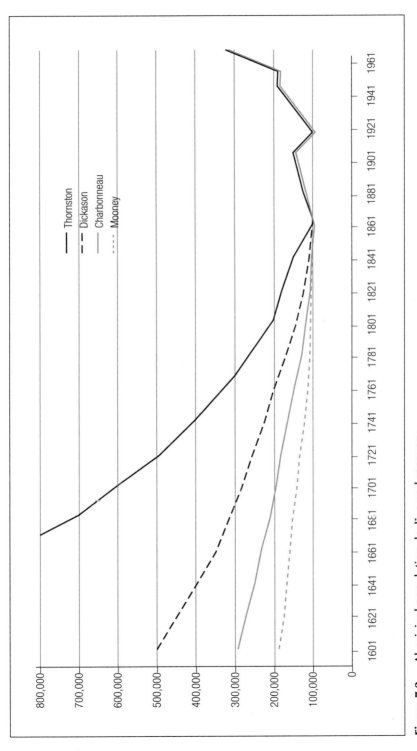

Figure 7.2   Aboriginal population decline and recovery.

Sources: Dickason 2002; Royal Commission on Aboriginal Peoples 1995; Mooney 1928; Charbonneau 1984; Thornston 1987.

decline, the late nineteenth century can be delineated as the beginning of a period of demographic stabilization and recovery. Although mortality remained very high, the most serious epidemics were eventually to subside, and the total number of Aboriginal births gradually began to surpass the total number of deaths. Toward the latter 1800s, the limited evidence available suggests that a negative rate of natural increase was gradually replaced by moderate growth. As a result, the Aboriginal population has been estimated to have grown from its nadir of about 100,000 to about 200,000 by the mid-twentieth century and to about 300,000 by the 1971 census (Goldmann and Siggner 1995).

Nevertheless, both mortality and fertility remained high. For example, mortality as documented among First Nations peoples in the early 1900s appears to have been comparable to that of the European population 100 years earlier (Romaniuc 2000). Similarly, fertility appears to have been quite high, with little evidence of anything other than natural fertility (that is, there is no evidence of any voluntary control over reproduction). While the Aboriginal population was eventually to experience major reductions in both fertility and mortality, the timing and pace of these changes departed significantly from that of other Canadians (Young 1994; Trovato 2000, 2001). An additional issue of uncertainty influencing all of our figures on the dynamics of population growth includes the extent to which Canada's Aboriginal population has evolved in isolation (or in demographic terms, as a 'closed' population). To an uncertain extent, these figures are influenced by intermarriage and assimilation to the larger society.

In research on the population growth of indigenous peoples in Latin America, Chackiel and Peyser (1993) refer to a fundamental 'demographic paradox' not easily explained by simple demographic accounting formulae. Even though many indigenous populations in both Central and South America had for many decades experienced high rates of natural increase for a variety of reasons, the available data on these populations indicate that they barely sustained their numbers from one census to the next. This research points to the constant loss of cultural identity, particularly the tendency to assimilate toward the dominant cultures and languages of these societies. In reference to this research, Romaniuc (2000), who draws a few parallels to Canada, speculates about the extent to which the same thing may have happened in Canada in the past. In the absence of direct empirical research, Romaniuc speculates that until fairly recently, losses of population as a result of shifts in cultural affiliation and assimilation have outweighed gains.

Consequently, we suggest that the Canadian census likely understated the actual size of Canada's Aboriginal population as defined by ancestry in the latter nineteenth and early twentieth centuries. The nadir of only about 100,000 persons in the 1871 census was likely an undercount, since many persons of Aboriginal descent were for a variety of reasons not reporting their ancestry. Similarly, the low figures as documented throughout the first half of the twentieth century were in all likelihood a serious understatement, a situation that has only recently corrected itself, to an uncertain extent. The number of Canadians reporting Aboriginal ancestry over recent censuses has climbed dramatically (a topic to which we now switch our attention). This growth is beyond what is possible through natural increase, and for this reason, we need to shift our attention to issues relating to how persons identify themselves on a census and to the associated difficulties of shifting cultural affiliation.

The Contemporary Situation

Defining the Aboriginal Population: Difficulties Due to Changing Identities

Most demographic research focuses on the nation-state or on populations as defined in terms of political boundaries and place of residence. Consequently, the definition of who is to be included in the target population is typically straightforward, relying on rules relating to citizenship or usual place of residence. In the study of Aboriginal peoples, it is much more complicated to define exactly who is to be included. Aboriginal peoples are spread throughout Canada, across provincial and territorial boundaries, and live in both rural and urban regions of the country. There are no clear residency rules that can be used in identifying this specific population, nor is there a clear legal status that can be used in identifying 'all' Aboriginal people.

At one point in Canada's history, the Aboriginal population could be defined easily on the basis of ancestry and way of life. In spite of the great variety among Aboriginal languages, customs, and material culture, there were recognizable common elements of culture and biology. Today, however, the situation has become far more complicated—owing to several centuries of cultural exchange, assimilation, intermarriage, and births of mixed ancestry. Though it may have been obvious to the seventeenth- or eighteenth-century observer who was Cree or Mi'kmaq, as opposed to British or French, today it is often far from obvious.

As an example of some of the difficulties involved, the question must be addressed as to how one classifies persons of mixed ancestry. This issue is not of minor consequence, since the majority of Canadians who currently report Aboriginal ancestry do so as part of a reported mixed ancestry. Of the 1,678,235 people who reported Aboriginal ancestry in the 2006 census (or about 5.4 per cent of Canada's population), well over half (997,715) also reported other, non-Aboriginal origins (Statistics Canada 2008b). Similarly, some people of Aboriginal ancestry report no particular affiliation or identification with their Aboriginal ancestry or culture (Siggner et al. 2001). Is it enough to rely upon the reported ancestry in the identification of this population, and if not, what are some of the other criteria that have been proposed?

The next section of this chapter will specifically address some of these issues. The census has historically defined the Aboriginal population by asking people their 'ancestry or cultural origins', their legal status under the Indian Act, and, more recently, whether they identify themselves as Aboriginal. Briefly, the data available in studying the demography of Aboriginal peoples is far from straightforward, and in essence it reflects definitions developed by government officials and researchers. The use of these definitions led demographers to document a very rapidly growing Aboriginal population over the last few decades of the twentieth century. Yet depending upon how the Aboriginal population is delineated, very different conclusions might be drawn about the dynamics of this growth and the corresponding demographic characteristics of this population.

The Canadian Census as a Source of Demographic Data

The Canadian census is the most comprehensive source of demographic data on Aboriginal peoples in Canada and is the exclusive source of demographic data for many Aboriginal groups. Historically, the census has calculated the number of Aboriginal people in Canada by asking respondents about their ancestry (as obtained through the 'ethnic or cultural origin' question). In the 2006 census, for example, respondents were asked 'to which ethnic or cultural group(s)' they belonged, with an encouragement to report as many origins as deemed appropriate. Whereas some respondents have answered that question with very specific responses (such as Objiway, Mohawk, or Cree), others have simply identified themselves as First Nations, North American Indian, Métis, or Inuit.

Although the census is perhaps the most comprehensive source of demographic data on Aboriginal peoples, there are several difficulties associated with this information. One of these problems relates to the fundamental issue of data comparability over time. Whereas the definition of Aboriginal has relied on the ethnic or cultural origin question in the census, there have been frequent changes in the wording involved, along with important changes in the way in which people answer these questions. Until the 1971 census, the ethnic origin was to follow only the male line of descent. Before 1986, multiple responses to the ethnic-origin question were either disallowed or at least discouraged, a situation that was completely reversed from 1986 onwards.

The encouragement of multiple origins has led to more people reporting Aboriginal ancestry compared to the situation when multiple or matrilineal origins were neglected. As demonstrated in Figure 7.3, the number of people reporting Aboriginal ancestry has increased dramatically over recent years—from only 496,500 in 1981, for example, to 1,678,235 in 2006 (Statistics Canada 2008b). In just 25 years, the size of this 'ancestry-based' population skyrocketed by more than 200 per cent. Underlying this change was an increase in the number of people who reported Aboriginal ancestry as part of a multiple response, increasing from 79,085 in 1981 to 997,715 in 2006. As Canada's population overall was growing at only about 1 per cent a year over this same period (with about half of this growth due to international migration), the growth of the Aboriginal population was obviously far beyond the pure demographics.

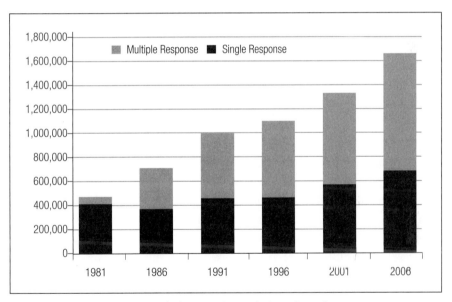

Figure 7.3   **Census counts of Aboriginal populations, based on ancestry, 1981–2006.**

Source: Statistics Canada. *Census of Canada*, 1981–2006; Statistics Canada. 2008b, Aboriginal Ancestry Population.

Nevertheless, it would quite wrong to suggest that all this growth was merely the result of this change in census methodology. It is also important to recognize the shifts in the propensity of Canadians to report Aboriginal ancestry independent of any other change. After documenting a similar situation in the United States among 'American Indians', Passel (1997) refers to a whole series of social changes that would have influenced the propensity on the part of

Americans to report American Indian heritage. Of particular importance was a new-found political awareness and self-confidence, which has contributed to a rising of North American Indian consciousness in a population that had previously not identified with this culture.

It has been argued that in societies such as Canada and the United States, most racial and ethnic identities are in a state of flux—that is, it is extremely difficult to establish fixed identities and stable boundaries in the delineation of ethnicity or cultural origins (Eschbach 1995; Hout and Goldstein 1994; Lieberson and Waters 1988). For example, among many Canadians of mixed ancestry, respondents to the census often change their declared ethnic affiliation from one census to the next in a manner that is often very difficult to predict. Consequently, the size of ethnic groups appears to change independently of natural increase or migration (Goldmann 1998; Guimond 2003). To the extent that subjectivity and choice enter into how populations report on their ancestry, one would expect reduced comparability of demographic data over time. With recent shifts in declared ethnic affiliation, Canadians appear to be far more likely to report their Aboriginal ancestry than was the case historically.

Aboriginal Populations

According to Section 25(2) of the Canadian Constitution, there are three major groups of Aboriginal peoples in Canada, including 'the Indian, Inuit and the Métis'. While some might suggest that such a classification obscures a virtual 'kaleidoscope of cultures and traditions' (Frideres 1998), this classification has had wide circulation among social scientists and has certainly had a strong influence on the character of most demographic research. While the Constitution recognizes these three broadly defined Aboriginal groups, it does not actually define what constitutes their populations. As a result, many researchers have merely relied upon information collected through the census on ancestry or cultural origins in classifying people into one of the above categories.

A further subdivision of this population into two additional groups is provided for in the Indian Act (first passed in 1867): North American Indians (First Nations Peoples), who hold legal Indian status, and those that do not (non-status). By virtue of the Indian Act, First Nations peoples (with status) have certain specified entitlements, including the right to elect representatives to negotiate with the federal government over land claim settlements and many other rights under treaties concluded with the Crown. According to the 2006 census, which also asked Canadians whether they are 'registered under the Indian Act', well under one-half (37.2 per cent) of the Aboriginal 'ancestry' population are in fact status Indians (623,780 people out of 1,678,235). This census count of the status population is widely considered an understatement of its true size owing to difficulties of data collection (see Box 7.1).

Box 7.1   What Is the True Size of the Status Poulation among First Nations Peoples in Canada?

According to the 2006 census, the size of the status population is 623,780 persons (Statistics Canada 2009b). This figure is noticeably lower than the official tally compiled by Indian and Northern Affairs Canada (INAC), which documents that the total number for roughly the same date (31 December 2006) is 763,555 (INAC 2008). Whereas INAC is the federal department responsible for meeting the national government's constitutional, treaty, political, and legal responsibilities to First Nations peoples, Statistics Canada is this country's official statistical agency. Although neither organization would appear to have any vested interest in misreporting the true size of this status population, neither has ever fully explained the reason for such a large discrepancy.

In reality, the true population likely falls somewhere between these two figures and is probably closer to the figure reported by Indian and Northern Affairs. Whereas Statistics Canada's figure is based on the 2006 census, Indian Affairs relies upon a population register, commonly referred to as the Indian Register. Whereas the census collects information by directly contacting and asking Canadians whether or not they are registered under the Indian Act, the population register is in essence a list of all persons who have at one point or another been registered as status and who continue to be classified as such according to the Indian Act. Whereas the census is conducted once every five years, the Indian Register is updated continually, documenting all new persons to be added to the register (predominantly through births) and all persons to be removed (predominantly through deaths).

Various factors are responsible for the discrepancy, including the fact that the 2006 census was not permitted or was interrupted on 22 First Nations before it could be completed. For largely political reasons, these communities refused access to Statistics Canada, arguing that the Government of Canada did not have the right to collect census information on their territories. In addition, the more general problem of census undercount has also served to reduce the overall population count (that is, both individuals and households are unintentionally missed in the census—well beyond the fact that certain First Nations refuse to be counted). The census is also not capable of documenting status Indians who are living abroad on Census Day (yet these persons are included in the register), nor are status persons who live in institutions or collectives included in the census count (as, for example, those who are living in long-term care facilities, hospitals, or federal or provincial correctional facilities). In combination, a correction for all these factors would bring the census count of the status population closer to the INAC figure. In addition, there may be inaccuracies in the INAC register—in particular, the late registration of deaths (and possibly births), which could lead to inaccurate population figures.

Although the Indian Act has undergone many revisions and iterations since the nineteenth century (Savard and Proulx 1982), it does provide for a specific but partial definition of Aboriginal peoples by setting the legal criteria for a person to be identified. As mentioned above, this is not the case for the other Aboriginal groups (the Inuit, Métis, and non-status persons), since the federal government has never specified exactly what constitutes these popula-tions. As suggested by Romaniuc (2000, 123), the status population can almost be thought of as 'de jure' members (or citizens, if you like) of Canada's First Nations. The non-status population with Aboriginal ancestry may exhibit many if not all the social, racial, and cultural attributes of Canada's First Nations but are not formally recognized by the federal government in a legal sense.

For a wide variety of reasons, non-status persons are not listed on the INAC registry. In some cases, their ancestors either may have refused or were not allowed to establish treaties or agreements with the Crown. Furthermore, throughout the nineteenth and twentieth centuries, thousands of Aboriginal people in Canada experienced 'enfranchisement' (that is, lost their status, some-times by choice but more often because of restrictions spelled out in the Indian Act). In fact, the 2006 census documented about 600,000 persons who reported some form of Aboriginal ancestry but were not registered under the Indian Act (Statistics Canada 2008b). It is noteworthy that much of the rapid growth of the Aboriginal population that has been recorded in recent censuses occurred among this 'non-status' population, while the number of persons reporting status has been much more stable and predictable from one census to the next.

The original inhabitants of Canada's Arctic regions, the Inuit, are clearly the least numerous of the three major groups. The question on ancestry in the 2006 census revealed about 60,000 people of Inuit ancestry. That figure is based on both single and multiple replies regarding ancestry (Statistics Canada 2008b). In Canada, the word 'Eskimo' has gradually been replaced by 'Inuit', the Inuktitut word used by the Inuit to refer to themselves. Largely situated in Nunavut, Yukon, and the Northwest Territories as well as in northern Quebec and Labrador, the Inuit have in many ways more in common with other Arctic groups in neighbour-ing countries than they do with other Aboriginal groups in Canada. With a very different history and culture, the Inuit of Canada's Arctic regions are quite distinct from the neighbouring Athabascan and Algonquin peoples to the south, and they have much more in common with many of the original inhabitants of Alaska and Greenland, not to mention the Chukotka of the northern regions of Russia.

The third Aboriginal group is the Métis; in the 2006 census, about 360,000 people reported Métis ancestry, either in single or multiple responses (Statistics Canada 2008b). The word 'Métis' has two different meanings: it has been used to denote any person of mixed Indian and European ancestry ('métis' just means 'mixed' in French), but perhaps more commonly, it is used to denote a sort of hybrid culture that developed primarily in western Canada from the marriages of Cree, Ojibway, and Saulteaux women to French and Scottish fur traders. In areas that were remote from European influence, a hybrid culture grew up under the influence especially of the fur trade, the Catholic Church, and the Hudson's Bay Company. Although the Métis were pivotal in the early history of the Prairie provinces, they do not hold the same legal status as status Indians. Whereas most people in the western provinces who describe themselves as Métis in the census do so in reference to this hybrid culture, an unknown number continue to use other meanings. Consequently, there are Aboriginal persons reporting Métis ancestry in all provinces of the country, including areas that are far removed from the traditional Métis homeland in the Prairie provinces.

Identity

To further complicate matters, Statistics Canada has evolved an additional definition of the Aboriginal population in the Canadian census, a definition based on 'identity' rather than 'ancestry'. As mentioned above, the use of 'ancestry' to define the Aboriginal population results in a total population count in 2006 of 1,678,235 (or about 5.4 per cent of Canada's population). Alternatively, the 'identity'-based definition produces a smaller total of 1,172,790 persons in 2006 (i.e., roughly 3.8 per cent of Canada's population). This latter, more restrictive definition has subsequently been used by Statistics Canada in most of its 2006 census releases (whereas information on the size and characteristics of the ancestry-based population was given less attention).

Efforts to establish time-series data on Aboriginal populations will always be hindered by the 'fluid or situational character' of such concepts as ancestry, cultural origins, and identity (Boxhill 1984; Lieberson and Waters 1993). Some people of Aboriginal ancestry may deny their origins, others may have a passionate commitment to these origins, and still others may be indifferent or simply unaware. It was in direct response to some of these difficulties that Statistics Canada introduced for the first time in 1996 a new question on Aboriginal identity (beyond the ethnic origin or ancestry question), with the ultimate goal of more narrowly focusing on Canada's First Nations. This new question, which was again used in 2001 and 2006, specifically asked Canadians whether or not they 'consider themselves as being Aboriginal, that is, North American Indian, Métis or Inuit' (Statistics Canada 1998a). Whereas one might argue that a count based on ancestry is more objective, the question on identity is arguably more meaningful, determining whether or not individuals feel an allegiance or association with Aboriginal culture. Not surprisingly, the numbers are somewhat smaller, with about 70 per cent of persons reporting Aboriginal ancestry stating that they 'consider themselves' to be Aboriginal.

If we use this narrower definition of the Aboriginal population, about 58 per cent of people with First Nations ancestry (or 698,025 people out of 1.2

million) say that they identify themselves as First Nations peoples, whereas among the Inuit, about 85 per cent identify themselves as Inuit (or 50,485 people out of 59,585). Among the Métis, curiously the census identity count was largely unchanged from the ancestry count, with 389,785 persons identifying themselves as Métis. In terms of the 'fluidity' of such an item in the census, not surprisingly Statistics Canada has again discovered considerable growth in the Aboriginal population over time, true of all populations defined in terms of their 'Aboriginal identity' (Table 7.1). Since 1996, when information was first collected on 'Aboriginal identity' in the census, this population has grown by roughly 45 per cent.

Table 7.1   Size and Growth of the Population by Aboriginal Identity, Canada, 1996 and 2006

	2006	Percentage Change from 1996–2006
Total Population	32,241,030	9
Aboriginal Identity Population	1,172,790	45
First Nations Peoples (North American Indian)	698,025	29
Métis	389,785	91
Inuit	50,485	26
Multiple and other Aboriginal Responses	34,500	34
Non-Aboriginal Population	30,068,240	8

Source: Statistics Canada, 2006 Census: Analysis series, 97-558-XIE2006001m 2008. www.statcan.gc.ca/bsolc/olc-cel/olc-cel?catno=97-558-XIE2006001&lang=eng.

Since Statistics Canada has subsequently used this 'identity population' in most of its data releases from the 2006 census, the implication is that it more accurately captures the essence of what one might define as a core Aboriginal population. Systematic comparisons have demonstrated that people who report a particular ancestry yet do not identify with it tend to be much more like the Canadian population in general than is the case with those who do identify with that ancestry. For example, Canadians of Aboriginal ancestry who do not report this identity are far less likely to speak an Aboriginal language, live in rural or more remote regions of the country, be registered, or live in a First Nations community (Norris 2000; Frideres 1998). Furthermore, whereas virtually all of the status population identifies with their ancestry, this is far less likely to be the case among persons who are non-status.

The growth of this population remains dramatic, suggesting problems in terms of temporal reliability regardless of whether we are working with the 'identity'-based or 'ancestry'-based figures. As a result, if in fact the census documents significant change in the socio-economic characteristics of either population, it remains difficult to discern how much of the change is due to real change in these characteristics of Aboriginal Canadians and how much is merely due to a different population reporting itself as Aboriginal identity or ancestry. This is a major problem in trying to document change over time in the socio-economic characteristics of Canada's First Nations, let alone the demographic change associated with trends in fertility, mortality, and migration.

The Dynamics of Population Change

Canada's population has moved through its demographic transition from the high mortality and fertility in the eighteenth and nineteenth centuries through to the relatively low birth and death rates of the present. Yet while Canadian mortality and fertility has dropped quite noticeably overall, the demographic history of Canada's Aboriginal population cannot easily be described in terms of what happened more generally for Canadian society. In other words, the demographic history of Canada's Aboriginal population is quite distinct and demonstrates the heterogeneity of experience that has characterized Canada's demographic history.

Mortality

In an overview of mortality patterns among Aboriginal peoples in both Canada and the United States, Trovato (2001) points to common problems that emerge out of recent research. While there have clearly been long-term gains in both life expectancy and infant mortality, Aboriginal North Americans continue to experience mortality conditions that are worse than that of the whole population. Whereas Canadian society in general is among the world leaders in the health of its population, current features of Aboriginal mortality and morbidity clearly indicate epidemiological patterns that are at odds with this overall situation.

Unfortunately, the information currently available on mortality is far from complete and can provide only a partial picture. Part of the reason is that Canada's system of vital statistics, which should document all births and deaths in this country (including cause of death), has never collected information on race, ancestry, or cultural origins. While there have been some recent attempts to link vital statistics with the Canadian census (Wilkins et al. 2008a), probably the best source of information currently available on the mortality of Aboriginal peoples remains the Indian Register, the population register maintained by INAC (2008). This register, which includes information exclusively on the status population, has been continuously updated in documenting births and deaths as far back as the nineteenth century. In addition, there is also the lesser-known population register on the Inuit of northern Quebec, which has documented births and deaths as far back as the 1940s (Robitaille and Choinière 1985). For both the Métis and non-status populations, there are currently no direct data on mortality, although some limited efforts have been made at indirect estimation (Norris, Kerr, and Nault 1995).

For the country as a whole, there have been some dramatic reductions in mortality, with average life expectancy at the end of the twentieth century about 30 years longer than it was at its beginning. This is a result of some rather important changes in the pattern of disease dominance. More specifically, in 1901 male life expectancy at birth was only about 47 years, and female life expectancy was only about 50 years (Statistics Canada 1999). While life expectancy was considerably shorter overall in Canada at this time, mortality was particularly high among the Aboriginal population. For example, in working with data from the INAC register, Romaniuc (1981) has estimated a life expectancy at birth in 1900 for First Nations of only 33 years, more than 15 years lower than the Canadian average at this same time (see Table 7.2).

Among the Inuit, the earliest direct evidence available, which was collected in the 1940s, indicated a life expectancy at birth of only about 35 years (Robitaille and Choinière 1985). Again, even by the standards of the day, this implies a very high level of mortality. Canadian life expectancy in the 1940s was almost 30 years longer (66 years for females and 63 years for males). Among First Nations, the situation was not much better, with only modest gains throughout the first several decades of the century. By 1941, the status population had an estimated life expectancy of only 38 years.

The epidemiological transition was delayed among both First Nations peoples and the Inuit; important changes were not to occur until the post-war period. By 2001, First Nations peoples in Canada continued to have life expectancy noticeably shorter than average, at 73 years (70.4 years for males and about 75.5 years for females). Among the Inuit, life expectancy is currently estimated at not much more than 65 years. For Inuit-inhabited areas of Canada's North, Wilkins et al. (2008b) estimate a male life expectancy of 64.4 years and a female life expectancy of 69.8 years. While mortality has declined, the longevity of First Nations remains about six to seven years shorter than that of other Canadians, while among the Inuit the discrepancy exceeds 10 years. To use a different comparison, the longevity as estimated for First Nations in 2001 is comparable to the longevity as reported for the Canadian population overall in the early 1970s. The life expectancy as estimated for the Inuit is in

Table 7.2 Estimated Life Expectancy at Birth for First Nations (status), Inuit, and Total Canadian Populationos, for Selected Periods and Years, Canada, 1900–2001

Year or Period	First Nations (Status) Both Sexes	Year	Inuit			Year	Total Canada
			Northern Quebec	Northwest Territories	Inhabited Areas		
1900	33					1901	47.0M/50.0F
						1921	58.8M/60.6F
1940	38	¯941–51	35	29		1941	63.0M/66.3F
		¯951–61	39	37			
1960	56	1961–71	59	51		1961	68.4M/74.2F
1960–64	59.7M/63.5F						
1965–68	60.5M/65.6F					1966	687.M/75.2F
1976	59.8M/66.3F	1971	52			1976	70.2M/77.5F
1981	62.4M/68.9F					1981	71.9M/79.0F
1982–85	64.0M/72.8F					1984–86	73.0M/79.8F
1991	66.9M/74.0F	1991	58M/69F				
1995	68.0M/75.7F						
2001	70.4M/75.5F	2001			64.4M/69.8F	2001	77.1M/82.2F

Sources: INAC 2005; Wilkins et al., 2008b; Romaniuc 1981; Medical Services Branch, Health and Welfare Canada, 1976; Hault et al 1993, Loh et al., 1998; Robitaille and Choinière; 1985; Norris, 2000; Statistics Canada 2005.

fact comparable to the longevity as documented for other Canadians as far back as the late 1940s.

Among the changes over the postwar period, particularly striking has been the reduction in infant mortality. As late as the 1940s, the infant mortality rate among First Nations was as high as 200 deaths per 1000 live births (Romaniuc 2000), a rate that was to drop dramatically to about 40 deaths per 1000 by the 1970s and to only about 12 deaths per 1000 by the 1990s (Loh et al. 1998). Among the Inuit, similar reductions have been documented, from at least 200 deaths per 1000 births down to about 28 deaths per 1000 by the early 1990s (Frideres 1998). Again, this decline lagged behind that among other Canadians; for example, the infant mortality rate for Canada overall has fallen to only about five deaths per 1000 (Statistics Canada 2008c). According to Health Canada (2003), among First Nations this rate has also continued to converge toward the rate observed nationally, at about 6.5 deaths per 1000 births. Among the Inuit, the current rate was about 15 deaths per 1000 by 2001, or roughly three times that observed among other Canadians (Healey et al. 2004).

Causes of Death

The epidemiological transition in Canada has involved important shifts in the pattern of disease dominance, particularly a decline in mortality associated with infectious disease. Currently, the big killers in Canada are no longer parasitic or infectious disease but degenerative disease, in particular cardiovascular disease and cancer. To a large extent, this shift in the pattern of disease dominance is a result of relative success in reducing the risk of premature death. With better diets, hygiene, and standard of living (and to a lesser extent through the inter-vention of modern medicine and antibiotics), major killers of the past have now been virtually eliminated or have become much less common.

While the risk of premature death has fallen for all Canadians, this is true to a lesser extent among Aboriginal people. For example, while smallpox has been eradicated, tuberculosis persists among Aboriginal people, albeit to a much lesser extent than in the past. According to epidemiological data col-lected by the Public Health Agency of Canada (2004), First Nations peoples and the Inuit are many more times likely than other Canadians to suffer from tuberculosis. Among the Canadian-born overall, the incidence recorded is very low at only 1.5 cases per 100,000, whereas among First Nations inci-dence rises to 37 cases per 100,000 and among the Inuit to 62 cases per 100,000. Although there has been much progress in this area, infectious and parasitic diseases associated with difficult living conditions and poverty still maintain a grip on Aboriginal peoples. This is a consequence of the inadequate housing conditions, water supply, and public sanitation, among other difficulties (Romaniuc 2000). As an example, Health Canada (2009) advised that as of October 2009, 119 First Nations communities across Canada were under a drinking water advisory.

In comparing the mortality of Aboriginal and non-Aboriginal Canadians, some of the largest differentials are found among children and infants. Among infants, most of the difference is due to post-neonatal mortality (beyond 28 days), which is suggestive of differences in lifestyle and socio-economic conditions (INAC 1999). As has become well established through epidemiological research, post-neonatal mortality is more sensitive to variations in socio-economic conditions and lifestyle than is neonatal mortality, which is often considered more sensitive to health care resources.

From birth to old age, mortality rates are consistently higher among Canada's Aboriginal peoples, and there are important differences in the profile of morbidity and injury in the two populations. The health of Aboriginal Canadians has long been compromised by what Trovato (2001) calls the 'geographic, socio-economic and even social psychological marginalization of many Aboriginal communities'.

While direct information is not available for all Aboriginal peoples, some striking differences emerge when we compare statistics on cause of death for First Nations and other Canadians. According to available statistics on 'cause of death' as collected by the First Nations and Inuit Branch of Health Canada (2003), the leading cause of death for First Nations peoples continues to be injuries and poisonings, followed by cardiovascular disease, cancer, and diseases of the respiratory system. For the Canadian population overall, cancer and heart disease are the two leading causes of death, responsible for about half (52.4 per cent) of all deaths, with stroke being a distant third at 6.5 per cent of all deaths (Statistics Canada 2008d). While injuries are responsible for about one-quarter of all deaths of First Nations peoples, Frideres (1998) has estimated that this proportion climbs to more than one-third when one considers the on-reserve population. Rates of injury death are from three to six times higher than the Canadian average, depending on type, with far greater risks of motor vehicle accidents, drowning, and death from fire. Suicide deaths rates are three to four times the Canadian average, with some major differences observed across different regions of the country (Health Canada 2001).

Since Canada's Aboriginal population is relatively young, these differences may be partly due to differences in the age structure of the population. More specifically, since First Nations have a much higher proportion of their population at ages the most at risk to injuries and accidental death (with many young adults), to what extent might deaths decrease if in fact they had the same age structure as that of Canadians overall? In standardizing for differences in age structure across Aboriginal and non-Aboriginal populations, Figure 7.4 summarizes results provided by Health Canada (2003) in terms of the ratio of age-standardized mortality rates by selected causes, comparing First Nations with the overall Canada total. A ratio greater than 1 indicates an excess risk of mortality among First Nations, while a ratio less than 1 suggests the opposite. As indicated, even after controls for differences in age structure, the apparent risk of dying from an injury is still about three times higher among First Nations peoples, while death due to digestive disease and endocrine disease both remain roughly two times higher than observed overall. The significantly higher risk of death from digestive and endocrine diseases is partly related to the very high incidence of diabetes among First Nations peoples.

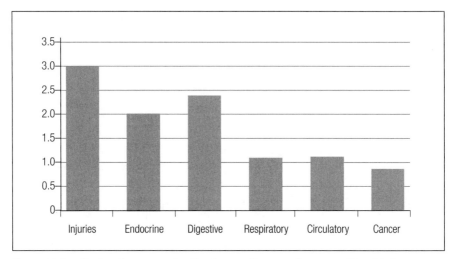

Figure 7.4   Ratio of age-standardized mortality rates by cause, First Nations (status) versus Canada, 2000.

Sources: Waldram, Herring, and Young 2006; Health Canada. First Nations and Inuit Branch. 2003.

Survey research into the living conditions and health status of Aboriginal peoples has further demonstrated the difficulties that this subpopulation experiences compared to other Canadians. According to evidence from the First Nations and Inuit Regional Health Survey, Aboriginal Canadians are significantly more likely to report a range of chronic health conditions. Diabetes is especially problematic in that it tends to be predominantly of the non-insulin-dependent type, with a relatively young age at onset and several complications, such as kidney disease and related endocrine and digestive diseases. As suggested by Romaniuc

(2000, 119), these relatively 'new illnesses' among Canada's Aboriginal population are due to factors that are at least partly 'poor men's afflictions' that can be attributable to an underprivileged status. Economic marginalization has widely been linked to poor diet, obesity, inactivity, and smoking, all linked to higher levels of morbidity and mortality.

Fertility

The evidence available on the childbearing behaviour of Aboriginal peoples early into the twentieth century suggests that fertility was high—although not anywhere close to the theoretical maximum that could occur if a population had absolutely no constraints on fertility. As was the case in most pre-modern societies, a wide assortment of factors explain a fertility level below the theoretical maximum. For example, involuntary infecundity was likely much more common than in present-day populations, owing to untreated disease as well as the nutritional constraints imposed by often difficult ecological conditions. In addition, overall fertility levels were reduced by the practice of prolonged breastfeeding, often for as long as two years. This contributed to effective reproduction by widening the spacing of births and maximized the chances of infant survival.

As with the epidemiological transition, there is relatively little evidence to suggest that fertility levels changed much among Aboriginal peoples before the postwar period of the twentieth century. Estimates of crude birth rates (the number of births expressed per 1000 persons) for First Nations peoples from 1900 to the 1940s suggest that the birth rate was about 40 births per 1000 population (Norris 2000). Among the Inuit, the crude birth rate was about 30 to 35 births per 1000 in 1941, somewhat lower than one might expect for a pre-transitional population (Robitaille and Chonière 1985). With this level of fertility, combined with high mortality, there was moderate growth. Among First Nations, the crude birth rate fell to about 22 births per 1000 by the 1990s (Frideres 1998) at a time when the overall rate was about 11 births per 1000 (Statistics Canada 2009a).

Whereas mortality declined in quite a pronounced and steady manner from the postwar period onward, fertility did not. The evidence currently available indicates that rather than dropping in the 1950s and 1960s (as did mortality), Aboriginal fertility actually increased somewhat over this period. For example, the crude birth rate among First Nations climbed to about 50 births per 1000 during the 1950s and 1960s, and fertility among the Inuit climbed to even greater heights. Although highly accurate data are not available, there is some evidence to suggest that fertility may have peaked at extremely high levels,

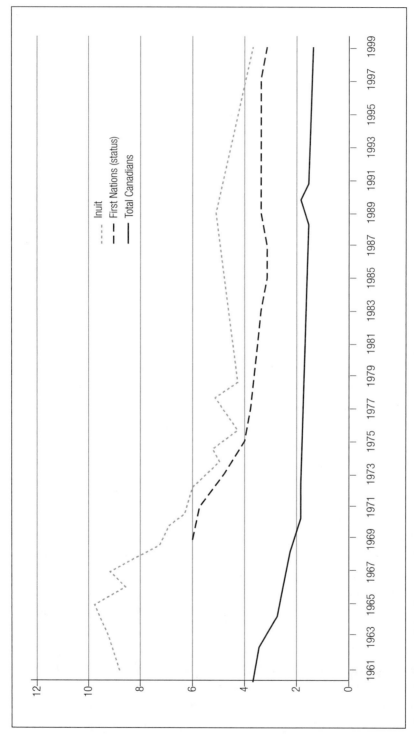

Figure 7.5   Total fertility rates for Inuit, First Nations (status), and total Canadian population, Canada, 1961–2001.

Sources: Statistics Canada 2008a; Nault et al. 1993; Loh et al. 1998; Robitaille and Choinière 1985; Norris 2000; Ram 2004.

approaching the phenomenal rate of almost 60 births per 1000. In explaining these levels, Romaniuc (1981; 2000) has argued that Aboriginal peoples experienced 'a rise in natural fertility' owing to rapid social change and modernization. Again, this is contrary to what one might expect in light of classical 'transition theory', since modernization is expected to introduce a period of fertility decline, following closely on the heels of mortality decline.

During the 1950s and 1960s, an increasing proportion of Canadians obtained comprehensive health care, which in conjunction with the introduction of various social assistance programs had a major impact on both the quality of life and general state of population health. In contrast to the situation historically, where medical intervention was often very limited, the risk of premature death for both mother and child was reduced. Among Aboriginal peoples, the very high rate of both neonatal and maternal mortality fell dramatically over this period. In addition, the likelihood of stillbirths, spontaneous abortions, and pregnancy accidents was also reduced. In view of these changes, one would expect a slight upturn in fertility. In providing a fuller explanation, Romaniuc (2000) also emphasizes a reduction in the likelihood of involuntary infecundity (owing to an improved diet and less disease) as well as changes in breastfeeding practices. During the 1950s and 1960s, health care professionals actively discouraged protracted breastfeeding among Aboriginal and non-Aboriginal women alike, which removed an important fertility-depressing factor in the absence of birth control. In addition, at least partly because of the geographic and social isolation of many First Nations communities, it is likely that many did not have easy access to efficient means of birth control.

Although the birth rate went up in the 1950s, this situation was relatively short-lived, and more recently fertility among Aboriginal peoples has dropped in quite a pronounced manner (Figure 7.5). From the early 1960s onward, the fertility of Aboriginal Canadians has been on a downward trajectory to such an extent that the climb in fertility of the postwar period has been more than offset by fertility decline. While the available time series on First Nations and the Inuit indicate that fertility has not fallen to levels as low as the below-replacement fertility of Canadians overall, fertility rates have fallen to levels of 2.7 and 3.2 births per woman, respectively, as measured by the total fertility rate (TFR). In many ways, both in terms of the timing and level of childbearing, the fertility outcomes of Aboriginal Canadians are increasingly coming to resemble those of other Canadians. While rates have stabilized somewhat over recent years, there is little evidence to suggest that fertility will not continue its downward trajectory into the future.

Demographic Differences by Aboriginal Group

Fertility and Mortality

As previously indicated, Canada's Aboriginal population can be divided into four major groups: (1) First Nations (status), (2) First Nations (non-status), (3) Métis, and (4) Inuit. In light of their distinct histories, it is not surprising that there are some important differences across these subpopulations. Whereas all four groups have witnessed both mortality and fertility decline, the evidence suggests that this is true to a lesser extent among the Inuit and the status populations.

Since the non-status and Métis populations have the highest level of intermarriage with other Canadians, it is not surprising that their demographic behaviour also more closely resembles that of the larger population. In examining census data, it has been shown that along a whole range of socio-economic variables, from education, labour-force participation, and language used to place of residence, the non-status population and the Métis have much more in common with other Canadians than do either status First Nations peoples or the Inuit. More specifically, a majority of the Inuit continue to live in remote northern regions, and a significant proportion of status First Nations peoples continue to live on reserves and in some of Canada's more remote settlements. In contrast, both the non-status population and the Métis are more likely to be living in urban areas or in non-Aboriginal communities and do not experience the same level of geographic and social segregation.

Past estimates of mortality and fertility have consistently ranked the Inuit as having the highest fertility and mortality. In turn, they are followed by the status population, who have higher fertility and mortality than either the Métis or non-status persons. According to a series of indirect estimates of fertility for 2001, the total fertility rate was about 3.21 children per woman for the Inuit, 2.68 for status First Nations peoples, and 2.15 for the Métis (Ram 2004). Life expectancy has been estimated at only 67.1 years for the Inuit, about 72.9 among the status population, and 74.8 among the Métis (Statistics Canada 2005). In terms of non-status First Nations peoples, Norris et al. (1996) have estimated birth and death rates comparable to Métis and closer to the Canadian average overall than those of other Aboriginal groups. A similar ranking is suggested in the limited information available on the state of population health, indicating that the Inuit and the status population are much more likely to suffer from an illness, disability, or chronic disease.

The census data also indicate that fertility is lower among the Inuit who live in southern Canada than among those in the North (Robitaille and Choinière

1985). Similarly, the mortality and fertility of First Nations peoples living on reserves is higher than among those living elsewhere (Loh et al. 1998). As a result, there are important differences in the demographic dynamics of the Aboriginal populations, not only varying by Aboriginal group but also by place of residence. Among the Inuit and First Nations peoples that have migrated from their home communities and more remote settlements into Canada's larger cities and towns, the demographic behaviour and experience more closely resemble those of the non-status and Métis populations.

Population Structure

In keeping with the differences in fertility, the age structure of Canada's Aboriginal population continues to be much younger than that of other Canadians. This implies a distinct set of challenges and priorities. Age and sex influence the working of society in important ways, and Canadian society overall has witnessed important changes over recent decades; for example, its population pyramid is no longer triangular but rather is becoming increasingly 'top heavy' in shape. This is in contrast to the population structure of the Aboriginal population, which has a large proportion of children and young adults (Figure 7.6, page 180).

According to the 2006 census, the median age in Canada in 2006 was 39.5 years—that is, 12.5 years older than that of the Aboriginal-identity population, which was only 27 years (Statistics Canada 2008a). Median age means the age at which half the population is older and half is younger. Furthermore, the median age of both First Nations peoples and the Inuit is even younger—about 24.9 among the First Nations and only about 21.5 among the Inuit. Among the Métis, the population is not quite as young (29.5) but still 10 years younger than for Canada overall. It is not an exaggeration to suggest that this situation has a fundamental impact on the social fabric of First Nations communities. A very young age structure (and a very high proportion of children) has important implications for many societal institutions, while potentially representing a major force for social change into the future.

Populations can also be classified as young or old depending on the proportion of people at different ages. For example, while only 17.7 per cent of Canadians are under the age of 15, among the Aboriginal-identity population, about 30 per cent are under 15. There are further differences among the various Aboriginal groups: among the Inuit, for example, 35 per cent are under the age of 15. At the other end of the age distribution, it is noteworthy that while about one in seven Canadians (13.7 per cent) was 65 or older in 2006, about one in 20 (4.8 per cent) of Aboriginal Canadians were in this age group; among the Inuit, the figure was 3.6 per cent (Statistics Canada 2008a).

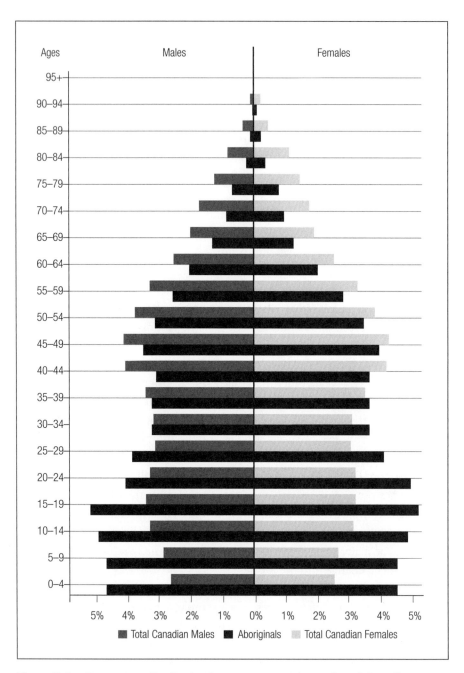

Figure 7.6   Percentage distribution by age group and sex of total Canadian and Aboriginal-identity populations, Canada, 2006.

Source: Statistics Canada. *Canadian Census, 2006*. These census counts of the Aboriginal-identity population and the total Canadian population are not adjusted for census undercount, which has been shown in past censuses to be particularly high among young adults (Kerr and Morissette 1997).

In public policy debates surrounding the impact of age structure in the Canadian context, the issue of population aging is typically highlighted, which speaks of the pressure on public resources represented by an older population. The large differences in population structures in this context are an excellent example of how issues of broader public concern in Canada are often completely out of line with the needs of Canada's Aboriginal peoples. The age structure of Aboriginal Canadians suggests a whole different set of priorities, from meeting the educational requirements of the young to assisting young adults and families as they attempt to establish themselves in the labour market or seek affordable housing. What is clear is that the role of the welfare state and government is very different in a young population than in a rapidly aging population. An acknowledgement of the underlying demographic situation of Aboriginal Canadians can assist in the development of informed policy.

Legislative Change as a Non-Conventional Growth Factor

With a history of higher-than-average fertility, the Aboriginal population is growing rapidly. As pointed out above, this rapid growth is due to a wide range of factors, not exclusively to high natural increase. For example, since populations are defined according to their cultural origins, the fact that people have become much more willing to report having Aboriginal ancestry is of fundamental importance in explaining past trends. Yet in defining Aboriginal persons according to legal status (status versus non-status), it is also necessary to consider a non-conventional growth factor—namely, legislative reform.

The federal government has introduced revisions to the Indian Act that have at times had an appreciable influence on the size and rate of growth of the First Nations population. The last legislative change of any importance in this regard was made in 1985 when the Act was amended to restore Indian status to people (and their children) who had lost their status under certain provisions of previous legislation (Bill C-31). The amending of the Act has had a dramatic impact, with 114,512 people reinstated as 'status' from 1985 through to 1 January 2001 (Library of Parliament 2003). Since the status population in the Indian Register totals about 792,000 according to 2006 figures, this legislative change is fundamental in explaining the rate of growth and composition of this population.

A significant share of these reinstatements were First Nations women (non-status) and their offspring. Before 1985, a woman who married a person not registered under the Indian Act lost her registered status, whereas a man who did so not only retained his status but also conferred eligibility on his wife. Similarly, only the children of registered men would acquire Indian status. The reason for amending the Act was to eliminate the discriminatory status-inherit-ance rules prescribed in the Indian Act. A whole new series of status-inheritance rules was subsequently introduced such that descent was no longer simply de-fined on a patrilineal basis.

Although legislative reform has substantially increased the total size of the status population, the number of reinstatements has since declined now that most of those who could qualify have been reinstated. In this regard, it is use-ful to think through some of the longer-term implications of Bill C-31, some of which are far from obvious. For example, according to recent projections, over the longer term it is quite possible that this legislative change will actually re-duce the total number of persons who qualify to be registered under the Indian Act, compared to what the situation would have been without this legislation (Clatworthy 2003).

In elaborating on this point, it is necessary to consider how Bill C-31 has reformed the status-inheritance rules. Further amendments to the Indian Act (specifically section 6 of Bill C-31) contained descent rules that specified two separate ways in which one could acquire status under the revised Indian Act: under either section 6(1) or section 6(2). Children born to parents who were both currently status Indians acquired entitlement under Section 6(1). Children with just one parent registered under section 6(1) and a non-registered parent acquired entitlement under section 6(2). But people with one non-registered parent and one parent registered under section 6(2) are, from 1985 onward, not entitled to Indian status. Therefore, to the extent that status Indians have children with persons without status, we can expect an increase in the number of children registered under section 6(2), as well as, over the longer term, an increase in the proportion not eligible for Indian status at all.

According to projections of the effects of out-marriage prepared for Indian and Northern Affairs Canada, by as early as 2010 a quarter of all children born to status Indians living off-reserve will no longer be eligible for Indian status (INAC 2000). With each subsequent generation, the proportion of all children who acquire entitlement under section 6(2) as opposed to section 6(1) is pro-jected to increase. This implies that a growing proportion of children will be liable not to qualify at all. Without further changes to the Indian Act, it is pos-sible that over several generations, the majority of children born will not be eligible. That is what will happen if there is little change in the propensity of First Nations peoples to have children with persons not registered. Intrinsic to the legislation are inheritance rules that can lead to a substantial reduction in the size of the status population.

Conclusion

This chapter began by observing that Aboriginal Canadians have not shared equally in the affluence of Canadian society. Unemployment remains very high, housing is often substandard, and health care and education are often inadequate. This chapter then charted the demography of Aboriginal Canadians in terms of population size, fertility, and mortality, as well as some of the implications of recent trends. Since other chapters of this book have examined the socio-economic conditions of Aboriginal peoples, we intentionally narrowed our scope by sketching what is known of the demography of Canada's Aboriginal population.

The focus on the demographic dynamics of the Aboriginal population of Canada demonstrates a few important points that are not always obvious when considering the overall Canadian population. One such point is the fact that the demographic behaviour and experience of Canadians is not always the same for all segments of the population. Whereas the overall demographic situation in Canada is such that fertility and mortality have fallen to unprecedented low levels (with the rate of natural increase steadily declining), Aboriginal peoples continue to have above-replacement fertility and relatively high mortality, along with a relatively high rate of natural increase. As a consequence, the age structure of Aboriginal peoples is also dramatically different from that of other Canadians, with important implications for both the internal dynamics of Aboriginal communities as well as the broader realm of public policy.

In addition, we have pointed out the enormous definitional challenges that demographers often face in conducting demographic research. The conventional practice by most users of census or demographic data is to accept the census definitions and categories and then to make sense of whatever data or time series are available. Nonetheless, it should be appreciated that most classifications used in the census and the federal statistical system are in fact socially constructed composites that have arisen from a variety of historical and contemporary influences. Definitions of Aboriginal have been incorporated into the legal infrastructure of Canadian society and have largely been imposed on Aboriginal peoples.

As indicated by Frideres (1998), the existence of the Indian Act implies a power relationship of sorts in that the federal government has long been involved in defining exactly who might be considered a North American Indian in a legal sense. This has significant economic and political consequences, since some Aboriginal people consider themselves well represented by this definition whereas others do not. Consequently, the demographic future of Aboriginal peoples holds much uncertainty, depending not only on demographic trends but also on various non-conventional growth factors (such as legislative reform, intermarriage, and the degree to which cultural continuity is maintained from one generation to the next). Various socio-economic, cultural, and political unknowns will have a direct impact on how people identify in the future, perhaps an even larger impact than strictly demographic factors. This observation is certainly of concern to many Aboriginal elders, teachers, and political leaders, with their interest in maintaining symbols of culture and group identity.

In the more recent trends, as identified in this chapter and others, there are grounds for both optimism and pessimism. Nonetheless, taking a longer-term view of the demographic development of Aboriginal peoples, the past half-century might be best labelled as a period of demographic recovery.

Discussion Questions

1. Why do you think, on average, Aboriginal peoples in Canada have not shared equally in the affluence of Canadian society?
2. We reported that the Aboriginal population is very young relative to Canada as a whole. As the Aboriginal population shifts from youth into working age groups over the next 15 years, what impact do you think this will have on the issues facing Aboriginal people?
3. Why do you think Aboriginal youth, especially those living outside reserves, tend to move or migrate much more than both the general population in Canada and their own counterparts in Aboriginal communities?
4. How might demographic factors have less of an impact on how Aboriginal identify themselves in the future than socio-economic, cultural, and political factors? Why do you think many Aboriginal elders, teachers, and political leaders are concerned about these possible future developments?
5. It is projected that as First Nations peoples have children with persons who are non-registered, a growing proportion of children of Aboriginal ancestry will eventually not to be able to qualify for Indian status. How is this possible, and what effects do you think it will have on First Nations in Canada?

Further Readings

Clatworthy, S.J. 2003. 'Re-assessing the population impacts of Bill C-31 Section 6'. In Jerry White, Paul Maxim, Paul Whitehead, and Dan Deavon, eds, *The Aboriginal Condition: Research Foundations for Public Policy*. Vancouver: University of British Columbia Press.

Guimond, Eric. 2003. 'Fuzzy definitions and population explosion: Changing identities of Aboriginal groups in Canada'. In David Newhouse and Evelyn Peters, eds, *Not Strangers in These Parts: Aboriginal People in Cities*, 35–50. Ottawa: Policy Research Initiative.

Romaniuc, Anatole. 2000. 'Aboriginal population of Canada: Growth dynamics under conditions of encounter of civilisations'. *Canadian Journal of Native Studies* 20: 95–137.

Statistics Canada. 2005. *Projections of the Aboriginal Populations, Canada, Provinces and Territories*. Catalogue 91-547-XIE. Ottawa: Statistics Canada.

———. 2008. *Aboriginal Peoples in Canada in 2006: Inuit, Métis and First Nations, 2006 Census*. Catalogue no. 97-558-XIE. Ottawa: Statistics Canada.

Waldram, James, Ann Herring, and T. Kue Young. 2006. *Aboriginal Health in Canada: Historical, Cultural and Epidemiological Perspectives*. 2nd edn. Toronto: University of Toronto Press.

References

Atleo, Shawn. 2009. 'AFN national chief responds to prime minister's statements on colonialism'. Press release. www.afn.ca.

Beavon, Daniel, and Martin Cooke. 2003. 'An application of the United Nations Human Development Index to registered Indians in Canada, 1996'. In Jerry White, Paul Maxim, Paul Whitehead, and Dan Deavon, eds, *The Aboriginal Condition: Research Foundations for Public Policy*. Vancouver: University of British Columbia Press.

Boserup, Ester. 1965. *The Conditions of Agricultural Growth*. Chicago: Aldine.

Boxhill, W. 1984. 'Limitations of the use of ethnic origin data to quantify visible minorities in Canada'. Working paper prepared for Statistics Canada, Housing, Family and Social Statistics Division.

Boyd, Robert. 1990. 'Demographic history, 1774–1874'. In W. Sturtevant, ed., *Handbook of North American Indians*, vol. 7, *Northwest Coast*, 135–48. Washington: Smithsonian Institution.

———. 1992. 'Population decline from two epidemics on the northwest coast'. In *Disease and Demography in the Americas*. Washington: Smithsonian Institution Press.

Chackiel, Juan, and Alexia Peyser. 1993. 'Indigenous population from Latin American national censuses'. Presented at the International Union for Scientific Study of Population Conference, Montreal, August.

Charbonneau, Hubert. 1984. 'Trois siècles de dépopulation amérindienne'. In L. Normandeau and V. Piché, eds, *Les populations amérindienne et Inuit du Canada*, 28–48. Montreal: Les presses de l'Université de Montréal.

Charbonneau, Hubert, and A. Larose. 1979. *The Great Mortalities: Methodological Studies of Demographic Crises in the Past*. Liège: Ordina.

Clatworthy, S.J. 2003. 'Re-assessing the population impacts of Bill C–31 section 6'. In Jerry White, Paul Maxim, Paul Whitehead, and Dan Deavon, eds, *The Aboriginal Condition: Research Foundations for Public Policy*. Vancouver: University of British Columbia Press.

Daniels, J. 1992. 'The Indian population of North America in 1492'. *William and Mary Quarterly* 49: 298–320.

Dickason, O. 2002. *Canada's First Nations: A History of Founding Peoples from Earliest Times*. Don Mills: Oxford University Press.

Dobyns, H. 1983. *Their Number Become Thinned: Native American Population Dynamics in Eastern North America*. Knoxville: University of Tennessee Press.

Eggertson, Laura. 2007. 'Physicians challenge Canada to make children, youth a priority'. *Canadian Medical Association Journal* 176 (12): 1693–4.

Eschbach, Karl. 1995. 'The enduring and vanishing American Indian: American Indian population growth and intermarriage in 1990'. *Ethnic and Racial Studies* 18: 89–108.

Frideres, James S. 1998. *Aboriginal Peoples in Canada: Contemporary Conflicts*. Scarborough, ON: Prentice Hall and Allyn and Bacon Canada.

Goddard, I. 1996. *Languages: Handbook of North American Indians*. Washington: Smithsonian Institution.

Goldmann, Gustave. 1998. 'Shifts in ethnic origins among the offspring of immigrants: Is ethnic mobility a measurable phenomenon?' *Canadian Ethnic Studies* 30: 121–48.

Goldmann, Gustave, and Andy Siggner. 1995. 'Statistical concepts of Aboriginal people and factors affecting the counts in the Aboriginal Peoples Survey'. In *Towards the Twenty-First Century: Emerging Socio-demographic Trends and Policy Issues in Canada*, 265–80. Ottawa: Federation of Canadian Demography.

Guimond, Eric. 2003. 'Fuzzy definitions and population explosion: Changing identities of Aboriginal groups in Canada'. In David Newhouse and Evelyn Peters, eds, *Not Strangers in These Parts: Aboriginal People in Cities*, 35–50. Ottawa: Policy Research Initiative.

Harris, M., and E. Ross. 1987. *Death, Sex and Fertility: Population Regulation in Pre-industrial and Developing Societies*. New York: Columbia University Press.

Healey, S., et al. 2004. *Nunavut Report of Comparable Health Indicators*. Iqaluit: Government of Nunavut.

Health Canada. 2009. *Drinking Water Advisories in First Nations Communities in Canada—A National Overview*. Catalogue H34-208/2009E. Ottawa: Health Canada.

Health Canada. First Nations and Inuit Branch. 2001. *A Statistical Profile on the Health of First Nations in Canada*. Ottawa: Health Canada.

———. 2003. *A Statistical Profile on the Health of First Nations in Canada*. Ottawa: Health Canada.

Hout, Michael, and Joshua Goldstein. 1994. 'How 4.5 million Irish immigrants became 40 million Irish Americans: Demographic and subjective aspects of ethnic composition of white Americans'. *American Sociological Review* 59: 64–82.

INAC (Indian and Northern Affairs Canada). 2000. *Registered Indian Population Project-ions for Canada and Regions, 1998–2008*. Ottawa: Indian and Northern Affairs Canada.

———. 2005. Basic departmental data 2004. Ottawa: Indian and Northern Affairs Canada.

———. 2008. *Registered Indian Population by Sex and Residence*. Ottawa: First Nations and Northern Statistics Section, Strategic Policy and Research Branch, Indian and Northern Affairs Canada.

Jain, A., and J. Bongaarts. 1981. 'Breastfeeding: Patterns, correlates and fertility effects'. *Studies in Family Planning* 12: 79–99.

Jenness, D. 1977. *The Indians of Canada*. Toronto: University of Toronto Press.

Kerr, Don, and Denis Morrisette. 1997. 'Census coverage evaluation and demographic analysis in Canada'. *Canadian Studies in Population* 24: 27–43.

Library of Parliament. 2003. *Indian Status and Band Membership Issues*. Ottawa: Library of Parliament, Political and Social Affairs Division.

Lieberson, Stanley, and Mary C. Waters. 1988. *From Many Strands: Ethnic and Racial Groups in Contemporary America*. New York: Russell Sage Foundation.

———. 1993. 'The ethnic responses of whites: What causes their instability, simplification, and inconsistency'. *Social Forces* 72: 421–50.

Loh, S., et al. 1998. 'Population projections of registered Indians, 1996–2021'. Working paper. Ottawa: Statistics Canada.

Mercredi, Ovide. 1997. Written transcript of conversation; subject: Royal Commission on Aboriginal Peoples. National Press Theatre, 30 April.

Meuvret, J. 1965. 'Demographic crisis in France from the sixteenth to the eighteenth century'. In D. Glass and D. Eversley, eds, *Population in History*. London: Edward Arnold.

Milan, Anne, and Laurent Martel. 2008. 'Current demographic situation in Canada, 2005 and 2006'. In *Report on the Demographic Situation in Canada*, 10–77. Catalogue no. 91-209-X. Ottawa: Statistics Canada.

Mooney, J. 1928. *The Aboriginal Population of America North of Mexico*. Washington: Smithsonian Miscellaneous Collections 80: 1–40.

Morrison, W. 1984. *Under One Flag: Canadian Sovereignty and the Native Peoples of Northern Canada*. Ottawa: Treaties and Historical Research Centre.

Nault, F., et al. 1993. *Population Projections of Registered Indians, 1991–2016*. Ottawa: Statistics Canada.

Norris, Mary Jane. 2000. 'Contemporary demography of Aboriginal peoples in Canada'. In David Long and Olive Patricia Dickason, eds, *Visions of the Heart: Canadian Aboriginal Issues*, 2nd edn. Toronto: Harcourt Brace Canada.

Norris, Mary Jane, Don Kerr, and François Nault. 1995. 'Technical report on projections of the population with Aboriginal identity, Canada, 1991–2016'. Report prepared by the Population Projections Section, Demography Division, Statistics Canada, for the Royal Commission on Aboriginal Peoples. Ottawa: Statistics Canada.

Passel, Jeffrey. 1997. 'The growing American Indian population, 1960–1990: Beyond demography'. *Population Research and Policy Review* 16: 11–31.

Public Health Agency of Canada. 2004. *Tuberculosis in Canada, 2001*. Ottawa: Public Health Agency of Canada.

Ram, Bali. 2004. 'New estimates of Aboriginal fertility, 1966–1971 to 1996–2001'. *Canadian Studies in Population* 31: 179–96.

Robitaille, N., and R. Choinière. 1985. *An Overview of Demographic and Socioeconomic Conditions of the Inuit in Canada*. Ottawa: Department of Indian Affairs and Northern Development.

Romaniuc, Anatole. 1981. 'Increase in natural fertility during the early stages of modernization: Canadian Indian case study'. *Demography* 18: 157–72.

———. 2000. 'Aboriginal population of Canada: Growth dynamics under conditions of encounter of civilisations'. *Canadian Journal of Native Studies* 20: 95–137.

Royal Commission on Aboriginal Peoples. 1995. *People to People, Nation to Nation: Highlights from the Report of the Royal Commission on Aboriginal Peoples*. Catalogue no. Z1-1991/1-6E. Ottawa: Indian and Northern Affairs Canada.

Saunders, S., P. Ramsden, and D. Herring. 1992. 'Transformation and disease: Precontact Ontario Iroquoians'. In J. Verano and D. Ubelaker, eds, *Disease and Demography in the Americas*. Washington: Smithsonian Institution Press.

Savard, R., and J. Proulx. 1982. *Canada: derrière l'épopée, les autochtones*. Montreal: L'hexagone.

Siggner, Andy, et al. 2001. 'New developments in Aboriginal definitions and measures'. Presented at the Canadian Population Society meetings, Quebec City.

Snipp, Matthew. 1989. *American Indians: The First of the Land*. New York: Russell Sage Foundation.

Statistics Canada. 1999. 'Life expectancy'. *Health Reports* 11: 9–24.

———. 2005. *Projections of the Aboriginal Populations, Canada, Provinces and Territories.* Catalogue 91-547-XIE. Ottawa: Statistics Canada.

———. 2008a. *Aboriginal Peoples in Canada in 2006: Inuit, Métis and First Nations, 2006 Census.* Catalogue no. 97-558-XIE. Ottawa: Statistics Canada.

———. 2008b. *Aboriginal Ancestry Population.* Special Interest Profiles, 2006 Census. Catalogue no. 97-564-XWE. Ottawa: Statistics Canada.

———. 2008c. CANSIM Table 051-0004.

———. 2008d. *Causes of Death.* Catalogue no. 84-208-XIE. Ottawa: Statistics Canada.

———. 2009a. *Births.* Catalogue no. 84F0210X. Ottawa: Statistics Canada.

———. 2009b. *Persons Registered under the Indian Act, by Province and Territory.* Census of Population Special Table. Ottawa: Statistics Canada.

Stewart, T. 1973. *The People of America.* New York: Scribner's.

Sturtevant, W.C. 1996. *Handbook of North American Indians.* Washington: Smithsonian Institution.

Thornston, R. 1987. *American Indian Holocaust and Survival: A Population History since 1492.* Norman: University of Oklahoma Press.

———. 2000. 'Population of Native North Americans'. In M. Haines and R. Steckel, eds, *A Population History of North America.* Cambridge: Cambridge University Press.

Trovato, Frank. 2000. 'Canadian Indian mortality during the 1980s'. *Social Biology* 47: 135–45.

———. 2001. 'Aboriginal mortality in Canada, the United States and New Zealand'. *Journal of Biosocial Science* 33: 67–86.

Ubelaker, D.H. 1976. 'Prehistoric New World population size: Historical review and current appraisal of North American estimates'. *American Journal of Physical Anthropology* 45: 661–6.

———. 2000. 'Patterns of disease in early North American populations'. In M. Haines and R. Steckel, eds, *A Population History of North America,* 51–98. Cambridge: Cambridge University Press.

UNDP (United Nations Development Programme). 2009. *United Nations Development Report 2009.* New York: UNDP.

Verano, J., and D. Ubelaker. 1992. *Disease and Demography in the Americas.* Washington: Smithsonian Institution Press.

Waldram, James, Ann Herring, and T. Kue Young. 2006. *Aboriginal Health in Canada: Historical, Cultural and Epidemiological Perspectives.* 2nd edn. Toronto: University of Toronto Press.

Weiss, K. 1973. 'Demographic models for anthropology'. Memoirs of the Society for American Archaeology, no. 27. *American Antiquity* 38 (2).

Wilkins, Russell, et al. 2008a. 'The Canadian census mortality follow-up study, 1991 through 2001'. *Health Reports* 19 (3): 25–43.

———. 2008b. 'Life expectancy in the Inuit-inhabited areas of Canada, 1989 to 2003'. *Health Reports* 19 (1): 7–19.

Young, K.T. 1994. *The Health of Native Americans: Towards a Biocultural Epidemiology.* New York: Oxford University Press.

Reclaiming Aboriginality: From Mainstream Media Representation to Aboriginal Self-Representation

Augie Fleras

Introduction: Framing the (Mis)representational Basis of Aboriginal Peoples–Media Relations

To say that Canada embraces a commitment to inclusiveness is trite but true. Canada is a multicultural society whose commitment to abide by the principles of multiculturalism has proved consequential. An official multicultural policy agenda not only secures the basis for living together with differences, it also sanctions institutional inclusion through the government's commitment to remove discriminatory barriers. With an official policy of multiculturalism, social institutions are under pressure to be inclusive, in part by improving workplace access, representation, and equity, in part by maintaining a workforce that reflects, respects, and is responsive to difference and diversities, and in part by providing services that are available, accessible, and appropriate to all (Fleras 2009).

Mainstream media are equally responsible for honouring and addressing the principles of inclusion. Both print and electronic entertainment media have responded to the challenge by improving the quality and quantity of minority representation, from TV programming to magazine advertising. But exceptions remain, most notably in media (mis)representation of Aboriginality. Mainstream news media, in particular, have been resistant to advancing the quality of Aboriginal peoples' coverage, preferring instead to embrace the hoary old cliché that 'the only good Indian is a bad Indian' (see also Friar and Friar 1972). In that the news media have historically embraced the newsworthiness principle of conflict and negativity, few should be surprised by their framing of Aboriginal peoples as 'troublesome constituents'—that is, little more than 'problem people' who are problems, who have problems, and who create problems (Miller 2006; Fleras 2007a, 2007b).

The cumulative impact of negatively framing Aboriginality within contexts of crime, crisis, or conflict is significant. The polarization of Aboriginal peoples into media frames of good or bad tends to gloss over the fact that their lives are complex, nuanced, evolving, and internally diverse. Simplistic narratives not only ignore the existence of many viewpoints on any given issue, they also compromise the collective reputation, self-esteem, and safety of an entire community by focusing exclusively on the extreme actions of a few while stripping events and circumstances of their context. Mainstream audiences are also affected by news media representations of Aboriginal peoples (Macpherson and Spoonley 2004). Insofar as people accept news media versions of reality as true, partly because they have no reason not to, the cumulative impact of this misrepresentation by misappropriation can be controlling—not in the sense of deliberate brainwashing but through coverage that is systemically biasing because of its consequences. And until they are challenged and/or superseded by other sources of information about Aboriginal peoples and politics, news media play a central role in defining public opinion, framing national discourses, and formulating government responses (also Sauvageau, Schneiderman, and Taras 2006).

But mainstream media are not the only storytelling narrative in town. This paper also argues that the emergence and popularity of Aboriginal media constitute a means by which Aboriginal peoples can counteract mainstream media hegemony. By using media to tell their own stories in their own ways, Aboriginal peoples illustrate how media technology can simultaneously serve as a handmaiden of colonialism yet provide a tool for dismantling it. In decolonizing the connections that colonial projects disrupted—namely, the communication corridors between, within, and among Aboriginal peoples' communities—Aboriginal media are striving to establish a new social order that productively links local groups to national bodies and international allies (Buddle 2005). Aboriginal media may also be understood as a form of social capital, since they serve both to *bond* (by cultivating ties within communities) and to *bridge* (by creating connections with others outside of communities). Or, to paraphrase Kathleen Buddle (2005), the goal of Aboriginal-authored media is to restructure relations between and within a variety of cultural groups by mediating neo-traditional (new-old) versions of Aboriginality.

To put these arguments to the test, the chapter begins by framing mainstream media as a principal means by which the hegemonic status of Eurocentric ideology is built and maintained. Insofar as the continued misrepresentation of Aboriginality is systemic—that is, structural rather than attitudinal, institutional rather than personal, and consequential rather than conspiratorial—Aboriginal media expose mainstream media for what they really are: a predominantly white Eurocentric discourse in defence of dominant ideology (Fleras 2007b). The chapter then looks at how news media routinely frame Aboriginal peoples as troublesome constituents through patterns of misrepresentation that are systematically biasing. Next, the chapter examines how Aboriginal peoples are reclaiming control over their lives by asserting authorship over the telling of their stories and demonstrates this in a case study showing how film images of Aboriginal peoples have evolved over time in both mainstream and Aboriginal media. The chapter concludes by addressing the significance of the shift from mainstream media stories of 'Aboriginal others' to 'self-representational' stories that are told by, for, and about Aboriginal peoples through media they control. The politics of Aboriginal media are shown to be critical not only in advancing a post-colonial social contract for living together differently but also for ensuring Aboriginal ownership of voices in speaking 'truth to power' (Buddle 2002; Graydon 2008; Himpele 2008; Knopf 2008).

Playing the Frame Game: Mainstream News as Discourses in Defence of Eurocentric Ideology

The politics of newscasting remains sharply contested. For some, news represents an empirically grounded mirror of social reality dispassionately uncovered and conveyed by impartial journalists who objectively uncover 'what's new' (but see Miller 2005). For others, instead of something 'out there' to be plucked for placement, news is defined as a socially created and culturally specific convention. According to this line of thinking, what passes for news reflects a socially constructed exercise involving individuals who make choices over what's on, what's not, who's quoted, what sources, and which spin (Weston 2003; Spoonley 2005). The assertion that news is socially constructed rather than uncovered and reported, and that journalists are culturally grounded rather than objectively detached, identifies the contradictions between what mainstream news says it is doing versus what it really is doing.

Despite paying lip service to the goal of speaking 'truth to power', mainstream news constitutes a socially constructed discourse in defence of Eurocentric ideology. As an ideological framework, mainstream news media are loaded with ideas and ideals that draw attention to some aspects of reality as natural and normal but 'frame' other dimensions as irrelevant or inferior (Henry and Tator 2002; Schuck and de Vreese 2006). Moreover, what is omitted by these ideological frames may prove just as informative in shaping public discourses as content that is included (Entman 1993; 2004). The centrality of framing is critical to this ideological work. Defined as a process of organizing information that makes sense or draws attention, news frames select, highlight, and interconnect snippets of reality to promote a particular interpretation of it. As a means of processing and organizing information that encourage a pre-ferred reading, frames also normalize what stories will appear, how issues will be framed, whose voices will prevail, the context in which events will appear, and the selection of approved images. Not surprisingly, the agenda-setting function of news frames promotes a media-centred view of how the world works, what is acceptable or not, and who gets what and why. As John Fiske (1994, 117) states:

> Social norms are realized in the day-to-day workings of the ideological state apparatuses. Each of these institutions is relatively autonomous . . . yet they all perform similar ideological work. They are all patriarchal; they are concerned with the getting and keeping of wealth and possessions; and they all endorse the individualism and competition between individ-uals. But the most significant feature is that they all present themselves as socially neutral, as not favoring one particular class over any other. Each presents itself as a principled institutionalization of equality: the law, the media, and education all claim, loudly and often, to treat all individuals equally and fairly.

In other words, media representations do not simply reflect some 'true' re-ality; rather, by selectively promoting one version of reality to the exclusion of others, they can be interpreted as a discourse involving institutionalized thought control.

How do mainstream news media reinforce their hegemonic[1] status as insti-tutionalized discourses in defence of Eurocentric ideology? First and foremost, news stories convey ideological assumptions that draw attention to some aspects of reality by normalizing the dominant ideas and ideals as natural or superior while problematizing as irrelevant and inferior ideas or actions of those who challenge convention (Abel 1997). This 'framing' experience is neither neu-tral nor objective; more accurately, it is driven by a news media culture that normalizes conformity while problematizing dissent (Henry and Tator 2002; Lambertus 2004). In reflecting and advancing the interests of the dominant group, a hegemonic news media play the 'frame game' by circumscribing the parameters of legitimate debate while marginalizing those outside the main frame (Mooney 2003; for discussion, see Henry and Tator 2003). Those who conform and comply receive favourable coverage; those who provoke or protest are framed as 'troublesome constituents' in need of control or correction.

News media are ideological in a second way. In addition to securing domin-ant ideologies, they themselves are loaded with ideological assumptions that influence the framing of news stories. What passes for news ('newsworthiness') reflects an institutional bias that is both routine and patterned as well as unintentional and inadvertent. News is essentially a 'medium of the negative' involving incidents of abnormality, negativity, crime, or conflict (as exemplified by a raft of clichés, such as 'the only good news is bad news', 'if it bleeds, it leads', 'if it scares, it airs'). The former editor of the *Globe and Mail*, Edward Greenspon (2003), spoke frankly of a profession enamoured with the abnormal:

> Let's not be coy here. Journalists thrive on the misery of others. It's not, as some have supposed, that the media dwell on the negative. It is that we dwell on the unusual and extraordinary. . . . If it happens everyday, it ain't news. Which creates a natural bias toward the negative since most of life actually unfolds as expected.

The centrality of conflict and the negative as ideological frames transforms news into an adversarial format that caters to those with loud voices, extreme views, strange appearances, and bizarre behaviour (Weston 2003; Editorial, *Christchurch Press* 2006). Compounding this negativity is the growing tabloidization of news that not only 'morselizes' reality into 'bitable' bits for easy consumption but also idolizes a kind of 'gotcha' journalism that sacrifices substance for scandal. The episodic framing of news over the thematic, the complex, or the contextual also reinforces shallower coverage that may conceal more than it reveals (Boykoff 2006).

Inasmuch as what passes for newsworthiness is driven by the prevailing news paradigm rather than by the needs of democratically informed citizenship, the news media are fundamentally 'mediacentric'.[2] A mediacentric bias prevails when newsworthiness is filtered through frames that encourage viewers or readers to 'see like the media' ('media gaze') and consider that normal, necessary, and as if it were no perspective at all (Fleras and Nelson, in press). By framing news around a mediacentric perception of reality, the media's capacity to convey accurate and impartial information is sharply compromised when they privilege the negative over the positive, deviance over normative, conflict over cooperation, the sensational over substance, the simplistic over context or complexity, and the episodic over the thematic (Keller 2006). Coverage of Aboriginal peoples and Aboriginality, and the framing of incidents involving Aboriginal protest, attests to this institutionalized slant (Comstock and Scharrer 2005; Ricard and Wilkes 2008).

Normalizing Eurocentricity and Problematizing Aboriginality

Mainstream news media personnel and organizations have long been reproached for their biased and sometimes insulting coverage of racialized minorities (Cottle 2000; Shaheen 2001). A similar critique applies to news media treatment of Canada's Aboriginal peoples (Ricard and Wilkes 2008). Despite modest improvements in the representational basis of media–Aboriginal relations, Aboriginal women and men continue to be ignored, stereotyped, and otherwise marginalized by negative images and (mis)information about who they are and what they want (Weston 2003). Simplistic stereotypes vilify Aboriginal peoples along racialized lines as: (a) a threat to Canada's territorial integrity or national interests; (b) a risk to Canada's social order and inter-group harmony; (c) an economic liability; (d) an irritant to the criminal justice system; and (e) pushers of privilege that undermine Canada's egalitarian norms and constitutional principles (Curry 2007). Compounding this negativity is the standard framing of Aboriginal peoples as social problems due in large part (or so the mainstream media story goes) to their excessive reliance on welfare, a predilection for alcohol and substance abuse, a pervasive laziness and lack of ambition, an inability to manage what little they have, and their tendency to justify questionable conduct by hiding behind the smokescreen of Aboriginal rights (Lambertus 2004; McCreanor 2006).

Admittedly, news norms involving a 'trafficking in the extreme' are not exclusive to Aboriginal coverage. Newsworthiness in general reinforces the media-centric notion that 'the only bad news is good news' (also ter Wal, d'Haenans, and Koeman 2005). But the framing of Aboriginality in exclusively negative terms exerts a different impact, in large part because Aboriginal peoples in Canada continue to lack the institutionalized power to deflect, absorb, and neutralize negative typecasts. The process in which Eurocentric media filters, historical lenses, and popular preconceptions combine to under-represent or distort Aboriginality has proven costly. Surveys indicate the vast majority of Canadians are generally misinformed about the history, circumstances, issues, and challenges that confront Aboriginal peoples. As well, most non-Aboriginal Canadians lack any meaningful contact with Aboriginal peoples, thus robbing them of the type of first-hand information necessary to critically evaluate and make sense of what is going on. What little they do know about Aboriginality is gleaned largely from mainstream media newscasts, television programs, and film. Nor surprisingly, media framing of Aboriginality and Aboriginal peoples as predominantly 'problem people' who impose costs or create inconvenience profoundly shapes public discourses regarding what is normal, acceptable, or desirable (Ricard and Wilkes 2008).

To be sure, news media coverage of Aboriginality has improved in recent years (Fleras and Kunz 2001; CRE 2004). Both research and anecdotal evidence attests to this shift (Task Force 2004). Crude stereotyping of Aboriginal peoples as victims, warriors, and ecologists has given way to more positive portrayals, at least in editorials, opinion columns, and investigative journalism (Spoonley and Trlin 2004). And yet paradoxes persist: while mainstream media are reluctant to say anything negative about Aboriginal peoples for fear of being branded as racist or attracting the wrong kind of publicity, mainstream messages continue to express a kind of disdain for Aboriginality. Aboriginal peoples and other racialized minorities are not necessarily labelled as inherently inferior; rather, they are stigmatized as incompatible with Canadian society because of their inappropriate cultural values (Fleras 2004a) and their inability to exercise control over themselves and their lives (Harding 2005).

Such negativity is hardly a simple error of perception or misjudgment. While no one should discount the tenacity of prejudice, ignorance, arrogance, indifference, ethnocentrism, or laziness, the logic behind negative coverage is structural. Aboriginal peoples are not necessarily victimized by news coverage that is deliberately misleading, consciously slanted, or wilfully malevolent. To the contrary, this misrepresentation arises from media coverage that is systemically biasing because of the cumulative if unintended effect of negatively one-sided representations. A one-size-fits-all portrayal of Aboriginality exerts a controlling effect by way of coverage that is systemic and institutionalized—institutionalized because the coverage is routine, repetitive, and impersonal rather than random and intentional; systemic because it supports the dominant, Eurocentric ideology as normal and superior, while Aboriginality is dismissed accordingly. In refusing to take Aboriginal peoples and their differences seriously, mainstream news media have proved to be both aversive and even hostile toward Aboriginality. This refusal also exerts a controlling effect since over time, stereotypical and misinformed representations contribute to the internalization of a colonized mindset (Tahmahkera 2008).

The net effect of this one-dimensional coverage constitutes a systemic ('soft') propaganda. The manipulation of this persuasion is not injected into the processing of information about Aboriginality and Aboriginal peoples but rather is inherent within the normal news media functioning. Coverage of Aboriginality reflects: (1) a pro-white news paradigm that normalizes ('privileges') whiteness/ Eurocentricity as the normative standard; (2) conventional news norms that focus on negativity and conflict as preferred frames for information process-ing; and (3) prevailing news values of a liberal universalism[3] that dismisses Aboriginal difference as inferior, irrelevant, or threatening. This normalizing of Aboriginal peoples as troublesome constituents is not without consequences, given the agenda-setting potential of media representations in defining 'who gets what, and why'. The refracting of Aboriginality through a monocultural, Eurocentric lens constitutes a form of institutionalized thought control known as soft propaganda (Fleras 2007a; also Herman and Chomsky 1988). This is not to say that news media *are* propaganda. Rather, mainstream news media may be interpreted *as if* they were systemic propaganda when judged by what they really do rather than by what they say they do.

Restoring Aboriginal Voices: From Media Gaze[4] to Aboriginal Gaze

Perception is as much of a threat as anti-sovereignty legislation. We have to regain control of our image.

Former principal chief of the Cherokee Nation,
Wilma Mankiller, cited in Corntassel and Witmer 2008

Aboriginal peoples have also used media institutions as a tool of empower-ment for linking the past with pathways into a globally integrated future (Meadows and Molnar 2001; Roth 2006). For many years, Aboriginal peoples have employed media technology (from print to radio to television to the Internet) as an alternative site for dialogue and representation, organizing resistance against colonization, preserving cultural values, nurturing a sense of community, providing direct links within and between communities, and fostering a shared agenda for continued advocacy of social justice goals (see also Hodgetts et al. 2005). But unlike the past when mainstream media mon-opolized the telling of Aboriginal stories, Aboriginal writers, producers, and directors now have the support and recognition to tell their own stories (Cobb 2003). In contrast to ethnic media, which provide an alternative ser-vice to that offered by mainstream news media, Aboriginal media strive to provide a first level of service, since mainstream media rarely service specif-ically Aboriginal audiences (Avison and Meadows 2000; Fleras 2007b). In rejecting a view of Aboriginal peoples as minorities with needs but rather seeing them as peoples with rights, Aboriginal media advance Aboriginal peoples' claims to sovereignty and a corresponding right to self-determining autonomy over land, identity, and political voice (Retzlaff 2008; Maaka and Fleras 2005).

Clearly, then, Aboriginal media seek to cultivate a counter-hegemonic discourse that challenges conventional wisdom and Eurocentric perspectives (Himpele 2008). Aboriginal media makers contest the ideological and imaginary Indian constructs of mainstream media (Knopf 2008). By assuming control over Aboriginal representations through Aboriginal storytelling frames and language, Aboriginal media provide a contrasting perspective on Aboriginal politics and culture while at the same time offering programs that are reflective of and responsive to local and cultural needs (Knopf 2008; Retzlaff 2008). As Kathleen Buddle (2005, 20) notes:

> Media production appears to represent a site where Native, Métis, and Inuit peoples render themselves worldly, as opposed to being globalized or assimilated by alien or impersonal forces . . . a place where individuals discern, import, and experiment with culture-making materials. By idiosyncratically combining and transforming these elements into something that is locally relevant, individuals compose for themselves a vision of their destiny, while drawing and redrawing the boundaries around their locality.

In other words, Aboriginal media cultivate a different set of 'media norms' to counteract and resist the dominant Euro-Canadian discourse, to combat stereotypes, and to ensure that histories and contemporary issues reflect Aboriginal perspectives and realities (Retzlaff 2008).

Case Study: Aboriginality and Film: From Playing Indian to Indigenous Storytelling

The movies loom so large for Indians because they have defined our self image as well as told the entire planet how we live, look, scream, and kill.

Comanche writer Paul Chaat Smith, cited in Wood 2008, 73

That Was Then: The Only Good 'Indian' Is a Bad 'Indian'

In 1975, McClelland and Stewart published a book entitled *Hollywood's Canada* in which the author, Pierre Berton, castigated the film industry for their misrepresentation of Canada and Canadians. From 1907 onward, Berton wrote, a total of 575 films were made about or specifically set in Canada and distributed worldwide. But the Canada that appeared on tinseltown celluloid differed sharply from the realities of Canada or that of Canadians. For Hollywood, Canada consisted almost exclusively of boundless forests and snow-swept mountains (no prairies), devoid of large cities (except Montreal), and peopled by happy-go-lucky French Canadians, savage Indians, wicked half-breeds, and grim-jawed Mounties in charge of policing an American-style wild-west frontier. These fabrications and caricatures did more than influence generations of movie-goers both in Canada and America and abroad (after all, what the world knew of Canada or Canadians was largely gleaned from the silver screen). In that film constitutes an extremely powerful form of representation and socialization (Gittings 1998), the refracting of these demeaning images and 'historical twaddle' through the lens of Hollywood's fantasy machine also aborted the attainment of a Canadian national identity.

This case study on Hollywood's depiction of Aboriginal peoples (called 'Indians' by Hollywood) and Métis (called 'half-breeds' by Hollywood) demonstrates the significance of a dominant media gaze in reflecting a reading of reality that is problematic and perverse. More than those of any other ethnic or racial group, images of Aboriginal/indigenous peoples have been shaped by a picture-based storytelling known as film/cinema/movies (Rollins and O'Connor 2003; Darian-Smith 2004; Wood 2008). Although all ethnic groups have been stereotyped or demeaned in one way or another by Hollywood storytelling, Aboriginal peoples proved reliable film 'fodder' for reeling in the audiences while perpetuating 'myth-conceptions' of the 'wild west' as the quintessential American proving ground. Hollywood capitalized on the winnable combination of non-stop action, arrows zipping through the air, blood-curdling shrieks, and high body counts to convey eye-popping images that proved appealing because they embraced rapid physical movement, exotic appearance, violent confrontations, and barbaric personalities ('It was in their blood') (Herzberg 2008). This focus on action and treachery reinforced the 'othering' of Aboriginal peoples as life-forms from a different time and place, with histories that began with the arrival of white people, whose current realities only made sense within the context of settler interaction (see also Razack 2002), and whose future could be crudely encrypted in the title of the acclaimed book by Ralph and Natasha Friar: *The Only Good Indian Is a Dead Indian*.

Aboriginal peoples in Canada may have been culturally and socially different peoples whose distinctiveness reflected variations in history, geography, and culture. But for Hollywood's 'injuns' (Buscombe 2006), a one-size-fits-all mindset prevailed. Regardless of where they lived or how they lived, Canadian

Indians—Blackfoot, Iroquois, Cree, Salish, or Ojibway—were bunched together as uniformly the same and largely indistinguishable from their American counterparts—in effect reinforcing a 'seen one Indian, seen them all' mentality. Film portrayals embraced a mythical image of an imaginary warrior who occupied the 'foothills' between 1825 and 1880 (Francis 1992) and whose generic appearance reflected a so-called Indian Identity Kit (Friar and Friar 1972). This identity kit consisted of a wig with hair parted in the middle into hanging plaits, a feathered warbonnet or headband (not an indigenous artifact but introduced by white actors to secure their wigs), buckskin leggings, moccasins, painted skin tipi, and armed with a spear, bow and arrow, or tomahawk. His actions conformed to a standard Primitive Savagery Kit—attacking wagon trains, swooping down on horseback to burn settler cabins, torturing prisoners, pounding on tom toms or whooping it up, fanning menacing smoke signals as a prelude to attack, and drinking uncontrollably.

Aboriginal women received more enlightened treatment under the weight of Hollywood's myth-making gaze. Nevertheless, their appearance and behaviour conformed to a Hollywood Female Indian Kit. With their beaded headbands, single eagle feathers, necklaces of beads or animal teeth, buckskin or leather skirts, and long black hair in braids, these celluloid maidens were portrayed as small, gentle creatures with an often fatal soft spot for captured white males (Marubbio 2006). In sharp contrast were their hot-blooded half-sisters ('half-breeds'), these sneaky spitfires would go to any length to snatch and secure hapless white males, in the process proving their immorality, innate savagery, and potential to destroy American society through miscegenation.

Half-breed males suffered worse indignities. Unlike the generally affable and likeable rogues that the French Canadians represented, the Métis were vilified as proof of the evils of miscegenation (Friar and Friar 1972)—although all Hollywood half-breeds were French (never English). These half-breeds were depicted as the worst sort of dirty no-good scoundrels and untrustworthy degenerates who coveted defenceless white women or sold bad whisky to Indians. But once again, what was filtered through the Hollywood gaze was opposite to what really happened. The Métis were not a lawless breed constantly pursued by Mounties, Berton writes, but a people whose code of honour and protocols established a degree of law and order in the West. Nor did they engage in the selling of bad whisky to other Indians—it was the white men who did, initially the large fur trading companies, then opportunistic American entrepreneurs.

The consequences of misrepresentation has proven costly. As Robert Berkhofer writes in *The White Man's Indian*, invented images of Aboriginal peoples have long influenced policy-makers in providing both moral and intellectual justification for policies and explanations for failures. The fact that Hollywood blamed Canada's indigenous peoples for a host of frontier misdemeanours is tantamount to the symbolic annihilation of a culture and society.

This Is Now . . . *Finding Dawn*: Finding Aboriginal Women's Voices

Finding Dawn is an award-winning 2006 National Film Board documentary about the violence inflicted on Aboriginal women in Canada. Produced and directed by the acclaimed Métis filmmaker Christine Welsh,[5] the film focuses on the fate of three Aboriginal women—Dawn Crey, Ramona Wilson, and Daleen Kay Bosse—of some 520 Aboriginal women murdered or missing in Canada over the past 30 years. In addition to honouring those who have passed, Welsh emphasizes how the living (from survivors of sexual violence to family and community members of the murdered and missing) are taking life-affirming steps to commemorate the forgotten, communicate beyond the silence of the silenced, and construct a society that respects Aboriginal women's rights to dignity and safety. Or as Welsh comments toward the end of the film, 'I set out on this journey to find Dawn. But I also found Faye, I found Janice, I found people who strike, who search and hope.'

In an effort to put human faces on this national disgrace, the title itself touches on the story of Dawn Crey, whose remains (numbered 23 by the authorities) were found on the property of serial killer Robert Pickton. But in Welsh's hands, Crey becomes more than a number but rather a daughter and sister in the throes of moving beyond a life of drugs and 'prostitution'. The film then moves from Vancouver's Skid Row to BC's Highway 16, or the Highway of Tears, which runs from Prince Rupert to Prince George. Nine women (all but one Aboriginal), including Ramona Wilson, have died or disappeared along that stretch of road since 1990. Filming in Saskatoon focuses on Daleen Kay Bosse, who disappeared in 2004 and whose disappearance or murder remains unresolved (her remains were discovered in 2008, and legal proceedings are now underway). Along the way, Welsh makes it clear that the tragedy of murdered and missing Aboriginal women persists because of (a) societal and institutional indifference to those who are poor and Aboriginal, (b) a belief by predators that nobody will miss the weakest and most vulnerable members of society, and (c) historical, social, and economic factors that conspire to inflame this epidemic of gendered violence.

But the documentary is more than a series of depressing vignettes about the dead or disappeared. On the contrary, the overriding theme is empowerment—Aboriginal women and men mobilizing to challenge, resist, and transform. Though painful at times to watch, *Finding Dawn* resonates with messages of resilience and strength rather than dwelling on the dark heart of Aboriginal women's experiences in Canada. There are rays of courage and outrage conveyed by Aboriginal rights activists Janice Acoose and Fay Blaney, each of whom is a survivor of abuse, violence, and the dangers of life on the streets. Hope and optimism are also demonstrated through the annual Women's Memorial March in Vancouver, community mobilization and vigils along the length of Highway 16, and local family commemoration of missing and murdered daughters and sisters. The film ends with a photo shoot of a large Aboriginal family, with Welsh's voice-over posing a beguiling question, 'What is it about numbers?'

Finding Dawn won a Gold Audience Award at the 2006 Amnesty International Film Festival in Vancouver. It was screened for the 2007 International Women's Day celebrations at the United Nations in New York. Hardly surprising: *Finding Dawn* is exemplary as a striking testimony to the power of images to highlight a worldwide culture of impunity that allows the murder of women who are poor, indigenous, and in high-risk occupations to go unsolved and unpunished. Its usefulness as an indictment of society is further sharpened by the eloquent testimonials of strong parents and caring siblings as they struggle to cope with the devastation of lost daughters and sisters. Welsh relies largely on interviews with family members and relatives who movingly talk about refusing to forget those who have gone missing or were murdered, about their own personal experiences as drug-addicted sex trade workers, and about the need to change attitudes that dismiss Aboriginal women as disposable. In demonstrating how Aboriginal women (and men) are organizing and demonstrating to combat violence, *Finding Dawn* shatters conventional media stereotypes of Aboriginal women as passive or victims. In the final analysis, however, as many have implored and as *Finding Dawn* implicitly pleads, women can march and demonstrate, but it is men who must change.

Models of Aboriginal Media

Buddle (2005) has identified four broad models (or categories) of Aboriginal media: mainstream media, community-access and university media, Aboriginal-owned and operated media, and Internet-based media. When Aboriginal media products are produced by or for Aboriginal peoples, the mainstream media may underwrite the funding of the program; however, Aboriginal control over these products varies according to the terms of the contract. Aboriginal use of community access facilities, such as university radio stations or local cable access channels, offers more freedom, although institutional regulations and organizational disruptions can compromise both quality and quantity of programming.

Radio

Aboriginal-owned and -operated radio, including officially licensed stations like Aboriginal Voices Radio Network (AVRN), provide another mediated context. As well, many reserves now operate their own version of a community radio station. Although these stations are subject to CRTC regulations, the general structure of the shows, content, and creative freedom tend to reflect, reinforce, and advance each community's sense of Aboriginal identity. Aboriginal radio also helps to promote collective activities among different groups by contributing to the creation of local action groups (Buddle 2005). It also links otherwise geographically dispersed individuals around common interests and helps to cultivate among them a pan-Aboriginal discourse on sovereignty.

Newspapers

Not all Aboriginal media are consciously politicized. Many incorporate informational and community agendas that provide Aboriginal peoples with one of the few places where they can see and hear stories that reflect their lived experiences (Raudsepp 1996). For example, consider the mission statement by *Anishnabek News*, an Aboriginal paper in Ontario, whose goal is 'to foster pride and share knowledge about Anishnabek current affairs, culture, goals, and successes'. Objectives include:

> Sharing: Provide opportunities for people from the four corners of the Anishnabek Nation to tell stories and record achievements, and to keep our citizens informed about the activities of the Union of Ontario Indians. Strength: To give voice to the vision of the Anishnabek Nation that celebrates our history, language, and culture, promotes our land, treaty, and aboriginal rights, and supports the development of healthy and prosperous communities.

Other Aboriginal media that share these objectives include the monthly print publication *Windwalker* and the Internet-based *Turtle Island News*.

Television

Canada's Aboriginal peoples may possibly possess one of the most advanced broadcasting systems in the world (Roth 2006). Nowhere is this more evident than in northern Canada, where Aboriginal communities have exercised control over the local media, largely by appropriating satellite technology to meet social and cultural needs. The Broadcasting Act in 1991 proved pivotal as well. It not only enshrined an Aboriginal right to control over their own communications but also instructed mainstream broadcasting to ensure 'the special place of aboriginal peoples' in its programming and employment. In keeping with the spirit of the Broadcasting Act, the CRTC approved the creation of a national Aboriginal network (APTN) in 1999 with an availability to 8 million Canadian homes (all cable companies are required to carry APTN as part of their basic consumer package, costing each subscriber about 15 cents a month, which is then allocated to APTN). As a national network by, for, and about Aboriginality, APTN provides a platform for the production of culturally and linguistically relevant programming for Aboriginal men, women, and children; in turn, Canadians are provided with a window into the Aboriginal world. Creation of Aboriginal media space also promises to counteract mainstream misrepresentation by promoting a positive and realistic portrayal of Canada's First People across a broad range of topics (Baltrushchat 2004; Retzlaff 2008). As Lorna Roth (2006, 327) put it when describing APTN as a symbolic meeting place for Aboriginal peoples and non-Aboriginals to communicate their common interests:

> APTN has enabled indigenous messages to be heard by constituency groups that might have never had access to a live person of Aboriginal descent; it provides an opportunity to share national imageries and histories, to build bridges of understanding, and to bridge cultural borders.

Film

Aboriginal filmmakers are no less active in constructing and advancing an Aboriginal mediascape (see below). In contrast to the past, when white people co-opted Aboriginal stories, the film industry is showing signs of indigenization with respect to who is charge, with a growing number of Aboriginal directors both in Canada and the United States. Films such as *Atanarjuat: The Fast Runner* or *The Journals of Knud Rasmussen* (both directed by the Inuit director Zacharias Kunuk) with their distinctive storytelling techniques attest to this shift. Films such as *Smoke Signals* and *Powwow Highway* were among the first feature films written, directed, acted, and co-produced by Native Americans (Cobb 2003). Of particular note are documentary films that explore Aboriginal issues from an insider perspective and from within their ranks (Knopf 2008). Foremost among Aboriginal documentarists is Alanis Obomsawin, whose works (including *Kanehsatake: 270 Years of Resistance*) privilege Aboriginal perspectives on political conflicts and challenge the perspective of films that simply legitimize colonial conquest.

Internet and Social Media

With the Internet, Aboriginal media creators are able to exercise significant control over form, content, and listenership (Buddle 2005). In response to the question of what the electronic frontier can deliver to peoples on the fringes of power and far from the centres of influence, the answer is increasingly clear: greater empowerment for the historically disenfranchised by changing the sub-jectivities and practices (both on-line and off-line) of the marginalized and dis-empowered (Landzelius 2006). This transformation goes beyond the simple 'use' or 'effects' of the new media. Emphasis instead is on how members of a community are making themselves a(t) home in a global communicative en-vironment.[6] As Valerie Alia (2010) observes, this new media nation is linking old traditions of storytelling with digital technology by taking control to chal-lenge misrepresentations by outsiders through images and stories that preserve language and culture ('looking inward') while communicating across borders ('looking outward'). Four patterns of use can be discerned, according to Kyra Landzelius: (1) appropriating and moulding information and communication technologies (ICTs) to reflect, reinforce, and advance their needs, interests, and identities—including the use of cyberactivism to promote their ends; (2) using ICTs as a forum for making claims in the name of ethnicity (or indigeneity or Aboriginality); (3) naming ethnicity or claiming ethnicity (or Aboriginality); and (4) shifting the boundaries by which the politics of Aboriginality is rethought, reworked, and revitalized.

Box 8.1   Insight: Aboriginality On-line

In 1994, a group of remote First Nations communities in northern Ontario launched an electronic bul-letin board that would eventually become Canada's largest Aboriginal broadband network and a model network for indigenous communications worldwide (this case study taken from Chan 2009). The bulletin board system was intended to establish lines of communication with the communities' children and encourage them to stay in school at a time when many were dropping out while living away from home. In less than a decade, the system expanded enormously into a telecommunications network known as K-Net (from the Oji-Cree word Kukkenah meaning everyone, everywhere). Through a satellite network, K-Net not only links about 70 Aboriginal communities in northern Ontario, Quebec, and Manitoba with each other and around the world but also interconnects to other regional networks to form a national broadband network that provides video conferencing and other applications across Canada. Throughout its evolutionary growth, however, addressing local needs by maintaining local ownership and fostering local development remains a prime objective. In remaining grounded, K-Net constitutes an Aboriginal success story in which even isolated communities seek out partnerships, leverage support, harness funding, and use ICTs to address local economic and social needs.

As well as protecting indigenous peoples' rights, ICTs are proving important for building economies through e-commerce, establishing workable governance patterns, and preserving language and culture (Chan 2009).

To date, Aboriginal peoples' engagement with ICTs stretches along two directional pulls: To one side, *reactive* (neutralizing negative mainstream coverage) and *proactive* (celebrating Aboriginal accomplishments and role models); to the other side, *in-reach* (bonding) and *outreach* (bridging) (Landzelius 2006; Fleras 2007b; also Alia 2010). In-reach orientations range from promoting localized interests and community services, including the dissemination of in-group information, to the importation of expert knowledge for community use. For example, Aboriginal leaders are turning to ICTs to deliver high-quality health care to remote Canadian communities (Gideon 2006). Telemedicine enables medical specialists to observe patients via real-time links, thus providing an affordable way to surmount the tyranny of distance across Canada's vast expanses while balancing Western medical knowledge with Aboriginal health beliefs and practices (Cooke and Long, this volume). Outreach orientations tend to focus on bridging the outside world, ranging in scope from simple tourist information to full-blown indigenous revolutionary movements. In short, far from being at odds with each other or cancelling each other out, in-reach and outreach functions are mutually reinforcing, in part by embedding the local with the global and their implications for the articulation of identities, experiences, and outcomes (Landzelius 2006).

Undoing the Bias: From 'Seeing Like Mainstream Media' to Aboriginal Self-Representation

Article 16. 1. Indigenous peoples have the right to establish their own media, in their own languages and to have access to all forms of non-indigenous media without discrimination. 2. States shall take effective measures to ensure that State-owned media duly reflect indigenous cultural diversity. States, without prejudice to ensuring full freedom of expression, should encourage privately owned media to adequately reflect indigenous cultural diversity.

UN Declaration on the Rights of Indigenous Peoples, 13 September 2007

In the hope of redefining how their stories are framed, Aboriginal peoples are seeking control of media representations of their 'selves'. The politics of perception are critical (Corntassel and Witmer 2008). In that media coverage of

Aboriginality tends to undermine both Aboriginal identities and claims to self-determining autonomy, mainstream media are structured around relationships of dominance (Hall 1980), involving a hierarchy of discourses that control the 'out there' by hegemonizing the 'in here'. And yet, despite dominant interests enjoying a significant advantage in framing issues and setting agendas, Aboriginal peoples can and do resist and react.

The challenge is formidable. Mainstream initiatives for improving the quality and quantity of Aboriginal coverage will remain mired in a monocultural rut if they fail to address the foundational principles of the news media's constitutional order. That is, the problem and solution are more fundamental than consciousness raising. Insofar as media bias is structural and systemic, proposed solutions cannot simply consist of add-ons; transformative changes that are integral and integrated from start to finish must be incorporated (Gallagher 2005). Proposed solutions must focus on 'interrogating' those paradigmatic rules that inform newsworthiness instead of simply tweaking the normative conventions that refer to these news rules. In other words, contesting media hegemony and institutionalized power must go beyond a splash of colour or a few Aboriginal hires. The transformation of the prevailing mainstream news paradigm must begin with problematizing dominant news norms—themselves often invisibly yet powerfully normative, seemingly natural yet socially constructed, and ostensibly neutral yet ideologically loaded (Jiwani 2006). Or, as eloquently expressed by the co-leader of Aotearoa New Zealand's Maori Party, to overcome the tyranny of mainstream media and their Eurocentric designs, Aboriginal (or indigenous) peoples must reclaim their Aboriginality (or indigeneity) by restoring the centrality of Aboriginal storytelling voices in speaking the truth of indigeneity to centralized power.

> We in the Maori Party are framing news from a different angle. The angle of our kaupapa [goal], the perspective of our people, their visions, their aspirations, their courage. We are talking about the determination of iwi [tribes] to stand strong, to preserve their land, to address the obstacles and challenges that confront us all. We are talking about collective force, about being true to the Treaty [of Waitangi signed in 1840 between the Crown and many north island Maori tribes] and about maintaining integrity in the face of diversity. This is our story. This is your story. We refuse to be marginalized, criticized, victimized, polarized. We refuse to be absent, silent, ignored. We are here to stay and we will be successful beyond our greatest expectations. We will be powerful beyond even the realms of possibility. We will be tangata whenua [peoples of the land], and

we are amazing (emphasis mine) (Tania Turiana, co-leader of the Maori Party, 2008).

At the core of this challenge is power. The politics of power addresses the issues of 'who is speaking', 'how often and in what contexts', 'whose voices predominate', 'whose voices vie and contend', and 'whose voices are marginalized or silenced' (Cottle 2000). Control over representations will remain rooted in power in that all representations are socially constructed by those with the power to create, circulate, and convince. Until the issue of power is resolved in terms of who controls what and how with respect to media representations and whose values will dominate in the sorting out process, the politics of Aboriginality will clash with Canada's stated commitment to restructuring its relationship with the 'nations within'. Improvements are likely only when mainstream media moves beyond the 'us versus them' framing of reality by embracing and working with Aboriginal peoples in Canada to tell the story of 'Aboriginality' as part of the national discourse for living together with differences (see Hodgetts et al. 2005).

Discussion Questions

1. Discuss some of the issues and debates associated with the misrepresentational basis of Aboriginality and Aboriginal peoples by Canada's mainstream media.
2. How and why are Canada's Aboriginal peoples claiming the right to tell media stories in their own voices rather than simply relying on mainstream media storytelling? Use the case study on film and Aboriginality as a starting point for analysis and debate.
3. In exploring the notion of media representations of Aboriginality, what the mainstream media *don't say* in terms of coverage and tone may be just as important as what they do say. Explain, with examples.
4. Explain what is meant when we say that a biased media is not the problem but that the problem lies in media coverage of Aboriginal peoples that is systemically biasing because of its one sidedness.
5. Mainstream media are often described as a discourse in defence of dominant ideology. Demonstrate the validity of this statement by reference to news media coverage of Aboriginal peoples' protest.

Further Readings

Alia, Valerie. 1999. *Un/Covering the North: News, Media, and Aboriginal People*. Vancouver: University of British Columbia Press.
———. 2010. *The New Media Nation: Indigenous Peoples and Global Communication*. New York: Bergahan Books.
Lambertus, Sandra. 2004 *Wartime Images, Peacetime Wounds: The Media and Gustafsen Lake Standoff*. Toronto: University of Toronto Press.

Miller, John. 2005. 'Ipperwash and the media: A critical analysis of how the story was covered'. www.attorneygeneral.jus.gov.on.ca/inquiries/ipperwash/policy_part/projects/pdf/ALST_Ipperwash_and_media.pdf.

Roth, Lorna. 2009. 'Canadian First Peoples' landscapes: A snapshot with three corners'. In L. Shade, ed., *Mediascapes: New Patterns in Canadian Communication*, 3rd edn. Toronto: Nelson.

Weston, Mary Ann. 2003. 'Journalists and Indians: The clash of cultures'. www.bluecorn comics.com/weston.htm.

Wilkes, Rima, and Danielle Ricard. 2006. 'Rebels, militants, or colonial insurgents? Canada news, media, and the framing of protest by Aboriginal people'. www.allacademic.com.

Notes

1. Hegemony is defined as the process by which those in positions of power achieve consent over those without by way of consensus rather than coercion so that people's attitudes experience change without their awareness of what is happening.

2. Mediacentrism can be defined as the tendency of mainstream media to interpret and frame reality according to their principles, logic, and priorities, to convey this framing as natural and unproblematic rather than constructed and contested, and to dismiss alternative perspectives as problematic.

3. Liberal universalism involves a belief that what we have in common as freewheeling and morally autonomous individuals is more important for purposes of recognition or reward than our differences or what divides us as members of racially distinct groups.

4. The expression *media gaze* refers to the distinctive way in which media represent reality. Reality is framed by media in ways that reflect and reinforce media interests and priorities as natural and normal, while other perspectives (gazes) are deemed to be irrelevant or inferior. Just as a male gaze reflects an androcentric view of reality (and a female gaze a gynocentric perspective), so too does a media gaze embrace and impose a *mediacentric* vision of the world out there (Fleras 2003).

5. Christine Welsh has written and directed films for 30 years, is an associate professor at the University of Victoria, and teaches courses in indigenous women's studies and indigenous cinema.

6. The uprising of the indigenous and metizo peasants of the Chiapas in their resistance against the Mexican government constitutes one example of an indigenous cyber-campaign against the new geopolitical order, thus reinforcing the Web's potential for local empowerment (Belausteguigoitia 2006).

References

Abel, Sue. 1997. *Shaping the News: Waitangi Day on Television*. Auckland: Auckland University Press.

Alia, Valerie. 2010. *The New Media Nation: Indigenous Peoples and Global Communication*. New York: Bergahan Books.

Avison, Shannon, and Michael Meadows. 2000. 'Speaking and hearing: Aboriginal newspapers and the public sphere in Canada and Australia'. *Canadian Journal of Communication* 25 (3).

Baltrushchat, Doris. 2004. 'Television and Canada's Aboriginal communities'. *Canadian Journal of Communication* 29: 47–59.

Belausteguigoitia, Marisa. 2006. 'On line, off line and in line: The Zapatista rebellion and the uses of technology by Indian women'. In K. Landzelius, ed., *Native on the Net*, 97–111. New York: Routledge.

Berkhofer, Robert. 1978. *The White Man's Indian*. New York: Vintage Books.

Boykoff, Jules. 2006. 'Framing dissent: Mass-media coverage of the global justice movement'. *New Political Science* 28: (2).

Buddle, Kathleen. 2002. 'Shooting the messenger: Historical impediments to the mediation of modern Aboriginality in Ontario'. *Canadian Journal of Native Studies* 22 (1): 97–160.

———. 2005. 'Aboriginal cultural capital creation and radio production in urban Ontario'. *Canadian Journal of Communication* 30 (1): 1–37.

Buscombe, Edward. 2006. *'Injuns!' Native Americans in the Movies*. Bodmin Cornwall: Reaktion Books

Chan, Cindy. 2009. 'Telecom network boosts development, support among Aboriginals'. *Epoch Times* 15–21 January.

Cobb, Amanda J. 2003. 'This is what is means to say *smoke signals*'. In Peter C. Rollins and John E. Connor, *Hollywood's Indian: The Portrayal of the Native American in Film*, 206–28. Lexington: University of Kentucky Press.

Comstock, George, and Erica Scharrer. 2006. *The Psychology of Media and Politics*. New York: Routledge.

Corntassel, Jeff, and Richard C. Witmer. 2008. *Forced Federalism: Contemporary Challenges to Indigenous Nationhood*. Norman: University of Oklahoma Press.

Cottle, Simon, ed. 2000. *Ethnic Minorities and the Media*. Philadelphia and Buckingham, UK: Open University Press.

CRE (Commission for Racial Equality). 2004. 'Guidance for journalists'. www.cre.gov.uk/media/guidetj/html.

Curry, Bill. 2007. 'Forces terror manual lists Natives with Hezbollah'. *Globe and Mail* 31 March.

Darian-Smith, Kate. 2004. 'Filming indigenous Australia'. *The Otemon Journal of Australian Studies* 30: 264–70.

Editorial, *Christchurch Press*. 2006. 'The good, the bad, and the ugly: News reflects life'. 27 January.

Entman, Robert. 1993. 'Framing: Toward a clarification of a fractured paradigm'. *Journal of Communication* 43.

———. 2004. *Projections of Power: Framing News, Public Opinion, and U.S. Foreign Policy*. Chicago: University of Chicago Press.

Fiske, John. 1994. *Media Matters: Everyday Culture and Political Change*. Minneapolis: University of Minnesota Press.

Fleras, Augie. 2003. *Mass Media Communication in Canada*. Toronto: Nelson.

———. 2004a. *The Conventional News Paradigm as Systemic Bias: Rethinking the Misrepresentational Basis of Newsmedia–Minority Relations*. Paper presented to the Media,

Minorities, and Integration Conference at Siegen University, Germany. Proceedings published under Rainer Geissler and Horst Pottker.

———. 2004b. *Social Problems in Canada.* 4th edn. Toronto: Prentice Hall.

———. 2007a. *Newscasting as Systemic Propaganda.* Paper presented to the 20 Years of Propaganda Model at the University of Windsor, Ontario, 16 May.

———. 2007b. *Ethnic and Aboriginal Media in Canada.* Paper presented to the Media and Integration Conference at the University of Dortmund, Germany, 22 June.

———. 2009. *Unequal Relations: Race, Ethnic, and Aboriginal Relations in Canada.* 6th edn. Toronto: Prentice Hall.

Fleras, Augie, and Jean Lock Kunz. 2001. *Media and Minorities: Representing Diversity in a Multicultural Canada.* Toronto: Thompson Publishing.

Fleras, Augie, and Adie Nelson. In press. *Seeing Like the Media.* Vancouver: University of British Columbia Press.

Francis, D. 1992. *The Imaginary Indian: The Image of the Indian in Canadian Culture.* Vancouver: Arsenal Pulp Press.

Friar, Ralph, and Natasha Friar. 1972. *The Only Good Indian . . . The Hollywood Gospel.* New York: Drama Book Publishers.

Gallagher, Margaret. 2005. 'Who makes the news'. Global Media Monitoring Project. London: World Association for Christian Communication.

Geissler, Rainer, and Horst Pottker, eds. 2006. 'Mass media-integration. Media and migration: A comparative perspective'. Transcript. *Medienumbruche/Band* 17.

Gideon, Valerie. 2006. 'Canadian Aboriginal peoples tackle e-health: Seeking ownership versus integration'. In K. Landzelius, ed., *Native on the Net,* 61–79. New York: Routledge.

Gittings, Christopher. 1998. 'Imaging Canada: The singing Mountie and other commodifications of nation'. *Canadian Journal of Communication* 23 (4): 1–13

Graydon, Jody. 2008. 'Aboriginal representation in the media'. http://canadian-aboriginal-peoples.suite101.com.

Greenspon, Edward. 2003. 'What passes for the normal in news'. *Globe and Mail* 10 May.

Hall, Stuart. 1980. 'Encoding/decoding'. In S. Hall, et al., eds, *Culture, Media, Language.* London: Hutchinson.

Hall, Tony. 1995. 'Manufacturing Contempt'. *Canadian Forum* November: 6–7

Harding, Robert. 2005. 'The media, Aboriginal people, and common sense'. *Canadian Journal of Native Studies* 25 (1): 311–25

Henry, Frances, and Carol Tator. 2002. *Discourses of Domination: Racial Bias in the Canadian English-Language Press.* Toronto: University of Toronto Press.

———. 2003. 'Racial profiling in Toronto: Discourses of domination, mediation, and opposition'. Final draft submitted to the Canadian Race Relations Foundation, Toronto.

Herman, Edward, and Noam Chomsky. 1988. *Manufacturing Consent.* New York: Pantheon Books.

Herzberg, Bob. 2008. *Indians in Motion Pictures.* Jefferson, NC: McFarland.

Himpele, Jeff D. 2008. *Circuits of Culture.* Minneapolis: University of Minnesota Press.

Hodgetts, Darrin, et al. 2005. 'Maori media production, civic journalism and the foreshore and seabed controversy in Aotearoa'. *Pacific Journalism Review* 11 (2): 191–208.

Keller, James. 2006. 'Journalism at risk, Jean says'. *Toronto Star* 26 May.

Jiwani, Yasmin. 2006. *Discourses of Denial: Mediations on Race, Gender, and Violence*. Vancouver: University of British Columbia Press.

Knopf, Kerstin. 2008. 'Introduction'. In K. Knopf, ed., *Aboriginal Canada Revisited*, 1–28. Ottawa: University of Ottawa Press.

Lambertus, Sandra. 2004. *Wartime Images, Peacetime Wounds: The Media and Gustafsen Lake Standoff*. Toronto: University of Toronto Press.

Landzelius, Kyra. 2006. 'Introduction'. In K. Landzelius, ed., *Native on the Net*, 1–42. New York: Routledge.

Maaka, Roger, and Augie Fleras. 2005. *The Politics of Indigeneity: Perspectives from Canada and New Zealand*. Dunedin: Otago University Press.

McCreanor, Tim. 2006. '"Sticks and stones may break my bones . . .": Talking Pakeha Identities'. In J.H. Liu et al., eds, *New Zealand Identities*, 52–68. Wellington: Victoria University Press.

Macpherson, Cluny, and Paul Spoonley. 2004. 'Mediated ethnicity: Media and the management of ethnic images in Aotearoa'. In P. Spoonley et al., eds, *Tangata Tangata: The Changing Ethnic Contours of New Zealand*, 221–46. Southbank Victoria: Dunmore Thomson.

Marubbio, M. Elise. 2006. *Killing the Indian Maiden: Images of Native American Women in Film*. Lexington: University Press of Kentucky.

Meadows, Michael, and Helen Molnar. 2001. *Songlines to Satellites: Indigenous Communication in Australia, the South Pacific, and Canada*. Halifax: Fernwood.

Miller, John. 2005. *Ipperwash and the Media: A Critical Analysis of How the Story Was Covered*. Paper prepared for the Aboriginal Legal Foundation, Toronto.

————. 2006. 'Media coverage of Ipperwash affair biased, untrue'. *News and Events*, Ryerson University. www.ryerson.ca/news/media.

Mooney, Chris. 'Winning the frame game'. *Utne Reader* July/August: 78–80 (from *The American Prospect* April 2003).

Raudsepp, L. 1996. 'Emergent media: The Native press in Canada'. In S. Nancoo and R. Nancoo, eds, *Mass Media and Canadian Diversity*. Toronto: Canadian Education Services.

Razack, Sherene. 2002. *Race, Space, and the Law: Unmapping a White Settler Society*. Toronto: Between the Lines.

Retzlaff, Steffi. 2008. 'The Elders have said: Projecting Aboriginal cultural values in contemporary news discourse'. In K. Knopf, ed., *Aboriginal Canada Revisited*, 330–59. Ottawa: University of Ottawa Press.

Ricard, Danielle, and Rima Wilkes. 2008. 'Newspaper framing of protest by indigenous peoples and the construction of national identity'. www.allacademic.com.

Rollins, Peter C., and John E. O'Connor, eds. 2003. *Hollywood's Indians: The Portrayal of the Native American in Film*. Lexington: University of Kentucky Press.

Roth, Lorna. 2009. 'Canadian First Peoples' landscapes: A snapshot with three corners'. In L. Shade, ed., *Mediascapes: New Patterns in Canadian Communication*, 3rd edn. Toronto: Nelson.

Sauvageau, Florian, David Schneiderman, and David Taras. 2006. *The Last Word: Media Coverage of the Supreme Court of Canada*. Vancouver: University of British Columbia Press.

Schuck, Andreas, and Claes H. de Vresse. 2006. 'Between risk and opportunity: News framing and its effects on public support for EU enlargement'. *European Journal of Communication* 21 (1): 5–32

Shaheen, Jack. 2001. *Reel Bad Arabs*. New York: Interlink Publishing Group.

Spoonley, Paul. 2005. 'Print media representations of immigration and immigrants, 1993–2003'. In A. Trlin, P. Spoonley, and N. Watts, eds., *New Zealand and International Migration: A Digest and Bibliography*, no. 4, 86–106. Palmerston North, NZ: Massey University.

Spoonley, Paul, and Andrew Trlin. 2004. *Immigration, Immigrants, and the Media: Making Sense of Multicultural New Zealand*. Palmerston North, NZ: New Settlers Programme, Massey University.

Tahmahkera, Dustin. 2008. 'Custer's last sitcom'. *American Indian Quarterly* 32 (3): 309–33

Task Force. 2004. *Cultural Diversity in Television*. Toronto: Solutions Research Group.

ter Wal, Jessika, Leen d'Haenans, and Joyce Koeman. 2005. '(Re)presentation of ethnicity in EU and Dutch domestic views: A quantitive analysis'. *Media, Culture, and Society* 27 (6): 937–50.

Turiana, Tania. 2008. 'Framing Maori: To do a Waitangi'. Speech, the Maori Party, 31 October. www.scoop.co.nz.

Weston, Mary Ann. 2003. 'Journalists and Indians: The clash of cultures'. Keynote speech on Symposium on American Indian Issues in the California Press, 21 February. www.bluecorncomics.com/weston.htm.

Wood, Huston. 2008. *Native Features: Indigenous Films from around the World*. New York: Continuum International Publishing Group.

9 First Nations Women in Canada

Cora J. Voyageur

Indian people must wake up! They are asleep! We were in touch but now we are not. Part of this waking up means replacing women to their rightful place in society. It's been less than one hundred years that men lost touch with reality. There's no power or medicine that has all force unless it's balanced. The woman must be there also, but she has been left out! When we still had our culture, we had the balance. The women made ceremonies, and she was recognized as being united with the moon, the earth and all the forces on it. Men have taken over. Most feel threatened by holy women. They must stop and remember, remember the loving power of their grandmothers and mothers![1]

The late Rose Auger, Cree Elder, Alberta

Wake up! This statement has been repeated by First Nations[2] women across Canada. They have been trying to get the attention of First Nations men, their chiefs and band councillors, the federal government, and mainstream society. They want to create awareness of, and subsequently change, the circumstances of Indian women in Canada. According to a Feminist Alliance for International Action report submitted to the United Nations, indigenous[3] women in Canada rank among the most severely disadvantaged groups in Canadian society (2008, 2).

Life has not been easy for First Nations women in Canada. Gender bias in the First Nations community and in Canadian legislation has a long history. Since Europeans contact, First Nations people, and most specifically First Nations women, have been placed in a precarious and subordinate situation by governments, both foreign and domestic.

In the more than 500 years since the 'Indians' discovered Columbus, the traditional role and status of First Nations women has changed dramatically. Even so, and despite all the changes endured by First Nations people, many aspects of the traditional indigenous women's role have remained constant. Indigenous women are still responsible for maintaining culture, stabilizing the community, and caring for future generations. Today, First Nations women have many of the concerns shared by women in general—concerns about children, family, economics, employment, and political rights. However, unlike mainstream Canadian women, they must also contend with the restrictive policies of the Indian Act, which governs many aspects of their lives.

The yoke of oppression had been lifted off the First Nations people[4] when some of the harshest policies governing them were removed with the 1951 Indian Act amendments. Policy changes allowed First Nations people to begin practising their traditional potlatch and the sundance ceremonies once again. They were also allowed to wear their traditional 'costume' at public dances, exhibitions, and stampedes. First Nations people could hire lawyers and bring legal proceedings against the government—a practice banned since 1927 (Venne 1981). In addition, 1951 saw First Nations women participate in band politics for the first time. They could vote in band elections and run for the elected offices of chief or councillor (Voyageur 2008).

First Nations women have had a tough battle in their pursuit of social and political equality. They have had many adversaries: government, mainstream society, and at times their own people. Sociologist Linda Gerber calls the situation of First Nations women 'multiple jeopardy'. She states:

> Native females suffer multiple jeopardy on the basis of a number of objective indicators of social and economic wellbeing. The fact that Indians as a group are disadvantaged and Indian females in particular suffer the greatest disadvantage suggests that Indian status, with its historical trappings of colonial dependency, does indeed create additional barriers to economic and social health. The position of Indian women with respect to labour force participation and income suggests that they are the most severely handicapped in their exchange relations with employers (1990, 72).

This multiple jeopardy manifests itself in ways that make First Nations women's lives more difficult. For example, in the economic realm, First Nations women generally hold fewer jobs and have a lower life expectancy. A Statistics Canada report entitled *Aboriginal Women in Canada* showed that Aboriginal women constituted 47 per cent of the Aboriginal labour force compared to 56 per cent for non-Aboriginal women (O'Donnell 2006, 198). The study also found that the life expectancy of Aboriginal women was about five years shorter than that of non-Aboriginal women (2006, 190).

This chapter examines the roles and concerns of First Nations women in contemporary Canadian society. It argues that specific events such as the creation of the Indian Act in 1876 and the passing of Bill C-31 in 1985 have greatly affected First Nations women.[5] To fully understand the present social, political, and economic position of First Nations women in Canada, one must first look at it in a historical context. It is certain that past events have laid the foundation for the current situation.

Regaining First Nations Women's Voice

Since the early 1970s, Indian women have organized and found their own political voice. Previously, Indian women had their voices appropriated by others and thus were essentially silenced. Their concerns and needs were determined and articulated by their husbands or fathers or by missionaries and government agents. This has changed; First Nations women no longer rely on the government or male-dominated political organizations to determine their fate. They are speaking for themselves collectively for the first time since European contact. Kenneth Lincoln, author of *Native American Renaissance*, refers to this articulation as a 'rebirth' (Tsosie 1988, 2).

The tenacity and relentless efforts of First Nations women like Sandra Lovelace, Jeanette Corbiere-Lavell, Yvonne Bedard, and the late Jenny Margetts have won them recognition as worthy adversaries. However, this political activity also brought them scorn and resentment. Nellie Carlson, an activist who worked alongside Margetts in Indian Rights for Indian Women, said that for 16 years the group lobbied the federal government to change the sections of the Indian Act that discriminated against women. Carlson recalled:

> This group of determined Indian women was not dissuaded when during a meeting the then Prime Minister Pierre Trudeau, told us, 'Go to [your] leaders. They will help you make the changes.' To this remark, we retorted, 'This legislation came from this building. What good can our leaders do about something that the government created? You must help us change it.'[6]

The women's persistence paid off when Bill C-31 amended the Indian Act on 17 April 1985. Bill C-31 attempted to eliminate the sex discrimination in the Indian Act by reinstating Indian status to women who had married non-Indian men and to others who had lost their Indian status for a variety of reasons. The Bill also stated that Indian status could not be gained or lost through marriage.

It was a long struggle for First Nations women to tell their own story. They have emerged from purely domestic roles to share in the rebuilding of their communities. For example, movement from the private realm into the public sphere is evident in the recent phenomenon of women being elected as chiefs. Women chiefs now lead more than 100 of Canada's 633 First Nations communities in Canada. The number of elected female chiefs has more than doubled in the past 15 years.[7]

First Nations women's concerns for community improvement has made them tireless workers and enduring advocates. In recent years, they have tackled such issues as matrimonial property issues and violence against indigenous women.[8] However, First Nations women still encounter many obstacles in their pursuit of a better community.

First Nations women must contend with many archaic notions that date as far back as first contact with Europeans. Racism and stereotyping of indigenous women illustrate this. First Nations scholar Janice Acoose speaks of the myth of indigenous women in the bifurcated role of either 'Pocahontas' or the 'Squaw' as illustrated in a series of Hollywood movies (1995, 2). Although some of these portrayals have diminished over time, the legacy of past attitudes is still being felt by indigenous women today.

Subordination of Indigenous Women

Many factors led to the lower social, economic, and political situation experienced by most First Nations women. These factors include the European hegemonic view of the New World, the historical unimportance of women in European society, the subjugation of indigenous people, ethnographic practices that misinterpreted or ignored women's issues, and the adoption of European values and governing systems by First Nations men in the community.

European Superiority

With colonization, the Europeans brought with them established opinions of cultural, intellectual, and structural[9] supremacy over those encountered in the new land. European ideology rested on the assumption that their civilization was superior to all others and involved the self-imposed burden of 'civilizing the barbarians'.[10] The European stance was simple: Indians were savages; women were socially and politically invisible; individualism and patriarchy[11] prevailed. These attitudes lay behind the Europeans' attempt to 'fix' whatever they viewed as unacceptable social conditions in the New World. They also guided the men who took it upon themselves to record and write history. Europeans viewed men, the holders of power and privilege, as the creators of civilization: analytical, logical, and inherently superior to women (Chalus 1990, 32).

Patriarchy: The Rule of the Father

History was, and some may argue still is, a man's world. Men were viewed as significant to the course of history. In public affairs, women were invisible, viewed as chattels owned by men. They were not given political or social rights. Thus, European women had little or no political or economic power.

European men set standards for women's decorum, which stated how a cultured woman should conduct herself. Restraint, modesty, submission, compliance, and piety all combined in the creation of a gender role for women (Chalus 1990, 38). Women were seen as psychologically unstable, physically fragile, and morally susceptible. It is not surprising that these attitudes and standards were transported to the New World and imposed upon indigenous women by European men.

Prior to colonization, women were a strong force in indigenous society.[12] Legal scholar Robert Williams states that in a number of North American Indian tribes, women traditionally selected male chiefs as political leaders and could also remove them (1990, 1034). Also, in many tribes, women owned substantial property interests, including the marital home, and exercised exclusive dominion over the means of production and the products of major subsistence activities such as farming (Williams 1990, 1034). Women in many tribes held the power to initiate or call off war.

The Iroquois Confederacy operated on a matriarchal system prior to the arrival of the Europeans (Native Women's Association of Canada 1991). This system was based on the concepts of equality between the genders. Iroquois women played a profound role in the political and economic life of the community. They also traditionally played important roles in their communities as nurturers, educators, and providers.

The Manipulation of History by the Literate

In Western society, the written word had long been considered the 'true medium' of historical accuracy, with oral history viewed as primitive, biased, and unreliable. As a result, history was left to the discretion of the literate and those with the ability and opportunity to write—whatever their agenda, philosophy, or predisposition.

Early accounts of the position of First Nations women in their cultures were written by male European fur traders and missionaries. These early accounts tell us as much about the ideological perspectives of the authors as they do about the subject at hand. Explorers and traders were part of the patriarchal and hierarchical structure that dominated women. As a result, they did not acknowledge the contributions made by First Nations women to everyday life. Patricia Albers writes that journalistic accounts ignore or trivialize women's activities and experiences by dealing with and writing about Indian men (Albers and Medicine 1983, 3). Much of the early literature on indigenous women was contradicted by what was discovered later. The early ethnographic record supplies ample evidence of a variety of roles for indigenous women. For example, anthropologist Judith Brown states that older women in the Wabanaki, Algonquin, Delaware, Powhatan, and Iroquois tribes had authority over kinsmen and had the right to exert power over them and extract labour (Brown 1982, 144). Females in the Wabanaki tribe achieved positions of leadership in both religious and political spheres when they reached middle age (Ezzo 1988, 141). Despite evidence from some early descriptions of women's authority, it is clear that reporting of Indian activities has often been based on purely ethnocentric interpretations. Anthropologist Alice Kehoe states that at the turn of the century, ethnographers were frustrated in their quest for data by the traditions of their discipline (1983, 53). However, because they viewed Indians as a 'dying breed', it became important that details of Indian life be collected for posterity. As a result, there was a big push for ethnographic information related to Indians. One example was work of Edward Sheriff Curtis and Ernest Brown, who amassed large portfolios of photographs of the indigenous people of the Canadian and American West in the nineteenth century.

Encounters between recorder and subject were limited in duration, frequency, and understanding. The resulting data were sometimes inaccurate and contained both gender and ethnocentric biases. For example, one such misinterpretation is the common explanation for a woman walking behind her husband. The assumption that it reflects the female's inferior status clouds the real reason: that it is the man's responsibility to protect his wife because she is the giver of life and more powerful than he.

Data collection was guided by conventions that did not allow for accurate depictions of either the role or the contributions of First Nations women. Ingrained biases were prevalent in all aspects of information-gathering. One reason was that anthropologists were predominantly male. Their scholarly custom was to speak exclusively to male subjects (Kehoe 1983, 54). Common practice dictated that the ethnographer and his male assistant interview a limited number of middle-aged and elderly men about life in the community. If and when indigenous women were interviewed, the situation was uncomfortable for the women, who were accustomed to being put down by European men. In addition, it was culturally inappropriate for indigenous women to discuss 'women's roles and practices' with men (Kehoe 1983, 54).

The hegemonic ideals of European traders and missionaries supplanted the indigenous perspective on women. In contrast to what was written about indigenous women in the historical record, indigenous customs held women in high regard; they were powerful, respected, and valuable within their communities.

Eliminating the People of the Terra Nullius

One of the primary reasons for the situation of First Nations women today is that First Nations people, in general, are subjugated by the immigrant European society. The subjugation is based on the myth of the 'savage Indian' who did not own land. Europeans viewed the land in the New World as Terra Nullius, or vacant land, and thus the land was free for the taking (Cumming and Mickenberg 1972, 18).

Missionary ideology and government policy held that the only way for First Nations to survive was to give up everything that defined them as a people: religion, language, lifestyle, and identity. For example, the residential school was created to convert the children from 'savages' to 'civilized' citizens for the betterment of the Indian and society as a whole (Voyageur 1993, 2). It was generally assumed that all First Nations people aspired to citizenship and would eventually embrace modernity.

Duncan Campbell Scott, assistant deputy superintendent of Indian Affairs, implemented an assimilation policy to rid Canadians and the government of the 'Indian Problem'. The Parliamentary Subcommittee on Indian Women and the Indian Act (1982) noted that:

> Between 1913 and 1930 the administration of Indian Affairs followed a rigid policy of forced assimilation. Traditional practises such as the Sundance and the Potlatch were prohibited and traditional languages were suppressed. Duncan Campbell Scott in explaining the rationale for changes to the legislation in 1920 said 'Our object is to continue until there is not a single Indian in Canada that has not been absorbed into the body politic. This is the whole object of this Bill' (McDonald 1987, 30).

The elimination of the Indian would occur through education and religious training in European customs and values. Separate legal Indian status was conceived as a stopgap measure by white legislators, who expected that Indians would gradually abandon their Native identity in order to enjoy the privilege of full Canadian citizenship—a state to which all would and should aspire (Francis 1993, 201).

When Indians met the minimal requirements for citizenship—literacy, education, and 'acceptable' moral character—they were allowed the rights of full citizenship through voluntary enfranchisement.[13] With citizenship came the ability to vote, to purchase alcohol, and to obtain land under the homestead system and no further requirement that they live under the aegis of the repressive Indian Act. It is ironic that enfranchisement, the right of full citizenship in Canadian society, was used as both a reward and a punishment for First Nations people. It was a reward for those who obtained a university degree, joined the military, or became a minister. But enfranchisement was a punishment for anyone who was caught in possession of alcohol or raised the ire of the Indian agent, who had the discretion to delete anybody from the band list for any reason.

The Yoke of Oppression: The Indian Act

The British North America Act of 1867, section 91(24) gave the power of legislative control over Indians and their lands to the federal government. Thus empowered, the Canadian Parliament began drafting provisions for what was to become the Indian Act. The Indian Act was, and perhaps still is, the most oppressive legislation in Canadian history. Prior to the Indian Act, the statutory definition of Indians was all persons of Indian blood, their spouses, and their descendants. This definition was to be applied to determine the right to possess or occupy lands. However, in 1869 the government passed the Gradual Enfranchisement Act,[14] which determined the scope of the government's responsibilities to those with whom it had entered into the treaty process and made a deliberate attempt to reduce the number of First Nations people for whom the government would be responsible.

The first Indian Act to bear the official title The Indian Act was passed in 1876. This Act redefined Indian as:

Firstly: any male person of Indian blood reputed to belong to a particular band;
    Secondly: any child of such person;
    Thirdly: any women who is or was lawfully married to such a person (Paul 1993, 19).

The Indian Act encompasses virtually every aspect of Indian life. It is primarily social legislation, but it has a broad scope, with provisions for liquor control, agriculture, education, bylaws, mining, Indian lands, and band membership (Paul 1993, 13).

Impact of Legislation on First Nations Women

The measure of depriving an Indian woman of her status when she married a non-Indian was first legislated in the 1869 Act for the Gradual Enfranchisement of Indians. This Act was also the first legislation that officially discriminated against Indian women by assigning them fewer fundamental rights than Indian men had. Section 6 stated: 'Provided always that any Indian woman marrying any other than an Indian shall cease to be an Indian within the meaning of this Act, nor shall the children issue of such marriage be considered as Indians within the meaning of this Act' (S.C. 1869, C6).

Gender-based, discriminatory provisions within the Indian Act limited Indian women's social and political rights and placed them in a subordinate position to men. This lesser position contributed to culture changes in many Indian tribes that had previously acknowledged the political power of the women. For example, the treaty process required that 'official' representatives be elected. This practice banned women from local and national politics. Thus, men were legally given more political power than they possessed under traditional politics.

Until 1951, the Indian Act denied First Nations women the right to vote in band elections, to hold elected office, and to participate in public meetings that decided band business (Voyageur 2008, xvi). The few administrative and political decisions allowed to First Nations people by the Indian Act were to be made by the men. Thus, First Nations women's traditional social and political powers were transferred to First Nations men.

The 1876 Indian Act determined legal status by patrilineal affiliation. First Nations women were not legal entities and had virtually no rights. The political status accorded them was that of a chattel of their husband, much like the political status accorded to European women in their patriarchal society. If an Indian man was enfranchised, then his wife and minor children were automatically enfranchised. At the time, Euro-Canadians thought that enfranchisement as British subjects was the most desirable goal for Indians to attain.

If an Indian woman married an Indian man from another reserve, then she became a member of her husband's band. The Act stated that a woman must follow her husband, so if her husband died or she divorced him, she could not return to her reserve. Other provisions stated that upon the death of an Indian man, his estate passed to his children, not to his wife.

The most troublesome portion of the Indian Act for women was Section 12(1) (b), which further illustrated the male bias in the Act. It pertained specifically to Indian woman losing their status by marrying a non-Indian man:

12. (1) The following persons are not entitled to be registered, namely . . .
    (b) a woman who married a person who is not an Indian, unless that women is subsequently the wife or widow of a person described in Section 11[15] (Jamieson 1978, 8).

If an Indian woman married a non-Indian man, she then became a non-Indian in the eyes of the government: she became one with her husband, who became in effect her owner under the patriarchal legislation. She was stripped of her Indian identity and not permitted to live on the reserve with her extended family or be buried there after her death. Many Indian women who married non-Indian men had no idea that they had lost their Indian status until they attempted to return to their reserves following the break-up of their marriages.

What made this section so discriminatory was that if an Indian man married a non-Indian woman, he did not lose his status. To add insult to injury, a non-Indian woman who married an Indian man became an Indian in the eyes of the law, was given band membership, and was able to live on the reserve. Non-Indian women did not lose their newfound Indian status when they were divorced or widowed; they and their children maintained band membership.

Under the Indian Act, Indian women lost their independence, were not legal entities unto themselves, and had no legal recourse to remedy the situation.

The Beginning of Change

Initial change to the restrictive legislation that governed First Nations people in Canada began after World War II. First Nations soldiers, although exempt from military duty by treaty, fought for Canada and made valuable contributions to the Canadian war effort both at home and on the battlefront (Sheffield 2005). However, upon returning home they were relegated to the subordinate social position in Canadian society they had occupied prior to leaving for war.

Legislative Changes

The 1960s brought a number of legislative changes that greatly affected the political position of First Nations people. As political organizations formed, they fought for and achieved many needed changes. And as demands for Aboriginal and treaty rights grew, so too did demands for equality by First Nations women.

The discriminatory treatment of First Nations women was chipped away by a number of legislative changes. The most significant were the Bill of Rights in 1960, the Charter of Rights and Freedoms in 1982, and Bill C-31 in 1985.

The Bill of Rights

The Bill of Rights was enacted by the federal government in 1960. Unlike the Bill of Rights in the United States, which was added almost immediately to its Constitution, Canada's Constitution Act of 1867 did not include any such statement. It was not until after World War II that Canada, like most developed countries, saw the need to protect civil liberties (Hogg 1992, 779). Section 1 of the Bill of Rights guaranteed equality to all under the law regardless of race or sex. Section 2 stated that any federal statutes or regulations that infringed any of the rights listed in the bill would be brought to Parliament's attention. However, there was a legal debate about the effect of this provision: Did section 2 render the infringing laws null and void, or was it merely to be used as a guide? This notion was not settled until *R. v. Drybones.*

Court challenges dealing with a variety of issues contributed to amendments to the Indian Act. The first important Indian case to challenge the Bill of Rights was the *Drybones* case in 1969.

Drybones was an Indian man charged with possession of alcohol. Under the Indian Act, Indians were not permitted to possess alcohol (Hogg 1992, 669). Since this rule did not apply to non-Indians, the basis for the legal argument was that the law discriminated against Indians. It was successfully argued that Indians and non-Indians were not treated equally under the law. Furthermore, the case gave the Supreme Court of Canada an opportunity to determine the effect of section 2 of the Bill of Rights. The Court held that any federal law that infringed on the Bill of Rights would be inoperative. Thus, section 2 was more than a guide.

The Lavell and Bedard case ([1973] S.C.R. 1349) dealt more specifically with Indian women. These were the first cases to attempt to win recognition as 'full persons' for Indian women, with the same rights and status as Indian men. Jeanette Corbiere-Lavell was an Ojibway woman who had lost her status after marrying a non-Indian man. She challenged the band administration's decision to strike her name from the band list. Yvonne Bedard, a Six Nations woman, tried to return to her reserve to live in a house that was left to her in her mother's will. Because she had married a non-Indian, her name was taken off the band list, and she and her children were ordered to leave the reserve (Atcheson 1984, 12).

Lavell and Bedard argued that section 12(1) (b) of the Indian Act discriminated on the basis of sex, which contravened the Canadian Bill of Rights. The two cases were heard together before the Supreme Court of Canada, which affirmed the validity of section 12(1) (b). The decision stated that the Canadian Bill of Rights meant equality only in the administration and enforcement of the law. The actual substance of the law could discriminate between men and women as long as the law was applied by its administrator in an even-handed way (Atcheson 1984, 12). Thus, the Supreme Court of Canada backtracked from the *Drybones* case by refusing to declare a discriminatory section of the Indian Act inoperative.

The Lovelace case of 1981 was another important case to challenge section 12(1) (b) of the Indian Act. Sandra Lovelace, a Maliseet woman, lost her status and band membership when she married a non-Indian man. She took the Canadian government to an international court, the United Nations Committee on Human Rights, because her rights as an Indian women were denied by section 12(1) (b) (Stacey-Moore 1993, 22). She won her case and brought international shame to the Canadian government. The Human Rights Committee found the government of Canada in breach of the International Covenant on Civil and Political Rights to Freedom from Sexual Discrimination (Silman 1987, 251). However, the government of Canada delayed amending this discriminatory legislation for four years. Meanwhile, other Indian women's groups were lobbying the government, national Native organizations, and local band administrations to deal with their concerns. For example, 200 Tobique women and children marched from their New Brunswick reserve to Ottawa, a seven-day trek, to protest housing conditions (Silman 1987, 149).

The Constitution and the Charter of Rights and Freedoms

The Bill of Rights lost most of its significance with the adoption of the Charter of Rights and Freedoms in 1982 as part of the Canadian Constitution Act, which ended the United Kingdom's imperial authority over Canada. The Charter protects certain fundamental rights and freedoms, one which is equality before the law. Indian organizations had to do some vigorous lobbying in the Canadian Parliament to have Aboriginal and treaty rights entrenched in the Constitution and put an end to the paternalistic attitude of the Canadian government.

Section 15(1) of the Charter of Rights and Freedoms states: 'Every individual is equal before and under the law and has the right to the equal protection and equal benefit of the law without discrimination and, in particular, without discrimination based on race, national or ethnic origin, religion, sex, age or mental or physical ability.' In addition, section 28 states: 'Notwithstanding anything in this Charter, the rights and freedoms referred to in it are guaranteed equally to male and female persons.'

Although both sections state that discrimination on the basis of sex and race would contravene the Charter of Rights and Freedoms, the Indian Act continued to do exactly that. It was not until three years later that the discriminatory provisions of the Indian Act would be amended.

Although section 35 of the Charter guarantees Aboriginal and treaty rights to Indian people and section 27 states that these rights apply equally to men and women, women were not assured by governments or their male leaders that they would speak to their concerns. As the Native Women's Association of Canada wrote about the process of entrenching Aboriginal rights in the Constitution: 'These arrangements are required to provide an arrangement that gives Native women and their children a destiny that they can participate in full and direct themselves' (Stacey-Moore 1993, 21).

The entrenchment of Aboriginal and treaty rights in the Charter of Rights was a major step toward ensuring the rights of indigenous women and would assist in fighting against gender-based discrimination.

Bill C-31

Bill C-31 came into effect on 17 April 1985 to rectify the infamous section 12(1)(b) of the Indian Act. Bill C-31 was also meant to restore Indian status to people who had been enfranchised. Some have argued that Bill C-31 is an Indian issue rather than solely an Indian women's issue, since enfranchisement occurred for a number of reasons: obtaining a university degree, joining the military or the clergy, or voluntary enfranchisement (Voyageur 2008). However, it is rightly seen as primarily a women's issue because women were the most affected in that they lost their status on marrying non-Indian men. Joan Holmes, researcher for the Canadian Advisory Council on the Status of Women, states that 12,305 of 16,980 losses of status, or 72.5 per cent, involved women who had married non-Indians (1987, 9). A United Nations Human Rights Committee report states that in Canada during the period 1965 to 1978, there were 510 marriages between Indian women and non-Indian men and 448 marriages between Indian men and non-Indian women (McDonald 1987, 28). However, only the Indian women who married non-Indian men lost their Indian status.

The Indian Act requires that Indians be registered on a central registry and that applicants apply for Indian status to the registrar. Bill C-31 states that those eligible to be registered as status Indians include:

(i)   women who lost status as result of marriage to non-status men;
(ii) individuals who lost status or were denied status through other discriminatory provisions of the Indian Act;
(iii) individuals who lost status through enfranchisement, a process that existed in the old Act whereby a person could voluntarily give up status; and
(iv) children of persons in any of the above categories (Paul 1993, 6).

In addition, Bill C-31 gave individual bands the authority to determine their own band membership. In other words, only First Nations governments should be able to decide who their members are and what their rights and responsibilities are to those members. This is where much of the present-day contention lies.

Although Bill C-31 was meant to rectify the past injustices of the Indian Act, it appears to have created new problems. For example, the law allows for a separation of status[16] and band membership.[17] The federal government determines status, while the individual First Nations administration (chief and council in most cases) determines band membership. Band councils, made up primarily of men, determine whether Indian women who married out can regain band membership.

Therefore, Bill C-31 has created new problems by stratifying Indian status into three possible scenarios: Indian status (determined by Indian Affairs in Ottawa), band membership (determined by chief and council), and both status and band membership (chief and council accept Indian Affairs' decision to confer Indian status to an individual and subsequently confer band membership).

First Nations Women's Concerns

Anthropologist Joanne Fiske studied the link between political and social life on a British Columbia First Nations reserve. She writes that First Nations women's domestic responsibilities are undifferentiated from community obligations (1990–1, 127): women are expected to share their surplus food, assist young people, and intervene in domestic disputes in an effort to restore harmony. Fiske concludes that First Nations women could not fulfil their domestic goals without political action (1990–1, 136).

The First Nations world is a political world, and there is no getting around that. As Karen Ilinik states, 'If you don't want to get involved, you really have to work at it' (1990, 37). Women of the New Brunswick Tobique reserve took some radical steps to improve their economic and political situation. They were desperate for housing, many of them finding themselves and their children out on the street with no place to go. Some women had been kicked out of their homes by their husbands.[18] Since the Indian Act gave men sole ownership of the family home through certificates of possession, their wives had no housing rights and no legal recourse (Silman 1987, 11). They took action by marching to Ottawa in 1979 to protest their situation. Indian women found themselves at the mercy of their husbands, the chief and council, and the federal government. Many factors brought about male domination in the First Nations community.[19]

Adoption of European Values

There is a discrepancy between the traditional respect accorded to First Nations women and the reality of gender tensions within the community (Fiske 1990–1, 130). In a submission to the Indian Circle on the Constitution, Mary Stanaicia speaks to the adoption of non-traditional leadership principles by Indians:

> The Indian Act imposed upon us a patriarchal system and laws which favoured men. By 1971, this patriarchal system was so ingrained the 'patriarchy' was seen as a 'traditional trait'. Even the memory of our matriarchal forms of government and descent was forgotten or unacknowledged. How can our Aboriginal leaders argue a case for traditional laws and customs when they continue to exclude women? Recognizing the inherent right to self-government does not mean recognizing and blessing the patriarchy created in our communities by foreign governments (Canada 1992, 34).

It would appear that First Nations men have adopted the attitude that First Nations women are dispensable. This probably stemmed from the indoctrination process in residential schools, the practices legislated by the Indian Act, and Euro-Canadian control of the socialization process of society in general. A submission to the First Nations Circle on the Constitution echoes the impact of the Indian Act on Indian government:

> Contrary to our traditional systems, the Indian Act system provides a political voice only to elected chiefs and councillors, normally residents on reserve and usually male. The Indian Act silences the voice of the Elders, women, and youth. We believe that true Aboriginal government must reflect the values on which our traditional governments were based (Canada 1992, 34).

First Nations leaders—that is First Nations men—must loosen their grip on the power given to them by the Department of Indian Affairs and other government departments. They must remember that they are in their positions to serve the people—which includes women. Men must be re-educated about the nature of their responsibilities in our efforts to abolish the subjugation of women in our communities (Monture-Okanee 1992, 260). First Nations women have suffered from the lack of respect and validity shown to them by those who were traditionally their protectors.

Community Conflict over Legislative Change

Another reason for the contemporary situation is the conflict raised in the communities over the legislative changes described above. Challenges by First Nations women to the non-status issue were attacked by the male-dominated First Nations political organizations, the largest being the National Indian Brotherhood (which later became the Assembly of First Nations, or AFN). They feared that if the Indian Act was struck down on the basis of discrimination, then all First Nations people might lose certain rights under the Indian Act. They also felt that the Indian Act should be kept intact for use as a bargaining tool with the federal government (Paul 1993, 31). The National Indian Brotherhood and other organizations lobbied the government to allow bands to deny women their full status. They wanted the authority to determine band membership. Noel Starblanket, then president of the National Indian Brotherhood, stated:

> The Canadian Government cannot change one section of the Indian Act without looking at the effect those changes will have on the Indian people of our communities. We feel the wrong being done to Indian women and their offspring cannot be undone by imposing further hardship on the rest of Indian people (Paul 1993, 31).

There was a general fear that the success of any equality argument would undermine the Indian Act's special protections and the White Paper's policy[20] could succeed through court decisions, even though it had been defeated politically. Chiefs and councillors were primarily concerned about the long-range cultural and economic impact in their community (Opekokiw 1986, 16).

There has been much conflict between the Bill C-31 First Nations people (those who regained their status under the Bill's provisions) and other band members over the distribution of already scarce resources. Conflict over housing is one example (Silman 1987, 11). Reserves usually have a long waiting list for housing, and the people already on the waiting list for housing began to resent the perceived 'special status' given to new Indians who wanted to move back to the reserve (Paul 1993, 68). Some believed that Bill C-31 Indians did not have to wait as long for housing or were placed at the top of the waiting list.

Some bands did not give band membership to people given status by the federal government because they did not have the desire, the resources, or the land base to do so. Most reserves were already overcrowded, and many felt that the conditions would only worsen if numerous reinstated Indians returned to the reserve. Pamela Paul, in her study of the impact of Bill C-31 on First Nations people, found that many reinstated people were not interested in returning to the reserve because they were established off the reserve and the reserve had nothing to offer them as far as housing or employment was concerned (Paul 1993, 108). They said that they were more interested in health and education benefits than in actually moving to the reserve (Paul 1993, 108).

There is a great deal of tension and conflict between reinstated members and band councils. In some cases, such as the Sawridge Band in Alberta, discriminatory practices have continued because the band implemented a rigorous and prying membership code so that few, if any, would qualify for membership.

First Nations women have not been welcomed back with open arms and warm hearts, which is the normal Native custom. Patriarchy cannot be solely blamed for this situation. Rather, it can be viewed more as an economic guarding of scarce resources by the band. However, continued discrimination by band administrations has left many First Nations women sceptical about whether male-dominated organizations and band councils are willing to ensure their political rights.

The reinstated Indians are referred to as 'C-31s' and sometimes scornfully called 'paper Indians' or 'new Indians' (Paul 1993, 94). Bill C-31 has further divided the First Nations community while giving rise to a negative attitude toward reinstated members. It seems that C-31s are being blamed for creating or exacerbating social problems on the reserves. One band administrator stated that the influx of C-31s was bringing about a change in the culture, a new set of ideas in the community. He also blamed them for increased drug, alcohol, and child abuse problems and even for a decrease in church attendance[21] (Paul 1993, 97). But this band administrator ignores the fact that First Nations culture is less likely to be retained if non–First Nations women become the mothers of their children. According to Kathleen Jamieson, a researcher for the Canadian Advisory Council on the Status of Women/Indian Rights for Indian Women from 1965 to 1976, the ratio of First Nations men marrying non–First Nations women was 0.8:1 (1978, 66). These data show a 136 per cent increase in First Nations men marrying non–First Nations women between 1965 and 1976.[22] It is sad that First Nations men feel obliged to protect their non–First Nations wives' newly found Indian status at the expense of alienating their own mothers, sisters, cousins, aunts, and grandmothers.

The fear of the influx of reinstated Indians to reserves has been unfounded to date. Gail Stacey-Moore, spokesperson for the Native Women's Association of Canada, states that of the 70,000 reinstated Indians, only 1400 (2 per cent) have moved back to the reserve (1993, 22).

Inequality

A third factor facing First Nations women is political inequality. Most of the elected leaders in the First Nations community are male. Although many leaders in the First Nations community were male in the past, women's input was sought in decision-making. This practice stopped when Indian agents and other Indian Affairs officials chose to deal exclusively with men. Today, locally elected individuals serve as intermediaries between the Indian and Northern Affairs Canada (INAC) and the people. INAC makes all the important and fiscal decisions. Sometimes the band is informed and consulted, and sometimes it is not. The band administration simply carries out initiatives given them by the department.

The chief and council allocate the scarce resources to band members. They determine which band members receive limited band employment opportunities, education funding, occupational training, housing, housing repairs, and other band-administered services (Voyageur 2008). This power, however limited, has a great impact on the day-to-day lives of band members. In some respects, the chief and council have taken over the powerful role of the Indian agent as intermediary between the government and the people. It is therefore in the best interest of band members to retain the favour of the allocaters.

Although women make up approximately 50 per cent of the Aboriginal population, they do not make up 50 per cent of the elected leadership. However, the number of women chiefs is increasing across the country.[23] Even with the building of a critical mass of women among elected leadership, there is no guarantee that women's concerns, such as child care, housing, education, family violence, and social programs, will be heard and acted upon. A high percentage of First Nations women are single parents. According to Statistics Canada, approximately one-third of First Nations children under the age of 15 live with a lone parent, the vast majority of whom are women (Statistics Canada 2008), which may lessen their influence with the male-dominated council. Single mothers may have less political influence in the community or less time to deal with community issues. If a woman cannot muster political power, she may be disregarded.

However, more women hold decision-making positions in the reserve community. In the past, women would normally do the preparatory work and would then have to receive approval from a superior, usually a male. However, this situation has changed over time because more women than men have a post-secondary education and more are opting to work in higher levels of band administration.

Speaking for Themselves

First Nations women have taken the initiative to protect their own rights and interests, since the past has shown that First Nations men have not always acted in their best interests. Bold moves on the part of First Nations women have ruffled a few feathers in the community. For example, the Native Women's Association of Canada (NWAC) attempted to block the 1992 national referendum on the Constitution because they were excluded from constitutional negotiations. They charged that the consultation process used by male First Nations leaders infringed on their right to freedom of expression (Stacey-Moore 1993, 21). First Nations women demanded a seat at the constitutional table to ensure that their issues would be addressed and demanded a portion of the funds given to male-dominated political organizations.

This action pitted First Nations men against First Nations women. The Native Women's Association of Canada was accused of placing individual rights over the rights of the collective and of going against tradition. It is ironic that the men who made these accusations live under the untraditional Indian Act. Women were also pitted against women, because NWAC was seen as dividing the First Nations community and wiping out the image of a 'united front' under the Assembly of First Nations.

By speaking on their own behalf, First Nations women have pursued their priorities and concerns. For example, matrimonial property rights (MRPR) was pursued by the Native Women's Association of Canada after the Supreme Court of Canada ruled that MRPR did not apply on the reserve. NWAC refers to matrimonial real property as 'the house or land that a couple lives on or benefits from while they are married or in a common law relationship' (2007, 1). NWAC proposed solutions to the government to deal with the issue. Minister of Indian Affairs Chuck Strahl announced on 2 February 2009 that a Family Homes on Reserves and Matrimonial Interests or Rights Act was being developed, which would protect individuals living on-reserve when their conjugal relationship breaks down (INAC 2009). Wendy Grant-John, a First Nations woman and Indian Affairs employee, had been appointed to examine the issue and made recommendations to the minister.

Another issue raised in recent years by indigenous women has been violence against women. Family violence is of great concern to indigenous women. Since women and children are usually the victims and men are the usually the perpetrators, women believe that male-dominated organizations and band councils will not give this issue priority. It has been pursued on a number of fronts. One was the Stolen Sisters initiative of Amnesty International (2006), which investigated the circumstances surrounding the more than 500 indigenous women who have been murdered or are missing in Canada. Amnesty International called for government and police forces to implement measures to protect indigenous women.

Conclusion

The tension between First Nations women and male-dominated organizations began when women decided that they would stand up for their rights as individuals. Indigenous women have reached a point in their political and individual growth at which they will not sit helplessly by while others negotiate their future. This tactic did not work for them in the past. So they are articulating their own needs and concerns. They must work against entrenched attitudes, because some leaders are not prepared to advance their cause.

First Nations women are moving ahead and continue to play a large role in the education of their children and in the promotion of a healthy lifestyle. They initiate and sustain many community programs and services and are prepared to deal with societal problems such as family violence, child abuse, unemployment, alcohol abuse, loss of cultural identity, and the decrease in language retention.[24]

First Nations women are bringing about social, educational, and economic change through their relentless efforts and unwavering commitment to their community. Some were in desperate situations and felt they had nothing to lose because their children's welfare and their cultural identity as First Nations women were at stake.

In many respects, First Nations women still play the traditional role they played prior to European contact; they are still the caregivers, the transmitters of culture, and the nurturers. They are ultimately responsible for the future of the community—only time and the conditions have changed. They are working their way toward becoming the social and political equals of First Nations men that they once were. First Nations women are earning the respect and recognition they deserve from First Nations men, the government, and society.

Discussion Questions

1. How did European society subjugate its women?
2. To what extent was the Canadian government responsible for the current situation of First Nations women?
3. What was the impetus for First Nations women to organize?
4. Why is it in First Nations men's best interest to maintain the status quo?
5. What are some of the benefits and some of the drawbacks of Bill C-31 status?
6. What steps are First Nations women taking to ensure equality?

Further Readings

Jamieson, Kathleen. 1978. *Indian Women and the Law in Canada: Citizens Minus*. Ottawa: Minister of Supply and Services Canada. This classic was commissioned by the Canadian Advisory Council on the Status of Women and Indian Rights for Indian Women. It laid the foundation for social and political arguments that are still cited more than 30 years later.

Kelm, Mary Ellen, and Lorna Townsend. 2006. *In the Days of Our Grandmothers: A Reader in Aboriginal Women's History in Canada*. Toronto: University of Toronto Press. This reader shows Aboriginal women's experience from a number of perspectives. It is well-written and well-documented. However, there is one only one indigenous scholar included in the selection.

Native Women's Association of Canada. 2009. *Voices of Our Sisters: A Report of Families and Communities*. 2nd edn. Ottawa: Native Women's Association of Canada. This document is the second edition of the work completed for the Sisters in Spirit project, a research, education, and policy initiative that focuses on the more than 500 missing or murdered Aboriginal women and girls in Canada. This edition features the life stories of murdered indigenous women: Debbie Sloss, Georgina Papin, and Terrie Ann Dauphinais.

Paul, Pamela Marie. 1993. 'The Trojan horse: An analysis of the social, economic and political reaction of First Nations people as a result of Bill C-31'. (University of New Brunswick, master's thesis). This thesis analyzes the social, economic, political, and cultural complexities as viewed by the people affected by Bill C-31. It is a candid review of the internal and external conflicts caused by this policy, which was intended to correct past wrongs.

Voyageur, Cora. 2008. *Firekeepers of the 21st Century: First Nation Women Chiefs*. Montreal: McGill-Queen's University Press. This book examines the experience of women who assume the traditionally male role of leadership in Canada's First Nations communities. It explores the experiences of female Indian chiefs as they negotiate the hierarchies of gender, race, and the sometimes unkind world of reserve politics.

Notes

1. Excerpt from Rose Auger's chapter in Diane Mieli, *Those Who Know: Profiles of Alberta's Native Elders*, p. 25. Edmonton: Newest Publishing, 1991.
2. I will use the terms First Nation and Indian interchangeably throughout this chapter.
3. I will use the terms indigenous and Aboriginal interchangeably throughout this chapter.
4. Some might not agree with this statement, since many equally oppressive rules still apply to First Nations people under the Indian Act.
5. The perspectives put forth in this chapter are based on the author's personal experiences as a First Nations woman, conversations with other First Nations women, and a survey of existing literature.
6. Personal interview with Nellie Carlson in Edmonton in June 2004.
7. According to Marie Frawley-Henry of the Assembly of First Nations Women's Secretariat, there are 109 women chiefs in Canada. That means that approximately 17 per cent of Canada's elected chiefs are women. For more information, see Cora J. Voyageur, *Firekeepers of the 21st Century: First Nations Women Chiefs*.

8. These issues will be discussed more fully later in the paper.
9. Structural supremacy means the hierarchical structure of European society at the time of contact.
10. This ethnocentric view may be shared by all people, but we are dealing specifically with the European view of Indian people and the results of that view.
11. Patriarchy is defined as a social system marked by the supremacy of the father and the legal dependence of wives and children and the reckoning of descent and inheritance in the male line. *Webster's Ninth New Collegiate Dictionary*, p. 863.
12. It must be understood that there is no 'pan-Indian' form of social structure or hierarchy with regard to the treatment of women. Tribes were individual in their customs and values and must not be viewed as a homogeneous group. The practice of viewing all Indians in the same light is one that exists to this day and must be resisted.
13. There is a distinction between voluntary enfranchisement, which a male person could apply for and be granted, and involuntary enfranchisement, which occurred when an Indian person lost his or her status through various offences, such as possession of alcohol.
14. The Gradual Enfranchisement Act of 1869 was the first to deal with Indians after Confederation, but there had been earlier Acts, such as the Act for the Gradual Civilization of the Indian Tribes of Canada, which was passed in 1857.
15. Section 11 states:
    11(1) Subject to Section 12, a person is entitled to be registered if that person
        (a) on the 26th day of May 1874 was, for the purposes of An Act providing for the organization of the Department of the Secretary of State of Canada, and for the Management of Indian and Ordinance Lands, being chapter 42 of the Statutes of Canada, 1868, as amended by section 6 of chapter 6 of the Statutes of Canada, 1869, and section 8 of chapter 21 of the Statutes of Canada, 1874, considered to be entitled to hold, use or enjoy the lands and other immovable property belonging to or appropriated to the use of the various bands or bodies of Indians in Canada:
        (b) is a member of a band
            (i) for whose use and benefit common lands have been set apart or since the 26th of May 1874 have been agreed by treaty to be set apart, or
            (ii) that has been declared by the Governor in Council to be a band for the purpose of the Act;
        (c) is a male person who is a direct descendent in the male line of the male person described in paragraph (a) or (b);
        (d) is the legitimate child of
            (i) a male person described in paragraph (a) or (b), or
            (ii) a person described in paragraph (c);
        (e) is the illegitimate child of a female person described in paragraph (a), (b) or (c);
        (f) is the wife or widow of a person who is entitled to be registered by virtue of paragraph (a), (b), (c), (d) or (e).
16. Status means registration on Main or Central Indian Registry in Ottawa.
17. Band membership means that the band accepts and recognizes you as a member.

18. In the Tobique community, some men had kicked their wives and children out of their family homes and moved their girlfriends in. Women had no place to live and resorted to living in abandoned shacks or tents.

19. Community means the reserve and the urban area.

20. In 1969, the Liberal government's *White Paper on Indian Policy* united Indian people in solidarity. The government was attempting to renege on its treaty obligations and dissolve the reserve system, a move that drew a storm of Indian protests from across the nation. The White Paper was subsequently withdrawn but not before it served as a catalyst for Indian political organization.

21. It is ironic that attendance at a Western-based church is viewed a measure of tradition in a First Nations community, especially since traditional religious rituals do not occur in a church.

22. In 1965, there were 258 marriages between First Nations men and non–First Nations women. This number increased to 611 in 1976.

23. Currently in Alberta, three of 46 Indian chiefs are female. There may be a number of reasons for this situation. Females running for chief may not have sufficient community support to attain the office. Additionally, women may choose not to venture into the primarily male domain until there are more females holding such posts.

24. The author drew this conclusion after attending a number of conferences dealing with First Nations women's issues.

References

Acoose, Janice. 1995. *Iskwewak—kah' ki yaw ni wahkomakanak: Neither Indian Princesses nor Easy Squaws*. Toronto: Toronto Women's Press.

Albers, Patricia, and Beatrice Medicine, eds. 1983. *The Hidden Half: Studies of Plains Indian Women*. New York: University Press of America.

Amnesty International. 2006. 'Stolen sisters'. Ottawa: Amnesty International. www.amnesty.ca/campaigns/sisters_overview.php.

Atcheson, M. Elizabeth. 1984. *Women and Legal Action: Precedents, Resources and Strategies for the Future*. Ottawa: Canadian Advisory Council on the Status of Women.

Brown, Judith. 1982. 'Cross cultural perspectives on middle-aged women'. *Current Anthropology* 23: 143–53.

Canada. 1992. *First Nations Circle on the Constitution*. Ottawa: First Nations Circle on the Constitution.

Chalus, Elaine H. 1990. 'Gender and social change in the fur trade: The Hargrave correspondence, 1823–1850'. (University of Alberta, master's thesis).

Cumming, Peter A., and Neil H. Mickenberg. 1972. *Native Rights in Canada*. Toronto: Indian–Eskimo Association of Canada and General Publishing.

Ezzo, David A. 1988. 'Female status and the life cycle: A cross cultural perspective from Native North America'. In *Papers of the Nineteenth Algonquian Conference*, 137–44. Ottawa: Carleton University.

Feminist Alliance for International Action. 2008. 'A failing grade on women's equality: Canada's human rights record on women'. Submission to the United Nations. www.fafia-afia.org.

Fiske, Joanne. 1990–1. 'Native women in reserve politics: Strategies and struggles'. *Journal of Legal Pluralism* 30–1: 121–37.

Francis, Daniel. 1993. *The Imaginary Indian*. Vancouver: Arsenal Pulp Press.

Gerber, Linda M. 1990. 'Multiple jeopardy: A socio-economic comparison of men and women among the Indian, Métis and Inuit peoples of Canada'. *Canadian Ethnic Studies* 22: 69–80.

Hogg, Peter W. 1992. *Constitutional Law of Canada*. Scarborough, ON: Carswell Thomson.

Holmes, Joan. 1987. *Bill C-31 Equality or Disparity: The Effects of the New Indian Act on Native Women*. Ottawa: Canadian Advisory Council on the Status of Women.

Ilinik, Karen. 1990. 'Breaking trail'. *Arctic Circle* 1 (3): 36–41.

INAC (Indian and Northern Affairs Canada). 2009. Minister Chuck Strahl speech: 'Government of Canada reintroduces legislation to provide matrimonial real property rights on reserves'. Ottawa: Indian and Northern Affairs Canada. www.ainc-inac.gc.ca/ai/mr/nr/j-a2009/nr000000176-eng.asp.

Jamieson, Kathleen. 1978. *Indian Women and the Law in Canada: Citizens Minus*. Ottawa: Minister of Supply and Services Canada.

Kehoe, Alice. 1983. 'The shackles of tradition.' In Patricia Albers and Beatrice Medicine, eds, *The Hidden Half: Studies of Plains Indian Women*, 53–76. New York: University Press of America.

McDonald, Michael. 1987. 'Indian status: Colonialism or sexism?' *Canadian Community Law Journal* 9: 23–48.

Meili, Diane. 1991. *Those Who Know: Profiles of Alberta's Native Elders*. Edmonton: NeWest Publishers.

Monture-Okanee, Patricia A. 1992. 'The roles and responsibilities of Aboriginal women: Reclaiming justice'. *Saskatchewan Law Review* 56: 237–66.

Native Women's Association of Canada. 1991. *Native Women and the Charter: A Discussion Paper*. Ottawa: Native Women's Association of Canada.

———. 2007. *Reclaiming Our Way of Being: Matrimonial Real Property Solutions Position Paper*. Ottawa: Native Women's Association of Canada.

O'Donnell, Vivian. 2006. 'Aboriginal women in Canada.' In *Women in Canada: A Gender-Based Statistical Report*, 5th edn. Ottawa: Statistics Canada.

Opekokiw, Delia. 1986. 'Self identification and cultural preservations: A commentary on recent Indian Act amendments'. *Canadian Native Law Reporter* 2: 1–25.

Paul, Pamela Marie. 1993. 'The Trojan horse: An analysis of the social, economic and political reaction of First Nations people as a result of Bill C-31'. (University of New Brunswick, master's thesis).

Sheffield, R. Scot. 2005. 'Aboriginal contributions to Canadian culture and identity in wartime Canada's image of the "Indian" and the fall of France, 1940'. In David Newhouse, Cora Voyageur, and Daniel Beavon, eds, *Hidden in Plain Sight: Contributions of Aboriginal Peoples to Canadian Identity and Culture*, 405–18. Toronto: University of Toronto Press.

Silman, Janet. 1987. *Enough Is Enough: Aboriginal Women Speak Out*. Toronto: Women's Press.

Stacey-Moore, Gail. 1993. 'In our own voice'. *Herizons: Women's News and Feminist Views* 6 (4): 21–3.

Statistics Canada. 2006. *Women in Canada: A Gender-Based Statistical Report*. Catalogue no. 89-503-XPE. Ottawa: Minister of Industry.

———. 2008. 'Aboriginal Peoples in Canada in 2006: Inuit, Métis and First Nations,

2006 Census'. http://www12.statcan.ca/census-recensement/2006/as-sa/97-558/p17-eng.cfm#02.

Tsosie, Rebecca. 1988. 'Changing women: The cross currents of American Indian feminine identity'. *American Indian Culture and Research Journal* 12 (1): 1–31.

Venne, Sharon. 1981. *Indian Act Amendments, 1868–1975.* Saskatoon: University of Saskatchewan Native Law Centre.

Voyageur, Cora J. 1993. 'An analysis of the University of Alberta's Transition Year Program, 1985–1992'. (University of Alberta, master's thesis).

——. 2008. *Firekeepers of the 21st Century: First Nation Women Chiefs.* Montreal: McGill-Queen's University Press.

Williams, Robert. 1990. 'Gendered checks and balances: Understanding the legacy of white patriarchy in an American Indian cultural context'. *Georgia Law Review* 24: 1019–44.

10 The Need for Radical Change in the Canadian Criminal Justice System: Applying a Human Rights Framework

Patricia A. Monture

Introduction

Millions of dollars and seemingly endless resources have been dedicated to studying the problem of overrepresentation of Aboriginal persons in the Canadian criminal justice system. Between 1967 and 1991, 30 major Aboriginal justice studies had been completed (RCAP 1996, 289). Studies continued until 1996 with the release of the justice report of the Royal Commission on Aboriginal Peoples (RCAP) titled *Bridging the Cultural Divide*.[1] Although a number of major, incident-specific inquiries have been commissioned since 1996, RCAP is the most comprehensive report in that it considered the experience of Aboriginal peoples in all Canadian criminal justice jurisdictions.[2] The RCAP report continues to be significant both because of its national scope and because of the attention it paid to issues that fall under federal, territorial, and provincial responsibilities. The RCAP justice report, however, actually offers little in the way of new information (RCAP 1996, 284). It is perhaps not surprising, then, that the report did not help to transform Canada's justice system. In fact, the next decade saw an increase in the rates of Aboriginal overrepresentation in Canada's criminal justice system. As noted in a report from the Office of the Correctional Investigator (2009, 6):

> Aboriginal over-representation has grown in recent years: between 1998 and 2008, the federal Aboriginal population increased by 19.7%. Moreover, the number of federally sentenced Aboriginal women increased by a staggering 131% over this period.

It is not clear from the historical record when exactly the overrepresentation of Aboriginal peoples in the Canadian criminal justice system first became a problem. Significant regional and historical differences in demographics and in law enforcement practices and a lack of uniformity in data collection all contribute to the somewhat murky picture. It is generally agreed that the release of the Canadian Corrections Association's report in 1967 was the first obvious sign that the government was aware of the problem. Almost 30 years after that report, the RCAP commissioners called on the government and others to commit themselves to examining the root causes of a problem that continued to oppress Aboriginal people.

> In a society that places a high value on equality before the law, docu-menting the appalling figures of over-representation might seem to be enough, without any further analysis, to place resolution of this problem at the very top of the national human rights agenda. However, as compel-ling as the figures are, we believe that it is equally important to under-stand what lies behind these extraordinary figures, which are a primary index of the individual and social devastation that the criminal justice sys-tem has come to represent for Aboriginal people. Understanding the root causes is critical to understanding what it will take by way of a national commitment to bring about real change (RCAP 1996, 33).

Citing the 1988 report of the Canadian Bar Association titled *Locking up Natives in Canada*, the RCAP concluded that 'without radical change, the problems will intensify' (1996, 29–30). The RCAP's study of the situation occurred almost a decade after the Canadian Bar Association penned their report, and now it is 15 years since the RCAP report. The question is, are there any signs that the 'rad-ical changes' called for in the many reports on criminal justice in Canada have occurred? How can we think differently from the way we have about how to address the problems and challenges identified in those reports? The following discussion is my response to these questions.

The Importance of Reading Aboriginal Justice Statistics Carefully

According to the Cawsey Commission report,[3] the multitude of justice-related reports between 1967 and 1990 contained more than 1800 recommendations for reforming the Canadian justice system. In commenting on the findings of the Cawsey report as well as their own commission, the final RCAP report states that

> despite this wealth of good ideas, the essence of the evidence we received for Aboriginal nations, communities, organizations and scholars is that there *has not been significant change in day-to-day realities facing Aboriginal people and their involvement with the criminal justice system*, except where

Aboriginal initiatives have taken hold. It is clear that the reason is not the lack of sound recommendations *but a lack of concrete implementation*. Our recommendations therefore focus on this lack of implementation—precisely because it is the primary stumbling block to reform of the existing system (RCAP 1996, 284–85; emphasis added).

Later in their report, the commissioners provide additional comments on the lack of implementation of the many recommendations. They first acknowledge that the problem is not due to a lack of understanding of what the problems are but rather the lack of political will and bureaucratic resistance to change. Commissioners also noted that recommendations for reform tend to focus on creating further accommodations within the existing criminal justice system, thereby failing to take into account Aboriginal justice traditions, which are arguably a clear component of the inherent right to self-government (RCAP 1996, 289). This is a clear failure of Canadian governments and their bureaucratic servants to be accountable both to Canada's constitutional structure and to Aboriginal peoples themselves. Unfortunately, very little has changed since 1996, and the challenge remains to find mechanisms for Aboriginal peoples to pursue the solutions that come from their languages, cultures, laws, and traditions. Clearly, the search for transformative change has been illusive. Accommodations and initiatives established to date have not contributed to even a small decline in the numbers of Aboriginal people who come into conflict with the justice system in Canada. This fact should force Aboriginal people (and the rest of Canada) to reconsider our approach to justice in Canada, especially those who see themselves as prisoner advocates and/or justice activists.

The final RCAP justice report outlined 15 major findings (1996, 309–15). It also provided 17 recommendations for change, the vast majority of which have yet to be implemented. In total, eight of the findings address the right of Aboriginal peoples to self-government, which includes authority over matters of criminal justice as well as the right to make laws. They also include the necessity, in their view, that the Canadian Charter of Rights and Freedoms must apply to Aboriginal governments. We can conclude from this that the commissioners believe that the solution to Aboriginal problems and issues within the Canadian criminal justice system lies primarily with Aboriginal peoples. Specifically, the source of radical change that is needed must come from Aboriginal traditions and governments, within the limits of Canada's Charter (a conclusion some Aboriginal peoples would dispute). Unfortunately, few initiatives currently exist in Aboriginal communities in Canada that could be described as truly self-governing justice processes. Because federal, provincial, and territorial Crowns control virtually all funds, resources, and administrative power, Aboriginal peoples' ability to realize their visions of justice are severely constrained (RCAP 309–11). Given the commissioners' assertion that Canada lacks both political will and bureaucrats who are committed to supporting transformative change, the lack of movement toward justice for Aboriginal people in this country is hardly surprising.

A disturbing aspect of RCAP's justice report is the certainty with which it concluded that Aboriginal people's overrepresentation is 'a product of high levels of crime among Aboriginal peoples and systemic discrimination' (309). Such a statement must be filtered through a systemic discrimination framework (since that would enable us to recognize, for example, that Aboriginal people are regularly overcharged and over-policed (RCAP 1996). It has long been noted by criminologists that we do not know how much crime exists in any society. We can accurately count the number of arrests made in Canada, but the total number of crimes committed, including those that are unreported, unrecorded, or undetected, is often referred to as a 'dark figure' (Linden 2004, 96).[4] What a given society defines as a crime is thus sometimes unclear and often reflects the interests of the ruling classes (Reiman 2007; Stern 2006).

One means of effecting positive change is to raise awareness and understanding. It is important in this respect to look back and understand the history of the desire to study the 'problem' of Aboriginal persons and the Canadian criminal justice system. Overrepresentation is one of the most significant problems, as was noted by the Supreme Court of Canada (Gladue 1999), and led to the majority of studies conducted since 1967. Additionally, the death of an Aboriginal person or persons in custody or at the hands of the police has been the lightning rod, which has coalesced Aboriginal political activists, thereby forcing individual provincial governments to act. One of the most comprehensive of these reports is the Aboriginal Justice Inquiry of Manitoba (Hamilton and Sinclair, 1991). The murder of Helen Betty Osborne in The Pas, a case that went unsolved for 15 years, and the death of J.J. Harper in a scuffle with a police officer were two critical incidents that resulted in the Manitoba government calling for the inquiry (Hamilton and Sinclair, vol. 2, 1991).

More than two decades ago, the Canadian Bar Association reported that an Aboriginal person in this country was more likely to go to jail than to university (1989). The reality is that despite all the good intentions, new initiatives, words written, and money spent, things have not changed in the area of Aboriginal justice in Canada. It is still more likely we will go to jail than to university,[5] and rates of Aboriginal overrepresentation in the criminal justice system have continued to grow. And far more money has been spent studying the lives of

Aboriginal men who are incarcerated than has been spent understanding the circumstances of women or youth.

Although most of these studies of Aboriginal overrepresentation focus on men, Aboriginal women constitute the fastest growing prison population in the world (CAEFS 2007; Stern 2006). Moreover, Aboriginal women have long faced multiple forms of discrimination within the Canadian justice system (Auditor General of Canada 2003; Canadian Human Rights Commission 2003; Office of the Correctional Investigator 2006–7). As noted previously, one of the defining incidents leading to the Aboriginal Justice Inquiry of Manitoba was the murder of Helen Betty Osborne. However, the 1996 RCAP justice report does not focus directly on gender issues, even though we know that racialized sexualized violence against Aboriginal women is a defining feature of our interactions with police.

A Question of Accountability: Who Holds the Powerful Accountable?

In light of the above facts, it seems vital that we begin to ask new, more fundamental questions if we hope to address the problem of the overrepresentation of Aboriginal people incarcerated in the Canadian criminal justice system. Specifically, how do we hold a criminal justice system accountable for the very real damage it is doing to Aboriginal people, communities, and nations? Further, what can those who are committed to transformational change do differently to create an energy that will transform a system that is not working into one that is fully responsible to the citizens of this country and to Aboriginal peoples? This kind of accountability—state to citizen—is, I believe, a basic requirement of true democracy. My belief in the value of democracy rests on my understanding of what it means to be Haudenosaunee (Iroquois). According to Johansen (1981; 1998), First Peoples, especially the Haudenosaunee, were the first to live and organize themselves democratically in North America. The question is, what kind of democracy was implemented by European colonizers, and how has this affected the lives of the original inhabitants of this land?

Much has been written about democracy, and confusion can arise around its definition, since it is both a form of government (or other organization) and a philosophy. The common Western understanding of democracy differs from the one I have experienced as a citizen of the Haudenosaunee, for majority rule is a common feature of Western democracy. Most contemporary democratic governments are based on electoral systems in which each person of legal age has one vote. Elections tend to be competitive, pitting parties and candidates against each other. In the Canadian context, liberal democracy is the prevailing norm and is a system based on political pluralism, equality of citizens, civil liberties, human rights, and the rule of law. Most people in the West have long believed that it is this approach to democracy that transforms primitive peoples into a civil society. Democracy among the Haudenosaunee is a complex and layered system, which is based on consensus being reached among the people.

This rudimentary and thoroughly Western understanding of democracy also grounds the claim made here that governments must be fully accountable to their citizens. This is in fact the basic feature of the electoral system. But between elections, what is it that citizens should expect from their elected leaders? Moreover, what actions are required to guarantee equality to all citizens and to protect their human rights and civil liberties? Not until the Supreme Court of Canada decision in *Martineau v.* [see CMS 15.45] *Matsqui Institutional Disciplinary Board* (1980), in which prison administrators were found to owe prisoners a 'duty to act fairly', did prisoners in Canada have any clear legal rights (see also Jackson 1983; 2002). Since that time, courts in Canada have been more willing to protect the liberty of prisoners as well as their Charter rights and human rights. From this perspective, a human rights framework is the appropriate prism through which to reflect on Canada's record in the area of justice and Aboriginal peoples.[6]

Broadening Our Human Rights Framework for Justice

The rights of all citizens is one of the foundations in which democratic countries such as Canada take great pride. Most frequently, a rights framework assumes that individual rights are granted by the state to its citizens. This is a minimalist construction of human rights. If a human rights lens were applied critically, it would focus our attention on the inadequacies inherent in and failures of a legal regime that is built on individual rights. Specifically, it would point to discrimination against (and even the exclusion of) 'types' of individuals based on certain social characteristics. As Australian scholar Chris Cunneen explains:

> The first point is that Indigenous people have been victims of profound historical injustices and abuses of human rights which can be at least partially understood as state crime. The second point is that contemporary justice systems are often seen in the context of the abuse of Indigenous people's human rights. The third strand is an analysis of how claims to specific Indigenous rights impact on current criminal justice processes, and how those claims might broaden our understanding of reform and change (2007, 244).

Criminologists and others who examine aspects of the justice system have been slow to accept a human rights framework in their work, and this has particular consequences for Aboriginal people. However, mechanisms do exist in a liberal democracy, as Cunneen points out, to think of the problem of Aboriginal over-representation in the Canadian criminal justice system differently. And we may find that a different way of thinking about long-standing problems such as over-representation of Aboriginal people in Canadian prisons points to different (or even new) solutions.

There are a number of aspects to the task of questioning accountability within Canadian systems of law and criminal justice. Part of the task is to understand the nature of the failings of the system of law and justice that lead to such a dramatic and continuous overrepresentation of Aboriginal persons. The perceptions and experiences of Aboriginal people must inform this understanding, since it is a fundamental principle of the Canadian legal system to guard against situations of unfairness and bias (*Wewaykum Indian Band v. Canada* 2003, para. 67). Situations of bias may be actual or perceived, and as such, perception matters. Throughout Canada, Aboriginal people do not view the criminal justice system as a system that represents or respects them (Hamilton and Sinclair 1991; RCAP 1996). The perceptions of Aboriginal peoples (while keeping in mind their diversity) thus thoroughly challenge the perspective of those who regard Canada to be a free and democratic state.

One of the consequences of the startling overrepresentation of Aboriginal persons as 'clients' of the Canadian criminal justice system is that it has become the focal point of research projects, program reforms, policy initiatives, and political discussion. However, equally important but almost fully neglected is the under-representation of Aboriginal people in the administration of the Canadian criminal justice system. Aboriginal persons are not wardens or correctional managers. We are not the lawyers or judges, high-ranking bureaucrats or police chiefs, commissioners of corrections or directors of institutions. This has some important consequences for the question of accountability, because it means that Aboriginal persons are not the policy-developers or decision-makers in the Canadian criminal justice system (Commission on First Nations and Métis Peoples and Justice Reform 2004, 1–15). It is senior policy-makers who are most able to influence systemic change, and Aboriginal persons have been systematically and continuously excluded from holding positions of authority and power in the system. As long as Aboriginal persons are systematically excluded from this group, it seems obvious that little, if any, meaningful change on their behalf will occur. This is especially true for Aboriginal women, for they are at least twice marginalized by race and gender. Even though equality of opportunity and equal access to employment is universally accepted as a primary component of international human rights, these are simply not principles that are defended in Canada.

There is another serious consequence to Aboriginal people not holding positions of power and authority in the criminal justice system. Sociologists have long noted that prisons are total institutions (Goffman 1961). As a result, the public has very little access to what happens within prisons (and prisoners have little access to 'civil society' beyond the prison walls). Without an accurate flow of information from inside the prison to the 'street', it is difficult if not impossible to establish a proper system of checks and balances. More and more in recent decades, there has been a demand by prisoners and their advocates for civilian oversight of closed 'correctional' regimes as a way of placing checks on state power. Madam Justice Louise Arbour was so concerned by her conclusions about the lack of the rule of law at the Prison for Women in Kingston, Ontario, that she recommended judicial oversight of the prison's administration of segregation decisions (Arbour 1996). But as Correctional Investigator Howard Sapers found, the challenge of effecting meaningful correctional reform goes much deeper than providing administrative oversight to one or two prisons. In his recent annual report, he wrote that

> [w]e cannot compel compliance with our recommendations. However, as a democratic institution established by Parliament, the OCI is well placed to conduct thorough and objective reviews and then cause the Correctional Service of Canada (CSC) to change decisions that do not comply with law and policy, or that raise issues of fairness (Office of the Correctional Investigator 2006–7, 3).

The Correctional Investigator has only the power of persuasion in their dealings with members of the Correctional Service of Canada. Because their office has no authority to mandate any ameliorative action on the part of government or correctional facility employees, there is no way of ensuring accountability for what is done in this country in the name of justice. Unfortunately for Aboriginal people in Canada, it would appear that their disproportionately high rates of incarceration and victimization as well as the problems they experience while in custody are likely to continue. That is, unless those who are responsible for ensuring that justice is done in Canada start listening and taking to heart the experiences and perspectives of Aboriginal people who are treated unjustly each and every day of their lives.

Systemic Elements of Injustice: Poverty, Race, and Gender

That the Canadian criminal justice system neither represents nor respects the rights of Aboriginal peoples in this country is demonstrated through an examination of the major factors that contribute to our oppression. Scholars and others have long noted the relationship between poverty and crime.[7] However, it is simplistic to say that poverty causes crime, since not all poor people are criminals and not all criminals are poor. Some scholars have nonetheless suggested that economically disadvantaged people are overrepresented in criminal justice systems because the laws of those countries are written to protect the interests of the rich (Reiman 2007). And if we find that poverty is highly correlated with crime and the state is complicit in creating and maintaining Aboriginal poverty, then the state in many respects must accept responsibility for addressing the problems of poverty if it is serious about addressing problems of overrepresentation. This is particularly the case in a 'free and democratic' society that prides itself on improving the quality of life of its citizens and protecting their human rights.

Drawing on 1996 census data, the Canadian Council on Social Development reported in 2000 that Aboriginal people were more than twice as likely to live in poverty as non-Aboriginal people and that certain groups of Aboriginal people experience greater rates of poverty than others (CCSD 2001). According to a report prepared for the Department of Indian Affairs using 2001 census data,

> Aboriginal women have lower incomes than Aboriginal men and a higher percentage of their income is derived from government transfer payments. In 2000 the average income of Aboriginal women was 75% of the average income of Aboriginal men (Hull 2006, 98).

Fully addressing issues of overrepresentation means addressing the systemic poverty that Aboriginal people (especially women) and nations survive. Continuing to judge Aboriginal women (and men) strictly on the basis of individual accountability, when in fact relatively high rates of incarceration are a consequence of such systemic issues as poverty and racism, must be seen as a societal failure. Aboriginal overrepresentation in the Canadian criminal justice system is not merely the result of a pathology found among poor and racialized individuals, which leads to the offending of the criminal law. The factors that contribute to criminal offending are systemic, yet the concern over accountability within the criminal justice system rarely if ever extends beyond the individual.

Making sense of Aboriginal peoples' relationship to the Canadian criminal justice system is far more complex, however, than showing clear connections between poverty and crime. Aboriginal peoples' distrust of Canadian law and criminal justice also extends far beyond the stark figures of their overrepresentation in the Canadian criminal justice system. As the commissioners of the Aboriginal Justice Inquiry of Manitoba (AJI) noted:

> From the perspective of Aboriginal people, the justice system has contributed to Aboriginal poverty by failing to provide them with the means to fight the oppressive conditions imposed upon them. It has not assisted Aboriginal peoples in defending their claim to their lands or in enforcing their treaty promises. In fact, at one time it was illegal for lawyers to represent Aboriginal persons without the consent of the federal government or for Aboriginal people to raise money to press their land claims. The loss of Aboriginal land is a clear contributor to poverty.
>
> Nor has the justice system assisted Aboriginal peoples in defending their freedoms of religion and association. The law forced Aboriginal parents, under threat of prosecution from the justice system, to send their children to residential schools. The justice system also failed to protect families from the child welfare practices of the 1960s and 1970s, which continue to create problems off reserve today. The separation of families, the oppression of culture and language, and the lack of Aboriginal control over decisions within their communities have contributed to inadequate education and to community breakdown, which in turn lead to poverty, as community resources are underdeveloped (Hamilton and Sinclair 1991, 94–5).

Although written in 1991, the conclusion and recommendations contained in the AJI report are fully applicable today, two decades later. Aboriginal peoples see clearly that the legal systems in this country have been part of their oppression as well as a fundamental source of their impoverishment. Clearly, poverty is not an individualized phenomenon in the case of Aboriginal peoples. It is a systemic source of oppression that is a direct result of colonization. Over the past 20 or more years, the state has taken small steps to settle outstanding grievances by Aboriginal people, particularly in the case of land claims. Clearly, however, it has been too little too late as poverty has continued to breed poverty and Aboriginal peoples still have disproportionately higher rates of contact with Canada's criminal justice system.

Individual struggles in the lives of Aboriginal people, such as substance abuse and poverty, are too often viewed as private troubles and not social issues that arise as the result of colonialism. When individual troubles are viewed as social issues, then the manner in which the state is directly implicated by its knowledge of Aboriginal overrepresentation becomes clear.

> . . . a break-and-enter may be the trigger event that leads us to restorative justice, but the restorative meeting has the potential to raise issues of age-ism (if, say, an elderly person was victimized), neighborhood poverty or economic disparities, youth disempowerment, or any number of issues. Unfortunately, it is too often the case that restorative justice programs fail to meet the standard that C. Wright Mills proposed for sociology; that is, they do not draw the link between 'private troubles' of crime commis-sion and victimization and 'public issues' of structural disadvantage and inequality (Woolford 2009, 39).

From a human rights perspective, the fact that Canadian courts and laws have not been pathways to justice and equality for Aboriginal persons further raises questions about state accountability. Despite report after report and a vir-tual mountain of statistics that provide a clear and detailed picture of Aboriginal overrepresentation as prisoners and under-representation as authority figures and employees in Canada's justice system, these realities are perpetuated by overt discrimination and oppressive practices in many institutional areas of Canadian life. For example, Bonita Lawrence (2004, 119) notes '65 to 70 per cent of the clients, criminal offenders, who use the services of the ALST (Aboriginal Legal Services of Toronto) were adopted out.' Child welfare is a state-sanctioned ap-paratus, and the connections between overrepresentation in the criminal justice system and problems within the child welfare system must be acknowledged if positive, transformative change is to occur on behalf of Aboriginal peoples in this country. Aboriginal peoples are also more likely to be taken from their families and placed in foster care—a fact that many understand to be a direct result of the loss of parenting skills because of experience in residential schools. As Bonita Lawrence (2004, 113) notes:

> The decision of the federal government to expand its role in funding social welfare services after phasing out residential schools suggests that welfare services became the chosen vehicle to deal with Aboriginal chil-dren in social need in the 1960s. . . . The removal of any child from his or her parents was seen as inherently damaging, while the effect of apprehension on Native children was understood to be more damag-ing because of the removal of the child from a tightly knit community of extended family members into a foreign, and often hostile culture;

nevertheless, social workers removed Aboriginal children from their communities in droves.

The apprehension of Aboriginal children through the 1960s 'child welfare scoop' has now been clearly linked to earlier experiences Aboriginal people had with residential schools.[8] In recent years, the federal government has supported efforts to help residential school survivors through the establishment of a residential school healing fund and the Truth and Reconciliation Commission. Although the abuses against Aboriginal children in these schools have long been well-documented, they are infrequently identified as crimes even though they clearly were (Chrisjohn 1997). Indeed, despite Prime Minister Stephen Harper's public apology on behalf of the government and people of Canada to Aboriginal people for the government's involvement in residential schools, the government has yet to accept full responsibility for the collective harms that were inflicted on families and communities—indeed entire nations—under the residential school regime. The collective suffering and losses of our communities are clearly evident in the figures of overrepresentation in the Canadian criminal justice system, a system that now complements the activities of child welfare authorities. Recognizing the significance of the connections between residential schools, the child welfare system, and the criminal justice system in Canada is critical if we are to find solutions not only to the overrepresentation but also to the more common experience of alienation and oppression that many Aboriginal people in Canada experience on a daily basis.

Politicians and senior civil servants have paid little attention to the AJI's 1991 findings or to the findings of the justice report for the Royal Commission on Aboriginal Peoples. Rather, we still regularly hear from many official quarters that Aboriginal peoples are treated fairly in Canada's justice system, despite the fact that not a single government-funded report has come to that conclusion. For example, in 2006 then–Minister of Public Safety Stockwell Day insisted in response to another condemnation of the Correctional Service of Canada by Correctional Services Investigator Howard Sapers that there was no 'empirical evidence that Aboriginal people are routinely disadvantaged once they are placed in the custody of the correctional service.'[9] In fact, statistics indicate that Aboriginal prisoners are more likely to be sent to solitary confinement, serve their sentences in maximum security, or be overlooked for early parole (Hamilton and Sinclair 1991; RCAP 1996). Reading between the lines, the position of the current Canadian government appears to reflect the belief that because Aboriginal peoples are more criminal than the 'white' citizens of this country, the government is excused from taking action to ameliorate the systemic discrimination against Aboriginal people that occurs at every level of the Canadian criminal justice system. Sadly, this is the same belief held for centuries by those who assumed that Aboriginal peoples must become civilized in order to be contributing members of society (Dickason 1997).

The practices of Canadian politicians and civil servants in relation to issues surrounding Aboriginal people and the Canadian criminal justice system often amaze and dishearten me. We have been extremely diligent on the one hand at counting the number of offenders and the growing number of Aboriginal gangs and reporting the public's increasing fears about 'Aboriginal gangs'. In contrast, information that could assist Aboriginal peoples in creating transformative opportunities is not always available. Statistics released in 2001 by the Prairie Region (Manitoba, Saskatchewan, and Alberta) of the Correctional Service of Canada indicated that the idea that Aboriginal women are overrepresented in Prairie prisons is an overgeneralization. Careful reading of the statistics shows that First Nations women (or in CSC's terms, North American Indians) are much more overrepresented than Métis or Inuit women. In May 2000, 119 women were in federal custody in the Prairie Region. Aboriginal women accounted for 67 of those inmates (53.6 per cent). Of those 67 Aboriginal women, 14 self-identified as Métis, three as Inuit, and 53 as 'North American Indian' (First Nations) (Borrowman 2000, 1). However, these statistics do not indicate whether the First Nations women were Cree, Saulteaux, Dakota, Lakota, or Nakota, Blackfoot, Dene, or so on. They also do not specify whether they were reserve residents or urban residents at the time of their arrest. Neither do they help us to know whether any particular First Nations communities were overrepresented or whether those in federal custody were from particular geographical areas. Failing to acknowledge and report these differences is another fundamental structural shortcoming that reflects the serious limitations of the conceptual framework the CSC has adopted to collect offender data. The consequence of this is serious, since the data collected by the CSC gives direction to governmental policy and program developers as well as to leaders of First Nation and other Aboriginal communities. Unfortunately, the CSC either does not recognize or is choosing to ignore that programs and services are more helpful and likely to effect positive change when they are developed with the characteristics and circumstances of those they are intended to support in mind.

Nation- and region-specific information is essential if policy and program development within corrections at both federal and provincial levels is to be effective. If policy and program initiatives fail to take such information into account, they will at best continue to address issues at the level of an individual's experience of incarceration. In other words, they will remain unable to contribute to the kind of transformative change in the criminal justice system that would meaningfully address Aboriginal rates of overrepresentation. The lack of attention to problems surrounding offender data is disturbing for another reason. Without specific information, it is difficult to hold First Nation bands or councils as well as other Aboriginal governments accountable or to get them involved in being part of the solution to the overrepresentation of their people in the justice system. This is particularly a problem for First Nations with disproportionately high rates of overrepresentation in Canada's prisons. The lack of detailed offender data prevents us from publicly acknowledging that many bands and communities continue to ignore what is happening to the women in their communities, both in terms of their involvement in the criminal justice system as well as their disproportionately high rates of victimization. Without the involvement of Aboriginal peoples' own governments, it is unlikely that transformative change will occur either within or outside of the Canadian criminal justice system.

As noted throughout this paper, Aboriginal peoples are those who are most likely to be accused and convicted of crimes as well as sentenced to incarceration by members of the Canadian criminal justice system. However, an equally disturbing fact that is overlooked by all is Aboriginal peoples' overrepresentation in the system in another significant way. Aboriginal persons are also much more likely to be the victims of crime. Given the focus by government and media on problems associated with Aboriginal crime, it is 'interesting' to note the silence of the media and the lack of governmental response to this aspect of overrepresentation. Aboriginal victim statistics are rarely if ever broken down by gender, for if they were, it would undoubtedly reveal that Aboriginal women are significantly overrepresented. A report prepared for the Department of Justice's Policy Centre for Victims Issues noted

> that 35 per cent of Aboriginal people (versus 26 per cent of non-Aboriginal people) tend to be victims, and that Aboriginal people are three times more likely to be victims of violent crimes. Sexual assault rates are five times higher for Aboriginal people and domestic violence is three times higher. Under reporting of crimes is more pronounced among Aboriginal peoples; in fact, one study found that 74 per cent of Aboriginal victims did not report the crimes. One reason for not reporting was lack of confidence in the system (Chartrand and McKay 2006).

A number of important questions these and other findings raise are: Of the 74 per cent of Aboriginal victims who did not call police, how many were women?

And how many of those women were surviving violence in their own homes? The failure to pay close attention to the social characteristics, circumstances, and experiences of victims unfortunately makes both race and gender invisible. Along with being victims of crime, Aboriginal women are further victimized by state representatives who are not made accountable for their (in)actions.

Not only do the above statistics reveal failures within Canada's justice system to protect Aboriginal women in this country, they also indicate that Aboriginal people are unwilling to report crime and engage the Canadian justice system. This further demonstrates the importance of paying attention to Aboriginal people's experience with and perception of the justice system in Canada. What is required are solutions that address the complexities of Aboriginal victims' and offenders' experiences of crime as well as the experiences and perspectives of those who are close to them. Such solutions require that we pay attention to the silence around the victimization of Aboriginal people, especially since silence in this case seems to serve a particularly destructive and at times deadly purpose. Fear of crime or reports in the media about increasing street violence facilitates the expenditure of more resources on policing and punitive justice measures (Garland 1996, 446–7). Thus, policing resources are more likely to be attached to high-crime areas (often the poorest areas in the city), and more police in an area means more arrests. As a result, such reports are more likely to contribute to the overrepresentation of Aboriginal persons in the Canadian criminal justice system than to decreasing it, and so in the end it becomes a self-fulfilling prophecy. Moreover, widespread attention to such reports increases the likelihood that Canadians will continue to see Aboriginal overrepresentation as deserved. Additionally, as increased police resources result in more arrests (whether or not crime is actually increasing), the continued expenditures on policing, punitive justice, and the extensive surveillance of Aboriginal people is seen as justified.

The duplicity of the state continues. If Aboriginal persons can be constructed as the 'problem'—that is, they are the 'criminals' and 'gang members'—then it reinforces the colonial myth that 'Natives' are dangerous and need to be controlled. This is in fact a form of racial profiling, a strategy that is older than the birth of the Canadian state. Colonialism in its modern form uses the justice system to construct Aboriginal persons, particularly First Nations, as 'criminal', 'bad', or 'dangerous' 'savages'. This is the same myth upon which institutions and practices like residential schools were built. Criminal justice statistics therefore appear on the surface to justify racist attitudes and practices, resulting in stereotypes about Aboriginal people becoming ever more deeply embedded in the Canadian psyche. Making the victims and their pain invisible also serves a social purpose for those in power. Consider carefully the last time you heard a Canadian criminal justice official ask for more money to assist Aboriginal victims of crime. As noted earlier, many of the Aboriginal persons who are victims of crime are women. Both Amnesty International and the Native Women's Association of Canada have worked very hard to make visible not only the number of murdered or missing Aboriginal women in this country—estimated minimally at 500 Aboriginal women since the 1970s—but also the ways in which the criminal justice has failed those women and their families (Amnesty International 2004). Focusing our attention on the overrepresentation of Aboriginal women as victims would make visible Canada's failure to deliver justice to Aboriginal persons in general and Aboriginal women in particular, thereby, one hopes, forcing the state to more adequately address the violence and injustice perpetrated against these people at the hands of the state.

Concluding Remarks

We live in times of political fundamentalism and increasing militarism, so the call to 'get tough on criminals' reverberates through each election campaign and in the halls of Canadian legislatures. This particular political climate obscures an important question, for while activists and prisoners have achieved a certain success in the journey to secure prisoners' rights, it is not clear what this has meant for the experiences of Aboriginal women, men, and youth in custody. In 2003, the Canadian Humans Rights Commission reviewed the progress made in women's corrections since the Task Force on Federally Sentenced Women reported in 1990. The commission reported that the gap between securing rights and seeing them implemented is vast (Canadian Human Rights Commission 2003). The lack of meaningful change in this area continues to be a significant frustration for many as the accountability of governmental leaders and justice representatives remains illusive. The 'law and order demand' that criminals be held accountable should also apply to those who are responsible for administering justice. That is, they should also be held accountable for their (in) action as it relates to the protection of the rights of all citizens, including prisoners. Quite simply, full accountability on the part of all who are responsible for administering justice in Canada means that they should be required to take responsibility for implementing as well as protecting human rights within the Canadian criminal justice system. It should not be left to activists and prisoners to fight for rights that are democratically owed to all citizens, including prisoners.

'Criminals must take responsibility for their misdeeds' is a popular mantra, particularly under the auspices of our current conservative government. Unfortunately, Canadian justice system representatives seem blind to the systemic patterns of injustice and oppression that exist within the Canadian criminal justice system. Changes to Canada's sentencing laws in 1995 and the creation of initiatives that accommodate Aboriginal persons in the Canadian criminal justice system effect insignificant change, largely because they ignore the need for communities to be empowered to control their own affairs. Tinkering with a racist and socially oppressive system will not begin to address the complexity of the issues involved in the relationship between Aboriginal peoples and the Canadian criminal justice system.

As noted throughout this chapter, academics, politicians, and senior government policy-developers in Canada have largely ignored the significance of race and gender in relation to victimization. As a consequence, neither factor is seriously considered by those responsible for ensuring the efficacy of the Canadian criminal justice system. Moreover, even though the issue of safety is a fundamental component of a law and order agenda, it is evident that only certain groups in Canada can hope to see their right to safety protected through meaningful access to justice. That is, safety appears to be a human right reserved for those with white privilege, a fact that clearly challenges Canada's reputation as a free and democratic society.

This chapter is intended as a challenge to the highly individualistic focus of criminal law and justice in Canada. By emphasizing individual accountability, the state and its citizens are able to ignore how the Canadian government, the Canadian criminal justice system, and society at large have failed Aboriginal people. It is our collective responsibility to ensure that all citizens have an equal right to safety, justice, and peace. None of these should be a matter of social, economic, or racial privilege. This examination of Aboriginal people and Canada's justice system indicates that a disproportionately high percentage of Aboriginal people in this country not only lack privilege, but they are also not guaranteed the safety, justice, and peace that is their right.

It is time for justice.

Discussion Questions

1. How do you see the problem of overrepresentation of Aboriginal people in Canada's criminal justice system?
2. In what ways would your social background and characteristics make a difference in how you view the criminal justice system in Canada?
3. What is your perception of the relationship between Aboriginal people and crime, and in what ways is your perception shaped by mainstream Canadian media?

4. Why do you think First Nations women in Canada experience disproportionately higher rates of incarceration when compared to women from other Aboriginal populations?
5. Why do you think the Canadian government, media, and a large number of Aboriginal leaders and communities ignore that First Nations women in this country experience high rates of victimization?
6. What would you like to see happen in response to any of the issues and problems discussed in this chapter?

Further Readings

Amnesty International. 2004. 'Stolen sisters—A human rights response to discrimination and violence against indigenous women in Canada'. Ottawa: Amnesty International. www.amnesty.ca/resource_centre/reports.
Canadian Human Rights Commission. 2003. *Protecting Their Rights: A Systematic Review of Human Rights in Correctional Services for Federally Sentenced Women.* Ottawa: Canadian Human Rights Commission.
Commission on First Nations and Métis Peoples and Justice Reform. 2004. *Legacy of Hope: An Agenda for Change—Final Report,* vol. 1. Regina: Saskatchewan Justice.
Office of the Correctional Investigator. 2009. *Good Intentions, Disappointing Results: A Progress Report on Federal Aboriginal Corrections.* Ottawa: Office of the Correctional Investigator.
Woolford, Andres. 2009. *The Politics of Restorative Justice: A Critical Introduction.* Halifax and Winnipeg: Fernwood.

Notes

1. Criminal justice is not a major topic in the six-volume final report tabled by the commission. The report on criminal justice was released in a separate volume earlier in the same year. I understand this decision was based on the commissioners' view that there was a particular urgency about matters of criminal justice in Canada and its impact on Aboriginal peoples.
2. Saskatchewan studied the problems in the Canadian criminal justice system, and this commission reported in 2004. See Commission on First Nations and Métis Peoples and Justice Reform, *Legacy of Hope: An Agenda for Change,* final report, Regina: Saskatchewan Justice. For recent incident-specific reports, see, for example, the Stonechild (Wright 2004) and Ipperwash (Linden 2007) inquiries. It is also important to note that there is a difference in power in the kinds of studies governments may commission. A task force is often used when the government wishes to study an issue without commitment to change. A task force report is not required to be published, nor does it generally have the power to subpoena. A royal commission generally has the power to subpoena witnesses, although RCAP did not use this power. A royal commission's report must be made public and is the government's strongest means to study a difficult problem, often a problem without a clear or easy solution. Other Canadian royal commissions include those that have studied national development (1949–51), health services (1961–4), bilingualism and biculturalism (1963–9), and the status of women (1967–70).

3. The Cawsey Commission was a task force appointed in 1990 by the government of Alberta to examine the criminal justice system in that province.
4. 'Darkness' is often synonymous with evil or not knowing, while 'whiteness' is light and purity. And thus the seeds of racialization are sown into our everyday language and the images we use.
5. Retrieved on-line at www.cssspnql.com/eng/documents/Rapportincarceration eng.pdf.
6. It is interesting to note that in Canada's legislative human rights regime, colonialism is not considered a violation of human rights.
7. Retrieved on-line at www.ccja-acjp.ca/en/abori4.html.
8. Retrieved on-line at www.originscanada.org/the-stolen-generation.
9. Retrieved on-line at www.cbc.ca/canada/story/2006/10/16/native-prisoners.html.

References

Amnesty International. 2004. 'Stolen sisters—A human rights response to discrimination and violence against indigenous women in Canada'. Ottawa: Amnesty International. www.amnesty.ca/resource_centre/reports.

Arbour, Louise. 1996. *Commission of Inquiry into Certain Events at the Prison for Women in Kingston*. Ottawa: Public Works and Government Services Canada.

Auditor General of Canada. 2003. *Report of the Auditor General of Canada to the House of Commons*. Ottawa: Minister of Public Works and Government Services.

Borrowman, Shelley. 2000. Memorandum provided to the Federation of Saskatchewan Indian Nations, dated 25 May 2000. Copy on file with author.

CAEFS (Canadian Association of Elizabeth Fry Societies). 2007. 'Criminalized and imprisoned women fact sheet'. www.elizabethfry.ca/eweek07/paf/crmwomen.pdf.

Canadian Bar Association (Michael Jackson, author). 1989. 'Locking up Natives in Canada'. Ottawa: Canadian Bar Association. *University of British Columbia Law Review* 23: 215–30.

Canadian Council on Social Development. 2001. '2000 poverty lines'. www.ccsd.ca/factsheets/fs_lic00.htm.

———. 2003. 'Aboriginal children in poverty in urban communities: Social exclusion and the growing racialization of poverty in Canada'. www.ccsd.ca/pr/2003/aboriginal.htm.

Canadian Human Rights Commission. 2003. *Protecting Their Rights: A Systematic Review of Human Rights in Correctional Services for Federally Sentenced Women*. Ottawa: Canadian Human Rights Commission.

Chartrand, Larry, and Celeste McKay. 2006. *A Review of Research on Criminal Victimization and First Nations, Metis and Inuit Peoples 1990–2001*. Ottawa: Department of Justice, Policy Centre for Victim Issues.

Chrisjohn, Roland. 1997. *The Circle Game: Shadows and Substance in Indian Residential School Experience in Canada*. Penticton, BC: Theytus Books.

Commission on First Nations and Métis Peoples and Justice Reform. 2004. *Legacy of Hope: An Agenda for Change*, final report, vol. 1. Regina: Saskatchewan Justice.

Correctional Service of Canada. 2006. 'Citizens' Advisory Committees portal: History of CAC's'. Ottawa: Correctional Service of Canada. www.csc-scc.gc.ca/text/partenair/ccc/resourcemanual/1_e.shtml.

Cunneen, Chris. 2007. 'Criminology, human rights and indigenous peoples'. In *Sociology of Crime Law and Deviance*, vol. 9, 243–65.

Dickason, Olive. 1997. *Canada's First Nations: A History of Founding Peoples from Earliest Times*. 2nd edn. Toronto: Oxford University Press.

Garland, David. 1996. 'The limits of the sovereign state: Strategies of crime control in contemporary society'. *British Journal of Criminology* 36 (4): 445–71.

Goffman, Erving. 1961. *Asylums: Essays on the Social Situation of Mental Patients and Other Inmates*. Garden City, NY: Anchor Books.

Hamilton, A.C., and C. Murray Sinclair (Commissioners). 1991. *Report of the Aboriginal Justice Inquiry of Manitoba: The Justice System and Aboriginal Peoples*, vol. I and II. Winnipeg: Queen's Printer.

Hull, Jeremy. 2006. *Aboriginal Women: A Profile from the 2001 Census*. Prepared for the Women's Issues Equality Directorate, Indian and Northern Affairs Canada. Ottawa: Minister of Public Works and Government Services.

Jackson, Michael. 1983. *Prisoners of Isolation: Solitary Confinement in Canada*. Toronto: University of Toronto Press.

———. 2002. *Justice behind the Walls: Human Rights in Canadian Prisons*. Vancouver: Douglas and McIntyre.

Johansen, Bruce E. 1981. *Forgotten Founders: Benjamin Franklin, the Iroquois and the Rationale for the American Revolution*. Ipswich, MA: Gambit.

———. 1998. *Debating Democracy: Native American Legacy of Freedom*. Sante Fe, NM: Clear Light Publishing.

Lawrence, Bonita. 2004. *'Real' Indians and Others: Mixed Blood Urban Native Peoples and Indigenous Nationhood*. Vancouver: University of British Columbia Press.

Linden, Rick. 2004. *Criminology: A Canadian Perspective*. Toronto: Nelson.

Linden, Sidney B. (Commissioner). 2007. *Report of the Ipperwash Inquiry*. Toronto: Ontario Ministry of the Attorney General.

Martineau v. Matsqui Institutional Disciplinary Board (No. 2) [1980]. 106 D.L.R. (3d) 385 (S.C.C.).

Office of the Correctional Investigator. 2006–7. *Annual Report of the Office of the Correctional Investigator*. Ottawa: Office of the Correctional Investigator.

———. 2009. *Good Intentions, Disappointing Results: A Progress Report on Federal Aboriginal Corrections*. Ottawa: Office of the Correctional Investigator.

R. v. Gladue [1999], 1 S.C.R. 688 (S.C.C.).

RCAP (Royal Commission on Aboriginal Peoples). 1996. *Bridging the Cultural Divide: A Report on Aboriginal People and Criminal Justice in Canada*. Ottawa: Minister of Supply and Services.

Reiman, Jeffrey. 2007. *The Rich Get Richer and the Poor Get Prison: Ideology, Class and Criminal Justice*. Boston: Pearson/Allyn and Bacon.

Stern, Vivien. 2006. *Creating Criminals: Prisons and People in a Market Society*. Halifax: Fernwood.

Wewaykum Indian Band v. Canada [2003] 2 *Supreme Court Reporter* 259.

Woolford, Andres. 2009. *The Politics of Restorative Justice: A Critical Introduction*. Halifax and Winnipeg: Fernwood.

Wright, D.H. (Commissioner). 2004. *Report of the Commission of Inquiry into Matters Relating to the Death of Neil Stonechild*. Saskatoon: Government of Saskatchewan.

From Paternalism to Partnership: The Challenges of Aboriginal Leadership

Brian Calliou

Introduction

Aboriginal leadership plays an important role in the struggles of Canada's in-digenous peoples to preserve their language and culture as well as in their aspir-ations for self-government and successful economic development. Sociologist Menno Boldt argues that 'Effective Indian leadership represents the only and final chance for Indian people to escape their destitution, despair, and frustra-tion, and it represents their only hope for survival and well-being as Indians' (Boldt 1993a, 117). In other words, if Aboriginal peoples in Canada are to have the freedom and capacity to develop their unique cultures and identities, they require strong, effective leaders who are dedicated to taking full ownership and control of their local affairs with the help and support of their own people as well as representatives of the state. In the following chapter, I explore a number of ways that Aboriginal leaders have long taken an active role in protecting their peoples' rights and cultures and in advocating for their place in Canadian soci-ety. I note how Aboriginal leaders have faced many challenges in their struggle to ensure that the people they represent are respected as unique peoples with a special relationship with Canada, as holders of special, inherent rights, and as partners who are the original owners of the natural resources on their traditional lands.

It is important to note that the context for current developments involving Aboriginal leadership in Canada is not confined to this country, for indigenous peoples throughout the world are increasingly demanding that the nation-states in which they live treat them more like partners in decision-making and in the development of their traditional lands. This is certainly the case in Canada, since Aboriginal issues are now a national concern and are being addressed by federal, provincial, and territorial governments, by many municipal and regional governments, and in every institutional area, including education, religion, and the justice system, as well as by the industrial and business sectors. Most provinces now have Aboriginal relations departments or units to address Aboriginal issues. Many colleges and universities have developed Native studies programs that are regarded as an important area of post-secondary curriculum. As a result of the active role of Aboriginal leaders, we also see land claims and self-government agreements being negotiated and settled across Canada (Saku and Bone 2000). Many Aboriginal communities and their agencies have entered into agreements with various levels of government to deliver their own educational, health, family and child welfare, and justice-related services. Aboriginal communities must now be consulted and their interests must be accommodated in the planning of any resource development or regulations that might infringe upon their rights. Resource development corporations are now concluding impact benefit agreements with Aboriginal communities whose traditional lands are affected, and many of these agreements result in opportunities for employment, sub-contracting, joint ventures, and equity ownership. All of these developments and many others are helping Aboriginal communities develop and grow their local economies. But all of these developments did not just happen; they required more than a century of struggle, resistance, and activism on the part of many Aboriginal leaders in a wide variety of informal and formal contexts. As a result of their dedication and hard work, Aboriginal issues are now taken sufficiently seriously that leaders are becoming increasingly recognized by representatives of the Canadian state as partners in future development.

But how has the present situation come about? Why are Aboriginal issues now on the national stage? What issues are being addressed today by Aboriginal leaders? This chapter addresses these questions by exploring the role of Aboriginal leaders in terms of their organization, activism, and aspirations for their people to become self-governing nations with their unique identities and cultures.

Before examining current developments, I need to make one further point about context. Leaders do not operate individually or in isolation. In order to understand indigenous peoples' relations with the Canadian state, it is important to understand the historical, political, economic, and legal context that drives state policies and practices. This will give us insight into why representatives of the state deal with its indigenous peoples the way it does. Specifically, we cannot fully understand indigenous–Canadian relations and the current status of indigenous peoples in this country unless we consider and examine the institutions and structures that have resulted in their marginalization and forced them into a state of underdevelopment and dependency (Voyageur and Calliou 2007). Frideres argues that 'the existence of external structural factors', such as the economic and legal systems, have impinged upon indigenous peoples with often negative consequences (Frideres 1988a, 83). However, as I discuss throughout this chapter, Aboriginal leaders have often used these very institutional structures, such as the legal and political systems, to protect their peoples' unique identities and rights (Calliou 1999–2000).

To set the stage for our discussion of current developments, this chapter begins with a brief outline of a number of stages the relationship between Aboriginal peoples and the Canadian state has gone through since the arrival of European explorers and settlers. In chronological order, these stages have been primarily characterized by: cooperation, especially during French–British wars and the fur trade; paternalism, particularly as it has been embedded in policy initiatives allegedly designed to protect indigenous peoples from the 'superior' European settler culture; coercion, whereby attempts were made through policy and a variety of institutionalized means to 'civilize' and assimilate indigenous peoples; and conflict, during which indigenous peoples began to organize more effectively in active resistance against the imposition of colonial policies, practices, and structures designed to destroy their culture or their rights (Tobias 1976; Miller 1989). The final section of the chapter addresses the current period, which the Royal Commission on Aboriginal Peoples (1996) envisions as a 'new relationship' that is moving much more toward a partnership between sovereign peoples.

The Institutional Context of Aboriginal–State Relations in Canada

Economic Institutional Structures

It is commonly understood that the ideology of liberalism underlies Canada's economic system. Liberalism is based on Western Enlightenment ideas that separate religion and science. This ideology contributes to particular views of nature and the environment that see humans as separate from nature and hold that it is the right and privilege of human beings to control nature. Liberalism is closely tied to capitalism, an economic system made up of structures and institutions that support and promote the unhindered accumulation of profit. Institutionalized legal support for the growth of capitalism is founded on private ownership of property, the rule of law, and contracts (North 1990). Liberal capitalism therefore supports the private ownership of lands and resources, which ensures that those who own or control resources can decide who has access to their use. This dominant ideology, combined with (an eventually secularized) Protestant religious ethic that values discipline, hard work, and thrift, pervades many Western democracies such as Canada. This world view emphasizes individual autonomy, private ownership of lands, and the accumulation of material goods and profits for personal wealth. The ideals embedded in this ideology also legitimize the exploitation of natural resources and the marginalizing of workers in a never-ending pursuit of progress. In liberal democracies such as Canada, the imposition of institutional structures and laws by the nation-state has also served to transform indigenous peoples into 'politically weak, economically marginal and culturally stigmatized members of national societies' (Dyck 1985, 1). In short, the combination of liberalism, industrial capitalism, and religious missionary zeal that equated Christianization with civilization all helped to fuel the development of colonialism in Canada.

Indigenous peoples in Canada have thus had to deal with the economic effects of colonialism ever since European immigrants began to settle on their traditional lands. As many Elders and scholars note, indigenous peoples have always adapted to their changing circumstances, including changes that occurred as a result of newly established trade relations. For example, First Nations people were significantly involved in the fur trade, and many even flourished under it as successful middlemen (Ray 1974). Steven High refutes the view that First Nations entered into an 'era of irrelevance' after the decline of the fur trade, arguing instead that they adapted well and 'not only participated in the capitalist economy during this [period] but did so selectively to strengthen their traditional way of life' (High 1996). Although efforts by indigenous people to adapt to changing economic conditions resulted in some successes, colonial settlers and state structures regularly interfered with Aboriginal peoples' traditional livelihood. For example, although many First Nations adapted successfully to the new agricultural economy, if they were too successful they often faced resistance from their white farming neighbours who complained to government, which in turn set policies and regulations that restricted First Nations people from leaving their reserve, from selling their products, and from using modern agricultural tools (Carter 1990). The expropriation of indigenous lands has also served capitalist interests and contributed to the development of what some scholars refer to as internal colonialism (Frideres 1988b), which is the process through which a dominant society imposes its ideology and institutional structures upon a racial group by implementing policies that constrain and in many instances destroy indigenous values and traditions (Blauner 1969). According to Parnell, the unfettered growth of capitalism facilitates the exploitation of indigenous peoples and destroys their traditional economies, thereby making them dependent on the state and turning indigenous communities into internal colonies (Parnell 1976).

Legal Institutional Structures

Crown representatives began to acquire open access to land in Canada by entering into treaties with the 'Indians' and by the issuance of scrip with the Métis. The motive behind Europeans trying to establish treaties with Aboriginal peoples was largely economic, for they were eager to gain access to lands for settlement and the exploitation of natural resources. Economist Irene Spry argued that the settlement of the west in the nineteenth century resulted in the 'disappearance of the commons', whereby indigenous peoples were dispossessed of their common property (Spry 1976). This property was then turned into an open access resource that led not only to private settler ownership but ultimately to indigenous peoples' economic degradation. Sanders argues that in order for internal state resource development to occur, the government and economic elite needed to obtain open access to indigenous lands and resources. Consequently, the 'treaties and the reserves were part of a fascinating piece of social planning designed to shift the economic basis of native people to facilitate non-native settlement' (Sanders 1973–4, 85).

Section 91(24) of the 1867 Constitution Act gave jurisdiction to the federal government over 'Indians and lands reserved for Indians'. The first official order of business for state representatives at this time was to exercise jurisdiction by enacting the Indian Act, a piece of legislation that gave the state full administrative control over virtually every aspect of the lives of Canada's First Nations. James Frideres argues that the Indian Act provided a 'mandate for government administrators to control the lives of Natives' (Frideres 1988a, 75). Furthermore, the legislation also imposed significant constraints on indigenous peoples in that they 'could not own land, could not develop it without the agent's consent, and could not hold or attend large gatherings' (Frideres 1988a, 75–6). This resulted in the devastation of personal and group autonomy, especially for traditional Native political and social organization. Indeed, this system enabled Indian agents to exercise almost complete control over First Nations, and many of them played the role of gatekeeper for the federal Department of Indian Affairs by selecting which concerns or complaints from First Nations would be passed along to senior government officials (Brownlie 2003). First Nations leaders did what they could to resist the imposition of such oppressive actions and structures. Milloy argues that when the Indian Act was passed in 1876, First Nations leaders strongly protested. Immediately upon publication of the Act, tribal councils recognized its intent and rejected it. Surely, one tribal leader noted accurately, it was an attempt 'to break them to pieces'. It did not, he continued, 'meet their views', since it was inconsistent with their desire to maintain tribal integrity within customary forms most recently expressed by their insistence on group rather than individual tenure of land (Milloy 1983, 59).

Other forms of social control were exercised by Indian agents who did what they could to keep First Nations people on their reserves in order to prevent them from continuing their traditional ways of supporting their livelihood through hunting, fishing, and trapping (Calliou 2000). These legal institutional structures worked together with federal government policies to impose an assimilative process upon indigenous peoples in Canada, which often had debilitating effects.

Government Policies

Early colonial ideology in Canada was also influenced by a combination of (eventually secularized) religious, social Darwinist, and economic thought that contributed to a form of racism that regarded European-born Canadians as the pinnacle of human evolution (Frideres 1988a, 87–8). Christian missionaries and government representatives worked together in a variety of ways in their attempts to assimilate indigenous peoples. Their purpose in doing so was to make it easier to get Aboriginal people off their traditional lands and settle them on small reserves in order to learn a more 'civilized', thoroughly colonized way of life (Frideres 1988a, 88).

Many of the early policies the federal government established were intended to address the declining numbers of Aboriginal people, which was largely a result of diseases to which they had no immunity. After the federal government's medical officer, Dr P.H. Bryce, revealed the atrocious health conditions in the residential and industrial schools, the deputy minister at the time acknowledged that 'fifty percent of the children who passed through these schools did not live to benefit from the education which they had received therein' (Scott 1914). As Wesley-Esquimaux argues, the death, destruction, and displacement caused by diseases contributed to an 'historical trauma' for all Aboriginal peoples in Canada.

> The intensive trauma from such massive death and destruction not only contributed a great deal to the inability of indigenous people to effectively protect their cosmological beliefs and social systems, it also rendered reconstruction of their devastated social and economic systems impossible. What followed, as the people turned their gaze away from their own powers . . . people, often out of necessity, begin to integrate ideals and concepts from another people and begin to incorporate aspects of those ideals into their own way of life (Wesley-Esquimaux 2009, 15).

The result of government and church policies was that many Aboriginal peoples became assimilated, leading to the loss of many traditional practices, languages, cultures, and whole Nations. A further result was that many communities ended up in a state of almost full dependency on the government of Canada. One well-documented case is the Fort Hope Band. In 1983, 90 per cent of the income in the community derived from program and transfer funds from the federal government (Driben and Trudeau 1983). Sadly, many Aboriginal communities have ended up in a similar state of dependency.

Despite such historical trauma and devastation, Aboriginal leaders have resisted the federal government's policy of assimilation in many different ways. Barron argues that First Nations leadership 'reacted to government measures by consciously persisting in their traditional institutions, and in some cases, by devising or adopting counter-innovative techniques as an assertion of Indianness' (Barron 1984, 31). It is in the character of indigenous people to adapt to changing conditions, and this is evident in the ways that Aboriginal leaders in Canada have fought throughout the history of their often economically, politically, and legally oppressive relations with representatives of the Canadian state. Although foreign values, attitudes, and institutional structures have been imposed upon them in many different ways, they have been anything but passive victims. Rather, they have long been active agents who have struggled to bring the concerns of their people to representatives of the Canadian state.

Aboriginal Leadership and Strategies for Change

Although research and writing on Aboriginal leadership in Canada is not extensive, indigenous leadership in this country has become an area of growing interest for scholars and other writers (Calliou 2006). A number of biographies of chiefs and other political leaders have been written in the past 40 years, often for a popular audience (Dempsey 1972, 1986, 1995; MacEwan 1973; Redsky 1972; MacFarlane 1993; Botting 2005). More scholarly are studies of Aboriginal leadership by ethno-historians (MacNeish 1956; Rogers 1959; Smith 1973; Smith 1979; Morantz 1982; Chute 1997). Sociologist Menno Boldt led a new wave of scholarly Aboriginal leadership studies in the 1980s (Boldt 1973, 1980, 1981a, 1981b, 1981c, 1982, 1993b; Long and Boldt 1987, 1988; Long 1990, 1991), although scholarly interest in that area waned during the 1990s (Hedican 1991). More recently, however, attention has once again begun to focus on Aboriginal leadership in Canada. A small and select list of recent scholarly work in this area includes research on female chiefs by sociologist Cora Voyageur; First Nations leaders in Saskatchewan by education scholar Jacqueline Ottmann; a critical analysis of contemporary Indian leaders and a call for the revitalization of traditional governance and leadership by political theorist Taiaiake Alfred; and a variety of studies on Aboriginal leadership by others (Voyageur 2002, 2003, 2005, 2008; Ottmann 2002, 2005, 2006; Alfred 1995, 1999; Crowfoot 1997; MacFarlane 2000; Calliou 2005, 2008; Anderson 2009). This emerging literature examines the attitudes, influences, training, experiences, and actions of Aboriginal leaders past and present.

Organizing

There were many factors, including institutional structures, that served as barriers in early attempts by indigenous leaders in Canada to organize. As noted previously, Indian agents often acted as gatekeepers in terms of any grievances. Further, the Indian Act was amended in 1927 to restrict both local Indian organizing as well as the raising of funds by Indians to pay the legal costs involved in bringing any kind of claim against the government. Indians were also not allowed to vote and thus had no voice in provincial or national politics. Such political isolation was coupled to geographic isolation in that many First Nations peoples were restricted to remote reserves located far from one another. High levels of poverty also meant that Aboriginal peoples could not afford the expense of travel.

Ironically, many of the early leaders who led Aboriginal peoples' resistance in Canada were educated in Christian mission schools (Miller 1989). Despite the negative impacts of the residential schools on their language, culture, and identity, many leaders were able to use the knowledge they gained of the colonists' ways to voice claims on behalf of their people. In the face of many institutional barriers, early Aboriginal leaders came together to organize and bring their communities' concerns to the attention of state representatives (Patterson 1978; Tennant 1982, 1983; Galois 1992). For example, the Indian Association of Alberta (IAA) was established in 1939 under the leadership of Johnny Callihoo. Under his leadership, the IAA organized to help status and non-status Indians achieve a level of equality with the rest of Canadian society by seeking changes within rather than by challenging the system or advocating for the priority of treaty rights (Meijer-Drees 2002). In contrast, John Tootoosis of Saskatchewan focused on the rights agenda—that is, on pressing for the inherent rights and treaty rights of First Nations (Goodwill and Sluman 1984). These two approaches to advocating on behalf of First Nations influenced a young Cree leader named Harold Cardinal, who eventually became the leader of the Indian Association of Alberta. Harold Cardinal led Aboriginal peoples' reaction to the government's infamous 1969 White Paper, including significantly influencing the National Indian Brotherhood's 'Red Paper' response to the White Paper. A young Cardinal also wrote a book that was a scathing indictment of Canada's treatment of Aboriginal peoples. He criticized the federal government's response to organized activities by First Nations leaders and argued that although there were a few Canadian politicians who 'worked to build up Indian competence and leadership qualities', the majority have 'contributed to a disastrous and calculated programme of leadership destruction' by seeking the complete disorganization of Native peoples through discrediting and destroying Indian leaders (Cardinal 1969). The words and actions of leaders like Harold Cardinal gave birth to the modern 'Indian movement'. Doug Elias observed that by the early 1970s, 'Indian political expression has moved away from the humble mutterings of complaint put forward at Treaty Day for the consideration of an inattentive and unheeding Indian agent to formal and often dramatic statements of concern and demand' (Elias 1976). He further noted that

> [t]he occupations of Indian Affairs offices in Ottawa, Kenora and Saskatoon, well-researched and powerfully written briefs and publications, application through the courts to have justice done for the Natives whose environments are being trespassed, the formation of national, provincial, and local native organizations are all clear indications of a political sophistication that is slowly winning for native people the ability to influence the form of public policy in Canada (1976, 36).

As noted above, the primary catalyst for the new movement to organize and push a rights-based agenda, including the preservation of indigenous identities, was the federal government's 1969 White Paper on Indian policy. The White Paper was a statement of policy by the Trudeau government to terminate Aboriginal identities and special rights. The intent of the policy was to ensure that 'Indians' would assimilate into mainstream Canada with rights equal to those of all other Canadians. Aboriginal leaders reacted swiftly and vehemently in opposition to the White Paper and in response issued their own Red Paper, which declared that 'Indians' were 'citizens plus'—that is, they were Canadian citizens with rights equal to those of all other Canadians, but they also had special status and rights as sovereign, indigenous peoples.

During the 1960s, First Nations and Métis leaders recognized that it made strategic sense to establish their own national-level organizations, since a primary concern of First Nations people was treaty rights, while the Métis were concerned with Aboriginal rights. The two groups decided to split from the National Indian Council, which had been founded in 1961 by Bill Wuttunee and others (Ponting and Gibbins 1980, 197–8). The National Indian Brotherhood (NIB), which later became the Assembly of First Nations (AFN), was then formed in 1968 by many First Nations chiefs across Canada. The NIB was first led by Walter Deiter of the Federation of Saskatchewan Indians, from 1968 until 1970. Because of a technicality having to do with the NIB not being officially incorporated and registered with the Department of Consumer and Corporate Affairs, a new election was held, and George Manuel, a British Columbia Shuswap Indian, was elected as the new leader. Manuel worked hard on the internal development of the National Indian Brotherhood. He had an open, consultative style of leadership that enabled him to build a 'relationship of trust between himself and the executive council members' (Ponting and Gibbins 1980, 201).

However, most leaders found the structure of the NIB unworkable, and that led to a complete restructuring, which in 1982 resulted in the official change of name to the Assembly of First Nations in which all First Nations chiefs would take part. Today, the Assembly of First Nations is led by an executive council comprised of regional chiefs and a national, grand chief. The AFN advocates on a variety of issues of concern to First Nations leaders, including rights, identity, culture, social issues, education, and economic development.

After the Métis broke away from their Aboriginal political allies in the 1960s to form the Canadian Métis Society, they concentrated on Métis-specific concerns focusing on their relations with provincial governments, since at the time the federal government refused to assume jurisdiction and responsibility for them. The organization was later renamed the Métis Nation of Canada (Sawchuk 1998; Weinstein 2007). After much lobbying, the Métis were included as one of the Aboriginal groups covered in the definition of Aboriginal peoples in section 35(2) of the Constitution Act, 1982. The Métis Nation of Canada supported and led the successful litigation of the Powley case in which the Supreme Court of Canada held in its 2003 decision that the Métis of northwestern Ontario had proved they were a Métis community with an existing Aboriginal right to hunt.

Two Aboriginal populations not represented by either the AFN or the Métis Nation of Canada were non-status and off-reserve Indians. Eventually, these groups came to be represented by the Congress of Aboriginal People (originally the Native Council of Canada). The Indian Act defined who was an Indian and who was not. Those who were not considered 'status Indians' under the Act were denied the benefits and protections it offered and thus became known as 'non-status' Indians. The Native Council of Canada (NCC), like the NIB, grew out of the failure of the National Indian Council and was formed in 1968 to represent the interests of the Métis and non-status Indians. The Métis broke away from the Native Council of Canada in 1982, but the NCC continued as a national organization representing non-status Indians. In 1994, the Congress of Aboriginal Peoples (CAP) was established as a national body to replace the NCC and to lobby on behalf of the interests of non-status as well as urban Indians. Since the federal government tended to fund only on-reserve Indians, many status Indians in cities and other off-reserve communities supported efforts by CAP to lobby on their behalf, but this has been a source of conflict between First Nations chiefs and CAP.

The Inuit Taparisit Katanami (ITK) was established in 1971 to work on behalf of and to lobby for Inuit people at the national level. The ITK represents the Inuit of Labrador, Nunavik (northern Quebec), Nunavut, and the Northwest Territories. It is made up of regional affiliates, which are the Inuvialiut Regional Corporation in the western Arctic, the Baffin Region Inuit Association, the Kitikmeot Inuit Association in the central Arctic, the Keewatin Inuit Association, the Makavik Corporation of northern Quebec, and the Labrador Inuit Association, as well as the Inuit women's association called Pauktuuit. The presidents of each of these regional affiliates make up the board of directors for ITK. They receive core funding from federal government departments such as Canadian Heritage and Indian and Northern Affairs. Much of the advocacy, lobbying, and petitioning done by the ITK is in relation to self-government for the Inuit, protection of Inuit language and culture, environmental conservation, and protection of natural resources. One of its major accomplishments was the establishment of the newest territory in Canada, Nunavut, which included a land claim settlement and a self-government agreement that is a hybrid public government.

First Nations women generally supported their male counterparts in the struggles and resistance movements. However, they have often had to struggle with their own community leaders and political organizations to get women's issues on the table. They eventually formed a national association of women leaders in 1974, the Native Women's Association of Canada (NWAC). It attempts to represent and advocate for all Aboriginal women: status Indians, non-status Indians, Métis, Inuit, on- and off-reserve, and urban. NWAC deals with a variety of issues affecting Aboriginal women, such as equality rights for women and protection against family violence. For example, one contemporary issue NWAC has brought to the attention of Aboriginal leaders and state representatives is matrimonial property rights for First Nations women so that these women and their children are not left without the means to survive after a marriage breakdown (NWAC 1991; Cornet and Lendor 2004).

Given the diversity of issues of concern to Aboriginal peoples in Canada, it should not be surprising that the federal government prefers to deal with national-level Aboriginal organizations when negotiating policy decisions (Sanders

2003). From the perspective of many Aboriginal leaders, there is greater power in numbers and in sharing knowledge, ideas, and strategies. However, this strategy can lead to tension or the need for a balancing act, because when community leaders focus on national issues, they have less time and energy for local issues. Furthermore, leaders face the challenge of working together under an overall Aboriginal identity for national lobbying purposes while acknowledging that they represent unique nations that are often very distinct from their allies within the organization.

These national organizations are also dependent on government funding to survive and carry out their work. Being dependent on government funding thus makes them vulnerable, since governments use funding cuts to punish organizations that are adversarial in their relations with government and other state representatives (Sawchuk 1998). The problem with being too dependent on government funding is that it may temper the message of leaders or allow their strategic direction to be set by the funders' priorities or funding constraints. One leaked internal government document cited by Sawchuk illustrates how representatives of the state prefer to support moderate or friendly leaders and their organizations. It stated that '[i]t was further agreed that the most productive course would be to . . . foster the Native associations and their moderate leadership in resolving outstanding issues' (Sawchuk 1998). Nonetheless, with what are now quite well-established organizations, Aboriginal leaders are able to use a variety of strategies to influence government policies and their relationship to the Canadian state. Two of their most effective strategies are litigation and lobbying.

Litigation and Lobbying

A major strategy used by Aboriginal leaders to effect social and political change on behalf of their people has been to bring claims before the courts. One famous case involved Nisga'a leader Frank Calder, who brought an Aboriginal title claim before the courts in British Columbia. The case was eventually heard by the Supreme Court of Canada, and in its 1973 decision, the Court decided for the first time in Canadian history that Aboriginal rights had full legal status in Canada. Although the Nisga'a lost the case on a technicality, it prompted the federal government to establish two claims policies: one for comprehensive claims for areas where no treaties had ever been entered into and one for specific claims to fulfill treaty promises or deal with unlawful surrenders.

Another significant development in support of Aboriginal rights in Canada occurred during the early 1980s negotiations between the federal and provincial governments to repatriate the Constitution. At the time, Aboriginal organizations lobbied for their leaders to be allowed to sit at the first ministers' meetings in order to ensure that Aboriginal and treaty rights became entrenched in the Constitution. When they encountered opposition, a delegation went to London, UK, to lobby the British Parliament and also to bring their concerns before the English courts (Sanders 1983). This resulted in a decision by Lord Denning of the British Court in January 1982, which held that the Canadian Crown rather than the Crown of England was responsible for Canada's First Nations. Lord Denning also ruled that this meant that the Canadian state was obliged to honour all Aboriginal and treaty rights. As a result of the lobbying efforts of the Aboriginal leaders, the Constitution was amended to include section 35(1), which stated that 'existing Aboriginal and treaty rights are hereby recognized and affirmed.' This was a major achievement, because existing treaty and Aboriginal rights would receive constitutional protection against government legislation and actions and any infringements on such rights required the governments to consult with them first and take their rights into account.

From the Calder case onward, the legal and political ideology of the Canadian government has changed, leading one commentator to state that 'while the law most often provides the foundation upon which powerful entrenched interests find support, at times it opens a pathway for change' (Asch 1999). As a result of more intense lobbying and the active use of litigation by Aboriginal leaders, the Supreme Court of Canada declared in the Van der Peet decision in 1996 that Canadian sovereignty must be reconciled with the existing sovereignty of Aboriginal nations. The court analyzed the meaning of the existing Aboriginal and treaty rights that were recognized and affirmed by section 35 of the 1982 Constitution Act and concluded that the parties had to work on the reconciliation of their rights, since there was now a 'new relationship' between the Canadian state and its Aboriginal nations. Fundamentally, this new relationship established Aboriginal peoples as partners in the Canadian federation.

Civil Disobedience

Civil disobedience and extra-legal action is another strategy that some indigenous leaders and organizations have used in the struggle for their rights. Civil disobedience is often used when there are feelings of alienation, deprivation, and frustration along with distrust toward government. It is also used by Aboriginal leaders to demonstrate their power to resist dominance by representatives of the state over Aboriginal peoples. As Anthony Long and Menno Boldt noted, both established and future Aboriginal leaders have not been afraid to engage in extra-legal action, especially when they have been committed to fighting for their peoples' right to political and cultural self-determination (Long and Boldt

1988; Boldt 1981b). During the past 20 years, civil disobedience has included everything from major public demonstrations and standoffs to road blocks, which have occurred at such places as Gustafson Lake, British Columbia; Lubicon Lake, Alberta; Old Man River Dam, Alberta; Ipperwash, Ontario; Oka, Quebec; and most recently at Caledonia, Ontario, and Teyendenaga, Ontario. Some have led to violence and even death, such as at Ipperwash in 1995 where an Ojibway man, Dudley George, was shot and killed and at Oka in 1990 where police officer Marcel Lemay was shot and killed (Edwards 2003; MacLaine and Baxendale 1991).

Lack of progress on land claims and the government's frequent unwillingness to consult with Aboriginal leaders before natural resource development occurs has contributed to growing militancy on the part of increasing numbers of Aboriginal peoples and organizations. Grand Chief George Erasmus gave such a warning publicly when he stated, 'Canada, we have something to say to you—we have a warning for you. We want to let you know you're playing with fire. We may be the last generation of leaders that is prepared to sit down and peacefully negotiate our concerns with you' (*Globe and Mail* 1988). That there is some truth to Erasmus's words was evidenced by the very vocal and active Aboriginal youth movement that opposed the 2010 Winter Olympics in Vancouver. In arguing that Aboriginal peoples' efforts to resist have constrained the federal government's exercise of power, Ponting and Voyageur state, 'The radicalization, actual and potential, of some First Nation youth is part and parcel of this constraining effect' (Ponting and Voyageur 2002, 293).

International Struggles

Indigenous peoples around the world have long struggled to preserve their cultures and protect their rights against neo-liberal states and resource development corporations. As far back as the 1920s, the Six Nations Confederacy, under the leadership of Chief Deskaheh, also known as Levi General, brought the concerns of the Six Nations before the League of Nations (Hauptman 2008). Since that time, indigenous leaders throughout the world have used an international forum to seek support for and protection of indigenous rights.

Recently, indigenous leaders have lobbied for support of article 27 of the International Covenant on Civil and Political Rights, which deals with the rights of minorities in nation-states and declares that minorities shall not be denied the right to enjoy their culture, religion, and language (Blades 1994). One Maliseet leader, Sandra Lovelace, used this article in the mid-1970s to bring a claim against the Canadian government before the United Nations Human Rights Committee. Her claim was against membership provisions in the Indian Act that deemed she was no longer an 'Indian' because she had married a non-Indian and therefore should be denied any privileges and benefits, such as her right to live on her native reserve. The lawyers for Sandra Lovelace argued that the provisions discriminated against Indian women because while Indian men did not lose their Indian status upon marrying non-Indian women, Indian women did. The Human Rights Committee found that there had been a breach of article 27 of the covenant because the denial of her right to live on the reserve was not a 'reasonable and necessary measure to preserve the identity of the tribe' (Blades 1994, 15). This ruling resulted in international embarrassment for the Canadian government, although it took the government almost 10 years to implement Bill C-31, which removed the offending provision from the Indian Act and allowed disenfranchised Aboriginal women and their children to apply for restoration.

Lubicon Cree leader Chief Bernard Ominayak also brought a claim against the Canadian government before the United Nations Human Rights Committee in the mid-1980s regarding the government's failure to protect traditional Lubicon lands from being expropriated by the Alberta government for oil and gas development. Chief Ominayak argued that the federal government's failure to protect Lubicon land had resulted in the Lubicon being unable to carry on their traditional livelihood. A significant and disturbing consequence of this was a marked deterioration in the health of band members. The Human Rights Committee found that these developments, along with historical inequities, 'threaten the way of life and culture of the Lubicon Lake Band, and constitute a violation of article 27 so long as they continue'. The committee accepted a promise by the federal government 'to rectify the situation' by offering a land claim settlement of approximately $45 million in benefits and programs as well as a 95-square-mile reserve that included 79 square miles of mineral rights for the Lubicon (McGoldtrick 1991). While these two examples illustrate how Canadian Aboriginal leaders have lobbied for international support to protect their rights, other Aboriginal leaders in this country have worked with indigenous leaders throughout the world to further international protection for indigenous rights.

Indeed, indigenous peoples from around the world have built a global movement in support of indigenous rights and have made inroads into the United Nations forum. The UN Working Group on Indigenous Peoples was established in 1982 by the Sub-Commission on Prevention of Discrimination and Protection of Minorities, and by 1993 it had completed the draft Declaration on the Rights of Indigenous Peoples (Sanders 1994). The UN General Assembly passed a resolution proclaiming 1993 as the International Year of the World's Indigenous People. The draft declaration contained language that required nation-states to protect and support indigenous peoples' right to self-determination, stating that 'Indigenous peoples have the right to self-determination' and therefore can 'freely determine their political status and freely pursue their economic, social and cultural development' (Sanders 1994, 12). Commenting on the draft declaration, legal scholar Mary-Ellen Turpel stated, 'In reading the draft, one is reminded of how long a struggle it has been to have indigenous voices reflected in any substantive fashion in a formal instrument at the United Nations' (Turpel 1994). She notes that 'many Indigenous people from Canada have participated in the years of lobbying, drafting and advocating for specific recognition of the human rights of Indigenous peoples' (Turpel 1994, 50). Indeed, several Canadian Aboriginal leaders played a significant role in these developments. One of the most prominent was Cree leader and lawyer Wilton Littlechild from the Ermineskin First Nation in central Alberta, who worked for many years on the draft declaration. His involvement also included a term as the North American indigenous representative.

A number of nation-state representatives within the working group objected to the language and therefore did not support calling indigenous groupings 'peoples' with a right of self-determination. When the draft declaration went to the UN General Council, four nation-states voted against it. Not surprisingly, all four have colonized their indigenous peoples: Canada, Australia, New Zealand, and the United States.

Coalitions

Aboriginal leaders and organizations have also used coalitions in their efforts to protect their peoples' rights and their land. They have formed numerous coalitions with NGOs such as environmental or church groups in their struggles for social and environmental justice (Davis, O'Donnell, and Shpuniarsky 2007). As one commentator noted in relation to the growth of 'organized dissent' in Canada at the end of the 1960s, 'growing numbers of Native and non-Native people joined forces in a strategically organized, spiritual, and cultural revolution against the unjust fate shared by a majority of Native people in this country' (Long 1997, 151). A middle- and upper-class coalition of socially conscious groups, especially environmentalists, have often been willing to join with Aboriginal peoples in opposing unfettered resource development. However, because they have their own particular interests, which may differ from those of the Aboriginal people involved, their support on the issues that concern Aboriginal peoples will vary. Indeed, as Hamel has argued, it is easier to mobilize people around a mega-project development such as a pipeline or dam than around unique constitutional rights (Hamel 1994). While environmentalists have aligned with Aboriginal peoples on numerous occasions in protesting against large-scale resource development projects, they have also been in conflict with Aboriginal communities who want to control and develop resources or to use parks for hunting or other uses (Clairman 1993). Yet despite the potential for such conflict, many Aboriginal leaders have willingly aligned with a wide variety of groups to seek social and environmental justice on behalf of their Aboriginal communities.

A couple of examples illustrate Aboriginal leaders' use of coalitions to good effect. From 1989, the James Bay Cree leaders used other groups as allies in their struggle to stop the new, huge Great Whale dam project on their traditional lands. They cooperated with a variety of groups such as the Maine group, No Thank Q Hydro-Quebec, the Audubon Society, the Natural Resources Defense Council, Greenpeace Quebec, and Les Amis de la Terre (Friends of the Earth), among others (Craik 2004). The Cree leaders maintained control over their strategies by making decisions that served their interests and by acting in ways that kept them at arm's length from their coalition partners. The leaders used a number of strategies, including intervening in the courts and before administrative tribunals, engaging in an ongoing public awareness campaign, and forming a variety of partnerships with other coalition members.

Another example is the Lubicon Cree of northern Alberta, who in their struggle in the late 1980s against industrial development on their traditional territories were able through their leadership to mobilize more than 100 local, national, and international organizations to support and work with them. These organizations included the Toronto-based Friends of the Lubicon (Long 1997). David Long argues that the coalition organizations used two master frames of reference to raise public awareness and understanding and to generate support for the Lubicon—support for indigenous peoples rights and protection of the environment (Long 1997). International organizations and groups that aligned with coalition partners in supporting the Lubicon came from Germany, Belgium, Netherlands, Britain, the United States, and Japan. Although the actions of the coalition resulted in some movement by representatives of the Canadian state to take Lubicon claims seriously, differences in values, beliefs, and interests, along with the length of the dispute, led to the eventual waning of support for the Lubicon. Nonetheless, their struggle lives on, and Chief Ominayak continues to lobby and seek support for the rights and future of his people.

Professionalization

One other area in which Aboriginal leadership is developing is the emerging Aboriginal professional class. Many advisors and consultants being hired by

Aboriginal and non-Aboriginal governments, corporations, and non-profit organizations are themselves Aboriginal. Today, there are Aboriginal persons in
positions of power in the Canadian political and legal systems as well as in the
educational, medical, and business sectors. There are Aboriginal members of
Parliament, members of legislatures, judges, lawyers and law professors, and
academics and professors with PhDs in many different disciplines. Many of these
people are leaders who have influenced public policy in areas such as claims and
legal and constitutional developments (Turpel 1995; 1992). There are Aboriginal
medical doctors, scientists, engineers, artists, and successful businesspersons.
Many of these leaders work within non-Aboriginal institutions and organizations to address the systemic discrimination and barriers embedded within them
and to improve our society for all Canadians (Newhouse, Voyageur, and Beavon
2005). One example of such leadership was the action of Elijah Harper, a Cree
leader and MLA in the Manitoba legislature, who stood firm in his refusal to give
an affirmative answer to the Meech Lake Accord constitutional amendment. The
Manitoba legislature required the consent of all MLAs in order for the premier of
Manitoba to give his province's support to the accord. Mr Harper, representing
Aboriginal leaders' concerns with the way the Canadian state was dealing with
Aboriginal issues, refused to give his consent.

Many Aboriginal professionals have established organizations to facilitate
collaboration among their colleagues on many common issues. Examples of
such organizations include the Indigenous Bar Association, the Council for
the Advancement of Native Development Officers, the Aboriginal Financial
Officers Association, the Aboriginal Forestry Association, the Indian and Inuit
Nurses Association of Canada, and the Native American and Indigenous Studies
Association. The new professional class also permeates local, regional, and national Aboriginal political organizations

This overview of the means that Aboriginal leaders have used to protect their
peoples' rights and their land and to develop positive relations with representatives of the Canadian state provides clear evidence that they have achieved significant results on behalf of their people. Their actions have resulted in Aboriginal
rights being enshrined in the Canadian Constitution, thereby securing stronger
protection for those rights. They have argued and won significant cases in support of Aboriginal and treaty rights at national and international levels. Not only
have their actions resulted in significant changes to federal 'Indian' policies,
but they also appear to have led to a paradigm shift in government thinking
about Aboriginal–state relations. Actions taken by Aboriginal leaders over the
years in their struggles to bring their concerns before the Canadian government
have prompted the government to change its relationship to Aboriginal people

in this country. Weaver argues that persistent lobbying and political pressure applied by Aboriginal leaders led to the federal government radically shifting its 'Indian' policy to a 'new paradigm of policy and decision making' (Weaver 1990). Weaver states, 'In terms of the overall ethos of the two paradigms, the old one is characterized by a preoccupation with law, formality, and control over Aboriginal peoples; while the new one is more concerned with justice, adaptation, and workable inter-cultural relations' (Weaver 1990, 151). But as all Aboriginal leaders know, the battle for respect, equality, and justice for their people is far from over. We therefore now turn our attention to an examination of a number of significant challenges facing today's Aboriginal leaders as well as to the aspirations many of these leaders have for the future of their people and Canada.

Contemporary Challenges for Aboriginal Leaders

Resistance to and struggle with representatives of the Canadian state is not the only matter that consumes indigenous leaders' time and energy. As noted in the following section, they spend much of their time and energy working for their community interests in community development and establishing successful and sustainable economic development.

Social Issues

Indigenous leaders in Canada today face many significant challenges. These challenges include social issues that are in large part the result of the trauma experienced by many of their people who lost their culture through the imposition of state-controlled schooling and child welfare practices (Milloy 1999; Fournier and Crey 2005). Through the hard work and leadership of their National Chief Phil Fontaine, the AFN recently negotiated a settlement agreement with the federal government to compensate all survivors of government- and church-run residential schools. The compensation package of almost $2 billion included a common experience amount of $10,000 for the first year a person was in a residential school and $3000 for each additional year. The agreement also allowed for further compensation to those who suffered physical and/or sexual abuse, as well as funding of a truth and reconciliation process for future healing and research initiatives. The Truth and Reconciliation Commission (TRC) was established as a result of efforts by the national chief and many other Aboriginal leaders to ensure that: all Canadians would be informed about what happened in Indian residential schools; the truth of the experiences of the survivors would be documented; a public historical record of the policies and operations of the schools would be created; and Aboriginal peoples and all other Canadians would receive guidance and inspiration to engage in a process of reconciliation and renewed relationship. On 11 June 2008, the federal government made a formal apology to all Aboriginal peoples for the imposition of the residential schools policy that removed approximately 150,000 Aboriginal children from their families and sent them to church-run boarding schools where they not only suffered cultural loss but also varying degrees of physical and/or sexual abuse. In his public statement of apology, Prime Minister Stephen Harper stated that he was before Parliament 'to offer an apology to former students of Indian residential schools' and to acknowledge that the primary objectives of the imposed policy were 'to remove and isolate children from the influence of their homes, families, traditions and cultures, and to assimilate them into the dominant culture' (CBC 2008b). This was a major event for Aboriginal peoples in Canada, for it was the first time a Canadian prime minister had officially acknowledged the trauma inflicted on Aboriginal people throughout this sad chapter in Canadian history. In response, most Aboriginal leaders viewed the official apology as a signal that a new era of Aboriginal–state relations had begun and that it was vital to make sure that clear and immediate action be taken to bring about continued healing and renewal (CBC 2008a). Indeed, some scholars have argued that healing is a fundamental component of any future initiatives in support of Aboriginal self-government (Monture-Angus 1999; Warry 1998).

Aboriginal leaders are also taking more control over their own social services. For example, the Blood Tribe, known as the Kainai of southern Alberta, have been in trilateral negotiations on a self-government agreement relating to a specific area—child welfare. The chief and council have been negotiating with the federal and provincial governments with the intent of 'regaining jurisdiction and law-making authority over Child, Youth and Family Services and formalizing certain aspects now occurring including elections, governance and membership' (Kainai Government Agreement n.d.). The negotiated Kainai Government Agreement seeks to ensure that the federal and provincial governments agree to vacate their powers, thus enabling the Kainai Government to exercise full jurisdiction over their own nation's interests.

Aboriginal leaders have also pressured governments in Canada for increased power over the education of their people. In British Columbia, an historic agreement was signed on 5 July 2006 between the federal government, the BC government, and the First Nations Education Steering Committee. The agreement was historic in that it recognized First Nations jurisdiction over First Nations education throughout all of British Columbia (BC Liberals n.d.).

Rights Litigation, Negotiation, and Consultation

As noted previously, Aboriginal leaders spend a considerable amount of time and energy on land claims negotiations and litigation. Many communities that do not have land claims requiring settlement are nevertheless often in consultation with government and industry representatives to negotiate benefits agreements regarding resource development on their traditional lands. And although state and industry stakeholders have a great deal of economic and political power, Aboriginal leaders have much more leverage today than they had prior to obtaining constitutional protection for their Aboriginal and treaty rights in 1982 (Henderson 2006; Wilkins 2004; McNeil 2001). Numerous legal cases over the past 30 years in support of Aboriginal sovereignty have also empowered and inspired more and more Aboriginal leaders and their people to fight in order to gain control over their lives and the future of their own nations.

The intense lobbying of Aboriginal leaders led the federal government in the 1970s to establish the Indian Claims Commission to evaluate claims and make recommendations on conditions of settlement. There has been much analysis and debate on the effectiveness of the Indian Claims Commission, and many Aboriginal leaders have voiced frustration with the way the commission has operated (Turpel 1995). The federal response was to work with the AFN and eventually introduce new legislation, which received royal assent in 2008, for a specific claims tribunal (INAC 2009). There is hope that this new claims tribunal will speed up the process of specific claims, since its terms specify that if no settlement has been reached in three years, then the First Nation can opt out of the negotiation process, and the tribunal will then establish a settlement determination that is binding for all parties.

Self-Government

One of the primary responsibilities that indigenous leaders in Canada have had throughout the history of indigenous–white relations in this country has been to express and fight for the rights and aspirations of their people. Their most fundamental aspiration has always been for self-government and limited interference by the Canadian state in their local affairs. Indeed, Cassidy argues that understanding Aboriginal governments in Canada requires more than seeing them as merely products of federal policies of constitutional reform. Rather, Aboriginal governments are best understood as

> products of aboriginal peoples living and working to form political structures they require to meet the challenges of economic development,

health, education, social services, resource management and any number of common concerns in their communities and on their lands' (Cassidy 1990, 84).

The majority of First Nations in Canada have had Indian Act forms of government imposed upon them (Crane, Mainville, and Mason 2006; Imai, Logan, and Stein 1993). The narrow law-making powers granted to Aboriginal peoples and the requirement for ministerial approval for sale or lease of lands and resources on the reserve have been major factors in First Nations being unable to establish local economic development initiatives. Many First Nations leaders agree with the sentiments of former National Chief of the AFN, Ovide Mercredi, who stated that the Indian Act is a 'colonial relic' that must be removed in order for genuine Aboriginal self-government to proceed (Mercredi and Turpel 1993). North of 60, the First Nations and Inuit do not have reserve lands. Rather, they have mixed communities, with some Inuit having negotiated a public government (Hicks and White 2000). The Métis have been viewed by both the federal and provincial governments as falling under provincial jurisdiction. However, since they were also recognized in the Constitution as an Aboriginal people with certain inherent rights, the federal government has entered into negotiations with them and funded certain programs for Métis. Currently, Alberta is the only province that has granted a land base to the Métis. This has enabled the Métis to establish eight settlements throughout the province and to operate with municipal-like powers over their settlement lands (Pocklington 1991; Bell and Robinson 2008).

The majority of First Nations leaders speak of exercising their inherent right to self-government even when they are forced to operate within the constraints of the Indian Act. The Royal Commission on Aboriginal Peoples acknowledged that some Aboriginal peoples could legitimately revitalize their traditional government structures (RCAP 1993, 41). Although the Indian Act structure was imposed upon First Nation leaders, it does not mean that traditional governments disappeared. For example, the Six Nations Confederacy retained their traditional government structure alongside the Indian Act structure of leadership (Johnston 1986). Because the federal government will only recognize leadership established under the terms of the Indian Act, state representatives will only deal with Aboriginal leaders who conform to those terms by holding 'legitimate' positions of leadership.

Another way that Aboriginal leaders are attempting to address problems with the Indian Act is through processes involving the negotiation of self-government agreements. The number of negotiations on Aboriginal self-government agreements has been increasing over the past 20 years or so, and many of them are part of land claim settlement discussions (Allen 2004). Self-government agreements establish that the federal and provincial governments acknowledge and accept the legitimacy of First Nations governments to exercise powers that normally fall under federal or provincial jurisdiction. One of the first self-government agreements in Canada involved the Sechelt First Nation in British Columbia. This agreement essentially released the Sechelt First Nation from many of the constraints of the Indian Act and provided them with expanded powers very much like those of a municipal government (Taylor and Paget 1991). A few other notable self-government agreements have involved the James Bay Cree, the Council of Yukon Indians, and the Tlitcho in the Northwest Territories.

When asserting their claims for self-government, Aboriginal peoples have often 'encountered the institutionalized political, legal and economic interests of the existing constituent governments', which functioned to 'limit the range of responses available to accommodate the demands of Indian peoples' (Long 1991, 193). Consequently, one former national chief of the AFN advocated for a limited form of sovereignty within the existing federal constitutional structure with powers akin to provinces when he stated, 'To us, it [self-government] means full autonomy and self determination within Canada and the Canadian Constitution' (Long 1991, 198). In other words, he advocated for autonomy as full as that of a province but within the legal state structure of the Constitution.

On the other hand, many indigenous leaders have taken a very strong nationalistic stand in asserting the sovereignty of their nations. However, most contemporary democratic nation-states are unwilling to amend their constitutions in order to grant sovereignty to the indigenous peoples within their borders. As Augie Fleras and Roger Maaka note, 'White settler dominions' such as Canada, New Zealand, and Australia have not been receptive to moving away from their colonial mindset in accepting the principle of 'indigeneity' and indigenous nationalism as grounds for reconstitutionalizing their relations with their indigenous peoples (Fleras and Maaka 2000). One example of an indigenous people who have taken a strong nationalistic stance recently in Canada is the Inuit, who developed the Inuit Declaration on Sovereignty in the Arctic. The declaration affirms Inuit sovereignty and states that any nation-state must consult and deal with them as a sovereign nation on any matters concerning the Arctic (ICC Canada Staff 2008).

Community Economic Development

A key area of concern for all Aboriginal leaders in Canada is community economic development. Many Aboriginal and non-Aboriginal commentators have argued that true self-government cannot be achieved unless Aboriginal communities attain a significant degree of economic independence (Helin 2006).

Despite the restrictive nature of the Indian Act, many First Nations leaders have exercised what powers they do have and brought about a certain amount of economic development in their communities. Examples include the Osoyoos First Nation in the BC Interior under the leadership of Chief Clarence Louie, the Membertou First Nation in Nova Scotia under the leadership of Chief Terence Paul, the Whitecap Dakota First Nation in Saskatchewan under the leadership of Chief Darcy Bear, and the Fort McKay First Nation in northeastern Alberta under the leadership of Chief Jim Boucher. Chief Clarence Louie led the development of Osoyoos reserve lands into a successful tourist destination with their golf resort, winery, and cultural interpretive centre. Chief Terrence Paul led the economic development of Membertou First Nation through many joint ventures with multinational corporations setting up projects to build maritime helicopters, provide engineering services and environmental technologies, offer onshore and offshore catering, and provide health records management services for military personnel. Chief Darcy Bear led the Whitecap Dakota economic development by developing a tourist destination with a casino and golf resort. Chief Jim Boucher led the economic development of the Fort McKay First Nation by taking advantage of the opportunities offered by oil sands mining in their region and setting up a number of companies providing oil sands services.

These successful First Nations leaders have taken a business approach to their leadership and the development of their business ventures. First Nations governments have also taken on broader powers through existing legislation such as the Land Management Act. Some First Nations have entered into joint venture agreements with one another. Examples include the Ktunaxa First Nation, the Rama First Nation, and the Samson Cree Nation, who are joint owners of a golf course and resort hotel in the British Columbia Interior. Rama First Nation also owns and operates its own casino in Ontario, while the Samson Cree Nation owns the money-lending Peace Hills Trust organization, the Samson Oil and Gas Company, and many other businesses. Aboriginal leaders have played a key role in the development of these organizations and initiatives, and as a result there continue to be increased opportunities for Aboriginal communities to benefit from diverse kinds of economic development on their traditional territories, including opportunities to enter into impact benefit agreements that include employment, business contracts, and sometimes equity ownership.

Lastly, Indian Act restrictions on land being used as security in loan applications has historically made it difficult for many First Nations to get loans. However, the creation of Aboriginal banking institutions such as the First Nations Bank of Canada, the Peace Hills Trust, and regional lending institutions such as the Alberta Indian Investment Corporation and the Métis lending institution Apeetigosan have made loans to Aboriginal nations and communities more accessible. Another economic development strategy increasingly used by Aboriginal communities and organizations has been the pooling of investment resources. One group that has succeeded by using this strategy is the Tribal Councils Investment Group in Manitoba (Wuttunee 2002).

Conclusion

There is much evidence to support the assertion that continued efforts by Aboriginal leaders have resulted in Aboriginal–state relations moving beyond conflict into partnership. It thus seems that the 'new relationship' with the Canadian state envisioned and recommended by members of the Royal Commission on Aboriginal Peoples is coming to fruition. However, this is not to say that Aboriginal leaders will now have things come easily to their communities. Many are convinced that Aboriginal people will have to continue to struggle for their fair share of what Canada has to offer, but there are also signs of hope that Aboriginal people in this country will increasingly realize their dreams of self-government and economic independence. In order to implement their visions of building economically independent, self-governing Nations and communities, Aboriginal leaders across Canada are committed to lobbying government as well as building the capacities of their peoples.

Despite the ongoing activism and laudable achievements of many Aboriginal leaders, Alfred argues that some leaders have internalized the Indian Act in ways that have shaped their attitude and behaviour. As noted by one leader cited by Alfred, 'The Indian Act had a profound effect on us in terms of identity, actual and for membership—and this effect can't be annulled by dismissing the Indian Act. It's like it's "in us" and we have consented to elements of it.' (Alfred 1995, 90). A fundamental problem with internalization is that it builds a barrier that gets in the way of the revitalization of traditional leadership and governance:

> Yet the imposition of this very particular set of Western values and institutions has been internalized to the degree that it now presents an obstacle to the re-implementation of a traditional form of government or even to the reform of Indian Act–mandated institutions currently existing within the community (Alfred 1995, 90).

The challenge is significant, for as one Blackfoot First Nations leader stated in challenging other indigenous leaders to get out of the colonial mindset:

[W]e need a paradigm shift in our thinking, away from the cynical, defensive, dependent, entitlement mindset that has been inculcated in us under the colonial Indian Act regime, and toward a more trusting, assertively proactive, persevering, visionary, affirming, meritocratic, and inclusive orientation. . . . If First Nations do not experience a drastic shift in leadership and followership . . . our very future as First Nations will be jeopardized (Crowfoot 1997, 323).

This is a far cry from the optimism of Boldt and Long, who stated rather optimistically in the mid-1980s that 'the emerging educated elite has the expertise to establish and staff the political and administrative infrastructures needed for Aboriginal self-government.' They did, however, recognize that 'one of the most urgent needs confronting Aboriginal peoples today is for personnel trained to facilitate economic and social development' (Boldt and Long 1985, 9). Borrows and Morales noted as recently as 2005 that there were still many gaps in the skills and competencies required for effective Aboriginal leadership: 'Recent trends imply major shortages of Aboriginal people educated in fields such as economics, community planning and development, business management, forestry, biology, resource conservation, wildlife management, geology and agriculture' (Borrows and Morales 2005). Furthermore, as Navajo scholar Manley Begay notes, the effects of colonialism continue to pervade the lives of Aboriginal people in this country, and it is the responsibility of Aboriginal leaders to 'rebuild, reunite, reshape, and revitalize their nations' (Begay 1997).

Calliou has also argued that in order for indigenous communities to effectively implement their vision of the inherent right to self-government, they must build the capacity to do so at the governance level as well as at the individual leader level (Calliou 2008). Professional development of Aboriginal leaders, managers, administrators, directors of boards, and entrepreneurs is vital if healthy and successful self-government and economic development arrangements are to be realized. Although there is much to be done, the many years of determined struggle by Aboriginal leaders in Canada on behalf of their people have resulted in countless positive developments in their Nations and communities. Their vision and efforts have led to a new era characterized by increasing opportunities for Aboriginal Nations, communities, organizations, and individuals to become equal partners in developing a new vision for Aboriginal–state relations in Canada.

Discussion Questions

1. What are some of the institutional and structural contexts that affect Aboriginal communities and influence how their leaders must respond?
2. What are some of the strategies Aboriginal leaders have used to represent their community's interests?
3. What were some of the issues that Aboriginal leaders have had to deal with in the past, and what issues are they dealing with now?
4. What are some of the organizations that Aboriginal leaders have established to represent their collective interests, what groups of Aboriginal peoples do they represent, and what types of issues do they deal with?
5. Regarding the relationship between Aboriginal peoples and the Canadian state, give some examples of the relationship of paternalism and some examples of the relationship of partnership.

Further Readings

Boldt, Menno. 1993. 'Leadership'. In Menno Boldt, *Surviving as Indians: The Challenge of Self-Government*. Toronto: University of Toronto Press.

Botting, Gary. 2005. *Chief Smallboy: In Pursuit of Freedom*. Calgary: Fifth House.

Calliou, Brian. 2005. 'The culture of leadership: North American indigenous leadership in a changing economy'. In Duane Champagne, Karen Jo Torjesen, and Susan Steiner, eds., *Indigenous Peoples and the Modern State*. Walnut Creek, CA: AltaMira Press.

Crowfoot, Strater. 1997. 'Leadership in First Nation communities: A chief's perspective on the colonial millstone'. In J. Rick Ponting, ed., *First Nations in Canada: Perspectives on Opportunity, Empowerment and Self-Determination*. Whitby, ON: McGraw-Hill Ryerson.

Dempsey, Hugh A. 1986. *The Gentle Persuader: A Biography of James Gladstone, Indian Senator*. Saskatoon: Western Producer Prairie Books.

Goodwill, J., and N. Sluman. 1984. *John Tootoosis*. 2nd ed. Winnipeg: Pemmican Publishing.

Long, J. Anthony. 1987. 'Leadership in Canadian Indian communities: Reforming the present and incorporating the past'. *Great Plains Quarterly* 7 (2): 103.

McFarlane, Peter. 1993. *From Brotherhood to Nationhood: George Manuel and the Modern Indian Movement*. Toronto: Between the Lines.

Ottmann, Jacqueline. n.d. 'First Nations leadership development'. www.banffcentre.ca/departments/leadership/aboriginal/library/First_Nations_Leadership_Ottmann.pdf.

Sawchuk, Joe. 1998. *The Dynamics of Native Politics: The Alberta Native Experience*. Saskatoon: Purich Publishing.

Tennant, Paul. 1982. 'Native Indian political organization in British Columbia, 1900–1969: A response to internal colonialism'. *BC Studies* 55: 3.

Voyageur, Cora. 2008. *Firekeepers of the 21st Century: Women Indian Chiefs*. Montreal: McGill-Queen's University Press.

John Weinstein. 2007. *Quiet Revolution West: The Rebirth of Métis Nationalism*. Calgary: Fifth House.

References

Alfred, Gerald (Taiaiake). 1995. *Heeding the Voices of Our Ancestors: Kahnawake Mohawk Politics and the Rise of Native Nationalism.* Toronto: Oxford University Press.

———. 1999. 'Leadership'. In Taiaiake Alfred, *Peace, Power, Righteousness: An Indigenous Manifesto,* 89. Don Mills, ON: Oxford University Press.

Allen, Edward. 2004. 'Our treaty, our inherent right to self-government: An overview of the Nisga'a Final Agreement'. *International Journal of Minority and Group Rights* 11: 233.

Anderson, Kim. 2009. 'Leading by action: Female chiefs and the political landscape'. In Gail Guthrie Valaskakis, Madeleine Dion Stout, and Eric Guimond, eds., *Restoring the Balance: First Nations Women, Community and Culture,* 99. Winnipeg: University of Manitoba Press.

Asch, Michael. 1999. 'From Calder to Van der Peet: Aboriginal rights and Canadian law, 1973–1996'. In Paul Havemann, ed., *Indigenous Peoples' Rights in Australia, Canada and New Zealand,* 428. Melbourne: Oxford University Press.

Barron, Laurie. 1984. 'Indian policy'. *Native Studies Review* 31.

BC Liberals. n.d. 'Historic agreement to improve First Nations education'. www.bc liberals.com/news/aboriginal_relations/historic_agreement_to_improve_first_nations_ education.

Begay, Manley, Jr. 1997. 'Leading by choice, not chance: Leadership education for Native chief executives of American Indian nations'. (Harvard University, Graduate School of Education, EdD dissertation).

Bell, Catherine, and Harold Robinson. 2008. 'Government on the Métis settlements: Foundations and future directions'. In Yale Belanger, ed., *Aboriginal Self-Government in Canada: Current Trends and Issues,* 260. Saskatoon: Purich Publishing.

Blades, Alexander B. 1994. 'Article 27 of the International Covenant on Civil and Political Rights: A case study on implementation in New Zealand'. *Canadian Native Law Reporter* 1:1.

Blauner, Robert. 1969. 'Internal colonialism and ghetto revolt'. *Social Problems* 16: 396.

Boldt, Menno. 1973. 'Indian leaders in Canada: Attitudes toward equality, identity, and political status'. (Yale University, Department of Sociology, PhD dissertation).

——— 1980. 'Canadian Native leadership: Context and composition'. *Canadian Ethnic Studies* 12 (1): 15.

———. 1981a. 'Enlightenment values, romanticism and attitudes toward political status: A study of Native Indian leaders in Canada'. *Canadian Review of Sociology and Anthropology* 18 (4): 545.

———. 1981b. 'Philosophy, politics, and extralegal action: Native Indian leaders in Canada'. *Ethnic and Racial Studies* 4 (2): 205.

———. 1981c. 'Social correlates of nationalism: A study of Native Indian leaders in a Canadian internal colony'. *Comparative Political Studies* 14 (2): 205.

———. 1982. 'Intellectual orientations and nationalism among leaders in an internal colony: A theoretical and comparative perspective'. *British Journal of Sociology* 33 (2): 484.

———. 1993a. 'Leadership'. In Menno Boldt, *Surviving as Indians: The Challenge of Self-Government,* 117. Toronto: University of Toronto Press.

———. 1993b. *Surviving as Indians: The Challenge of Self-Government.* Toronto: University of Toronto Press.

Boldt, Menno, and J. Anthony Long, eds. 1985. *The Quest for Justice: Aboriginal Peoples and Aboriginal Rights*. Toronto: University of Toronto Press.

Borrows, John, and Sarah Morales. 2005. 'Challenge, change and development in Aboriginal economies'. In Dwight Dorey and Joseph Magnet, eds., *Legal Aspects of Aboriginal Business Development*, 147. Markham, ON: Nexis Butterworths.

Botting, Gary. 2005. *Chief Smallboy: In Pursuit of Freedom*. Calgary: Fifth House.

Brownlie, Robin. 2003. *A Fatherly Eye: Indian Agents, Government Power, and Aboriginal Resistance in Ontario, 1918–1939*. Don Mills, ON: Oxford University Press.

Calliou, Brian. 1999–2000. 'The imposition of state laws and the creation of various hunting rights for Aboriginal peoples of the Treaty 8 territory'. In Duff Crerar and Jaroslav Petryshyn, eds., 'Treaty 8 revisited: Selected papers on the 1999 Centennial Conference'. Special premier issue, *Lobstick: An Interdisciplinary Journal* 1 (1): 151.

———. 2000. 'Losing the game: Conservation and the regulation of First Nations hunting, 1880–1930'. (University of Alberta, Faculty of Law, master's thesis).

———. 2005. 'The culture of leadership: North American indigenous leadership in a changing economy'. In Duane Champagne, Karen Jo Torjesen, and Susan Steiner, eds., *Indigenous Peoples and the Modern State*, 47. Walnut Creek, CA: AltaMira Press. 2006. 'Indigenous leadership bibliography'. www.banffcentre.ca/departments/leadership/aboriginal/library/pdf/Indigenous_Leadership_Bibliography-Brian_Calliou.pdf.

———. 2008. 'The significance of building leadership and community capacity to implement self-government'. In Yale Belanger, ed., *Aboriginal Self-Government in Canada: Current Trends and Issues*, 3rd edn, 332. Saskatoon: Purich Publishing.

Cardinal, Harold. 1969. *The Unjust Society: The Tragedy of Canada's Indians*. Edmonton: Hurtig Publishers.

Carter, Sarah. 1990. *Lost Harvests: Prairie Indian Reserve Farmers and Government Policy*. Montreal and Kingston: McGill-Queen's University Press.

Cassidy, Frank. 1990. 'Aboriginal governments in Canada: An emerging field of study'. *Canadian Journal of Political Science* 23 (1): 73.

CBC. 2008a. 'Aboriginal leaders look to future after historic apology'. www.cbc.ca/canada/story/2008/06/11/apology-future.html.

———. 2008b. 'Prime Minister Stephen Harper's statement of apology'. www.cbc.ca/canada/story/2008/06/11/pm-statement.html.

Chute, Janet E. 1997. 'Ojibwa leadership during the fur trade era at Sault Ste. Marie'. In *Papers of the Seventh North American Fur Trade Conference*. East Lansing: University of Michigan.

Clairman, Cara L. 1993. 'First Nations and environmental groups in Ontario's parks—conflict or cooperation?' *Canadian Native Law Reporter* 1: 1.

Cornet, Wendy, and Allison Lendor. 2004. 'Matrimonial real property issues on-reserve'. In Jerry White, Paul Maxim, and Dan Beavon, eds., *Aboriginal Policy Research: Setting the Agenda*, vol. II, 143. Toronto: Thompson Educational Publishing.

Craik, Brian. 2004. 'The importance of working together: Exclusions, conflicts and participation in James Bay, Quebec'. In Mario Blaser, Harvey Feit, and Glenn McRea, eds., *In the Way of Development: Indigenous Peoples, Life Projects and Globalization*, 166. London: Zed Books.

Crane, Brian A., Robert Mainville, and Martin W. Mason. 2006. 'Band governance under the Indian Act'. In Brian A. Crane, Robert Mainville, and Martin W. Mason, *First Nations Governance Law*, 101. Markham, ON: LexisNexis, Butterworths.

Crowfoot, Strater. 1997. 'Leadership in First Nation communities: A chief's perspective on the colonial millstone'. In J. Rick Ponting, ed., *First Nations in Canada: Perspectives on Opportunity, Empowerment and Self-Determination*, 299. Whitby, ON: McGraw-Hill Ryerson.

Davis, Lynne, Vivian O'Donnell, and Heather Shpuniarsky. 2007. 'Aboriginal–social justice alliances: Understanding the landscape of relationships through the Coalition for a Public Inquiry into Ipperwash'. *International Journal of Canadian Studies* 36.

Dempsey, Hugh A. 1972. *Crowfoot: Chief of the Blackfeet*. Norman: University of Oklahoma Press.

———. 1986. *The Gentle Persuader: A Biography of James Gladstone, Indian Senator*. Saskatoon: Western Producer Prairie Books.

———. 1995. *Red Crow: Warrior Chief*. Saskatoon: Fifth House.

Driben, Paul, and Robert S. Trudeau. 1983. *When Freedom Is Lost: The Dark Side of the Relationship between Government and the Fort Hope Band*. Toronto: University of Toronto Press.

Dyck, Noel. 1985. *Indigenous People and the Nation State: Fourth World Politics in Canada, Australia and Norway*. St. John's: Memorial University of Newfoundland.

Edwards, Peter. 2003. *One Dead Indian: The Premier, the Police, and the Ipperwash Crisis*. Toronto: McClelland and Stewart.

Elias, Doug. 1976. 'Indian politics in the Canadian political system'. In Marc-Adelard Tremblay, ed., *The Patterns of 'Amerindian' Identity*, 35. Laval: Les Presses de l'Université Laval.

Fleras, Augie, and Roger Maaka. 2000. 'Reconstitutionalizing indigeneity: Restoring the "sovereigns within"'. *Canadian Review of Studies in Nationalism* 27: 111.

Frideres, James S. 1988a. 'Institutional structures and economic deprivation: Native people in Canada'. In B. Sing Bolaria and Peter S. Li, eds., *Racial Oppression in Canada*, 2nd edn, 71. Toronto: Garamond Press.

———. 1988b. 'The political economy of Natives in Canadian society'. In James Frideres, *Native Peoples in Canada: Contemporary Conflicts*, 3rd edn, 366. Scarborough, ON: Prentice-Hall.

Fournier, Suzanne, and Ernie Crey. 2005. *Stolen from Our Embrace: The Abduction of First Nations Children and the Restoration of Aboriginal Communities*. Vancouver: Douglas and McIntyre.

Galois, Robert. 1992. 'The Indian Rights Association, Native protest activity and the "land question" in British Columbia, 1902–1916'. *Native Studies Review* 8 (2): 1.

Globe and Mail. 1 June 1988.

Goodwill, J., and N. Sluman. 1984. *John Tootoosis*. 2nd edn. Winnipeg: Pemmican Publishing.

Hamel, Peter. 1994. 'The Aboriginal Rights Coalition'. In Christopher Lind and Joe Mihevc, eds, *Coalitions for Justice: The Story of Canada's Interchurch Coalitions*. Ottawa: Novalis.

Hauptman, Laurence M. 2008. 'The idealist and the realist: Chief Deskaheh, attorney George Decker, and the Six Nations' struggle to get to the World Court, 1921–1925'. In George M. Hauptman, *Seven Generations of Iroquois Leadership: The Six Nations since 1800*, 124. Syracuse, NY: Syracuse University Press.

Hedican, Edward J. 1991. 'On the ethno-politics of Canadian Native leadership and identity'. *Ethnic Groups* 9: 1.

Helin, Calvin. 2006. *Dances with Dependency: Indigenous Success through Self-Reliance.* Vancouver: Orca Spirit.

Henderson, James (Sakej) Youngblood. 2006. *First Nations Jurisprudence and Aboriginal Rights: Defining the Just Society.* Saskatoon: Native Law Centre, University of Saskatchewan.

Hicks, Jack, and Graham White. 2000. 'Nunavut: Inuit self-determination through a land claim and public government?' In Jens Dahl, Jack Hicks, and Peter Jull, eds, *Nunavut: Inuit Regain Control of Their Lands and Their Lives*, 30. Denmark: International Working Group for Indigenous Affairs.

High, Steven. 1996. 'Native wage labour and independent production during the "era of irrelevance"'. *Labour/Le Travail* 37: 244.

ICC Canada Staff. 2008. 'Arctic sovereignty begins with Inuit'. *Drum* 1 (2): 1.

Imai, Shin, Katherine Logan, and Gary Stein. 1993. 'Band powers under the Indian Act' and other chapters in Shin Imai, Katherine Logan, and Gary Stein, *Aboriginal Law in Canada.* Toronto: Carswell Thomson Professional Publishing.

INAC (Indian and Northern Affairs Canada). 2009. 'The proposed Specific Claims Tribunal Act'. www.ainc-inac.gc.ca/al/ldc/spc/jal/fct3-eng.asp.

Johnston, Darlene. 1986. 'The quest of the Six Nations Confederacy for self-determination'. *University of Toronto Faculty Law Review* 44: 1.

Kainai Government Agreement. n.d. Brochure. www.kainaigovernment.org/pdfs/ 600285%20 Kainai%20Brochure%20LR.pdf.

Long, David Alan. 1997. 'The precarious pursuit of justice: Counter hegemony in the Lubicon First Nation Coalition'. In William K. Carroll, ed., *Organizing Dissent: Contemporary Social Movements in Theory and Practice*, 2nd edn, 151. Toronto: Garamond Press.

Long, J. Anthony. 1990. 'Political revitalization in Canadian Native Indian societies'. *Canadian Journal of Political Science* 23 (4): 751.

———. 1991. 'Federalism and ethnic self-determination: Native Indians in Canada'. *Journal of Commonwealth and Comparative Politics* 29 (2): 192.

Long, J. Anthony, and Menno Boldt. 1987. 'Leadership in Canadian Indian commun-ities: Reforming the present and incorporating the past'. *Great Plains Quarterly* 7 (2): 103.

———. 1988. 'Self-determination and extra-legal action: The foundations of Native Indian protests'. *Canadian Review of Studies in Nationalism* 15 (1–2): 111.

MacEwan, Grant. 1973. *Sitting Bull: The Years in Canada.* Edmonton: Hurtig Publishing.

McFarlane, Peter. 1993. *From Brotherhood to Nationhood: George Manuel and the Modern Indian Movement.* Toronto: Between the Lines.

———. 2000. 'Aboriginal leadership'. In David A. Long and Olive Patricia Dickason, eds, *Visions of the Heart: Canadian Aboriginal Issues*, 2nd edn, 49. Toronto: Harcourt Canada.

McGoldrick, D. 1991. 'Canadian Indians, cultural rights and the Human Rights Committee'. *International Covenant Law Quarterly* 40: 658.

MacLaine, C., and M. Baxendale. 1991. *This Land Is Our Land: The Mohawk Revolt at Oka.* Montreal: Optimum Publishing.

McNeil, Kent. 2001. *Emerging Justice: Essays on Indigenous Rights in Canada and Australia.* Saskatoon: Native Law Centre, University of Saskatchewan.

MacNeish, J.H. 1956. 'Leadership among the northeastern Athabascans'. *Anthropologica* 2: 131.

Meijer-Drees, Laurie. 2002. *The Indian Association of Alberta: A History of Political Action.* Vancouver: University of British Columbia Press.

Mercredi, Ovide, and Mary-Ellen Turpel. 1993. *In the Rapids: Navigating the Future of First Nations*. Toronto: Viking.

Miller, J.R. 1989. 'The beginnings of political organization'. In J.R. Miller, *Skyscrapers Hide the Heavens: A History of Indian–White Relations in Canada*, rev. edn, 211. Toronto: University of Toronto Press.

Milloy, John S. 1983. 'The early Indian Acts: Developmental strategy and constitutional change'. In Ian A.L. Getty and Antoine S. Lussier, eds, *As Long as the Sun Shines and Water Flows: A Reader in Canadian Native Studies*, 56. Vancouver: University of British Columbia Press.

———. 1999. *A National Crime: The Canadian Government and the Residential School System*. Winnipeg: University of Manitoba Press.

Monture-Angus, Patricia. 1999. *Journeying Forward: Dreaming First Nations Independence*. Halifax: Fernwood.

Morantz, Toby. 1982. 'Northern Algonquian concepts of status and leadership reviewed: A case study of the eighteenth-century trading captain system'. *Canadian Review of Sociology and Anthropology* 19: 482.

Newhouse, David, Cora J. Voyageur, and Dan Beavon, eds. 2005. *Hidden in Plain Sight: Contributions of Canada's Aboriginal Peoples*. Toronto: University of Toronto Press.

North, Douglas. 1990. *Institutions, Institutional Change and Economic Performance*. Cambridge: Cambridge University Press.

NWAC (Native Women's Association of Canada). 1991. *Matrimonial Property Rights*. Ottawa: NWAC.

Ottmann, Jacqueline. 2002. 'First Nations leadership and spirituality within the Royal Commission on Aboriginal Peoples: A Saskatchewan perspective'. (University of Saskatchewan, Department of Educational Administration, master's thesis).

———. 2005. 'First Nations leadership development within a Saskatchewan context'. (University of Saskatchewan, Department of Educational Administration, PhD dissertation.)

———. 2006. 'First Nations leadership development'. www.banffcentre.ca/departments/leadership/aboriginal/library/First_Nations_Leadership_Ottmann.pdf.

Parnell, Ted. 1976. *Disposable Native*. Edmonton: Alberta Human Rights and Civil Liberties Association.

Patterson, E. Palmer. 1978. 'Andrew Paull and the early history of British Columbia Indian organizations'. In Ian A.L. Getty and Donald B. Smith, eds, *One Century Later: Western Canadian Reserve Indians Since Treaty 7*. Vancouver: University of British Columbia Press.

Pocklington, T.C. 1991. *The Government and Politics of the Alberta Métis Settlements*. Regina: Canadian Plains Research Centre, University of Regina.

Ponting, J. Rick, and Roger Gibbins. 1980. 'History of the National Indian Brotherhood'. In J. Rick Ponting and Roger Gibbins, *Out of Irrelevance: A Socio-political Introduction to Indian Affairs in Canada*, 195. Toronto: Butterworths.

Ponting, J. Rick, and Cora Voyageur. 2001. 'Challenging the deficit paradigm: Grounds for optimism among First Nations in Canada'. *Canadian Journal of Native Studies* 21 (2): 275.

Ray, Arthur J. 1974. *Indians in the Fur Trade: Their Role as Hunters, Trappers and Middlemen in the Lands Southwest of Hudson Bay, 1660–1870*. Toronto: University of Toronto Press.

Redsky, J. 1972. *Great Leader of the Ojbway: Mis-quona-queb*. Toronto: McClelland and Stewart.

Residential Schools Settlement Official Court Notice. www.residentialschoolsettlement.ca/summary_notice.pdf.

Rogers, E.S. 1959. 'Leadership among the Indians of eastern subarctic'. *Anthropologica* 7: 263.

Saku, James C., and Robert M. Bone. 2000. 'Modern treaties in Canada: The case of northern Quebec agreements and the Inuvialuit Final Agreement'. *Canadian Journal of Native Studies* 20 (2): 283.

Sanders, D.E. 1973–4. 'Native people in areas of internal national expansion'. *Saskatchewan Law Review* 38: 85.

———. 1983. 'The Indian lobby'. In Keith Banting and Richard Simeon, eds, *And No One Cheered: Federalism, Democracy and the Constitution Act*, 301–32. Toronto: Methuen.

———. 1994. 'Developments at the United Nations: 1994'. *Canadian Native Law Reporter* 4: 12.

Sanders, Will. 2003. 'From unorganized interests to nations within: Changing conceptions of indigenous issues in Australia and Canada'. *Australian Canadian Studies* 21 (1): 125.

Sawchuk, Joe. 1998. *The Dynamics of Native Politics: The Alberta Native Experience*. Saskatoon: Purich Publishing.

Scott, D.C. 1914. 'Indian Affairs, 1867–1912'. In A. Short and A.G. Doughty, eds, *Canada and Its Provinces*, vol. VII, 16. Toronto: Glasgow Brook.

Smith, Donald B. 1973. *Leadership among the Southwestern Ojibwa*. Ottawa: National Museum of Canada.

Smith, James G.E. 1979. 'Leadership among the Indians of the northern woodlands'. In R. Hinshaw, ed., *Currents in Anthropology: Essays in Honor of Sol Tax*. The Hague: Mouton.

Spry, Irene. 1976. 'The great transformation: The disappearance of the commons in western Canada'. In Richard Allen, ed., *Man and Nature on the Prairies*, 21. Regina: Canadian Plains Research Centre.

Taylor, John, and Gary Paget. 1991. 'Federal/provincial responsibility and the Sechelt'. In David C. Hawkes, ed., *Aboriginal Peoples and Government Responsibility: Exploring Federal and Provincial Roles*, 297. Ottawa: Carleton University Press.

Tennant, Paul. 1982. 'Native Indian political organization in British Columbia, 1900–1969: A response to internal colonialism'. *BC Studies* 55: 3.

———. 1983. 'Native Indian political activity in British Columbia, 1969–1983'. *BC Studies* 57: 112.

Tobias, John. 1976. 'Protection, civilization, assimilation: An outline of Canada's Indian policy'. *Western Canadian Journal of Anthropology* 6 (2): 13.

Turpel, Mary Ellen. 1992. 'Further travails of Canada's human rights record: The Marshall case'. In J. Mannette, ed., *Elusive Justice: Beyond the Marshall Inquiry*. Halifax: Fernwood.

———. 1994. 'Commentary'. *Canadian Native Law Reporter* 1: 50.

———. 1995. 'A fair, expeditious, and fully accountable land claims process'. In Indian Claims Commission, Special Issue on Land Claims Reform, *Indian Claims Commission Proceedings*, 2. Ottawa.

Voyageur, Cora J. 2002. 'Keeping all the balls in the air: The experience of Canada's women chiefs'. In A. MacNevin et al., eds, *Women and Leadership*. Ottawa: Canadian Research Institute for the Advancement of Women.

———. 2003. 'The community owns you: Experiences of Canada's women chiefs'. In Meryn Stuart and Andrea Martinez, eds, *Out of the Ivory Tower: Taking Feminist Research to the Community*, 228. Toronto: Sumach Press.

———. 2005. 'They called her Chief: A profile of Dorothy McDonald'. In Sarah Carter et al., eds, *Unsettled Pasts: Reconceiving the West through Women's History*. Calgary: University of Calgary Press.

———. 2008. *Firekeepers of the 21st Century: Women Indian Chiefs*. Montreal: McGill-Queen's University Press.

Voyageur, Cora J., and Brian Calliou. 2007. 'Aboriginal economic development and the struggle for self-government'. In Les Samuelson and Wayne Antony, eds, *Power and Resistance: Critical Thinking about Canadian Social Issues*, 4th edn, 135. Halifax: Fernwood.

Warry, Wayne. 1998. *Unfinished Dreams: Community Healing and the Reality of Self-Government*. Toronto: University of Toronto Press.

Weaver, Sally. 1990. 'A new paradigm in Canadian Indian policy for the 1990s'. *Canadian Ethnic Studies* 22 (3): 8.

Weinstein, John. 2007. *Quiet Revolution West: The Rebirth of Métis Nationalism*. Calgary: Fifth House.

Wesley-Esquimaux, Cynthia. 2009. 'Trauma to resilience: Notes on decolonization'. In Gail Guthrie Valaskakis, Madeleine Dion Stout, and Eric Guimond, eds, *Restoring Balance: First Nations Women, Community and Culture*, 13. Winnipeg: University of Manitoba Press.

Wilkins, Kerry, ed. 2004. *Advancing Aboriginal Claims: Visions/Strategies/Directions*. Saskatoon: Purich Publishing.

Wuttunee, Wanda. 2002. 'Partnering among Aboriginal communities: Tribal Councils Investment Group (TCIG)'. *Journal of Aboriginal Economic Development* 3 (1): 9.

12 Moving Beyond the Politics of Aboriginal Well-being, Health, and Healing

Martin Cooke and David Long

Introduction

The [Royal] Commission recommends that . . . Governments, in formulating policy in social, economic or political spheres, give foremost consideration to the impact of such policies on the physical, social, emotional and spiritual health of Aboriginal citizens, and on their capacity to participate in the life of their communities and Canadian society as a whole (RCAP 1996, section 3.3.4).

In the following examination of well-being, health and illness, and healing in the lives of First Nations, Inuit, and Métis, we take our lead from the Royal Commission on Aboriginal Peoples (RCAP). Our chapter begins with a brief introduction on the history and politics surrounding Aboriginal health in Canada to illustrate how the development of Aboriginal health policy and legislation has reflected a power imbalance between Aboriginal peoples and the Canadian state. This is followed by our presentation of two perspectives on well-being and health that at first glance appear to be significantly at odds with one another. After noting certain contrasts between the 'Western' scientific, biomedical approach to health/illness research and its indigenous counterpart, we examine how the adoption of the 'social determinants of health' perspective is bringing about a new understanding of Aboriginal health and facilitating more promising dialogue among those involved in Aboriginal health research as well as legislative, policy, and program development. The chapter concludes with a discussion of how we see these two perspectives coexisting, albeit with a certain amount of tension, in the field of Aboriginal health.

We argue that this tension must be recognized by the variety of stakeholders committed to bringing healing, wellness, and health not only to the lives of Aboriginal individuals and communities but also to relations between Aboriginal and non-Aboriginal peoples in Canada. Before we present our brief account of a number of key developments in Aboriginal health legislation and policy, a few introductory comments on how the RCAP framed the relationship between health and healing are in order.

RCAP: Clarifying a Vision for Aboriginal Health and Healing

If we were to summarize the goals of the RCAP, we might say that the commission was struck to instigate change in policies, practices, outcomes, and most fundamentally the relationships between Aboriginal peoples and Canadian institutions (RCAP 1996). One of the critical domains that the commission identified as being in need of change was health. Volume 3, Chapter 3 of the RCAP report, *Health and Healing*, was a document that addressed all aspects of Aboriginal peoples' health: physical, social, emotional, spiritual, and environmental. Not surprisingly, the findings of the research reported in that volume were that First Nations, Inuit, and Métis peoples continued to experience much poorer than average health than other Canadians. This was the case whether Aboriginal people lived in urban areas or on reserves, in Inuit communities in the North, in Métis settlements, in parkland areas in the south, in rural areas, or in any other type of community across the country.

Accounts presented by Aboriginal individuals to the RCAP testified not only to the ways that the historical legacy of European colonization had continued to affect their individual health and well-being but also to how it had torn apart the interpersonal, cultural, structural, and spiritual fabric of their families and communities. And the Indian Act was consistently named as the most destructive means through which colonization secured control over virtually every aspect of Aboriginal life from birth to death (RCAP 1996). The authors of the RCAP report detailed how everything from loss of Aboriginal traditions and languages, family and community disruption, political corruption among Aboriginal leaders, serious economic disparity and unemployment in many communities, addiction, suicide, disease, disability, and shorter life spans for Aboriginal peoples was clearly linked to the colonizing attitudes, policies, and practices of Europeans. To their credit, however, the report is anything but a litany of harsh experiences and desperate circumstances. Rather, it embodies a vision of reconciliation and hope that promises to bring healing to past, present, and future generations of Aboriginal peoples through the establishment of a 'new relationship' with the Canadian state (RCAP 1996; Long 2004).

Like the commission's recommendations in other areas, those related to the well-being and health of Aboriginal peoples were wide-ranging and systemic. They involved strengthening community control over health service delivery and training sufficient numbers of Aboriginal health professionals to reduce reliance on non-Aboriginal experts (Long 2009). They focused on empowering communities to define the content of their own health care services, partly in order to honour and maintain culturally specific conceptions of illness and disease, wellness, and healing. Western science and medicine clearly had a role to play in the understanding and treatment of poor health, but the RCAP recommendations related to health specified that all scientific research should be of direct benefit to the individuals and communities that take part. As we note in the following section, the final RCAP report followed roughly 150 years of often heated 'negotiations' between Aboriginal peoples and representatives of the Canadian state. And for good reason, health has always been a central issue in these negotiations.

Jurisdiction and Responsibility for Aboriginal Health

Although the RCAP brought national attention to the need for a fundamental restructuring of Aboriginal–state relations, there is longstanding debate over these relations in general and the role of the state in supporting Aboriginal health in particular. Central to these debates has been a lack of clear understanding regarding the administration and delivery of Aboriginal health services. While the 1867 Constitution Act placed 'Indians and lands reserved for Indians' under full legislative authority of the federal government, the same Act placed responsibility for the administration and delivery of health and social services under the jurisdiction of the provinces. Consequently, although the Act decreed that each provincial government was to be responsible for providing health care to Canadian citizens within their boundaries, administrative oversight of health care delivery to status[1] First Nations peoples and the Inuit lay mainly with the federal government. In this way, the historical process of treaty-making and changing legal definitions of 'status' eligibility have divided Aboriginal populations into those for whom social and health care services are the responsibility of the federal government and those for whom these services are provided, as they are for other Canadians, by provincial or territorial governments.

Even for those whose health clearly falls under federal jurisdiction, the question of what kind of health care the federal government should provide has been the subject of much discussion and disagreement. Only Treaty 6, signed in 1876 by the Government of Canada and the Cree of central Alberta and Saskatchewan, specifically mentions government provision of health care in its terms:

> In the event hereafter of the Indians . . . being overtaken by any pestilence or by general famine, the Queen . . . will grant to the Indians assistance . . . sufficient to relieve them from the calamity that shall have befallen them. . . . A medicine chest shall be kept at the house of each

Indian Agent for the use and benefit of the Indians at the discretion of such Agent.[2]

Despite the fact that the 1876 Indian Act states that the government would accept responsibility to 'prevent, mitigate and control the spread of diseases on reserves . . . and to provide for sanitary conditions . . . on reserves', there has nonetheless been much dispute over the meaning of 'the medicine chest' and government responsibility for Aboriginal health care. According to many First Nations peoples who signed treaties, rights bestowed by those treaties were intended to include comprehensive health care (RCAP 1993, 42; Littlechild and Littlechild 2009).

Unfortunately for many Aboriginal people in Canada, it has often been assumed that Aboriginal health refers to the health of those defined as having proper legal status and who live on First Nation reserves or in distinct Aboriginal communities, despite the fact that nearly two-thirds of Aboriginal people in this country now live in urban areas or other non-reserve communities and that only about half have 'status' (Fitzmaurice and McCaskill, this volume). One consequence of this is that the majority of Aboriginal health research has focused on First Nations reserves and Inuit communities, which by default has resulted in a lack of information about as well as attention to the health of non-status First Nations, Métis, and other Aboriginal people (Young 2003; Wilson and Young 2008).

Although most of the government funding for health services and research has been directed toward First Nations peoples living on reserves and members of Inuit communities, the federal government does provide some health care services and benefits to Aboriginal people living off-reserve, including those in cities. The Non-Insured Health Benefits program (NIHB) administered by Health Canada provides some services such as eyeglasses, some mobility aids, and a few others that are not covered by provincial health care programs (Health Canada 2009). However, these benefits are only available to status First Nations people or to those who are part of a recognized Inuit land claims agreement. To this point, non-status First Nations, Métis, and Inuit people not covered by such agreements have no such additional health benefits coverage.[3]

It seems that there has always been some confusion among government representatives surrounding the question of which department and level of government ought to be responsible for Aboriginal health in Canada. Although the Department of Indian Affairs (DIA) had been originally charged with the administrative responsibility to provide health services for on-reserve Aboriginal people, this changed in 1945, the year after Parliament passed the National

Health and Welfare Act and Indian health services were transferred to the newly established Department of Health and Welfare, now known as Health Canada. While there was some wisdom in transferring Aboriginal health into this minister's portfolio, it nonetheless contributed to somewhat of a fragmentation of Aboriginal health policy and program initiatives, since the DIA retained authority over health-related areas that included housing, education, welfare, and even sewage, sanitation, and safe drinking water.

A 1979 federal Indian health policy paper was the beginning of the end of full federal control over Aboriginal health care. Much like the 1969 White Paper served as a catalyst for the building of coalitions by Aboriginal people and their supporters to engage in large-scale resistance (Caillou, this volume), the 1979 health policy paper generated heated debate over who should control Aboriginal health care in Canada. By the mid-1980s, Aboriginal leaders were in full agreement that the Canadian government must allow First Nation and Inuit communities to have greater control over their own health services. Their negotiations with government representatives resulted in the development of health transfer agreements that would enable First Nations and Inuit communities to have greater control over their own health-related services.[4] By 2002, roughly 47 per cent of eligible communities had signed such an agreement. These communities, combined with 151 others that had established community-based health services agreements and 41 that were involved in the pre-transfer phase, added up to more than 80 per cent of all eligible Aboriginal communities in Canada (Waldram, Herring, and Young 2006, 270).

Ultimately, however, the health of Aboriginal populations in Canada cannot be separated from the history of colonialism and the relationships between Aboriginal peoples and the Canadian state. The provision of health care services has long been a contentious issue, and while support for health transfer agreements reflects a growing recognition of the benefits of Aboriginal control over Aboriginal health, understanding what needs to happen next is a complex question. One of the more significant challenges facing those who are committed to addressing this question is the deep cultural differences between Aboriginal and non-Aboriginal understandings of well-being, health, and illness.

Perspectives on Aboriginal Health

Part of the dispute regarding control over Aboriginal health and health care is rooted in different conceptions of health, illness, and well-being. As we note later on in this chapter, RCAP recommendations related to health sought to articulate a way of addressing the conflict between these two quite different cultural perspectives. It has long been recognized that in very basic terms, the Western, 'allopathic' approach to human health is based on a biomedical model that views the human body as an organic system of interrelated physical parts. Given that the 'ideal state' of this system is for all body parts to function smoothly and in well-coordinated fashion, human health is a matter of whether or not the parts of our bodies function properly, individually and within complex systems. Those involved in health research and diagnosis are thus essentially responsible for identifying what is wrong with the parts that are not working so that physicians and other health professionals can properly intervene and treat, remove, or replace the diseased or improperly functioning part. Health practitioners and policy-makers who operate from this perspective tend to conceptualize health as mainly a physical state, characterized by the absence of physical disease. Even mental illnesses such as depression tend to be considered from within a 'physical framework' of malfunctioning neurotransmitters, receptors, and parts of the brain itself. The result is that treatment of sickness and disease is primarily focused on physical interventions aimed at sick individuals, who for the most part are seen in isolation from their relationships in families, communities, or society at large.

By comparison, an indigenous conception of health and well-being emphasizes that the life of each individual human being is deeply connected to all of 'creation' in the past, the present, and the future.

> Health is the core of the well-being that must lie at the centre of each healthy person and the vitality that must animate healthy communities and cultures. Where there is good health in this sense, it reverberates through every strand of life (RCAP 1993, 51).

Physical manifestations of illness are important, but Aboriginal peoples' much more broad and holistic perspective on health assumes that the emotional and spiritual dimensions of life must also be given consideration when 'diagnosing' the potential causes of empirically measurable ailments.

Although there is a great deal of diversity in health and healing practices among Aboriginal cultures, Aboriginal 'healing' is therefore generally focused not only on the body but more fundamentally on restoring relationships with the whole self and others and with understanding through tradition and ceremony one's relation to all of creation—past, present, and future. Health from an indigenous perspective is thus more than the absence of physical disease in an individual. Rather, it is a 'measure' of the spiritual, mental, emotional, and physical well-being of individuals, communities, and 'all their relations'.

It is in the context of this holistic perspective that we are able to see many of the health problems experienced by Aboriginal peoples as being directly related to the profound disruption and destruction of their cultures and communities. As noted throughout this edition of *Visions of the Heart*, the long history of colonization and its (continued) devaluation of Aboriginal experiences and world views lies at the root of such destruction. Many have argued that minor tinkering with health legislation and/or social policies and programs will thus remain largely ineffective, since they do little to address the root causes of exclusion and racism that have become normalized through the Indian Act and hundreds of years of colonization (Blackstock 2003). As representatives of the Nechi Institute (1988, 4) noted:

> Attempting to heal isolated Aboriginal individuals apart from their family and their community cannot heal abuse and other imbalances of life. To get to the root cause of abuse and neglect, the entire system that allowed it to occur must be restored to balance. This means that the accumulated hurt of generations, carried to our families and our communities, needs to be released through a healing process.

Exactly what this healing process ought to look like in relation to Aboriginal health remains open to discussion and debate. A common idea expressed in statements to the RCAP was that resources and social change efforts need to be directed toward community-based programs and initiatives that are responsive to the diversity of experience and circumstance between as well as within Aboriginal communities (Ferris et al. 2005). As Saulis (2003, 291) notes:

> It is important to underscore that social policy decision-making in the Aboriginal process is rooted in the perceptions of the people in the communities, and that they play an active role in interpreting, priority setting, and evaluating the directions of policy. It is not a process isolated from people and located in the bureaucracy, as we see in the mainstream process.

If we look to developments in public health over the past 20 or 30 years, we can see evidence that there may be points of convergence between these two perspectives, even though on the surface the 'Aboriginal process' and mainstream public health initiatives appear to be grounded in two very different worlds.

The Changing View of (Public) Health in Canada

It is clear that the RCAP occurred at an important time in the history of pub-lic health, for by the mid-1990s significant changes had occurred in govern-ment and scientific perspectives on health and well-being. In Canada and other wealthy countries, ideas around the 'new public health' that had begun to take shape in the 1960s and 1970s had contributed to two significant shifts in health policy thinking. The first was a move away from a primary concern with those who were already ill or who were most at risk of becoming ill to more general prevention of disease. It was recognized that although treating the sick and those likely to become sick would always be a primary role of the health care system, much greater emphasis needed to placed on the prevention of disease among the broader population. As epidemiologist Geoffrey Rose (1985) explained, for many types of health problems there might be a greater overall reduction in the 'burden of illness', achieved by focusing on the health of the population as a whole rather than on only those at 'high risk'.

A second shift was that health researchers began to pay greater attention to the social and economic correlates of health and well-being. It had long been recog-nized that those with lower education, income, and social standing tended to be in poorer health and to live shorter lives (Richmond and Ross 2009). However, explanations had traditionally been on the direct, or what researchers referred to as 'proximal', causes of illness such as poor food and water quality, smoking and excessive drinking, and poor housing, to name a few. In contrast, population health research in the 1960s and 1970s began to focus on the broader relation-ships between social, economic, and political contexts and poor health. The land-mark Whitehall Studies in the UK identified what they termed a 'reliable status gradient in health', meaning that they found a direct relationship between lower social status and higher mortality, regardless of the adequacy of diet or other physical conditions. This contributed to a wide-ranging research effort to investi-gate the ways that socio-economic conditions contributed to some groups experi-encing poor health and others experiencing much better health. These studies were therefore very influential in moving academic and policy attention from the biological causes of disease to what became known as the 'social' determinants of health and to balancing the traditional clinical focus on the health of individuals with a much broader focus on the health of communities and societies.

Canada has also had international influence in relation to the develop-ment of this new direction for public health through the publication of two documents. The first was the Lalonde Report (Lalonde 1972), which is widely cited as the first government articulation of a social determinants approach to public health. A decade later, the *Ottawa Charter for Health Promotion* was published as the outcome of the World Health Organization's First International Conference on Health Promotion (World Health Organization 1986). The charter identified the prerequisites for health as peace, shelter, education, food, income, stable ecosystem, sustainable resources, social justice, and equity. Population health research added critical health determinants, including healthy child development; adequate incomes; a small gap between rich and poor; the absence of discrimination based on gender, culture, race, and sexual orientation; life-long learning opportunities; healthy lifestyles; meaningful work opportunities with some control over decision-making; social relationships that respect diversity; freedom from violence or its threat; freedom from exposure to infectious disease; protection of humans from environmental hazards and protection of the environment from human hazards. The charter also drew on a number of values that are explicitly supported throughout RCAP reports, including that:

- individuals are treated with dignity, and their innate self-worth, intelligence, and capacity of choice are respected;
- individual liberties are respected, but priority is given to the common good when conflict arises;
- participation is supported in policy decision-making to identify what constitutes the common good;
- priority is given to people whose living conditions, especially a lack of wealth and power, place them at greater risk;
- social justice is pursued to prevent systemic discrimination and to reduce health inequities;
- health of the present generation is not purchased at the expense of future generations.

The strategic principles articulated in the charter further specify that:

1. Health promotion addresses health issues in context. It recognizes that many individual, social, and environmental factors interact to influence health. It searches for ways to explain how these factors interact in order to plan and act for the greatest health gain.
2. Health promotion supports a holistic approach that recognizes and includes the physical, mental, social, ecological, cultural, and spiritual aspects of health.
3. Health promotion requires a long-term perspective. It takes time to

create awareness and build understanding of health determinants. This is true for organizations as well as for individuals.

4. Health promotion supports a balance between centralized and decentralized decision-making on policies that affect people where they live, work, and play.

5. Health promotion is multi-sectoral. While program initiatives often originate in the health sector, little can be done to change unhealthy living conditions and improve lifestyles without the support of other people, organizations, and policy sectors.

6. Health promotion draws on knowledge from a variety of sources. It depends on formal knowledge from the social, economic, political, medical, and environmental sciences. It also depends on the experiential knowledge of people.

7. Health promotion emphasizes public accountability. Those providing health promotion activities need to be accountable and to expect the same commitment from other individuals and organizations.

The social determinants of health approach promoted through the Lalonde Report and the Ottawa Charter has gained strength over the past three decades and as recently as 2005 became institutionalized through the creation of the Public Health Agency of Canada (PHAC) and the position of the Chief Medical Officer for Canada. Given that the interim and final RCAP reports were written in the early and mid-1990s, it should not be surprising that many of those involved were familiar with and sympathetic to the values and principles that informed the new public health perspective. What might be surprising to some is that the authors of the RCAP report noted that the fundamental principles underlying the 'newly discovered' public health perspective had long been part of indigenous teachings. Consequently, the RCAP report invited representatives of Aboriginal, federal, provincial, and territorial governments to endorse the fundamental principles of:

- holism—that is, attention to whole persons in their total environment;
- equity—that is, equitable access to the means of achieving health and rough equality of outcomes in health status;
- control by Aboriginal people of their lifestyle choices, institutional services, and environmental conditions that support health;
- diversity—that is, accommodation of the cultures and histories of First Nations, Inuit, and Métis people that make them distinctive within Canadian society and that distinguish them from one another (RCAP 1996, section 3.3.1).

It was in the context of this broad perspective that RCAP recommendations directed at improving the health of Aboriginal populations focused on better education and income, as well as on reducing social and economic inequality between Aboriginal peoples and non-Aboriginal Canadians. Since the 1990s, there have been other directions within public health and health research that parallel and reinforce some of the recommendations of the RCAP. They have included an increased focus on the relationship between community and neighbourhood characteristics and individual health as well as increased attention to culture, notably the movement from 'cultural awareness' to 'cultural competence' in delivery and design of health care programs.[5] In all, these developments indicate support for a more socially inclusive perspective on public health initiatives.

One way the RCAP helped to advance a more socially inclusive approach to Aboriginal health was to promote a new kind of dialogue between Western and Aboriginal health researchers. The RCAP challenged those with a fairly narrow, empirically scientific approach to research by both articulating and utilizing in its own reports an indigenous perspective that supports a more holistic, locally based, and culturally relevant approach to the gaining of new knowledge. In particular, it highlighted the benefits of 'participatory' action research (PAR) for those engaged in community-based health research (Episkenew and Wheeler 2002). The most notable of these benefits was that PAR sought to change the dynamics of power between the researcher and the 'subjects' of research such that research is the outcome of an ongoing relationship between researchers and communities (Flicker et al. 2008; McCaulay et al. 1999). Whereas most Aboriginal health research in the past involved non-Aboriginal researchers studying the health status of Aboriginal peoples, Aboriginal organizations and communities now increasingly demand control over the way research is conceived, conducted, reported, and used by potential stakeholders (Long and LaFrance 2004; McNaughton and Rock 2004; O'Riley 2004). That RCAP participants and non-Aboriginal stakeholders interested in Aboriginal health were of a similar mind on this was evident when the Canadian Public Health Association, in the same year that the final RCAP report was released, expressed support for increased collaboration between government and those involved in community-based research, as well as for the promotion and development of research projects that combined different methodologies (Canadian Public Health Association 1996). This was in line with the call by many to support grassroots developments in Aboriginal communities (RCAP 1993, 59). A particularly challenging call was for Aboriginal and non-Aboriginal people to accord proper respect for and inclusion of ceremony and Elder wisdom in addressing the roots of brokenness and ill-health experienced by many Aboriginal people in Canada (Nuu-chah-nulth Tribal Council 1989).

Aboriginal health research conducted since the release of the final RCAP report suggests that we are witnessing the bridging of two traditions of thought about well-being and health. The resulting new knowledge about Aboriginal health and well-being is contributing to the development of a wide variety of practical as well as policy-related initiatives that directly benefit Aboriginal communities. This is not to say that we are ignoring a number of significant, some would say fundamental and perhaps even irreconcilable, differences between the perspectives and approaches used by scientific, epidemiological health researchers and locally focused, community-based researchers. Notwithstanding their differences and the challenges and tensions they present, which we address in our concluding remarks, the following sections illustrate how interaction and collaboration between health science, social epidemiological, and community-based research appear to be contributing to a more holistic understanding of the well-being and health of Aboriginal peoples in Canada.

The Demography and Social Epidemiology of Aboriginal Health

One of the ways that the social determinants of health perspective has affected practices related to Aboriginal health is the changing of research topics. Although the majority of Aboriginal health research continues to focus on empirical indicators of physical health and illness, by the early 1990s Aboriginal health research in Canada had begun to slowly incorporate the social determinants of health perspective. From this perspective, the health of individuals is viewed in relation to their social characteristics and the contexts in which they live. In contrast to research that focuses almost solely on the physical health (problems) of individuals, research on the social determinants of health examines the ways that social circumstances contribute in positive or negative ways to the physical health and well-being of individuals, families, and whole communities. In academic and medical research circles, this approach is sometimes referred to as 'social epidemiology'. Given that social epidemiological health research draws a great deal upon physical health data, the following section begins with our analysis of data on the general health status of Aboriginal populations, including trends in mortality and self-rated health. Also included is our examination of more specific aspects of physical health, including the diseases to which Aboriginal peoples are particularly at risk. We conclude the section by discussing certain points of convergence between social epidemiological research and research that is focused on the health and well-being of particular communities.

General Health Status

For those interested in the health of Aboriginal populations, it is important to consider the dynamics of those populations and how they have been changing in recent years. One of the important characteristics of Aboriginal populations, and one that is related to health, is that they are growing much more rapidly than is the general population of Canada. Since the Second World War, Aboriginal populations that had been severely affected by disease, starvation, and violence associated with colonization have rebounded (Waldram, Herring, and Young 2006). The number of people identifying themselves as 'members of an Aboriginal group' in the 2006 census, including Métis, First Nations, and Inuit, was more than 1.1 million (Statistics Canada 2008b). Measuring this growth has been made somewhat challenging by changing patterns of ethnic self-identification (Guimond, Kerr, and Beaujot 2004; Norris, this volume), but a greater willingness to identify oneself as Aboriginal in response to the census question can also be seen as a positive sign and perhaps an indication of an improving position of Aboriginal peoples in Canadian society.

Beyond the changing patterns of identification, the growth of Aboriginal populations has been due to changing patterns of mortality and fertility, broadly following what is known as a 'demographic transition' (Caldwell 2006). Following the course that was first set by European populations, populations in well-developed and less-developed countries have moved through several stages of population growth. Historically, demographers hypothesize that populations remained a fairly constant size, with high birth rates roughly balanced by high mortality due to periodic famines and plagues. According to the theory of the demographic transition, improved conditions result in lower mortality and especially in more children surviving infancy. However, despite more children surviving, fertility remains high for a certain period before eventually declining. The intervening period of high fertility and low mortality is one of relatively high population growth (Caldwell 2006).

Mortality in Aboriginal populations has indeed fallen in recent decades and appears to be continuing to improve, although there are important exceptions. Life expectancy at birth is in some sense the single most comprehensive measure of general health status. Despite some methodological problems, it seems that life expectancy has been improving; however, there are reasons for concern.

Table 12.1 presents the best available life expectancy estimates for registered

Indians, Métis, and Inuit. The registered Indian figures show an increasing life expectancy over the period. Life expectancy at birth in 1980 for registered Indian males and females was, respectively, 60.9 and 68.0 (Table 12.1). This was roughly 10 years lower than life expectancy rates for the Canadian population as a whole (Indian and Northern Affairs Canada 2005). By 2001, life expectancy for the general population had risen to 77 years for men and 82.1 years for women, with the gap between the general and registered Indian populations decreasing to less than seven years (Verma, Michalowski, and Gauvin 2003).

Life expectancy estimates are difficult to arrive at for Métis and Inuit, and there are no reliable estimates for non-status First Nations. However, it appears that Métis had higher life expectancy in 2001 than did the registered Indian population. The Aboriginal population with the lowest life expectancy was the Inuit. Wilkins et al. (2008) have estimated that Inuit life expectancy at birth was about 10 years lower than that of Canadians in 1991. Disturbingly, these authors find that Inuit life expectancy may have *decreased* between 1991 and 2001 and that this gap had widened to 12 years by 2001 (Table 12.1).

While life expectancy at birth is perhaps the most common summary measure of overall population health, it can obscure important age patterns in mortality. Naturally, risk of mortality is enormously influenced by age, with those at the youngest and oldest ages typically most at risk of dying. One of the major factors contributing to increased life expectancy is therefore an improvement in infant mortality. This is a particularly important measure for social epidemiologists, since it is affected by maternal and infant nutrition, housing conditions,

Table 12.1 Estimated Life Expectancy at Birth (Years) for Aboriginal Populations and Canada, 1981, 1991, 2001

	1981 (1980)		1991 (1990)		2001	
	Male	Female	Male	Female	Male	Female
Registered Indians[1]	60.9	68.0	66.9	74.0	70.4	75.5
Métis[2]	–	–	–	–	72.4	79.9
Inuit[3]	–	–	66.0	69.6	64.4	69.8
Canada[4]	72.0	79.2	74.6	80.9	77.0	82.1

[1] Source: INAC (Indian and Northern Affairs Canada). 2005. *Basic Departmental Data* 2004. Ottawa: INAC. Note: Registered Indian life expectancies estimated for 1980, 1990, and 2001.
[2] Source: R. Wilkins, S. Upal, P. Finès, S. Senécal, E. Guimond, and R. Dion. 2008. 'Life expectancy of the Inuit-inhabited areas of Canada, 1981–2003'. *Health Reports* 19 (1). Note: Estimates calculated using geographic areas with high concentrations of Aboriginal peoples rather than ethnic identifiers on mortality data.
[3] Source: R. Wilkins, P. Finès, S. Senécal, and E. Guimond, 2006. *Mortality in Urban and Rural Areas with High Proportion of Aboriginal Residents in Canada*. Presentation at the annual meeting of the Population Association of America, 31 March. Note: See note above.
[4] Source: Statistics Canada. 2009. 'Life tables, Canada, provinces and territories'. Catalogue no. 84-537-XIE. www.statcan.gc.ca/bsolc/olc-cel/olc-cel?catno=84-537-XIE&lang=eng.

the risk of infectious disease, and access to health care facilities (Reidpath and Allotey 2003). There is solid evidence that infant mortality among Aboriginal populations has indeed improved dramatically over the past 30 years in Canada. Among registered Indians, the numbers of infants dying in their first year has declined considerably, from about 24 per 1000 in 1980 to 7.2 per 1000 in 2001 when the comparable Canadian rate was 5.2 per 1000 (Indian and Northern Affairs Canada 2005).

As predicted by demographic transition theory, falling mortality and high fertility have contributed to the growth of Aboriginal populations in Canada. The infant mortality rate began to decline rapidly in the 1960s when the fertility rate of Aboriginal peoples was high. Since its peak around 1967 when Aboriginal fertility was more than four times that of the general Canadian population, the fertility of Aboriginal populations has declined considerably, to about one and a half times the Canadian rate (Statistics Canada 2003). These population dynamics have contributed to the growth of Aboriginal populations as well as to a younger age profile. First Nations, Inuit, and Métis populations have a considerably higher proportion of young people relative to the general Canadian population, and this will continue to be the case for years to come (Steffler 2008).

An Aboriginal Epidemiological Transition? The Changing Causes of Mortality

As noted previously, low infant mortality is typical of populations that have undergone the transition from a pattern of high mortality to low mortality. Along with this demographic transition in mortality generally comes an *epidemiological transition*, or a change in the most important causes of death in a population (Omran 1971). Very high mortality in pre–demographic transition populations is broadly caused by epidemics of contagious disease, which are enabled by poor sanitation and insufficient nutrition. Western populations have, it is argued, moved from this early stage through the 'age of receding pandemics' and into a third stage characterized by chronic diseases, such as cardiovascular disease and cancer, as increasingly important causes of death. One reason is that with a greater proportion of the population surviving infancy and living into their adult and older adult ages, people simply live long enough to be at risk to these chronic conditions. Some epidemiologists have proposed that many Western populations have now moved into a fourth stage in which these degenerative diseases occur even later in life (Olshansky and Ault 1986). Others have characterized the current stage differently, as one in which 'lifestyle' diseases have taken on an increasingly important role in mortality (Rogers and Hackenberg 1987). These authors have observed that at the same time that deaths from degenerative disease in older ages have become more likely, so too have deaths in mid-adulthood due to increasing obesity and sedentary lifestyles. Diabetes and heart disease therefore coexist with delayed degenerative diseases as important causes of death in what Rogers and Heckenberg (1987) refer to as a 'hybristic' stage of the epidemiologic transition.

Figure 12.1 offers a comparative picture of mortality rates across ages for registered Indian males and females in 1980 and 2000. It shows the decline in infant mortality over those years but also a reduction in the risk of death at all ages. The changes that Western countries have experienced in the ages at which people are likely to die have been called the 'compression of mortality'. Essentially, the risk of dying becomes considerably lower in youth and young adult years, and mortality therefore becomes 'compressed' into the older years of life. It is particularly notable that this seems to have also happened in Canadian Aboriginal populations in recent decades, or at least among those registered under the Indian Act. Note that this compression seems to have become more pronounced for registered Indian women than for men (Figure 12.1), which is

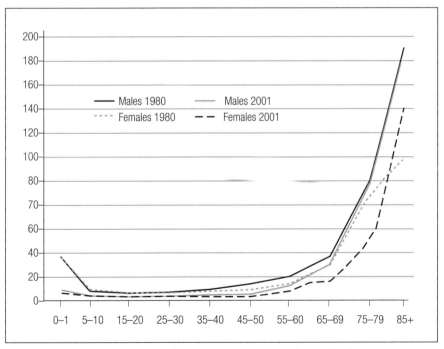

Figure 12.1   Age-specific mortality rates (per 1000), registered Indian males and females, 1980 and 2001

Source: Statistics Canada. Verma, R. , M. Michalowski, and R.P. Gauvin. 2003. 'Abridged Life Tables for Registered Indians in Canada, 1976–80 to 1996–2000', in annual meeting of the Population Association of America.

similar to changes that have occurred among ethnic minority populations in other Western contexts (Go et al. 1995).

However, it is not entirely clear that the changing birth, mortality, and health patterns among Aboriginal populations in Canada are following the same pattern that other Western populations, including the general Canadian population, have already followed. In relation to the causes of death for Aboriginal and non-Aboriginal populations (Table 12.2), three things are worth pointing out. First, although Canadians in general may have passed through the 'age of receding pandemics', Aboriginal peoples continue to be much more at risk to diseases causing death such as pneumonia and influenza than are other Canadians. Second, rates of cancer and other chronic 'degenerative diseases' such as ischemic heart disease have risen among Aboriginal people such that the relative risk of mortality due to these causes is now nearly the same for Aboriginal and non-Aboriginal peoples. Third, it is of particular concern to many that the burden of diseases related to 'lifestyle' such as diabetes mellitus is also far greater for Aboriginal people than for the Canadian population as a whole. Moreover, the contribution of 'accidents, violence, and poisonings', including suicides, to Aboriginal mortality is much higher than that of other Western populations (Table 12.2) and also higher than that of indigenous populations in other countries (Trovato 2001).

It is therefore somewhat doubtful that Aboriginal populations in Canada are simply following the progress of the Canadian population through the stages of the epidemiologic transition. In fact, Aboriginal peoples in Canada appear to be suffering from relatively high rates of all of the major causes of death—infectious,

Table 12.2 Age-Standardized* Mortality Rates (Per 100,000) by Primary Cause of Death, Aboriginal and Non-Aboriginal Canadians, 1990

	Aboriginal	Non-Aboriginal	Risk Ratio**
Malignant Neoplasms (cancer)	98.9	143.0	0.7
Ischemic Heart Disease	83.8	89.6	0.9
Cerebrovascular Disease	28.1	30.9	0.9
Other Chronic Obstructive Pulmonary Disease	10.8	16.1	0.7
Pneumonia and Influenza	24.4	17.7	1.4
Diabetes Mellitus	19.5	13.3	1.5
Assault	8.1	1.5	4.5
Intentional Self-Harm	27.8	12.2	2.3

Source: Bramley et al. 2004.
*Age-standardization accounts for the fact that the two populations have different age structures and makes the rates directly comparable.
**The ratio of the Aboriginal rate to the non-Aboriginal rate. This can be interpreted as the relative risk of mortality. For example, the risk of death due to cancer for Aboriginal people is 0.7 times that of Non-Aboriginal people.

chronic, and 'lifestyle' diseases—simultaneously. Moreover, this review has included only discussions of patterns of mortality and the major causes of death. If we also consider morbidity, including illness and disease that does not necessarily cause death, Aboriginal peoples may have higher rates of nearly all chronic and infectious diseases than the non-Aboriginal population (Young 1994). Understanding these differences and the reasons behind them is obviously of critical importance. However, the reasons for differences in health status and in the patterns of disease among Aboriginal populations in Canada are complex and multifaceted, and various researchers have focused on quite different explanations.

Explanations for Health Inequalities: Biology, Behaviour, and Society

Academic health researchers investigate an incredibly wide range of possible causes of disease and poor health in Aboriginal populations. However, there have generally been two emphases, each focusing on different ends of a causal chain that extends from the most direct causes, such as smoking behaviour or lack of health care, to more systemic 'distal' causes including colonialism and institutional racism. Epidemiological approaches to understanding patterns of health and disease have often been positioned near the direct end of the causal chain. In general, 'risk factor epidemiology' has used correlational methods to predict health status at the individual level on the basis of various personal behaviours, characteristics, or life conditions (McDowell 2008; Susser 1998).

The risk factor that has received the most attention from academic and policy researchers is the lack of health care, especially on remote reserves or in other Aboriginal communities (MacMillan et al. 2003; Newbold 1998; Shah, Gunraj, and Hux 2003). Clearly, the lack of health care services can have an immediate and dramatic impact on health. However, it is not immediately obvious how this explains most of the disparity between the health status of Aboriginal peoples and that of other Canadians, particularly the differences that are evident even in urban and otherwise well-served areas.

There has been some interest in the role of genetic differences between Aboriginal populations and the general Canadian population, especially with regard to the role these might play in the very high rates of diabetes in Aboriginal populations (Dyck, Klomp, and Tan 2001; Young et al. 2000). The 'thrifty genotype' hypothesis (Neel 1962) suggests that genetic adaptation to conditions of food insecurity have led Aboriginal peoples to perhaps be more at risk of high birth weight and then of diabetes later in life (Dyck, Klomp, and Tan 2001). However, it should be noted that these explanations remain contested on empirical grounds as well as from those who point out rather critically that these explanations reintroduce 'race', an analytical concept with little relation to the reality of genetic diversity (Fee 2006).

Regardless whether or not genetic differences are real, it seems unlikely that they could provide sufficient explanation for the significant differences between the Aboriginal and general populations in terms of the prevalence of diabetes and other major health issues. For example, there is good evidence that health-related behaviours, including diet and exercise, smoking, alcohol and other substance abuse, as well as help-seeking behaviour, are also important factors. Aboriginal people exhibit higher rates of smoking and alcohol use than other Canadians (Retnakaran et al. 2005), and research indicates that the prevalence of diabetes in Aboriginal populations is related to their lower levels of physical activity and their higher percentage of body fat (Liu et al. 2006). Although these tendencies may be affected to some degree by genetic propensities, it seems that more useful explanations can be found by examining the social and economic conditions in which Aboriginal peoples live.

Social Determinants of Health

Although many researchers remain interested in examining the proximal factors affecting health, a major development over the past two decades has been the widespread incorporation of the social determinants of health perspective to many areas of health research. This approach has encompassed a broad range of theories and models that focus on how the social and economic contexts in which people live directly and indirectly produce certain health outcomes. And because this approach examines the relationships between health and the conditions in which people live, including the social and economic conditions that are aspects of *societies* rather than merely characteristics of individuals, this type of research goes well beyond the study of behavioural or biomedical factors that contribute to disease, illness, and even death.

A number of social determinants frameworks have been developed. Recent compilations by Raphael (2006) and the Public Health Agency of Canada (2003) are reproduced in Box 12.1. Although there are differences, such as the inclusion of biology and gender in the PHAC framework, these two frameworks contain many similar determinants. Notably, Raphael includes Aboriginal identity as the first determinant, indicating its importance in the Canadian context. But including Aboriginal identity as a determinant of health slightly obscures the fact that the health of Aboriginal peoples is negatively affected by the other determinants listed in Box 12.1 as well. For example, Aboriginal children may be subject to a variety of conditions in early life, such as poor maternal nutrition, that put them at higher risk of poor health at older ages. Moreover, Aboriginal youth are more likely to begin engaging in risky behaviours, such as smoking and alcohol use, earlier in life than their non-Aboriginal counterparts (Munro 2004). Lastly, Aboriginal peoples also continue to have lower educational attainment than other Canadians (Hull 2001), and there is some evidence that education gaps are not closing very quickly (Clement 2008).

Box 12.1   Components of Social Determinants of Health Frameworks

Raphael (2006): Social Determinants of Health	PHAC (2003): Key Determinants of Health	Aboriginal-Specific Determinants (Wilson & Rosenberg, 2002; Richmond and Ross 2009)
• Aboriginal Status	• Healthy child development	• Participation in traditional activities
• Early Life	• Education and Literacy	• Balance
• Education	• Employment/working conditions	• Life control
• Employment and working conditions	• Health services	• (Environmental) education
• Unemployment and employment security	• Physical environments	• Material resources
• Health care services	• Income and social status	• Social resources
• Housing	• Social support networks	• Environmental/cultural connections
• Income and income distribution	• Social environments	
• Social safety net	• Personal health practices and behaviours	
• Social exclusion	• Biology and genetic endowment	
• Food security	• Gender	

The health of Aboriginal peoples is also affected by food insecurity, which indicates an unreliable supply of nutritious food, as well as by poor housing. Willows and colleagues (2009) have found that Aboriginal households are more than five times as likely to experience food insecurity as non-Aboriginal households. Moreover, this finding merely refers to those living off-reserve and does not include those living in remote or northern communities where fresh fruits and vegetables or other healthy food may be prohibitively expensive (Willows 2009). Housing has also been a long-standing issue in urban areas as well as in

First Nations and Inuit communities (Walker 2008) and has been linked to the spread of a variety of infectious diseases, including tuberculosis (Clark, Riben, and Nowgesic 2002; Rosenberg et al. 1997).

Although environmental health might not be strictly seen as a 'social' determinant of health, some frameworks have included a clean and healthy environment as a key determinant, partly on the grounds that environmental degradation is an outcome of social processes and also because the risk of living in unhealthy environments is unevenly distributed. Aboriginal communities, and First Nations in particular, have had long-standing issues related to water quality and sanitation, as identified in the RCAP report. These problems continue, putting First Nations at risk to *E.Coli* and *Helicobacter* infections, which can then be transmitted in other ways (Eggertson 2006; Sinha et al. 2004). Although Indian and Northern Affairs Canada representatives have repeatedly stated that providing adequate and safe water supplies to First Nations is a priority, as of February 2008 there were 93 First Nations communities with boil-water advisories or 'do not consume' orders (Eggertson 2008).

Many of these issues are related, directly or indirectly, to low income and poverty, which continue to disproportionately affect Aboriginal peoples throughout Canada. According to the 2006 census, the 2005 median incomes for North American Indians, Métis, and Inuit were $13,700, $19,200, and $16,300, respectively, compared to $25,600 for all Canadians (Statistics Canada 2008c). The unemployment rate for the Aboriginal identity population in the census was nearly 15 per cent in 2005, while only 6.6 per cent of all Canadians reported being out of work (Statistics Canada 2008d). According to the census, 8.6 per cent of Canadians who were living in economic families were living with low income in 2005. For First Nations (registered Indians), this rate was a staggering 29 per cent. Métis and Inuit had a somewhat lower prevalence of low income, with 11 and 10 per cent, respectively (Statistics Canada 2008a).

The role of income, and income inequality, in producing population health is a complex and much-contested area of research. Psycho-social explanations focus on the distribution of income and the physical effects of low social status (Wilkinson 1999). Other epidemiological approaches focus on social resources, such as social capital, and their implications for health. For example, low-income individuals or communities may have social networks that are less able to deliver the kind of social or material support that can lead to better health outcomes (Hawe and Shiell 2000). Other social epidemiologists argue that income directly affects health, since income improves access to services, better housing, better food, and other goods (Muntaner and Lynch 1999; Muntaner, Lynch, and Smith 2001).

There have been some attempts to explicitly apply social determinants frameworks to Aboriginal health (see Anderson 2007). Whereas Raphael has included Aboriginal identity itself as a determinant of health and the other determinants in these frameworks are also clearly important for Aboriginal health, some researchers have suggested that there may be important determinants that are *unique* to Aboriginal peoples (Box 12.1). For example, Wilson and Rosenberg (2002) suggest that participation in traditional activities such as hunting or fishing as well as ceremonies and other cultural activities may have independent effects on health. Richmond and Ross (2009) identify six determinants that are important for First Nations and Inuit health and which are related to the experience of environmental dispossession, or the separation of Aboriginal peoples from their natural environments (Box 12.1). The importance of traditional lands for Aboriginal peoples and communities means that these factors are unique determinants of their health; they are not experienced by non-Aboriginal peoples, and they are not easily included in general social determinants frameworks.

Sorting out the causal links has been a challenge for social determinants researchers. Although Raphael (2006) claims that the social determinants approach enables health researchers to focus beyond behaviour and risk factors, much of the social determinants research has been of the 'risk-factor' variety (McDowell 2008). As Susser (1998) notes, examining correlations between various conditions and health does not provide clear understanding of the actual processes that produce inequalities in health. Although epidemiologists are increasingly making use of more technically sophisticated models that include contextual factors and longitudinal data to examine complex causal processes, other 'process-sensitive' approaches are providing an alternative to strictly quantitative, epidemiological research on Aboriginal health.

Indigenous and Community-Based Health Research

Although there is no clear definition of Aboriginal or indigenous research methodology, in general terms it is part of a movement to regain control over the production of knowledge by those whose lives are most directly affected by the research (Newhouse 2004). Support for indigenous research is based on the recognition that Aboriginal research in general and Aboriginal health research in particular has been a means by which colonial relations have been built and maintained (Tuhiwai Smith 1999). For both Aboriginal and non-Aboriginal peoples and organizations in Canada, control over Aboriginal research has become an important political priority (Episkenew and Wheeler 2002; McNaughton and Rock 2004; McPherson 2005; O'Riley 2004).

Practically speaking, Aboriginal health research has often taken the form of 'participatory action' or 'community-based' research (PAR). The popularity of PAR is due in large part to the way it seeks to balance the power relations between the researchers and 'the researched' by involving members of the studied communities in all stages of the planning and execution of the research (Flicker et al. 2008; Macaulay et al. 1999). Whereas 'traditional' academic research has often been criticized for providing little of practical value to participating individuals and communities, participatory designs consider the benefits of the research to the community as important as or even more important than any possible contribution to the scientific literature. Research may be designed to produce outcomes that are of practical value to the community, such as need assessments or program designs (Steenbeck 2004). PAR does not discount that there may also be academic outputs potentially useful to academic research partners, although these outcomes are usually deemed less important than those that directly benefit the community.

In general, indigenous approaches to research involve consultation between community members and researchers throughout all stages of the research. Some proponents of 'indigenous' methodologies also claim that traditional scientific research processes are inherently incompatible with indigenous world views and that only Aboriginal communities can legitimately institute and carry out research involving members of their communities (Tuhiwai Smith 1999; McPherson 2005). Quantitative, statistical research is sometimes singled out as particularly at odds with an indigenous approach to research, since it reduces the complexity of people's lives and situations to numbers and can be linked to government attempts to define and control indigenous peoples (O'Neil, Reading, and Leader 1998; Rowse 2009). There are those who assert that research that isolates individuals from their local, cultural, and historical contexts, or that frames health in terms of a narrow, 'Western' definition of well-being, simply does not serve the interests of Aboriginal peoples (Michelle and Lemyra 2006; Salée 2006).

Whereas traditional 'risk-factor' epidemiology examines statistical correlations between various predictors and morbidity or mortality, indigenous health research tends to focus on understanding processes associated with the progress of disease or with healing. An example of research that incorporates aspects of local geography and cultural factors is Cammer's work on the experiences of older northern First Nations adults with mainstream dementia care (Cammer 2006). Other research that seeks to integrate Aboriginal conceptions of health into mainstream health research includes the work of Richmond and Ross (2009), which produced the Aboriginal determinants of health framework we mention above (Box 12.1). Using data collected through interviews with community health representatives from First Nations and Inuit communities, these researchers conclude that historical dispossession of Aboriginal peoples from their traditional environments had an enormous negative impact on the health of these people because of the fundamental interrelationship between Aboriginal cultures and the environment. They therefore propose that a social determinants framework for Aboriginal health should include 'balance', life control, education, access to material resources, and social resources, as well as the maintenance of environmental and cultural connections. Similarly, Adelson (1998) found that ideas of well-being among the Cree in northern Quebec were intimately tied to their access to traditional foods, land, hunting, and lifestyles. This type of research suggests that support for traditional ways and resistance to the threats posed by settler culture and political domination are essential to regaining control over community health.

From an indigenous research perspective, the history of Aboriginal health in Canada has been less about a failed epidemiological transition and more about a history of domination and colonization. Understanding how these relations of domination have affected health was one of the primary goals of the RCAP and has remained of central concern to many involved in Aboriginal research since that time. According to the authors of the RCAP report, the articulation of an indigenous health research paradigm would play a vital role in changing the way Aboriginal health research was viewed and conducted. Evidence that attitudes and perspectives on Aboriginal research have indeed changed since that time can be found in the recent draft of the revised *Tri-Council Policy Statement* on research ethics (TCPS), the document that guides university research ethics boards across Canada (Interagency Advisory Panel on Research Ethics 2008). Chapter 9 of the draft revision deals exclusively with research involving First Nations, Inuit, and Métis peoples and insists that researchers must consult with all stakeholder organizations and communities prior to engaging in any research involving Aboriginal people. The TCPS asserts that academic researchers need to be aware that all research involves relations of power and domination and that research projects involving Aboriginal people should result in research that is *for* rather than simply *about* Aboriginal peoples. The TCPS honours the principles of 'ownership', 'control', 'access', and 'possession' (OCAP) that were developed to govern the First Nations Regional Longitudinal Health Survey (RHS). This survey is the first major source of health-related quantitative data ever produced through an Aboriginal-directed process, and the OCAP guidelines were developed to ensure that the communities participating in that survey controlled how their data would be used (National Aboriginal Health Organization 2006;

O'Neil, Reading, and Leader 1998). According to the guidelines, access to RHS data is given only to researchers who design projects that will serve the interests of the communities that take part and who have been approved through a consultation process with the communities involved.

Changing Relationships and Continuing Tensions

As we have presented it, the epidemiological evidence gives a somewhat mixed picture of how the health status of First Nations, Inuit, and Métis peoples in Canada has changed since the final report of the RCAP was submitted to Parliament in 1996. Although life expectancy has improved, Aboriginal peoples are still at significantly higher risk of disease and premature mortality than other Canadians. Focusing as it does on patterns of disease in the population, epidemiological research indicates that Aboriginal peoples have not necessarily followed the same health and disease path as other Western populations and that they are in a unique position of being at high risk to all types of disease. Behavioural and genetic explanations for these patterns, although still the subject of some research and debate, have largely given way to social determinants of health research. Research findings from this perspective highlight not only that Aboriginal people in Canada continue to be more at risk to poorer social, economic, and environmental conditions but also the many negative ways that socially constructed and maintained conditions affect their health and well-being. Specifically, it clearly supports the view that the significantly lower than average levels of education and income experienced by Aboriginal peoples are directly related to much poorer living conditions, on average, than those of other Canadians. It also helps us understand how and why their living conditions are in turn directly related to a wide variety of health and social problems experienced by Aboriginal people.

It is important to note that the relative lack of success in improving Aboriginal peoples' health is not confined to Canada. The legacy of colonization is evident in the poorer health outcomes of indigenous populations the world over, and progress in virtually every locale has been almost universally slow (Cooke et al. 2007; Stephens et al. 2005). Whereas epidemiological research tends to focus on more direct or causal factors, proper understanding of the well-being and health of Aboriginal peoples in Canada requires critical examination of the entirety of the relationships between Aboriginal peoples and the state. Although Canadian governments have worked with many First Nations communities and organizations to improve conditions on reserves and in urban settings, efforts and initiatives have been by and large piecemeal and lacking the transformative vision of the RCAP (Canadian Institute for Health Information 2003). Not surprisingly, then, most RCAP recommendations had still not been implemented a full 10 years after the commission's final report (Assembly of First Nations 2006).

Admittedly, Aboriginal health research is a messy business. Although researchers, communities, and ethics review bodies may agree that open consultation between all research stakeholders is necessary, what this means in practice is often unclear. Indeed, there are a number of factors that challenge those committed to carrying out healthy, community-based projects that fully engage with communities in research that responds to the needs that are defined by those communities. First, for a number of reasons, not all communities are easily defined. Whether this is due to amendments to Indian Act legislation, changes to band membership rules by newly elected band councils, or mobility to and from reserves, the fact is that there is a certain 'permeability' of Aboriginal communities. Furthermore, along with Aboriginal populations in Canada being very culturally, socially, politically, and economically diverse, they are now mainly urban and have been so for some time (Peters 2000). If defining the membership of a discrete First Nation or other Aboriginal community is difficult, defining a 'community' in an urban setting is even more so.

It is also the case that every community, whether Aboriginal or not, is comprised of groups and individuals with divergent interests (Fox and Long 2000). In a community of any type there may be groups or individuals who themselves feel marginalized or ill-represented by the formal or informal power structures in their communities. For researchers in partnerships with those communities, it may be unclear how the 'community' and its interests can be best defined. In all, the complexity of Aboriginal communities presents a significant challenge to those who support the view that there is one 'way' to understand and address Aboriginal health issues. This applies equally to those engaged in epidemiological research and to those involved in community-based participatory action research.

Despite the various sources of tension between the different approaches to Aboriginal health research discussed above, we are convinced that there are numerous reasons to support their use and coexistence. Although research that focuses on the lived realities of individuals is important and necessary, population-level statistics and traditional epidemiological approaches remain critical to understanding the overall patterns of disease and, crucially, whether conditions are improving or getting worse. This means collecting data on the incidence and prevalence of diseases, vital statistics on mortality, and survey data on health-related questions. This standard epidemiological approach to research may not produce immediate results for communities or individuals, but it does provide important information and direction to policy developers and service providers. Moreover, quantifiable and comparable health outcome research has provided important statistical profiles and trends that have been invaluable for advocacy and for political action. As important as it is to recognize a distinctly Aboriginal conception of health and well-being, objective measures of life expectancy and prevalence of particular diseases and other health-related problems provide invaluable information on the lives of Aboriginal people in particular social, economic, and political circumstances. Conversely, data that do not allow comparison to other populations, or that include quite specific measures of health, may end up not providing proper and full understanding of certain health issues that affect Aboriginal people within as well as outside a given community.

Ultimately, though, the tension between an indigenous approach to health research and the traditional epidemiological approach is not only epistemological or ontological; it also reflects the different interests of all who have a stake in understanding some aspect of Aboriginal health. For example, academics and other researchers are often constrained by certain occupationally related pressures. Research that does not generate the kind of information that can be easily presented in a peer-reviewed academic publication or which requires a lengthy process of community involvement and relationship-building may therefore be considerably less attractive to even the most well-meaning researcher. Moreover, although there are some initiatives within universities that value products other than academic articles or books as vehicles of 'knowledge mobilization', there remain significant institutional barriers to academic researchers who are interested in engaging in community-based Aboriginal health research. There are also divergent perspectives and interests within as well as between members of specific Aboriginal organizations, communities, and Nations. Consequently, while the tensions and 'politics' of Aboriginal health research have much to do with divergent world views, they are also reflective of struggles for power and control between Aboriginal stakeholders (Long and Fox 2000).

Conclusions: Living with Contradictions

In this chapter, we have sought to address two themes that relate to the health of Aboriginal peoples in Canada. The first is the current health situation of Aboriginal peoples in Canada and the factors that contribute to ongoing disparities in health outcomes. The second has involved discussion about the way that 'health knowledge' is produced, including how health is defined and who controls the research process. The question of what counts as evidence is vitally important in the production of policy and for ultimately improving health outcomes. However, the politics of Aboriginal health research also reflects the changing relationship between Aboriginal people and Canadian institutions and changing power relations. The health of Aboriginal peoples has clearly not improved in the ways envisioned and called for in the final RCAP report, although it cannot be denied that there have been significant and positive changes to health research involving Aboriginal peoples in Canada over the past 20 years.

These discussions regarding control over research, the procedures used in research, and the ownership of the process of research are not limited to the Canadian context but are part of a broader discourse regarding the relationships between research and power. In general, this literature focuses on how scientific ways of knowing have maintained unequal social relations by systematically erasing from the accepted evidence the perspectives of racialized and colonized peoples (Bonilla-Silva and Zuberi 2008; Tuhiwai Smith 1999) and of women (Eichler 1997). Although there are important arguments about the particular role of statistical methods in reproducing these relations (e.g., Zuberi 2008), in some ways the choice of an 'indigenous methodology' may be less about the type of research conducted and more about the relationships that underlie research activities.

There are a number of problems with presuming to address any and all Aboriginal health issues by a strictly indigenous, community-based approach to research. Although local and qualitative research is necessary and important, as is supporting community control over research, many also agree that epidemiological data tells an important part of the story of Aboriginal health in Canada (RCAP 1996). Challenges related to the defining of communities, the diversity and complexity of Aboriginal populations, and the need for ongoing and comparable population-level measures of health all suggest that social epidemiological research can and should continue to play as important a role in understanding and addressing Aboriginal health issues in Canada as qualitative, community-based research.

It is tempting, then, to conclude that we need to invite the use of multiple approaches to understanding Aboriginal health, since each contributes an important part of the total picture of Aboriginal health in Canada. However, to accept this middle position and continue on with the 'research business as usual' attitude is to ignore the real political, ontological, and epistemological issues at stake. It is the case that many Aboriginal people and communities may have fundamentally different conceptions of health and well-being and that traditional epidemiological measures may give a rather narrow and even potentially misleading picture of the whole of their lives. The use of statistical techniques and the data they generate may not be very useful for improving our understanding of the processes that relate social conditions to health outcomes, which is important to note, since these processes may be very different for Aboriginal peoples and other Canadians. Not only may the statistical picture be misleading, but strict use of statistical data to tell the story of Aboriginal health may contribute to the ongoing reproduction of colonial relations, as official statistics have in the past. On the other hand, to assume that all health-related experiences and processes that affect Aboriginal peoples are unique is equally narrow and limiting, since it would lead us to discard decades of fruitful theoretical and empirical work that bears directly on the health and well-being of Aboriginal people in Canada. Moreover, ignoring disproportionately high rates of particular illnesses and morbidity across the life span would result in a less clear understanding of the very concrete ways that colonization continues to make its presence felt in the lives of Aboriginal people in this country.

Rather than suggesting that we therefore simply adopt a multiplicity of research practices, we have another suggestion: that diverse people learn to live somewhat *uncomfortably* with the coexistence of these research paradigms. This would mean accepting that research as a fundamentally human endeavour is constantly changing and that we therefore need to be both respectful as well as honest and sceptical about the foundations of any research practice. Although we recognize that this might not be the most satisfying position to take regarding Aboriginal health research, our sense is that it may be the most honest and will therefore bear the most useful fruit.

All of this suggests that in the end, health and healing have everything to do with people being in right relationships. If the relationships between Aboriginal health research stakeholders are in any way unhealthy, then any and all research findings may do more harm than good, since they will serve to perpetuate the unhealthiness within and between the people in those relationships. It is our view that any and all stakeholder relationships must therefore be healthy and good for this or any other kind of research to serve a healthy and healing purpose. Consequently, until relations between Aboriginal and non-Aboriginal people in Canada are based on a shared commitment to treat each other with respect and dignity, we perhaps have little choice but to remain open to the challenges and possibilities of walking 'uncomfortably' together in this new and ever-changing relationship.

Discussion Questions

1. The chapter suggests that traditional indigenous approaches and Western medical approaches to health have some fundamental differences. Briefly describe these differences.
2. What do you think are currently the most important healing and health-related issues facing Aboriginal people in Canada? In what ways might these be similar to and different from the healing-related issues facing non-Aboriginal people in this country?
3. Aboriginal people in Canada currently have shorter life expectancy than other Canadians. However, some have suggested that it is inappropriate to focus research only on reducing the 'gaps' between Aboriginal and non-Aboriginal Canadians (Salée 2006), arguing that it inappropriately sets the non-Aboriginal standard as the benchmark and the goal to which Aboriginal peoples should aspire. What do you think about this argument?
4. The 'social determinants of health' perspective focuses attention on the 'upstream' factors that affect health, such as the distribution of income in society, rather than the 'downstream' factors, such as individual behaviour or genetics. Does this correspond with the way you generally think about health and health policy?
5. What do you think are the most significant personal, cultural, and structural obstacles faced by Aboriginal and non-Aboriginal people who want to bring healing and health to the lives of Canada's Aboriginal people?
6. The authors of this chapter state that the two different perspectives on health and health research can coexist, although uncomfortably. What do you think are the prospects for this coexistence?

Further Readings

Assembly of First Nations. 2006. *Royal Commission on Aboriginal Peoples at 10 years: Report Card*. Ottawa: Assembly of First Nations.

Browne, Annette J., Victoria L. Smye, and Colleen Varcoe. 2005. 'The relevance of post-colonial theoretical perspectives to research in Aboriginal health'. *Canadian Journal of Nursing Research* 37 (4): 16–37.

Salée, Daniel. 2006. 'Quality of life of Aboriginal people in Canada: An analysis of current research'. *IRPP Choices* 12 (6).

Waldram, James B., D. Ann Herring, and T. Kue Young. 2006. *Aboriginal Health in Canada: Historical, Cultural, and Epidemiological Perspectives*. Toronto: University of Toronto Press.

Notes

1. 'Status' is the term most often used to refer to those registered under the Indian Act of Canada and who are also known as 'registered Indians'. According to the 2006 census, about 53 per cent of Aboriginal people in Canada were registered under the Act. Most First Nations people living on-reserve are status, while a majority of Aboriginal people living off-reserve in rural or urban areas are non-status (Statistics

Canada 2008b). This includes most Métis and Inuit, as well as a large proportion of First Nations ('American Indian') people.

2. www.canadiana.org/view/30387/0353.

3. Developments at the national AFN meetings in the summer of 2009 suggest this may change in the future, since one of the issues discussed at the meeting had to do with the role the AFN should play in advocating on behalf of non-status and off-reserve Aboriginal people.

4. According to Health Canada, devolution gives communities the ability to respond to locally defined needs rather than to federal priorities and is part of the recognized inherent right of self-government (Health Canada 2005).

5. See Long 2009 for an extended discussion of the important distinctions between cultural awareness and cultural competence, particularly for those involved in the design and delivery of health policy and program initiatives.

References

Adelson, Naomi. 1998. 'Health beliefs and the politics of Cree well-being'. *Health 2* (1): 5–22.

Anderson, Ian. 2007. 'Understanding the processes'. In Bronwyn Carson, et al., eds, *Social Determinants of Indigenous Health*, 21–40. Crows Nest, New South Wales: Allen and Unwin.

Assembly of First Nations. 2006. *Royal Commission on Aboriginal Peoples at 10 years: A Report Card*. Ottawa: Assembly of First Nations.

Blackstock, C. 2003. Interview at Canadian Council on Social Development Social Inclusion and Social Policy Conference.

Bonilla-Silva, E., and T. Zuberi. 2008. 'Toward a definition of white logic and white methods'. In T. Zuberi and E. Bonilla-Silva, *White Logic, White Methods: Racism and Methodology*, 3–30. Plymouth, UK: Rowman and Littlefield.

Bramley, D., et al. 2004. 'Indigenous disparities in disease-specific mortality, a cross-country comparison: New Zealand, Australia, Canada, and the United States'. *New Zealand Medical Journal* 117 (1207): U1215.

Caldwell, John. 2006. *Demographic Transition Theory*. Dordrecht: Springer.

Cammer, Alison Lee. 2006. 'Negotiating culturally incongruent healthcare systems: The process of accessing dementia care in Northern Saskatchewan'. In *College of Community Health and Epidemiology*, 116. Saskatoon: University of Saskatchewan.

Canadian Institute for Health Information. 2003. *Seven Years Later: An Inventory of Population Health Policy Since the Royal Commission on Aboriginal Peoples 1996–2003*. Ottawa: Canadian Institute for Health Information.

Canadian Public Health Association. 1996. 'Action statement for health promotion in Canada'. www.cpha.ca/en/programs/policy/action.aspx.

Clark, M., P. Riben, and E. Nowgesic. 2002. 'The association of housing density, isolation and tuberculosis in Canadian First Nations communities'. *International Journal of Epidemiology* 31: 940–5.

Clement, J. 2008. 'University attainment of the Registered Indian population, 1981–2001: A cohort approach'. *Horizons* 10 (1): 34–48.

Cooke, M., et al. 2007. 'Indigenous well-being in four countries: An application of the UNDP's

Human Development Index to indigenous peoples in Australia, Canada, New Zealand, and the United States'. BMC *International Health and Human Rights* 7: 9.

Dyck, R.F., H. Klomp, and L. Tan. 2001. 'From "thrifty genotype" to "hefty fetal phenotype": The relationship between high birth weight and diabetes in Saskatchewan registered Indians'. *Canadian Journal of Public Health* 92: 340–4.

Eggertson, Laura. 2006. 'Safe drinking water standards for First Nations communities'. *Canadian Medical Association Journal* 174: 1248.

———. 2008. 'Despite federal promises, First Nations' water problems persist'. *Canadian Medical Association Journal* 178: 985.

Eichler, M. 1997. *Family Shifts: Families Policies and Gender Equality*. Toronto: Oxford University Press.

Episkenew, Jo-Ann, and Winona Wheeler. 2002. *A Brief to Propose a National Indigenous Research Agenda*. Presented to the Social Science and Humanities Research Council.

Fee, Margery. 2006. 'Racializing narratives: Obesity, diabetes and the "Aboriginal" thrifty genotype'. *Social Science and Medicine* 62: 2988–97.

Ferris, P., et al. 2005. *Promising Practices in First Nations Adolescent Child Welfare Management and Governance*. Weechi-it-te-win Family Services. September.

Flicker, Sarah, et al. 2008. 'A snapshot of community-based research in Canada: Who? What? Why? How?' *Health Education Research* 23: 106–14.

Fox, T., and D. Long. 2000. 'Struggles with the Circle: Violence, healing and health on a First Nations reserve'. In D. Long and O. Dickason, eds, *Visions of the Heart: Canadian Aboriginal Issues*, 2nd edn., 271–301. Toronto: Harcourt Canada.

Go, C.G., et al. 1995. 'Ethnic trends in survival curves and mortality'. *Gerontologist* 35: 318–26.

Guimond, Eric, Don Kerr, and Roderic Beaujot. 2004. 'Charting the growth of Canadian Aboriginal populations: Problems, options and implications'. *Canadian Studies in Population* 31: 33–82.

Hawe, P., and A. Shiell. 2000. 'Social capital and health promotion: A review'. *Social Science and Medicine* 51: 871–85.

Health Canada. 2005. 'Ten years of health transfer First Nation and Inuit control'. Ottawa: Health Canada. www.hc-sc.gc.ca/fniah-spnia/pubs/finance/_agree-accord/10years_ ans_ trans/index-eng.php.

———. 2009. 'Non-insured health benefits for First Nations and Inuit'. /www.hc-sc.gc.ca/ fniah-spnia/nihb-ssna/index-eng.php.

Indian and Northern Affairs Canada. 2005. *Basic Departmental Data 2004*. Ottawa: First Nations and Northern Statistics Section, Corporate Information Management Directorate, Information Management Branch.

Interagency Advisory Panel on Research Ethics. 2008. *Draft 2nd Edition of the Tri-Council Policy Statement: Ethical Conduct for Research Involving Humans*. Ottawa: Interagency Secretariat on Research Ethics.

Lalonde, Marc. 1972. *A New Perspective on the Health of Canadians*. Ottawa: Department of National Health and Welfare.

Littlechild, Wilton, and Danika Littlechild. 2009. *The Treaty Right to Health: The Case of Treaty No. 6 in Alberta and Saskatchewan*. Brief presented to the Assembly of Treaty Chiefs. February.

Liu, Juan, et al. 2006. 'Lifestyle variables, non-traditional cardiovascular risk factors, and the metabolic syndrome in an Aboriginal Canadian population'. *Obesity* 14: 500–8.

Long, D. 2004. 'On violence and healing: Aboriginal experiences, 1969–1993. In Jeffrey Ian Ross, ed., *Violence in Canada: Socio-political Perspectives*, 2nd edn, 40–77. Toronto: Oxford University Press.

———. 2009. 'All dads matter: Towards an inclusive vision for father involvement initiatives in Canada'. www.fira.ca/cms/documents/176/April7.Long.pdf.

Long, D., and B. LaFrance. 2004. 'Pursuing the truth with care: Aboriginal research issues'. *Canadian Journal of Native Studies* spring: 1–5.

Macaulay, A., et al. 1999. 'Participatory research maximises community and lay involvement'. *British Medical Journal* 319: 774–8.

McDowell, I. 2008. 'From risk factors to explanation in public health'. *Journal of Public Health* 30: 219–23.

MacMillan, H.L., et al. 2003. 'The health of Ontario First Nations people: Results from the Ontario First Nations Regional Health Survey.' *Canadian Journal of Public Health* 94: 168–72.

McNaughton, Craig, and Darrel Rock. 2004. 'Opportunities in Aboriginal research: Results of SSHRC's dialogue on research and Aboriginal peoples'. *Canadian Journal of Native Studies* spring: 37–60.

McPherson, Dennis. 2005. 'Indian on the lawn: How are research partnerships with Aboriginal people possible?' *American Philosophical Association Newsletter* 5 (2): 1–12.

Michelle, Chino, and DeBruyn Lemyra. 2006. 'Building true capacity: Indigenous models for indigenous communities'. *American Journal of Public Health* 96: 596.

Munro, Gordon. 2004. 'Comparing risk behaviours among urban and rural youth by grade, Grades 7 to 12: The Alberta Youth Experience Survey 2002'. *Canadian Research Index*.

Muntaner, C., and J. Lynch. 1999. 'Income inequality, social cohesion, and class relations: A critique of Wilkinson's neo-Durkheimian research program'. *International Journal of Health Services* 29: 59–81.

Muntaner, C., J. Lynch, and G.D. Smith. 2001. 'Social capital, disorganized communities, and the third way: Understanding the retreat from structural inequalities in epidemiology and public health'. *International Journal of Health Services* 31: 213–37.

National Aboriginal Health Organization. 2006. *First National Regional Longitudinal Health Survey (RHS) 2002/3: Report on Process and Methods*. Ottawa: National Aboriginal Health Organization.

Nechi Institute, Four Worlds Development Project, Native Training Institute, and New Direction Training. 1988. *Healing Is Possible: A Joint Statement on the Healing of Sexual Abuse in Native Communities*. Alkalai Lake, BC: Nechi Institute.

Neel, J.V. 1962. 'Diabetes mellitus: A "thrifty" genotype rendered detrimental by "progress"?' *American Journal of Human Genetics* 14.

Newbold, K. Bruce. 1998. 'Problems in search of solutions: Health and Canadian Aboriginals'. *Journal of Community Health* 23: 59–74.

Newhouse, David. 2004. *Ganigonhi:oh: The Good Mind Meets the Academy*. Department of Indigenous Studies, Trent University. 1–15.

Nuu-chah-nulth Tribal Council. 1989. *Nuu-chah-nulth First Family Proposal*. Vancouver: Nuu-chah-nulth Tribal Council.

Olshansky, S.J., and A.B. Ault. 1986. 'The fourth stage of the epidemiologic transition: The age of delayed degenerative diseases'. *Milbank Quarterly* 64: 355–91.

Omran, Abdel R. 1971. 'The epidemiologic transition: a theory of the epidemiology of population change'. *The Milbank Memorial Fund Quarterly* 49: 509–38.

O'Neil, John, Jeffrey R. Reading, and Audrey Leader. 1998. 'Changing the relations of surveillance: The development of a discourse of resistance in Aboriginal epidemiology'. *Human Organization* 57: 230–7.

O'Riley, Patricia. 2004. 'Shapeshifting research with Aboriginal peoples: Toward self-determination'. *Canadian Journal of Native Studies* spring: 83–102.

Peters, Evelyn. 2000. 'Aboriginal people in urban areas'. In D. Long and O. Dickason, eds, *Visions of the Heart: Canadian Aboriginal Issues*, 2nd edn, 237–70. Toronto: Harcourt Canada.

Public Health Agency of Canada. 2003. 'Population health approach: What determines health?' www.phac-aspc.gc.ca/ph-sp/determinants/determinants-eng.php#social.

Raphael, D. 2006. 'Social determinants of health: Present status, unanswered questions, and future directions'. *International Journal of Health Services* 36: 651–77.

RCAP (Royal Commission on Aboriginal Peoples). 1993. *Public Hearings: Focusing the Dialogue. Interim report of the Royal Commission on Aboriginal Peoples*. Ottawa: Supply and Services Canada.

———. 1996. *Looking Forward: Looking Back. Report of the Royal Commission on Aboriginal Peoples*. Ottawa: Canadian Communication Group.

Reidpath, D.D., and P. Allotey. 2003. 'Infant mortality rate as an indicator of population health'. *Journal of Epidemiology and Community Health* 57 (5): 344–6.

Retnakaran, Ravi, et al. 2005. 'Cigarette smoking and cardiovascular risk factors among Aboriginal Canadian youths'. *Canadian Medical Association Journal* 173: 885–9.

Richmond, C.A., and N.A. Ross. 2009. 'The determinants of First Nation and Inuit health: A critical population health approach'. *Health and Place* 15: 403–11.

Rogers, R.G., and R. Hackenberg. 1987. 'Extending epidemiologic transition theory: A new stage'. *Social Biology* 34: 234–43.

Rose, Geoffrey. 1985. 'Sick individuals and sick populations'. *International Journal of Epidemiology* 1985: 32–8.

Rosenberg, T., et al. 1997. 'Shigellosis on Indian reserves in Manitoba, Canada: Its relationship to crowded housing, lack of running water, and inadequate sewage disposal'. *American Journal of Public Health* 87: 1547–51.

Rowse, Tim. 2009. 'Official statistics and the contemporary politics of indigeneity'. *Australian Journal of Political Science* 44: 193–211.

Salée, Daniel. 2006. 'Quality of life of Aboriginal people in Canada: An analysis of current research'. *IRPP Choices* 12 (6).

Saulis, M. 2003. 'Program and policy developments from a holistic Aboriginal perspective'. In Anne Westhues, ed., *Canadian Social Policy*, 3rd edn, 285–300. Waterloo, ON: Wilfrid Laurier University Press.

Shah, B.R., N. Gunraj, and J.E. Hux. 2003. 'Markers of access to and quality of primary care for Aboriginal people in Ontario, Canada'. *American Journal of Public Health* 93: 798–802.

Sinha, Samir K., et al. 2004. 'The incidence of *Helicobacter pylori* acquisition in children of a Canadian First Nations community and the potential for parent-to-child transmission'. *Helicobacter* 9: 59–68.

Statistics Canada. 2003. *Aboriginal Peoples of Canada: A Demographic Profile*. Catalogue no. 96F0030XIE2001007. Ottawa: Statistics Canada.

———. 2008a. 'Aboriginal ancestry (14), area of residence (6), age groups (8), sex (3) and selected demographic, cultural, labour force, educational and income characteristics (227A), for the total population of Canada, provinces and territories, 2006 census—20% sample data'. File No. 97-564-XCB2006001.IVT. Ottawa: Statistics Canada.

———. 2008b. *Aboriginal Peoples in Canada in 2006: Inuit, Métis and First Nations, 2006 Census*. Ottawa: Statistics Canada.

———. 2008c. 'Income statistics (4) in constant (2005) dollars, age groups (5A), Aboriginal identity, registered Indian status and Aboriginal ancestry (21), highest certificate, diploma or degree (5) and sex (3) for the population 15 years and over with income of Canada, provinces, territories, 2000 and 2005—20% sample data'. File 97-563-XCB2006008.IVT. Ottawa: Statistics Canada.

———. 2008d. 'Labour force activity (8), Aboriginal identity (8B), age groups (13A), sex (3) and area of residence (6A) for the population 15 years and over of Canada, provinces and territories, 2001 and 2006 censuses—20% sample data'. File 97-559-XCB2006008.IVT. Ottawa: Statistics Canada.

Steenbeeck, Audrey. 2004. 'Empowering health promotion: A holistic approach in preventing sexually transmitted infections among First Nations and Inuit adolescents in Canada'. *Journal of Holistic Nursing* 22: 254–66.

Steffler, Jeanette. 2008. 'Aboriginal peoples: A young population for years to come'. *Horizons* 10 (1): 13–20.

Stephens, C., et al. 2005. 'Indigenous peoples' health—why are they behind everyone, everywhere?' *Lancet* 366: 10–13.

Susser, M. 1998. 'Does risk factor epidemiology put epidemiology at risk? Peering into the future'. *Journal of Epidemiology and Community Health* 52: 608–11.

Trovato, F. 2001. 'Aboriginal mortality in Canada, the United States and New Zealand'. *Journal of Biosocial Science* 33: 67–86.

Tuhiwai Smith, Linda. 1999. *Decolonizing Methodologies: Research and Indigenous Peoples*. London: Zed Books.

Verma, R., M. Michalowski, and R.P. Gauvin. 2003. 'Abridged life tables for registered Indians in Canada, 1976–80 to 1996–2000'. Presentation at the annual meeting of the Population Association of America, Minneapolis.

Waldram, James B., D. Ann Herring, and T. Kue Young. 2006. *Aboriginal Health in Canada: Historical, Cultural, and Epidemiological Perspectives*. Toronto: University of Toronto Press.

Walker, Ryan. 2008. 'Aboriginal self-determination and social housing in urban Canada: A story of convergence and divergence'. *Urban Studies* 45: 185–205.

Wilkins, R., et al. 2008. 'Life expectancy in the Inuit-inhabited areas of Canada, 1989 to 2003'. *Health Reports* 19: 7–19.

Wilkins, R., P. Finès, S. Senécal, and E. Guimond. 2006. 'Mortality in urban and rural areas with high proportion of Aboriginal residents in Canada'. Presentation at the annual meeting of the Population Association of America, 31 March.

Wilkinson, R.G. 1999. 'Health, hierarchy, and social anxiety'. *Annals of the New York Academy of Sciences* 896: 48–63.

Willows, N.D. 2005. 'Determinants of healthy eating in Aboriginal peoples in Canada: The current state of knowledge and research gaps'. *Canadian Journal of Public Health* 96 supp. 3: S32-6, S36-41.

Willows, N.D., et al. 2009. 'Prevalence and sociodemographic risk factors related to household food security in Aboriginal peoples in Canada'. *Public Health Nutrition* 12 (8): 1150–6.

Wilson, Kathi, and M.W. Rosenberg. 2002. 'The geographies of crisis: Exploring accessibility to health care in Canada'. *Canadian Geographer* 46 (3): 223–34.

Wilson, Kathi, and T. Kue Young. 2008. 'An overview of Aboriginal health research in the social sciences: Current trends and future directions'. *International Journal of Circumpolar Health* 67:179–89.

World Health Organization. 1986. *Ottawa Charter for Health Promotion*. Ottawa: World Health Organization.

Young, T.K. 1994. *The Health of Native Americans: Toward a Biocultural Epidemiology*. New York: Oxford University Press.

———. 2003. 'Review of research on Aboriginal populations in Canada: Relevance to their health needs'. *British Medical Journal* 327: 419–22.

Young, T. Kue, et al. 2000. 'Type 2 diabetes mellitus in Canada's First Nations: Status of an epidemic in progress'. *Canadian Medical Association Journal* 163: 561–6.

Zuberi, T. 2008. 'Deracializing social statistics: Problems in the quantification of race'. In T. Zuberi and E. Bonilla-Silva, *White Logic, White Methods: Racism and Methodology*. Plymouth, UK: Rowman and Littlefield.

13 Urban Aboriginal People in Canada: Community Trends and Issues of Governance

Kevin FitzMaurice and Don McCaskill

Aboriginal people are increasingly living in urban areas in Canada. The 1951 census recorded that only 6.7 per cent of the Aboriginal population resided in Canadian cities; by 2006 this number had increased to between 53 and 60 per cent, depending on how one defines the term Aboriginal. In spite of popular stereotypes and misconceptions about Aboriginal people living primarily on remote reserves far beyond the pale of urban civilization, they actually have a long-standing connection to Canadian cities. Former Aboriginal settlements and gathering places have been transformed over time into cities, and many continue to be contested under outstanding land claims.[1]

Urban Aboriginal communities today are extremely complex; they are generally young, culturally diverse, highly mobile, and home to an increasing number of new 'ethnic drifters'. Many members of urban Aboriginal communities experience varying degrees of poverty, while an emerging minority is increasingly affluent. Recent statistical trends have pointed to improvements in educational levels, income, and employment rates. However, when compared to the overall population, urban Aboriginal residents trail behind on most indicators of community health. As well, urban Aboriginal communities are engaging in diverse practices of community organizational development and governance, which appear to present many opportunities as well as challenges.

Organized into two major sections, this chapter provides an overview of some of the major trends in urban Aboriginal communities and governance in Canada. Beginning with a demographic overview from the 2006 census, we then move on to discuss the implications of these data in relation to issues of urban Aboriginal governance in Canada. More specifically, Part 2 of this paper explores questions relating to urban Aboriginal identity politics, culture and community, Aboriginal rights, and the present challenges to political representation.

Part 1: Urban Aboriginal Community Profiles in Canada

In spite of some limitations to the use of census data,[2] it is nonetheless very helpful in providing some initial demographic insights into the complex and dynamic nature of urban Aboriginal communities in Canada.

In excess of 1 million people (1,172,790) now self-identify as Aboriginal persons, comprising 3.8 per cent of the total Canadian population (see Box 13.1 below for Statistics Canada definitions of terms of identity). Notably, of those who identify as Aboriginal in Canada, a minority (26 per cent) live on a reserve, while the remaining 74 per cent live off-reserve in both rural (21 per cent) and urban (53 per cent) settings. The on-reserve population is comprised primarily (97.5 per cent) of registered Indians,[3] while they account for only 50 per cent of the urban Aboriginal population, with Métis and Inuit populations making up 43 per cent and 7 per cent of the remaining urban population, respectively.

The census further provides for the possibility of someone indicating Aboriginal ancestry/origins without having to indicate a corresponding Aboriginal identity. In other words, a person may indicate having an Aboriginal ancestor (perhaps distant) without feeling that she or he is in fact an Aboriginal person, with an Aboriginal identity. As indicated in Table 13.1, if we add this group (people of Aboriginal ancestry but not identity) to those having only Aboriginal identity, we then see that the proportion of Aboriginal people living in urban areas increases from 53 to 60 per cent, and the proportion of those living on reserves decreases to just 18 per cent. However, as published census data tabulations focus exclusively on those reporting Aboriginal identity, it is

Table 13.1 Location of Residence, Aboriginal Ancestry/Origins, and Identity Population, Census 2006

	Total	On-Reserve	Rural	Urban
Aboriginal Ancestry/Origin[1]	1,678,235 (100%)	308,490 (18%)	367,120 (22%)	1,022,635 (60%)
Aboriginal Identity[2]	1,172,790 (100%)	308,490 (26%)	240,825 (21%)	623,470 (53%)
Registered Indians[3]	698,025 (100%)	300,755 (43%)	85,210 (12%)	312,055 (45%)
Métis	389,780 (100%)	4,320 (1%)	114,905 (29%)	270,555 (70%)
Inuit	50,480 (100%)	435 (.1%)	31,065 (62%)	18,980 (37.9%)

[1] Aboriginal ancestry/origin refers to those persons who reported at least one Aboriginal origin (North American Indian, Métis, or Inuit) on the ethnic origin question in the census. The question asks about the ethnic or cultural group(s) to which the respondent's ancestors belong.
[2] Aboriginal identity refers to those persons who reported identifying with at least one Aboriginal group, i.e., North American Indian, Métis, or Inuit. Also included are individuals who did not report an Aboriginal identity but did report themselves as a registered or treaty Indian and/or did report band or First Nation membership.
[3] Registered, status, or treaty Indian refers to those who reported they were registered under the Indian Act of Canada. Treaty Indians are persons who are registered under the Indian Act of Canada and can prove descent from a band that signed a treaty. The term 'treaty Indian' is more widely used in the Prairie provinces (Statistics Canada, 2006).

Source: Statistics Canada, 2006 Census.

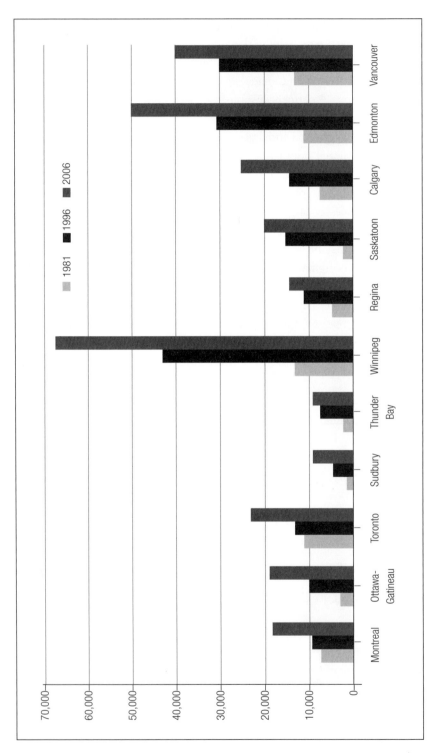

Figure 13.1 Urban Aboriginal population counts in selected CMAs: 1981, 1996, 2006

therefore this population of urban Aboriginal people (1,172,790) upon which we have based this initial community demographic profile.

Focusing on the 11 census metropolitan areas (CMAs)[4] from across Canada in which significant numbers of Aboriginal people reside, we see from Figure 13.1 a considerable and sustained growth of Aboriginal people in urban areas over the past 25 years.

Moreover, the western cities of Winnipeg, Edmonton, Vancouver, and Calgary have the highest populations of Aboriginal people in Canada. In eastern Canada, Toronto is home to the largest number of Aboriginal people, followed by Ottawa-Gatineau, Montreal, and Thunder Bay.

From Table 13.2, we see that in the three prairie cities of Winnipeg, Saskatoon, and Regina, Aboriginal people now make up between 9 and 10 per cent of the total population. Moreover, Winnipeg, Sudbury, and Calgary have the highest proportions of Métis people among their Aboriginal populations, at 60, 57, and 56 per cent respectively, while Thunder Bay and Regina have the highest proportion of registered Indians. Notably, Ottawa-Gatineau, Montreal, and Calgary have the lowest proportion of registered Indians, at 30, 32, and 34 per cent respectively.

All of the selected cities have experienced significant (104 per cent at minimum) growth rates in Aboriginal population numbers over the past 25 years. The Aboriginal identity population has quadrupled in Saskatoon and Ottawa-Gatineau and has more than tripled in Sudbury and Winnipeg.

What is particularly interesting about these exceptionally high levels of growth in the urban Aboriginal population over the past 25 years is that in

Table 13.2 Census 2006 Aboriginal Identity Population Characteristics per CMA

Selected CMAs	Aboriginal Identity Population	(%) of City Population	(%) of Métis	(%) of Registered Indians	Growth Rate (%) 1981 to 2006
Winnipeg	68,385	10	60	39	325.3
Edmonton	52,100	5	53	40	287.9
Vancouver	40,310	2	37	44	162.1
Toronto	26,575	.5	29	37	279.9
Calgary	26,575	2	56	34	104.2
Saskatoon	21,535	9	45	51	412.1
Ottawa-Gatineau	20,250	2	39	30	408.2
Montreal	17,865	.5	35	32	128.2
Regina	17,105	9	42	57	167.7
Thunder Bay	10,055	8	24	69	233.5
Sudbury	9970	6	57	36	365.9

Source: Statistics Canada, 2006 Census.

contrast to the early years, or the 'first wave' of movement from reserves to urban centres from 1951 to 1971, these increases are not the result of the emigration of Aboriginal people from reserves to cities, nor are they a result of natural increases relating to birth rates of a younger Aboriginal population already living in the city (Norris 2003b, 62).

Rather, they are the implications of both legislative changes within Indian Act definitions of status Indians and a marked change in the politics of identity, which are contributing to the overall phenomenon of 'ethnic mobility'. In response to the effective political activism of Aboriginal women in the late 1970s and early 1980s, the rules governing entitlement to Indian status (section 12 of the Indian Act) were amended in 1985 with the passing of Bill C-31.[5] Broadly speaking, Bill C-31 was an attempt to end sexual discrimination within the Indian Act through the re-instatement of status to formally denied Aboriginal women and their children and through the equitable amendment of the legal requirements for determining Indian status. In terms of its implications on the growth of the urban Aboriginal population, roughly 114,700 people were registered under Bill C-31 from 1985 to 1999, accounting for a 35 per cent increase in the national population of registered Indians at that time (Clatworthy 2003, 86). Moreover, as the previous loss of Indian status under the old section 12 provision often meant a corresponding loss of the right to reserve housing, the majority of these 're-instated' status Indian women and their children were living at that time (and continue to live today) in urban centres (Peters 2006, 319).

In addition to these legislative amendments, there has also been a significant upward trend in 'intergenerational ethnic mobility' such that, for a diversity of personal reasons, individuals are increasingly choosing to change their ethnic identity over time. Throughout the decade of 1986 to 1996, this particular form of ethnic mobility accounted for 41 per cent and 56 per cent of the proportional growth of the North American Indian and Métis population growth, respectively (Guimond 2003, 43).

A second type of 'intergenerational ethnic mobility' occurs in families of mixed Aboriginal–non-Aboriginal-parent families whereby the Métis identity of one or more of the children comes to be acknowledged only later in their life (Guimond 2003, 43). The recent 2006 census indicates that the general Métis population—the majority (69 per cent) of whom live in cities—is on the rise and is surpassing the growth of the other Aboriginal groups. In 2006, an estimated 389,785 people reported that they were Métis, doubling the population (increasing by 91 per cent) since 1996. This phenomenon of Aboriginal people marrying non-Aboriginal people is not new. A study of Aboriginal people in four major cities in the 1970s found that 50 per cent of respondents in Toronto and 39 per cent in Edmonton had brothers or sisters married to non-Aboriginal people (McCaskill 1981, 85).

It is, however, important to note that Aboriginal population growth due to ethnic mobility does not affect all cities with the same degree of intensity. In the western cities of Regina, Saskatoon, Winnipeg, and Edmonton, population growth is largely attributed to natural (net birth rate) increases. In Vancouver, Calgary, as well as the cities of eastern Canada, on the other hand, ethnic mobility plays a much larger role in the recent growth of the Aboriginal population (Siggner and Costa 2005, 14). Overall, however, given the possible socio-economic differences between those recently deciding to identify as an Aboriginal person and those who have always been Aboriginal, questions relating to the longer-term demographic trends of the total urban Aboriginal community becomes increasingly complex. In other words, as key social indicators of health in urban areas have historically been lower for Aboriginal people relative to the general urban population, there is therefore a real possibility that the significant number of newly identifying Aboriginal people has positively affected recent upward trends in urban Aboriginal census data. The impact of ethnic mobility, although difficult to measure, should therefore be taken into account when critically assessing recent census analysis, which highlights many significant improvements in the general well-being of urban Aboriginal people in Canada.

In their recently released long-term (1981 to 2001) study of census data, Siggner and Costa indicate that high school completion rates for urban Aboriginal youth have increased, as have post-secondary completion rates for young urban Aboriginal adults. These increases, however, did not correspond equally across gender. Aboriginal women had higher completion rates for both high school and post-secondary education (2005, 6).

Across selected CMAs, Table 13.3 highlights the significant differences in university completion rates between urban Aboriginal people and the general urban population. In terms of differences across cities, although Ottawa and Toronto had the highest proportion of Aboriginal people with university degrees at 16 per cent and 13 per cent, respectively, we can see from Table 13.3 that the cities with the lowest differences across the Aboriginal and general population with university degrees are Thunder Bay, Sudbury, and Saskatoon.

Employment rates improved during this 20-year period for urban Aboriginal people in most major cities, Regina being the exception. However, the gap in employment rates between Aboriginal and non-Aboriginal people did not improve significantly over this time, except in Winnipeg, Edmonton, and Sudbury where the difference narrowed by 7 to 10 per cent (2005, 7). The discrepancy between Aboriginal and non-Aboriginal people in terms of median income derived from employment also narrowed in most cities over the 20-year period.

From Table 13.3, we can see that when compared to the total population in each of the selected CMAs (except Ottawa-Gatineau), the urban Aboriginal population has lower employment rates, percentages of university degrees, and median incomes. The differences between median incomes for urban Aboriginal people and the general population are lowest in Toronto, Montreal, Ottawa-Gatineau, and Calgary, corresponding with lower differences in mobility and employment rates. When compared to the overall population, Aboriginal people living in Thunder Bay, Sudbury, and Saskatoon have relatively low median incomes in spite of having the highest proportion of university degrees.

Mirroring national income distribution trends in Canada, the 20-year period from 1981 to 2001 further marked the movement toward economic polarization within urban Aboriginal communities (Heisz 2007, 6). During this time, there was a 281 per cent growth in the number of Aboriginal employment income earners making $40,000 or more. At the same time, however, the number of those employed and making less than $15,000 grew by 550 per cent (Siggner and Costa 2005, 39). From Figure 13.2, we see that in 2006, compared to the total population, Aboriginal people in large urban areas were significantly more likely to either not have an income or earn less than $20,000 a year than to earn more than $40,000 a year. Moreover, Figure 13.2 reveals a similar income distribution

Table 13.3 Census 2006 Selected Demographics: Comparing Aboriginal and Overall Populations Per CMA

Selected CMAS	Ages 0–24 % Difference	Employment Rate % Difference	Median Income Aboriginal as % of Overall	University Degree % Difference	5-Year Mobility % Difference
Winnipeg	17	7	70.7	11	9
Edmonton	16	6.3	67.6	12	16
Vancouver	12	2.9	72.7	16	7
Toronto	6	0.4	909.2	14	7
Calgary	13	0.6	78.9	16	13
Saskatoon	19	12.9	63.1	8	22
Ottawa-Gatineau	6	−0.2	80.2	13	9
Montreal	4	1.8	80.8	11	7
Regina	22	11.8	60.9	10	24
Thunder Bay	18	8.7	60.7	6	22
Sudbury	11	3.4	71.9	7	15

Source: Statistics Canada, 2006 Census.

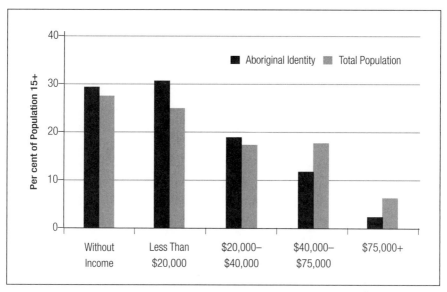

Figure 13.2   Census 2006 employment distribution in CMAs

Source: Statistics Canada, 2006 Census.

pattern to that of the rest of the Canadian CMA population in that the majority of residents (60 per cent of Aboriginal population and 56 per cent of total population) were either without an income or were part of the working poor, earning less than $20,000 per year. The middle class—those earning between $40,000 and $75,000 per year—occupy a minority position (15 per cent of Aboriginal population and 18 per cent of total population) within total CMA populations.[6]

Employment income distribution for urban Aboriginal people is not evenly distributed across gender. In spite of having higher completion rates for both high school and post-secondary education, urban Aboriginal women are 1.4 times more likely than Aboriginal men to be without an income or making less than $20,000 per year. Aboriginal women also make up only 42 per cent of the middle class of Aboriginal people earning between $40,000 and $75,000 and only 27 per cent of those earning more than $75,000 per year (Census 2006).

Moreover, it is within cities with the greatest discrepancy of relative advantage that we see Aboriginal people continue to be involved with the criminal justice system. Significantly overrepresented in correctional institutions in Canada are those who are young, male, poor and unemployed, and less educated (La Prairie 2003, 182).

Winnipeg, Saskatoon, and Regina have some of the largest discrepancies between the Aboriginal and overall populations (see Table 13.3) and also have the largest percentage of Aboriginal people living in extremely poor neighbourhoods (La Prairie 2002, 197). These cities, as well as Thunder Bay, are the highest urban contributors to the overrepresentation of Aboriginal people in Canada's prisons (2002, 197).

Two additional and related demographic considerations for urban Aboriginal people in Canada are language use and transmission and disproportionately high rates of population mobility. Although younger generations are learning their Aboriginal language as a second language, many languages are endangered as a consequence of the long-term effects of the residential school system. For a variety of reasons, including ethnic mobility, cultural diversity (Aboriginal as well as non-Aboriginal), and living as a minority population within a vast majority of non-Aboriginal residents, Aboriginal language use is declining dramatically in Canadian urban areas. From Figure 13.3, we see that relative to reserve communities, the engagement with Aboriginal languages is significantly lower in urban areas.

The use of a language at home is essential to its transmission to the next generation as a mother tongue. In their work on protecting languages under threat, UNESCO suggests that languages that are not learned by at least 30 per cent of the children in that community are endangered (Norris 2003a, 95). From 1996 to 2006, there was an overall decline in already low language use in urban areas and a greater proportion of use in reserve communities. Moreover, the percentage of those speaking an Aboriginal language at home dropped during this time from 4 to 2 per cent, signalling a major concern for Aboriginal language transmission in urban areas.

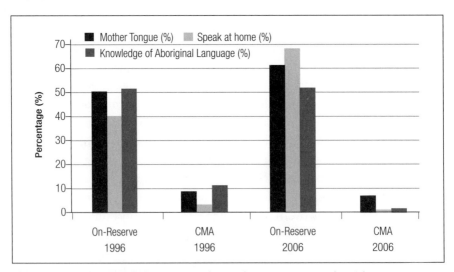

Figure 13.3 Aboriginal identity population, language use, and residency: 1996 and 2006

Source: Statistics Canada, 2006 Census.

Given the prevalence of language use within reserve communities, it is perhaps not surprising that those with the ability to speak an Aboriginal language are much more likely to move between reserve and urban areas, contributing to what as been described as the 'churn effect' of high rates of Aboriginal mobility (Norris 2003a, 112).

Unique to urban Aboriginal populations are high rates of mobility between urban centres and reserves and within and between urban centres. Table 13.3 points to a higher rate of mobility for urban Aboriginal people relative to the overall population across all selected CMAs, with the most significant rates occurring in Regina, Thunder Bay, Saskatoon, and Edmonton. Registered Indians are more likely to move generally and account for the majority of Aboriginal people who move between reserves and urban centres (Norris 2003b, 64). Moreover, although some of the larger cities have experienced slight increases in 'net migration' over recent years, this movement is generally understood as reciprocal (2003b, 63).

Another important characteristic of urban Aboriginal people that has remained consistent over time is their continued connection to their community of origin, mainly First Nations or Métis communities. A study conducted in Vancouver, Edmonton, Winnipeg, and Toronto in the 1970s found that more than two-thirds of Aboriginal people returned home 'sometimes' or 'often' annually (McCaskill 1981, 88). Similarly, a study of five cities in Ontario (Ottawa, Barrie/Midland/Orillia, Sudbury, Thunder Bay, and Kenora) in 2007 discovered that the majority of individuals in all the cities continue to maintain a strong relationship to their community of origin (McCaskill and Fitzmaurice 2007, 65). The most common reasons for visiting the community of origin were to visit family and friends and for cultural reasons such as attending powwows, socials, or ceremonies (2007, 66). The maintenance of links with the community of origin is a reflection of such factors as the proximity of First Nations and Métis communities to cities, the history of mobility of Aboriginal people, the fact that the land is such a fundamental source of traditional and contemporary Aboriginal culture, and the continuance of strong family and social ties to the communities.

Part 2: Urban Aboriginal Identities, Community, and Governance

Structural Prospects of Urban Aboriginal Governance

The possibility of urban Aboriginal governance raises a diversity of both theoretical questions surrounding identity, culture, and community and practical

questions concerning rights, jurisdiction, and Aboriginal–non-Aboriginal governmental relations. The reality of an urban land base shared by Aboriginal
and non-Aboriginal residents requires a different approach from the land-based
models most often associated with First Nations and 'modern day' treaty governments established through land claim settlements. In a commentary provided to
the Royal Commission on Aboriginal Peoples (RCAP), Dan Smith, then president
of the United Native Nations of British Columbia, argued for the need to

> emphasize that there is an urgent need for non-reserve Aboriginal people
> to be treated equally and fairly. After all, we are working toward the same
> end . . . whether [we] reside on- or off-reserve. The majority of bands,
> tribal councils and treaty areas do not have the capacity or infrastructure
> to address off-reserve Aboriginal issues and concerns. . . . Historically, off-
> reserve Aboriginal people have had to look after themselves individually,
> and then over a period of time to organize into groups for mutual sup-
> port. Self-determination for individuals and families is the foundation of
> Aboriginal people both on- and off-reserve (RCAP 1996, 580).

In response to submissions from Aboriginal people across the country, RCAP
proposed two possible models of urban Aboriginal governance. The 'reform
of urban government and public authorities' model called for greater involvement of urban Aboriginal people in mainstream urban governments through the
establishment of permanent Aboriginal political representation on municipal
councils and related political bodies and the co-management of urban programs
and services.

Alternatively and with the understanding that enhanced Aboriginal participation in mainstream urban governance structures would fall short of community
expectations for greater autonomy through meaningful self-government, urban
Aboriginal governance could emanate out of a 'community of interest' model.
Broadly stated, urban Aboriginal governance based upon a 'community of interest' would entail the voluntary association of a diversity of urban Aboriginal
organizations. Governance in this way could take the form of a specific service
sector and/or act through an array of agencies and institutions that would establish a larger city-wide politically representative body (RCAP 1996).

The Basis of Governance: Identity, Community, and Culture

In helping us to understand the aspirations for urban Aboriginal governance
and some of the related questions of race, power, jurisdiction, and rights, it
is important to begin with a brief exploration of the fundamental ideas of

identity, community, and culture. At the core of our identity (the Self) is a desire to exist as an individual as well as a member of a group, whether that be
a family, clan, community, nation, and/or nation-state. It is through our ever-
changing relationships with others that we are able to find meaning as part of
an ongoing process of defining our individual and collective identities. How
we live our lives personally, intimately, and reflexively to some degree relates to
how we choose to organize and govern ourselves collectively/politically. What
is critical to this process, however, is the power to be able to decide for oneself
who one is in relation to others. In a collective sense, it is the power to define
the boundaries of who we are in relation to others, between who is the same
and who is different. Having organized and created the collective agency to
define and maintain the parameters of our associations—the boundaries of
our communities—we can then begin the process of self-governance, but always in relation to those 'others' understood as being on the outside of one's
communities. To some degree, this collective identity is expressed through
institutions created by members of the group that are designed to protect,
maintain, and enhance group solidarity and express the group's culture and
identity. For example, groups develop a network of organizations and informal
social relationships, which permit and encourage the members of that group
to support and sustain the group. The degree to which a group develops its
own institutions varies. Within some groups, individuals can meet all of their
needs within the group's institutional structures. On the other hand, some
groups consist primarily of a network of interpersonal relationships with no
supporting formal institutions.

Within the context of individual and collective identities, culture may be
thought of as the medium of understanding through which all of this can happen. It is what provides members with 'meaningful ways of life across the full
range of human activities, including social, educational, religious, recreational,
and economic life, encompassing both the private and public spheres' (Schouls
2003, 5). Moreover, it is in the need for recognition and respect from others that
we then come together into larger groups and communities, creating multiple,
dynamic, and interwoven individual and group identities and cultures that involve ongoing, complex negotiations of power in defining the boundaries of
where we belong and find meaning and where we are strangers and do not.

Colonial Racism: A Background to Contemporary Urban Aboriginal Governance

As one of the central ways in which culture is expressed, language plays a critical
role in individual and collective identity formation and the negotiation of power.

In her submission to the Royal Commission on Aboriginal People, Dawna Le Blanc of the Anishnaabe Language Teachers Association offered:

> Languages reflect fundamental differences in culture in ways that specific language groups perceive their world, their family relationships, kinship structure, relationship to other cultures, and to the land. Language impacts on our cultural, educational, social, economic, and political life, therefore language has a direct bearing on how we see ourselves as a people and our role in self-government, on land claims and our claim to a distinct society (RCAP 1996, 534).

Different languages can therefore be significant markers/boundaries of cultural distinctiveness. Within the same language, however, cultural as well as political differences can still be negotiated through the reproduction of specific discourses and not others.[7] The meaning of Aboriginal rights and in particular the Aboriginal right to self-government are central sites of Aboriginal and state discursive struggles that can be understood as part of a critical engagement with the power relations that have shaped, and continue to shape, the politics of urban Aboriginal identity and community governance.

For example, it can be argued that in limiting the Aboriginal identity questions in the census to that of ancestry, identity, registered status, and First Nations membership and then deciding on related demographic topics of interest, Statistics Canada has some degree of influence in shaping how we understand urban Aboriginal identity, community, and governance. The vast majority of, if not all, scholarly and governmental publications and reports (including this one) that engage with urban Aboriginal issues refer to aspects of the demographic view provided to us by Statistics Canada. In a significant way, the census attempts to define the boundaries of urban Aboriginal identities and communities for Aboriginal people and establish the parameters of what can be discussed in terms of urban Aboriginal governance. And importantly, as noted earlier in this paper, there are some Aboriginal individuals and communities that recognize this use of power and choose to resist the process altogether. At the same time, Statistics Canada has, since the 2001 census, attempted to gain a consensus with Aboriginal people as to the nature of the questions to be asked on the census and Aboriginal Peoples Survey by convening a series of consultative workshops involving a wide range of Aboriginal people with a view to ascertaining their opinions.

Although Statistics Canada functions to reproduce and consolidate these categories of Aboriginal identity for Aboriginal people, they did not independently create them. Rather, they are participating in a long-standing legal discourse in Canada that began when the country began, with the separation of powers between the federal and provincial governments under section 91 and 92 respectively.[8] In the eyes of the then newly configured nation-state of Canada, former international, 'nation to nation' relations between Aboriginal people and the British Crown became domestic affairs of colonial control. Informed by the popularized, racist notions of Aboriginal cultural inferiority,[9] section 91(24) transformed diverse nations of Aboriginal allies and trading partners and their lands into uniformly defined 'Indians'[10] and 'Indian lands' within the sphere of federal jurisdictional authority (Carter 2007, 101–31). As a foundational state perspective, section 91(24) has had profound implications for Aboriginal people, since it provided the legal (in fact constitutional) basis behind early policy and programs designed to assimilate Aboriginal people and their land into the Canadian body politic. After the 1969 White Paper's blatant attempt to assimilate status Indians met with widespread Aboriginal resistance, the federal government formally repudiated its assimilationist policy direction in favour of increased consultation and the establishment of self-government and land claim initiatives. Nonetheless, many Aboriginal people continue to suspect that more subtle forms of colonial policy continue to inform contemporary government programming.

Although many of the features of early colonial relations are beyond the scope of this paper, it is important to mention here that in spite of (or perhaps because of) this early federal policy of assimilation, many Aboriginal nations continued to negotiate formal, nation-to-nation treaty relations with the Canadian government from 1871 to 1891. And it was during this time of negotiation and from within this overarching policy of assimilation that the reserves were created as separate places away from urban centres where 'Indians' were isolated from mainstream society and other members of their diverse nations. Moreover, this post-Confederation time of assimilation marked the passing of the Indian Act of 1876, a law that severely repressed almost all aspects of Aboriginal cultural, spiritual, and political life and also marked the beginning of the residential school system, which is now widely recognized as a large-scale devastation[11] that has led to much personal and collective hardships in many reserve and urban Aboriginal communities today.

After many generations of colonial repression, the Indian Act was significantly amended in 1951 to allow for increased civil rights. Able to now move freely off reserves, many Indians after the Second World War began moving to urban centres seeking education, employment, and housing and in the process creating new identities, families, communities, and formal associations and institutions. Beginning as Indian and Métis clubs during the 1950s, friendship centres first began as Aboriginal community-building organizations and developed into social services organizations. Since these early years, the number of friendship centres and related urban Aboriginal agencies have grown in step with an expanding urban Aboriginal population and have participated in the creation of Aboriginal community life in the city (Newhouse 2003, 252).

The history of Aboriginal urban institutions in Canada is quite distinct from one city to another. Each major city has more than 50 Aboriginal organizations. The vast majority of urban Aboriginal organizations are health and social service–oriented, focusing on services in such fields as health, justice and corrections, policing, poverty, child welfare, social housing, homelessness, troubled youth, family counselling, education and training, and alcohol and drug counselling, as well as providing shelters, drop-in centres, and street patrols in order to meet the substantial needs of the urban Aboriginal population. These organizations often function in ways significantly different from those of non-Aboriginal social service agencies in that they attempt to provide services and structure in a culturally based manner (McCaskill and Fitzmaurice 2007, 87). There are other types of Aboriginal organizations in cities as well, such as arts and business organizations, and a number of more informal programs and activities such as powwows, social and cultural events, Elders conferences, and sports events. But the predominance of social service organizations has led to a negative stereotype that the majority of urban Aboriginal people are poor and possess a number of negative traits. Aboriginal individuals who have attained economic success in cities may sometimes feel that there is little institutional support for their Aboriginal identity, and thus they may not conceive of themselves as part of the urban Aboriginal community as it currently exists. Research in Ontario cities suggests that factors such as negative stereotypes, the lack of relevant programs and facilities to meet their needs, as well as divisions within the urban Aboriginal community contribute to an alienation of the emerging urban Aboriginal middle class (2007, 171). This has significant implications for any broad-based participation in urban Aboriginal governance.

The broader context of urban Aboriginal governance today, however, has its roots in the early period of colonization when Aboriginal identities and communities were systematically created, segregated, and oppressed. Much of the legal and ideological infrastructure of this early period persists today. Indians and their lands continue to be both a federal responsibility in accordance with section 91(24) and heavily regulated by the Indian Act. Racism today plays a significant role in the creation of disadvantage for urban Aboriginal people and is experienced in both personal and systemic ways that discriminate against and exclude Aboriginal people from positions of power and privilege (McCaskill and FitzMaurice 2007, 103). Moreover, conceiving Aboriginal culture in this racialized way as static, exclusively traditional, and reserve-based makes it irreconcilable with urban modernity. According to this view, one cannot be both urban and Aboriginal; moving to the city becomes a process of shedding one's Aboriginal cultural distinctiveness and becoming fully integrated into urban Canadian life as one resident among many.

At the same time, it is important to recognize the agency of urban Aboriginal people. They have not been passive recipients of racialized legal structures and policy initiatives. Significant efforts by members of the urban Aboriginal community to create a type of governance have been made through the creation of boards of directors that attempt to be representative of the larger urban Aboriginal community. Indeed, many Aboriginal organizations believe that the most effective model of urban governance is the formal recognizing and expanding of their role in representing Aboriginal people.

Jurisdictional Uncertainty in Urban Areas

A major impediment in the development of urban Aboriginal communities is policy and programming uncertainty and confusion stemming from disagreements over legislative authority for urban Aboriginal people between the federal and provincial governments. Mirroring the racialized view of Aboriginal culture as static and reserve-based, the federal government's position is that through the application of the Indian Act, it is exclusively responsible for Indians within reserve boundaries (Hanselmann and Gibbins 2002, 3). According to this view, Indians stop being Indians once they leave the reserve. The implication of this position has been that the federal government focuses almost exclusively on reserve-based policy development and programming for status Indians at the expense of urban Aboriginal people. However, some administrative and funding links have been established between the federal government and the urban Aboriginal community. Post-secondary education funding, some social services programming, and the provision of non-insured health benefits are examples of continued off-reserve federal support for status Indians. Moreover, the federal government has initiated the Office of the Federal Interlocutor within Indian and Northern Affairs Canada (INAC), which is mandated to implement the Urban Aboriginal Strategy, 'an approach based on problem-solving partnerships with provincial governments, urban Aboriginal organizations, municipalities and other federal departments'.[12]

The provinces, for their part, have consistently put forward a position that Aboriginal people are legally the same as other urban people and that once they take up residence in urban areas, provincial responsibilities to them parallel those for non-Aboriginal residents and are thus 'needs-based' rather than contingent upon a unique legal or cultural status. According to this view, any specific policy or programming development relating to urban Aboriginal people falls under the jurisdiction of the federal government (Hanselmann and Gibbons 2002, 4). Provinces nonetheless maintain Aboriginal units, in some cases ministries, that focus on Aboriginal communities and the co-ordination of provincial policies and programs toward all Aboriginal people, including those in urban centres (Malloy 2001, 134–6).

The implication of these divergent positions is the creation of what is often referred to as 'policy confusion' for urban Aboriginal people, resulting in inconsistencies and inequities in the provision of programs and services. As a result, urban Aboriginal agencies attempting to provide services to their clients are faced with short-term, unpredictable programming, chronic underfunding, and ambiguity in available programs and services (McCaskill and FitzMaurice 2007, 90).

> Most of us are always fighting over dollars, to keep our administration going, to house ourselves, and look after our administration costs, whether we're Métis, Treaty, whatever. . . . [W]e give people the runaround now when they come into the city. Well, you're Treaty and you've not been here one year so you go to this place. But, oh no, you've been here a year already so you go to this place. Well, you're Métis, you have to go somewhere else. It's too confusing for people (RCAP 1996, 538).

What is missing from both federal and provincial discourses on urban Aboriginal people and their institutions is any mention of the inherent right to urban Aboriginal self-government or the provision of programs and services as a function of that right.

First Nations Land Claims and the Urban-Reserve

Broadly speaking, based on a static, pre-contact understanding of Aboriginal cultural distinctiveness, the past 30 years of Aboriginal rights litigation has produced a common-law discourse that restricts Aboriginal rights to guidelines on hunting and fishing access, a *sui generis* title to the land, and most recently, a duty to consult.

This discourse, however, was legally bolstered in 1982 with the inclusion of section 35 in the Constitution, which 'recognizes and affirms existing Aboriginal and treaty rights for Aboriginal people' while defining Aboriginal people as Indians, Inuit, and Métis. Moreover, since 1995 the federal government has explicitly recognized Aboriginal self-government as an inherent section 35 Aboriginal right and has negotiated the meaning of this constitutional right as part of land claim agreements with First Nations communities and with the Inuit as part of the creation of Nunavut.

An important dimension of the land claim process that directly affects urban Aboriginal communities has been the creation of the 'urban-reserve'. In accordance with the federal 'Additions to Reserves' and 'Treaty Land Entitlement' policy, several land claim negotiations (primarily in Saskatchewan) have included the creation of reserve land within city limits. Governed as part of rural-based First Nations reserve lands, albeit situated within city limits, urban-reserves have thus far been created primarily as economic development initiatives for First Nations members and are considered a growing trend in First Nations governance within urban communities (Loxely and Wien 2003, 222).

Concluding Questions and Challenges: Urban Aboriginal Governance, Aboriginal Rights, and Cultural Diversity

Competing discourses on Aboriginal rights, whether they be the Aboriginal assertion of full political sovereignty or the state's more restricted view, have therefore focused exclusively on land, natural resources, and governance arrangements for First Nations communities outside of urban-based organizations and communities. Moreover, it appears that although there are many examples of urban Aboriginal agency co-ordination in the interest of local governance,[13] there is uncertainty as to the usefulness or applicability of the concept of Aboriginal rights in the pursuit of urban Aboriginal community interests. In response to the Aboriginal rights focus of the most recent Prime Minister's Roundtables on Aboriginal People, Peter Dinsdale (president of the National Association of Friendship Centres [NAFC]) commented on the concerns of an Aboriginal rights discourse for urban Aboriginal communities:

. . . rights are necessarily nation-based, focusing on nations and governments. But what about those who fall through the cracks? The NAFC would prefer that the discussion centered more on needs. This may not be as politically exciting or as persuasive as the rights-based approach, but it is what is needed to ensure that all are included. The NAFC operates on a 'status blind' basis, is pan Aboriginal, and focuses on needs. So far, the NAFC has not had great success in advocating a needs-based approach to Aboriginal issues. But there is tremendous need for homeless services, and to deal with kids who have dropped out of school. Talk about rights will not solve these issues (Institute on Governance 2005, 9).

One of the key questions relating to urban Aboriginal governance in Canadian cities is whether or not pursuing an Aboriginal rights discourse, based on section 35, would be more productive then the present 'needs-based' approach. As discussed above, the present situation is fraught with jurisdictional inconsistency, funding uncertainty, and unmet social service needs. The demographic profile outlined in Part 1 of this paper documented a community that experiences significantly lower levels of education, income, and labour force participation and higher levels of instability and criminal activity than the overall urban population. Urban Aboriginal people are more likely to live in lone-parent families, have poorer health status, have higher rates of homelessness, have greater housing need, and experience domestic violence (Hanselmann and Gibbins 2002, 2). Will increased Aboriginal control over the provision of services to their community members, their clients, as a section 35 right lead to an enhanced alleviation of these disparities?

Could Aboriginal political representation within municipal governing bodies be made mandatory as an Aboriginal right of governance? Could an urban Aboriginal rights agenda, based on the identities (Indian, Inuit, and Métis) and the authority of section 35 as a constitutional check on the policy and program development for all levels of government, provide the foundation for consistent and supportive urban Aboriginal–state relations and comprehensive political representation within a 'community of interest' political framework?

The present complexity of urban Aboriginal political relationships poses some important challenges to these possibilities. As discussed above, power is foundational to questions of identity, culture, and community. As part of efforts to move toward urban Aboriginal governance, who will decide on community membership and the meaning of 'Indian, Inuit, and Métis'? Will Indian mean status Indians only, excluding all those who have lost their status, or will it be an inclusive term to include all those of Indian/Aboriginal ancestry? In terms of political representation, who within the urban community will be empowered to participate in this process? Will it be exclusively those with a long family history of identifying as Aboriginal people, or will the new ethnically mobile Aboriginal population also be included? In the eastern cities of Montreal, Ottawa, and Toronto, the Aboriginal ancestry–only populations (people with Aboriginal ancestry but not identity) are more than twice as numerous as the Aboriginal identity populations (Census 2006). Are those with Aboriginal ancestry and not identity part of the urban Aboriginal community and thus potentially empowered under a section 35 urban Aboriginal rights paradigm?

Moreover, there are several structural divisions within the urban Aboriginal community that will inhibit a movement toward more formal political associations. As stated in the RCAP report, existing urban Aboriginal social service agencies are key to the possibility of an urban Aboriginal 'community of interest' governance structure in that they would voluntarily come together to form a larger city-wide, politically representative body. However, the vast majority of these organizations are not politically accountable by design. In spite of having boards of directors based within the community, they are structured around a non-politically representative client–worker relationship. The primary organizational goal, then, is not to retain clients as though they were members of a political party but rather to help and provide services to them until they are no longer in need of assistance. In other words, the basis of the client–worker relationship is professional, confidential support rather than public, political association. In order to preserve confidentiality, social service workers often do not publicly acknowledge or associate with their clients. Is it possible to develop broad-based, non-service organizations that are representative of the majority of members of the urban Aboriginal community, many of whom, as discussed earlier in the case of the emerging middle class, feel disenfranchised from that community?

As previously discussed, culture plays an important role in the formation of identity, community, and governance. Although culture is ever-changing across relationships and time, it can nonetheless point to the boundaries between community members and non-members at any given moment. In Part 1 of this chapter, we noted the decline in the use of Aboriginal languages in urban centres as an important marker of declining cultural meaning and distinction. Moreover, the complex diversity of Aboriginal and non Aboriginal cultures in urban centres presents a challenge to community-building in the interests of urban Aboriginal governance. In addition, the predominance of Aboriginal social service institutions, combined with a lack of cultural and political organizations in urban areas, can work against the formation of broad-based urban Aboriginal community formation and political association.

Nonetheless, new identities, communities, and hybrid Aboriginal cultures are developing around the urban Aboriginal social services agencies. Generally speaking, these agencies attempt to respond to both the social service and the cultural needs of their clients through the intentional incorporation of Aboriginal cultural expression into their services. These social service communities are not, however, for everyone, and an important finding in Ontario has been that although many of the urban Aboriginal social services staff are part of the emerging middle class, a segment of this middle-class population has moved away from the social service community. Instead, they consider themselves Aboriginal individuals who for various reasons do not participate in Aboriginal agency–sponsored cultural events and do not feel that they belong to the urban Aboriginal community per se (McCaskill and FitzMaurice 2007, 193).

Finally, an important challenge to creating urban Aboriginal communities in the interests of fostering inclusive and representative governing structures can be found in the high rates of Aboriginal mobility within urban areas. High rates of population turnover or 'churn' within and between urban centres and between First Nation and urban communities inhibit the possibility of finding a common identity, sharing cultural experiences, and working toward political association and governance. Nonetheless, as noted in Part 1, when income, education levels, and labour force participation increase, mobility rates appear to decrease proportionally, suggesting a gradual lessening of this challenge over time as the emerging urban Aboriginal middle class expands. Ultimately, creatively imagining and fostering urban Aboriginal communities inclusive of a diversity of identities and cultures, as well as socio-economic experiences, will be essential to the future development of urban Aboriginal governance in Canada

Discussion Questions

1. What does it mean to be part of a community, and what are some of the key features of urban Aboriginal communities in Canada?
2. What are some of the challenges to the recognition and respect of Aboriginal rights, particularly the right to self-government, in urban centres in Canada?
3. What is the difference between 'needs-based' and 'rights-based' approaches to Aboriginal policy and programming, and does this distinction matter in urban centres?
4. What do you feel might be the reasons that some members of the emerging Aboriginal middle class are moving away from social service–based urban Aboriginal communities, and what are the implications of this trend for urban Aboriginal identity, community, and governance?

Further Readings

McCaskill, D., and K. FitzMaurice. 2007. *Urban Aboriginal Task Force: Final Report*. Ontario Federation of Indian Friendship Centres, Ontario Métis and Aboriginal Association, and Ontario Native Women's Association. In addition to the Ontario-wide final report, five UATF reports have been completed for Sudbury, Ottawa, Thunder Bay, Kenora, and Barrie-Midland. All UATF reports can be found in pdf format at www.ofifc.org/ofifchome/page/index.htm.

Peters, E. 2006. 'We do not lose our treaty rights outside the . . . reserve: Challenging the scales of social service provision for First Nations women in Canadian cities'. *GeoJournal* 65: 315–27.

Newhouse, D., and E. Peters, eds. 2003. *Not Strangers in These Parts: Urban Aboriginal Peoples*. Ottawa: Policy Research Initiative.

Notes

1. Including areas within and/or adjacent to the cities of Vancouver, Edmonton, Saskatoon, Thunder Bay, Sudbury, Toronto, and Ottawa.

2. The Assembly of First Nations reports that the 2006 census for the on-reserve population undercounts by at least 200,000 compared to the official federal Indian Registry. As well, the Ontario Urban Aboriginal Task Force highlights undercounting as a result of urban Aboriginal resistance to the census and the mobility of some members of the urban Aboriginal community. Statistics Canada indicated in a recent census publication that in 2006, there were 22 incompletely enumerated Indian reserves, down from 30 in 2001 and 77 in 1996 and that 2006 and comparative figures have been adjusted to account for these discrepancies. For further reading see Brian Edward Hubner, 'This Is the Whiteman's Law': Aboriginal Resistance, Bureaucratic Change and the Census of Canada, 1830–2006 (Springer Science+Business Media B.V., 2007).

3. For consistency in meaning across the demographic profile and analysis sections of this paper, we have adhered to Statistics Canada definitions of Aboriginality.

4. CMAs have an urban core population of 50,000 or more with a total population of 100,000 or more (Census 2006).

5. For further reading, see Janet Silman's *Enough Is Enough: Aboriginal Women Speak Out*.

6. For further readings on Canada's diminishing 'middle class', see Andrew Heisz's 'Income inequality and redistribution in Canada: 1976 to 2004', Analytical Studies Branch Research Paper Series, Statistics Canada.

7. For further reading on the power of language and its role in creating and the maintenance of identity please see Gerald Vizenor's *Manifest Manners: Narratives on PostIndian Survivance*, Greg Sarris's *Keeping Slug Woman Alive: A Holistic Approach to American Indian Texts*, as well as Michel Foucault's *The History of Sexuality*.

8. Broadly speaking, the federal government maintained authority for matters of national concern while the provincial jurisdiction revolves around matters of social policy for its residents.

9. For further reading on the many dimensions of stereotypes of Aboriginal people, see Daniel Francis's *Imaginary Indian: The Image of the Indian in Canadian Culture* and Berkhofer's *The White Man's Indian: Images of the American Indian from Columbus to Present*.

10. A Supreme Court decision in 1939 (*In re Eskimos*) also brought the Inuit within federal responsibility. Métis, with the exception of those living in Métis settlements in Alberta, were not subject to special federal or provincial legislation.

11. For further reading on the residential schools, see John Milloy's 'A national crime' in the report of the Royal Commission on Aboriginal Peoples, vol. 1, ch. 10, and

Roland Chrisjohn's *The Circle Game: Shadow and Substance in the Residential School Experience in Canada.*

12. For more information, see INAC website at www.ainc-inac.gc.ca/ai/ofi/uas/index-eng .asp.

13. Some prominent examples include the Toronto Aboriginal Support Services Association, the Aboriginal People's Council in Vancouver, the Ottawa Aboriginal Coalition, the Aboriginal Council of Winnipeg, Barrie Area Native Advisory Circle, and the Aboriginal Council of Lethbridge.

References

Carter, S. 2007. *Aboriginal People and Colonizers of Western Canada to 1900.* Toronto: University of Toronto Press.

Clatworthy, S. 2003. 'Impacts of the 1985 amendments to the Indian Act on First Nations populations'. In J.P. White, P. Maxim, and D. Beavon, eds, *Aboriginal Conditions: Research as a Foundation for Public Policy,* 63–90. Vancouver: University of British Columbia Press.

Guimond, E. 2003. 'Fuzzy definitions and population explosion: Changing Aboriginal groups in Canada'. In D. Newhouse and E. Peters, eds, *Not Strangers in These Parts: Urban Aboriginal Peoples,* 35–48. Ottawa: Policy Research Initiative.

Hanselmann, C., and R. Gibbins. 2002. *Another Voice Is Needed: Intergovernmentalism in the Urban Aboriginal Context.* Kingston, ON: Institute of Intergovernmental Relations.

Heisz, A. 2007. *Income Inequality and Redistribution in Canada: 1976 to 2004.* Ottawa: Statistics Canada.

Institute on Governance. 2005. *Roundtable on Urban Aboriginal Governance: Summary of the 5th IOG Aboriginal Governance Roundtable.* Ottawa.

La Prairie, C. 2002. 'Aboriginal over-representation in the criminal justice system: A tale of nine cities'. *Canadian Journal of Criminology* April: 181–208.

———. 2003. 'Exile on Main Street: Some thoughts on Aboriginal over-representation in the criminal justice system'. In D. Newhouse and E. Peters, eds, *Not Strangers in These Parts: Urban Aboriginal Peoples,* 179–91. Ottawa: Policy Research Initiative.

Loxely, J., and F. Wein. 2003. 'Urban Aboriginal economic development'. In D. Newhouse and E. Peters, eds, *Not Strangers in These Parts: Urban Aboriginal Peoples,* 217–42. Ottawa: Policy Research Initiative.

McCaskill, D. 1981. 'The urbanization of Indians in Winnipeg, Toronto, Edmonton and Vancouver: A comparative analysis'. *Culture* 1 (1): 82–9.

McCaskill, D., and K. FitzMaurice. 2007. *Urban Aboriginal Task Force: Final Report.* Ontario Federation of Indian Friendship Centres, Ontario Métis and Aboriginal Association, and Ontario Native Women's Association.

Malloy, Jonathan. 2001. 'Double identities: Aboriginal policy agencies in Ontario and British Columbia'. *Canadian Journal of Political Science* 34 (1): 131–55.

Newhouse, D. 2003. 'The invisible infrastructure: Urban Aboriginal institutions and organizations'. In D. Newhouse and E. Peters, eds, *Not Strangers in These Parts: Urban Aboriginal Peoples,* 243–52. Ottawa: Policy Research Initiative.

Norris, M.J. 2003. 'Aboriginal languages in Canada's urban areas: Characteristics, considerations, and implications'. In D. Newhouse and E. Peters, eds, *Not Strangers in These Parts: Urban Aboriginal Peoples*, 93–110. Ottawa: Policy Research Initiative.

———. 2003. 'Aboriginal mobility and migration within urban Canada: Outcomes, factors, and implications'. In D. Newhouse and E. Peters, eds, *Not Strangers in These Parts: Urban Aboriginal Peoples*, 51–78. Ottawa: Policy Research Initiative.

Peters, E. 2006. 'We do not lose our treaty rights outside the . . . reserve: Challenging the scales of social service provision for First Nations women in Canadian cities'. *GeoJournal* 65: 315–27.

RCAP (Royal Commission on Aboriginal Peoples). 1996. *Report of the Royal Commission on Aboriginal Peoples*. Ottawa: Canada Communications Group.

Schouls, T. 2003. *Shifting Boundaries: Aboriginal Identity, Pluralist Theory and the Politics of Self-Government*. Vancouver: University of British Columbia Press.

Siggner, A.J., and R. Costa. 2005. *Trends and Conditions in Census Metropolitan Areas: Aboriginal Conditions in Census Metropolitan Areas, 1981 to 2001*. Ottawa: Statistics Canada.

14 The Canada Problem in Aboriginal Politics

David Newhouse and Yale Belanger

Introduction

This chapter examines Aboriginal politics through the lenses of the 'Indian problem' and the 'Canada problem', since the politics surrounding Aboriginal peoples is conducted within the dual paradigms of 'the Indian problem' and 'the Canada problem'.

More than a decade ago, the Royal Commission on Aboriginal Peoples (RCAP) presented its final report. The report set out the principles of a new relationship between Aboriginal peoples and Canada and proposed a way to achieve it. The RCAP report also set out a vision of a Canada that contained Aboriginal peoples as full and equal partners in Confederation, a Canada comprised of 10 provinces, three territories, and 40 to 60 Aboriginal Nations, as well as a First Nations House as part of Parliament, all confirmed and given expression by treaties. The vision was dismissed as unworkable and costly, although to be fair, the cost was mainly related to the cost of dealing with the colonial legacy—i.e., cleaning up the past.

Until recently, the conversation about Canada has been framed by, dominated by, and led by the English and French. Others who might wish to speak have been overshadowed by the loud and raucous conversation between these two ancient rivals who transported their rivalry from the old country to the New World. These elites saw Canada as a European creation. It is only recently that the original inhabitants of the country have been seen as having a role in the creation of country, if not at Charlottetown in 1864 then in other ways.

John Ralston Saul, writing in *Reflections of a Siamese Twin: Canada at the Beginning of the Twenty-First Century* (1998), argues that Canada is founded upon three pillars: English, French, and Aboriginal. He argues that there has been little recognition of Aboriginal people as a pillar or as a foundational group. Canada has not come to terms with its Aboriginal heritage. In popular Canadian history books until recently, Aboriginal peoples appear at the beginning, then disappear, only to pop up again like prairie gophers. Yet despite their relative invisibility, Aboriginal people are a constant presence in Canadian policy history.

In a more recent book, *A Fair Country: Telling Truths about Canada* (2008), Saul contends that the foundational ideas of Canada are Aboriginal in origin and that Canada is a Métis country. The ideas of inclusivity and fairness are based, he argues, in indigenous political philosophy, not in European philosophy. If Saul's ideas are valid, then his is a unique contribution and represents a fundamental change in how Canadians might see themselves.

Aboriginal peoples in Canada now constitute distinct cultural and political communities with a set of rights that have been gradually evolving and expanding since the 1970s' decisions of the Supreme Court of Canada. This is a remarkable turn of events for a people who for so long have been seen through the lens of the 'Indian problem' (Dyck 1991).

For Canada, the Indian problem has been about the transformation of Indians into Europeans—more particularly, into either British or French peoples—and the absorption and assimilation of Aboriginal peoples into the Canadian body politic. Canada followed this policy from Confederation until 1971 when the proposed Statement of Indian Policy of the Government of Canada (Canada 1969), known iconically as the White Paper, was withdrawn. Over the next three decades, the policy of assimilation was slowly replaced by a policy of self-determination and self-government and more recently by one of reconciliation, following the work of the Royal Commission on Aboriginal Peoples in 1996.

For Aboriginal peoples, the Canada problem is about the transformation of Canada into a territory that enables them to live as Aboriginal peoples in distinct communities with the ability to make decisions on the important aspects of their lives and which lives up to its many promises. Some Aboriginal leaders have framed their work as the continuation of Confederation to include them in the federation in a distinct and recognizable fashion. The *Canadian Encyclopedia* expands the definition 'Fathers of Confederation' to include Inuit leaders who negotiated the creation of Nunavut.

Aboriginal peoples were not part of the original discussions surrounding Confederation, were not consulted in any fashion at the time, and saw their relationship with the British and French colonial powers transformed from one of nation-to-nation to that of a dependent wardship within the new country called Canada. Aboriginal political objectives revolve around correcting this mistake.

While Canada has followed a consistent Indian policy until recent decades, Indians have been consistent all along in their approach to Canada, time and again proposing the creation of a harmonious relationship with the newcomers and their institutions through nation-to-nation agreements. This strategy was based on a political philosophy rooted in Aboriginal political ideals of cooperation, sharing, and harmonious relationships. Robert Williams, in *Linking Arms*

Together: American Indian Visions of Law and Peace, 1600–1800 (1997), argues
that the treaty literature is a primary source for examining indigenous political
thought. A successful relationship between peoples was based on a foundation
of mutual reliance and trust. It required visible signs that human beings could,
in a multicultural world, trust each other: sharing a peace pipe, exchanging
hostages, and presenting valuable gifts like land and hunting grounds to each
other were seen as signs of linking arms and creating a circle of security, peace,
and happiness.

These ideas also animate contemporary Aboriginal political action. Yale
Belanger, in *Seeking a Seat at the Table: A Brief History of Indian Political Organizing
in Canada, 1870–1951* (2006), describes their use in indigenous political organizing in Canada after Confederation. Ovide Mercredi and Mary Ellen Turpel,
in *In the Rapids: Navigating the Future of First Nations* (1993), propose the same
ideas as the basis for the relationship between Aboriginal peoples and Canada,
and the final report of the Royal Commission on Aboriginal Peoples (1996)
proposes an Aboriginal political vision of Canada based on ideas of mutual respect, mutual responsibility, and sharing. The First Nations Leadership Council
of British Columbia (2006) articulated these ideals as well.

Starting in the 1960s, Aboriginal peoples have been consistently advocating
for increased self-determination and self-government and a return to the nation-
to-nation relationship as originally envisioned by the Royal Proclamation of
1763. This has stimulated an animated discussion about Aboriginal citizenship.[1]

This chapter lays out some of the changes that have occurred over the past
half century, changes that made it possible for Saul to conceive of Canada as a
Métis country—a remarkable idea that would have been inconceivable in 1960,
the year that the Progressive Conservative government of John Diefenbaker
granted Indians the right to vote in federal elections for the first time. At that
time, Indians were barely citizens, and Canada treated them as problems. In
1995, Aboriginal peoples, a group considerably larger and broader than Indians
alone, were recognized as having an inherent right to govern themselves within
the Canadian federation. The chapter focuses on the contemporary period, beginning with the move away from a policy of assimilation as articulated in the
White Paper to one of self-government as expressed in the 1995 statement on
the inherent right to self-government. This period was a time of transformation
for both Indians and Canada, with the development of Aboriginal governments
emerging as a key objective for Aboriginal leaders.

It is important to recognize and acknowledge that Aboriginal peoples
occupy a unique place within Canadian history, the Canadian imagination, and
Canadian citizenship. By virtue of section 35.1 of the Canada Constitution Act,

Aboriginal people enjoy a legal status that is different from that of ordinary Canadian citizens. The jurisprudence of the last century has clearly established a solid foundation of rights that accrue to Aboriginal peoples, both as individuals and as collectivities. The treaties, constitutional status, and law all come together to endow Aboriginal peoples with a different status as citizens within a modern liberal democratic society. International covenants add moral authority to this position. Aboriginal peoples are not simply another member of the ethnocultural community struggling to create 'peace, order, and good government' in Canadian society.

Aboriginal peoples, by virtue of treaties, legislation, and jurisprudence are, to put it in the words of the 1966 Hawthorn Report, 'citizens plus' and charter members of Canadian society. This status implies that a new approach is called for in discussions about the Canadian federation.

As a first step, a move away from the dominant paradigm that has informed Aboriginal policy since Confederation is necessary. This is the paradigm of the 'Indian problem'. Even though such language is no longer used, its legacy lives on in the continuing efforts to solve the 'Indian problem'.

Since the arrival of Europeans and the establishment of governments in Canada after 1763, government officials have been trying to decide what to do with the original inhabitants: each government over the years has had a particular view of the 'Indian problem'. At one time or another, the problem would be framed as whether or not Aboriginals were human and had souls; how they could be turned into good Christians; how to coexist with them; how to induce them into military alliances; how to civilize them; how to assimilate them; and now how to transform them into an ethnic group as part of the multicultural environment of Canada. Each of these views of the Indian problem has led to a particular policy solution and a set of actions by government officials.

The Colonial Legacy

The legacy of Canada's colonial Indian policy is reflected in the position of Aboriginal peoples at the social, economic, and political margins of the country: lower levels of education and income, poor housing, and poor health. Initially confined to reserves and remote areas as a result of the original Indian policy, a majority now live in urban centres throughout the country. The vast majority live in the western provinces, although Ontario has the largest Aboriginal population.[2] Several studies[3] over the past two decades have also shown that a disproportionate number have encountered problems with the justice system, resulting in higher levels of incarceration. These studies highlight the racism that many have encountered within the justice system, while others[4] demonstrate the difficult relationship that many Canadians have with the original inhabitants.

Another aspect of the colonial legacy that continues to dominate the political landscape is the Indian Act, originally adopted in 1876 as a consolidation of pre-colonial legislation and the policy ideas underlying it. While the Act has been amended from time to time, its basic underlying premises have not changed. John Tobias, a historian of Aboriginal peoples, argues that there has been a consistency to Canada's Indian policy over the past 100 years or so. Protection, civilization, and assimilation have always been the goals of Canada's Indian policy.[5] The three policy pillars, he argues, were in place by the time of Confederation. What changed over time was the relative emphasis placed on each.

Indians were seen as inferior to Europeans and in need of protection from exploitation by them. This policy idea required that Indians be given a special status within Canada whereby the state would take special measures to protect them. Protected status would also make it easier for the state to civilize them— i.e., convert them to Christianity and teach them to live and work in the manner of Europeans. Becoming civilized would then make it easier for Indians to leave their old ways of life behind and assimilate into Canadian society. This, one could argue, was the core government policy until retraction of the 'White Paper' in 1970.

Addressing the Indian Problem in the Second Half of the Twentieth Century

The Hawthorn–Tremblay Commission Report of 1966

During the 1950s, there was a growing feeling that the integration of Indian people into the greater Canadian society was progressing too slowly, and granting the franchise was viewed as one method of accelerating the assimilation process. In 1960, the federal government extended the franchise and full citizenship to all Indian people in Canada without abolishing Indian status. For the first time, Indian people had the right to vote in all provincial and federal elections. It was a step toward the type of Indian political/societal participation politicians had long envisioned for Aboriginal peoples—citizens absorbed into Canadian society and practising Canadian norms. A joint parliamentary committee, struck in 1959 and reporting in 1961, concluded that Indians were still viewed as a racial minority and that the time had come for Indian people to 'assume the responsibility and accept the benefit of full participation as Canadian citizens': 'Your committee has kept this in mind in presenting its recommendations which are designed to provide sufficient flexibility to meet the varying stages of development of the Indians during the transition period.'[6]

In response to growing concerns about the poor social and economic situation of the new citizens, the federal government launched a number of studies, with Harry Hawthorn and Marc Tremblay preparing the most influential report. Appointed in 1963, they presented their report in two parts: Part I in 1966 and Part II in 1967. Commissioned to study the socio-economic situation of Indians in Canada, they made a series of recommendations for improving Indian lives. The report lays the foundation for modern Indian policy, presenting the radical idea that Indians ought to be 'citizens plus'. In doing so, it rejected the idea of assimilation into mainstream society and created within the Canadian polity the notion that Indians had more rights than other citizens 'by virtue of promises made to them and expectations they were encouraged to hold, and from the simple fact that they once used and occupied a country to which others came to gain enormous wealth in which the Indians shared little.'[7] In short, Indians were now to be included as 'charter members of the Canadian community'.[8] The commissioners stressed 'a common citizenship as well as the reinforcement of difference'.[9]

The notion of 'citizens plus' would prove extremely powerful, so much so that the Indian Chiefs of Alberta (1970) chose the name for its response to the 1969 federal Indian policy proposals.

Hawthorn and Tremblay recognized the need for Indians to govern themselves and for the Canadian system to accommodate Indian governments. Recommendations 67 and 68 state: 'Continuing encouragement should be given to the development of Indian local government'[10] and 'The problem of developing Indian local government should not be treated in the either/or terms of the Indian Act or the provincial framework of local government. A partial blending of the two frameworks within the context of an experimental approach which will provide an opportunity for knowledge to be gained by experience is desirable.'[11] Hawthorn and Tremblay proposed that Indian governments would be rooted in the Indian Act while blended into the provincial–municipal framework: a federal–provincial–Indian hybrid. Recommendation 72 states: 'The integration of Indian communities into the provincial municipal framework should be deliberately and aggressively pursued while leaving the organization, legal and political structure of Indian communities rooted in the Indian Act.'[12]

The White Paper[13] of 1969

The 1969 Statement of Indian Policy of the Government of Canada rejected the Hawthorn–Tremblay idea of Indians as 'citizens plus'. Based upon Pierre Trudeau's notion of a 'just society', the proposal envisioned Indians as ordinary citizens of Canada with neither special status nor any entitlement to different administrative arrangements or legal relationships. The central ideas of the proposed policy were the notions of 'equality' and 'equity', expressed in its overall goal of enabling Indian people 'to be free to develop Indian cultures in an environment of legal, social and economic equality with other Canadians'.[14] The White Paper went even further, proposing that programs and services be transferred to provincial jurisdiction and delivered accordingly. Indians would become the responsibility of the province in which they resided. It also recommended that Indians should receive government services from the same agencies as other Canadians.

The Canadian government argued that it was the policy of a separate legal status for Indians that 'kept the Indian people apart from and behind other Canadians' and that this 'separate road cannot lead to full participation, to better equality in practice as well as theory.' The Indian Act of 1876 was to be repealed, since it was viewed as the source of this separate legal status. The Department of Indian Affairs would be dismantled within five years. The government would appoint an Indian land claims commissioner to deal with issues resulting from treaties under a land claims policy. The treaties, described as 'historic documents', would be interpreted as containing only 'limited and minimal promises' that had in most cases been fulfilled. Indian reserve lands would be turned over in fee simple to Indian bands, which could then determine ownership among members. Indians should assume the responsibilities of citizens, have the same legal status and rights as all other citizens, and move away from the policy regime of protection and special rights.

The Hawthorn Report and the White Paper, while not explicitly about Canada, did contain ideas about Canada. The Hawthorn Report envisioned Indians as charter citizens—citizens plus, to use its terminology. The White Paper rejected this idea and saw Indians as citizens like any others, arguing that special citizenship status for Indians was incompatible and inconsistent with the values of a modern democratic society and in particular with the vision of the 'just society'. The solution to the Indian problem was to do away with Indian status.

Addressing the Canada Problem

The Red Paper of 1970

The White Paper proposals were unacceptable to Indian leaders and to many others in Canadian society. They ignored or minimized treaties, dismissed separate legal status for Indians, and pointed to a future that envisioned Indians as a part of an emerging multicultural society.

The Indian Chiefs of Alberta (ICA) presented their position entitled *Citizens Plus*, now called the Red Paper, in 1970. Presenting an Indian political vision of the nature of the relationship between Indians and Canada, they argued that Indians had special status within Canada, a status similar to Hawthorn's notion of 'citizens plus' but rooted in the treaties. The preamble to the Red Paper states: 'To Us who are Treaty Indians there is nothing more important than our Treaties, our lands and the well being of our future generation.' The statement also argues for the continuation of Indian status, saying that it is essential for justice, for continuation of Indians as Indians: 'The only way to maintain our culture is for us to remain as Indians. To preserve our culture it is necessary to preserve our status, rights, lands and traditions. Our treaties are the basis of our rights. . . . The intent and spirit of the treaties must be our guide, not the precise letter of a foreign language.'[15]

On Indian lands, it says: 'The Indians are the beneficial (actual) owners of the lands. The legal title has been held for us by the Crown to prevent the sale and breaking up of our land. We are opposed to any system of allotment that would give individuals ownership with rights to sell.'

On services, the Red Paper says: 'The federal government is bound by the BNA Act . . . to accept legislative responsibility for Indians and Indian Lands. In exchange for the lands . . . the treaties ensure the following benefits:

'a. to have and to hold certain lands called "reserves" for the sole use and benefit of the Indian people forever and assistance in the social, economic, and cultural development of the reserves; b. the provision of health services . . . at the expense of the Federal government; c. the provision of education of all types and levels to all Indian people; d. the right of the Indian people to hunt, trap and fish for their livelihood free of governmental interference and regulation and subject only to the proviso that the exercise of this right must not interfere with the use and enjoyment of private property.'

The Red Paper described the basic political philosophy used to guide Aboriginal leaders over the next 30 years. It was based on indigenous notions of reciprocity and respect: we give you these lands in return for these rights and guarantees and services. These promises of reciprocity are set out in treaties. It is also based on the idea of a nation-to-nation relationship that confers a 'citizenship plus' status for Aboriginal peoples.

The Union of British Columbia Indian Chiefs issued *A Declaration of Indian Rights* the same year, and in 1971 the Association of Iroquois and Allied Indians in Ontario presented their position paper. They rejected all the proposals and, more importantly, set out their own vision of their place in Canadian society and the steps that needed to be taken to move forward.

While the Red Paper was foundational to political reaction to the federal government's Indian policy proposal, the emerging Aboriginal vision was best captured by the response of the Manitoba Indian Brotherhood (MIB) (1971): *Wahbung: Our Tomorrows*: 'The Indian Tribes of Manitoba are committed to the belief that our rights, both aboriginal and treaty, emanate from our sovereignty as a nation of people. Our relationships with the state have their roots in negotiation between two sovereign peoples. . . . The Indian people enjoy special status conferred by recognition of our historic title that cannot be impaired, altered or compromised by federal–provincial collusion or consent.' *Wahbung* recommended a comprehensive approach to development of Indian communities, both economically and as central to Indian life. Development should proceed not in bits and pieces but according to a comprehensive plan on several fronts. There were three elements to this plan: (1) helping individuals and communities recover from the pathological consequences of poverty and powerlessness; (2) protection of Indian interests in lands and resources; and (3) improved and sustained support for human resource and cultural development. The MIB plan rested on the idea that development and change ought to be directed by Indian people themselves so that Indians could consider both individual and communal interests.

The White Paper was formally withdrawn in 1971, although it remains a potent political icon within Aboriginal politics. The Indian reaction to the White Paper was informed by ideas expressed in the 1968 consultations around revisions to the Indian Act. While there was no consensus among Indians during the consultations about all the change needed, there was consensus about the way forward: recognize the special rights of Indians, recognize the historical grievances over lands and treaties, deal with them in an equitable fashion, and give them direct and meaningful participation in the making of policies that affect their future.

In 1973, a decision by the Supreme Court of Canada about Aboriginal land title involving the Nisga'a on the west coast of the country would alter the political landscape forever. In the *Calder* decision (*Calder v. The Attorney General of British Columbia* 1973),[16] as it came to be known, six of the seven Supreme Court justices determined that Aboriginal rights were in fact pre-existing, albeit relegated to a lesser position in Canadian society.[17] This judgment entrenched Aboriginal rights within the country's political legal landscape and laid the foundation for the renewal of the treaty process and the contemporary land claims policy. It also forced the government to reflect upon the position expressed in the Red Paper and *Wahbung*, among other Aboriginal positions, that not only did Aboriginal rights exist but that these rights in certain cases entailed self-government. *Calder* also laid the foundation for changing the view of the history of Indians, finding that prior to the encroachment of settlers onto Native territories, 'Indians were there, organized in societies occupying the land as their forefathers had for centuries.'

The *Calder* case represented a turning point in addressing the Canada problem in that it brought the judiciary and the law clearly into the politics of Aboriginal peoples in a large and important way. Aboriginal people began to use the courts to pursue land claims, redress past mistreatments, and further define their legal rights. Over the next two decades, the courts proved to be good allies, and favourable rulings emanated from all levels: *Sparrow*, *Delgamuukw*, and *Marshall* among them (*R. v. Sparrow* 1990; *Delgamuukw v. British Columbia* 1997; *R. v. Marshall* 1999).

Shortly before the *Calder* decision, the Council for Yukon Indians (CYI) presented its plan, *Together Today for Our Children Tomorrow*, for regaining control over lands and resources that included a comprehensive approach to development in its land claims statement to Prime Minister Trudeau. The CYIs ought to 'obtain a settlement in place of a treaty that will help us and our children learn to live in a changing world. We want to take part in the development of the Yukon and Canada, not stop it. But we can only participate as Indians. We will not sell our heritage for a quick buck or a temporary job.'[18]

The CYI also promoted the importance of retaining a land base: 'Without land Indian people have no soul—no life—no identity—no purpose. Control of our own land is necessary for our cultural and economic survival. For Yukon Indian People to join in the social and economic life of Yukon we must have specific rights to lands and natural resources that will be enough for both our present and future needs.'[19] Land was seen not as a repository of resources awaiting exploitation but rather as a significant component of who Indians are and important to any form of self-government.

The Push for Aboriginal Self-Government

Aboriginal self-government appears as part of the measures advanced to solve the Canada problem in the mid-1970s as self-determination morphs into self-government. Contemporary ideas about Indian government were articulated by the Federation of Saskatchewan Indians (FSI) (now the Federation of Saskatchewan Indian Nations [FSIN]) in 1977. The FSI was the first Aboriginal organization to formally articulate the principles of Aboriginal self-government in a paper entitled *Indian Government* (1977). The principles advanced represent a position that has become familiar to public policy–makers throughout Canada.

Indian Government starts by articulating a foundational set of beliefs, immutable to refutation: 'No one can change the Indian belief. We are Nations; we have Governments. Within the spirit and meaning of the Treaties, all Indians across Canada have the same fundamental and basic principles upon which to continue to build their Governments ever stronger.' It establishes eight fundamental and basic principles: (1) Indian nations historically are self-governing; (2) section 91(24) of the Indian Act gives the federal government the authority to regulate relations with Indian nations but not to regulate their internal affairs; (3) Indian government powers have been suppressed and eroded by legislative and administrative actions of Canada; Indian government is greater than what is recognized or now exercised and cannot be delegated; (4) treaties reserve a complete set of rights, including the right to be self-governing and to control Indian lands and resources without federal interference; (5) treaties take precedence over provincial and federal laws; (6) the trust relationship imposes fiduciary obligations on the trustee; (7) the federal government has mismanaged this relationship; and (8) Indians have inalienable rights, including the 'inherent sovereignty of Indian Nations, the right to self-government, jurisdiction over their lands and citizens and the power to enforce the terms of the Treaties'.

The FSI saw sovereignty as 'the right to self-government. It is inherited and it comes from the people. We have never surrendered this right and we were never defeated militarily.' Sovereignty is both 'inherent and absolute': Indian governments traditionally exercised the powers of sovereign nations, and the most fundamental right of a sovereign nation is the right to govern its people and territory under its own laws and customs. 'Inherent' means that Parliament or any other branch of any foreign government did not grant the right of self-government. Indians have always had that right, and the Treaties re-enforce this position.

The FSI further argued in a 1979 paper *Indian Treaty Rights: The Spirit and Intent of Treaty* (Federation of Saskatchewan Indians 1979) that between 1817 and 1929, more than 20 major international treaties were signed between the Crown and the Indian and Dene Nations. In return for these treaty rights, the Indian Nations agreed to cede certain lands for use and settlement. The FSI advanced a view of treaties as recognizing the powers of Indian nations and establishing sovereign relationships between Indian nations and Canada.

The discussion on Indian self-government broadened over the next few years to include Métis, non-status Indians, Inuit, and urban Aboriginal peoples as talks about repatriation of Canada's Constitution got underway, with the terminology changing to 'Aboriginal' self-government. The self-government discussion came to be dominated by the FSIN view of Aboriginal self-government, grounded in a view of Aboriginal peoples as constituting self-governing nations with a broad and deep right to self-government guaranteed by treaty. This view resonated throughout the country and captured the political imagination of Aboriginal peoples far beyond those with treaties. Aboriginal peoples solidly rejected the idea of a universal citizenship[20] as articulated by the White Paper and firmly accepted and developed the idea of 'citizens plus' as articulated in the Hawthorn Report. What remained was to convince others of this position—in particular, the government of Canada.

In 1982, the Constitution of Canada was repatriated and recognized Aboriginal peoples as including[21] Indian, Inuit (formerly Eskimo), and Métis. The Constitution also affirmed existing Aboriginal rights but left them indeterminate. The first amendment called for a series of constitutional conferences between Canada, the provinces, and Aboriginal peoples to try and determine what these rights were and what self-government meant.[22] These televised meetings brought the self-government discussions into the homes of Canadians and introduced them to contemporary Aboriginal leaders in conversation with members of the federal cabinet and the provincial premiers. The idea of self-government was hotly debated, its legitimacy and foundations questioned.

While the discussions were underway, the House of Commons established a special committee to deal with Indian self-government. The committee's 1983 report, now named after the committee chair, Keith Penner, advanced a view of Indian government as enhanced municipal-style government within a federal legislative framework, with three important differences: (1) Indian government should be a 'distinct order' of government within Canada with a set of negotiated jurisdictions and fiscal arrangements; (2) the right of Indian self-government should be constitutionally entrenched with enabling legislation to recognize Indian governments; and (3) the areas of authority for Indian governments could be education, child welfare, heath care, membership, social and cultural development, land and resource use, revenue-raising, economic and commercial development, justice and law enforcement, and intergovernmental relations.

The Penner Report argued for a new relationship with Aboriginal peoples based on Prime Minister Trudeau's comments at the First Ministers' Conference on Aboriginal Constitutional Matters (Ottawa, March 1983):

> Clearly, our aboriginal peoples each occupied a special place in history. To my way of thinking, this entitles them to special recognition in the Constitution and to their own place in Canadian society, distinct from each other and distinct from other groups who, together with them comprise the Canadian citizenry (Penner, 1983).

The report recommended that 'the federal government establish a new relationship with Indian First Nations and that an essential element of this relationship be recognition of Indian self-government'. It also recommended that

> the right of Indian peoples to self-government be explicitly stated and entrenched in the Constitution of Canada. The surest way to achieve permanent and fundamental change in the relationship between Indian peoples and the federal government is by means of a constitutional amendment. Indian First Nations would form a distinct order of government in Canada, with their jurisdiction defined.

The report indicated that 'virtually the entire range of law-making, policy, program delivery, law enforcement and adjudication powers would be available to an Indian First Nation government within its territory.'

The Government of Canada responded to the Penner Report in March 1984, indicating acceptance of the report: 'The Committee's recommendations have a special importance because they were unanimously supported by Committee members of all Parties.' It agreed with the need to establish a new relationship with Indian peoples: 'The effect . . . is to call for the Government and Indian First Nations to enter into a new relationship. . . . Many of the details of the restructured relationship will have to be worked out after careful consideration and full consultation with Indian people.'

Importantly, the response said:

> The Government agrees with the argument put forth by the Committee that Indian communities were historically self-governing and that the graduate erosion of self-government over time has resulted in a situation which benefits neither Indian people nor Canadians in general.

The government did not accept the idea of constitutional entrenchment, but a decade later it would read the Constitution in such a way as to include the right to self-government within it:

> The Government of Canada recognizes the inherent right of self-govern-ment as an existing Aboriginal right under section 35 of the Constitution Act, 1982. It recognizes, as well, that the inherent right may find expres-sion in treaties, and in the context of the Crown's relationship with treaty First Nations. Recognition of the inherent right is based on the view that the Aboriginal peoples of Canada have the right to govern themselves in relation to matters that are internal to their communities, integral to their unique cultures, identities, traditions, languages and institutions, and with respect to their special relationship to their land and their resources (Canada 1995).

What makes the Penner Report important in the history of the development of Aboriginal government is that it accepted and reinforced the FSIN argument that Indian nations have always been self-governing and presented historical evidence for it. The acceptance of the report in the House of Commons and the detailing of a plan for recognition of Aboriginal self-government represent the end of a phase in the debate about Aboriginal self-government. The first phase of the debate focused on the question: do Aboriginal peoples have the right to govern themselves? In 1984 the federal government responded: Yes, but within the Canadian federation[23] (details to follow over the next several lifetimes, as is the nature of federal systems).

The debates around the Meech Lake and Charlottetown constitutional pro-posals in the late 1980s and early 1990s, ostensibly to deal with Quebec, then took on a different significance in relation to the debate about Aboriginal self-government. These discussions were concerned with the details of Aboriginal self-government. The Charlottetown Accord in particular, with its proposal of a distinct order of Aboriginal government, foreshadowed the recommendations of the Royal Commission on Aboriginal Peoples. It is also important to point out that these self-government discussions involved not just the federal government but provinces and municipalities as well. Provincial involvement is particularly important in discussions around natural resources, social services, and educa-tion. The debates included not only issues of government authority, jurisdiction, and funding but issues of service delivery as well.

Not satisfied with reluctant acceptance of Aboriginal self-government, Aboriginal leaders then pushed for an acknowledgement of the idea that self-government was not granted but recognized and as such could not be taken away. In this regard, they insisted on use of the term 'inherent'. Canada accepted this position in the 1995 Federal Statement on the Inherent Right to Aboriginal Self-Government, now known as the Inherent Rights Policy (IRP). Although there is now much debate about the effect of the term 'inherent', a key element of the Canada problem has been addressed.

In the interim, however, Aboriginal peoples in the late 1980s and early 1990s were not satisfied with the progress toward self-government. Discontent resulted in a series of confrontations across the country. In response to a confrontation over Aboriginal lands at Oka, Quebec, the Conservative government of Brian Mulroney in 1991 established the Royal Commission on Aboriginal Peoples to investigate the evolution of the relationship between Aboriginal peoples, the government of Canada, and Canadian society as a whole. The 4000-page five-volume report tabled in 1996 recommended a restructuring of the relationship between Canada and Aboriginal peoples and set out the details of the 'third pillar'. It contained an Aboriginal political vision of Canada in which Aboriginal peoples comprise distinct political communities as Aboriginal Nations and have a place within the governing structure of the country as Aboriginal governments with defined jurisdictions and authorities as well as a role in relation to Parliament through a First Peoples House. The report also called for a major effort, similar to *Wahbung* recommendations, to improve the social and economic conditions of Aboriginal peoples.

The RCAP models of Aboriginal governments as 'national governments' or 'Aboriginal public governments' or 'community of interest governments' go far beyond the limited municipal-style governments proposed by Hawthorn and envisioned by the Indian Association of Alberta in the 1960s and early 1970s. It envisions Aboriginal governments as informed by a distinct Aboriginal political culture rooted in local Aboriginal traditions of governance. It also envisions a continuing confederation of Canada with Aboriginal peoples occupying a distinct and constitutionally protected place within it. A new round of treaty-making would give shape, form, and substance to it. The RCAP embraces the notion of complexity in its vision, rejecting a one-size-fits-all view of Aboriginal governance.

These ideas were not developed in a vacuum but arose through various land settlements and agreements over the previous two decades that gave concrete expression to the idea of Aboriginal self-government: The Cree-Naskapi Act (1975), Sechelt Indian Self-Government Act (1986), Yukon Settlement (1993). Post-RCAP agreements such as the Nisga'a Treaty (2000) and the creation of Nunavut (1999) and Nunavik (2005), to name a few of the more prominent ones, lend further substance to the RCAP narrative. Further, numerous agreements in areas such as health, education, child care, and economic development give some sense of how Aboriginal governance might proceed in program and service areas. There is now a large body of experience and literature in contemporary Aboriginal governance that can be explored to describe contemporary practice and to build Aboriginal governance theory for use in educating the next generation of Aboriginal peoples.

The treaty process has started in British Columbia and has been restarted in Saskatchewan. In British Columbia, the process, facilitated by the BC Treaty Commission, is a joint undertaking of Canada and the First Nations Summit. The commission is an independent agency overseeing the negotiations of new treaties in this part of Canada, an area that was part of the historic treaty process and was thought to have been dealt with when British Columbia entered Confederation in 1871. In Saskatchewan, the treaty process, a joint federal FSIN initiative with the province as an official observer, focuses on developing a contemporary interpretation of Saskatchewan's four treaties and using them as the basis for building a new relationship, including self-government. The treaty process, arising out of the land claim policy as well as the Royal Proclamation of 1763, includes discussion not just on lands and resources but on self-government as well.

In summary, the idea of self-government has broadened considerably over the past three decades. It has grown from an initial conception as local municipal-style government rooted in the Indian Act to a constitutionally protected inherent right, with its most recent expression in the idea of 'Aboriginal national government' as a distinct order of government within the Canadian federation. The range of people affected by the discussions has grown considerably. The initial focus of self-government was on status Indians residing on reserves, but this has now broadened to include Métis, Inuit, and urban Aboriginal peoples. The basis of self-government has fundamentally changed. Aboriginal self-government is no longer seen as rooted in the Indian Act but as an 'inherent' right, rooted in history and treaties. The scope of authority and jurisdiction for self-government has also enlarged considerably. Aboriginal governments are now seen as more than municipalities, as encompassing federal, provincial, and municipal authorities as well as some unique Aboriginal authorities. In the federal system, this means that the range of actors that need to be involved has also broadened.

The debate over self-government has fundamentally changed. It is now about 'how' rather than 'why'. In a short period of 26 years—from the White Paper of 1969 to the Statement of Inherent Right of 1995—Canada has moved from an official government policy of termination and assimilation to a reluctant acceptance of the inherent right of self-government. Aboriginal leaders have succeeded, at least philosophically and in some practical ways, in addressing a key aspect of the Canada problem.

Into the Twenty-first Century

The end of the twentieth century and the start of the twenty-first have seen Canada starting to come to terms with its colonial heritage. In particular, the nation has begun to publicly acknowledge its past actions, atone for them, and make promises that it will not engage in the same actions again.

On 7 January 1998, the Minister of Indian Affairs and Northern Development, the Honourable Jane Stewart, stood up in a room in the House of Commons and read a statement of reconciliation. We can debate whether or not it was an apology and what the words meant. We can also debate whether or not she should have said it, whether it was sincere, whether it went far enough, and what its effect, if any, might be. It's quite legitimate to debate and discuss these things. However, if we step back a bit and look at the statement in another light, we could see it this way: It is the first statement by a government of the New World that acknowledges that it has been wrong in its treatment of the people that it encountered:

> The Government of Canada today formally expresses to all Aboriginal people in Canada our profound regret for past actions of the federal government which have contributed to these difficult pages in the history of our relationship together.

No other government in the New World—the United States of America, Mexico, Brazil, Argentina, Peru—or any government of the Old World—England, Spain, France, Portugal—had, to that time, expressed such sentiments.

The statement also contained a view of Aboriginal and Canadian history. It said explicitly that Aboriginal peoples had lived here for thousands of years, had their own forms of government, were organized into nations with distinct national cultures, and had made contributions to the development of Canada. It also said that there had been a deliberate attempt, based on attitudes of racial and cultural superiority, to suppress Aboriginal cultures and values and to dispossess Aboriginal peoples of their lands and territories and that these actions were wrong. It contained a vow to change that. It also painted a picture of Aboriginal peoples as having remarkable strength and endurance.

The statement goes on to say:

Reconciliation is an ongoing process. In renewing our partnership, we must ensure that the mistakes, which marked our past relationship, are not repeated. The Government of Canada recognizes that policies that sought to assimilate Aboriginal people, women and men, were not the way to build a strong country. We must instead continue to find ways in which Aboriginal people can participate fully in the economic, political, cultural and social life of Canada in a manner which preserves and enhances the collective identities of Aboriginal communities and allows them to evolve and flourish in the future. Working together to achieve our shared goals will benefit all Canadians, Aboriginal and non-Aboriginal alike.

We can be cynical about the statement, but we should know that at least in its ideas it conforms to the position held by many Aboriginal peoples. We should also know that Aboriginal peoples, working within one of the major Aboriginal political organizations, were the ones primarily involved in preparing it. It is a remarkable statement, yet it has been much ignored by Canadians and Aboriginal peoples alike. Aboriginal peoples ignored it because they saw it not as a real apology but merely a statement of regret. Many Canadians ignored it because they thought that the Indian problem was now on the way to a speedy once-and-for-all resolution.

Even more remarkable, another statement followed Minister Stewart's profound declaration a decade later. On 10 June 2008, the prime minister of Canada stood in the House of Commons to deliver a formal apology, not a statement of reconciliation. It stated in part:

In the 1870's, the federal government, partly in order to meet its obligation to educate aboriginal children, began to play a role in the development and administration of these schools. Two primary objectives of the residential schools system were to remove and isolate children from the influence of their homes, families, traditions and cultures, and to assimilate them into the dominant culture. These objectives were based on the assumption aboriginal cultures and spiritual beliefs were inferior and unequal. Indeed, some sought, as it was infamously said, 'to kill the Indian in the child.'

Today, we recognize that this policy of assimilation was wrong, has caused great harm, and has no place in our country. . . . The government now recognizes that the consequences of the Indian residential schools policy were profoundly negative and that this policy has had a lasting and damaging impact on aboriginal culture, heritage and language. . . . The legacy of Indian residential schools has contributed to social problems that continue to exist in many communities today. It has taken extraordinary courage for the thousands of survivors that have come forward to speak publicly about the abuse they suffered. . . .

The government recognizes that the absence of an apology has been an impediment to healing and reconciliation.

Therefore, on behalf of the government of Canada and all Canadians, I stand before you, in this chamber so central to our life as a country, to apologize to aboriginal peoples for Canada's role in the Indian residential schools system. . . . We now recognize that it was wrong to separate children from rich and vibrant cultures and traditions, that it created a void in many lives and communities, and we apologize for having done this. . . . The burden of this experience has been on your shoulders for far too long.

The burden is properly ours as a government, and as a country. The government of Canada sincerely apologizes and asks the forgiveness of the aboriginal peoples of this country for failing them so profoundly.

We are sorry.

These are extraordinary statements, and they begin to address the Canada problem. They are the outcome of a confident, aggressive, savvy, educated, and experienced leadership that has emerged in Aboriginal communities over the past four decades. This leadership is highly skilled, knows how to push hard, and knows how to get what it wants. Behind the leadership is an ever-growing cadre: thousands of Aboriginal professionals who have gained post-secondary credentials and workplace experience in mainstream and Aboriginal communities. These professionals are slowly moving into decision-making positions and are effecting change.

Behind them are thousands of students currently enrolled in post-secondary educational institutions across the country. Over the next few decades, these individuals will also be moving into leadership positions. As a whole, these people are determined, well-educated, and courageous; they want a better world for themselves and for their children.

Many of the upcoming generation see Aboriginal self-government within their grasp. They have experienced aspects of self-government in education, in health care, in economic development, in social work, in housing, in cultural programs, in education, and in language training.[24] They work to ensure that federal and provincial policy, in particular, are consistent with Aboriginal principles and visions. For example, they worked hard to ensure retraction of the First Nations Governance Act (FNGA) in 2003, which was introduced by the federal government to provide a legislative basis for Indian band councils. Aboriginal leaders condemned the Act as incongruent with their principles about the foundations of Aboriginal self-government. The new generation of leaders is well-versed in their own political history and is proving adept at crafting and putting forward positions that reflect their ideals.

The members of this highly educated group have an understanding of the world different from that of those who came before them. They are imbued with an understanding of the fundamental condition of modern Aboriginal society—post-colonial consciousness. It is a society well aware that it has been colonized in many ways, a society aware of the implications of its colonization and choosing deliberately, consciously, and systematically to deal with that colonization, a society coming to terms with what has happened to it, and a society determined to overcome its colonial legacy. It is a society that is gathering strength and determined to address the Canada problem using this newfound pride.

Post-colonial consciousness will be the defining political and social force within Aboriginal society over the next generation. Post-colonial Indians want to renovate the master's house with the master's tools so that it can accommodate their desires more easily. This desire for change, arising out of post-colonial consciousness, brings a number of challenges for Canadians.

Over the past four decades, an Aboriginal modernity has emerged that forms the context and foundation of modern Aboriginal societies: confident, aggressive, assertive, insistent, desirous of creating a new world out of Aboriginal and Western ideas, and self-consciously and deliberately acting out of Aboriginal thought. This desire and the actions of the past three decades have shaped modern Aboriginal society: it has also shaped Canada as the nation has sought to accommodate Aboriginal peoples in a variety of ways.

We have seen the creation of a new territory: Nunavut, which is by reputation and design an Aboriginal territory. We have seen the signing of the Nisga'a treaty and the creation of the Nisga'a government. Prior to that, we have seen the Sechelt First Nation Government District created in British Columbia. We have seen the amendment of the Constitution in the early 1980s to recognize something called 'Aboriginal rights'. We have seen the emergence of a social affairs infrastructure that delivers social services and education to Aboriginal peoples throughout the country. We are witnessing the signing of many agreements that acknowledge Aboriginal jurisdiction in health care, education, and economic development. We are also seeing the emergence of a class of Aboriginal entrepreneurs who are creating wealth using funds derived from land claim settlements. In many ways, Aboriginal peoples are changing Canada.

These political developments have a parallel in other areas. A recognized genre of art known as Aboriginal art includes a wide variety of expression: Inuit stone carving, Iroquoian soapstone, Haida masks, Mi'kmaq baskets, Ojibway quill work (the quills belong to the porcupines), post-modern Aboriginal expressionism. Particularly inspiring is the Woodland School's development based on the techniques of the late Norval Morriseau, as are the emergent forms of carving, painting, and pottery.

There also has been an explosion in Aboriginal music. In 2008, the Canadian Aboriginal Music Awards celebrated its tenth year as part of the 15-year-old Canada Aboriginal Arts Festival.

Aboriginal literature has similarly grown. There are writers galore: Thomas Highway, Jeannette Armstrong, Drew Hayden Taylor, Thomas King, and Eden Robinson, to name a few of the most prominent ones. CBC-TV produced two regular series featuring Aboriginal characters: 'North of 60' and 'The Rez'. CBC Radio 2 and Thomas King produced the 'Dead Dog Café', a weekly comedy show featuring Aboriginal peoples. In September 1999, with the approval of the CRTC, the new Aboriginal Peoples Television Network was launched and is today available on basic service in every cable viewer's home across Canada.

The National Aboriginal Achievement Foundation (formerly the Canadian Native Arts Foundation) gives out annual awards to Aboriginal peoples who have made outstanding contributions to their communities. It has no difficulty in finding nominees and regularly receives many more nominees than it can possibly give awards to.

In education, there is now one Aboriginal university and 49 Aboriginal-controlled post-secondary institutions.[25] The last federally run Indian residential school was closed in 1985. Virtually all public schools on Indian reserves are now under Indian control.

In large urban centres, there is an extraordinary array of service and cultural organizations serving large urban Aboriginal populations. The first edition of the *Arrowfax* (1991) directory of Aboriginal organizations identified close to 6000 Aboriginal organizations, split evenly between the profit and not-for-profit sectors, including First Nations governments. This number has grown every year since then. Currently, there are about 14,000 Aboriginal businesses, nearly 3000 Aboriginal organizations, and 117 Aboriginal Friendship Centres serving urban populations across Canada.

An increasing number of Aboriginal people now choose mainstream careers, working as professors and teachers in the secondary and post-secondary sectors, serving as public servants in the federal, provincial, and Aboriginal public sectors. Others pursue careers as lawyers, health care professionals, social workers, and business people, among many other professionals. Some academic studies point to an Aboriginal middle class emerging.[26] In the area of health and healing, a widespread healing movement has emerged, reaching almost every Aboriginal person in this country and resulting in the establishment of Aboriginal health centres across the country. In the midst of these developments a strong desire has emerged to bring forward, and interpret for a contemporary world, traditional teachings and philosophies. Thus, a new category of human knowledge, traditional indigenous knowledge, has appeared on a broader stage and is beginning to be presented in mainstream school systems.

Aboriginal peoples have also developed international linkages and worked in collaborative efforts with indigenous people around the world, helping to foster a worldwide movement focused on gaining recognition of indigenous rights and improving the quality of indigenous lives. The World Council of Indigenous Peoples (1974–1996) was founded by George Manuel, former president of the National Indian Brotherhood (now the Assembly of First Nations).[27] In September 2007, after two and a half decades of lobbying, the United Nations adopted the Declaration of the Rights of Indigenous Peoples (without Canada's support), stating clearly that indigenous peoples have the right to the recognition, observance, and enforcement of treaties concluded with states or their successors, a position advocated by the ICA in 1970.

Unfortunately, the remarkable political achievements of this period have not yet resulted in an overall improvement in the quality of life for Aboriginal peoples. Concurrent with efforts to solve the Canada problem, Aboriginal peoples advocate for additional measures to address social and economic disparities. These aspirations are advanced in a collective and powerful fashion through Aboriginal political and civil sector organizations funded by governments. Between 1965 and 1992, for example, these organizations produced hundreds of reports containing thousands of recommendations on how to improve Aboriginal socioeconomic conditions nationally.[28] Today, Aboriginal issues are on the agenda of virtually every government agency, including the Supreme Court of Canada. Governments, civil sector organizations, and members of the private sector have had to adjust to the continuing legal presence of Aboriginal peoples. For example, in 2007 the BC government created the position of Aboriginal physician as a senior public officer responsible for Aboriginal health. Ontario that same year created a new cabinet portfolio to deal with Aboriginal affairs. *Time* magazine on 15 February 1997 described the Canadian lands claim process as 'one of the boldest experiments in social justice in Canada's history'.[29]

Two fundamental aspects of the Canada problem need addressing. The first is overcoming poverty and its effects that envelop many Aboriginal communities, both rural and urban. Despite the political developments, many Aboriginal people still live in very difficult circumstances. That they remain so is the legacy of colonialism that needs urgent addressing.

Meeting this challenge requires state assistance in a variety of ways, resource sharing, the development of an ethos of generosity toward Aboriginal peoples that is not always evident and present, and a willingness to share. We have seen the development of an economic infrastructure of businesses and business support that is an important aspect of the addressing this problem. We have also seen a reawakening of the entrepreneurial spirit among many Aboriginal peoples, but the challenge is too great to leave it to the Aboriginal private sector. Overcoming poverty, increasing education levels, improving housing, and increasing employment levels will benefit Canada as well.

The second set of challenges is finding ways of changing the governing structures and institutions of Canada to accommodate Aboriginal governance—to tackle founding error head on.

At first glance, this would seem to be a difficult and immense task. And it is. Where to start? We start first by recognizing that Aboriginal peoples have ideas about Canada, about how it ought to be governed, and about their place within the governance structure. We also start by recognizing that Aboriginal peoples have ideas about their own governments—the principles and ideas that ought to inform them. In many cases, these ideas are based in traditional political thought.

The Guswenteh, or two row-wampum, has been put forward as one of the ways that we can do this. The Guswenteh symbolizes two nations, separate and distinct, engaged in a relationship of mutual friendship and non-interference. The wampum, which represents these ideas, depicts two solid blue or purple parallel lines separated by a row of white space. The public discourse focuses on the ideas of separateness, distinctiveness, and non-interference. What is missing from the discourse is the idea of dialogue and learning. The spaces between the rows are not empty spaces. They are and can be places of conversation, dialogue, debate, discussion, and sharing. They are places where one can learn from the other. This is the place where we can use our 'good minds'.

The dialogue in this space is not about cultural diversity, ethnocultural accommodation, or multiculturalism and how to support it. The dialogue in the space is how to recognize and embody Aboriginal governance within Canada in a meaningful and significant way.

In October 1983, the House of Commons Special Committee on Indian Self-Government reported to the House that 'contrary to the view held by non-Indians that political structures were unknown to Indian people prior to contact with Europeans, most First Nations have complex forms of government that go far back into history and have evolved over time.' The committee then goes on to recommend 'that the federal government establish a new relationship with Indian First Nations and that an essential element of this new relationship be recognition of Indian self-government'. The committee's report was accepted by the House in a rare all-party agreement.

This event represented, in our view, the end of the philosophical debate about whether Indian people had a right to govern themselves: we had convinced Canadians that we have this right. The debate now moved on to details of implementation. The implementation of this right is proving to be challenging for both Aboriginal and newcomers alike. Strangely enough, it is proceeding somewhat along the lines suggested by the special committee.

The debate about details has now been fully engaged and currently rages passionately within our communities. The first part of the debate lasted from 1867 until 1985: 118 years. The second part of the debate may be with us forever. We should not be afraid of that. After all, European societies have been debating similar issues for at least the last few hundred years. And so we now join in a long tradition of debate about the origins, nature, structuring, uses, and limits of political authority.

It is important that we turn our attention to examining the process of government development within Aboriginal communities and bring to bear the accumulated insight and understanding of both our own traditions and those of the rest of the world. Aboriginal people bring their own political thought to the table and want to see it reflected in the governance of Canada. They want recognition that the dialogue about Canada is no longer just between the English and the French.

A major challenge is fostering the development of positive public attitudes toward Aboriginal peoples and their governments. The Royal Commission on Aboriginal Peoples recommended the establishment of a significant public education effort aimed at educating Canadian citizens about Aboriginal aspirations, cultures, communities, and ways of living. An important part of this education would be creating an understanding of the colonial context, including the racism that created the current situation as well as ways of eliminating it. This is an area that is all too often neglected. Canadians do not like to think of themselves as having a colonial past that extends into the present. The current debate about Aboriginal governance is taking place within a context in which many Canadians have a hard time coming to terms with a continued Aboriginal presence, let alone a modern, educated Aboriginal presence that challenges non-Aboriginals, asserts itself, insists on its own place at the table, and possesses the legal clout to achieve it. An Angus Reid poll commissioned by Indian and Northern Affairs in 2000 indicated that only 25 per cent of Canadians believed Aboriginal peoples have a historic right to self-government.[30] But only 16 per cent believed that Aboriginal people have 'no claim to any more land in Canada', while a similar percentage believed that Indian land claims were 'legitimate and should be fully compensated in land, money or both'. At the same time, support for the honouring of treaties increased from 75 per cent in 2006 to 80 per cent in 2008.[31]

In solving the Canada problem, Aboriginal leaders are challenging the foundations of the nation-state but are doing it in a way that is based on indigenous political philosophies that argue for collaboration and cooperation, that seek accommodation and coexistence and acceptance of diversity.

Aboriginal peoples are transforming Canada as they work to address the Canada problem. The constitutional recognition of Aboriginal peoples and the recognition of an inherent right to self-government, even though they remain contentious in some places, have been transformative, both for Aboriginal peoples and the Canadian nation. Slowly but surely, Canada is transforming itself into a post-colonial state:[32] a state that recognizes its foundations in the political thought of its indigenous inhabitants and that enables its original inhabitants to live with dignity and respect as indigenous peoples.

Discussion Questions

1. Do you think that the Canada problem has changed over time? If so, what important elements have changed, and what are its current elements?
2. What do you see as elements of the solution to the Canada problem?
3. From the perspective of Canada, what are the contemporary aspects of the Indian problem?
4. If you were the prime minister of Canada, how would you address the Indian problem?
5. If you were an Aboriginal leader, how would you address the Canada problem? How might your response to this question differ if you were a leader of First Nation, Métis, or Inuit people?

Further Readings

Belanger, Yale D., ed. 2008. *Aboriginal Self-Government in Canada: Current Trends and Issues*. 3rd edn. Saskatoon: Purich Publishing.

Cairns, Alan. 2000. *Citizens Plus: Aboriginal Peoples and the Canadian State*. Vancouver: University of British Columbia Press.

Mercredi, Ovide, and Mary Ellen Turpel. 1994. *In the Rapids: Navigating the Future of First Nations*. Toronto: Penguin Books.

Saul, John Ralston. 2008. *A Fair Country: Telling Truths about Canada*. Toronto: Viking Canada.

Notes

1. A literature on Aboriginal citizenship and its possible meanings within a nation-state has emerged over the past two decades. For example: R. Maaka and A. Fleras, *The Politics of Indigeneity: Challenging the State in Canada and Aotearoa New Zealand* (Dunedin: University of Otago Press, 2005) and Gerald Kernerman, *Multicultural Nationalism Civilizing Difference, Constituting Community* (University of British Columbia Press, 2005).

2. Statistics Canada. 'Aboriginal Peoples in Canada in 2006: Inuit, Métis and First Nations, 2006 Census'. On-line catalogue no. 97-558-X2006001.

3. See Royal Commission on Donald Marshall, Jr., *Prosecution* (Nova Scotia: Queen's Printer, December 1989); Public Inquiry into the Administration of Justice and Aboriginal People, *Report of the Aboriginal Justice Inquiry of Manitoba* (Winnipeg: Queen's Printer, 1991); *Report of the Task Force on the Criminal Justice System and its Impact on the Indian and Metis People of Alberta* (Alberta: 1991); Commission of Inquiry into Matters Relating to the Death of Neil Stonechild (Saskatchewan: Queen's Printer, 24 September 2004).

4. *Report of the Ontario Task Force on Aboriginal Peoples in the Urban Centres* (1982, 2008); 'Debwewin: Three City Anti-Racism Initiative' www.debwewin.ca (2005).

5. For a discussion of the historic origins of Canada's Indian policy, see John Tobias, 'Protection, civilization, assimilation: An outline history of Canada's Indian policy', in Ian Getty and Antoine Lussier, eds, *As Long as the Sun Shines and Water Flows: A Reader in Canadian Native Studies* (Vancouver: University of British Columbia Press, 1983); and John Milloy, *A Historical Overview of Indian–Government Relations, 1755–1940* (Ottawa: Indian and Northern Affairs Canada, 1992).

6. Canada, *The Report of the Joint Parliamentary-Senate Committee Hearings on Indian Affairs in Canada*, p. 605 (Ottawa: Queen's Printer, 1961).

7. H.B. Hawthorn and M.-A. Tremblay, *A Survey of the Indians of Contemporary Canada: A Report on Economic, Political, and Educational Needs*. Ottawa: Queen's Printer, 1966 [vol. 1], 1967 [vol. 2]).

8. Ibid.

9. Ibid.

10. Ibid.

11. Ibid.

12. Ibid.

13. A government white paper is a policy proposal released to invite comment and stimulate discussion. In this case, it did just that. In addition, the government proposal achieved iconic status within Aboriginal communities by proposing that for all intents and purposes, Indians become white.

14. Canada, 'Statement of the Government of Canada on Indian Policy' (1969). www.fcpp.org/publications/worth_a_look/spr/native.html.

15. See, for instance, the Supreme Court's determination that the treaties must be

interpreted in a liberal way so as not to harm or denigrate the Aboriginal interpretation of events. *R. v. Sparrow* (1990) 1 S.C.R. 1075.

16 An excellent examination of the importance of the *Calder* decision is contained in Hamar Foster, *Let Right Be Done: Aboriginal Title, the Calder Case, and the Future of Indigenous Rights* (Vancouver: University of British Columbia Press, 2008).

17. Mark S. Dockstator, *Toward an Understanding of Aboriginal Self-Government: A Proposed Theoretical Model and Illustrative Factual Analysis* (York University, PhD dissertation, 1993).

18. Council for Yukon Indians, *Together Today for Our Children Tomorrow: A Statement of Grievances and an Approach to Settlement by the Yukon Indian People*, p. 18 (Whitehorse: 1973).

19. Ibid.

20. For a discussion on the concepts of universal versus differentiated citizenship, see R. Maaka and A. Fleras, *The Politics of Indigeneity: Challenging the State in Canada and Aotearoa New Zealand* (Dunedin: University of Otago Press, 2005).

21. The word 'includes' led to much speculation by Aboriginal leaders that perhaps there were other, yet undiscovered Aboriginal peoples.

22. The provinces have an interest in the discussion as it involves land, natural resources, and possible amendments to the Constitution, all issues that are within their purview. Over the next two decades, provinces became increasingly involved in Aboriginal affairs, in many cases establishing ministries and departments to deal with Aboriginal peoples within their borders. Aboriginal leaders were initially reluctant to include provinces, since they saw their relationship as one with the Crown, refusing to accept the fanciful notion of the division of the Crown.

23. Yale D. Belanger and David R. Newhouse. 'Emerging from the shadows: The pursuit of Aboriginal self-government to promote Aboriginal well-being'. *Canadian Journal of Native Studies* 24 (2004) 1: 129–222.

24. Saul Alinksy, in *Rules for Radicals* (Toronto: Vintage Books, Random House of Canada, 1971), argues that it is the 'have a little, want more' group who lead societal change.

25. *Aboriginal Institutes of Higher Learning: A Struggle for the Education of Aboriginal Students, Control of Indigenous Knowledge and Recognition of Aboriginal Institutions* (Toronto: Aboriginal Institutes' Consortium and Canada Race Relations Foundation, 2005).

26. *Report of the Ontario Task Force on Aboriginal Peoples in the Urban Centres* (1982, 2008); 'Atlas of Urban Aboriginal People', on-line resource by Evelyn Peters, Department of Geography, University of Saskatchewan. http://gismap.usask.ca/website/Web_atlas/AOUAP.

27. For a good history of this effort, see Peter McFarlane, *Brotherhood to Nationhood: George Manuel and the Making of the Modern Indian Movement* (Toronto: Between the Lines, 1993).

28. Katherine Graham, Carolyn Dittburner, and Frances Abele, 'Soliloquy and dialogue: The evolution of public policy discourse on Aboriginal issues since the Hawthorn Report', in *For Seven Generations: An Information Legacy of the Royal Commission on Aboriginal Peoples* (Ottawa: Canada Publications Group, 1996); and Katherine Graham, Carolyn Dittburner, and Frances Abele, 'Summaries of reports by federal

bodies and Aboriginal organizations', in *For Seven Generations: An Information Legacy of the Royal Commission on Aboriginal Peoples* (Ottawa: Canada Publications Group, 1996).

29. Andrew Purvis, 'Whose home and Native land?' *Time* (Canadian edn) 15 February 1997, 18.

30. Quoted in Yale D. Belanger, *Aboriginal Self-Government in Canada: Current Trends and Issues*, 3rd edn, p. 403. (Saskatoon: Purich Publishing, 2008).

31. Ibid.

32. For the emerging discussion on post-colonial states, see for example Taiaiake Alfred, *Wasase: Indigenous Pathways of Action and Freedom* (Peterborough, ON: Broadview Press, 2005); John Borrows, *Recovering Canada: The Resurgence of Indigenous Law* (Toronto: University of Toronto Press, 2002); Gerald Kernerman, *Multicultural Nationalism Civilizing Difference, Constituting Community* (University of British Columbia Press, 2005); James Tully, *Strange Multiplicity: Constitutionalism in an Age of Diversity* (Cambridge: Cambridge University Press, 1995); and Dale Turner, *This Is Not a Peace Pipe: Towards a Critical Indigenous Philosophy* (Toronto: University of Toronto Press, 2006).

References

Belanger, Yale D. 2006. 'Seeking a seat at the table: A brief history of Indian political organizing in Canada, 1870–1951'. (Trent University, PhD dissertation).

Calder v. The Attorney General of British Columbia (1973) 34 D.L.R. (3d) 145.

Canada. 1961. *The Report of the Joint Parliamentary–Senate Committee Hearings on Indian Affairs in Canada*. Ottawa: Queen's Printer.

———. 1995. *Federal Policy Guide Aboriginal Self Government: The Government of Canada's Approach to Implementation of the Inherent Right and the Negotiation of Aboriginal Self Government*. Ottawa: Queen's Printer.

Delgamuukw v. British Columbia (1997) 3 S.C.R. 1010.

Dyck, Noel. 1991. *What Is the Indian Problem? Tutelage and Resistance in Canadian Indian Administration*. St. John's, NL: Institute of Social and Economic Research.

Federation of Saskatchewan Indians. 1977. *Indian Government*. Saskatoon: Federation of Saskatchewan Indians.

———. 1979. *Indian Treaty Rights: The Spirit and Intent of Treaty*. Saskatoon: Federation of Saskatchewan Indians.

First Nations Leadership Council. 2006. *Progress Report* vol. 1, issue 1 (April). Vancouver: First Nations Leadership Council.

Indian Chiefs of Alberta. 1970. *Citizens Plus*. Edmonton: Indian–Eskimo Association of Canada.

Manitoba Indian Brotherhood. 1971. *Wahbung: Our Tomorrows*. Winnipeg: Manitoba Indian Brotherhood. www.manitobachiefs.com/amc/history/Wahbung.pdf.

Mercredi, Ovide, and Mary Ellen Turpel. 1994. *In the Rapids: Navigating the Future of First Nations*. Toronto: Penguin Books.

Penner, Keith. 1983. *Special Committee on Indian Self-Government (Task Force)*. Ottawa: Queen's Printer.

R. v. Marshall (1999) 3 S.C.R. 533.

R. v. Sparrow (1990) 1 S.C.R. 1075.

Saul, John Ralston. 1998. *Reflections of a Siamese Twin: Canada at the Beginning of the Twenty-First Century*. Toronto: Penguin Group Canada.

———. 2008. *A Fair Country: Telling Truths about Canada*. Toronto: Viking Canada.

Williams, Robert A. 1997. *Linking Arms Together: American Indian Treaty Visions of Law and Peace, 1600–1800*. New York: Oxford University Press.

15 Rekindling the Fire: Indigenous Knowledge and New Technologies

Simon Brascoupé

A cross the Americas, indigenous peoples are 'rekindling the fire' of revitalization through the innovative use of indigenous knowledge and new technologies to achieve sustainable and healthy communities. Fire may have been the first technology, a gift of the creator. It enabled our ancestors to be warm, manage large territories, and connect spiritually. Many Aboriginal communities are on journeys searching for the fire of their ancestors that will reawaken their values, ceremonies, and teachings. Aboriginal peoples are on a journey back to the fire.

Sometimes, when there is so much change all around us, we do not notice the innovations bringing indigenous knowledge and technology together to solve problems. In the 1970s, when I first started work on my PhD in Native Studies, my supervisor Oren Lyons asked, 'What role does spirituality play in economic development?' This put me on a long journey to answer the question, which this chapter partially addresses. In 1991, in a preparatory meeting leading up to the 1992 Earth Summit, I posed the same question to a young man from a First Nation in the Northwest Territories. He said they had asked their elders the same question. The elders deliberated on the question for two weeks before they came back with their answer. They said that economic development is when the birds they harvest for country food return cyclically each year. Therefore, for Aboriginal peoples, economic development is the sustainable use of renewable resources. We will examine here how Aboriginal communities are developing models of sustainable development that exemplify their reigniting of that sacred fire.

Only in the past century has the locus of Aboriginal peoples' economic activity shifted from the land to the service sector. This transformation has occurred largely over the past 50 years. The end result is that Aboriginal peoples across Canada have been pushed to the margins economically, culturally, socially, and spiritually. Will this pattern continue in the future? Will Aboriginal people manage to transform their economies? Since the 1970s, Aboriginal peoples' economic, political, cultural, and spiritual influence has grown nationally and internationally. This new, although limited, autonomy provides Aboriginal peoples with an opportunity to build a new economic, cultural, and socially sustainable future. This chapter argues that through education, training, health and healing, community planning, and indigenous knowledge, Aboriginal peoples can build upon a sustainable economic, environmental, and cultural strategy that consists of seven elements:

1. education based on science, indigenous knowledge, technology, and language;
2. training directed toward the environment, leading-edge technologies, and resource management;
3. development of indigenous knowledge institutions controlled by Aboriginal peoples;
4. policy and development support for Aboriginal environmental employment strategies;
5. sharing stories, knowledge, and experience of innovative initiatives built on collaborative use of technologies and indigenous knowledge;
6. development of partnerships between Aboriginal indigenous knowledge institutions, governments, universities, colleges, and the private sector; and
7. expansion of transition/bridging, access, and internship programs supported by federal, provincial, and territorial governments, the private sector, and Aboriginal governments to recruit and retain Aboriginal people in the environmental field, including development, business, resources management, research, and science.

For the next generation of Aboriginal peoples, the coming changes will be as dramatic as the transition from the fur trade to the industrial area, although this time there appear to be some favourable conditions for Aboriginal peoples. First, they have growing political autonomy (self-government and land claims) to negotiate greater control over their lives and resources. Second, a massive restructuring of the world economy is underway, as well as greater awareness of the world environmental crisis, with a place for indigenous knowledge. Ancient prophesies say this is a time when the world will turn to indigenous peoples for help. Third, food security is an emerging issue. With a focus on locally grown food, there is a place for traditional foods and practices. Fourth, there is an urgent need to educate and train young Aboriginal leaders in both traditional and Western knowledge.

The challenge for Aboriginal peoples is to regain control of their economy and traditional territories through strategies that include sustainable resource harvesting and restoration of the environment built on indigenous knowledge and leading-edge technologies. One emerging sector is traditional food, building on the interest in organic, healthy foods among Aboriginal communities and consumers. Other sectors of the New Traditional Economy that could revitalize Aboriginal communities are forestry, tourism, fishing, and resource and land management.

There are several barriers to realizing the New Indigenized Economy. Misunderstanding and stereotypes about indigenous knowledge are rife among the public, governments, and academia. One such stereotype is that indigenous cultures are backward, savage, and uncivilized. Think of newspaper stories in Canada about someone finding a 'stone age culture in the jungles of Amazonia'. Another shocking example is the many stereotypes and misconceptions in a book written recently by two political scientists. The authors made dozens of pronouncements on the basis of old stereotypes drawn from fields in which they had no expertise, such as anthropology and sociology. Yet surprisingly, the book received serious consideration because it conformed to present-day stereotypes to the effect that Aboriginal peoples are primitive and need to be civilized. In contrast, other scientists have found that indigenous peoples possess sophisticated knowledge systems and cultures that can benefit the world. For example, it was Haudenosaunee (Iroquois) leaders who first introduced the idea of making decisions for the seven generations to come and that Mother Earth is alive. These ideas took hold and are now commonplace in the imagination of industrialized society. Some of the major barriers to indigenous peoples moving forward include:

1. lack of understanding of the indigenous knowledge of Aboriginal peoples, their culture and way of life;
2. lack of awareness of how to blend indigenous environmental knowledge with Western science;
3. lack of awareness of models of successful sustainable indigenous economies and projects.

Moving forward will require participatory research, scholarship, and education directed at improving understanding of how indigenous peoples historically adapted to environmental change, validating indigenous knowledge methodologies, and studying sustainable indigenous economies and projects. The most successful innovative approaches are those that are community-controlled, with public and private partnerships. There is a growing body of evidence that this approach is effective in restoring the environment as well as indigenous cultures and way of life, resulting in sustainable communities.

Learning from Aboriginal Peoples

This section argues that the world will have to change its basic value system to save the planet. We now know that global warming will affect lives around the world, forcing people to adapt to change and perhaps listening to indigenous peoples, because they have knowledge of how their ancestors adapted to change in their territory over the millennia. I remember speaking with a Tuscarora chief who was recalling a time when winter lasted for several years. We talked about how they survived through this challenging time. This is not to say that industrialized societies should become indigenous peoples. But they need to learn from indigenous peoples about respecting and living harmoniously with Mother Earth. We have to find a way to talk about respect for Mother Earth that finds its way into government policy, industrial strategies, religious practice, and people's ways of life. This process of reflection could become a dialogue between industrialized society and indigenous peoples based on respect for the environment.

Without a fundamental change in value systems, culture, and social relations, the survival of human beings is threatened. Evidence abounds, such as global warming, more violent storms, flooding, and species loss. At the end of the last century, Vaclav Havel identified the following threats: overpopulation, AIDS, depletion of biodiversity, nuclear terrorism, television culture, racism, and regional wars. He recently argued that:

> If humanity is to survive and avoid various potential catastrophes, then the global political order must be accompanied by mutual respect of different civilizations, cultures, nationalities and continents and their genuine efforts to look for and find values or basic ethical imperatives that are common to everyone and use them as the basis, on which stand and will stand their shared co-existence in a globally connected world. In practical politics that means devising a common minimum that is respected by all cultures and religions and use it as the basis for co-existence in the 21st century (Havel 2007).

Unfortunately, industrialized societies and thinkers have long lost their connection with their own ancestors who had the original sustainable-living values. All cultures have had values that connected people with the environment, resulting in lifestyles that relied on the continuous harvesting of plenty from Mother Earth rather than the destruction of Mother Earth, which results in scarcity. Industrialized societies can learn about sustainability from indigenous societies, as envisaged by Gro Harlem Bruntland, but they can also take a close look within themselves to find farmers, fishers, and harvesters with ancient values and connections with the natural world. Again, we have to overcome the intellectual barrier and recognize that farmers, fishers, and harvesters have something important to say about sustainability. Indigenous peoples and a growing number of consumers insist on their right to healthy food, a healthy environment, and a lifestyle that does not threaten their culture, language, or traditions.

Parents and grandparents may find it disquieting that we live in a world that is not safe for the seven generations to come. Oren Lyons talks about making responsible decisions and actions as if we were walking on the faces of children seven generations into the future. So today, we measure our energy footprint, eat locally and organically, and talk about a green world, but will this be enough? Part of the answer lies in making fewer trips in our car, using less energy, and in general consuming less: one day there will be a tipping point at which we find our love for Mother Earth is greater than our love for that next purchase.

The Seventh Generation

The Seventh Generation teaching has had a significant impact in the international dialogue on the environment. Just a few decades ago, economists argued that society was ethically responsible for a five-year planning period; no one talks this way today. The dialogue is about Mother Earth, Gaia, Earth Day, and the Seventh Generation. We must think about future generations, the seven generations to come. Society is morally, ethically, and philosophically responsible not only for our future generations but for Mother Earth and all life that shares the Earth. The Brundtland Report mimics the Seventh Generation principle: 'Sustainable development is development that meets the needs of the present without compromising the ability of future generations to meet their own needs' (Brundtland Report 1987).

Indigenous culture is endowed with a rich diversity of values, teachings, and ceremonies that reach back thousands of years to the time when humans first became hunters, fishers, gatherers, and farmers. This way of life, which survived over the millennia, reminds us of our original responsibilities to creation and to Mother Earth. When I was a young boy, I had a garden at our home on Tuscarora Indian Nation. In midsummer of 1958, it was dry and hot; I watered my growing small garden every day from my Uncle Percy's well. I asked my Grandmother Sarah if she knew how to make it rain. She said to go and sing in my garden; it did not matter what song I sang. I understand now she was teaching me about the relationship we as humans have with the natural world. When I sang to my plants, I felt a connection to the hot sun, the breeze that sang through the corn, the insects that pollinated the plants, and the smell of the earth. I remember this as if it was yesterday. I also remember it raining and me carrying water into August.

Years later I learned from a friend that Seneca women sing a song to Mother Earth apologizing for disturbing her skin, giving thanks, explaining that they need to cultivate in order to survive. And so it is for indigenous peoples all around the world, giving thanks by offering sacred plants to creation as part of their original sustainable way of life. They give thanks to water, fish, Mother Earth, medicines, insects, plants, four-legged creatures, the sky, and birds; they do not take what they do not use, and they use everything. So when my father hunted, he gave thanks to the creator with tobacco and a prayer for the deer that gave its life for us to survive.

Brundtland saw some hope for industrial society in looking to indigenous people, but what was that hope? First, indigenous people have a lifestyle that has proved sustainable over thousands of year. Industrialization is only a couple of hundred years old and is proving to be unsustainable. Second, industrial society has created an image of indigenous peoples as uncivilized and savage and their way of life as short and brutal. The opposite is true: indigenous peoples of the Americas lived healthy lives free of Western diseases such influenza and smallpox. Third and most difficult, we live in a 'use it or lose it world' when it comes to land and resources; indigenous peoples' lands are being overrun for 'development'. By the end of this century, half the indigenous cultures of the world will no longer exist—this is a real threat to sustainability. Brundtland said that 'Indigenous Peoples teach us about the values that have permitted human kind to live on this planet for thousands of years without desecrating it' (Brundtland 1999). 'They teach us about holistic approaches to health that seek to strengthen the social networks of individuals and communities, while connecting them to the environment in which they live. And they teach us about the importance of a spiritual dimension to the healing process.' Some world leaders have the insight and understanding to know that the world has much to learn from indigenous peoples.

Nature and indigenous peoples' ways may provide direction and lessons for everything from food production, transportation, and manufacturing to human rights. 'Nature—whose designs are inherently efficient, effective, and beautiful—offers us models of abundant, healthy production,' write Bill McDonough and Michael Braungart (2002), illustrating the point with a cherry tree: 'Its fruit becomes food for animals and insects; its bounty of lovely leaves degrades naturally into the earth. Nothing is wasted; nothing is toxic. In terms of nature, growth is in fact good. So why can't the same be said about the growth of human settlement?' Promising lessons may come from the architects who, like indigenous peoples, try to mimic nature. They design structures founded on the principles of the natural world—for example, buildings constructed like trees, with shade to keep things cool and roots that keep the tree cool in the summer and warm in the winter. Architects are collaborating with chemists, biologists, ecologists, and psychologists to learn Mother Earth's secrets and apply them to design (McDonough and Braungart 2002). A leading Aboriginal architect, Douglas Cardinal, has pioneered these ideas in his 'organic' designs in buildings such as the Canadian Museum of Civilization.

Case Study: Unama'ki Institute

The vision of Aboriginal management of natural resources utilizing indigenous knowledge, science, and technology can be found in the Mi'kmaq communities located in the Bras d'Or Lakes, Cape Breton Island, Nova Scotia. Under the leadership of their Elders, they developed new institutions and partnerships to address dwindling fishing stocks, a declining environment, and cultural loss.

Since 1999, Unama'ki Institute of Natural Resources (UINR) has been the voice of Cape Breton's five Mi'kmaq communities on natural resources and environmental sustainability. UINR works closely with other levels of government and other First Nations to meet its three objectives:

1. to provide resources for Mi'kmaq equal participation in natural resource management in Unama'ki and its traditional territory;
2. to strengthen Mi'kmaq research and natural resource management while maintaining their traditions and world views;
3. to partner with other groups sharing the same desire to protect and preserve their resources for future generations.

The institute is unique in that it has its own wet and dry labs on-site run by six Mi'kmaq scientists. Through its partnership with the Aboriginal Science Program at Cape Breton University, they train the next generation of Aboriginal scientists based on science and indigenous knowledge. UINR calls this approach 'Two-Eyed Seeing', which brings together the best of Western science and traditional knowledge. Its research program is guided by the Mi'kmaq community's Elders. Its program addresses Mi'kmaq concerns such as oyster, lobster, eel, gaspereau, and other food fishing species. Its research interests include species at risk and invasive species resulting from pollution and global warming. The Mi'kmaq communities depend on clean drinking water and marine water quality and are responsible for monitoring drinking water weekly in four communities.

Unama'ki Institute of Natural Resources has partnered with provincial, federal, and municipal governments to address environmental and water concerns. It plays a lead role in organizations such as Pitu'paq and the Bras d'Or Lakes Collaborative Environmental Planning Initiative to improve the environment in the region. UINR has partnerships with Parks Canada, Fisheries and Oceans Canada, Cape Breton University, Georgia Pacific, New Page, the province of Nova Scotia, Cape Breton municipalities, and a host of other government departments and organizations to ensure that Mi'kmaq perspective and knowledge are an integral part of many projects. UINR's partnerships with other organizations are critical to achieving success in restoring the natural environment, assuring cultural continuity, and maintaining a way of life.

Case Study: Traditional American Indian Farmers Association

Since the 1950s, Aboriginal peoples' health has deteriorated as a result of adopting poor Western diets and a sedentary lifestyle. Aboriginal farmers, chefs, academics, and leaders are promoting a return to traditional foods as a way of improving health and restoring traditions. Recently, the slow food and food security movements have focused attention on indigenous peoples as a means of providing healthy foods to a population that suffers from a shortage of food and from malnutrition. The Traditional American Indian Farmers Association is active in education and the return to traditional foods, cooking, and diet.

In 1991, Native Seed/SEARCH of Tucson, Arizona, surveyed Native American farmers in Arizona and New Mexico. The survey revealed that Native American farmers faced a startling lack of interest on the part of their own communities. At that time, the farmers felt that few young people saw farming as a viable profession. But with growing awareness of the dietary causes of diabetes in recent years, interest has grown in the health benefits of traditional foods.

The Native American Farmers Association (TNAFA) was formed in 1992 in response to the needs of 'traditional' family-scale farmers. TNAFA has seen an increased interest in traditional agriculture from all sectors of Native communities, especially youth. Its mission is to revitalize traditional agriculture for spiritual and human need by creating awareness and support for Native environmental issues. Through community research programs, TNAFA has found that a sound agriculture base is needed to build healthy communities, including both physical and spiritual health. Hence, TNAFA has created projects that address social, economic, and health problems in its members' communities.

It has witnessed major advances in the way local communities think and care for the Earth and the food they eat. Each growing season, TNAFA helps existing farmers and interests new young farmers in the tradition of agriculture, land care, and healthy lifestyles. Even though the US southwest has experienced 10 years of drought, there has been a growing demand for TNAFA services, particularly traditional foods and organic farming.

TNAFA Objectives

1. revitalize the decline in traditional, family-scale farming among the community by developing educational programs that demonstrate sustainable agriculture;
2. demonstrate and train communities and youth in a holistic approach to sustainable agriculture based upon community ethics and traditions;
3. help the community access heirloom/traditional seeds;
4. educate the community on traditional seed saving and the GE, GMO threat to our traditional seed heritage;
5. identify local resources for agriculture, compost materials, local plants, local herbs, water supplies, local farmers, local markets, etc.;
6. revive and restore a sustainable economic base through organic agriculture for our youth;
7. increase use and consumption of 'traditional' foods for higher nutritional value.

TNAFA Programs

- youth in agriculture (developing youth garden projects);
- traditional agricultural/permaculture design course (12-day course on sustainable community design in July);
- corn-processing for home use (traditional foods/nutrition);
- community seed 'library' workshops (methods of storing and growing seed);
- seed distribution (free seed and information about seed);
- home gardening workshops (garden design, composting, organic methods, irrigation, drip irrigation, etc.);
- other workshops (marketing traditional crops, packaging, value-added crops, growing herbs);
- indigenous outreach program designed to assist and exchange

agricultural and cultural knowledge with other indigenous peoples outside the southwestern United States.

Pre-contact agriculture was the foundation of traditional community health,
culture, and economy. Through socio-economic changes over the past 60 years,
Native agriculture has seen a rapid decline. Most government agricultural programs focus on agri-business-type models, often overlooking farmers already in
the community and not developing the interest of our youth. In the US, for example, Native American farmers have been undercounted and have not received
appropriate federal support to develop. TNAFA focuses on family-oriented farming as the best approach to building a sound sustainable future for agriculture.
The promotion of traditional agriculture ensures economic, social, and health
stability in our communities. The decline in traditional farming mirrors the
decline in Native American social, cultural, and physical health. Health issues
such as diabetes and heart ailments are on the rise and have become a major
focus of concern. TNAFA's goal is to reverse this trend by developing educational
programs that will demonstrate sustainable agriculture. Educating farmers and
youth in traditional, community-scale organic farming will help to ensure a
future for agriculture and healthy communities.

Nationally, TNAFA sees communities being ruined by corporate farming,
which also destroys environmental integrity. Internationally, TNAFA has worked
with Mayan communities in Belize through training and partnerships. Their
vision is to demonstrate the value of local, family-scale farming for people, the
economy, and the environment. In traditional culture, each person plays an important role in the health of their community, and this strengthens the community. When each person fulfills their responsibility, harmony exists in the
community. TNAFA trains community members and youth to become teachers,
guides, and examples within their own families and communities. By working
with key individuals in communities, TNAFA can help to restore and maintain
an unbroken tradition of agriculture. TNAFA is proud of its alumni who have
returned to their communities to become leaders and teachers of the benefits of
traditional farming.

Case Study: Waswanipi Cree Model Forest

Another issue is cultural dissonance. Indigenous knowledge has proved very
effective in managing natural resources sustainably, but Elders do not speak in
ways that planners and scientists can understand. The Waswanipi Cree model
forest is an innovative project that asks the question: can the Cree way of life

survive forestry operations by developing a forest management plan using indigenous knowledge and Western science? Cree traplines in northwest Quebec completely cover the same area of land as forestry operations. Historically, forestry operations destroyed the habitat, making trapping and a traditional way of life impossible. In many other parts of Canada, First Nations and Métis communities have been devastated by forestry. The model forest project is one step in breaking new ground toward a sustainable economy, culture, and way of life.

Begun in 1998, Waswanipi model forest management is based on a research model that integrates indigenous knowledge and Western science. The Cree's trapping way of life was threatened by clear-cutting and habitat destruction, but during the past couple of decades, industrial forestry has come under pressure to move to a new sustainable forestry model and to recognize the needs and rights of indigenous peoples. As a result, the Cree model forest developed an innovative forest management system called 'Ndoho Istchee'—one of the first practical models of integrating Aboriginal participation and knowledge in forestry planning.

The Cree model forest's research created new scientific understanding of wildlife habitat built on indigenous knowledge and a new effective model of consultation. Forestry engineer Martin Pelletier framed the problem:

> Most consultation used the downstream approach: First you have a plan, then you consult, and nothing would change in the end. The system was like a game of Battleship: Everyone was hiding their game. We wanted to build a land-use study that could be shared (with developers), would be understandable to planners and would recognize both sides' knowledge (Waswanipi Cree Model Forest 2009).

The Cree developed an approach that relies on three kinds of maps:

1. Family maps: maps of a family's trapline that include important areas such as portages, trails, camps, burial sites, animal habitats, lakes and rivers, even simply beautiful landscapes; the family shares only the information it chooses with companies and authorities.
2. Conservation value maps: created by the model forest team that translates family map data into the technical language of the forestry planners, to be incorporated into forestry plans.
3. State of the trapline maps: created for each family's hunting ground, which evaluate animal habitat using Cree knowledge, forest conditions

based on Cree knowledge, government and forestry data, and how trees will be harvested.

The model forest demonstrated that it is more productive to start with the Cree trappers' questions to successfully integrate Cree knowledge and Western science. One of the major challenges is to first build trust with indigenous peoples. In the case of Cree trappers, historically their indigenous knowledge was misused or ignored.

Another major problem is the capacity of Aboriginal peoples to exercise the rights they have won in courts because of the technical challenges of managing resources within a Western system, and this is particularly true in forestry. Aboriginal peoples understand sustainable development using indigenous knowledge but cannot translate it into the highly technical language and systems of contemporary forestry management. The lesson of Waswanipi is that through the innovative use of knowledge translation, Aboriginal peoples can exercise their rights and break down the cultural dissonance barrier.

Case Study: Health Sector

Remarkable achievements have occurred through cooperation and collaboration in health employment development. In 1996, the Royal Commission on Aboriginal Peoples (RCAP) recommended the development of a comprehensive human resources strategy and a federal, provincial, and territorial commitment to train 10,000 Aboriginal professionals over a 10-year period in health and social services. In 1996, there were approximately 5000 Aboriginal health care workers, and that numbers nearly tripled by 2006. In addition, more than 40,000 Aboriginal people work in the health care sector in other positions.

So how did this remarkable achievement come about? First, a clear objective and strategic direction was set by the Royal Commission on Aboriginal Peoples. 'Upstream' programs were established to promote careers in health care to Aboriginal youth at primary and secondary schools. Recently, organizations such as the National Aboriginal Achievement Foundation have promoted careers in health care and provided awards to Aboriginal students entering the field. Medical and nursing schools created access programs that have been successful in attracting and retaining Aboriginal students, similar to programs instituted earlier in law schools. Remember, it wasn't long ago that medical schools were saying that they could not attract qualified Aboriginal students, but this attitude has now changed. Deans of medical schools have made it a priority to attract and retain Aboriginal students and to develop a strategy to incorporate cultural competency into their curricula. Medical and nursing schools have partnered with Aboriginal physician and nursing organizations to develop strategies and achieve joint objectives.

A federal, provincial, and territorial committee was formed to oversee the growing problem of shortages in health care human resources. The committee made Aboriginal health care human resources a priority and focused on increasing the numbers and addressing the issues of Aboriginal health care workers. Provinces and territories have also developed strategies, some more successful than others, such as Saskatchewan's pioneering work in access programs, cross-cultural training, and improving the workplace for Aboriginal peoples. It is an excellent model of a strategy to increase the number of Aboriginal people employed in a particular labour market and is resulting in increased numbers of Aboriginal health care workers, not only in Aboriginal communities but in rural, remote, and urban areas as well. The challenge will be to continue increasing the number of Aboriginal health care professionals, provide cultural competency training in schools, and develop policy for the complementary delivery of traditional and Western medicine.

Aboriginal Employment Strategies

The environment is an important emerging field for Aboriginal employment. Employment in traditional territories could help stem the tide of migration of Aboriginal peoples to urban centres. In this regard, the BEAHR[1] project expects environmental employment to grow by 4.6 per cent per year, with 200,000 new jobs in the environment labour market over the next 15 years (BEAHR n.d.). It is anticipated that 600,000 Aboriginal youth will be entering the workforce during the period to 2026. The 2006 census indicated that there has been a 25 per cent increase in the number of Aboriginal persons with a university degree,[2] although the proportion still lags far behind that of the non-Aboriginal population (23 per cent). If Aboriginal communities could double the number of university graduates over the next decade, they could be near what Malcolm Gladwell (2002) calls a tipping point for positive change. Gladwell writes that communities in which more than 15 per cent are professionals create an environment where more youth complete high school. This is a tremendous challenge, which must be addressed for a healthy community, because education leads to employment, which leads to improved health outcomes. This section examines ways in which communities could increase employment in various sectors.

Paul Hawkens (1993) and others argue that managing and improving the environment means increased employment. The fear in the past and in some quarters today is that protecting the environment will result in a loss of jobs and slowing of the economy. We now know that environmental restoration is good for employment and the economy. The growing concern today is that the economy is not sustainable and is having catastrophic affects on the environment. Greed and exploitation are destroying the environment and threatening humankind. Today, big industrialized countries see the need to move from unsustainable exploitation of the Earth to a sustainable revolution. The advantage Aboriginal peoples have is their indigenous knowledge and values, combined with new technologies such as Geographic Information Systems (GIS), organic and perma-culture agriculture, sustainable resource planning, and co-management.

For Aboriginal peoples, the best opportunities are linked to the environment, regional economy, health, sustainable development, and local government. Of course, Aboriginal employment will be shaped by the economy and outside forces. In a strange twist caused by global warming, Canada has created a north-ern strategy promising more investments to ensure Canadian sovereignty. But the extent to which Aboriginal communities can benefit will be determined by their capacity to stay ahead of the curve and create sustainable development. There is growing evidence that Aboriginal communities can compete and contribute to the economy using their indigenous knowledge and culture. The case studies in this chapter demonstrate how Aboriginal communities are developing the tools and knowledge to control and manage their own resources and economies.

To be successful, Aboriginal communities must develop community-based strategies that are socially, culturally, economically, and politically sustainable. Plans must be built on a community vision based on their values, culture, and spirituality. Community development is one model that Aboriginal communities are familiar with and that works. When I was on the board of CANDO,[3] we learn-ed that communities that had strategic plans were successful and communities that did not were struggling. Through the good work of the Aboriginal Healing Foundation, we learned that struggling communities can revitalize and trans-form through healing initiatives rooted in their culture and spirituality. Finally, the marriage between indigenous knowledge and technologies can be a power-ful employment and economic tool.

There has been a major shift in the Aboriginal labour force away from the primary sector of the economy, such as forestry, fishing, trapping, and farming, over the past 40 years. In 1966, 80 per cent of First Nations people were em-ployed in the primary sector. By 1991, only 11 per cent on-reserve workers were employed in the primary sector. In 2006, 8 per cent of the Aboriginal labour force worked in resource-based industries. Aboriginal communities are moving away from the primary sector of the labour force just when successes are being achieved in traditional agriculture, medicine, hunting, and fishing. The traditional strategy is based on the fact that Mother Earth provides an endless flow of food, medicine, and goods to meet all our human needs if approached sustainably. Western economic strategy, on the other hand, is based on the production, distribution, and consumption of scarce resources, which become depleted as a result of overexploitation. While indigenous economics has proved sustainable over thousands of years, Western economics is proving unsustainable.

Table 15.1 2006 Census Aboriginal Labour Force Participation

Industry	Total	Per cent
Agriculture and other Resource-based industries	39,705	8
Construction	43,880	9
Manufacturing	39,770	8
Wholesale Trade	11,995	2
Retail Trade	51,465	10
Finance and Real Estate	14,970	3
Health Care and Social Services	58,160	12
Educational Services	32,955	7
Business Services	69,900	14
Other Services	134,480	27
Total Experienced Labour Force	497,280	100

Source: Statistics Canada, 2006 Census.[4]

Data in Table 15.1 indicate major areas of the labour force in which Aboriginals participate. We acknowledge that change does not happen overnight, and a shift back to the primary labour market and traditional economies will take time. Aboriginal communities need a whole new generation of environmental managers, workers, and entrepreneurs. To create employment and shift toward a sustainable economy, Aboriginal communities need to think about the following:

1. Become an active player in the regional economies, focusing on the restoration and sustainable use of natural resources. This strategy should be based on indigenous knowledge, sustainable practice and science, and use of technologies such as GIS. Examples are multi-use forestry strategies, which focus on forestry, trapping, non-timber forest products, cultural tourism, and so on.
2. Identify initiatives that build on indigenous knowledge and can strengthen culture, create employment, build partnerships, and be sustainable. The use of technology such as GIS facilitates knowledge transfer between indigenous and Western practitioners.

3. Develop education and training strategies that focus on the next generation of community leaders, managers, and administrators and on such fields as health, education, business, science, and mathematics. Because of the large number of Aboriginal students who have not completed high school, there is a need for a new generation of high school equivalency and access programs. In addition, indigenous knowledge should be taught in all training and education programs.

4. Develop community retail and cultural centres that provide local goods and services, such as grocery, pharmaceutical, and other retail outlets; health, social, child, and other services; and cultural and tourist centres. These market-based centres will help to reduce economic leakages and increase employment and wealth in Aboriginal communities.

5. Develop an economic development strategy that facilitates control over management of natural resources based on indigenous knowledge and sustainable technologies. The strategy should shift on the continuum from conventional to sustainable development.

6. Develop partnership(s) with post-secondary institutions to deliver education and training that incorporates indigenous knowledge at all levels and in all fields. These partnerships should develop capacity in Aboriginal communities in resource management, science and technology, business and entrepreneurship, based on lifelong learning, capacity-building, and skill development.

7. Develop local technical and manufacturing capacity in new and emerging environmental industries. Technologies such as Geographic Information Systems are powerful tools for managing, planning, and administering Aboriginal lands and resources.

8. Develop community-based participative planning mechanisms based on local culture and knowledge to ensure strategies reflect community needs, values, vision, and goals. These comprehensive strategies should include healing and wellness strategies focused on building healthy communities.

9. Develop a community's ability to gain access to capital for financing business and community projects.

10. Develop a long-term plan to facilitate development of community leadership in social, cultural, economic, and spiritual areas. Strategies could include youth development, exchanges, training, and mentorships, all focused on investing in future leadership.

We know that successful Aboriginal communities have developed comprehensive community development strategies. This includes a good economic development strategy that captures all available business and employment opportunities. However, there are two mistakes communities sometimes make. First, economic development without a strategic focus amounts to chasing one project after another without results, and second, betting on one large project or industry can also end badly. Yogi Berra once said, 'If you don't know where you are going, you might wind up someplace else.' The following briefly summarizes the broad employment opportunities available in most Aboriginal communities in the context of sustainability, self-determination, and the future.

Areas for potential employment growth in Aboriginal communities can be divided into six categories:

1. community services and administration;
2. natural resources;
3. cultural tourism;
4. environment and traditional economies;
5. emerging technologies;
6. business and entrepreneurial development.

Community Services and Administration

Community governance and services are a major source of full-time stable employment in Aboriginal communities. Communities should focus some resources on training and educate a well-qualified Aboriginal public service. The health labour market is one good example, where 90 per cent of on-reserve health services are provided by Aboriginal employees. For the remaining 10 per cent, more Aboriginal students are entering health professions as doctors, nurses, dieticians, therapists, and so on. In addition, the health field presents an opening for Elders and healers in the area of healing and wellness that is growing in response to the trauma of residential schools. Local government employs people in accounting, administration, project management, social work, child care, data processing, and many other areas. Currently, employment in this sector is significant in Aboriginal communities and could represent up to 50 per cent of local jobs (2006 Census, *Aboriginal Labour Force Participation*). Aboriginal communities need to partner with educational institutions to develop education and training plans to build capacity and leaders in this field. The training should be based on indigenous knowledge, technologies like GIS, and future employment opportunities.

Natural Resources

Forestry is arguably the most significant economic opportunity for Aboriginal people because many Aboriginal communities are located in northern forested areas. For others, fishing, tourism, traditional foods, and non-timber forest products (maple syrup, berries, teas, for example) offer tremendous opportunities. A forest is harvested once every few decades, but natural products can be harvested year after year. There are some good examples of sustainable forestry, even some with multiple uses, such as the Waswanipi Cree model forest. Markets are developing for timber products accredited as sustainable. A mixed-use strategy is important in maintaining a traditional economy such as trapping, hunting, fishing, and gathering. To achieve sustainable forestry, planning must incorporate indigenous knowledge and GIS mapping. Today, most Aboriginal communities are utilizing indigenous knowledge, but they must now develop the tools, practices, and technical knowledge to devise useful natural resource plans. Communities need to learn from others' successes by working with other Aboriginal communities that have instituted innovative approaches.

Cultural Tourism

Tourism continues to be a growth sector in the international economy, with a projected growth of 6.4 per cent per year, according to the World Tourism Organization (Ling 2010). Tourists are interested in Aboriginal culture and communities. Tourism strategies could be built on indigenous knowledge, skills, and culture in support of cultural revitalization. Ecotourism and cultural tourism attracts people who are seeking new experiences and have an interest in the natural environment. Employment in the tourism sector includes jobs in operations, visitor centres, museums, travel services, lodges, and restaurants and as artists, artisans, performers, and cultural interpreters. Most communities cannot afford to build tourism centres but could invest in multi-use facilities, such as cultural centres that house museums, shops, workshop space, and services that would serve as a destination for tourists visiting the community.

Environment and Traditional Economies

There are growing opportunities in the environmental industry for the Aboriginal workforce. Education and training strategies such as the BEAHR project could generate opportunities for high-paying and rewarding employment. BEAHR's goal is to increase Aboriginal environmental employment by 6000 positions over a 15-year period. Most Aboriginal communities need workers with expertise in water and natural resource management. Communities would benefit from youth with both scientific and traditional knowledge. This knowledge and the attendant skills could be leveraged in other areas, such as natural resource management and restoring traditional activities such as hunting, fishing, and gathering.

Emerging Technologies

Over the past decade, a number of new technologies have emerged with the potential for future employment opportunities in Aboriginal communities. For example, the use of satellites for telemedicine whereby patients in isolated northern First Nations can be cared for by a doctor in a major urban centre in the south holds great promise for improved health outcomes. Students could take high school courses with Aboriginal content via the Internet. The information highway is available in most Aboriginal communities, and it could be used to market traditional arts, foods, and teas around the world. The Internet has already had a major impact on Aboriginal communities' ability to communicate at a community, personal, and business level. It provides an opportunity for Aboriginal communities to promote local businesses and services. As the use and local availability of information technology increases, there will be a growing need for technologists, service and sales personnel, programmers, repair people, and administrators. The demand for knowledgeable workers will also grow as governments deliver more and more of their programs and services via the Internet.

Business and Entrepreneurial Development

The area with perhaps the greatest economic opportunity in Aboriginal communities is the business sector. An increase in the number of businesses could result in a multiplier effect, creating more jobs in the community and helping to prevent wealth from 'leaking' out of the community. In the non-Aboriginal community, businesses are started by entrepreneurs and managers who come from business families. But this is not a tradition in Aboriginal communities, where there are few entrepreneurs and a need for strategies to create home-grown solutions. Business development requires long-term attention. Some communities are focusing programs on youth who are interested in business, giving them opportunities to learn business management and gain experience and skills. Some communities have created opportunities for budding entrepreneurs by forming enterprise centres, economic development corporations, and Aboriginal–private sector partnerships. Because this approach is new for most communities, it will take political will and leadership to make things happen. Economic development needs to be part of a comprehensive community plan.

Conclusion

Aboriginal peoples once had sustainable economies; every person in the community had employment as a hunter, fisher, gatherer, healer, leader, and so on. These economies and communities survived over thousands of years, adapting to change and new technologies. The Americas were alive with trade networks that provided goods, seeds, and services over thousands of kilometres.

Aboriginal communities everywhere are revitalizing their culture, values, and ways—they are 'rekindling the fire'. This is a tremendous challenge, and one of the first questions communities ask is: where to start? A good place to start is community healing and wellness to recover from the trauma of colonization and residential schools. Two dramatic examples are Alkali Lake First Nation and Hollow Water First Nation, who revitalized their severely dysfunctional communities. Other communities have focused on issues such as education, health, economic development, or land claims to begin the process of building healthy communities. What has been learned is that healing from colonization must occur before or as part of community renewal.

Decolonization is a process of moving away from colonial institutions, thought, and attitudes toward healthy approaches based on traditional values, culture, and spirituality. The Harvard Project calls this getting the right cultural match, which can be realized through community-based development. Thus begins the work of decolonizing key functions in the community, including governance, institutions, culture, and leadership. In the healing and wellness experience, there are important clues on how to transform Aboriginal government and communities. But it is a long process. There are many examples of the healing process beginning in Aboriginal communities through cultural, child and youth, elders, education, and training programs. These are all starting points, when members of a community recognize that the source of their dysfunction is colonization and that they have the power, courage, and leadership to make changes.

Discussion Questions

1. Can Aboriginal values, culture, and spirituality be adapted to contemporary economic and resource development? Can indigenous knowledge and science be harmonized to create sustainable development plans? For example, how can values such as 'respect for nature' inform resource development decisions?
2. What is the linkage between environmental employment, new technologies, and sustainable development? How can these factors be integrated in sustainable resource development plans?
3. How can communities overcome the barriers to sustainable development? One barrier is the lack of understanding of how to integrate indigenous knowledge with Western knowledge.
4. How can industrialized societies learn from Aboriginal peoples about living sustainably?
5. How will Aboriginal communities develop sustainable economies based on indigenous knowledge and new technologies?

6. Where are the economic opportunities in new and emerging economies that can help Aboriginal peoples develop sustainable economies?

Further Readings

Battiste, Marie, ed. 2000. *Reclaiming Indigenous Voice and Vision*. Vancouver: University of British Columbia Press. This book by Mi'kmaq scholar Marie Battiste is about cultural restoration of oppressed indigenous peoples. The contributors, mostly indigenous, explain how colonization resulted in the oppression of indigenous peoples. By understanding this process, one can understand the impact historical trauma has had on the health, education, and employment of indigenous peoples.

Cajete, Gregory, ed. 1999. *A People's Ecology—Explorations in Sustainable Living: Health, Environment, Agriculture, Native Traditions*. Santa Fe, NM: Clear Light Publishers. A collection of essays from the perspective of indigenous peoples edited by Pueblo scholar Gregory Cajete. They write about indigenous ways of seeing health, ecology, and sustainable living. The writers clarify the indigenous concept of 'healthy environment, healthy culture, healthy people'. For example, Clayton Brascoupé describes his life as a farmer in northern New Mexico, and John Mohawk and Yvonne Dion-Buffalo report on a program dedicated to assisting Six Nations Iroquois farmers grow and market white corn.

———. 2000. *Native Science: Natural Laws of Interdependence*. Santa Fe, NM: Clear Light Publishers. Discusses indigenous knowledge and how it is acquired, transmitted, and retained. This is an excellent book for beginning to understand science from an indigenous perspective.

Cornell, Stephen, Joseph P. Kalt, et al. n.d. 'The Harvard Project on American Indian economic development'. Harvard University. www.hks.harvard.edu/hpaied/index.htm. The project began in 1984 and continues to this day, focusing on the main issues of indigenous economic development, which include sovereignty, institutions, culture, and leadership. A number of research papers and studies are available on-line.

Jorgensen, Miriam, ed. 2007. *Rebuilding Native Nations: Strategies for Governance and Development*. Tucson: University of Arizona Press. This is an excellent book for examining strategies to rebuild indigenous communities that have been affected by colonization. The book's themes include starting points, rebuilding foundations, reconceiving and decolonizing key functions, and making it happen.

Waswanipi Cree Model Forest. 2009. 'Waswanipi Cree model forest milestone report: 2008'. Canadian Forest Service's Model Forest Program, Natural Resources Canada. www.modelforest.net/cmfn/en/forests/waswanipi/publications.aspx. The Waswanipi Cree model forest was a unique experiment in cooperation among a diverse range of people who rely on forests for their livelihood and way of life. This report tells the story of the only Aboriginal model forest and the innovative way indigenous knowledge is translated and incorporated into forestry plans.

Wesley-Esquimaux, Cynthia C., and Magdalena Smolewski. 2004. *Historic Trauma and Aboriginal Healing*. The Aboriginal Healing Foundation. Cynthia Wesley-Esquimaux is an indigenous scholar who unravels the impact of colonization and historical trauma to explain how healing and wellness works in Aboriginal communities. This is an important study for understanding historical trauma and the healing and wellness movement.

Healing and wellness is an important part of successful comprehensive community-based development planning.

Notes

1. Building Environmental Aboriginal Human Resources (BEAHR); see www.beahr.com.
2. The Aboriginal population aged 25 to 64 with a university degree has increased slightly since 2001 (from 6 per cent to 8 per cent); see www.ainc-inac.gc.ca/ai/mr/is/cad-eng.asp.
3. Council for the Advancement of Native Development Officers (CANDO); see www.edo.ca/home.
4. www12.statcan.gc.ca/census-recensement/2006/dp-pd/prof/92-594/details/page.cfm?Lang=E&Geo1=PR&Code1=24&Geo2=PR&Code2=01&Data=Count&SearchText=quebec&SearchType=Begins&SearchPR=01&B1=All&Custom=.

References

BEAHR Project. n.d. 'Building Environmental Aboriginal Human Resources: Round table discussion paper'. Aboriginal Human Resources Development Council of Canada and Canadian Council for Human Resources in the Environment Industry. http://www.beahr.com/documents/roundtablediscussionpaper.pdf.

Brundtland, Gro Harlem. 1999. *International Consultation on the Health of Indigenous Peoples*. World Health Organization, Geneva, 23 November.

Brundtland Report. 1987. *Our Common Future: Report of the World Commission on Environment and Development*. World Commission on Environment and Development. Published as Annex to General Assembly document A/42/427, Development and International Co-operation: Environment August 2, 1987.

Gladwell, Malcolm. 2002. *The Tipping Point: How Little Things Can Make a Big Difference*. Boston: Little Brown.

Havel, Vaclav. 2007. *To the Castle and Back*. tr. Paul Wilson. New York and Toronto: Alfred A. Knopf.

Hawken, Paul. 1993. *The Ecology of Commerce*. New York: Harper Business.

Ling, P. 2010. UNWTO—World Tourism Will Grow 3–4% in 2010, Uptake. 18 January. http://travel-industry.uptake.com/blog/2010/01/18/unwto-world-tourism-2010.

McDonough, Bill, and Michael Braungart. 2002. 'Cradle to cradle: Remaking the way we make things'. North Point Press. www.czech.cz/en/current-affairs/getting-to-know-czech-republic/vaclav-havel-%E2%80%9Cwe-are-at-the-beginning-of-momentous-changes%E2%80%9D.

Statistics Canada. 2006. 'Census of Canada'. www12.statcan.gc.ca/census-recensement/2006/dp-pd/prof/92-594/details/page.cfm?Lang=E&Geo1=PR&Code1=24&Geo2=PR&Code2=01&Data=Count&SearchText=quebec&SearchType=Begins&SearchPR=01&B1=All&Custom=.

Waswanipi Cree Model Forest. 2009. 'Waswanipi Cree model forest milestone report: 2008'. Canadian Forest Service's Model Forest Program, Natural Resources Canada. www.modelforest.net/cmfn/en/forests/waswanipi/publications.aspx.

Conclusion: Reconciliation and Moving Forward

A Dialogue between David Newhouse and David Long

It is our hope that readers of this edition of *Visions of the Heart* will appreciate the challenges involved in trying to capture the 'life' of ongoing dialogue in writing. We also hope they will recognize that the preceding articles and the following dialogue embody a particular way forward in relations involving Aboriginal and non-Aboriginal people in Canada, a way that reflects a commitment to walk together on a post-colonial path that seeks truthfulness and reconciliation. Those who walk this path understand that truthfulness and reconciliation are anything but abstract, unadorned principles or points of view. Rather, we understand them to be essential to the development of healthy, whole relationships. And while genuine commitment to truthful, reconciling dialogue and action may be challenging to all involved, it is our conviction that such commitment is both a sign as well as a means of healing and hope for those who seek a positive way forward in our relations with one another.

This is not to say that the post-colonial way forward is clear and straight, for truthful, reconciling dialogue and relations take many twists and turns. Such dialogue inevitably shifts and even jars taken-for-granted thought and behaviour, and it affects different people in many different ways. Post-colonial dialogue and action is thus not about wanting to be or become the same. It reflects an attitude of heart and mind that acknowledges and welcomes the wisdom that informs our different ways of being and doing. Consequently, although moving forward is no easy task, we are confident that it will become more inviting and hopeful to the extent that those involved are as committed to *listening humbly* as they are to *speaking truthfully* and *acting wisely* as we learn to treat ourselves and others with dignity, honesty, and respect. We understand that the post-colonial way forward is no simple task, and we agree with National Chief of the Assembly of First Nations Phil Fontaine (2008), who noted to members of the Standing Senate Committee on Aboriginal Peoples that:

> We need to try and create the same kind of transformative change when it comes to First Nations and Aboriginal people so all Canadians can be proud of us, so all Canadians can know that we are being treated fairly

and that all Canadians will know that we are being treated with respect. Here I come to you this evening; I am the National Chief for the Assembly of First Nations, representing First Nations people, distinct peoples with rights that are unique to us. We are the only peoples in this land that have treaties with the federal Crown, yet I have to convince the federal government year after year of the legitimacy of the community I represent, the legitimacy and validity of this organization to represent all First Nations people. If I speak out of turn, I will get punished.

David L. I was fortunate in that I was raised to treat all others with respect, dignity, and kindness. I was also taught that being mindful of the wisdom of others would enable me to learn from them. But as I read the comments by National Chief Phil Fontaine, I am struck not only by the difference between my world of experience and the experience of Canada's First peoples but also by how little I know of your experience and perspective. Perhaps we could begin our 'moving forward' dialogue by you sharing a bit about how you as an Aboriginal person living in Canada experience and make sense of your life.

David N. For Aboriginal peoples, educated in historical and traditional understandings and experiences, the world is in a state of constant flux and change. Movement is the central aspect of life. Things change constantly; new understandings emerge; new relationships need to be formed, and old relationships renewed or discarded. Living in a world of contingencies and negotiated spaces requires a constant attention to the big picture as well as a mindfulness of the details of relationship. While one may have a desire for stability and certainty, it is rare for them to be achieved for any lengthy period of time. The stability that one desires emanates from inside rather than outside. Spirituality provides a groundedness that allows one to successfully live in an ever-changing world. We live in the world as the last created, dependent upon the lives of others for continued existence, and as the least powerful in a web of beings.

We live our lives in relationship. We are defined through relationship. A good life is one that is filled with good relationships. We are expected to create good relationships, to cultivate them, to find ways of accommodating those who enter into one's life. We give our lives meaning through the relationships we create. We uphold the world through relationship. The idea of living in relationship to all of creation is a central theme of indigenous philosophies throughout the world. Surrounding this idea is a moral imperative that speaks to the requirement to accommodate one's existence to those who enter one's world and to find ways to live harmoniously together, to find mutual benefits in the world and to help each other to achieve them.

David L. While my parents raised me to live in light of the moral imperative you mention, I have to say that my experience as a second-generation Canadian of Irish–British descent has been quite different from yours. My involvements with school, media, church, sports, work, and countless leisure pursuits in my communities have socialized me to take 'living dominantly' for granted. Apart from rather superficial social studies lessons I had on the value of multicultural-alism, I cannot honestly say that I have been encouraged, let alone challenged, to accommodate my life to those who are not part of my privileged, dominant world. It seems to me that those of us who inhabit and move within and around the privileged centre of the dominant culture are taught in countless ways throughout our lives that Canada is *our people's* world and that even if we don't really know who *our people* are, we can rest assured that the way things are organized means that most of life should go well for us. In other words, dominant living teaches us that while we can work toward social justice with others if we want to, that would be our individual prerogative and isn't neces-sary (or particularly attractive), since there are many privileged opportunities at our disposal. Indeed, dominant living reinforces the 'dangers' of promoting social justice in that doing so may well result in us having to give up certain privileges we have learned to largely take for granted.

Your comment 'Living in a world of contingencies and negotiated spaces requires a constant attention to the big picture as well as a mindfulness of the details of relationship' thus brought to mind a line from Margaret Atwood's *The Handmaid's Tale* that reads something like: 'the slave always understands the master better than the master understands the slave, since for the slave such understanding is a matter of survival.' I was reminded of this because in many ways, dominant and disadvantaged people living in Canada face very different challenges in coming to terms with where 'we' go from here. I know from our discussions that you and I are both committed to moving forward, but I wonder what you mean by paying constant attention to the big picture as well as how you see 'being mindful of the details of our relationship'? I ask this because while I agree that 'we' are in this together, I honestly wonder if 'we' as different people need, at least for a time, to walk different paths on our way forward? Put another way, how exactly do you see moving forward?

David N. Indigenous philosophies are profoundly transformative; all human beings are capable of change and want to live well together. All human beings desire peace and are capable of working to create peace. A destructive relation-ship can be transformed. Harmony, while not the natural order of things, requires effort and attention, not just to one's own existence but to the existence of others; it requires an acknowledgement that others have a right to live and to pursue their idea of a good life. Achieving harmony may require that one help others to live in ways that one does not agree with.

These are some of the ideas that we as indigenous peoples come to the table with. We come always with a sense of profound hope and goodwill because we believe in this idea of transformation. We have much experience in living with beings more powerful than us.

In the early part of the twenty-first century, as Aboriginal peoples, the public discourse centres on healing and reconciliation in the context of the post-colonial. We talk of the need to move forward, away from the colonial legacy that continues to define the existence of many Aboriginal peoples. The question that ought to preoccupy us is how to move forward. This raises the question of what are we moving forward to? What does moving forward entail? Will healing get us there? How will we know when we are healed and when we are recon-ciled? What is the desired state of affairs that we wish to create for ourselves, as Aboriginal and otherwise[1] peoples in this nation-state we call Canada? This process of imagining a desired future, then interrogating the present to see how we might move toward it, and then engaging in actions designed to move us toward it is what I call reconciliation. It is a process directed toward creating new relationships and ultimately intended to foster good lives.

We have been made to feel uncomfortable in our own land. To continue to live in our traditional territories, to use its resources to sustain us in this new world, we have to launch a land claim; we have to prove to the satisfaction of the state that we have lived here since time immemorial, have had effective control and stewardship over the land, and had not given it up voluntarily. This state of existence, of being exiles in one's own house, so to speak, confined in a sense to a small space, has profound effects upon one's psyche. We are caged, imprisoned forever in the past, reluctant participants in the contemporary world. We begin to long for the past, for a world that no longer exists and that can no longer be. It is a dispiriting existence.

David L. To be honest, I don't think I can begin to personally understand your experience of living a 'dispiriting existence'. Neither was I raised to experience my relationship with the land in the same way you were. I have always identi-fied closely with an indigenous way of knowing and being, and so the spiritual connection that you and I have to 'our land' may perhaps not be as different as one might think. Personally, I experience 'the land' as a sacred gift, and as such I recognize that it is more than a resource to be cared for and/or used for my benefit. We are all part of creation, and so I see and feel and know all my relations to other humans, the land, and all else as sacred. However, since identifying with the land involves both a spiritual connection as well as the time a people spends inhabiting the land, it seems to me that the time that Aboriginal people have inhabited this land has provided opportunity to cultivate a much deeper and more intimate and respectful relationship with it. I thus don't see any of us as 'strangers in a strange land'; we are inhabitants of the same land, with diverse experiences, perspectives, and relationships to it. Along with what this means for the relationship that I along with many 'other' relatively recent immigrants have with this land, this as well as other differences between you and me pose a challenge for me in relation to my scholarship.

While I am not Aboriginal (though as an aside, neither have I ever seen myself as merely 'otherwise'), I have long been committed to walking humbly, loving mercy, and seeking reconciliation and social justice. I grew up knowing and learning that human beings flourish individually and collectively when we treat one another with respect, dignity, and love. I have also personally experienced a good deal of poverty, addiction, abuse, and lack of comfort in this land that is presumably mine. As a sociologist who continues to be fascinated and often disturbed by social difference, I have interrogated the present by examining statistics as well as countless stories told by people whose circumstances, experiences, and opportunities are not only different from mine but whose lives have also been much more negatively affected by colonialism. At times my scholarly pursuits have not only enabled me to listen to the stories of 'others' but also to tell at least parts of stories that I connect with even though they are not fully my own. I often wonder what to do with this and am starting to question whether it is possible for 'us' to move forward unless 'we' acknowledge our differences by telling our own stories. I thus wonder what you mean when you talk about reconciliation as a process that involves imagining a desired future, interrogating the present to see how we might move toward it, and then engaging in actions designed to move us toward it? Can you elaborate?

David N. We have, I think, moved beyond the point where the questions can be answered only by the Canadian state and otherwise peoples within it. Our common conception of Canada is that it is a state that can accommodate many within a tent held up by common values. We have lived with the English–French dialogue on this for many years and have learned that the set of relationships that comprise Canada does not fall apart when the distinctiveness is recognized.

In fact, English Canadians have begun to learn that Canada is strengthened when distinctiveness is recognized and celebrated, a finding that the founders of the Iroquoian Confederacy encountered half a millennium ago. The newcomers to our land, while technologically and materially advanced in many ways, have yet to learn how to accommodate themselves to their new landscape and to learn from it. We must constantly remember that transformation is possible.

David L. I agree, though I wonder how you envision transformation in light of the entrenchment and deep divides cultivated by colonialism that affect Aboriginal people in Canada as well as many 'others'? I am particularly interested in how you envision transformation and reconciliation in the context of relations between and among Aboriginal people. As contributors to this edition and many others note, colonialism has far more devastating effects than merely contributing to material and social inequality. Specifically, much has been written on the ways that internal colonialism has benefited some Aboriginal people at the expense of others in their families and communities. In what ways do you think reconciliation between and among Aboriginal people is an important part of reconciliation, and what will that process look like? And in what ways, if any, do you envision others in Canada being involved in this process?

David N. The question of reconciliation in my own mind is no longer a question of whether but when and how. Let me explain why I'm optimistic about the outcome of this project and offer some cautions and concerns.

In my half century of life, I have seen incredible changes in the way in which we think about Canada and Aboriginal peoples. The two founding nations thesis is receding, and emerging to take its place is a more complex thesis involving pillars and influences. The three pillars (Aboriginal, French, and English) are seen as contributory, influential, and interactive. The idea of Aboriginal peoples as a burden on the state, as represented by the assignment of constitutional responsibility for Indians to the federal rather than the provincial governments, is waning. State action regarding Aboriginal peoples is more likely to be seen through the lens of accommodation and investment rather than as responsibility and expense, although there has emerged in jurisprudence over the past three decades a set of 'Aboriginal rights' that occupies a unique place in Canadian constitutionalism. The state itself has moved, somewhat reluctantly and slowly, to accommodate Aboriginal interests particularly around self-government. Canada has apologized, twice, for an official state policy of assimilation and has taken some, albeit limited, steps to make reparations for this century-long policy. The Truth and Reconciliation Commission has the potential to make important contributions to healing and moving forward. On the economic front, the land claims policies and treaty process are concrete efforts that can do much to assist in improving the economic status of some Aboriginal peoples.

We have also seen incredible changes in the way in which we see ourselves as indigenous peoples living within nation-states. Canada itself has been transforming itself to accommodate Aboriginal peoples. There is now constitutional recognition, a set of rights arising from this, and a record of jurisprudence, as well as a sense that something more needs to be done. The issue is no longer whether change will come but when.

At the same time as these incredible changes at the state level, overall living conditions of Aboriginal peoples have not improved much. Some would argue that Aboriginal peoples are having a tough time holding their own in the modern capitalist, pluralistic society that Canada has become. There is considerable evidence that this view may turn out to be wrong. Witness the incredible explosion of Aboriginal entrepreneurial activity over the past decade, the care with which land claim settlements are being used, and the debate about the role of Aboriginal governments in fostering good business and economic climates. What we tend to forget is that overcoming the colonial legacy is a long, multi-stage, complex process. We cannot consider the post-colonial project complete but only in its early stages.

The colonial legacy is more than its material effects. We are familiar with the colonial marginalization and dispossession that has resulted in lower levels of education, low incomes, poor housing, and poor health, both physical and mental. These are real problems that need to be addressed. As you note, the effects of colonialism go much further and deeper. Colonialism steals the spirit of a people as it seeks to replace an indigenous sense of self with a different one: one that is premised upon the idea of inferiority. Colonialism creates a sense of boundary, limitedness, and powerlessness. It robs one of the ability to imagine a transformative future consistent with one's own cultural teachings. It forces one to live in an eternal present with no future other than that imagined by the colonial masters. The psychological and spiritual effects are the most long-lasting and require the most effort to overcome.

When I look around for signs of post-colonial activity, I see tremendous effort underway at addressing this central aspect of the colonial legacy. Let me explain what I see and why I am optimistic about the reconciliation project.

What is new and different from the situation four decades ago is the emergence of what I call 'post-colonial consciousness' not just within Aboriginal peoples in Canada and elsewhere but within some Canadians. This consciousness is an important foundation for what is to come. What I mean by this particular type of consciousness is a keen awareness of the history and effects of colonization upon Aboriginal peoples, a strong desire to take steps to ensure that the policies and actions of the past are not repeated, the gathering of skills and knowledge to deal with its contemporary effects and inoculate society as much as possible against any future recurrence. It is also desirous of creating a world out of indigenous thought and Western thought. Central to indigenous post-colonial consciousness is this desire, and it has led to a set of actions across all levels of society: local, regional, provincial, and national. We could conceive of the establishment of National Aboriginal Day at the national level or the various Treaty Days as examples arising out of post-colonial consciousness. Similarly, we could see examples in the land claims process, although some would see the process as the continued exercise of power by a colonial state. I think we have to allow for multiple interpretations of actions, acknowledging that decolonization is a complex task, not prone to simplicity.

Post-colonial consciousness is driving much of the Aboriginal effort at reconciliation.

I think that it is important to see reconciliation as an ongoing process rather than an end-state. Reconciliation is the process by which we mutually accommodate our own disparate ideas about how to live well together. It also means that we will always be involved in reconciliation in some way or another; to a large extent, this is the essence of Canada: negotiation and accommodation and reconciliation.

Reconciliation means that Canadians need to think differently about their country and come to terms with a continuing significant presence of Aboriginal peoples as distinct peoples with a distinct legal status confirmed in jurisprudence. It also means that Aboriginal peoples need to find ways of presenting themselves as part of Canada, albeit with so much difference that Canadians openly question the reconciliation project. There is also a need to recognize and honour the differences within each group. We cannot present ourselves to each other with so many incommensurate differences that we cannot find common ground.

As Supreme Court Justice Lamer remarked in *Delgamuukw* (1997): 'Let's face it. We are all here to stay.' This makes reconciliation an important and central part of moving forward. The Leadership Council of British Columbia in 2006 defined reconciliation as building a positive, enduring relationship based on trust and mutual respect. The report of the Royal Commission on Aboriginal Peoples a decade earlier uses similar terms to define the characteristics of a reconciled relationship between Aboriginal peoples and other Canadians.

Indeed, Aboriginal peoples have been laying out for Canadians for more than a century the nature of the relationship that they wish to establish with them and the new Canadian state.

Reconciliation is a difficult political project because it involves power and accommodation. Canada as a state is a powerful actor and has almost unlimited power to influence the political and social reality of Aboriginal peoples. There is a long history of the use of this power in ways that have not been beneficial to Aboriginal peoples, that create mistrust, and we now live with its consequence. Part of reconciliation means agreeing not to use the power of the state against Aboriginal people and to use it to support Aboriginal initiatives as well as create spaces of dignity and respect that enable Aboriginal and other peoples to live well with each other.

Reconciliation is dealing with the sense of grievance and unfairness that has dominated Aboriginal–state relations over the past few decades, particularly since 1969. The land claims process requires one to negotiate with Canada for a share of what were once homelands and to use its methods to prove historic use and ownership. Getting Canada to fulfill the terms of its treaties without litigation causes a sense of real grievance. Canada exhibits a grudging reluctance to fulfill its responsibilities.

Reconciliation is dealing with the sense of inequity that continues to exist: economic, social, and political. There are real inequities, with serious consequences, that fuel this sense. Part of reconciliation also involves helping Canadians to understand the roots of these inequities, that they do not have origins in Aboriginal moral character, that they are the result of a century-long assault on Aboriginal lands and livelihoods.

Reconciliation is fostering a real sense of belonging to the Canadian nation among Aboriginal people by demonstrating a willingness to accommodate their interests; at the present time, accommodation is a reluctant act; it is not an act that is carried out with any sense of enthusiasm or joy; accommodation is arrived at only after a long and arduous confrontational process, often involving litigation. The land claims process places the onus upon Aboriginal peoples to justify claims.

Reconciliation is changing the founding myth of the country, recognizing that Canada is founded upon three primary pillars and that its political and cultural institutions have some Aboriginal aspects to them. Making these elements visible in the ceremonial life of the country is an important element in creating a sense of inclusion.

Reconciliation is healing the wounds resulting from past actions. There is also a sense of loss that has not been addressed and needs to be addressed.

Often, loss is expressed as 'anger'; the emotional aspects of the relationship have not been recognized.

We are doing some of these things, but most of it is out of the sight of ordinary Canadians. Many who frequent Tim Horton's or Holt Renfrew all share a basic lack of understanding of this aspect of the reality of Canadian–Aboriginal relationships; for them, issues involving Aboriginal peoples are framed in social justice terms if they are liberal or if they are conservative. For them, the issues are far away and of little consequence. Aboriginal peoples are part of the past or people who have not been able to adjust to modern times. I spent a year sitting in coffee shops listening to conversations about Aboriginal peoples. It was an interesting exercise to discover just how much is not known and how much blame is placed on Aboriginal peoples themselves for the current state of affairs. 'If only they would become like us' was a constant theme of these conversations.

I am heartened by the efforts underway in many parts of the country to change this situation through the public school curriculum. Perhaps in a generation the coffee shop conversations will be different, and more things will be in plain sight.

Moving Forward

How do we move forward, or perhaps we should ask an even more basic question: what does it mean to move forward? What are we moving forward to? It is clear what we are moving away from. It is simple to say that we are moving from a colonized world to a decolonized world. What does a decolonized world or, to be more specific, what does a decolonized Canada look like?

Talking about moving forward is difficult because of the wide range of things that could be talked about and the dominance of the legal political framework in public discourse. It might be easy to describe a bureaucratic framework and process that we could say, if followed, would lead us to a reconciled state. I'm going to resist this easy route, because I think that while framework and process are important aspects of moving forward, they can only take us so far. They have the air of panacea and promise, again important to keep us going through the difficult times.

Moving forward means that we turn our eyes from the past to the future. I think that this means we have to let go of the past. What I mean by this is that we cannot let the past dominate our lives and trap us. We can use the past to guide our actions, to learn what not to do, and to remember what we are moving away from. It can become our moral compass, a way to gauge our actions. I am reminded of a 'Star Trek Next Generation' episode in which the *Enterprise* crew become caught in a time warp and only get out of it by learning what has happened and then finding ways to not do what got them into the fix in the first place. Not knowing kept them trapped in an endless loop. Letting go is a fearful act, for we can forget completely. Moving forward is finding ways to collectively remember what has happened and to remind us regularly of what not to do to recreate the iniquitous world that we inhabit as Aboriginal peoples and Canadians.

Moving forward requires that we articulate a vision of a future state of affairs, that we imagine a future that we can work toward, that we articulate a set of principles for our relationship on this land, how we will share, how we will live next to each other and among each other, and how we will treat each other. I am reminded of the vision of Canada put forward by Aboriginal peoples in the report of the Royal Commission on Aboriginal Peoples and the negative reaction by the Canadian government that ignored it. I am reminded of the story of the Peacemaker in bringing the Great Law to Atatarho, lead Chief of the Onondagas. Each time he presented the ideas, Atatarho says: It is not yet. The story concludes with his acceptance of the Great Law and his transformation from a twisted mind to a good mind.

Moving forward requires conversation and dialogue between Aboriginal peoples and the Canadian state, between Aboriginal peoples and their neighbours, and between Aboriginal individuals and their friends. Conversation and dialogue identify commonalities, bring out differences, and can help us find ways to live together with mutual respect. Conversation and dialogue can prevent problems from becoming larger and perhaps even from starting. Conversation and dialogue can be both structured and formal and unstructured and informal, occurring in both the expected and the unexpected places.

Each time I think about these issues, I am reminded of a conversation I had a few years ago with a colleague when we working on a report on Aboriginal policy. We had concluded our review of the literature and were talking about how to approach the 'Indian problem'. He remarked at one point in the conversation: 'I have thought about these issues using all of the intellectual tools of my profession as a political scientist. I cannot find a solution to them using these tools. Perhaps we need new tools.'

Moving forward means that we have to start from the place that states, 'we are all here to stay.' We have to find ways that foster and nurture our collective selves, that foster a sense of connectedness and belonging, that honour our histories and engage us in creating a collective future of mutual benefit. I am reminded of the Iroquoian ideal of the good mind. Perhaps this idea could help us to move forward. A good mind is one that is balanced of reason and passion and that is filled with a yearning for peace between peoples. I am also reminded of the Guswentah, the two-row wampum that sets out a relationship between peoples and allows for a way for them to conduct a dialogue that fosters a sense of joint enterprise. And the spaces between the two rows is a space we create that enables us to learn from one another. Perhaps if we conceive of Canada as a huge Guswentah space we might be able to move forward differently. Bringing indigenous ideas to the discussion may be the tools that we need. We are all here to stay, which means that we need to recognize the legitimacy of all those who speak.

David L.   Thank you for your words, and I have one last observation and question. There is much talk about post-colonial consciousness and lots of apparent evidence of post-colonial conditions. After thinking about it for quite some time, I introduced this edition of *Visions of the Heart* by questioning the validity of the statement I made in the previous edition that we live in a 'post-colonial era'. As you know, while the vestiges of colonialism still leave many with much pain and even suffering, there is growing consensus that transformation is happening and that we cannot go back to 'colonial times'. What I hear from you and what I see happening in many different contexts and ways is the precarious, though apparently somewhat inexorable, movement and growth of post-colonial relations. I am not saying that we should stop talking about post-colonial consciousness or stop interrogating post-colonial conditions. I am, however, wondering whether you think it would help move us forward if more people committed to truth and reconciliation began speaking much more deliberately, honestly, and respectfully about the challenges we face and the substance of the hope we envision?

David N.   Certainly I think that a commitment to truth is important, as is a commitment to speak truths. These are the foundations of moving forward. A commitment to act upon these truths so that the colonial past is not repeated is also critical. Our good words have to be translated into political action that changes the present and future. This is the difficult challenge. We live in a world of realpolitik where those who have power get to make the rules and need to be reminded or forced to think about and act for others. Witness the Kelowna Accord, agreed to in 2005 by Aboriginal peoples, provincial premiers, and the Government of Canada after an 18-month set of negotiations and then simply cancelled without discussion or consultation with any of the partners. Similarly, the New Relationship approach started by British Columbia in 2005, which culminated in the proposed Recognition and Reconciliation Act in 2009, has now stalled. Despite good intentions, the New Relationship is at a standstill because those involved cannot agree on the legal or political meanings of these terms. It appears that the New Relationship may be too threatening to certain powerful interests. The treaty processes underway in Saskatchewan and British Columbia are also examples of the difficulty of reconciliation. We have difficulty in translating truths into action.

We have, however, been able to translate truths into action in the establishment of the Nunavut Territory and the creation of the Nisga'a nation and treaty, as well as in various land claims and self-government agreements around the country. There is a history that suggests that positive, transformative change is possible. There is also a history that suggests that Canada does not fall apart when Aboriginal peoples come into the body politic in substantive and meaningful ways. In fact, if we look closely we can see that we are all better off as a result. Am I hopeful? Yes, at times. I am occasionally overwhelmed by the enormous scale of the task that looms ahead: the transformation of Canada and this land into a place where Aboriginal peoples live with respect and dignity again. We sustain ourselves through continually renewing our commitment to these lands and their spirits.

Note

1. We encounter at the very start this problem of how to speak of the collectives that we are part of. The use of 'non' doesn't sit well with me, nor does ROC (rest of Canada), since it evokes the English–French rivalry. I like Sherman Alexie's term 'Native American or otherwise' and have adjusted it here for a Canadian context. Even this is not ideal, since 'othering' can result in a loss of human characteristics.

References

Delgamuukw v. British Columbia (1997) 3 S.C.R. 1010.
Fontaine, Phil. 2008. Speech to the Standing Senate Committee on Aboriginal Peoples. Issue 11—Evidence—16 April.

Glossary

Glossaries are comprised of particular definitions of terms specified by the author(s) of a given text. It is therefore important to recognize that each definition contained in this (or any other) glossary reflects the particular perspective and focus of its contributors and that definitions of many terms often change over time as they are informed by new experiences, attitudes, and understandings. It is also important to note that the following definitions were arrived at through dialogue among various contributors to this as well as previous editions of *Visions of the Heart* and that in the end, the definitions that follow are those that appealed most to the majority of discussants.

Aboriginal people (also indigenous peoples) — Descendents of the original occupants of the land. Aboriginal people remain a fundamentally autonomous and self-determining political community that continues to possess a special relationship with the colonizers, together with the rights and entitlements that flow from their unique relational status. Legal categories for Aboriginal people in Canada include registered or status Indians, Métis, Inuit, and non-status Indians. However, many Aboriginal people prefer to identify themselves by their cultural community of origin (e.g. Gwitchin, Cree, Métis, Nisga'a).

Aboriginal Peoples Survey (APS) — Statistics Canada has conducted this national survey every five years since 1991. Survey results reflect the responses of individuals who identify themselves as Aboriginal people, in contrast to general census data comprised of responses from individuals who have Aboriginal ancestry but may or may not identify themselves as Aboriginal people. The APS is a national survey of Aboriginal peoples (First Nations people living off-reserve, Métis, and Inuit) living in urban, rural, and northern locations throughout Canada. The purpose of the survey is to identify the needs of Aboriginal people and focus on issues such as health, language, employment, income, education, housing, and mobility.

Aboriginal revitalization — Growing support for Aboriginal spirituality and cultural traditions in a wide variety of modern social and political contexts.

Aboriginal rights (also indigenous rights) — By virtue of their status as the descendents of the original occupants, Aboriginal peoples possess both inherent and collective claims (rights) over those jurisdictions related to land, identity, and political voice that have never been extinguished but continue to serve as a basis for entitlement and engagement.

Aboriginal self-government — The ideal of parity between Aboriginal, provincial, and federal political authorities and powers.

Aboriginality (also indigeneity) — A nominalization of the adjective 'Aboriginal' in the same way that ethnicity nominalizes the adjective 'ethnic'. Aboriginality refers to a shared awareness of original occupancy as a catalyst for challenging the status quo with respect to who gets what and why.

Age Specific Suicide Mortality Rates (ASSMR) — Statistical measure of suicide rates according to the age of the deceased.

Alberta Métis Settlements Accord — An agreement between the Métis Settlements Councils and the Alberta provincial government that was formally legislated in November 1990. The agreement established Métis land ownership rights (fee simple ownership of 1.28 million acres) and a reorganized form of governance for the Métis of the eight Alberta settlements. The Alberta government also agreed to pay $310 million over 17 years and to establish the Transition Commission, which consisted of a membership tribunal, a revenue trust fund, and other groups to work with provincial government and settlement representatives to assist in implementation and maintenance.

American Indian Movement (AIM) — Organization initiated and controlled by American

Indian people, dedicated to grassroots, social, and political revitalization of Indian people.

Amerindian — Inclusive term that denotes individuals from all groups of indigenous peoples of North America.

Assembly of First Nations (AFN) — National organization established in 1982 to represent the perspectives and interests of status Indians in Canada.

Assimilation — Process through which a dominant group seeks to undermine the cultural distinctiveness of a subordinate group by subjecting them to the rules, values, and sanctions of the dominant group and by then absorbing the 'de-cultured' minority into the mainstream.

Band council — Elected body of representatives including a chief and band councillors, which is responsible for administering the affairs of a First Nation band.

Band councillor — Member of a First Nation band elected (every two years) by fellow band members to develop band-related policies and administer community resources.

Band members — First Nations people who belong to a particular band. Before 1985, all registered Indians belonged to a band. Since Bill C-31 was passed, status and band membership were separated, and bands were given jurisdiction over band membership. Only band members have rights to live on the reserve held in trust for a band, run for band council, vote in band elections, or participate in decision-making about how band resources are to be dispensed.

Biculturalism — Two nations with two distinct cultures existing within the context of a single, overarching political/legal framework.

Bilingualism — Government policy that grants equal, official status to two distinct languages.

Bill C-31 — In June 1985, Parliament enacted a series of amendments to the Indian Act, known as Bill C-31: Act to Amend the Indian Act. The legislation brought the Indian Act into line with the provisions of the Canadian Charter of Rights and Freedoms. The three principles that guided the amendments were: the removal of sex discrimination; restoring Indian status and membership to women; and increasing the control Indian bands have over their own affairs.

Burden of illness — Also known as 'burden of disease', refers to the impact a disease or illness has on a population, based on a series of indicators of mortality and morbidity.

Bureaucratic paternalism — Formalized, ideologically grounded relationship between superordinate and subordinate peoples, which controls all aspects of the subordinate peoples' lives.

Charter of Rights and Freedoms — The Charter adopted when the Canadian Constitution Act, 1982, terminated the United Kingdom's imperial rule over Canada. The Charter protects certain fundamental rights and freedoms of Canadian citizens, such as equality before the law.

Clans — Extended family groups related by blood or marriage.

Colonization — The establishing of imperial rule over foreign territories and peoples through economic, social, and political policies. Colonizing policies and practices are often informed by racist and ethnocentric beliefs and attitudes.

Comprehensive land claims — Process of clarifying Aboriginal peoples' legal relationship with the land as a basis for cultural renewal, economic development, and political control.

Compression of mortality — A pattern in which deaths in a population occur over an increasingly narrower range of years, typically in older ages.

Constitutionalism — The political and moral framework (or first principles) that govern a society or country and provide a blueprint for defining internal relationships among the governed.

Constructive engagement — The process by which central authorities such as the Crown and Aboriginal peoples establish a non-dominating, co-determining relationship in a spirit of cooperative coexistence.

Cooptation — Process through which socially, organizationally, and/or politically powerless people come to support the perspectives of those who have power and control over them.

Council of Elders — A group that provides direction to the Assembly of First Nations by developing the rules and procedures for members and by overseeing the individual and collective activities of AFN members.

Counter-hegemony — Ideas and practices designed to challenge and/or subvert processes and structures that support those in positions of power and dominance.

Crown sovereignty — The power and right of a monarch to rule over people and resources in a given territory.

Cultural awareness — An understanding of how an individual's culture may influence their values, beliefs, and behaviour.

Cultural competence — The ability to communicate effectively with individuals from other cultures. Competence entails one's attitude toward and knowledge and awareness of different cultural practices and beliefs.

Cultural genocide — Destruction of a people's cultural ways and means, often through colonial policies, legislation, and practices.

Curriculum — Contents, sequence, and scope of material taught in formal educational contexts.

Decolonization — Process of restructuring relations between indigenous and colonizing peoples, often through efforts to establish Aboriginal right to ownership of land and control by Aboriginal people over social and economic development.

Demographic transition — A model that helps explain how a country with high birth and death rates has transitioned to low birth and death rates as a result of economic developments in that country. The model consists of three stages, with stages 1 and 2 often representing developing countries and stage 3 representing developed countries.

Department of Indian Affairs and Northern Development (DIAND) — Federal government department established in 1966. Also referred to as Department of Indian Affairs (DIA), Department of Indian and Northern Affairs (DINA), and Indian and Northern Affairs Canada (INAC). Previous Indian affairs branches had resided in the Secretary of State, Department of the Interior, Department of Health and Welfare, and Department of Citizenship and Immigration.

Devolution — Colonial governmental policies and practices designed to decrease governmental responsibility and simultaneously increase indigenous peoples' responsibility for the administration of their people's own affairs.

Distal causes of illness — Factors indirectly related to the causal pathways of a specified health outcome. For example, while smoking can be defined as a proximal or direct cause of lung cancer, education or employment can be a distal or indirect cause.

Dualism — The view that the world consists of fundamental entities. In the case of human existence, it is the view that human life is comprised of two distinct entities: the soul and the body.

Epidemiologic transition — A generalized pattern of historical changes in the major causes of death in populations. These changes are thought to have occurred as a result of demographic, economic, and sociological factors, as well as technological change.

Ethno history — Use of written historical materials and/or a people's oral literature or memory to reconstruct a people's cultural history.

Ethnocentrism — The view that a people's cultural and institutional ways are superior to those of other peoples.

Existentialism — Philosophical perspective that asserts that human experience is the ultimate reality and that humans are ultimately both free to act as they choose and responsible for the actions they take.

Families of the heart — Marlene Brant Castellano describes a growing trend, especially in urban areas, whereby families are formed and grow based on choice, reaching out to and incorporating individuals who may or may not be related biologically or through legal unions.

Food insecurity — The availability of food and an individual's access to it. Food security is considered to exist when an individual does not live in hunger or fear of starvation.

Fourth World — Concept describing the phenomenon that emerges as a people develop customs and practices that wed them uniquely to their own land.

Global cultural pathology — Set of perspectives, attitudes, and actions that are contributing to the destruction of the Earth's ecology.

Hegemony — Ideological as well as political processes and structures through which one class or people achieve domination over others.

Holism — The perspective that the inner and outer states of existence are profoundly connected and that the purpose of all of life is harmony and balance between all aspects and dimensions of reality.

Holistic healing — The view that healing involves the harmonious restoration of physical, psychological, emotional, and spiritual dimensions of human life.

Indian Act Indian — Any male person of Indian blood reputed to belong to a particular band; any child of such person; or any woman who is or was lawfully married to such a person.

Indian Acts (1876, 1951) — Bodies of federal legislation that specified who, legally, was an Indian, what Indian peoples were entitled to under the government's legal obligation, who could qualify for enfranchisement, what could be done with Indian lands and resources, and how Indian peoples were to be governed (through Indian agents and elected band councils).

Indian control of Indian education — Policy initiated by the National Indian Brotherhood in 1972 that sought to shift control of First Nations education into the hands of First Nations people, including increasing the involvement of Aboriginal parents in the education of their children.

Indian Register — A list of all Indians registered according to the Indian Act. The register carries information about the name, date of birth, gender, marital status, and place of residence (on- or off-reserve) of all registered Indians. The Indian Register was centralized in 1951. Previously, individual Indian agents were responsible for lists of individuals eligible for registration.

Indian reserve — Land, the legal title to which is vested in the Crown, that has been set apart for the use and benefit of an Indian band and that is subject to the terms of the Indian Act.

Indigenization — Process through which colonial laws, policies, and organizational practices are reformulated according to indigenous peoples' perspectives and interests.

Indigenous — People who were born in or are natural to a specified territory or land.

Indigenous people's movement — Global effort dedicated to protecting the rights of indigenous people by seeking to redress injustices committed against them and ensuring their social, economic, and political well-being.

Indigenous (or Aboriginal) **sovereignty** — Based on the principle that (a) Aboriginal peoples are sovereign in their own right regardless of formal recognition, (b) they possess a right of sovereignty if not necessarily the right to sovereignty, and (c) Crown sovereignty can be shared by way of multiple yet joint jurisdictions.

Indoctrination — Process through which individuals are socialized to see and act in exclusive, narrowly defined ways.

Internal colonialism — Context and process through which: one ethnic group or coalition rules the affairs of others living within the state; there is territorial separation of the subordinate ethnic groups in 'homelands', 'native reserves', and the like; land tenure rights for subordinate groups are different from those of members of the dominant group; an internal 'government within the government' is established by the dominant group to rule the subordinate groups; unique legal status is granted to the subordinate group and its members, who are then considered to have a corporate status that takes precedence over their individual status; members of the ruling ethnic groups are considered individuals in the eyes of the state; economic inequality is ensured, since subordinate peoples are relegated to positions of dependency and inferiority in the division of labour and the relations of production.

Inuit — Relatively recent Aboriginal immigrants who share genetic similarities with certain Asian peoples and who are the majority inhabitants of Canada's northern regions.

Jurisdiction — The right of authority to have final say or control over a territory, its inhabitants, and activities within that domain. Implies some degree of non-interference from external authorities.

Land claims — Process of negotiating agreements that specify the rights of occupation in relation to a particular territory, as well as arrangements between governments, private enterprises, and Aboriginal peoples to control the resources available on lands or other places designated sacred by Aboriginal groups.

Marginality — Personal experiences and social designation of those with subordinate social, economic, and political status.

Métis — Individuals who identify themselves as being Métis. The history of the Métis is complex, but many people who identify with this Aboriginal group trace their origins to combined Indian and non-Indian parentage. Distinct Métis and 'mixed-blood' cultures emerged in various areas of Canada, the community at Red River being probably the best known. In 1982, the repatriated Canadian Constitution identified the Métis as one of the three Aboriginal groups officially recognized by the Government of Canada.

Morbidity — An epidemiological term referring to the experience of disease or illness.

Multiple jeopardy — The fact that Aboriginal women are disadvantaged in relation to both their social and their economic well-being.

Mysticism — The belief that becoming/being is rooted or grounded in one's relationship to all immanent and transcendent aspects or dimensions of reality.

Nation — A people whose shared awareness of their distinctiveness in history, culture, and homeland provides a catalyst for collective action to preserve or enhance self-determination over their lives, destiny, and life chances.

National Indian Brotherhood (NIB) — National organization established in 1968 by Aboriginal people to represent the perspectives and interests of status Indians.

Native Council of Canada (NCC) — National organization established in 1968 by Aboriginal people to represent the perspectives and interests of the Métis and non-status Indians.

Native Women's Association of Canada (NWAC) — National organization established in 1973 by Aboriginal women to represent the perspectives and interests of non-status Indian, status Indian, Métis, and Inuit women.

Nepotism — Context in which those in positions of power use their position to provide social, political, and/or material benefits primarily to their own relatives or close friends.

New Public Health — Concept encompassing two new approaches in public health. One is the shift from treating to preventing illness or disease. The second is the development of social and economic determinants in addition to biological factors in order to better understand health outcomes.

New traditionalists — Aboriginal people committed to combining traditional Aboriginal and modern Western ways of thinking and acting.

Non-status Indian — Individuals who identify culturally as Indian but who do not have legal status as such either because they or their ancestors gave up that status or because their ancestors were never registered initially.

Nunavut — Canada's third territory, stretching from Hudson Bay to the northernmost parts of Ellesmere Island. Under the terms of the Nunavut land claim settlement agreement, signed on 25 May 1993, the government of Nunavut has powers like those of other territorial governments, established and maintained in the context of a very close working relationship with the federal government. The basic land claim settlement gives the Inuit outright ownership of about 18 per cent of the land—353,610 square kilometres, including 36,257 square kilometres of subsurface mineral rights. The remaining 82 per cent of Nunavut remains Crown land, although the Inuit keep the right to hunt, fish, and trap throughout Nunavut. The federal government also agreed to pay Nunavut $1.15 billion, intended for economic development and social revival.

Organized dissent — Strategically organized

social activity focused on challenging status quo arrangements and practices.

Participatory Action Research — A research approach that includes community members and researchers as collaborators and that usually has the goal of producing some concrete outcomes for the community, perhaps in addition to research reports. Participatory Action Research is now often referred to as Community-Based Participatory Research and is a popular method within minority populations because of its ability to empower communities while research is being conducted.

Paternalism — A 'father knows best' ideology that views those who maintain power and control over the affairs of others as legitimately deserving of their authority and power and that has served to perpetuate inequality and the oppression of Aboriginal people in Canada.

Patriarchy — A social system marked by the supremacy of the father, the reckoning of descent and inheritance according to male lineage, and the dependent legal status of wives and children.

Pedagogy — Methods of teaching based on one's perspective of how and why humans learn.

Plausibility structures — Organized set of beliefs and practices that explain and legitimize a particular way of thinking about one's place in the world and one's relationship to other human beings.

Population health — An approach to public health and epidemiology that considers the health of the entire population rather than individuals already ill or most 'at risk' to disease.

Post-colonialism — Deconstructing analysis/critique of the social ideas, policies, everyday practices, and organizational structures that perpetuate the subordination of indigenous and other marginalized peoples. In Canada, the most egregious forms of colonialism have been addressed, although systemic aspects of colonialism such as Crown authority have yet to be explored or explained. A post-colonizing constitutionalism privileges the idea of Aboriginal models of self-determination over land, identity, and political voice.

Power brokers — The role played by the chief and council members on some First Nations reserves, since they have the power to determine who

receives the limited band resources such as band employment opportunities, educational funding, occupational training, housing allocation, housing repairs, and other band-administered benefits and services.

Primordial experience — The connection of Elders (as well as shamans and others) to the pervasive, all-encompassing reality of the life force, which reveals to them the oneness of all that has been, is, and is to come.

Proximal causes of illness — Factors that are closely related to a specified health outcome. For example, genetic makeup can be a direct causal pathway in developing diabetes.

Racism — Assumption that psycho-cultural traits and capacities are determined by biological race, coupled with the belief in the inherent superiority of a particular race and the right of its people to have domination over others.

Residential schools — Government-established facilities, often run by religious groups, that housed Aboriginal children for the purpose of providing them with a European education.

Resolution 18 — A resolution introduced by Premier Peter Lougheed of Alberta in 1982 that represented a formal commitment by the government to negotiate a renewed relationship between the province and the eight Métis settlements in Alberta. It eventually led to the Métis Settlements Accord and to land ownership for the Métis.

Resource mobilization — Processes through which individuals and organizations bring human and material resources together to achieve collective goals.

Self-determination — Essentially a political and politicized assertion about autonomy and control, the right of a people to exercise control over political, cultural, economic, and social issues that are of concern to them.

Self-government — Predicated on the premise that a people have the authority to create and maintain the organizational structures necessary for administering the daily affairs of their community.

Shaman — Intermediary to the spirit world.

Includes individual men and women who, because of dreams, visions, illness, or some inborn sensitivity or need, directly experience the presence of spirits and who therefore may receive sacred knowledge and/or possess special power to guide and cure others.

Social capital — A resource of individuals or communities that is hypothesized to affect health. Aspects of social capital can include social networks, trust, and reciprocity between community members and links to various institutions.

Social determinants of health — Social and economic factors that influence an individual's health and well-being. These factors include, but are not limited to, income, employment, education, housing, gender, age, culture, and social support networks. They can influence health outcomes either collectively or independently.

Social epidemiology — The branch of epidemiology that looks at social factors such as education, employment, and housing and their effects on health outcomes within a population.

Social infrastructures — Groups, organizations, policies, legislation, and practices established to address the diverse cultural, health, justice, and education-related needs of individuals living in a given community.

Social movement ideology — Set of beliefs that inform the experiences as well as legitimize the actions of a diverse body of people committed to reorganizing society or any of its major components.

Specific land claims — Land claims based on perceived violations by federal authorities of their treaty obligations.

State — A set of politically dominant institutions that has a monopoly on the legitimate use of violence and that is formally comprised of the legislature, executive, central and local administration, judiciary, police, and armed forces.

Status — The relative position of a person on a publicly recognized scale or hierarchy of social worth.

Status Indians — First Nation individuals whose membership in a First Nation band is formally recognized by the federal government.

Structural supremacy — The hierarchical structure of European society at the time of contact between First Nation and European peoples.

Tradition — Any human practice, belief, institution, or artifact that is regarded as the common inheritance of a social group.

Traditional — Anderson and Ball (Chapter 4) use 'traditional' to signify communities that live in close relationship with the land and with the wisdom of the ancestors of their particular cultural group. It is important to note that traditions and traditional ways are not static and that many of the values, principles, and practices that come from 'traditional' Aboriginal ways still operate in contemporary communities. Many traditional ways are also now being reclaimed to suit current generations.

Treaties (numbered) — Written documents signed by representatives of the Crown, the federal government, and First Nation leaders, which outline the conditions of the formal relationship between the sovereign peoples designated in the document.

Unemployment rate — Percentage of the total labour force (individuals 15 or older) who were, during the week prior to enumeration: (a) without work, actively looked for work in the past four weeks, and were available for work; or (b) were on lay-off and expected to return to their job and were available for work; or (c) had definite arrangements to start a new job in four weeks or less and were available for work.

Wahkohtowin — A word defined as 'the act of being related to each other' in the *Alberta Elder's Cree Dictionary* (N. LeClaire and G. Cardinal, 1998). However, it carries a bigger bundle than the definition implies, since it speaks to a world view in which everything is understood to be interrelated: humans, animals, plants, the land, and the spirit world. The health and well-being of one is thus dependent on the other.

Welfare dependency — Social, economic, and political conditions cultivate an apparently inescapable cycle of poverty in which individuals and communities become dependent on regular government handouts.

White Paper (1969) — Federal government policy designed to phase out federal responsibilities toward First Nations people and to eventually remove the special status of 'Indian' peoples in Canada.

Wisdom — A holistic understanding of what is true, right, and lasting.

Women's issues — Issues of concern to Aboriginal women, including, to name a few of the more prominent ones, child care, housing, education, family violence, social programs, spirituality, political representation, and legal status.

World view — A particular social group's set of beliefs, which constitute their outlook on humanity and the world.

Index